Competition Law and Policy in the EC and UK

Competition law, at both the EC and UK levels, plays an important and ever-increasing role in regulating the conduct of businesses. Based on the premise that open and fair competition is good for both consumers and businesses, competition law prevents businesses from entering into anti-competitive agreements and from abusing a dominant market position.

Competition Law and Policy in the EC and UK looks at how competition law affects business, including: co-ordinated action; pricing behaviour; takeovers and mergers; and state subsidies. It provides a clear guide to and outline of the general policies behind, and the main provisions of EC and UK competition law. Information is presented within a structured framework, complete with a glossary of useful terminology.

This fourth edition has been revised and updated to take into account developments since publication of the previous edition, including expanded coverage of the regulation of cartels, the development of private enforcement, the consideration of IP issues in *Microsoft*, and extended discussion of UK competition law.

Barry J Rodger is a Professor at the Law School, University of Strathclyde.

Angus MacCulloch is a Senior Lecturer at the Law School, Lancaster University.

Competition Law and Policy in the EC and UK

Fourth Edition

Barry J Rodger and
Angus MacCulloch

Routledge·Cavendish
Taylor & Francis Group
LONDON AND NEW YORK

Fourth edition published 2009
by Routledge-Cavendish
2 Park Square, Milton Park, Abingdon, Oxon, OX14 4RN

Simultaneously published in the USA and Canada
by Routledge-Cavendish
270 Madison Avenue, New York, NY 10016

*Routledge-Cavendish is an imprint of the Taylor & Francis Group,
an informa business*

© 2009, 2004, 2001, 1998 Rodger, BJ and MacCulloch, A

Previous editions published by Cavendish Publishing Limited

First edition   1998
Second edition   2001
Third Edition   2004

Typeset in Times by
RefineCatch Limited, Bungay, Suffolk
Printed and bound in Great Britain by
CPI Antony Rowe, Chippenham, Wiltshire

British Library Cataloguing in Publication Data
A catalogue record for this book is available from the British Library

Library of Congress Cataloging-in-Publication Data
Rodger, Barry J.
   Competition law and policy in the EC and UK / Barry J Rodger and
Angus MacCulloch.—4th ed.
      p. cm.
1. Restraint of trade—European Union countries.   2. Antitrust
law—European Union countries.   3. Restraint of trade—Great Britain.
4. Antitrust law—Great Britain.   I. MacCulloch, Angus.   II. Title.
III. Title: Competition law and policy in the European Community and
United Kingdom.
KJE6456.R625 2008
342.24′072–dc22   2008021871

ISBN 13: 978-0-415-45848-1 (hbk)
ISBN 10: 0-415-45848-X (hbk)

ISBN 13: 978-0-415-45847-4 (pbk)
ISBN 10: 0-415-45847-1 (pbk)

ISBN 13: 978-0-203-92658-1 (ebk)
ISBN 10: 0-203-92658-7 (ebk)

To Susan, Lucy, Kirsty, Euan, Coll and Baby Mac

Contents

Table of cases	xv
Table of legislation	xxvii
Table of statutory instruments	xxxi
Table of EC legislation	xxxiii
Table of decisions	xxxix
Abbreviations	xlvii
Preface	xlix

1	**Introduction to competition policy and practice**	**1**
	Competition law background	1
	Monopoly	2
	Cartels	2
	Mergers	3
	'Pure competition' objective	3
	State regulation – State aid	4
	Economics of competition law and terminology	11
	Politics of competition law	14
	Competition policy objectives	16
	Prevention of the concentration of economic power	16
	Regulation of excessive profits and fairer distribution of wealth	17
	Protection of consumers	17
	Regional policy	18
	Creation of unified markets and prevention of artificial barriers to trade	19
	Small is beautiful	19
	US antitrust law and policy	20
	Development of Community competition law	22
	Development of UK competition law	24
	Criminal law	24
	Statutory development	27

Comparison of competition law objectives under Community
  and UK law and policy   29
    Community competition policy objectives   29
  UK competition policy objectives   31
  Further reading   33
    Competition policy general   33
    The consumer interest and competition policy   33
    EC competition policy development   33
    UK competition policy development   34
    US background   34
  Discussion   34

2   Enforcement of Community and UK competition law   35

  Introduction   35
  EC enforcement framework   36
    Outline   36
    Decentralised Community competition enforcement   39
    Relationship between Community and national law   43
    The European Commission   46
    Initiation   48
    Decision-making   56
    Rights of the defence   60
    Review of Commission decision-making   62
    Ancillary enforcement issues   65
  Administrative enforcement in the UK   66
    Introduction   66
    The Competition Act 1998   67
    Competition Appeal Tribunal (CAT)   74
    The Enterprise Act 2002   76
    Initiation   76
    Investigation and reporting   79
    Enforcement   80
    Cartel offence investigations and director disqualification   81
    Private enforcement of EC and UK competition law   83
    Co-operation between courts and authorities   89
  Globalisation and extraterritoriality   90
    Extraterritoriality   90
    Subject matter jurisdiction   91
    Community competition law and extraterritoriality   92
    Resistance to extraterritorial application   94
  International co-operation and global competition rules   95

Further reading   97
   Regulation 1/2003, The Network Notice and the ECN   97
   UK competition law reform, the Competition Act 1998 and the
      Enterprise Act 2002   97
   Private enforcement   98
   Globalisation   98
Discussion   98

3 The control of dominance   101

Introduction to Art 82 of the EC Treaty   101
Undertakings and the effect on trade between Member States   102
Dominant position   104
   The relevant market   104
   Dominance   110
   Barriers to entry   112
   Criticism   116
Abuse   117
Exploitative abuses   119
   Excessive prices   119
   Unfair conditions   120
   The quiet life   121
Exclusionary abuses   121
   Export bans   123
   Pricing strategies   123
   Tying and leverage   128
   Mergers   129
   Refusal to supply   130
   Intellectual property rights   134
Collective dominance   136
Control of dominance in the UK   141
   Introduction   141
   Reform of UK anti-monopoly laws   141
   The Competition Act 1998 – the Chapter II prohibition   143
   Consistency with Community law   145
   Guidelines on the prohibition   146
   Practice and case-law to date   147
The Enterprise Act 2002   155
   Investigation and information gathering   155
   Market investigation references   156
   The reference test: prevention, restriction or distortion of
      competition   157
   The reporting stage   158

The competition test	159
Consumer protection	165
Remedial action	166
Further reading	168
Article 82	168
Chapter II prohibition	169
The Enterprise Act 2002, Pt 4	169
Discussion	169
4 Control of anti-competitive agreements	**171**
Introduction to Art 81 of the EC treaty	171
Article 81(1)	172
Agreements, decisions of associations and concerted practices	173
Undertakings	178
Effect on interstate trade	179
Prevention, restriction or distortion of competition	180
Agreements of minor importance	189
Within the Common Market	190
Article 81(2)	190
Article 81(3)	192
The exception rule	193
The four conditions for inapplicability	194
Block exemptions	196
Article 81 and the national courts	199
Introduction to UK controls on anti-competitive agreements	200
The 1976 Restrictive Trade Practices legislation	200
Reform of UK restrictive trade practice laws	202
The Competition Act 1998	203
The Chapter I prohibition – an outline	203
The operation of the prohibition	204
Practice and case law to date	211
Notification/Exemption	212
Resale price maintenance	214
Vertical restraints	217
The effects of vertical restraints	217
General Commission approach to vertical restraints under	
Art 81(1)	220
Particular types of restriction	221
US rule of reason	223
The Court and the rule of reason	224
Article 81(3) – the old Block Exemption Regulation 1983/83	226
The reform of vertical restraints policy	226

The Vertical Agreements Regulation   227
    Introduction   227
    Vertical agreements   228
    Market share threshold   228
    Hard core restraints   229
    Other excluded obligations   230
    Withdrawal of the Block Exemption Regulation 230
The Guidelines   230
Impact of the reform package   231
    Exclusive distribution   231
    Exclusive purchasing or single-branding agreements 234
    Conclusion   236
UK competition law and vertical restraints   236
    Introduction   236
    Reform and the 2004 Order   237
Further reading   238
    Article 81   238
    The Competition Act 1998; the Chapter I prohibition 238
    Vertical restraints, the US rule of reason and the Vertical
      Agreements Regulation   239
Discussion   239

5   Cartels: deterrence, leniency and criminalisation   241

Introduction   241
    The history of European cartels   242
    The early history of the EC provisions   244
    Cartel wars: the cartel strikes back   245
The contemporary view of cartels   246
    Optimal deterrence   247
Punishment   249
    Administrative corporate fines in the EC   249
    Administrative corporate fines in the UK   252
    The problem with corporate fines   253
    Increasing financial penalties: damages   254
    Individual penalties: criminalisation and disqualification 258
    Increasing punishment   261
Increasing the likelihood of catching cartels   261
    Leniency policies   262
    Direct settlement   269
The future of cartel regulation   271
Further reading   272
    General   272

Fines	273
Private actions	273
Criminalisation	273
Leniency	273
Discussion	273

6 Control of mergers 275

Introduction	275
Historical background to the Community controls	277
The Merger Regulation	280
The scope of the Regulation	280
The 'Community dimension' and case allocation	282
Mandatory notification and suspension	288
Appraisal procedure	289
Basis of the appraisal	295
Joint ventures	304
International mergers	306
Background to UK merger control	307
The Fair Trading Act 1973 and reform	308
Part 3 of the Enterprise Act 2002	312
The referral stage	313
The Competition Commission (CC) investigation and report	326
Remedial action	335
Review	337
Further reading	338
General	338
Merger regulation	338
UK merger control	339
Discussion	339

7 State aid and State regulation 341

Introduction to State aid	341
Article 87(1): the Prohibition of State Aid	344
What constitutes 'aid'?	344
Effect on intra-Community trade	347
Distortion or potential distortion of competition	348
The market economy investor principle	349
Services of General Economic Interest	352
Exemptions	354
Article 87(2): mandatory exemptions	354

Article 87(3): discretionary exemptions   355
Frameworks and guidelines   356
Procedure and remedies   360
Notification   361
Competitors' remedies   364
Recent and future developments   367
State regulation and intervention   370
Measures adopted by the State   372
Article 81   372
Article 82   373
Article 86(3)   375
The State entities as undertakings   375
State regulation and undertakings   378
Further reading   380
General reading   380
State aid   380
State regulation   381
Discussion   381

8 Overview: policy developments and practical implications   383

Introduction   383
Policy level   384
Laissez-faire competition laws?   384
Certainty and predictability v economic analysis   385
*Globalisation and international co-operation in
  competition law enforcement*   386
Changes in substantive Community competition law   388
*Developments in the enforcement of Community
  competition law*   392
New directions for competition law   394
*The revised UK competition regime post-Competition and
  Enterprise Acts*   397
Practical implications   398
Instituting an effective compliance programme   398
Pigeon-holing in market analysis   400
Whistle-blowing and leniency   401
The position of competitor and customer complainants   403
Discussion   407

Glossary of key competition related terms   409
Index   417

Table of cases

A, M & S Europe Ltd v Commission (Case 155/79) [1982] ECR I575;
[1982] 2 CMLR 264 54
Aberdeen Journals v DGFT [2002] CAT 6; [2003] CAT 11 .... 72, 75, 149
Abertis/Autostrade Case COMP/M.4249, 22 September 2006 288
ABTA v DGFT (1004/2/1/01) 17 September 2001 212
ACF Chemifarma v Commission (Quinine) (Cases 41/69, 44/69, 45/69)
[1970] ECR 661; [1970] CMLR 8083 .... 173, 182, 245
Adria-Wien Pipeline GmbH, Wietrsdorfer & Peggauer Zementwerke GmbH
und Finanzlandesdirektion fur Karnten (Case C-143/99) [2002]
ECR I-8365; [2002] 1 CMLR AEG 347
Aéroports de Paris v Commission (Case T-128/98) [2000] ECR II-3929 379
Ahlstrom (A) Oy v Commission (Wood Pulp) (Cases C-89/85, C-104/85,
C-114/85, C-116/85, C-117/85, C-125/85, C-129/85) [1988] ECR 5193;
[1988] 4 CMLR 901; [1993] ECR I-1307;
[1993] 4 CMLR 407 .... 93, 94, 177, 178, 190, 208, 246
Ahmed Saeed Flugreisen v Zentrale zur Bekämpfung Unlauteren
Wettbewerbs (Case 66/86) [1989] ECR 803; [1990] 4 CMLR 102 138
Air France v Commission (Case T-358/94) [1996] ECR II-2112;
[1997] 1 CMLR 492 .... 348, 351, 359
Air France/KLM (Case IV/M3280) OJ 2004, C60/5 292
Airtours v Commission (Case T-342/99) [2002] ECR II-2585;
[2002] 5 CMLR 7 .... 140, 141, 301, 302, 320, 332, 391
AKZO Chemie BV v Commission (Case 53/85) [1986] ECR I965;
[1987] 1 CMLR 231 61
AKZO Chemie BV v Commission (Case C-62/86) [1991] ECR I-3359;
[1993] 5 CMLR 215 .... 112, 116, 126–128, 148, 149
Akzo Nobel Chemicals and Akcros Chemicals v Commission
(Cases T-125, T-253/03) [2007] ECR II-00479 .... 54, 55, 64
Akzo Nobel Chemicals and Akcros Chemicals v Commission and others
(Case C-550/07P) pending 54, 55
Albany (Case C-67/96) [1999] ECR I-5751 376
Alitalia v Commission (Case T-296/97) [2001] All ER (EC) 193 349
Alrosa v Commission (Case T-170/06) judgment of 11 July 2007,
[2007] 5 CMLR 7 64

Altmark Trans GmbH v Nahverkehrsgesellschaft Altmark GmbH
(Case C-280/00) [2003] ECR I-7747; [2003] 3 CMLR 12 .... 345, 353
Amalgamated Industries/Herbert Morris (1975/76) HCP 434 316
Amministrazione delle Finanze dello Stato v Denkavit Italiana (Case 61/79)
[1980] ECR 1205; [1981] 3 CMLR 694 344
AOK Bundesverband v Ichthyol-Gesellschaft Cordes, Hermani and Co
(Cases C-264/01, C-306/01, C-354/01, C-355/01)
[2004] 4 CMLR 22 .... 103, 151, 377, 378
Apex Asphalt and Paving Co Limited v OFT [2005] CAT 4 .... 175, 207
Application des Gaz v Falks Veritas [1974] 1 Ch 381 191
Argos, Littlewoods and JJB v OFT (Replica Kits) [2006] EWCA Civ 1318
on appeal from [2004] CAT 24, [2005] CAT 13, [2004] CAT 17
[2005] CAT 22 .... 8, 18, 72, 75, 175, 207, 216
Argyll v Distillers 1987 SLT 514; [1986] 1 CMLR 764 84
Associated Press v United States, 326 US 1 (1945) 132
Attheraces Ltd v British Horseracing Board [2005] EWHC 3015 (Ch);
[2005] All ER (D) 336 (Dec) 154, 213, 214
Attheraces Ltd v The British Horseracing Board Ltd [2007] EWCA Civ 38;
[2007] UKCLR 309, CA 17, 120, 154, 213, 214
Automec srl v Commission (No 2) (Case T-24/90) [1992] ECR II-2223;
[1992] 5 CMLR 431 .... 49, 83, 403, 404

B & I Line plc v Sealink Harbours Ltd and Sealink Stena Ltd
[1992] 5 CMLR 255 133
BAI and Commission v Bayer (Cases C-2/01 and C-3/01) [2004] ECR I-23;
[2004] 4 CMLR 13 .... 123, 174
BASF & Others v Commission (PVC) (Cases T-79/89 etc)
[1992] ECR II-315 246
BAT v Commission (Philip Morris case) (Case 142/84 and 156/84)
[1986] ECR 1899; [1987] ECR 4487; [1988] 4 CMLR 24 .... 64, 278
Bayer v Commission (Case T-41/96) [2000] ECR II-3383; [2001] 4 CMLR 4 123
Beguelin Import v GL Import Export (Case 22/71) [1971] ECR 949;
[1972] CMLR 81 .... 103, 178
Belgium v Commission (Case 142/87) [1990] ECR I-959;
[1991] 3 CMLR 213 .... 350, 364
Belgium v Commission (Case C-5/01) ('Cockerill Sambre')
[2002] ECR I-11991 344
Benedeti v Munari (Case 52/76) [1977] ECR I63 354
Benzine Petroleum Handelmaatschappij BV v Commission (Case 77/77)
[1978] ECR I513 .... 109, 130
Bertelsmann and Sony v Impala (Case C-413/06P) judgment of
10 July 2008 .... 291, 391
BetterCare Group Ltd v DGFT (Case 1006/2/1/01) [2002] CAT 6;
[2002] CAT 7; [2002] Comp AR 226 .... 74, 75, 150, 376–378
BNIC v Yves Aubert (Case 136/86) [1987] ECR 4789; [1988] 4 CMLR 331 372
Boeing/McDonnell Douglas (Case IV/M877) OJ 1997, L336/16 .... 307, 387
BPB and British Gypsum v Commission (Case T-6/89) [1993] ECR II-389;
[1993] 5 CMLR 32 .... 111, 115

Brasserie de Haecht SA v Wilkin (No 1) (Case 23/67) [1967] ECR 407;
   [1968] CMLR 26 .... 84, 185
Brasserie de Haecht SA v Wilkin (No 2) (Case 48/72) [1973] ECR 77;
   [1973] CMLR 287 84
Brasserie du Pêcheur v Germany (Factortame III) (Cases C-46–49/93) [1996]
   ECR I-1029; [1991] ECR I-5357; [1996] 1 CMLR 889; [1996] 2 WLR 506;
   [1996] All ER (EC) 301 .... 84, 366, 404
British Aggregates Association v Commission (Case T-210/02)
   [2006] ECR II-2789 347
British Aggregates Association v Commission (Case C-487/06P) on appeal,
   OJ 2007, C42/8 347
British Airways v Commission (Case C-95/04P) [2007] [2007] 4 CMLR 22;
   ECR I-02331 .... 5, 112, 125
British Airways v Commission (Case T-219/99) [2004] 4 CMLR 19;
   [2003] ECR II-5917 .... 5, 112, 125
British Airways and British Midland Airways v Commission (Joined Cases
   T-371/94, T-394/94) [1998] ECR II-2405; [1998] 3 CMLR 429 .... 359, 365
British Airways Board v Laker Airways Ltd [1985] AC 58;
   [1984] 3 All ER 39 .... 7, 94
British Leyland v Commission (Case 226/84) [1986] ECR 3263;
   [1987] 1 CMLR 185 146
British Sugar v Commission (Case C-359/01P) [2004] ECR I-4933 .... 104, 128
BRT v SABAM (Case 127/73) [1974] ECR 313; [1974] ECR 51;
   [1974] 2 CMLR 238 .... 83, 120, 379
Bundesanstalt für den Güterfernverkehr v Gebruder Reiff (Case C-185/91)
   [1993] ECR I-5801 373
Burgess and Sons v OFT [2005] CAT 25 .... 5, 152, 153

Calor Gas Ltd v Express Fuels (Scotland) Ltd [2008] CSOH 13 235
Camera Care v Commission (Case 792/79R) [1980] ECR II9;
   [1980] 1 CMLR 334 56
Carlo Bagnasco and Others v Banco Polare di Navara and Others
   (Joined Cases C-215/96 and C-216/96) [1999] ECR I-135 180
Celesio v OFT (Boots/Unichem merger) [2006] CAT 9 .... 314, 321, 337, 398
CELF and Others v SIDE (Case C-199/06) judgment of 12 February 2008 366
Cementhandelaren v Commission (Case 8/72) [1972] ECR 977;
   [1973] CMLR 7 .... 176, 180
Chemidus Wavin v Société pour la Transformation et L'Exploitation des
   Resines Industrielles SA [1978] 3 CMLR 514 191
Cimenteries v Commission (Noorwijks Cement Accord) (Cases 8–11/66)
   [1967] ECR 75 245
Claritas (UK) Ltd v The Post Office and Postal Preference Service Ltd [2001]
   UKCLR 2 .... 88, 153
Claymore/Express Dairies v DGFT [2003] CAT 3 74
CNSD v Commission (Case T-513/93) [2000] ECR II-1807 372
Coditel II (Case 262/81) [1982] ECR 3381; [1983] 1 CMLR 49 221
COFAZ and Others v Commission (Case C-169/84) [1986] ECR 391;
   [1986] 3 CMLR 385 365

Comité Central d'Enterprise de la Société Anonyme Vittel v Commission
(Case T-12/93) [1995] ECR II-1247 299
Comite d'Entreprise de la Société Française de Production v Commission
(Case C-106/98) [2000] ECR I-3659 365
Commercial Solvents v Commission (Cases 6/73, 7/73) [1974] ECR 223;
[1974] 1 CMLR 309 .... 93, 104, 108, 131, 152
Commission v AKZO (Case C-62/86) *See* AKZO Chemie BV v Commission
(Case C-62/86)
Commission v Anic Partecipazioni SpA (Case C-49/92P)
[1999] ECR I-4125 .... 173, 181, 184, 206
Commission v France (Case 290/83) [1985] ECR 439; [1986] 2 CMLR 546 345
Commission v Germany (Case 5/89) [1990] ECR I-3437;
[1992] 1 CMLR 117 364
Commission v Germany (Case 70/72) [1973] ECR 813; [1973] CMLR 741 346
Commission v Greece (Case 226/87) [1988] ECR 3611; [1989] 3 CMLR 569 375
Commission v Italy (Case C-35/96) [1998] ECR I-3851 372
Commission v Tetra Laval (Case C-12/03P) [2005] ECR I-987 302
Compagnie Maritime Belge Transports SA v Commission of the
European Communities (C-395 and 396/96) [2000] ECR I-1365;
[2000] 4 CMLR 1076 .... 111, 127, 139
Compagnie Nationale Air France v Commission (Air France)
(Case T-358/94) [1996] ECR II-2112; [1997] 1 CMLR 492 .... 10, 345
Compagnie Maritime Belge Transport NV v Commission
(Case T-24–26, 28/93) [1996] ECR II-1201; [1997] 4 CMLR 273 149
Consten and Grundig v Commission (Case 8/72) [1972] ECR 977;
[1973] CMLR 7 193
Consten and Grundig v Commission (Cases 56/64 and 58/64) [1966] ECR 299;
[1966] CMLR 418 .... 174, 183, 209, 222, 223, 229, 233, 245
Consumers' Association v JJB Sports plc (Case No 1078/7/9/07)
CAT Order of 14 January 2008 .... 76, 89, 257, 397, 406
Continental Can v Commission (Case 6/72) [1973] ECR 215;
[1978] 1 CMLR 199 .... 105, 106, 109, 115, 129, 277
Continental TV Inc v GTE Sylvania 433 US 36 (1977) 224
Cook v Commission (Case C-198/91) [1993] ECR I-2486;
[1993] 3 CMLR 206 365
Co-operative Group (CWS) Limited v OFT [2007] CAT 24 .... 325, 337
Corbeau (Case C-320/91) [1993] ECR I-2533; [1995] 4 CMLR 621 .... 375, 379
Costa v ENEL (Case 6/64) [1964] ECR 585; [1964] CMLR 425 43
Courage Ltd v Bernard Crehan (Case C-453/99) [2001] ECR I-6297;
[2001] 5 CMLR 28 .... 84, 85, 192, 208, 255, 256, 393, 404
Crehan v Inntrepreneur Pub Co (CPC) [2003] UKCLR 834; [2003] EWHC
1510 (Ch); [2004] EuLR 693 CA; [2004] EWCA Civ 637, CA
[2006] UKHL 38; [2007] 1 AC 333;
[2006] 4 All ER 465, HL 84, 86, 90, 186, 200, 255, 403, 404
Criminal Proceedings v Manuele Arduino (Case C-35/99) [2002] ECR I-1529 373

Days Medical Aids Ltd v Pihsiang Machinery Manufacturing Co
[2004] EWHC 44 (Comm) 27

Delimitis v Henniger Bräu (Case C-234/89) [1991] ECR I-935;
   [1992] 5 CMLR 210 .... 180, 185–187, 207, 225, 228, 230, 235
Déménagements-Manutention Transport SA (DMT) (Case C-256/97)
   [1999] ECR I-3913; [1999] All ER (EC) 601 345
Deutsche Post AC v Gesellschaft für Zahlungssysteme mbH and Citicorp
   Kartenservice GmbH (Joined Cases C-147/97 and C-148/97)
   [2000] ECR I-825; [2000] 4 CMLR 838 380
Devenish Nutrition Ltd and others v Sanofi-Aventis SA and others (Vitamins)
   [2007] EWHC 2394 (Ch) 89, 258
DGFT v Smiths Concrete Ltd [1991] 4 All ER 150 201
Distillers Co Ltd v Commission (Case 30/78) (Johnny Walker Red Label case)
   [1980] ECR 2229; [1980] 3 CMLR 121 .... 7, 30
Dr Miles Medical Co v John D Park & Son Co 220 US 373 (1911) 220

Emerson Electric Co and others v Morgan Crucible Company plc,
   [2007] CAT 28 89
Enirisorse SpAv Ministero delle Finanze (Case C-34–38/01)
   [2004] 1 CMLR 10 353
ERT v DEP (Case C-260/89) [1991] ECR I-2925 375
Erven Warnink BV v J Townend and Sons (Hull) Ltd (No 1) [1979] AC 731 26
Esso Petroleum Co Ltd v Harper's Garage (Stourport) Ltd [1968] AC 269;
   [1967]1 All ER 699 .... 26, 236
ETA Fabriques d'Ebauches v DK Investments SA (Case 31/85)
   [1985] ECR 3933; [1986] 2 CMLR 674 221
Etablissement Consten SA and Grundig Verkaufs-GmbH v Commission
   (Cases 56/64 and 58/64) See Consten and Grundig v Commission
   (Cases 56/64 and 58/64)
European Night Services v Commission (Cases T-374, 375, 384, 388/94)
   [1998] ECR II-3141 182
Executif Regional Wallon v Commission (Case 62/87) [1988] ECR I573;
   [1989] 2 CMLR 771 364

FENIN v Commission (Case C-205/03P) [2006] ECR I-6295, OJ 2003,
   C184/19 .... 103, 151, 376, 378
FENIN v Commission (Case T-319/99) [2003] ECR II-357;
   [2003] 5 CMLR 1 .... 103, 151, 376, 377
FFSA (Case C-244/94) [1995] ECR I-4013 376
FNCE v France (Salmon) (Case C-354/90) [1991] ECR I-5505 363
Ford Werke v Commission (Cases 25/84, 26/84) [1985] ECR 2725;
   [1985] 3 CMLR 528 174
France v Commission (Cases 188–90/80) [1982] ECR 2545;
   [1982] 3 CMLR 144 375
France v Commission (Case C-301 /87) (Boussac) [1990] ECR I-307 363
France v Commission (Cases C-68/94, C-30/95) [1998] 4 CMLR 829 300
France v Commission (Case C-241/94) (Kimberly-Clark)
   [1996] ECR I-3203 .... 344, 346
France v Commission (Case C-17/99) [2001] ECR I-2481 359
France v Commission (Case C-261/99) [2001] ECR I-2537 364

France v Commission (Case C-482/99) ('Stardust Marine')
  [2002] ECR I-4397; [2002] 2 CMLR 41 ....346, 349
France Télécom v Commission (Case T-340/03) [2007] 4 CMLR 21.
  On appeal Case C-202/07 P, pending 128
France Télécom v Commission (Case T-339/04) [2007] ECR II-521 389
France Télécom v Commission (Case C-202/07P) on appeal, pending 128
Francovich v Italian State (Cases C-6/90, C-9/90) [1991] ECR I-5357;
  [1993] 2 CMLR 66 ....84, 85
Freeserve.com v DGFT [2002] CAT 8; [2003] Comp AR 1 74
Freistaat Sachsen and Others v Commission (Cases T-132/96; T-143/96)
  [1999] ECR II-3663 348
FRUBO v Commission (Case 71/74) [1975] ECR 563;
  [1975] 2 CMLR 123 ....50, 182
Funke v France (A/256-A) [1993] 1 CMLR 897; (1993) 16 EHRR 297 55

Garden Cottage Foods v The Milk Marketing Board [1984] AC 130 84
GE v Commission (Case T-210/01) [2005] ECR II-5575 ....302, 307, 320
GE/Honeywell Judgment (Case IV/M/2220) OJ 2004, L48/1
  [2007] ECLR 52 ....10, 307, 320, 387
Gebr Lorenz GmbH v Germany (Case 120/73) [1973] ECR I471 362
Geigy v Commission (Case 52/69) [1972] ECR 787; [1972] CMLR 557 93
Gencor/Lonrho Case IV/M619 307
Gencor Ltd v Commission (Case T-102/96) [1999] ECR II-753;
  [1999] ECR II-879; [1999] 4 CMLR 971; [1999] ECLR 334 .....93, 94, 140, 190, 208
General Electric Co v Commission (Case T-210/01) [2005] ECR I-5575 ....10, 94
General Motors v Commission (Case 26/75) [1975] ECR I367;
  [1976] 1 CMLR 95 ....119, 149
Genzyme Ltd v OFT [2004] CAT 4 ....151, 152, 155
Gestevision Telecinco SA v Commission (Case T-95/96) [1998] ECR II-3407 365
Gibbs Mew v Gemmell [1998] EuLR 588, CA 85, 192, 208
GIL Insurance v Customs & Excise (Case C-308/01) [2004] ECR I-4777 347
Giovanni Carra and Others (Case C-258/98) [2000] ECR I-4217 374
Guerin Automobiles v Commission (Case C-282/95P) [1997] ECR I-1503;
  [1997] 5 CMLR 447 ....49, 365
GVL v Commission (Case 7/82) [1983] ECR 483; [1983] 3 CMLR 465 146

Haig and Co Ltd v Forth Blending Ltd 1954 SC 35 26
Hamburger Hafen- und Lagerhaus Aktiengesellschaft and Others v
  Commission (Case T-69/96) [2001] ECR II-1037 366
Hanover Shoe v United States Shoe Machinery Corp 392 US 481 (1968) 256
Hasselblad (GB) Ltd v Orbinson [1985] QB 475 49
HealthCare at Home Ltd v Genzyme Ltd [2006] CAT 29 ....75, 89, 155, 406
Hercules Chemicals NV v Commission (Polypropylene) (Case C-51/92P)
  [1999] ECR I-4235; [1999] 5 CMLR 976 ....61, 173, 184, 246
Hercules Chemicals NV v Commission (Polypropylene) (Case T-7/89)
  [1991] ECR II-1171; [1992] 4 CMLR 84 ....61, 173, 184, 401
Hercules NV v Commission (Case C-49/920) [1991] ECR II-1711;
  [1992] 4 CMLR 84 181

Hilti AG v Commission (Case T-30/89) [1991] ECR II-1439;
[1992] 4 CMLR 16 114
Hilti AG v Commission (Case C-53/92P) [1994] ECR I-666;
[1994] 1 CMLR 590 129
Hoechst v Commission (Cases 46/87 and 227/88) [1989] ECR 2859;
[1991] 4 CMLR 410 .... 44, 53, 61
Hoffmann-La Roche v Centrafarm (Case 102/77) [1978] ECR II39;
[1978] 3 CMLR 217 125
Hoffmann-La Roche v Commission (Case 85/76) [1979] ECR 461;
[1979] 3 CMLR 211 .... 112, 114, 124, 125, 138, 152
Hoffmann-La Roche Ltd, Hoffmann-La Roche Inc, Roche Vitamins Inc,
BASF AG, BASF Corp, Rhône-Poulenc Animal Nutrition Inc,
Rhône-Poulenc Inc v Empagran SA 124 S Ct 2359 (2004) 91, 92, 216
Höffner and Elser v Macrotron (Case C-41/90) [1991] ECR I-1979;
[1993] 4 CMLR 306 373–376
Honeywell International Inc v Commission (Case T-209/01)
[2005] ECR I- 5527 94

IBA Health Ltd v OFT [2003] CAT 28; [2003] CAT 27;
on appeal [2004] EWCA Civ 142 .... 76, 313, 321, 337, 398
Iberian UK Ltd v BPB Industries plc [1996] 2 CMLR 601 403
IBM v Commission (Case 60/81) [1983] ECR 3283; [1981] 3 CMLR 635 64
Illinois Brick Co v Illinois 431 US 720 (1977) 256
Impala v Commission (Case T-464/04) [2006] ECR II-2289 .... 291, 391
Imperial Chemical Industries v Commission (Dyestuffs)
(Cases 48/69, 49/69, 51–57/69) [1972] ECR 619; [1972] CMLR 557;
[1972] ECR 704 .... 92, 175–177, 182, 190, 245
Imperial Chemical Industries plc v Commission (Cases T-36 and 37/91)
(Soda Ash Case) [1995] ECR II-1847, II-1901 .... 61, 62
IMS v Ofcom [2008] CAT 13 .... 186, 235
IMS Health GmbH v NDC Health GmbH (Case C-418/01)
[2004] 4 CMLR 28 .... 134, 136, 389
Industria Vetrana Alfonso Cobelli v Societa Italiana Vetro (Italian Flat Glass
case) OJ 1989, L33/44; [1990] 4 CMLR 535 181
Industrie Aeronautiche e Meccaniche Rinaldo Piaggio v International
Factors Italia SpA (IFITAL1A) (C-295/97) [1999] ECR I-3735;
[2000] 3 CMLR 825 346
Inno v ATAB (Case 13/77) [1977] ECR 2115; [1978] 1 CMLR 283 372
Inntrepreneur Estates Ltd v Mason [1993] 2 CMLR 293 .... 50, 191
Inntrepreneur Pub Company (CPC) and others v Crehan See Crehan v
Inntrepreneur Pub Co (CPC)
Interbrew SA v Competition Commission and Secretary of State for Trade
and Industry [2001] UKCLR 954 338
Intermills v Commission (Case 332/82) [1984] ECR 3809;
[1986] 1 CMLR 614 364
IRB v DGFT (1002/2/1/01(IR)); (1003/2/1/01) 17 September 2001 212
Irish Sugar plc v Commission (Case T-228/97) [1999] ECR II-2969;
[1999] 5 CMLR 1300 .... 111, 125, 127, 148, 149, 388–389

Italy v Commission (Textiles) (Case 173/73) [1974] ECR 709;
    [1974] 2 CMLR 593 .... 345–347, 348

Jones v North (1875) LR 19 Eq 426 244

Kobler v Austria (C-224/01) [2003] 3 CMLR 28 85
Kruidvat BVBA v Commission (Case C-70/97) [1998] ECR I-7183;
    [1999] 4 CMLR 68 63

La Cinq v Commission (Case T-44/90) [1992] ECR II-1; [1992] 4 CMLR 449 56
Ladbroke Racing Ltd v Commission (Case C-83/98P) [2000] ECR I-3271 345
Laker Airways v Pan American World Airways [1984] ECC 296,
    District of Columbia 7
Lancome v Etos (Case 99/79) [1980] ECR 2511; [1981] 2 CMLR 164 50
Land Rheinland Pfalz v Alcan Deutschland (Case C-24/95)
    [1997] ECR I-1591; [1997] 2 CMLR 103 .... 364, 367
Langnese-Iglo GmbH v Commission (Case T-7/93) [1995] ECR II-1533;
    [1995] 5 CMLR 602 186
Langnese-Iglo GmbH v Commission (Case C-279/95P) [1998] ECR I-5609;
    [1998] 5 CMLR 933 186
Leegin Creative Leather Products Inc v PSKS Inc. 127 SCT 2705 US
    (2007) 220, 224, 395
Leeuwarder Papierwarenfabriek v Commission (Case 296/82)
    [1985] ECR 809; [1985] 3 CMLR 380 349
Lenzing AG v Commission (Case T-36/99) [2004] ECR II-3597 350
Leyland DAF v Automotive Products [1994] 1 BCLC 245 130
Louis Erauw-Jacquery v La Hesbignonne (Case 27/87) [1988] ECR I919;
    [1988] 4 CMLR 576 221
Lucazeau v SACEM (Case 110/88) [1989] ECR 2811; [1991] 4 CMLR 248 119

Mackprang v Commission (Case 15/71) [1971] ECR 997; [1972] CMLR 52 64
Manfredi v Lloyd Adriatico Assicurazioni SpA (Cases C-295/04–298/04)
    [2006] ECR I-6619 .... 86, 255, 405
Mannesmannröhren-Werke AG v Commission (Case T-112/98)
    [2001] ECR II-729; [2001] 5 CMLR 1 55
Masterfoods Ltd v HB Ice Cream (Case C-344/98)
    [2001] 4 CMLR 14 .... 90, 200, 403
Matra SA v Commission (Case C-225/91) [1993] ECR I-3203 365
Merci Convenzionali Porto di Genova SpA v Siderurgica Gabrielli SpA
    (Case C-179/90) [1991] ECR I-5889; [1994] 4 CMLR 422 .... 121, 374
Metro v Commission (No 1) (Case 26/76) [1977] ECR I875;
    [1978] 2 CMLR 1 .... 63, 188, 194
Métropole Télévision (M6) v Commission (Case T-112/99)
    [2001] ECR II-2459; [2001] 5 CMLR 1236 .... 182, 188
Michelin NV v Commission (Case 322/81) [1983] ECR 3461;
    [1985] 1 CMLR 282 .... 108, 116, 118, 121, 124, 130, 152
Michelin NV v Commission (Case T-203/01) [2003] ECR II-4071;
    [2004] 4 CMLR 18 .... 125, 126

Microsoft v Commission (Case T-201/04)
[2007] 5 CMLR 11 .... 59, 111, 117, 122, 129, 135, 136, 387–389, 396
Midland Bank plc v Laker Airways plc [1986] 1 All ER 526 94
Millar and Bryce v Keeper of the Registers of Scotland
1997 SLT 1000 (OH) 84, 103
Miller International Schallplatten GmbH v Commission (Case 19/77)
[1978] ECR I31; [1978] 2 CMLR 334 221
Mogul Steamship Co Ltd v McGregor Gow and Co [1892] AC 25 25
Montecatini v Commission (Case C-235/92P) [1999] ECR I-4539 182
Montedipe SpA v Commission (Case T-14/89) [1992] ECR II-1155 182
Municipality of Almelo v Energicbedrijf Ijsselmij NV (Case C-393/92)
[1994] ECR I-1477 139
Musique Diffusion Francaise SA, C Melchers and Pioneer Electronic
(Europe) and Pioneer High Fidelity (GB) Ltd v Commission; Pioneer,
Re (Cases 100/80–103/80) [1983] ECR I825; [1983] 3 CMLR 221 .... 58, 223

Napp Pharmaceutical Holdings Ltd v DGFT (No 5) [2002] CAT 1;
[2002] ECC 13; [2002] EWCA Civ 796; [2002] 4 All ER 376;
[2002] UKCLR 726 .... 71, 75, 146, 148, 149
Nederlandsche Banden-Industrie Michelin NV v Commission, See Michelin
NV v Commission (Case 322/81)
Nestlé/Perrier (Case IV/M190) OJ 1992, L356/1; [1993] 4 CMLR M17 300
Netherlands and Others v Commission (Cases C-48/90; C-66/90)
[1992] ECR I-565 375
Neue Maxhutte Stahlwerke v Commission (Cases T-129/95, T-2/95 and
T-97/96) [1999] ECR II-17; [1999] 3 CMLR 366 349
Norris v Government of the United States of America
[2008] UKHL 16 .... 24, 25, 29, 244, 259
North Western Salt Co v Electrolytic Alkali Co Ltd [1913] 3 KB 422 244
Nungesser (LC) KG and Kurt Eisele v Commission (Case 258/78)
[1982] ECR 2015; [1983] 1 CMLR 278 .... 188, 225
NV Algemene Transport en Expeditie Onderneming Van Gend en Loos v
Netherlands Administratie der Belastingen (Case 26/62)
[1963] ECR I; [1963] CMLR 105 43

OFT v IBA Health Ltd [2003] CAT 28; [2004] EWCA Civ 142 313
Ohra Schadeverzekeringen (Case C-245/91) [1993] ECR I-5851;
[1995] 5 CMLR 145 373
Orkem v Commission (Case 374/87) [1989] ECR 3283; [1994] 4 CMLR 502 55
Oscar Bronner GmbH and Co KG v Mediaprint Zeitungs und
Zeitschriftenverlag GmbH and Co KG (Case C-7/97) [1998] ECR I-7791;
[1999] 4 CMLR 112 .... 132–136, 152, 389

Panayiotou and Others v Sony Music Entertainment (UK) Ltd
[1994] 1 All ER 755 27
Parke, Davis and Co v Probel (Case 24/67) [1968] ECR 55; [1968] CMLR 47 134
Passmore v Moreland and Others [1999] 3 All ER 1005;
[1999] 1 CMLR 1129 .... 187, 192

Pearle BV and others v Hoofdbednifschap Ambachten (Case C-345/02)
   [2004] ECR I-7139 345
Pernod Ricard SA and Campbell Distillers Ltd v OFT [2004] CAT 10 74
Petra Kirsammer-Hack v Nurhan Sidal (Case C-189/91) [1993] ECR I-6185 345
Phillip Morris Holland BV v Commission (C-730/79) [1980] ECR 2671;
   [1981] 2 CMLR 321 348
Portugal v Commission (Case C-163/99) [2001] ECR I-2613 375
Poucet and Pistre (Cases C-159/91, C-160/91) [1993] ECR I-637 376
Preussenelektra AG v Schleswag AG (Case C-379/98) [2001] 2 CMLR 36 346
Pronuptia de Paris GmbH v Pronuptia de Paris Irmgard Schillgalis
   (Case 161/84) [1986] ECR 353; [1986] 1 CMLR 414 .... 188, 221, 225, 234
Provimi Ltd v Aventis Animal Nutrition SA and others [2003] EWHC 961
   (Comm) [2003] 2 All ER (Comm) 683; [2003] ECC 29 .... 86, 89, 103, 405

R v Customs & Excise ex p Lunn Poly Ltd and Another [1998] 3 CMLR 369;
   [1998] 2 CMLR 560; [1999] EuLR 653, CA 347, 363
R v Dennis O'Neill and Others (2006) SFO Press Release 24, 29
R v Ghosh [1982] 2 All ER 689, CA 259
R v Monopolies and Mergers Commission ex p South Yorkshire
   Transport Ltd [1993] 1 All ER 289 .... 317, 328
R v Secretary of State for Trade and Industry ex p Anderson Strathclyde plc
   [1983] 2 All ER 233, DC 335
Racecourse Association (The) and others v OFT [2005] CAT 29 .... 75, 189, 213
Radio Telefis Eireann v Commission (Case T-68/89) [1991] ECR II-485;
   [1991] 4 CMLR 586 153
Rawlings v General Trading Co [1921] 1 KB 635 244
Remia BV and Nutricia v Commission (Case 42/84) [1985] ECR 2545;
   [1987] 1 CMLR 1 .... 187, 225
Rhône-Poulenc v Commission (Polypropylene) (Cases T-1/89 etc)
   [1991] ECR II-867 246
Roberts v Commission (Case T-25/99) [2001] ECR II-1881 .... 185, 186
Roquette Freres SA v Directeur General de la Concurrence, de la
   Consommation et de la Repression des Fraudes (Case C-94/00)
   [2002] ECR I-9001; [2003] 4 CMLR 1 53
RTE and Others v Commission (Cases C-241/91P, C-242/91P)
   [1995] ECR I-743; [1995] 4 CMLR 718 .... 134, 135
RTT v GB-Inno (Case C-18/88) [1991] ECR I-5941 .... 374, 375

Sacchi (Case 155/73) [1974] ECR 409 373
Salmon (Case C-354/90) [1991] 1 ECR 5505 366
Saunders v UK (1997) 23 EHRR 313 55
Schneider Electric SA v Commission (Case T-351/03) [2008] 4 CMLR 22.
   On appeal Commission v Schneider Electric (Case C-440/07) pending 293, 391
Schroeder Music Publishing Co Ltd v Macauley [1974] 3 All ER 616 27
Scottish Milk Marketing Board v Dryborough and Co Ltd 1985 SLT 253 26
Sepia Logistics Ltd & Precision Control Ltd v OFT [2007] CAT 13 179
Sloman Neptun Schiffahrts AG v Seebetriebstrat Bodo Zeisemer der Sloman
   Neptun Schiffahrts (Cases C-72/91, C-73/91) [1993] ECR I-887 345

Smalbach-Lubeca v Carnaud IP/88/14; [1988] 4 CMLR 262 278
Società Italiana Vetro SpA and Others v Commission (Italian Flat Glass
    case) (Cases T-68/89, T-77/89, T-78/89) [1992] ECR II-1403;
    [1992] 5 CMLR 302 .... 139, 182
Société Générale v Commission (Case T-34/93) [1995] ECR II-545;
    [1996] 4 CMLR 665 55
Societe Stenuit v France (Application 11598/85) (1992) 14 EHRR 509 60
Société Technique Minière v Maschinenbau Ulm GmbH (Case 56/65)
    [1966] ECR 235; [1966] CMLR 357 .... 103, 179, 233
Soda Ash Cases See Solvay v Commission and ICI v Commission
Solvay v Commission (Case 27/88) [1989] ECR 3355; [1991] 4 CMLR 502 55
Solvay v Commission (Cases T-30–32/91) (Soda Ash Case)
    [1995] ECR II-1775, II-1821, II-1825 .... 61, 62, 104
Somerfield plc v Competition Commission [2006] CAT 4 .... 338, 398
Spain v Lenzing AG (Case C-525/04P) 22 November 2007 350
Stagecoach Holdings plc v Secretary of State for Trade and Industry
    1997 SLT 940 (OH) 317, 328
Ste Colas Est v France (37971/97) (2002) (unreported) April 16, ECHR 53
Steinike and Weinlig v Germany (Case 78/86) [1977] ECR 595;
    [1977] 2 CMLR 688 349
Stericycle International LLC and others v Competition Commission
    [2006] CAT 21 .... 338, 398
STM v Maschinenbau Ulm (Case 56/65) [1966] ECR 235;
    [1966] CMLR 357 .... 181, 191, 208
Suiker Unie v Commission (Sugar) (Cases 40–48/73, 50/73, 54/73–56/73,
    111/73, 113–114/73) [1975] ECR 1663; [1976] 1 CMLR 295 175
Supply of Ready Mixed Concrete (No 1) Re; Director General of Fair
    Trading v Smiths Concrete Ltd [1991] 4 All ER 150 201
Supply of Ready Mixed Concrete (No 2) Re; Director General of Fair
    Trading v Pioneer Concrete UK Ltd and Another
    [1995] 1 All ER 135 .... 24, 201
Suretrack Rail Services Ltd v Infraco JNP Ltd [2002] All ER (D) 261 216
Syndicat Francais de l'Express International (SFE1) and Others v La Poste
    and Others (La Poste) (Case C-39/94) [1996] ECR I-3547;
    [1996] All ER (EC) 685; [1996] 3 CMLR 369 .... 363, 366, 367
Sytraval v Commission (Case T-95/94) [1995] ECR II-2651 365

Tate & Lyle plc, British Sugar plc and Napier Brown and Co Ltd
    (Cases T-202/98, T 204/98, T-207/98) [2001] ECR II-2035 .... 180, 182
Tele-Marketing v CLT (Case 311/84) [1985] ECR 3261; [1986] 2 CMLR 558 114
Tetra Laval v Commission (Case T-5/02) [2002] ECR II-4381 302
Tetra Pak International v Commission (Case 333/94P) [1996] ECR I-5951;
    [1997] 4 CMLR 662 .... 127, 149, 152, 154
Tetra Pak International v Commission (Case T-51/89) [1990] ECR II-309;
    [1991] 4 CMLR 334 114
Tetra Pak International v Commission (Case T-83/91) [1994] ECR II-755;
    [1997] 4 CMLR 726 .... 149, 152
Texaco Ltd v Mulberry Filling Station Ltd [1972] 1 All ER 513 26

Thermenhotel Stoiser Franz Gesellschaft mbH & Co KG v Commission
(Case T-158/99) [2004] ECR II-1 350
Tierce Ladbroke v Commission (Case T-504/93) [1997] ECR II-923 135
TNT Traco SpA v Poste Italiane SpA (Case C-340/99) [2001] ECR I-4109 380
Tokai Carbon v Commission (Cases T-236/01, T-239/01, T-244–246/01,
T-251–252/01) [2004] ECR II-1181 58
Trefilunion SA v Commission (Case T-148/89) [1995] ECR II-1063 182
TWD Textilewerke Deggendorf GmbH v Germany (Case C-188/92)
[1994] ECR I-833; [1995] 2 CMLR 145 366

Umbro and Othrs v OFT (Toys) [2005] CAT 22 75
Unichem Ltd v OFT [2005] CAT 8 .... 337, 398
Unilever Bestfoods (formerly Van Den Bergh Foods) v Commission
(Case C-552/03P) [2006] ECR I-9091 .... 8, 194, 235
United Brands Continental BV v Commission (Case 27/76) [1978] ECR 207;
[1978] 1 CMLR 429 .... 107, 109, 110, 112, 115, 119, 120, 123, 131
United States v Aluminium Co of America (Alcoa) 148 F 2d 416
(1945) 2 Circ 92, 94
United States v El Du Pont de Nemours and Co 118 F Supp 41 (D Del 1953);
aff'd 351 US 377 (US Sup Ct 1956) 106
United States v Terminal RR Ass'n, 224 US 383 (1912) 132

Van Den Bergh Foods Ltd v Commission (Case T-65/98) [2003] ECR II-4653;
[2004] 4 CMLR 1 .... 8, 186, 194, 235
Van Eycke (Case 267/86) [1988] ECR 4769; [1990] 4 CMLR 330 372
Van Vliet Kwasten and Ladderfabriekev Fratelli Dalle Crodc (Case 25/75)
[1975] ECR 1103; [1975] 2 CMLR 549, 223
Vereeninging van Cementhandelaren v Commission (Noorwijks Cement
Accord) (Case 8/72) [1972] ECR 977 245
Vereniging van Vlaamse Reisbureaus v Sociale Dienst (Case 311/85)
[1987] ECR 3801; [1989] 4 CMLR 213 372
Verizon Communications v Law Offices of Curtis V Trinko, 540 US 398, 408
(2004) 271
Viho Europe v Commission (Case T-102/92) [1995] ECR II-17;
[1997] 4 CMLR 469 103
Viho Europe v Commission (Case C-73/95P) [1996] ECR I-5457;
[1997] 4 CMLR 419, CA 103, 178
Viscido and Others v Ente Post Italiane (Cases C-52–54/97)
[1998] ECR I-2629 346
Völk v Ets Vervaecke Spr1 (Case 5/69) [1969] ECR 295; [1969] CMLR 273 189

Walt Wilhelm v Bundeskartellamt (Case 14/68) [1969] ECR I;
[1969] CMLR 100 .... 44, 46
Wolf Meng (Case C-2/91) [1993] ECR I-5751 373
Wouters v Algemene Raad van de Nederlandse Orde van Advocaten
(Case C-309/99) [2002] ECR I-1577, [2002] 4 CMLR 913 .... 188, 214, 390

Table of legislation

UK Legislation

Communications Act 2003 311
  ss 375–388 311
Companies Act 1989 .... 309, 324, 325
Company Directors
  Disqualification Act 1986 ..... 260, 266
  s 9A 260
Competition Act 1980 ... 28, 67, 141, 143
Competition Act 1998 .... 2, 24–29,
                    32, 35, 42, 43, 46, 66–76, 78,
                85, 88, 89, 92, 97, 98, 120,
         141–143, 145, 147–150, 153,
           154, 156–159, 161, 200,
         202–206, 208–212, 216,
     236–239, 260, 266, 309, 310,
     312, 378, 383, 394, 396–399,
             401, 403, 406, 414
Pt 1 (ss 1–60) .. 143, 145, 203, 204, 237
s 2 .... 92, 203, 205–207
s 2(1) 208
s 2(1)(b) 212
s 2(3) 207
s 2(4) 208
s 4 .... 208, 213
s 6 .... 209, 212
s 9 .... 208, 213
s 10 .... 43, 205, 209
ss 12–16 208
s 18 .... 92, 143, 144, 147, 238
s 18(1) 143
s 25 .... 42, 69, 203
ss 26–28 .... 69, 144, 203, 211
s 29 .... 69, 144, 203
ss 31, 33–35 .... 144, 203

s 36 .... 70, 144, 203
s 36(8) 70, 71
s 38 .... 144, 203
s 39(1) 215
s 40 145
ss 42–44 .... 144, 203
s 46 43
s 46(1) 74
s 47 .... 43, 74, 406
s 47A 75, 89, 153, 155
s 47B 75, 89, 257
s 49 75
s 50 237
s 50(1) 237
s 52 .... 42, 69, 144, 147, 204, 205
s 52(1) 146
s 54 73
s 54(1) 42
s 54(4) 73
s 54(5) 74
ss 55, 56, 58, 58A 88, 145, 204
s 59 147
s 60 .... 43, 144, 146, 147, 149,
               203, 205, 208, 212
s 60(1) 145, 204
s 60(2), (3) 146
s 60(6)(b) 208
s 72 25
Sched 1 210
Sched 1, para 1(1) 312
Sched 1, para 1(2) 210, 312
Sched 2 210
Sched 3 210
Sched 4 210
Sched 5 208

Sched 6A 69, 209
Sched 8 .... 145, 204
Sched 8, para 3(2) 75

Deregulation and Contracting Out
Act 1994 309
s 39 324
Sched 11, para 2 324

Enterprise Act 2002 .... 9, 18, 25, 26,
28, 29, 32, 33, 35, 42, 66, 74,
76–82, 89, 97, 98, 101, 141,
143, 145, 155, 157–159, 161,
163–167, 170, 210, 238, 260,
266, 308–313, 315–318, 320,
323–326, 330, 332–336, 338,
339, 383, 394, 397, 406
s 1 67
s 2 .... 66, 67, 203
s 5 .... 155, 157
s 11 .... 18, 66, 156
s 11(1) 77
Pt 2 (ss 12–21) 74
s 12 .... 74, 145, 204
ss 13, 14 74
s 17 393
ss 18, 19 .... 75, 89, 393
s 20 .... 89, 393
Pt 3 (ss 22–130) 32, 76, 210, 277,
308, 310, 312, 313, 337
s 22 .... 18, 313, 319, 321
s 22(1) 318
s 22(2)(a) 322
s 23 314
s 23(2)–(5) 317
s 25 144
s 25(2)–(4) 315
s 26(1) 315
s 29 316
s 30 .... 18, 322
s 33 .... 18, 313, 321, 325
s 33(1) 318
s 33(2)(c) 322
s 34A 314
s 35(1) 327
s 36(1) 327
s 41 335
s 41(2), (4) 335

ss 71, 72 327
s 73 .... 323, 324
s 75 324
s 75(5) 327
ss 80, 81 327
ss 82, 84, 96, 97 335
s 97(1) 325
s 106 314
s 120 .... 81, 313, 321
s 129(1) 315
Pt 4 (ss 131–184) 32, 76, 141,
143, 155, 163, 165, 168, 169
s 131 156
s 131(2) 156, 158
s 134 165
s 134(1) 160, 161
s 134(2) 160
s 134(5) 161
s 134(6) 167
s 134(7) 167, 336
s 134(8) 167, 336
s 137 158
s 138 167
s 154 157
ss 159, 162 166
s 174 156
s 179 81
Pt 6 (ss 188–202) 25
s 188 .... 25, 41, 66, 81, 82, 258
s 188(1) 258
s 188(2) 25, 259
s 189 258
s 190 .... 81, 259
s 190(4) 268
s 204 81
s 209 209
s 528A 311
Sched 1 311
Sched 2 .... 74, 145, 204
Sched 8 .... 167, 335
European Communities
Act 1972
ss 2(1), 3(1) 43

Fair Trading Act 1973 .... 18, 27, 28,
32, 66, 76–78, 80, 141–143,
155–162, 165, 166, 168, 200,
238, 308–313, 315–319, 323,

325, 328–332, 335–337, 397,
400, 406
s 6(2) 157
s 56 .... 80, 166
Pt V (ss 57–77) 308
s 66A 316
s 73 80
ss 75A–75F 325
ss 75G–75K 324
s 76 312
s 84 .... 16, 159, 165, 308,
318, 329
s 84(d) 329
s 88 80
s 90 .... 80, 166
ss 91, 93 80
Sched 8 80
Sched 9 80

Monopolies and Mergers Act
1965 .... 27, 308
Monopolies and Restrictive
Practices (Inquiry and Control)
Act 1948 .... 27, 307

Profiteering Act 1919 27
Protection of Trading Interests
Act 1980 95
ss 1–6 95

Resale Prices Act 1964 27
Resale Prices Act 1976 .... 28, 67, 200
Restrictive Practices Court
Act 1976 .... 28, 67
Restrictive Practices (Inquiry and
Control) Act 1948 244
Restrictive Trade Practices
Act 1956 .... 27, 244, 308
Restrictive Trade Practices Act
1976 .... 28, 67, 76, 200–202
s 21 201
s 35(2) 88

Theft Act 1968 259
Trade Marks Act 1994
s 56(2) 26

Water Industry Act 1991
Sched 4ZA 311

US Legislation

Clayton Act 1914 20

Federal Trade Commission Act
1914 20

Sherman Act 1890 ... 17, 19–21, 224, 409
s 1 .... 20, 223
s 2 .... 2, 20

Table of statutory instruments

Competition Act 1998 and Other Enactments (Amendment) Regulations
2004 (SI 2004/1261) 24, 29, 67
  Reg 3 42
  Sched 1, paras 2, 9 .... 69, 205, 209
  Sched 1, paras 10–14 69
  Sched 1, para 18 .... 69, 209
Competition Act 1998 (Concurrency) Regulations 2004 (SI 2004/1077) 74
Competition Act 1998 (Determination of Turnover for Penalties) Order 2000
(SI 2000/309) 70
Competition Act 1998 (Determination of Turnover for Penalties)
(Amendment) Order 2004 (SI 2004/1259) 67, 70, 73
Competition Act 1998 (Director's rules) Order 2000 (SI 2000/293)
  r 14 .... 144, 203
Competition Act 1998 (Land Agreements Exclusion and Revocation) Order
2004 (SI 2004/1260) 67, 206, 210, 237
  Art 3 210
  Art 4 210
Competition Act 1998 (Land and Vertical Agreements Exclusion) Order 2000
(SI 2000/310) 206, 210, 237
  Art 5 210
Competition Act 1998 (Office of Fair Trading's Rules) Order 2004
(SI 2004/2751) 67, 68, 144, 203
Competition Act 1998 (Public Transport Ticketing Schemes Block
Exemption) (Amendment) Order 2005 (SI 2005/3347) 209, 212
Competition Act 1998 (Public Transport Ticketing Schemes Block
Exemption) Order 2001 (SI 2001/319) 209, 212
Competition Act 1998 (Small Agreements and Conduct of Minor
Significance) Regulations 2000 (SI 2000/262) 204
Competition Appeal Tribunal Rules 2003 (SI 2003/1372) 75
  r 60 75
Competition Commission Appeal Tribunal Rules 2000 (SI 2000/261) 75

EC Competition Law (Articles 88 and 89) Enforcement Regulations 1996
(SI 1996/2199) 314

Enterprise Act 2002 (Commencement No. 3, Transitional and Transitory
Provisions and Savings) Order 2003 (SI 2003/1397) 143, 310

Foreign Package Holidays (Tour Operators and Travel Agents) Order 2000
(SI 2000/2110) 81

Restriction on Agreements and Conduct (Specified Domestic Electrical
Goods) Order 1998 (SI 1998/1271) 80, 164

Supply of Beer (Loan Ties, Licensed Premises and Wholesale Prices) Order
1989 (SI 1989/2258) 80, 162
Supply of Beer (Tied Estate) (Amendment) Order 1997 (SI 1997/1740) 162
Supply of Beer (Tied Estate) Order 1989 (SI 1989/2390) 80, 162
Supply of Beer (Tied Estate) (Revocation) Order 2002 (SI 2002/3204) 80, 162
Supply of New Cars Order 2000 (SI 2000/2088) 164, 166

Table of EC legislation

European Coal and Steel
Treaty (Treaty of Paris)
1951 .... 22, 244, 277, 370
Art 3(1)(g) 370
Art 65 244
Art 65(5) 250
European Convention on the
Protection of Human Rights
and Fundamental Freedoms
1957 .... 60, 395
Art 6 .... 55, 60, 395
Art 8 53
European Economic Area
Agreement 96
Arts 53, 54, 57 .... 38, 61
Art 61 358

Geneva Declaration on Cartels
1927 243

Single European Act 1986 62

Treaty of Amsterdam 1997 87
Arts 65, 67 87
Treaty of European Union 1992
(EC Treaty) 22, 29, 43, 63, 64,
138, 190, 244, 278, 287,
341, 342, 344, 364, 365,
370, 371, 374, 414
Art 1 23
Art 2 .... 23, 30, 118, 299
Art 3 (old Art 3) 23, 372
Art 3(1)(g) 23, 101, 118, 122
Art 4 23

Art 10 (old Art 5) 209, 371, 372
Art 10(2) 371
Art 12 371
Art 81 (old Art 85) 23, 24, 27,
28, 33, 35–46, 49–51, 53,
61, 65–67, 69, 73–75, 82–86,
88–90, 102, 103, 123, 138,
139, 143, 144, 147, 171–176,
178–180, 183, 185, 187, 189,
191, 193, 196, 197, 199, 200,
202–210, 222, 232, 234,
236–238, 245, 260, 264, 266,
268, 278, 279, 287, 296, 302,
304–306, 314, 345, 365,
371–373, 377, 378, 390, 392,
397, 399, 402–404, 412, 414
Art 81(1) 50, 147, 172–174,
179–182, 186–192, 194,
197–199, 205–207, 209,
215, 220–225, 227, 228,
231, 233–235, 239, 304,
306, 390, 402
Art 81(2) 190, 191, 278
Art 81(3) 17, 37–39, 44, 48, 50,
181, 185, 187, 188, 192–199,
209, 217, 221, 222, 224, 226,
227, 230, 231, 234–236, 239,
241, 278, 304, 306
Art 82 (old Art 86) 2, 23, 24, 28,
33, 35, 36, 38–46, 49, 50, 53,
58, 61, 65–67, 69, 73–75, 82,
84, 85, 88–90, 101–104, 110,
111, 113, 117, 118, 121–123,
126, 129–131, 133–136,
138–144, 147, 150, 154, 161,

168, 169, 178–180, 185, 189,
199, 200, 203–206, 209, 260,
277–279, 287, 296, 297, 300,
301, 314, 365, 371–374,
378–390, 392, 397, 399, 401,
404, 409, 411
Arts 83, 84 .... 65, 371
Art 85 .... 37, 65, 220, 371
Art 85(1) 182
Art 86 (old Art 90) 23, 37, 371,
375, 378–381
Art 86(1) 371, 373, 374, 375, 379
Art 86(2) 371, 375, 379
Art 86(3) 375
Art 87 (old Art 92) 23, 341, 352,
355, 361, 362, 366, 371
Art 87(1) 342, 344–346,
348, 354, 361
Art 87(2) 343, 354
Art 87(2)(a) 354
Art 87(2)(b), (c) 355
Art 87(3) 343, 354–356, 368
Art 87(3)(a), (b) 355
Art 87(3)(c) 356, 359
Art 87(3)(d), (e) 356
Art 88 (old Art 93) 23, 39, 66,
314, 341, 352, 367, 371
Art 88(2) 362, 366
Art 88(3) 348, 361, 363, 366, 367
Art 89 (old Art 94) 23, 39, 66,
314, 341, 360, 361, 371
Art 92 358
Art 92(3)(a), (c) 355
Art 93 358
Art 157 29
Art 158 299
Art 211 .... 46, 48
Art 220 63
Art 226 .... 371, 375
Art 229 64
Art 230 .... 62, 63, 74, 365, 403
Art 230(2) 63, 364
Art 232 .... 64, 365, 403
Art 234 (old Art 177) 36, 44, 65,
75, 90, 120, 139, 186,
188, 192, 193, 200, 255,
363, 366, 367, 372
Art 235 65

Art 287 61
Art 288(2) 293
Art 295 .... 350, 370
Art 296 .... 287, 314
Treaty of Lisbon 2007
(Reform Treaty) 23, 101, 371
Treaty of Nice 62
Treaty of Rome 1957
(EEC Treaty) 22, 277
Treaty on the European Union
1991 (Maastricht Treaty)
Art 2 299

Secondary Legislation

Directives

93/38/EEC (coordinating the
procurement procedures of
entities operating in the water,
energy, transport and
telecommunications sectors)
OJ 1993, L199/84 373
2006/111/EC (on the transparency
of financial relations between
Member States and public
undertakings as well as on
financial transparency within
certain undertakings (Financial
Transparency Directive))
OJ 2006 L318/17 354

Regulations

17/62/EEC (First Regulation
implementing Arts 85 and 86 of
the Treaty) OJ, sp ed,
1959–62, 87 .... 24, 36–38, 48, 52,
54, 56, 83, 172, 181, 187,
192–196, 199, 221, 231, 245
Art 15(2) 250
19/65/EEC (on application of Art
85 (3) of the Treaty to certain
categories of agreements and
concerted practices) OJ 1965,
Spec Ed 35 197
1983/83/EEC (Block Exemption
Regulation) OJ 1983, L173/1,
as corrected by OJ 1983,
L281/24 .... 226, 229, 233, 234, 369

4056/86/EEC (laying down
detailed rules for the application
of Articles 85 and 86 of the
Treaty to maritime transport)
OJ 1986, L378/4 139
4064/89/EEC (Merger Regulation
on the control of concentrations
between undertakings) OJ 1990,
L257/13 .... 24, 26, 88, 94, 140,
141, 279, 280, 286, 290,
292–296, 298, 299–301,
305, 332, 339, 410, 412
Art 2(3) 295
1310/97/EC (Revised Merger
Regulation amending
Regulation 4064/89 on the
control of concentrations
between undertakings) OJ 1997,
L180/1 .... 279, 280, 339, 410, 412
447/98/EC (on remedies acceptable
under the Merger Regulation)
OJ 2001, C68/3 .... 292, 294
994/98/EC (on the application of
Arts 92 and 93 of the EC Treaty
establishing the European
Community to certain
categories of State aid) OJ 1998,
L142/1 .... 348, 361, 367
Art 2 348
659/99/EC (on the procedural
rules for the application of the
State aid provisions) OJ 1999,
L83/1 .... 66, 342, 343, 361–363, 365
Art 2(1) 361
Art 6 362
Arts 7(6), 10(3) 363
Art 11(1), (2) 363
Art 14 363
Art 20(1), (2) 365
Art 22 361
2790/99/EC (on the application of
Art 81(3) of the Treaty to
categories of vertical
agreements and concerted
practices) OJ 1999 L336/21,
[2000] 4 CMLR 398 .... 102, 187,
189, 197, 198, 217, 220, 221, 224,
226–231, 233–239, 390, 400, 401

Art 1(a), (b) 235
Art 2(1) 228, 234
Art 2(2)(b) 234
Art 2(3), (4) 228
Art 3 .... 228, 235
Art 3(c), (d) 234
Art 4 .... 228, 229
Art 4(a) 229
Art 4(b) 229, 234
Art 5 230
Art 5(a) 235
Arts 6, 7 230
Art 8 235
Arts 9–11 228
2658/2000/EC (on the application
of Art 81(3) of the Treaty to
categories of specialisation
agreements) OJ 2000, L304/3 197
2659/2000/EC (on the application
of Art 81(3) of the Treaty to
categories of research and
development agreements)
OJ 2000, L304/7 .... 185, 197, 241
Art 5 242
68/2001/EC (on the application
of Arts 87 and 88 of the EC
Treaty to training aid) OJ 2001,
L10/20 .... 343, 348
70/2001/EC (on the application of
Arts 87 and 88 of the EC Treaty
to State aid to small- and
medium-sized enterprises)
OJ 2001, L10/33 343
1400/2002/EC (on the application
of Art 81(3) of the Treaty to
categories of vertical
agreements and concerted
practices in the motor vehicle
sector) OJ 2002, L203/30 197,
217, 224, 226, 227, 238
2204/2002/EC (on the application
of Arts 87 and 88 of the EC
Treaty to State aid for
employment) OJ 2002, L337/3 343
1/2003/EC (Competition
Regulation) OJ 2003 L1/1 24,
35, 36, 38–42, 45–48, 52, 56, 57,
65, 66, 73, 82, 86, 97, 98, 102,

103, 144, 147, 172, 178, 179, 187,
193–196, 199, 204–206, 208,
209, 234, 236, 237, 251, 271,
385, 390, 392, 403
Art 3 .... 82, 103, 179
Art 3(1), (2) 45, 103
Art 3(3) 45
Art 7 .... 57, 178, 269
Art 7(2) 49, 404
Art 8 56
Art 9 .... 57, 64
Art 10 .... 50, 209
Art 11 .... 40, 41
Art 11(3), (4), (6) 41
Art 12 41
Art 13 .... 40, 41
Art 13(1) 49
Art 14 .... 41, 57
Art 15 .... 89, 90
Art 15(3) 90
Art 16 .... 89, 90
Art 17 .... 48, 51
Art 18 .... 51, 55, 144, 203
Art 18(2), (3) 52
Art 19 .... 51, 52, 144, 203
Art 20 .... 51–53, 55, 144, 203
Art 20(6) 53
Art 21 .... 51, 53, 144, 203
Art 22 .... 41, 51
Art 23 .... 51, 52, 58, 269
Art 23(2) 59, 251, 393
Art 23(2)(a) 250–252
Art 23(5) 55
Art 24 .... 52, 58
Art 27 57
Arts 27(2), 28 61
Art 29(2) 238
358/2003/EC (on the application
of Art 81(3) of the Treaty to
certain categories of
agreements, decisions and
concerted practices in the
insurance sector) OJ 2003,
L53/8 197
139/2004/EC (on the control of
concentrations between
undertakings The EC Merger
Regulation) OJ 2004 L24/1 24,

30, 38, 45, 51, 61, 65, 88,
94, 102, 129, 140, 141, 277,
280–282, 284, 286, 287,
289–292, 295, 296, 299, 301,
302, 304–306, 310, 314, 339,
390, 391, 410, 412
Art 1 .... 45, 282, 285, 287, 314
Art 1(2) 283
Art 1(3) 283, 284
Art 1(5) 283
Art 2 295
Art 2(1) 296
Art 2(3) 295
Art 2(4) 296, 306
Art 3 281
Art 3(1), (2) 281
Art 3(4) 305
Art 4 .... 285, 314, 339, 390
Art 4(1), (3) 288
Art 4(4) 284, 285, 287, 314
Art 4(5) 284, 285
Art 5 283
Art 6 295
Art 6(1)(a), (b) 291
Art 6(2) 292
Art 7 289
Art 7(3) 289
Art 8 .... 286, 295
Art 8(1), (2) 293
Art 8(3) 293, 294
Art 8(4) 293
Art 9 .... 284–287, 289, 314,
339, 390
Art 9(2), (4)–(6), (8) 286
Art 10 294
Art 10(1) 286, 289, 292
Art 10(4) 290
Art 10(6) 293
Art 11 51
Art 11(1), (3), (7) 290
Arts 12, 13 .... 51, 290
Art 14(1) 290
Art 14(2) 293, 294
Art 14(2)(a) 288
Art 15(1) 290
Art 15(2) 293, 294
Art 21 .... 45, 288, 390
Art 21(1) 282, 314

Art 21(2) 45
Art 21(3) 45, 282, 314
Art 21(4) 287, 314
Art 22 .... 284–286, 339
772/2004/EC (on the application
    of Art 81(3) of the Treaty to
    categories of technology
    transfer agreements) OJ 2004,
    L123/11 .... 187, 197, 198, 225,
                                      227, 228
773/2004/EC (relating to the
    conduct of proceedings by the
    Commission pursuant to Arts
    81 and 82 of the EC Treaty)
    OJ 2004, L123/18 .... 38, 57, 269
    Art 14 .... 57, 60
794/2004/EC implementing
    Council Regulation (EC) No
    659/99/EC laying down detailed
    rules for the application of Art
    93 of the EC Treaty) OJ 2004,
    L 140/1 361
802/2004/EC (implementing

Council Regulation (EC) No
    139/2004 on the control of
    concentrations between
    undertakings) OJ 2004, L133/1 290
2204/2002/EC (on the application
    of Arts 87 and 88 of the EC
    Treaty to State aid for
    employment) OJ 2002, L337/3 343
1998/2006/EC (on the application
    of Arts 87 and 88 of the EC
    Treaty to de minimis aid)
    OJ 2006, L379/5 ..... 343, 348, 362, 364
    Art 2 348
271/2008/EC (amending
    Regulation (EC) No 794/2004
    implementing Council
    Regulation (EC) No 659/1999
    laying down detailed rules for
    the application of Article 93 of
    the EC Treaty) OJ 2008, L82/1 361
622/2008/EC (amending
    Regulation (EC)
    No 773/2004) 59, 269, 393

Table of decisions

Commission Decisions

Commission Decision 64/556/EEC (Constcn and Grundig) OJ 1964, 2545;
[1964] CMLR 489 174
Commission Decision 77/327/EEC (ABG) OJ 1977, L117/1;
[1977] 2 CMLR D1 .... 109, 130
Commission Decision 78/516/EEC (RAI/UNITEL) OJ 1978, L157/39;
[1978] 3 CMLR 306 102
Commission Decision 80/1334/EEC (Italian Cast Glass) OJ 1980, L383/19;
[1982] 2 CMLR 61 182
Commission Decision 82/1283/EEC (ANSEAU/NAVENA) OJ 1982, L167/39;
[1982] 1 CMLR 221 102
Commission Decision 84/380/EEC (Synthetic Fibres) OJ 1984,
L207/17 .... 195, 196, 246
Commission Decision 85/77/EEC (Uniform Eurocheques) OJ 1985, L35/43 379
Commission Decision 86/398/EEC (Polypropylene) OJ 1986, L230/1;
[1988] 4 CMLR 347 .... 173, 181, 183, 246, 401
Commission Decision 87/500/EEC (BBI/Boosey and Hawkes (Interim
Measures)) OJ 1987, L286/36; [1988] 4 CMLR 67 .... 56, 130, 131
Commission Decision 88/518/EEC (Napier Brown/British Sugar)
OJ 1988, L284/41; [1990] 4 CMLR 196 128
Commission Decision 88/589/EEC (London-European/SABENA)
OJ 1988, L317/47; [1989] 4 CMLR 662 132
Commission Decision 89/93/EC (Italian Flat Glass) OJ 1989, L33/44;
[1990] 4 CMLR 535 .... 139, 181
Commission Decision 89/191/EC (LdPE) OJ 1989, L74/21 173
Commission Decision 89/205/EC (Magill TV Guide/ITP, BBC & RTE)
OJ 1989, L78/43; [1989] 4 CMLR 757 .... 134–136, 389
Commission Decision (Case IV/M025) (Arjomari/Wiggins Teape Appleton)
OJ 1990, C321/16; [1991] 4 CMLR 854 281
Commission Decision (Case IV/M010) (Conagra/Idea) OJ 1991, C175/18;
[1991] 4 CMLR 580 282
Commission Decision 91/555/EC (SABENA) OJ 1991, L300/48 358
Commission Decision 91/619/EC (Aerospatiale/Alenia/de Havilland)
(Case IV/M53) OJ 1991, L334/42, [1992] 4 CMLR M2 300

Commission Decision (Case IV/M160) (Elf Atochem/Rohm and Haas)
OJ 1992, C201/27 305
Commission Decision (Case IV/M229) (Thomas Cook/LTU/West LB)
OJ 1992, C199/16 282
Commission Decision 92/213/EC (British Midland/Aer Lingus)
OJ 1992, L96/34 .... 122, 132, 134
Commission Decision 92/553/EC (Nestlé/Perrier) (Case IV/M190)
OJ 1992, L356/1; [1993] 4 CMLR M17 300
Commission Decision 93/82/EC (Cewal) OJ 1993, L34/20;
[1995] 5 CMLR 198 139
Commission Decision 94/19/EC (Sea Containers v Stena Sealink – interim
measures) OJ 1994, L15/8 .... 131, 133
Commission Decision 94/118/EC (Aer Lingus) OJ 1994, L54/30 351
Commission Decision 94/208/EC (Mannesmann/Valourec/Ilva)
(Case IV/M315) 0] 1994, L102/15 300
Commission Decision 94/449/EC (Kali and Salz/MdK/Treuhand)
(Case 1V/M308) OJ 1994, L168/38 300
Commission Decision 94/559/EC (PVC) OJ 1994, L239/14 173
Commission Decision 94/601/EC (Cartonboard) OJ 1994, L243 173
Commission Decision 94/653/EC (Air France) OJ 1994, L254/73 359
Commission Decision 94/696/EC (Olympic Airways) OJ 1994, L273/22 357
Commission Decision 94/810/ECSC, EEC, OJ 1994, L330/67 57
Commission Decision (Case IV/M511) (Texaco/Norsk Hydro)
OJ 1995, C23/3 305
Commission Decision 95/188/EEC (COAP1) OJ 1995, L122/37;
[1995] 5 CMLR 468 176
Commission Decision 95/354/EC (Mercedes/Benz/Kassbohrer)
(CaseIV/M477) OJ 1995, L211/1 298
Commission Decision (Case IV/M722) (Téneo/Merill Lynch/Bankers Trust)
OJ 1996, C159/4 305
Commission Decision (Case IV/M764) (St Gobain/Poliet) OJ (1996) C-225/08 281
Commission Decision (Case IV/M777) (Mercedes Benz/Kassbohrer)
(1996) unreported 298
Commission Decision 96/435/EC (Kimberly-Clark/Scott Paper)
(Case IV/M623) OJ 1996, L183/01 294
Commission Decision 96/478/EEC (Adalat) OJ 1996, L201/1;
[1996] CMLR 416 123
Commission Decision 97/26/EC (Gencor/Lonrho) (Case IV/M619)
OJ 1997, L11/30 307
Commission Decision 97/610/EC (St Gobain/Wacker-Chemie/NOM)
(Case IV/M774) OJ 1996, L247/1 298
Commission Decision 97/624/EC (Irish Sugar plc) OJ 1999, L258/11 .... 125, 127
Commission Decision 97/816/EC (Boeing/McDonnell Douglas)
(Case IV/M877) OJ 1997, L336/16 .... 9, 307, 387
Commission Decision 98/531/EC (Van Den Bergh Foods) OJ 1998, L246/1 8
Commission Decision (Case IV/JV15, IP/99/209) (BT/AT&T) 30 March 1999 305
Commission Decision (Case 1V/M1430) (Vodafone/Airtouch)
OJ 1999, C295/2 292

Commission Decision 2000/74/EC (Virgin/British Airways) OJ 2000, L30/1,
    confirmed on appeal in Case T-219/99 [2003] ECR II-5917, and
    subsequently by the ECJ in Case C-95/04 P [2007] ECR I-2331 5
Commission Decision 2000/276/EC (Airtours/First Choice) (Case IV/M1524)
    OJ 2000, L93/1 ....294, 300, 302
Commission Decision 2000/475/EC (CECED) OJ 2000, L187/47 ....194, 195
Commission Decision 2001/418/EC (Amino Acids) OJ 2001, L152/24 173
Commission Decision 2001/462/EC, OJ 2001, L162/21 57
Commission Decision 2001/718/EC (AOL/Time Warner) (Case IV/M1845)
    OJ 2001, L268/28 ....295, 307, 387
Commission Decision 2002/165/EC (NDC Health/IMS Health: Interim
    Measures) OJ 2002, L59/18, subsequently withdrawn 135
Commission Decision 2002/405/EC (Michelin) OJ 2002, L143/1 125
Commission Decision (Case IV/M3003) (Electrabel/Energia Italiana/
    Interpower) OJ 2003, C25/2 305
Commission Decision 2003/2/EC (Vitamins) OJ 2003, L6/1 59
Commission Decision 2003/174/EC (NDC Health/IMS Health: Interim
    measures) OJ 2003, L268/69 135
Commission Decision 2003/675/EC (Video Games/Nintendo)
    OJ 2003, L255/33 183
Commission Decision (Case IV/M3333) (Sony/Bertelsmann) (4064)
    OJ 2004, C13/15 ....293, 302
Commission Decision 2004/134/EC (GE/Honeywell) (Case IV/M/2220)
    OJ 2004, L48/1 ....10, 94, 302, 307, 320, 387
Commission Decision 2004/393/EC (Advantages Granted by the Walloon
    Region and Brussels South Charleroi Airport to the Airline Ryanair in
    Connection with its Installation at Charleroi) OJ 2004, L137/1 ....10, 342
Commission Decision 2004/420/EC (Carbon & Graphite) OJ 2004, L125/45 252
Commission Decision 2004/900/EC (Microsoft) 5, 117, 122, 399
Commission Decision Case COMP/M.3986 (Gas Natural/Endesa)
    15 November 2005 288
Commission Decision 2005/842/EC (on the application of Article 86(2) of the
    EC Treaty to State aid in the form of public service compensation granted
    to certain undertakings entrusted with the operation of services of general
    economic interest) OJ 2005, L312/67 354
Commission Decision (Case COMP/M.3916) (T-Mobile Austria/Tele.ring)
    C (2006) 1695 final, 26 April 2006 297
Commission Decision (Case COMP/M.4110) (E.ON/Endesa) 25 April 2006,
    and Case COMP/M.4197, 20 December 2006 288
Commission Decision 2006/460/EC (Specialty Graphite) OJ 2006, L180/20 252
Commission Decision (C (2007) 512 final) (PO/Elevators and Escalators)
    21 February 2007 ....7, 264
Commission Decision 2007/53/EC (Microsoft)
    OJ 2007, L32/23 ....5, 59, 129, 135, 136, 387

DGFT Decisions

DGFT Decision CA98/2/2001 (Napp Pharmaceutical Holdings Limited and
    Subsidiaries (Napp)) 30 March 2001, [2001] CAT 1 ....75, 120, 148

DCFT Decision CA98/4/2001 (Consignia plc and Postal Preference Service
    Ltd) 15 June 2001 153
DGFT Decision CA98/5/2001 (Case CF/99/1200/E) (Predation by Aberdeen
    Journals Ltd) 16 July 2001 71
DGFT Decision CA98/11/2002 (Case CP/0829–01) (North & West Belfast
    Health and Social Services Trust) 30 April 2002 377
DGFT Decision CA98/12/2002 (Case CP/0717/01) (John Bruce (UK) Ltd,
    Fleet Parts Ltd and Truck and Trailer Components) 13 May 2002 .... 214, 215
DGFT Decision CA98/14/2002 (Predation by Aberdeen Journals Ltd)
    16 September 2002 .... 71, 149
DGFT Decision CA98/16/2002 (General Insurance Standards Council)
    13 November 2002 .... 168, 213
DGFT Decision CA98/2/2003 (Case CP/0480–01) (Hasbro UK Ltd, Argos
    Ltd and Littlewoods Ltd) 19 February 2003 215
DGFT Decision CA98/3/2003 (Case CP/0488–01) (Exclusionary Behaviour
    by Genzyme Ltd) 27 March 2003 151
DGFT Decision CA98/04/2003 (Case CP/0809–01) (Lladró Comercial SA
    and UK retailers) 31 March 2003 215
DGFT Decision CA98/06/2003 (Case CP/0871/01) (Price-Fixing of Replica
    Football Kit) 1 August 2003; on appeal, reduced JJB's fine to £6.7m,
    Manchester United's fine to £1.5m, and Umbro's fine to £5.3m
    ([2005] CAT 22). 72

OFT Decisions

OFT Decision CA98/9/2002 (Case CP/1163–00) (Market Sharing by
    Arriva plc and FirstGroup plc) 30 January 2002 205
OFT Decision CA98/04/2003 (Case CP/0809–01) (Agreements between
    Lladro Comercia SA and UK Retailers Fixing the Price of Porcelain and
    Stonework Figurines) 31 March 2003 215
OFT Decision CA98/06/2003 (Case CP/0871/01) (Price-Fixing of Replica
    Football Kit) 1 August 2003; on appeal on appeal from [2004] CAT 24,
    [2005] CAT 13, [2004] CAT 17 [2005] CAT 22 .... 18, 215, 216
OFT Decision CA98/07/2003 (Case CP/1761/02) (El Du Pont de Nemours &
    Co and Op Graphics (Holography) Ltd) 9 September 2003 148
OFT Decision CA98/08/2003 (Case CP/0480/01) (Agreements between
    Hasbro UK Ltd, Argos Ltd and Littlewoods Ltd Fixing the Price of
    Hasbro Toys and Games) 21 November 2003; on appeal CAT Cases
    1014/1/1/03 and 1015/1/1/03 (Argos Ltd and Littlewoods Ltd v OFT)
    [2004] CAT 13 .... 72, 215, 216
OFT Decision CA98/09/2003 (Case CE/1836–02) (BetterCare Group Ltd/
    North & West Belfast Health & Social Services Trust)
    18 December 2003 .... 151, 377
OFT Decision CA98/05/2004 (Case CP/0361–01) (First Edinburgh/Lothian)
    29 April 2004 148
OFT Decision CA98/01/2006 (Joined Cases CE/3123–03 and CE/3645–03)
    (Collusive Tendering for flat roof and car park surfacing contracts in
    England and Scotland) OFT press release 34/06, 23 February 2006 72

OFT Decision CA98/05/2006 (Exchange of information on future fees by certain independent fee-paying schools) 20 November 2006 .... 262, 270
OFT Decision CA98/00/2007 (Lloyds Pharmacy/Pharmacy Care Centres) 18 January 2007 317
OFT Decision CA98/00/2007 (Flybe Group/BA Connect) 7 February 2007 320

Competition Commission Reports

Lloyds TSB/Abbey National Cm 5208, 2001 319

Monopolies and Mergers Commission Reports

Eurocanadian Shipholdings/Furness Withy/Manchester Liners (1975–76) HCP 639 316
South Yorkshire Transport Ltd Acquisitions, Cm 1166, 1990 317
Stagecoach Holdings plc/Lancaster City Transport Ltd, Cm 2423, 1993 315

Press Releases

Commission Press Releases

Commission Press Release IP/99/209 (BT/AT&T) (Case IV/JV15) 30 March 1999 305
Commission Press Release 1P/00/1145 (AOL/Time Warner) (Case IV/M1845) OJ 2000, C73/4 307
Commission Press Release IP/01/939, 3 July 2001 10
Commission Press Release IP/01/1625 (Vitamins) OJ 2003, L6/1 .... 59, 216
Commission Press Release IP/04/157 (Ryanair v Commission) pending 10, 342
Commission Press Release 1P/04/194 (Case IV/M3280) (Air France/KLM) OJ 2004, C60/5 292
Commission Press Release IP/04/200 (Sony/Bertelsmann) OJ 2004, C13/15 .... 293, 302
Commission Press Release IP/04/382 (Microsoft) 24 March 2004 111
Commission Press Release IP/04/856, 7 July 2004 360
Commission Press Release IP/04/959 (Sony/Bertelsmann) OJ 2004, C13/15 302
Commission Press Release IP/05/680 7 June 2005 .... 368, 391
Commission Press Release IP/06/1418 (Abertis/Autostrade) 18 October 2006 288
Commission Press Release IP/07/209 (PO/Elevators and Escalators) 21 February 2007 .... 7, 59, 264
Commission Press Release IP/07/1437 (Sony/Bertelsmann) 292
Commission Press Release IP/07/1572, 23 October 2007 352
Commission Press Release IP/07/1608 (Antitrust) 26 October 2007 .... 59, 270
Commission Press Release, IP/07/1609, 26 October 2007 363
Commission Press Release IP/07/1667 (Financial Transparency Directive) 9 November 2007 354
Commission Press Release IP/07/1802, 29 November 2007 371
Commission Press Release IP/07/1859, 5 December 2007 .... 10, 371
Commission Press Release IP/08/24, 10 January 2008 353
Commission Press Release IP/08/49 (Antitrust) 16 January 2008 48

Commission Press Release IP/08/318 (Antitrust) 27 February 2008 .... 5, 399
Commission Press Release IP/08/1110, 7 July 2008 .... 343, 355, 368

Competition Commission Press Releases

Competition Commission Press Release 70/05, Robert Wiseman Dairies
    4 November 2005 323
Competition Commission Press Release 33/06, 15 June 2006 159
Competition Commission Press Release 57/07, BAA Airports Market
    Investigation – Issues statement, 9 August 2007 159
Competition Commission Press Release 61/07, Groceries Market –
    Provisional Findings, 31 October 2007 159
Competition Commission Press Release 18/08, PPI – Provisional Findings,
    5 June 2008 159

DTI Press Releases

DTI Press Release, P/90/576 324
DTI Press Release, P/96/408 324
DTI Press Release, P/97/293 330
DTI Press Release, P/98/397, 20 May 1998 80
DTI Press Release, P/98/713, 23 September 1998 331
DTI Press Release, P/99/018, 11 January 1999 319
DTI Press Release, P/99/309, 9 April 1999 .... 8, 17, 331
DTI Press Release, P/99/690, 6 August 1999 309
DTI Press Release, P/99/1036, 16 December 1999 326
DTI Press Release, P/99/1054, 22 December 1999 324
DTI Press Release, P/2000/509, 20 July 2000 166
DTI Press Release, P/2000/549, 1 August 2000 164
DTI Press Release, P/2000/863, 22 December 2000 .... 168, 337
DTI Press Release, P/2001/11, 3 January 2001 331
DTI Press Release, P/2001/362, 10 July 2001 319
DTI Press Release, P/2003/500, 14 November 2003 332
DTI Press Release, P/2003/561 332

OFT Press Releases

OFT Press Release, 12/99, 19 April 1999 211
OFT Press Release, 46/00, 21 November 2000 211
OFT Press Release, 03/01, 26 January 2001 212
OFT Press Release, 101/04, 28 June 2004 69
OFT Press Release 29/05, 16 February 2005 286
OFT Press Release 144/05, 2 August 2005 324
OFT Press Release 34/06, 23 February 2006 72
OFT Press Release 88/06, 19 May 2006 270
OFT Press Release 162/06, 20 November 2006 324
OFT Press Release 166/06, 23 November 2006 73
OFT Press Release 16/07, 7 February 2007 320
OFT Press Release 49/07, 22 March 2007 73

OFT Press Release 113/07, 1 August 2007 .... 7, 72, 82, 267, 270
OFT Press Release 162/07, 26 November 2007 .... 89, 406
OFT Press Release 170/07, 7 December 2007 .... 7, 73, 270
OFT Press Release 178/07, 19 December 2007 396
OFT Press Release 180/07, 20 December 2007 322
OFT Press Release 8/08, 16 January 2008 322
OFT Press Release 16/08, 4 February 2008 322
OFT Press Release 52/08, 17 April 2008 69
OFT Press Release 54/08, 23 April 2008 260
OFT Press Release 72/08, 11 June 2008 .... 81, 259, 394
OFT Press Release 82/08, 11 July 2008 .... 72, 73, 270

Abbreviations

Journals

All ER (EC)	All England Law Reports (EC)
CLP	Current Legal Problems
CMLR	Common Market Law Reports
ECLR	European Competition Law Review
ECR	European Court Reports
Harv L Rev	Harvard Law Review
JL and Econ	Journal of Law and Economics
LIEI	Legal Issues of European Integration
OJ	Official Journal
Ox YEL	Oxford Yearbook of European Law

Statutes

RTPA	Restrictive Trade Practices Act

Terms

ACRPDP	Advisory Committee on Restrictive Practices and Dominant Positions
CC	Competition Commission
DG Comp	Directorate General for Competition
DGFT	Director General of Fair Trading
DTI	Department of Trade and Industry
ECN	European Competition Network
MMC	Monopolies and Mergers Commission
NBA	Net Book Agreement
NCA	National Competition Authorities
OFT	Office of Fair Trading
RPM	resale price maintenance

Courts

CAT	Competition Appeal Tribunal
CFI	Court of First Instance
DC	Divisional Court
ECJ	European Court of Justice
RPC	Restrictive Practices Court

Preface

Competition law, at both the Community and UK levels, plays an ever-increasing role in regulating the conduct of businesses. Competition law can affect business contracts, takeovers and mergers, co-ordinated actions, pricing behaviour, incentives to innovate and State subsidies. Competition law has assumed a crucial role in monitoring national and European markets, seeking to ensure workable competitive markets and, to a limited extent, 'fair play' on the level playing field created in the European single market. As businesses struggle to come to terms with the implications and impact of competition law, they require graduates aware of the significance and effect of the provisions of both national and European competition law. As competition law is loosely based on a mixture of economics and politics, and has tended, historically at least in a European context, to be enforced administratively, its basic tenets have proved difficult for students to understand and apply with confidence. This book seeks to provide a clear guide to, and outline of, the main provisions and policies shaping Community and UK competition law, in a structured framework. The book is designed to be user-friendly by encouraging the examination of competition law in context. It incorporates a glossary of useful terminology and sections at the end of each chapter for discussion and further reading. The book is aimed principally at any competition law students – BA and LLB – as a course textbook and will also be of assistance (as an introductory guide) for postgraduate students and practitioners of competition law.

Both authors have gained experience from their teaching of the subject, and have been particularly aware of the difficulty students have in grasping and understanding the core issues in competition law. The text places the law in context, using clear and relevant examples of the application of the competition rules. Understanding should be fostered by the provision of discussion issues and further reading at the end of each chapter. The glossary of terms is particularly important in an area of law which has links with economics. Students often find it difficult to come to terms with the technical language and terminology adopted, and the glossary aims to provide a helpful starting point for that process. The definitions and meanings provided are not intended to be technical or definitive statements on each term.

The text analyses both Community and UK competition law developments. Slightly greater emphasis will be placed on the former, due to its relative importance and burgeoning case law. However, no competition law text in a UK context would be complete without analysis of UK competition policy and legal provisions. This is particularly important since the principal provisions of the Competition Act 1998 and Enterprise Act 2002 came into force in March 2000 and June 2003, respectively; the developing UK practice under both will be detailed in this edition.

The book is not intended to be a competition law encyclopaedia. It is designed to be an accessible introduction to Community and UK competition law, which will provide suitable coverage for a full undergraduate competition law course. The focus is on key areas of policy and practice in order to enhance student awareness of the substance, importance and effect of the competition rules. The fourth edition maintains this focus and introduces more topical cases and issues to highlight the practical significance of competition law and its impact on daily life. After the introductory chapter, Chapter 2 deals with the enforcement of EC and UK competition law. We consider that, prior to dealing with the substantive competition rules, it is necessary for students to understand the basic enforcement structures, which regime will have jurisdiction, the bodies involved in enforcement under each system, and an outline of the powers and procedures involved. This is even more important, given the fundamental reforms introduced by Regulation 1/2003, to the way Community competition law is to be enforced in the future. One other point to note is that we have reversed the normal practice of dealing with anti-competitive agreements before the controls on monopoly. This reflects the concentration on the pure competition policy objective, based on its concern with monopolies, as a focus for all competition laws. There may be a minimal degree of repetition across chapters but this is on the assumption that students will read chapters to follow lectures and topics, and avoids the need to make constant cross-references.

Competition law develops and adapts ever more rapidly and there are considerable amendments in the fourth edition. A number of key developments have been covered, including, in particular: the operation of the European Competition Network (ECN) following Regulation 1/2003 and the ancillary Commission notices and the debate on ways to further facilitate and encourage private enforcement under both EC and UK law (Chapter 2); the developing law and practice under the Competition Act 1998 (Chapters 3 and 4) and market investigations and merger control under the Enterprise Act 2002 (Chapters 2, 3 and 6); the modernisation of State aid enforcement following the adoption of the State Aid Action Plan in 2005

(Chapter 7); and, developing practice under the revised EC Merger Regulation (Chapter 6). The most significant change has been the reduced focus on vertical restraints; coverage of this area is now contained in Chapter 4 on anti-competitive agreements rather than in a separate chapter. Following the increased focus by competition authorities worldwide, and the European Commission and OFT in particular, on cartels, including the enhanced significance of deterrence through the adoption of leniency programmes, the ratcheting up of the level of fines, and the introduction of criminal offences for participation in cartels (at least in the UK), we consider it appropriate and timely, in this edition, to include a new Chapter 5: 'Cartels: Deterrence, Leniency and Criminalisation'. There appear to be no quiet periods for competition law and policy and, inevitably, the law will develop further in the next few years, but this edition will provide students with a foundational knowledge of competition law and policy and assist them in understanding developments which will, no doubt, occur after the publication of this edition. It is intended that this edition will state the law as of 1 April 2008, although some later developments have been incorporated at proof stage.

Finally, certain stylistic comments regarding the book's content are appropriate. Generally, the competition rules of the EC Treaty and, for example, the Merger Regulation, will be referred to as Community competition law. In that context, where references are made to the Court, this will refer generically to the European Court of Justice unless it is appropriate to make specific reference to either the Court of First Instance or the Court of Justice. Similarly, in the book we generally utilise the term 'companies' in a non-technical and generic sense to refer to commercial enterprises. However, where appropriate, we use the terminology of 'undertakings', which is used in both Community and UK competition law and has a specialised meaning, outlined in Chapter 3, although it should be noted that the term 'undertakings' can also be used to refer to binding commitments under some aspects of UK competition law. In making references to Community case law, we have adopted the form of giving the case number followed by the case name and then reference to the *European Court Reports* where available. In the context of UK Government publications, students should be aware of the different citations which were adopted over the years in relation to Command publications, formerly referred to as Cmnd and latterly as Cm documents, although all relevant Competition Commission reports and other documents are now available on its website. The Office of Fair Trading is referred to generally as the OFT. The Directorate General for Competition within the European Commission is referred to generally as DG Comp. Finally, throughout this edition, the post-Amsterdam Treaty numbering system has been adopted; however, direct quotations and citations may still refer to the old Treaty numbering system. The table of comparison below provides the reader with a simple conversion of the Treaty Articles in this context:

New numbers	Old numbers
Article 3	Article 3
Article 10	Article 5
Title VI	Title V
Article 81	Article 85
Article 82	Article 86
Article 86	Article 90
Article 87	Article 92
Article 88	Article 93
Article 89	Article 94
Article 234	Article 177

In relation to the first edition, the authors thanked, and continue to thank, the following people for their support, advice and assistance: Cavendish Publishing and, in particular, Jo Reddy, for having faith in our project; research assistants David McGowan and, especially, Joanne McDowall for their invaluable help in checking text and citations; Professor Alan Paterson at Strathclyde University Law School for his kind provision of funds to secure quality research assistants; Professor David Milman, Professor Martin Loughlin and John Tillotson for their support at the University of Manchester; David McLean, computer assistant at Strathclyde University, for helping to revive many crashed files; Lorna Balfour, of Clifford Chance, and Madame Anne Houtmann and Adinda Sinnaeve, at the European Commission, for their co-operation on, respectively, Chapter 5, vertical restraints, and Chapter 7, State aids; John Huntley and Richard Whish who, successively at the University of Strathclyde and Oxford University, inspired Barry Rodger's interest in competition law.

Similarly, in relation to the second edition thanks were due to Cavendish Publishing, particularly Cara Annett, for helping, cajoling and supporting in equal measure, and to research assistants Michelle Calvert, Steven Kennedy and Sarah-Jane Fowler for their help in updating the book.

For the third edition, we again thanked Cavendish Publishing, particularly Sanjeevi Perera for her understanding in extending our deadlines to accommodate the many late developments as a result of the changes introduced on 1 May 2004; and research assistant, Jonathon Galloway, for his dedication in sourcing material and checking drafts.

The fourth edition requires further thanks to Routledge-Cavendish, particularly Fiona Kinnear and Kate Murphy who accommodated our tardiness with good grace. We would like to thank Bob Banbury and Chris Smith for RefineCatch's work. Barry Rodger is also grateful to Catriona Skinner for her assistance in collating materials. In this edition the vast majority of Chapters were prepared jointly; the exception being Chapter 5 which is the work of Angus alone. He, therefore, accepts sole responsibility for its errors or omissions.

Finally, we would like to thank all our colleagues and, particularly, those nearest and dearest, Susan and Lucy, for their encouragement and patience during this project.

Barry J Rodger
Angus MacCulloch

Chapter 1

Introduction to competition policy and practice

Competition law background

Competition law concerns intervention in the marketplace when there is some problem with the competitive process or when there is 'market failure'. This broad generalisation needs to be clarified in two respects.

First, public authority intervention has traditionally been the dominant mode of competition law enforcement. However, although competition law has generally been enforced administratively by national or European Community regulatory authorities intervening in markets, there has been a more recent development, particularly at the European Community level,[1] towards private enforcement of competition laws through regular court processes.[2] Nonetheless, it is difficult to equate competition law with other areas of law, such as the law of contract or delict/tort, which rely almost exclusively on adjudication by normal court processes. Administrative enforcement of competition law is currently still the norm, although we have to be aware of developments in private enforcement of competition law 'rights' in the courts, particularly following the 'modernisation' of Community law and recent reforms under UK competition law.

Secondly, the broad definition does not really clarify exactly what kinds of ills competition law seeks to remedy. In order to explain and understand the role of competition law more fully, one should assess what is meant by a failure in competition or the competitive process. This must also be considered in its appropriate context. We must ask whether all systems of competition law consider the same types of conduct or market result to be a 'market failure' and anti-competitive. The basic answer is no; this will become apparent on closer analysis of the respective roles that economics and politics play in competition law, as well as the different concerns of the principal legal systems to be considered.

---

1 The law of the European Community will hereinafter be referred to as Community law.
2 See, further, in Chapter 2. US antitrust law is particularly distinctive in that it relies more heavily on private enforcement in the courts.

However, it is possible at this introductory stage to broadly outline the types of issues that competition law will be concerned with, although the policies and specific rules adopted in various legal systems may differ. The following are the key issues concerning competition law which will be addressed in this book.

Monopoly

In purely economic terms, a monopoly is a market in which one company or business controls 100% of the market.[3] In practice, this situation is very rare. However, competition law is also interested in businesses with smaller, but still significant, market shares which enable such businesses to have power or influence over the market. For instance, the term adopted in Community law and the Competition Act 1998 is that of an 'undertaking' with a 'dominant position',[4] whereas s 2 of the Sherman Act 1890 in the USA applies to 'every person who shall monopolise, or attempt to monopolise' trade or commerce. The general concern in these situations is that the 'monopolist' will exploit its power over the market and act anti-competitively.[5]

Cartels

This is a non-technical term for various forms of co-operation between companies, which may be prohibited by competition law. In everyday use, 'cartel' signifies a group of conspirators pooling their production resources. Readers may be aware of the OPEC oil cartel as an example of such behaviour. The 'cartel' phenomenon is usually dealt with under competition law provisions regarding anti-competitive agreements, although looser collaborations[6] are also considered under this broad heading.[7] The main concern, in relation to competition, is that a group of producers will conspire or agree to act together and, in effect, will carry the same threat to the market as a monopolist. In recent years, supported by the moral argument that cartelisation be equated with theft where companies are effectively stealing from consumers by fixing high prices, competition authorities worldwide have focused their enforcement on major cartels and imposed very considerable fines.

---

3 We shall return to the complex issue of the determination of what constitutes a particular market in Chapter 3.

4 See, further, in this chapter and also the detailed consideration of Art 82 under 'Community law' and the Chapter II prohibition under UK law in Chapter 3.

5 The economic concern with monopolies will be addressed more fully in this chapter. The idea of what constitutes exploitation or anti-competitive behaviour will also be addressed in outline in this chapter and further reference should also be made to consideration of the particular Community and UK rules in Chapter 3.

6 See, further, Chapter 4.

7 See, further, Chapters 4 and 5.

Mergers

This covers the situation where two companies, and their respective share-holders, have agreed on some form of union between them. It also includes hostile takeovers, where the takeover by a 'predator' company has been resisted. Competition law is not concerned with shareholder welfare or inter-ests. There are a wide variety of types of merger which may provoke differ-ent concerns but there is a general consensus that the principal focus of competition law should be on the effect that the merger has on competition in the market. The basic idea is that two or more companies can achieve a position akin to that of a monopolist by formally merging their companies. It should be noted here that, probably to a greater extent than with either monopoly or cartel control, mergers may directly impact on politically sensi-tive 'public interest' issues, such as the resultant loss of jobs and, accordingly, competition law merger controls may not focus solely on the competitive impact of any merger.

'Pure competition' objective

Monopoly, cartels and mergers are the three principal issues of interest for most competition law systems. The concern with the potential anti-competitive market consequences of a monopoly situation is the unifying link between the three issues. In other words, the primary concern with cartels and mergers between competitors is that they will in effect achieve a monopoly position, dominate the market and exploit their position as an anti-competitive monopolist would be expected to do.[8] We consider the 'pure competition' objective in competition law to be this concern with monopoly and economic theory's prediction of the negative consequences of a monopolistic market.

However, things are not as simple as they may seem. First, virtually no competition law system bans monopolies outright. Such an outcome would seem to be the logical consequence of reliance on the pure competition objective. Indeed, debate has focused on the situations under which a mon-opolist's behaviour may be declared anti-competitive and unlawful. As very few companies have a true monopoly position, reliance on the pure competi-tion objective is not realistic. A key factor in many jurisdictions is whether or not the monopolist's behaviour is efficient. This is certainly not the same as the pure competition objective although, particularly in the US, efficiency has been developed as the primary criterion for judging monopolists' conduct. Cartels tend to be prohibited, particularly where they fix prices between com-petitors, even where the companies combined do not have monopoly power. In addition, some restrictions placed upon a retailer by a producer of goods

8 The economic analysis of monopoly will be discussed shortly in this chapter.

may be caught by some competition law systems even though they do not seek to create a traditional type of monopoly. These are known as vertical restraints. Merger control can appear to reflect the pure competition objective in that a merger may be blocked when it threatens to create a greater degree of concentration in the market. Nonetheless, pro-efficiency arguments in favour of the merger may counterbalance such concerns. Furthermore, there are also a range of other objectives that may be embodied in the legal rules.[9] To conclude, the core concern with the pure competition objective still exists through analysis of the degree of concentration in markets, but it may also be applied in tandem with other policy objectives. The potential for economic analysis and political input into the competition controls shall be examined in more detail later in this chapter.

In addition to these three core issues in any competition law system – monopoly, cartel and mergers – Chapter 7 of this book will focus on two related areas which are specific to Community law, the application of the Community competition laws to State regulation or activity, and the rules on State aid.

State regulation – State aid

This area is exclusively related to Community competition law. The coverage of State regulation and State aid reflects particular concerns of the Community system within which the Community competition rules operate. State regulation broadly covers involvement by the governments of Community Member States in the market, thereby affecting competition within the Community. State aid is an important and distinct aspect of the competition rules regulating the financial assistance which Member States may afford to companies. Both of these areas reflect the general Community aspiration that there should be a level competitive playing field between businesses situated across the various Member States within the Community.

Practical examples

Understanding these basic problem issues is assisted by a consideration of practical examples, and readers may note that competition-related issues are reported daily in the press, particularly in the *Financial Times*. Readers should be aware that competition law has directly affected the pricing and availability of goods and services, such as petrol, milk, electrical and electronic goods, ice cream, bananas, beer, contraceptive sheaths, breakfast cereals, perfume, tampons, estate agents, air travel, travel agents, banking services, Coca-Cola, whisky, cars, CDs and DVDs, TV rights for football, replica

---

9 See, further, below in this chapter.

football strips, children's board games, video games and vitamins. Competition law and policy, therefore, have a direct impact upon all our daily lives.

Monopoly

This concept could be more readily associated with the pre-privatisation nationalised industries, such as British Gas and British Telecom. Although competition has been introduced in both industries, both remain in a particularly strong position in their markets.[10] In recent years there have also been allegations that British Airways has used its strong market position unfairly to competitors' detriment. For instance, BA was fined by the European Commission in respect of its unlawful incentive scheme for travel agents.[11] Microsoft has been the subject of antitrust law litigation in the US and was fined €497m (£332m) by the European Commission in relation to its Windows operation system and required to provide vital interoperability information to its competitors.[12] On a more localised level, UK competition law authorities have in the past monitored the behaviour of Stagecoach Holdings plc in various local areas, particularly in regard to allegations of price-cutting to force out actual and potential competitors.[13] More recently, the Competition Appeal Tribunal (CAT) in the UK held that refusal to allow access to a rival local firm of funeral directors to a crematorium constituted an abuse of a dominant position.[14]

Cartels

The most obvious historical examples, in a UK context, concern agreements to fix prices of two products: books and drugs. The Net Book Agreement (NBA) raised particular controversy in 1995. The NBA was a long-standing agreement by book publishers to set prices for their titles for up to six months after their publication. This agreement had been approved by the UK competition authorities under the restrictive trade practices legislation. Although

---

10 Regulation of the privatised utilities forms a distinct set of regulatory controls which will not be dealt with in this book. See, generally, Ogus, A, *Regulation: Legal Form and Economic Theory*, 1994, Oxford: Clarendon. See, also, Robinson, C, *Utility Regulation in Competitive Markets: Problems and Progress* (2007) London: Edward Elgar.

11 Commission Decision 2000/74/EC *Virgin/British Airways*, OJ 2000, L30/1. Confirmed on appeal by the CFI in Case T-219/99, [2003] ECR II-5917, and subsequently by the ECJ in Case C-95/04 P [2007] ECR I-2331.

12 Commission Decision 2007/53/EC *Microsoft*, OJ 2007, L32/23. Because of Microsoft's failure to comply with the 2004 Decision the penalties have now increased to €1.4bn; see Commission Press Release IP/08/318, Antitrust: Commission imposes €899 million penalty on Microsoft for noncompliance with March 2004 Decision, 27 February 2008.

13 See discussion of this tactic, known as 'predatory pricing', in Chapter 3.

14 *Burgess and Sons v OFT* [2005] CAT 25.

its approval would appear to be contrary to anti-cartel type laws, the approval highlights the different interests and policies that can operate under competition law in different periods. In this case, the cultural argument was that price-fixing under the NBA allowed a wide range of books to be stocked by small as well as by large shops, thus encouraging new writers. In 1995, certain publishers withdrew from the NBA and the NBA was subsequently declared unlawful by both the UK[15] and Community authorities. Similar arguments and developments were noted in relation to the resale price maintenance agreement for non-prescription drugs, which Asda breached in 1996 to sell cut-price branded drugs.

Over the last 10 years Community competition law enforcement has focused on cartels, which increase prices considerably for consumers across the European market. The European Commission has fined companies involved in cartels in a number of industries, particularly those with homogeneous products, in which there is no difference between the products of different suppliers, where price fixing is easier to maintain. For example, it began an investigation, in May 1999, into eight distinct cartels concerning market sharing and price-fixing agreements in vitamin markets. On 21 November 2001,[16] the Commission found that 13 companies had participated in these cartels between September 1989 and February 1999 with the aim of eliminating competition. As a result, eight of the companies were fined a total of €855.22m. Hoffmann-La Roche and BASF were subject to particular criticism for their roles and individually fined €462m and €296.16m, respectively. The same companies were also subject to antitrust investigation in the US, resulting in fines for the companies, and individual fines and imprisonment for several senior level directors involved in the cartel.

The case also serves to illustrate the use of a key tool in competition law enforcement by the European Commission (and the US antitrust authorities), namely by encouraging whistle-blowing by the offer of leniency in the calculation of fines for infringements of competition law.[17] In the vitamins case, Aventis (formerly Rhône-Poulenc) was granted full immunity with regard to its participation in two of the eight cartels because it was the first company to co-operate with the Commission and it provided decisive evidence relating to those two cartels. By encouraging whistle-blowing, the Commission can destabilise ongoing cartels and potentially become a more effective and efficient enforcer, while using less resources. However, the Commission cannot offer immunity from civil proceedings instigated by private parties as a result of the cartel activity; there is still litigation ongoing in relation to the Vitamins cartel in various jurisdictions, including the UK. A

---

15 This illustrates the change in emphasis on different policy goals within the same framework of competition rules over a period of 30 years.

16 IP/01/1625.

17 See Commission Notice, OJ 2006, C298/1, replacing its earlier Leniency Notice of 2002.

recent high-profile example of the combined impact of the Commission's fining and leniency policies to police cartels was the fine of over €900m imposed in February 2007 on a number of companies involved in a European-wide cartel in relation to lifts and elevators, following a successful leniency application by one of the companies involved.[18]

In the late 1970s, there was prominent coverage of an alleged cartel in the airline industry. Sir Freddie Laker began operating a cheap rate, cost-cutting service between the UK and the US, a forerunner to today's budget airlines. Several years later, his company was forced out of business and he claimed that this was as a result of a conspiracy amongst other carriers, including British Airways, to collectively drop their fares. Litigation ensued in both the English and American courts.[19] Interestingly, British Airways was fined considerable sums during 2007 by both the US and UK competition authorities for its part in a cartel relating to fuel surcharges for consumers.[20] Given that Laker Airways was the forerunner to Richard Branson's Virgin Airways, it was somewhat ironic that the latter used the OFT leniency programme to confess, gain immunity from fines and ensure that BA was considered the blameworthy party in a cartel in which both were involved. Another recent example of UK cartel enforcement arose in September 2007, when a number of supermarkets and dairy processors admitted their participation in anti-competitive prices in dairy products to the OFT and agreed to pay fines of over £116m in total.[21]

Vertical restraints are not strictly a cartel-type problem, but such agreements between companies have been subject to scrutiny by competition authorities and intense debate by competition practitioners and academics. A clear early example arose under Community law in relation to the marketing of Johnny Walker Red Label whisky in the 1970s. Distillers plc, who produced Johnny Walker, wanted to sell Red Label in France and, in order to protect distributors there, imposed an export ban on its UK distributors. This ban was declared contrary to the competition rules by the Community authorities,[22] and reflected a particular Community interest in maintaining the free flow of trade across Member State borders.[23] As a result, Distillers decided that Johnny Walker Red Label would no longer be sold in the UK in order to protect Distillers' overseas distributors. This highlighted

---

18 Commission Decision, 21 February 2007, *PO/Elevators and Escalators*, C (2007) 512 final. See Commission press release IP/07/209, 21 February 2007.

19 *British Airways Board v Laker Airways Ltd* [1985] AC 58; and *Laker Airways v Pan American World Airways* [1984] ECC 296, District of Columbia.

20 See OFT Press Release 113/07, 'British Airways to pay record £121.5m penalty in price fixing investigation', 1 August 2007.

21 See OFT Press Release 170/07, 7 December 2007.

22 Case 30/78 *Distillers Co Ltd v Commission* [1980] ECR 2229; [1980] 3 CMLR 121.

23 See, further, below in this chapter, regarding Community competition law objectives, and Chapter 4, on vertical restraints.

the dramatic effect that competition laws can produce. A more recent example was the condemnation by the Commission of the practice of 'freezer exclusivity' in Ireland, which restricted the access of potential competitors to the market for the supply of 'impulse' ice cream.[24] Generally, Community competition law now tends to focus less on vertical restraints, although price-fixing in the form of resale price maintenance is still condemned in the Community. There have been a number of examples of such practices being prohibited and fined in the UK by the OFT, for instance in relation to price-fixing of replica football shirts by the manufacturer Umbro, and a number of retailers, and an agreement between the UK retailers Argos and Littlewoods and toy manufacturer Hasbro to fix the prices of toys and games.[25] Interestingly, the latter case involved the board game 'Monopoly'!

Mergers

Examples of competition law authorities' interest in mergers are numerous and can range from very localised alliances to mergers on a global scale. In the late 1980s, controversy arose, for a variety of reasons, during the protracted takeover by Guinness plc of Distillers plc, Guinness and Distillers being two major UK drinks companies. The UK merger controls played a significant, though ultimately limited, role in the process and eventually led to the takeover being permitted, subject to conditions. The affair also highlighted the potential conflict between a 'pure competition' policy and other policy reasons for prohibiting mergers and takeovers.[26]

The 'old' UK system of merger control was also seen working during the late 1990s when the proposed takeover by BSkyB of Manchester United, arguably the largest football club in the world, was blocked controversially following the recommendation of the Competition Commission (CC) that it would be against the public interest by limiting competition and exacerbating the unequal share of wealth in English football.[27]

In 2003 alone there were two high-profile UK merger investigations, one involving the proposed merger of Carlton Communications plc and

---

24 Commission Decision 98/531/EC Van Den Bergh Foods, OJ 1998, L246/1, approved on appeal by the Court of First Instance in Case T-65/98 *Van Den Bergh Foods Ltd v Commission* [2004] 4 CMLR 1.
25 See Chapter 4 *infra*. The OFT Decision was ultimately upheld by the Court of Appeal although the fines had been reduced, *Argos, Littlewoods and JJB v OFT* [2006] EWCA Civ 1318 on appeal from [2004] CAT 24, [2005] CAT 13, [2004] CAT 17 [2005] CAT 22.
26 In this instance, there was a strong, but insufficient, 'pro-regional policy' lobby that sought to prevent the takeover on the basis that indigenous control of a major Scottish-based company would be lost from Scotland.
27 See *British Sky Broadcasting Group plc and Manchester United plc: A Report on the Proposed Merger*, Cm 4305, 1999 and DTI Press Release, P/99/309, 9 April 1999.

Granada plc, both ITV broadcasters, and in the other the Competition Commission (CC) investigated the proposed takeover of the supermarket chain Safeway by a number of other supermarket chains, including Asda, Morrisons, Sainsbury's and Tesco. Following advice on the proposed acquisition from the OFT, the Secretary of State accepted the conclusions of the CC report and, on 26 September 2003, prohibited the proposed acquisition by Asda, Sainsbury's or Tesco.[28] The proposed acquisition by Morrisons was given conditional clearance on the proviso that it could successfully negotiate undertakings, relating to the divestment of 53 stores, with the OFT. Without such a divestment, the CC concluded that the acquisition would operate against the public interest. The three prohibited acquisitions were expected by the CC to operate against the public interest at both a national and local level, which, it was decided, could not be remedied by any divestiture. The UK authorities are often concerned with the competitive effects in localised markets, as exemplified by the Commission's report in February 2006 into the acquisition of six multiplex cinemas in the UK by Vue Entertainment Holdings (Ltd) ('Vue'). The Commission concluded that Vue would be required to sell one of two cinemas in Basingstoke, one it already owned and one it had acquired, to avoid the higher prices and reduced choice for consumers in that area as a result of the merger.[29] A more recent example of the application of the Enterprise Act merger control provisions involved the joint venture between Stagecoach, with its megabus brand, and Scottish Citylink. In October 2006, the Commission considered that this was likely to lead to a substantial lessening of competition on the 'Saltire Cross' routes (Glasgow–Aberdeen and Edinburgh–Inverness routes, which cross at Perth). The removal of competition between megabus and Scottish Citylink could lead to higher fares and reduced service levels, and the sale of certain services was required.[30]

During the late 1990s, Community merger controls also made headlines in relation to the airline industry. The Community authorities were involved in extensive and well-publicised negotiations concerning the proposed merger involving Boeing and McDonnell Douglas in an attempt to alleviate competition-related concerns arising from the proposed merger.[31] Subsequently, the Directorate General for Competition (DG Comp) controversially blocked the proposed conglomerate merger between General

---

28 *Safeway plc and Asda Group Limited (owned by Wal-Mart Stores Inc); Wm Morrison Supermarkets plc; J Sainsbury plc; and Tesco plc – A Report on the Mergers in Contemplation*, Cm 5950, 18 August 2003.

29 Competition Commission, *Vue Entertainment Holdings (UK) Ltd and A3 Cinema Limited*, 24 February 2006.

30 Competition Commission, *Stagecoach and Scottish Citylink*, 23 October 2006.

31 See Case IV/M877, Commission Decision 1997/816/EC *Boeing/McDonnell Douglas*, OJ 1997, L336/16.

Electric and Honeywell, which provoked tension with the US antitrust authorities that had earlier approved the deal.[32]

State aid

The most notable examples of Community competition law intervention using the State aid rules have occurred in the airline industry. There were numerous instances, during the 1980s and 1990s, in which the State aid rules were applied to the financing of airlines by Member State governments. In most Member States there exists one prominent airline, generally known as a 'flag-carrier', such as British Airways or Air France. Problems have arisen in the past, partly because some, if not all, of these airlines have, at some time, been State-owned or controlled, and also because no Member State wants to see its flag-carrier going out of business. Accordingly, there have been numerous instances in which Member States have financed and, indeed, 'bailed out' their flag-carrying airline when it was in difficulty. These instances have been regulated to a certain extent by the Community authorities. One of the most prominent State aid disputes became apparent in the early 1990s as a result of subsidies to Air France by the French Government.[33] Furthermore, in 2003 the European Commission investigated the legality of the arrangements between the low-cost airline Ryanair and the publicly owned Charleroi airport in Belgium. The Commission considered that the 'incentives' offered to induce Ryanair to use the airport, principally in the form of subsidised rates, were to be prohibited even though Ryanair argued such a move could effectively destroy the low-cost airline industry.[34] The application of the State aid rules in a UK context is recently exemplified by the Commission's authorisation of a support package of temporary rescue measures provided to Northern Rock bank by the UK Government. This case also illustrates the potential for exemption from the application of the State aid prohibition, in this instance to allow for rescue aid.[35]

---

32 See, Commission Press Release, IP/01/939, 3 July 2001; Case IV/M2220, Commission Decision 2004/134/EC *GE/Honeywell*, OJ 2004, L48/1; and, Case T-210/01 *GE v Commission* [2005] ECR I-5575. For discussion see, Burnside, A, 'GE, honey, I sunk the merger' [2002] ECLR 107 and Killick, J, 'The *GE/Honeywell* judgment – in reality another merger defeat for the Commission' [2007] ECLR 52.

33 See, for example, Case T-358/94 *Air France v Commission* [1996] ECR II-2112; [1997] 1 CMLR 492.

34 See Commission Decision 2004/393/EC *Advantages Granted by the Walloon Region and Brussels South Charleroi Airport to the Airline Ryanair in Connection with its Installation at Charleroi*, OJ 2004, L137/1, and Commission Press Release, IP/04/157. See Chapter 7.

35 See Commission press release IP/07/1859, 5 December 2007.

Economics of competition law and terminology

In order fully to appreciate the objectives of competition law and, indeed, the debate on the aims and objectives of competition law across differing legal systems, it is helpful to be aware of the economic background to competition policy. It is important to understand the significant role that both economics and politics play in the formation of competition policy. For competition law students, it is sufficient to gain a relatively simplistic appreciation of economic theory in relation to market structures, but some form of understanding is a necessity, given that it forms the basis of the pure competition strand of competition policy. In addition to outlining the pure competition objective, this section will give an introduction to some economics-based concepts, which have a bearing on competition policy, and a brief account of developments that challenge the application of basic economic theory to competition law.

Neoclassical economic theory plays a crucial role in competition policy, and is based on the presumption that society, or consumer welfare to use a more technical term, is better off when a state of perfect competition exists in a market. Perfect competition under economic theory has certain prerequisites. There must be identical[36] products; there must be an infinite number of buyers and sellers; there must be free entry and exit from the market; and full information must be available to all buyers and sellers allowing them to make rational decisions. The perfect competition model is abstract and unlikely to arise in practice due to the improbability of all these conditions existing simultaneously. The reader could, nonetheless, consider the degree of competition between individual fruit sellers within a large fruit market to reflect the main ideas in the theory. The theory is based on the prediction of different market outcomes from perfect competition at one end of the spectrum and monopoly at the other.

The theory predicts that perfectly competitive markets will result in both allocative efficiency and productive efficiency.[37] Allocative efficiency is achieved when resources are allocated in accordance with consumer demand. This arises under perfect competition because the producer is a 'price-taker', the price of the product being determined by aggregate industry output and consumer demand through the law of supply and demand. The individual company has a minimal effect on aggregate output and, hence, is a price-taker. On the other hand, where a monopolist controls the output of the

---

36 The technical term is 'homogeneous'.

37 See economic textbooks for a general description: Scherer, FM and Ross, D, *Industrial Market Structure & Economic Performance*, 3rd edn, 1990, Boston: Houghton Mifflin; and Livesey, F, *A Textbook of Core Economics*, 4th edn, 1995, London: Longman. For more specific reading on antitrust economics, see Bishop, S and Walker, M, *The Economics of EC Competition Law: Concepts, Application and Measurement*, 2nd edn, 2002, London: Sweet & Maxwell (3rd edn forthcoming, 2008, W Greens); and Wils, W, *The Optimal Enforcement of EC Antitrust Law: A Study in Law and Economics*, 2002, The Hague: Kluwer Law International.

market, the monopolist can manipulate output, thereby determining the price. The monopolist is a 'price-maker'. Perfect competition, according to the theory, results in the most efficient allocation of resources – 'allocative efficiency'. Alternatively, it is predicted that a monopolist will create a scarcity of the product in order to make excess or monopoly profits, and resources are, thus, misallocated. In addition, the theory predicts that there will be productive inefficiency on the part of the monopolist because there will be neither the incentive nor the competitive pressure to keep down production costs as would exist under perfectly competitive conditions.

What must be remembered is that the models of perfect competition and monopoly are best used as tools to provide us with an understanding of how markets would operate under such theoretical conditions. They are useful as a point of reference when considering real market conditions. Indeed, real market conditions reflect a range of competitive structures between perfect competition and monopoly. The theory is a useful starting point when identifying a core concern in competition policy – the pure competition objective – which is based on the degree of power or control that a firm or firms exert on the market. The concern with monopolies, as alluded to earlier, also explains the attention that competition law pays to cartels and mergers. However, because the theoretical true monopoly situation is likely to be very rare in practice, competition policy has generally tended to use the tenets of the theory in relation to high degrees of concentration in a particular market. Another way of describing this is that competition law is concerned with increasing concentration in markets, that is, when there are few competitors. Thus, a company with a high market share may be able to act in a similar way to a monopolist, through the exercise of their 'market power', but without achieving true monopoly. Furthermore, a high degree of concentration may lead to the problem of oligopoly[38] where the limited number of market competitors may facilitate collusion, whether intentionally or tacitly.

A further argument is that the models may not necessarily be accurate. The theory suggests that perfect competition caters best for society's needs through satisfying consumer demands, but it is difficult to prove empirically. First, the ideal state of perfect competition is in reality an unattainable goal. Secondly, although the theory predicts that monopolists will be inefficient in their production, as there is no pressure of competition, this has not been proven conclusively. Indeed, it may be argued that powerful firms are in that position simply because they are more efficient and responsive to consumer demands. Thirdly, although competition policy may be shaped on the basis of this theory and termed a pro-competition policy, its influence has waned, particularly in the US. Certain scholars in the US have adopted the concept of 'workable competition' as a means to counter the argument that the theoretical model could not work in practice. In effect, this means that competition

---

38 This will be discussed briefly towards the end of this chapter.

law should adopt rules that are not abstract, but which attempt to ensure an appropriate and adequate level of competition. This is, of course, a generalisation of the 'workable competition' school and it also begs the question as to what level of competition is appropriate.[39] This issue has stimulated a great deal of debate, notably in the US, where a particular approach to competition policy based on the analysis of the efficiency of conduct has been especially prominent. In effect, this approach seeks to assess company behaviour and is based not strictly on analysis of the effects of market power but rather on whether the particular behaviour is efficient. This will be outlined further in this chapter, but this different economic view of the function of competition law as an alternative to the traditional theory is noteworthy.

Traditional economic theory is static in that it predicts the effect of competitive markets but does not consider competition as a process. For instance, the theory is generally considered to be laissez-faire in that it allows competitive forces to have a free role. The pure competition objective has, thus, been taken to connote 'let the free market operate'. However, competition law looks to intervene when markets do not perform according to the competitive ideal. The paradox inherent in this simplistic outline of competition law objectives is clear. Competition law should seek to encourage the free play of competitive forces in the market on a neutral basis – Darwinian-style survival of the fittest. Yet, in certain conditions, competition law will seek to interfere with these forces, for example, where there may be 'detrimental behaviour', such as a cartel agreement or a monopolist exploiting its position in some way. Accordingly, neoclassical economic theory predicts the best outcome if there are many competitors. But what should happen if in the 'process of competition' one competitor wins fairly and then makes excess profits out of the unwitting consumer? This highlights that the theory may not be pro-competitive, in that it may not encourage companies to compete, and also that different policy goals are likely to exist in any system in order to help to determine when the law should intervene.

It is interesting to note here the confusion of the pure competition objective with support for a pro-competitive free market stance, which would advocate minimal market intervention. One extreme of this latter stance is termed 'creative destruction' and is related to the Austrian school of economics. This group of economists regarded competition as a process rather than a desirable end, and believed, particularly, that innovation would result from nonintervention in the competitive process. Similar ideas have been expressed through the Chicago school in the US and in UK competition policy, particularly during the 1980s.

To sum up, neoclassical theory is a guide – albeit an imperfect one – to basic analysis of competition law problems. It can be criticised as being too abstract, and alternative modern economic theories have sought to marginalise its

39 See Easterbrook, FH, 'Workable antitrust policy' (1986) 84 Michigan L Rev 1696.

basic concerns. In addition, competition law is not solely about the fulfilment of economic ideals. These economic ideals would not relate directly to rules on, for instance, State aid; also, economic theory is combined with other political and social goals to form competition policy. Indeed, an interesting debate concerns the role of economics in competition law. The next section outlines the problems of relying solely on economic theory, which it is suggested can be distinguished from economic analysis. General economic theory has problems in dealing with real world market situations, but economic analysis of particular markets and predicted outcomes may be useful for competition law enforcers. Economic analysis can be used to aid enforcement of existing competition laws and policies, but we should be wary of uncritically accepting economic theory as a pure science to guide competition policy. The politics of competition law should not, and cannot, be ignored.

Politics of competition law

It is clear that in all developed competition law systems competition policy does not seek solely to fulfil the pure competition objective of competitive markets, with cartels outlawed, no monopolistic companies and mergers between competing companies prohibited. For instance, in the Community one must note the important link between competition law and industrial policy. There have been instances when the Community authorities have approved what appeared to be highly anti-competitive agreements – market sharing or price-fixing cartels. These have been justified on various grounds, for instance, that these were 'crisis cartels' and were allowed in order to protect the continuing existence of an industry within the Community. Similar trends can be identified in both Community mergers and State aid policy. In relation to the former, there was an early debate as to whether Europe-wide alliances should be encouraged to foster pan-European businesses able to compete in the global market. Certain Member State governments have made financial contributions to major companies which have been permitted under the State aid rules, for both industrial and overtly political reasons. It could also be argued that US antitrust's more lenient approach to 'monopolistic' abuses, compared to the more interventionary European Commission line, is consistent with the very different socio-political background in the US, sometimes expressed as the 'American dream' of an individual's entrepreneurial route to success and wealth. Also, among the variety of interests that have been relevant considerations in UK merger policy, regional policy was at one stage a particularly important factor.

Accordingly, a discussion of the political goals and policy objectives forming the basis of a system of competition laws is necessary. Furthermore, these objectives are linked to the interpretation given to the concepts used in competition law. Terms are, therefore, only given meaning or content in the context of the particular competition law system.

Subsidiary questions, here, concern whether we have a scientific understanding of markets, what ideal competition is, and the extent to which we can define the role of competition law? As discussed above, there are economic theories defining and delimiting what is termed perfect competition, monopoly or oligopoly, but the fundamental flaws or deficiencies in these theories limit their applicability in real world situations, although they are extremely useful reference points.

The limitations are exemplified by the work of Robert Bork, an influential American economist and antitrust lawyer associated with the Chicago school and renowned for his important contribution to economic theory and competition policy in his book, *The Antitrust Paradox: A Policy at War with Itself*.[40] In this book he advocates that one economic theory should be at the core of antitrust policy – the efficiency of a monopolist's behaviour or the enhanced efficiencies derived from a merger. Nonetheless, it is clear that his work is based on his own beliefs as to the success of markets and the limited scope for intervention in markets by competition authorities. It has been suggested by John Flynn[41] that all scientific models, whether political, economic or other, must be aware of the 'ought assumptions' that underlie them. Furthermore, these 'ought assumptions' form the basis of key terms, such as consumer welfare, as defined by various economic and competition policy scholars. In other words, they seek to implement ideological beliefs through supposedly scientific economic models, but antitrust/competition law has to be clear and specific about its socioeconomic and political goals.[42]

Looking, for instance, at the US, we can see that there have been two dominant schools of antitrust thinking in the last 60 years, namely those associated with the Harvard and Chicago schools. The models of competitive analysis associated with each school[43] are, in essence, related to the academics' fundamental beliefs as to what is meant by the competitive process and the role of the State via the law in that process. In other words, what ends does competition law serve? This academic debate in the US can be referred to as the 'battle for the soul of antitrust'.

Importantly, this is also part of the free market/government interference dichotomy[44] as to what legitimate role the State should play in interfering

40 Bork, R, *The Antitrust Paradox: A Policy at War with Itself*, 1993, Oxford: Maxwell Macmillan.

41 In Flynn, J, 'Legal reasoning, antitrust policy and the social sciences of economics' (1985) 62 Antitrust Bulletin 713.

42 Helm, D, *The Economic Borders of The State*, 1999, Oxford, New York: OUP, pp 1–45, uses corresponding terminology of underlying value assumptions and suggests that political arguments about economic policy tend to start with ideology and progress to search for an economic rationale.

43 To be discussed, briefly, later in this chapter.

44 Discussed by Helm, above, fn 42.

to correct perceived market failures. However, again we fall back on the as-yet-unresolved issue of what constitute the legitimate competition policy goals upon which the role of the State is dependent. For instance, is the aim of competition law to protect the public interest, and how is this to be defined and quantified?[45] This leads to a discussion of the various potential aims and objectives which competition policy may wish to include.

Competition policy objectives

The 'pure competition' objective or ideal has already been outlined. However, in practice there are a number of different economic, social and political objectives which may also form part of any particular competition policy. It is often the extent to which these other policies should and do play a role that causes greatest debate among practitioners, competition administrators and academics. Some of these other policies may be termed 'extra-competition' policies or 'non-competition law proper' policies and it has often been suggested that competition law should not be concerned with them. However, this argument often comes from those, particularly academics associated with the Chicago school, who consider that efficiency should be the only criterion of legality, ignoring the politically biased basis of that preference. Also, as this introduction suggests, competition law or policy is not fixed, but is dependent, to a great extent, upon the particular political and social emphases of the legal system in which it operates. It can, therefore, be justifiably stated that, in applying the core economic thesis which informs competition law, any set of appropriate principles and policies may play a part in a coherent competition law system. Indeed, it has been recognised that the fundamental rationale for the introduction of a set of competition policies has been to promote the economy of a given country and the wellbeing of both its consumers and its industries generally. The appropriate balance must be sought between industry and the consumer, but this illustrates that the incorporation of any set of extra-competition policy objectives will be to further national interest, irrespective of the outcome predicted by economic theory. The following are examples of political objectives which may form part of competition policy.

Prevention of the concentration of economic power

This is a political ideal that relates to the pure competition objective. It is based on the idea that economic corporations should not become more powerful and influential than elected democratic governments, an influential idea at the time of the introduction of the first US antitrust statute at

---

45 For instance, the public interest test which existed in UK competition law under s 84 of the Fair Trading Act 1973.

the end of the nineteenth century[46] and in Europe following the Second World War.[47]

Regulation of excessive profits and fairer distribution of wealth

Again, this is essentially derived from the neoclassical theory's concern with monopolies. The general idea was fairly topical in 1997, with discussion in the UK surrounding the introduction of windfall taxation of the regulated utilities, and was a traditional concern of anti-monopoly laws, particularly evident during the 1970s in the UK. However, this concern has been more generally less well regarded in recent times, partly because of the advanced debate on incentives to new market entrants created by excessive profits and the ongoing criticism that redistribution of wealth should not be a concern of competition law. However, it was prominent in the CC's criticism of the proposed BSkyB/Manchester United merger concerning the potential worsening of the distribution of wealth in English football.[48] More generally, the post-1997 Labour Government introduced a high-profile 'Rip-Off Britain' campaign, which resulted in subsequent referrals to the CC concerning perceived excessive pricing in supermarkets and of new cars in the UK.[49] Similarly in the *Banking* report in 2002, the CC was highly critical of the excessive prices charged to small- and medium-sized enterprises by major banks. Nonetheless, more recently, in *Attheraces Ltd v British Horseracing Board*, the Court of Appeal rejected an excessive pricing claim and rejected the idea that competition law should regulate prices and redistribute wealth.[50]

Protection of consumers

This seeks to further the basic pure competition objective by providing the extent to which competition law should have regard to the interests of the consumer. Indeed, competition laws often seek to balance competing gains to balance the competing demands of industry and the consumer.[51] The consumer interest and the protection of consumers from anti-competitive abuses by cartels and firms with market power has been stressed as the primary objective of competition law by the competition authorities in recent years.

46 Sherman Act 1890.
47 See Amato, G, *Antitrust and the Bounds of Power*, 1999, Oxford: Hart.
48 See *British Sky Broadcasting Group plc and Manchester United plc: A Report on the Proposed Merger*, Cm 4305, 1999 and DTI Press Release, P/99/309, 9 April 1999.
49 *Supermarkets: A Report on the Supply of Groceries from Multiple Stores in the United Kingdom*, Cm 4842, 2000 and *New Cars: A Report on the Supply of New Motor Cars within the UK*, Cm 4660, 2000.
50 [2007] EWCA Civ 38, CA.
51 See, for instance, the conditions for gaining an exemption under Art 81(3) in Community law.

The recent focus on the consumer in competition policy signifies a move away from the thinking of the Chicago School who could be categorised as equating consumer interests with price competition. Post-Chicago thinking sees the consumer as wanting more than simple price competition; they also desire choice and innovation in markets. The link between consumer policy and competition policy is highlighted in the UK by the existence of one body, the OFT, which supervises both areas and champions the interests of consumers. The link is also highlighted under Community law by the appointment of a Consumer Liaison Officer within the DG Comp. The importance of the consumer is exemplified by the investigation into replica football strips by the OFT, which resulted in a number of companies, including Umbro and Manchester United, being fined for their role in a resale price maintenance scheme that clearly harmed the consumer.[52] The importance of the consumer has been further demonstrated by the introduction, under the Enterprise Act 2002,[53] of a system where super-complaints are made to the OFT by designated consumer bodies. The emphasis on the impact on consumers and the requirement to consider customer benefits in designing appropriate remedies, together with the innovation of the consumer super-complaints procedure which has kick-started a number of inquiries already, demonstrates that consumer protection has been a key focus of the CC's assessment under the market investigation provisions of the Enterprise Act.

Regional policy

This may seem to be a strange component of competition policy, but it can be understood given that competition law is part of an overall policy to promote the national, or regional, economy. Thus, regional policy formed a clear part of UK competition policy under the Fair Trading Act (FTA) 1973. Furthermore, regional policy constituted an overriding consideration in the analysis of a series of mergers, which might have proven detrimental to the Scottish economy and which were ultimately prohibited under this regional policy criterion.[54] Regional policy is also important under Community law, specifically in relation to State aid, where financial assistance may be allowed for a deprived region of the Community.

---

52 OFT Decision CA98/06/2003 *Price-Fixing of Replica Football Kit*, 1 August 2003. See *Argos, Littlewoods and JJB v OFT* [2006] EWCA Civ 1318 on appeal from [2004] CAT 24, [2005] CAT 13, [2004] CAT 17 [2005] CAT 22.

53 Section 11. In addition, ss 22 and 33 of the 2002 Act allow the OFT to decide against referring mergers if relevant 'customer benefits' outweigh the substantial lessening of competition concerned. Section 30 outlines the relevant customer benefits to be considered, such as lower prices, higher quality or greater choice of goods or services.

54 See Rodger, BJ, 'Reinforcing the Scottish "ring-fence": a critique of UK mergers policy vis à vis the Scottish economy' [1996] 2 ECLR 104.

Creation of unified markets and prevention of artificial barriers to trade

This is a political objective peculiarly related to Community competition policy, and is known as the policy of 'market integration'. It is derived from the overall aim of integrating the markets of Member States to create a more united Europe.[55] Historically, it was crucial to the development of European competition policy but is now of diminishing significance.

Small is beautiful

This is indirectly related to the pure competition policy objective in that competition policy may seek to foster the ability of smaller companies to compete more directly with established, powerful companies. This appears to have been one of the rationales which lay behind the adoption of the Sherman Act in the US. One way that this competition can be achieved is by responding more leniently to forms of co-operation between smaller firms, which might involve the sharing of technology. Competition authorities may also adopt the concept of 'countervailing power', based on the need for strength on one side of the market in order to counteract strength on the other side, the general consensus being that this may ultimately benefit the consumer. The promotion of small- and medium-sized enterprises (SMEs) has been a particular goal of the Community authorities, on the basis that such companies may start to compete across national frontiers and, hence, indirectly support the market integration policy.

These are some of the individual objectives which may form part of competition law and policy. Once we have identified the particular objectives that form part of a particular system's competition policy, one of the difficulties for competition law enforcement lies in assessing the priorities and trade-offs among the various objectives in a concrete case.[56] These political objectives inevitably have a spillover effect into the types of competition rules employed by the particular system. We will see, for instance, in the Community context how important the principle of market integration has been. Indeed, it has appeared to override many other objectives, such as efficiency.

During different periods in a competition law system's development there will be changes in the emphasis given to the various policy objectives. For instance, the last decade has witnessed many developments under both Community and UK law to emphasise the importance of the consumer interest in competition law, both substantively and procedurally. Changes in preoccupations are also evidenced by a brief consideration of the situation in the US, where the fear of big business was obvious, particularly when

---

55 This will be assessed in fuller detail later in this chapter.
56 This is often the matter which is debated most strongly.

antitrust law was introduced at the end of the nineteenth century, and in the UK, where collusive practices were encouraged in the postwar era. The marked change in approach over the last 30 years to the NBA, which was prohibited in the 1990s after over 30 years in existence, is also clear evidence of trends in competition policy, reflecting the greater emphasis on the evils of collusion.

Community competition law in practice reflects many of the above comments. There are a number of policy objectives that may be identified in Community competition law and the emphasis given to each may vary over time. These objectives inevitably affect the interpretation of specific legal provisions.

The inclusion of political objectives or extra-competition policies raises two further issues, as it suggests the necessity of some degree of discretion within the rules to accommodate flexible objectives. First, their inclusion may have repercussions on the type of remedies that will be available under the competition rules. Should the remedies be public or private remedies and should they be retroactive and punitive, or prospective? Secondly, the flexible nature of the administrative intervention in advancing those political objectives has led to calls for greater certainty and predictability in the enforcement of competition law. Indeed, criticism over the inclusion of extra-competition policies is essentially due to the unpredictability of administrative intervention in the market. Accordingly, there is a clear link between the substantive content of competition law and its enforcement. It should also be noted that, particularly under UK competition law, there has been a recent move to 'depoliticise' competition law, for instance, by discarding the focus on the public interest test, enforcing the law through fines, and enhancing the availability of private rights of redress through court processes. More generally, there have also been developments at the Community and UK level seeking to further facilitate and encourage private enforcement of competition law. This will lead competition law further away from the traditional policy-oriented administrative enforcement framework.

US antitrust law and policy

In this book we shall be focusing on the competition law and policy of the Community and the UK. However, some reference will be made to US antitrust law and policy due to its influence on the competition policy of other jurisdictions. The US was the first jurisdiction to introduce a coherent competition system, known as 'antitrust', and it produces a vast amount of academic literature on the topic. The substantive provisions of US law are notable for their brevity. Essentially, legislative provision is made in three statutes: the Sherman Act of 1890, the Clayton Act and the Federal Trade Commission Act, both of 1914. The Sherman Act is the most important. The core provisions of the Sherman Act are in ss 1 and 2, and there has been intense debate throughout the history of the Sherman Act as to the role of antitrust policy and the ensuing implications for the interpretation of those provisions.

The history and traditions of US antitrust law form an essential backdrop to the continuing debate over its role and purpose. It has been argued that 'American antitrust law is not only "law" but also a socio-political statement about our society'.[57] The political consensus reflected in the law during the early years of antitrust, and for a considerable period thereafter, was that high concentration of industry lessened competition. This mainstream antitrust tradition was also sceptical of the notion that the competitive process adequately controls market power.

The Harvard school of antitrust law and economics had its origins in the 1930s. Harvard school economists placed great emphasis on market structure as the root of market failure and, particularly, on poor performance, primarily in the form of high profits, as the result of excessive concentration of market power, which is detrimental to the consumer. Parallel to the academic prominence achieved by the Harvard school, the US Supreme Court, in the 1960s and 1970s, appeared to adopt a similar concern for increasing market concentration.

The Chicago school of antitrust law and economic analysis began its development in the 1950s and is particularly associated with the work of Robert Bork. The Chicago school tends to focus on two 'truths'. The first is that the Chicago school are 'efficiency advocates'. The goal of markets is the efficient allocation of resources and the only concern of antitrust, therefore, is to intervene to prevent the inefficient allocation of resources. The second 'truth' is that there is very little scope for antitrust law and, consequently, for government intervention in the functioning of markets. This is perhaps a logical consequence of the Chicago school's presumption as to the efficiency of firms and the functioning of markets. The Chicago school's aim would appear to be to 'keep government out' and to seek the least disruptive way to correct market failures. In any event, with the inauguration of President Reagan in 1981, the Chicago school approach was adopted by the US Government with Reagan's promise to curtail the Government's role in business. As a result of adherence to the Chicago school policy, government enforcement of antitrust was at a low ebb, although the Supreme Court never fully embraced the concept that efficiency was the only concern. The Chicago school also encouraged a black letter approach to competition law, based on the importance of legal certainty and predictability. Although the Chicago school's beliefs are still important in the US, there has been constant debate and criticism of the Chicago school's approach. In addition, there has been a

---

57   Sullivan, T, *The Political Economy of the Sherman Act: The First One Hundred Years*, 1991, Oxford: OUP, p 3; but it has also been referred to as 'humbug based on economic ignorance': Wendel Holmes, O, 'Privilege, malice and intent' (1894) 8 Harv L Rev 1.

recent rise in the prominence of a new school of industrial economics, in response to the Chicago school, which seeks to analyse strategic behaviour affecting competition, emphasising in-depth analysis of the particular market involved.[58] Nonetheless, there is a sense that, generally, US antitrust embodies an optimism about how markets work and that the 'hope for monopoly' is a driver of competition as allowing monopolies, with limitations, may create incentives to innovate. Despite differences in approach on the two sides of the Atlantic, it is clear that the focus of Community and UK competition law and its reform has been greatly inspired by a number of fundamental aspects of US antitrust law and its enforcement, namely: the prominence of private enforcement, notably involving consumers in class actions; the dramatic increase in fines imposed on cartels; and, the adoption of antitrust leniency programmes for cartel 'whistleblowers', a driver of the US DOJ Antitrust Division's cartel work.

Development of Community competition law

The earliest Community competition controls were introduced in the Treaty of Paris 1951, which established the European Coal and Steel Community. However, these were specialised rules pertaining only to limited markets and shall not be considered further in this text. The main competition provisions were introduced in the Treaty of Rome 1957. This established the European Economic Community (EEC). This is now known as the European Community, following the adoption of the Treaty of European Union in 1992.[59] Community law is a separate legal order which applies throughout the European Community. Accordingly, both governments and private citizens, including companies that operate within the Community, are required to comply with the legal rules established by Community law.

It is useful to be aware of the Treaty background, in addition to the specific provisions on competition law, partly because of what is known as the teleological system of interpretation which is used in Community law. This means that, in interpreting any particular or specific provision of the Treaty or Community rule, regard should be had to the spirit of the Treaty as well as to

---

58 For an interesting discussion on the relationship between the Harvard and Chicago Schools in the development of US antitrust see, Kovacic, WE, 'The Intellectual DNA of Modern US Competition Law for Dominant Firm Conduct: The Chicago/Harvard Double Helix' [2007] Columbia Bus LRev 1.

59 The EEC was originally formed with six Members and the EU has now grown to have 27 Member States. For further detail on the background to the European Union and European Community law, see, for example: Craig, P and de Búrca, G, *EU Law: Text, Cases and Materials*, 4th edn, 2007, Oxford: OUP; and Steiner, J and Woods, L, and C Twigg-Flesner *EU Law*, 9th edn, 2007, Oxford: OUP.

its strict wording. The following is a brief review of the introductory Articles of the Treaty.

Article 1 establishes the European Community and Art 2 sets out the central tasks for the Community as follows:

> The Community shall have as its task, by establishing a common market and an economic and monetary union and by implementing common policies or activities referred to in Articles 3 and 4, to promote throughout the Community a harmonious, balanced and sustainable development of economic activities, a high level of employment and of social protection, equality between men and women, sustainable and non-inflationary growth, a high degree of competitiveness and convergence of economic performance, a high level of protection and improvement of the quality of the environment, the raising of the standard of living and quality of life, and economic and social cohesion and solidarity among Member States.

Article 3 lists the means necessary to achieve the goals of Art 2, which include, in para (1)(g):

> . . . the institution of a system ensuring that competition in the internal market is not distorted.

It is very interesting to note that, following intervention by the French Government, the EU Reform Treaty will, if ratified by the Member States, remove the reference to 'free and undistorted competition' from the objectives of the Treaty and relegate it to a legally binding protocol annexed to the Treaty. One of the objectives of the establishment of the European Community was to prevent a reoccurrence of a war in Europe. Therefore, in order to unite the people, at least economically, the EEC was established. The Common Market, known since 1992 as the Internal Market, was intended to create interdependence between the States of Europe. However, it was considered that, in order to make the Common Market operate successfully, it would be necessary to ensure that more or less equivalent competitive opportunities existed throughout this 'integrated market'. Accordingly, competition rules were included in the Treaty to assist in the creation of a unified competitive environment and partly in an attempt to prevent companies from re-erecting trade barriers. The main competition law rules, which readers should be aware of, are as follows.

Articles 81 and 82 are the principal substantive rules dealing with anti-competitive agreements and the activities of the powerful, respectively. Article 86 contains specialised provisions relating to undertakings where there is some form of State regulation or involvement. Articles 87–89 provide the rules on State aid. Merger control was introduced in 1990, through Regulation

4064/89. The current Merger Regulation, Regulation 139/2004,[60] provides a specific set of Community merger control provisions.

Regulation 17/62 introduced a set of measures for enforcement of Arts 81 and 82, affording the European Commission responsibility for investigating and fining companies for breach of the substantive rules. Regulation 17/62 was superseded by Regulation 1/2003, which revised the powers available to the Commission and provided for a decentralised network involving National Competition Authorities (NCAs) and national courts to assist the Commission in its regulatory tasks.[61] Accordingly, as of 1 May 2004, the OFT has been a member of the European Competition Network (ECN), the network of national competition authorities applying Arts 81 and 82 of the EC Treaty alongside the Commission.[62] The modernised enforcement regime introduced by Regulation 1/2003 also includes private enforcement of competition law in the national courts, albeit with limited success to date.

Development of UK competition law

Current competition law in the UK is essentially statute-based. It was a notable feature of the development of the common law that it abstained from competition issues. The common law has tended to reflect the philosophy of Adam Smith, the famous Scottish economist, an advocate of the free market and laissez-faire in the early nineteenth century. Attempts to develop methods of dealing with competition problems in three common law areas have met with little success.

Criminal law

The criminal law is not generally considered to be the best venue in which to pursue anti-competitive behaviour, although breach of the former UK restrictive trade practices legislation, which was repealed by the Competition Act 1998, constituted a contempt of court with the possibility of fines and imprisonment for senior managers.[63] There also existed the possibility of prosecuting those involved in price-fixing or bid-rigging for conspiracy to defraud.[64] Breach of Community law may lead to 'administrative' fines of

---

60 Regulation 139/2004/EC on the control of concentrations between undertakings, OJ 2004, L24/1.
61 Regulation 1/2003/EC on the implementation of the rules on competition laid down in Arts 81 and 82 of the Treaty, OJ 2003, L1/1.
62 See Competition Act 1998 and Other Enactments (Amendment) Regulations 2004, SI 2004/ 1261, para 3; OFT Guidance, Modernisation, OFT 442.
63 *Re Supply of Ready Mixed Concrete (No 2), Director General of Fair Trading v Pioneer Concrete UK Ltd and Another* [1995] 1 All ER 135.
64 An attempt to prosecute nine individuals and five companies for conspiracy to defraud in relation to pharmaceuticals in *R v Dennis O'Neill and Others*, see SFO Press Release, 'Fraud

up to 10% of a company's annual turnover. Similarly, breach of either prohibition under the Competition Act 1998 may result in a fine imposed by the OFT; the fine may not exceed 10% of the relevant turnover of the undertaking in the last financial year. Debate exists as to whether these fines should be considered penal in nature.[65] It is worth noting that the Competition Act 1998 includes particular provision, in s 72, in respect of bodies corporate and partnerships for offences committed under the Act, such as destroying or falsifying documents to be attributed to individual officers, directors or partners. In addition, following Community law, a number of classes of individuals (for example, opera singers) can be considered to be undertakings and are, therefore, likely to face the full range of penalties. Furthermore, the Enterprise Act 2002 created a criminal offence, punishable by a fine or imprisonment, for individuals involved in cartels in order to increase the deterrent effect of the law.[66]

Delict/tort

The law of delict or tort is also of limited application to competition matters, being designed to regulate personal and property interests. However, there are various forms of competition-related delictual or tortious action, under both UK legal systems, which may be collectively termed the 'economic delicts'.[67] The most relevant, for this discussion, is the action based on conspiracy to injure. The classic example, in *Mogul Steamship Co Ltd v McGregor Gow and Co*,[68] highlights the limitations of this action. A shipping conference regulated freight in the China tea trade. Mogul joined the trade and managed to transport tea at lower rates. The reaction of its competitors was to drop their rates to such a level that Mogul went out of business. This was a classic predatory pricing case and Mogul sued for conspiracy to injure. There was a clear intention to restrain trade, but the action would only succeed if the conspiracy was to fulfil an improper purpose. Although there was abundant evidence of a cartel, there was no liability as the protection of legitimate trade

---

on the National Health Service', 5 April 2006, were thrown into doubt following the ruling by the House of Lords, in *Norris v Govt of the USA* [2008] UKHL 16 in relation to extradition proceedings, that price fixing did not constitute a crime in the UK from 1989 to 2000.

65 As in the US where the principal method of enforcement is through private actions for 'treble damages' in which the aggrieved litigant will be awarded three times the amount of their alleged loss as a result of the anti-competitive action.

66 See Pt 6, ss 188–202 of the Enterprise Act 2002. Section 188 creates a criminal offence for those who dishonestly agree with others to make or implement an agreement of the same nature as those outlined in s 188(2), such as price-fixing. See Chapter 5.

67 See Thomson, J, *Delictual Liability*, 3rd edn, 2004, Edinburgh: Tottel; Murphy, J, *Street on Torts*, 12th edn, 2007, Oxford: OUP; and Carty, H, *An Analysis of Economic Torts*, 2001, Oxford: OUP.

68 [1892] AC 25.

interests was not deemed to be an improper purpose, even if it restricted competition.

In the UK legal system, before the enactment of the 1998 Act, the most important competition action under delict/tort was that of passing off. The basic premise is that it is not permissible to confuse the public into thinking one company's goods are, in fact, those of another company. This allows an action to be brought if the public associates particular goods, or the way they are marketed, with one company and another company misrepresents their goods in such a way as to confuse the public and seeks to benefit from the goodwill of the other.[69] Passing off is one area of the present law which may be considered as falling under the general principle against unfair competition, an area of law which is more developed in, for example, the German legal system.[70] It should be noted that the Competition Act 1998 and Enterprise Act 2002, as discussed more fully in Chapter 2, facilitate claims being brought before the courts or the Competition Appeal Tribunal for breach of the prohibitions in the 1998 Act. These claims will be determined on normal principles of delictual/tortious liability as breaches of a statutory duty. Similar claims can also be made on the basis of a breach of the Community prohibitions.

Restraint of trade

The third area of common law involvement in competition law is through the contract-based remedy of unreasonable restraint of trade. This is a fairly limited doctrine which allows a party to escape a contract that unreasonably restrains their ability to trade. The remedy relies on two tests: first, reasonableness as between the parties; and, secondly, reasonableness in the public interest. The doctrine was given importance in *Esso Petroleum Co Ltd v Harper's Garage (Stourport) Ltd*[71] where purchasing agreements, which required the purchase of petrol exclusively from Esso, were considered. Although the effect is limited,[72] the restraint of trade doctrine still has vitality. In particular, restraint of trade actions has been taken in recent years by individuals claiming that long-term agreements have been in restraint of trade due to the inequality of bargaining power between the parties. Notable in this context have been claims by various recording artists, for instance,

---

69 See, for example, *Erven Warnink BV v J Townend and Sons (Hull) Ltd (No 1)* [1979] AC 731; *Haig and Co Ltd v Forth Blending Ltd* 1954 SC 35; and *Scottish Milk Marketing Board v Dryborough and Co Ltd* 1985 SLT 253. Also, note the related remedies under s 56(2) of the Trade Marks Act 1994 in respect of the proprietor of a 'well-known' trademark.

70 See, for example, Willimsky, S, 'Aspects of unfair competition law in Germany' [1996] ECLR 315.

71 [1968] AC 269.

72 See *Texaco Ltd v Mulberry Filling Station Ltd* [1972] 1 All ER 513.

George Michael's claim against Sony.[73] That action failed, although it was noted that agreements of lesser duration involving Holly Johnson and the Stone Roses were held to be invalid in earlier litigation. In practice, it appears that parties often make alternative claims under Art 81 of Community law or the 1998 Act Chapter I prohibition or the common law restraint of trade doctrine in order to seek to avoid their contractual obligations.[74]

Statutory development

As noted above, competition policy objectives can change. This can be observed in the changing attitudes towards differing competition concerns, such as cartelisation and pricing, which are reflected in the statutory developments and their enforcement. It should also be stressed at this stage that the content and enforcement of UK competition law has altered dramatically in recent years.

The first competition-related statute was the Profiteering Act 1919, which was aimed at excessive pricing following the First World War. The 1944 White Paper on Employment Policy led to the Monopolies and Restrictive Trade Practices (Inquiry and Control) Act 1948. A major concern of the administrative body established by the 1948 Act, the Monopolies and Restrictive Practices Commission, was with the activities of trade associations, which were prevalent in the UK. Following upon the Monopolies and Restrictive Practices Commission's 1956 report, *Collective Discrimination*,[75] the Restrictive Trade Practices Act 1956 was introduced, and later extended by the Resale Prices Act 1964. The only other major statutory development before 1973 was the Monopolies and Mergers Act 1965, which introduced merger controls for the first time.

The UK entered the European Community in 1973 and, in that year, the Fair Trading Act 1973 was enacted and came into force. This statute was not a response to membership of the Community, but was a consolidating piece of legislation adding a major new feature to the UK competition law regime. This was the creation of the post of the Director General of Fair Trading (DGFT), who would be assisted in their task of overseeing competition law enforcement in the UK by the Office of Fair Trading (OFT). The 1973 Act covered monopolies, in the loosest possible sense, and mergers. Further

73 *Panayiotou and Others v Sony Music Entertainment (UK) Ltd* [1994] 1 All ER 755. See, also, the earlier case of *Schroeder Music Publishing Co Ltd v Macauley* [1974] 3 All ER 616.

74 See *Days Medical Aids Ltd v Pihsiang Machinery Manufacturing Co* [2004] EWHC 44 (Comm) where it was considered that the common law doctrine did not have a different objective from Art 81 and indeed the court would be precluded from applying it to the extent that it was inconsistent with the application of Art 81.

75 Monopolies and Restrictive Trade Practices Commission, *Collective Discrimination: A Report on Exclusive Dealing, Collective Boycotts, Aggregated Rebates and Other Discriminatory Trade Practices 1955–56*, Cmnd 9504, 1956.

consolidating legislation was introduced in 1976, regulating anti-competitive agreements: the Restrictive Trade Practices Act 1976, the Restrictive Practices Court Act 1976 and the Resale Prices Act 1976. The only competition legislation introduced by successive Conservative Governments from 1979 to 1997 was the Competition Act 1980. This Act extended the powers of the DGFT to regulate 'anti-competitive practices' and also introduced a measure, latterly of limited significance, providing for efficiency audits of nationalised industries.

From the late 1980s, there was continuous debate on whether UK competition law should be reformed to mirror the Community competition law provisions.[76] In 1996, the outgoing Conservative Government published a consultation document[77] followed by a draft Competition Bill.[78] This would have introduced an Art 81-type provision in place of the 1976 Acts and added newer enforcement powers for the DGFT under the FTA 1973 and Competition Act 1980. The Labour Government, following the 1997 election, introduced the Competition Bill, subsequently passed as the Competition Act 1998. This radically altered UK competition law by repealing the 1976 Acts and the Competition Act 1980. In their place, the Competition Act 1998 introduced, as of 1 March 2000, new controls known as the Chapter I and Chapter II prohibitions, essentially modelled on Arts 81 and 82, respectively. The FTA 1973 was retained at that stage, subject to certain modifications.

It appeared at that stage that major competition law reform in the UK occurred on a 25-year cycle. However, in 2001, the Government proposed further changes to the UK competition law structure.[79] The Enterprise Act 2002 was subsequently introduced and has further reformed UK competition law, repealing the monopoly and merger provisions of the FTA 1973 and making the following changes, *inter alia*: transfer of the functions of the DGFT to a new corporate body, the OFT; reform of merger control and the replacement of the public interest test with a new competition test; introduction of a market investigation scheme to replace the FTA 1973 'monopoly' provisions; enhanced rights for consumer bodies to complain

---

76 *Opening Markets: New Policy on Restrictive Trade Practices*, Cm 727, 1989, following the earlier Green Paper, *Review of Restrictive Trade Practices Policy*, Cm 331, 1988; *Abuse of Market Power*, Cm 2100, 1992; House of Commons Trade and Industry Committee, Fifth Report, HC 249-I, 1995; see, also, *Government Observations on the Fifth Report from the Trade and Industry Committee (Session 1994–95) on UK Policy on Monopolies*, HC 748, 19 July 1995.

77 Department of Trade and Industry, *Tackling Cartels and the Abuse of Market Power: Implementing the Government's Policy for Competition Law Reform, a Consultation Document*, March 1996, London: DTI.

78 Department of Trade and Industry, *Tackling Cartels and the Abuse of Market Power: A Draft Bill, An Explanatory Document*, August 1996, London: DTI.

79 HM Treasury and DTI, *Productivity in the UK: Enterprise and the Productivity Challenge*, June 2001, and *Productivity and Enterprise: A World Class Competition Regime*, Cm 5233, 31 July 2001.

('super-complaints'); creation of a specialist competition tribunal, the Competition Appeal Tribunal (CAT); and, the creation of a criminal offence for involvement in cartels.[80] In April 2004 the OFT appointed a Scottish representative to strengthen links with consumers, businesses and other enforcement agencies in Scotland. Finally, as of 1 May 2004, a number of important changes were made to domestic competition law to mirror the changes introduced following modernisation of EC competition law, including notably the abolition of the notification system originally introduced under the Competition Act 1998.[81]

Comparison of competition law objectives under Community and UK law and policy

Community competition policy objectives

The market integration objective is a general aim of the EC Treaty and became a crucial goal of Community competition policy. Most commentators accept that market integration has traditionally been the unifying aim of Community competition policy; however, it is difficult to discern the other policy objectives that should be pursued by competition policy. Nonetheless, certain objectives have become clear in the jurisprudence of the Commission and Court in applying Community competition law, such as: the diffusion of economic power; the protection of the economic freedom of market participants, specifically of small- and medium-sized firms; and the assurance that economic resources are efficiently allocated. More generally, and in contrast to the US, the social value of 'fairness' has also been incorporated. The Community's refusal to adopt the Chicago school approach, based solely on efficiency, can be linked to these broad objectives.

Furthermore, Art 157 of the EC Treaty gives legal basis to the link between competition law and industrial policy. Similar links exist with other tangential policy objectives pursued by the Commission. Competition law does not exist in a vacuum and this is clearly recognised by the Commission. Indeed, it is instructive each year to examine the *Annual Report on European Competition Policy*, compiled by the Commission, to gain an insight into the Commission's views on the objectives of competition law. The *XXVIth Report* (1996) is particularly informative and states that:

80 The Enterprise Act introduced the first specific competition law offence but there have been attempts, for instance in *R v Dennis O'Neil and Others*, to use the common law crime of conspiracy to defraud in respect of participation in a cartel. See SFO Press Release, 'Fraud on the National Health Service. Appearance at Magistrates Court', 27 April 2006. The continuation of that prosecution has been thrown into doubt by the House of Lords judgment in *Norris v Govt of the USA* [2008] UKHL 16.

81 See, generally, the Competition Act 1998 and Other Enactments (Amendment) Regulations 2004, SI 2004/1261.

(1) . . . competition policy interacts with most other broadly based policies such as the development of the internal market, the policy on growth and competitiveness, the policy on cohesion, research and development policy, environmental policy and consumer protection.

(2) Competition policy is thus both a Commission policy in its own right and an integral part of a large number of Union policies and with them seeks to achieve the Community objectives set out in Art 2 of the Treaty.[82]

In particular, that report identified a positive link between competition policy and employment policy. In addition, it stressed that before Community competition policy could function fully it should be required to 'take account of globalisation' and 'help to develop the full potential of the internal market'.

During the process of reforming the Merger Regulation, the Commission highlighted the potential for an increased role for efficiency arguments.[83] In addition, the importance of the interests of consumers has also been stressed as a key factor in Community competition policy generally,[84] bolstered by the appointment of a Consumer Liaison Officer within DG Comp. In the future, market integration may struggle to be the predominant principle in Community competition policy. In any event, from analysis of Community jurisprudence, it is apparent that market integration is not an issue in all, or even most, cases involving the application of the competition rules, notwithstanding its persuasive effect in early cases such as the *Johnny Walker Red Label* case,[85] but even its application in this context has been limited to a great extent by recent developments in EC vertical restraints policy.[86] More recently, the Commission has focused its enforcement effort on international cartels affecting the Community market and consumers, such as the vitamins and the escalators and lifts cartels, both discussed above. It is instructive to read the foreword to the Report on Competition Policy 2006 by Neelie Kroes, the Commissioner responsible for Competition, as it provides a flavour of the current Community competition law agenda:

---

82 *European Community Competition Policy – 1996*, 1997, Brussels: OOPEC.
83 *XXXIInd Report on Competition Policy 2002*, p 4: 'A further objective of the . . . proposal is to take greater account of the efficiencies that can result from mergers.'
84 *Ibid*, p 12: 'One of the main purposes of European Competition Policy is to promote the interests of consumers, that is, to ensure that consumers benefit from the wealth generated by the European economy . . . the Commission thus takes the interest of the consumers into account in all aspects of its competition policy.' See, also, various speeches by Neelie Kroes, emphasising the importance of the impact of competition law on consumers can be found on the DG Comp website at http://ec.europa.eu/comm/competition/index_en.html.
85 Case 30/78 *Distillers v Commission* [1980] ECR 2229; [1980] 3 CMLR 121.
86 See Chapter 4 for further detail.

The experience of the past fifty years of European integration shows that fair and undistorted competition in a single market works to the benefit of everyone in terms of prosperity, consumer choice, and sustainable employment.

'Free competition' is not an end in itself – it is a means to an end. When we strive to get markets working better, it is because competitive markets provide citizens with better goods and better services, at better prices. Competitive markets provide the right conditions for companies to innovate and prosper, and so to increase overall European wealth. More wealth means more money for governments to use to sustain the fabric of our societies and to guarantee social justice and a high-quality environment for generations to come.

When companies fix prices in markets like beer or elevators, customers pay higher prices and the economy at large picks up the bill. When companies abuse a dominant position, they not only exclude competitors but also dampen innovation since other companies know that however good their products are, they cannot compete on the merits. So our European antitrust rules outlaw such behaviour throughout the Union, to the benefit of consumers.

European companies need to be able to take advantage of an open internal market, by creating efficiencies of scale and diversifying. Our merger control rules allow European champions to grow on their merits, developing into global players, provided that consumers are not harmed through reduced competition.

Our properly balanced state aids discipline prevents undue state intervention, which would distort competition on the merits, but also increasingly helps Member States to target support where it is most effective in filling genuine gaps in the overall public interest, and so get real added value for taxpayers' money.

The spirit and objectives underlying the European competition rules, and the need to enforce them effectively, remain as pertinent today as ever before. But of course the environment in which competition policy functions, changes and develops over time. European companies, employees and consumers are increasingly part of a global economy, and are having to adjust to reap the benefits globalisation has to offer.[87]

UK competition policy objectives

This section aims to give a brief background to the history of UK competition law and the approach adopted by the UK authorities involved. At no time have the objectives of UK competition law been clearly stated and defined. However, general directions about competition policy and law in

87 Available at http://ec.europa.eu/comm/competition/annual_reports/2006/en.pdf.

action in the past can be derived from the reports of the DGFT, policy statements by the Secretary of State and various policy review documents. More recently, the OFT has adopted a more transparent approach, notable by its publication of an Annual plan, preceded by a period of consultation on a draft. The UK legislative materials provide a useful example of how competition law objectives can differ, even within the context of the same domestic setting. Under the FTA 1973, conformity of market structure and conduct with the public interest test was the basic benchmark, but this broad test comprised a variety of vague economic and sociopolitical concerns. Its flexibility allowed markets to be investigated without the requirement for blame and, consequently, a variety of factors that may have led to market failure could be assessed. The utilitarian model of public interest assessment was central to a statutory framework, which concentrated on market failure and not necessarily on some form of reproachable behaviour. The public interest test was certainly not based on the need for certainty and predictability.

There was debate in the UK regarding the suitability of the public interest test and its concern with non-competition issues. The tension was noted by Sir Geoffrey Howe, as the Minister for Trade and Consumer Affairs, after the 1973 Act was passed, in relation to merger control:

> If a merger seemed likely to cause significant redundancies or to be incompatible with the Government's regional policies, the case for full investigation would be strengthened ... What I have deliberately not attempted to do is to say what weight is to be attributed, for all time, to any particular aspect. Our national priorities change. The Government's powers must be sufficiently flexible to reflect these changing priorities.[88]

Subsequently, in July 1984, the then Secretary of State for Trade and Industry, now Lord Tebbit, issued a statement now known as the 'Tebbit Doctrine'. He stated, in relation to merger control, that the merger referral policy would be based 'primarily on competition grounds'. Although retained when the Competition Act 1998 was introduced, the FTA 1973 and its public interest test have now largely been consigned to historical interest following the coming into force of the Enterprise Act 2002. The 2002 Act sought to depoliticise UK competition law by in effect removing the Secretary of State's role in merger control, and also by replacing the public interest test with a competition-based test for market and merger investigations.[89]

The Competition Act 1998 has already clearly become the predominant statute in UK competition law and policy. It is suggested that there were two principal objectives behind this legislation. The first was to harmonise

---

88 'Government policy on mergers' (1973) 13 (1 November) Trade and Industry 230, p 235.
89 Enterprise Act 2002, Pts 3 and 4, more fully discussed in Chapters 3 and 6.

domestic controls with those under Arts 81 and 82 of Community law, partly in order to avoid the imposition of a double compliance burden on UK business. The second, perhaps paradoxical, object has been to increase the deterrent effect of UK competition law by providing enhanced investigatory and fining powers. The Enterprise Act 2002, with the introduction of criminal sanctions and a specialist competition court (CAT), was also clearly designed to enhance the deterrent effect of the new prohibition-based system in the UK, while the subsequent reforms introduced as of 1 May 2004 reflect the harmonisation objective. In addition, many of the reforms introduced by the 2002 Act make promotion of the consumer interest an explicit objective of the system, both substantively and institutionally. The OFT's Annual Report for 2007/08 emphasised that the OFT is saving consumers £326m per year.

Further reading

Competition policy general

Amato, G, *Antitrust and the Bounds of Power*, 1997, Oxford: Hart.
Jebsen, P and Stevens, R, 'Assumptions, goals and dominant undertakings: the regulation of competition under Art 86 of the European Union' (1996) 64 Antitrust LJ 443.
Willimsky, S, 'The concept(s) of competition' [1997] 1 ECLR 54.

The consumer interest and competition policy

Ahdar, 'Consumers, Redistribution of Income and the Purpose of Competition Law' [2002] ECLR 341.
Averitt, NW and Lande, RH, 'Using the "Consumer Choice" Approach to Antitrust Law' (2007) Antitrust Law Journal 175.
Marsden, P and Whelan, P, ' "Consumer Detriment" and its Application in EC and UK Competition Law' [2007] ECLR 569.

EC competition policy development

Frazer, T, 'Competition policy after 1992: the next step' (1990) 53 MLR 609.
Gerber, D, *Law and Competition in Twentieth Century Europe*, 1998, Oxford: Clarendon.
Venit, J, 'Brave new world: the modernisation and decentralisation of enforcement under Articles 81 and 82 of the EC Treaty' (2003) 40(3) CML Rev 545.
Weitbrecht, A, 'From Freiburg to Chicago and Beyond – The First 50 Years of European Competition Law' [2008] ECLR 81.

UK competition policy development

Lawrence, J and Moffat, J 'A dangerous new world – practical implications of the Enterprise Act 2002' [2004] 25(1) ECLR 1.

Maher, I, 'Juridification, codification and sanction in UK competition law' (2000) 63 MLR 544.

Middleton, K, 'The Americanisation of UK competition law' 2003 SL PQ 27.

Rodger, BJ and MacCulloch, A (eds), *The UK Competition Act: A New Era for UK Competition Law*, 2000, Oxford: Hart.

US background

Bork, R, 'Introduction: the crisis in antitrust', in *The Antitrust Paradox: A Policy at War with Itself*, 1993, Oxford: Maxwell Macmillan.

Fox, E, 'The new American competition policy – from antitrust to pro-efficiency' [1981] ECLR 439.

Kovacic, WE, 'The Intellectual DNA of Modern US Competition Law for Dominant Firm Conduct: The Chicago/Harvard Double Helix' [2007] Columbia Business Law Review 1.

Pitofsky, R, 'The political content of antitrust' [1979] 127 UPLR 1051.

Schwartz, L, 'Justice and the non-economic goals of antitrust' [1979] 127 UPLR 1076.

Sullivan, L, 'Antitrust, microeconomics and politics: reflections on some recent relationships' [1980] 68 Calif LR 1.

Discussion

> Antitrust policy cannot be made rational until we are able to give a firm answer to one question: what is the point of the law – what are its goals?
> (Robert Bork, *The Antitrust Paradox: A Policy at War with Itself*, 1993, Oxford: Maxwell Macmillan)

Discuss the possible goals of antitrust/competition law and, in particular, the development of Community and UK competition law and policy objectives.

Chapter 2

Enforcement of Community and UK competition law

Introduction

This chapter deals with the ways in which Community and UK competition laws are administered and enforced. The chapter will review the administrative framework for enforcement in each system, the bodies involved in enforcement, and outline the relevant rules for investigation, decision-making and judicial review. The starting point is the European Competition Network (ECN) and the Community framework of enforcement led by the Commission. In particular, we shall address the modernisation of Community competition law introduced by Regulation 1/2003.[1] In the UK context, the enforcement structure introduced by the Competition Act 1998 and the Enterprise Act 2002 will be outlined. It should be stressed that the primary enforcement authority in the UK, the Office of Fair Trading (OFT), is entrusted with enforcing the Competition Act 1998 prohibitions and Articles 81 and 82 EC, as the UK's National Competition Authority in the ECN; these will be considered together as the OFT's investigative and fining powers for both are identical. The enforcement structure for market and merger investigations under the Enterprise Act 2002 will be considered, followed by the developing trends in private enforcement at the EC and UK level, together with the attempts and proposals to facilitate private competition litigation, to act as a complement to public enforcement and further enhance competition law deterrence. Markets, and hence the application of competition rules in relation to market behaviour, are not necessarily confined to the territorial boundaries of either the Community or the UK, particularly given the increasing tendency towards the globalisation of markets. Accordingly, the potential for the extraterritorial application of the competition rules will be considered together with steps towards international co-operation in competition law enforcement.

---

1 Regulation 1/2003/EC on the implementation of the rules on competition laid down in Arts 81 and 82 of the Treaty, OJ 2003, L1/1.

EC enforcement framework

Outline

The Community enforcement system has undergone significant reform. While the majority of this text will focus on the framework introduced by Regulation 1/2003, it is still necessary to have a basic understanding of the previous regime, under Regulation 17/62,[2] to appreciate the reasons for, and importance of, the reform. The European Commission (the Commission), based in Brussels, has an important central role in the enforcement of Community competition law, but it is also assisted by a network of National Competition Authorities (NCAs) at the national level across the Community. There are also two Community judicial bodies, which may be involved in Community competition law. First, appeal from a Commission Decision may be made to the Court of First Instance (CFI), and thereafter a further appeal on a point of law may be made to the European Court of Justice (ECJ). The ECJ may also deal with Art 234 EC references for preliminary rulings, which are received from domestic courts and tribunals seeking authoritative rulings on matters of Community competition law and which will assist them in resolving disputes that involve competition issues. Such domestic cases are the final important aspect of the enforcement system. An individual's ability to directly enforce Community competition law in their domestic courts bolsters the effectiveness of the administrative enforcement system.

The former regime under Regulation 17

From 1962 until 2004 the Commission was, to most practical extents, solely entrusted with enforcement of the Community competition rules. This was known as centralised enforcement. This task was carried out within the Commission by the Directorate General for Competition (DG Comp, formerly Directorate General IV 'DGIV'). Regulation 17 set up the framework for the enforcement of Arts 81 and 82 EC and contained provisions for investigation procedures, the Commission's conduct of infringement proceedings, general rules for hearings, and gave the Commission power to take other decisions. The Commission had the central enforcement role under Regulation 17, but its powers were subject to certain limitations. Procedural fairness and other general principles of Community law, such as a right to a hearing, proportionality and fundamental freedoms, had to be ensured, particularly in the exercise of its fining powers. The Commission's role was central to the system as the Commission retained sole control over a number of

---

2 Regulation 17/62/EEC First Regulation implementing Arts 85 and 86 of the Treaty, OJ, sp ed, 1959–62, 87.

important powers, particularly the power to grant exemptions from the prohibition contained in Art 81 EC. In the early years of the Community competition regime the central role of the Commission was useful as the Commission gained valuable experience of the way in which business was organised across the Community. In many situations the parties to potentially anti-competitive agreements would have to notify their agreements to the Commission and seek an exemption. The Commission used the notification process to gain insight and experience, and then used its decision-making powers to shape the future of the system; however, the centralised notification procedure also had other effects. Because of the importance of the power of exemption, the NCAs and the domestic courts found it very difficult to enforce effectively the competition rules; often the domestic courts would have to stop their proceedings to wait for a Commission ruling. The procedure also created a heavy administrative burden for the Commission, which considered that it spent too much of its time and resources dealing with a large number of relatively benign agreements rather than investigating more serious, and more covert, competition infringements. In the late 1990s it became abundantly clear that the administrative arrangements that had served the embryonic Community well in the 1960s were increasingly unable to deal with the pressures of a much larger and more integrated Community of 15 Member States. With the prospect of imminent enlargement, it was evident that reform was necessary.

The Commission began a process of consultation, which led to the recent modernisation reform, by publishing its *White Paper on Modernisation of the Rules Implementing Articles 85 and 86 of the EC Treaty*.[3] The White Paper highlighted the problems with the Regulation 17 regime and suggested various options which the Commission might have been able to adopt. It also sparked an enormous amount of debate.[4] The Commission's preferred option was to move towards a 'directly applicable' system whereby it would give up its sole power to grant exceptions under Art 81(3). This would allow NCAs and national courts, alongside the Commission, to enforce the whole of Art 81.[5] After further consultation on the issue, the Commission put forward proposals for a new governing regulation, to replace Regulation 17, based on

---

3 Commission Programme No 99/027, OJ 1999, C132/01.
4 See, for example, Forrester, I, 'Modernisation of EC competition law' (2000) 23 Fordham Int LJ 1032; Ehlermann, CD, 'The modernisation of EC antitrust policy: a legal and cultural revolution' (2000) 37 CML Rev 537; Rodger, BJ, 'The Commission White Paper on modernisation of the rules implementing Articles 81 and 82 of the EC Treaty' (1999) 26 EL Rev 653; Wesseling, R, 'The Commission White Paper on modernisation of EC antitrust law: unspoken consequences and incomplete treatment of alternative options' [1999] ECLR 420; and, Odudu, O, *The Boundaries of EC Competition Law*, Oxford, OUP, 2006.
5 See Todino, M, 'Modernisation from the perspective of national competition authorities: impact of the reform on decentralised application of EC competition law' [2001] ECLR 349.

the 'directly applicable' model.[6] The debate in Council, leading up to the adoption of Regulation 1/2003, was heated with several Member States having concerns about various aspects of the new regime.[7] While the main focus of the debate was on the direct application of Art 81(3), the new Regulation was also devised to update various aspects of the enforcement regime, and introduce several innovations that were not part of Regulation 17, including the introduction of structural remedies and sectoral investigations. The new Regulation was eventually adopted by Council in December 2002 and came into force on 1 May 2004.[8] The Commission has also adopted a number of other procedural Regulations and Notices in order to facilitate the operation of the new system.[9]

It may not necessarily be coincidental that Regulation 1/2003 came into force on the same day that the Community enlarged to 25 Member States. Nonetheless, the impact of enlargement, combined with the new role of the NCAs within the competition regime, creates a unique set of problems. The majority of accession States have, within a relatively short timescale, moved from planned economies to a liberalised market economy model. This made their adaptation to the modernised competition regime potentially more difficult. Some of the accession States were better prepared for their role within the ECN, as they had existing NCAs that have experience of operating prohibitions that are based on Arts 81 and 82 EC,[10] but others were not as well developed.

---

6 Proposal for a Council Regulation on the implementation of the rules on competition laid down in Articles 81 and 82 of the Treaty, C(2000) 582. See, also, Jones, T, 'Regulation 17: the impact of the current application of Article 81 and 82 by the National Competition Authorities on the European Commission's proposals for reform' [2001] ECLR 405.

7 In particular a debate concerning whether Art 81(3) EC is capable of having direct effect; see, Odudu, O, 'Article 81(3), discretion and direct effect' [2002] ECLR 17.

8 Regulation 1/2003/EC, OJ 2003, L1/1. See, also, Riley, A, 'EC antitrust modernisation: the Commission does very nicely – thank you!' Part 1 [2003] ECLR 604; Part 2 [2003] ECLR 657. Cf Pijetlovic, K, 'Reform of EC antitrust enforcement: criticism of the new system is highly exaggerated' [2004] ECLR 356.

9 Regulation 773/2004/EC relating to the conduct of proceedings by the Commission pursuant to Arts 81 and 82 of the EC Treaty, OJ 2004, L123/18, Commission Notice on co-operation within the Network of Competition Authorities, OJ 2004, C101/43, Commission Notice on the co-operation between the Commission and the courts of the EU Member States in the application of Arts 81 and 82 EC, OJ 2004, C101/54, Commission Notice on the handling of complaints by the Commission under Arts 81 and 82 of the EC Treaty, OJ 2004, C101/65, Commission Notice on informal guidance relating to novel questions concerning Arts 81 and 82 of the EC Treaty that arise in individual cases (guidance letters), OJ 2004, C101/78, Commission Notice, Guidelines on the effect on trade concept contained in Arts 81 and 82 of the Treaty, OJ 2004, C101/81, Commission Notice, Guidelines on the application of Art 81(3) of the Treaty, OJ 2004, C101/97, and Commission Notice on the rules for access to the Commission file in cases pursuant to Articles 81 and 82 of the EC Treaty, Articles 53, 54 and 57 of the EEA Agreement and Council Regulation (EC) No 139/2004, OJ 2005, C325/7.

10 For example, Poland.

Decentralised Community competition enforcement

The institution of a decentralised network of National Competition Authorities enforcing Community competition law is at the core of Regulation 1/2003.
Enforcement by the Commission alone is no longer plausible and the difficulties encountered in facilitating widespread recourse to national courts, as
discussed below, suggested that an alternative and more radical solution was
required. The solution proposed during the early 1990s was to institute a
system of NCAs enforcing Community competition law in each Member
State. The NCAs were to enforce Community competition law on a decentralised basis. Most Member States had a body which could fulfil the NCA
role and several Member States had adopted rules enabling their NCAs
to apply Community competition law.[11] In 1997 the Commission Notice on
Co-operation between National Competition Authorities and the Commission, on handling cases falling within the scope of Arts 81 and 82 of the
Treaty, was published.[12] The crucial feature of the Notice was the provisions
on the allocation of competencies for applying Community competition law
both between the Commission and the Member States and between the
Member States themselves. The Notice also provided advice to NCAs as to
how they should proceed in enforcing the Community competition rules.
Although the intention was to reduce the workload of the Commission
the impact of the Notice in practice was minimal. The value of the Notice
was particularly limited by the absence of a provision by all Member States
affording their NCAs the competence to apply Arts 81 and 82 EC. Nonetheless, the Notice did set the platform for the more detailed provisions
subsequently introduced in Regulation 1/2003.

Probably the most important aspect of Regulation 1/2003 was the provision for an increased level of co-operation between all the authorities
involved in the enforcement of Community competition law.[13] This operates
through the network of competition authorities, known as the 'European
Competition Network' (ECN), incorporating the Commission and all the
NCAs. The direct applicability of Art 81(3) EC means that many of the
barriers to the enforcement of Community competition law by nationally
based authorities have been removed, but it is still vital that the Commission
plays a central role in order to co-ordinate the enforcement activities of
the separate NCAs and oversee the activities of the national courts. The
Commission's role will now focus on co-ordinating and developing policy,

---

11 See, for further discussion of the limited UK provision, Kerse, CS, 'Enforcing Community
competition policy under Articles 88 and 89 of the EC Treaty – new powers for UK competition authorities' [1997] ECLR 17.
12 OJ 1997, C313/3.
13 See Dekeyser, K, and Jaspers, M, 'A New Era of ECN Cooperation, Achievements
and Challenges with Special Focus on Work in the Leniency Field' (2007) 30(1) World
Competition 3.

rather than on day-to-day enforcement;[14] however, it will still play a role in enforcing the most serious infringements. Article 11 of Regulation 1/2003 establishes the principle of close co-operation between the Commission and NCAs to enable the system of parallel competences within the ECN to function smoothly. It sets out the basic information exchange and consultation mechanisms, and is supplemented by the Network Notice.[15] Article 13 of the Regulation seeks to ensure effective case allocation and to avoid duplication of effort by allowing an NCA or the Commission to suspend or terminate proceedings where a case is being, or has been, dealt with by another authority; although, it is clear that the ECN has not instituted a formal system of case allocation.[16] The Network Notice sets out that most cases should be dealt with by a single 'well-placed' authority. The Notice envisages three possibilities: enforcement by a single NCA; enforcement by several NCAs acting in parallel; or enforcement by the Commission. Cases will normally remain with the authority that begins the proceedings, either of its own initiative or as the result of a complaint,[17] but some proceedings will need to be reallocated. Where reallocation is required, the proceedings will preferably go to 'a single well-placed' authority.[18] There are three key factors in determining which authority is most appropriate, and they are as follows: (a) the area in which the anti-competitive practice has substantial, actual or foreseeable effects, is implemented, or originated; (b) which authority is most able to effectively bring the infringement to an end and impose an appropriate sanction; and (c) which authority can gather the evidence required to prove the infringement.[19] The Commission will usually be best placed to deal with a practice that has effects in more than three Member States[20] or the Community interest requires a decision to develop competition policy.[21] To ensure this division of work operates effectively Regulation 1/2003 provides, in Art 11, for the exchange of information between all the authorities. This seeks to ensure that where related practices are being examined by more than one authority this should be identified quickly. When a case has been allocated to an authority, any other authorities that have received similar

---

14 As Dekeyser and Jaspers *supra* note, between 1 May 2004 and 31 December 2006, 670 cases were pursued under the Community competition rules, and the Commission was involved in investigation in less than 25% of cases.

15 Commission Notice on co-operation within the Network of Competition Authorities, OJ 2004, C101/43.

16 For a detailed discussion, see Brammer, S, 'Concurrent Jurisdiction under Regulation 1/2003 and the issue of case allocation' (2005) 42(5) CMLRev 1383.

17 Commission Notice on the handling of complaints by the Commission under Articles 81 and 82 of the EC Treaty, OJ 2004, C101/65.

18 Network Notice, para 7.

19 Network Notice, para 8.

20 Network Notice, para 14.

21 Network Notice, para 15.

complaints are empowered by Art 13 of Regulation 1/2003 to reject those complaints and terminate their investigations.

To assist in the cross-border investigation of possible infringements, Regulation 1/2003 also provides, under Art 12, for the exchange of information between authorities. In addition to the exchange of existing material, an authority can ask another authority, under Art 22, to assist it in gathering material. The information that can be exchanged includes confidential information gathered by an authority for the purpose of applying the Community prohibitions. The power to exchange information does not always include information that has been gathered in relation to proceedings under national law, if the application of national law leads to an outcome different from that of Arts 81 and 82 EC, or where sanctions could be imposed on individuals.[22] This will obviously include material gathered in the UK in relation to a potential prosecution of the cartel offence under s 188 of the Enterprise Act 2002. There are several provisions that seek to ensure consistency and uniformity in the application of Community law within the ECN. Article 11 of Regulation 1/2003 sets out situations in which the NCAs must inform the Commission of their activities. Article 11(3) requires the NCAs to inform the Commission as soon as they commence an investigation. They are also required to inform the Commission, at least 30 days in advance, of any decision being made. The information passed to the Commission may then be shared with other NCAs. These procedures ensure that the Commission should be aware of the ongoing investigations across the ECN and will be able to intervene to ensure consistency. Article 14 of Regulation 1/2003, on the other hand, consolidates the existing role of the Advisory Committee on Restrictive Practices and Dominant Positions (ACRPDP), which is made up of representatives from the NCAs, by requiring the Commission to consult with it prior to taking decisions.

The final way in which the central role of the Commission in the ECN is retained is through the operation of Art 11(6) of Regulation 1/2003. If, after being informed of the initiation of an investigation by one or more NCAs under Art 11(3) or (4), the Commission decides that the Community interest would benefit from action by the Commission, the Commission can 'call in' the investigation under Art 11(6). When the Commission initiates proceedings it has the effect of relieving any NCA from dealing with that case and reserving all future action in the case to the Commission. This has the dual effect of ensuring that the Commission retains the central 'policy-making' role, and allows the Commission to act decisively if there is a concern that NCAs may not deal consistently with an anti-competitive practice.[23]

When investigating an infringement of Community law, the NCA must rely upon the powers granted to it within domestic law as neither Regulation

22 Network Notice, para 28.
23 Network Notice, para 54.

1/2003 nor the Network Notice sought to harmonise domestic rules on enforcement procedures and powers of the various NCAs. At one stage it was considered that a future Modernisation II package, involving some form of harmonisation of national NCA powers, procedures and remedies in cases of Community law infringements, would be required. However, the ability to exchange information and engage in dialogue within the ECN has facilitated a certain degree of convergence already;[24] particularly in relation to leniency where virtually all Member States now have some form of leniency programme, and the ECN has developed a Model Leniency Programme.[25]

Enforcement of Community law in the UK

Prior to the adoption of Regulation 1/2003, the Office of Fair Trading, the NCA within the UK, was not empowered to enforce Community law within the UK; only the domestic provisions which were based on Community law were within its competence. The Enterprise Act 2002 contained a number of provisions that gave the Government powers to adapt the competition regime to fit in with the final shape of the modernised Community regime. In order to participate in the ECN, a number of measures were adopted in early 2004 and the OFT published new guidance setting out its role and responsibilities.

Paragraph 3 of the Competition Act 1998 and Other Enactments (Amendment) Regulations 2004[26] designates the OFT[27] as the authority that will exercise the relevant powers and functions of a Member State NCA under Regulation 1/2003. In addition, s 25 of the 1998 Act was amended to provide the necessary powers to the OFT to enable it to carry out the necessary investigations under both the Competition Act 1998 prohibitions and Arts 81 and 82 EC. The OFT can also impose fines for breaches of the Community prohibitions, and the Guidance on Fines has been revised in this respect to allow the OFT to take into account anti-competitive effects in other Member States when determining a penalty. Section 52 of the 1998 Act was amended to require the OFT to produce guidance on the new powers; the revised guidance, including 'Modernisation',[28] 'Agreements and Concerted Practices',[29]

---

24 See ECN Working Group on Cooperation Issues, 'Results of the questionnaire on the reform of the Member States national competition laws after EC Regulation No. 1/2003', as of May 18, 2007, at http://ec.europa.eu/comm/competition/ecn/index_en.html which demonstrates the increasing degree of convergence in Member States' procedural and remedial rules.

25 See Dekeyser, K, and Jaspers, M, 'A New Era of ECN Cooperation, Achievements and Challenges with Special Focus on Work in the Leniency Field' (2007) 30(1) World Competition 3. The ECN Model programme is published on the ECN website, http://ec.europa.eu/comm/competition/ecn/index_en.html. See further discussion in Chapter 5.

26 SI 2004/1261.

27 And any other UK regulator mentioned in s 54(1) of the 1998 Act.

28 OFT 442.

29 OFT 401.

and 'Abuse of a Dominant Position',[30] was published during 2004. Sections 46 and 47 of the 1998 Act were also amended to give the Competition Appeal Tribunal (CAT) the role of hearing appeals from OFT decisions regarding the Community prohibitions. It should be noted that there have been very few decisions to date in which the OFT, or a sectoral regulator, has applied Articles 81 or 82 EC in combination with the Competition Act prohibitions.[31]

Relationship between Community and national law

An important question concerns the relationship between national, or domestic, competition rules and Community competition law. Of course, the UK provisions under the Competition Act 1998 are modelled on the Community provisions and there are measures to ensure consistency in ss 10 and 60; therefore, disharmony is less likely. How, then, is the general potential dilemma of the dual application of domestic and Community competition rules resolved? The EC Treaty establishes an independent legal order capable of affecting Member States' governments and of conferring rights on individuals in certain instances. The basic rule regarding the relationship between the Community legal system and national laws is that of the supremacy of Community law. Directly applicable Community rules, such as Community competition law, take precedence over national law. This principle of supremacy of Community law, or the doctrine of 'precedence', was established in Community law by the important ECJ judgments in *Van Gend en Loos*[32] and *Costa v ENEL*[33] and was given effect in the UK by ss 2(1) and 3(1) of the European Communities Act 1972, upon the UK accession to the European Community.[34] Accordingly, when a conflict exists with UK domestic

---

30 OFT 402.
31 To date, the OFT has only applied the EC rules in two cases, *Mastercards UK Members Forum Limited*, 6 September 2005, in which it considered that an agreement infringed both the Chapter I prohibition and Article 81, although this decision was subsequently set aside by the CAT; and in relation to British Airways, which was fined £121.5 m for price-fixing in relation to 'long-haul passenger fuel surcharges', where a final OFT decision is awaited. There have been a number of cases in which OFCOM has found that practices have infringed neither the Chapter II prohibition nor Article 82, for instance in relation to BT's pricing of digital cordless phones, 7 August 2006, and BT Wholesale Calls, 17 June 2005. However, the Office of Rail Regulation imposed a penalty of £4.1 m on English Welsh and Scottish Railways, 17 November 2006, for behaviour which infringed the Chapter II prohibition and Article 82.
32 Case 26/62 [1963] ECR 1; [1963] CMLR 105.
33 Case 6/64 [1964] ECR 585; [1964] CMLR 425.
34 The European Communities Act 1972, s 2(1) provides: 'All such rights, powers, liabilities, obligations and restrictions from time to time created under . . . Treaties . . . are without further enactment . . . to be treated as law in the UK.' Section 3(1) provides that if there is any question as to the meaning or effect of the Treaty such a question of law will go to the Court or be dealt with in accordance with the principles laid down by it.

competition law it follows that Community competition law is treated as supreme and that the provisions of UK law cannot be relied upon.

The respective roles for the application of national and Community competition laws were laid down in *Walt Wilhelm v Bundeskartellamt*,[35] a case that involved a company that was allegedly involved in a price-fixing cartel in the aniline dyes industry. Parallel proceedings were commenced in Germany, under German law, and by the European Commission under the Community competition rules. The German court made a reference under Art 234, asking the Court if the company could be subject to penalties under national rules in respect of the same conduct that could be penalised under Community law. The Court confirmed that this was possible but that, in imposing the penalties, the national authorities must bear in mind the penalties that may be imposed by the Community authorities. The Court also confirmed the following points: (a) any conflicts between Community and domestic law would be resolved by the principle of supremacy of Community law; (b) if an NCA decision is incompatible with a Commission decision, the national authority needs to take proper account of the Commission decision; and (c) if, during the national proceedings, it appears possible that the Commission may adopt a conflicting decision then it is for the national authority to take the appropriate measures to avoid such a conflict. However, the national authorities can still apply national rules, even where the same issues are under investigation by the Commission, provided that the national decision does not prejudice the full and uniform application of Community law. For instance, the national authorities cannot condemn agreements that fall within an Art 81(3) block exemption.

The basic rule, confirmed by the *Walt Wilhelm* case, of the supremacy of Community law was fairly straightforward in principle. However, in practice, it could lead to a degree of uncertainty. The Community rules in Arts 81 and 82 only apply when there is an effect on interstate trade as a result of the conduct in question. Otherwise, only national competition rules may be applicable to the potentially anti-competitive activity. However, the effect on the interstate trade criterion has been interpreted widely by the Community authorities. As a result there was a great degree of potential overlap between the applicability of national and Community competition rules to the same potentially anti-competitive activity. The statements by the Court in *Walt Wilhelm* compounded this problem, resulting in a vague separation between the powers of the national and Community authorities. The rule in *Walt Wilhelm* has been described as a procedural precedence rule that concentrated on the status of administrative decisions, providing that national authorities should have regard to Community law decisions that are issued or expected; this may cause both delay and confusion.

---

35 Case 14/68 [1969] ECR 1; [1969] CMLR 100. See, also, Cases 46/87 and 227/88 *Hoechst v Commission* [1989] ECR 2859; [1991] 4 CMLR 410.

An alternative, and clearer, way of separating the competencies of national and Community authorities, by providing a clear line between the application of national and Community competition controls, is provided in the Merger Regulation.[36] The approach provided by the Regulation seeks to avoid the difficulties involved where two systems of law may apply to the one issue. The Merger Regulation establishes a basic rule that provides for the exclusive application of Community law above a certain threshold. Through a combination of the provisions of Arts 1 and 21, the Regulation established a system of exclusive and separate competencies for the Community and national authorities based on the concept of a 'Community dimension'. The Regulation applies to all concentrations with a Community dimension as defined quantitatively under Art 1, based on the turnover of the relevant organisations. Article 21(2) provides that the Commission alone is to have jurisdiction under the Regulation, and more importantly, Art 21(3) provides that '[n]o Member State shall apply its national legislation on competition to any consideration that has a Community dimension'. The Regulation sets clear and separate competencies for national and Community authorities to apply national and Community merger control measures in the event of a takeover or merger.

Although the White Paper on Modernisation rejected the arguments for reform of enforcement of Community law based on subsidiarity, Regulation 1/2003[37] seeks to avoid potential problems arising from the procedural precedence rule outlined above. Article 3(1) provides that, where there is an effect on interstate trade, national courts and authorities shall, in applying domestic competition law rules, also apply Arts 81 and 82.[38] This seeks to ensure a clearer substantive rule of precedence in the application of Community law and national law. Nonetheless, Art 3(3) limits the scope of the rule as follows:

Without prejudice to general principles and other provisions of Community law, paragraphs 1 and 2 do not apply when the competition authorities and the courts of Member States apply national merger control laws nor do they preclude the application of provisions of national law that predominately pursue an objective different from that pursued by Articles 81 and 82 of the Treaty.

The first part of this provision is straightforward; the second is more complicated and allows scope for the application of laws which are, for example,

36 Regulation 139/2004/EC on the control of concentrations between undertakings, OJ 2004, L24/1.
37 OJ 2003, L1/1.
38 Article 3(2) notes that agreements, etc, which comply with Art 81, are not to be prohibited by domestic law whereas domestic competition law may apply stricter standards to that which constitutes unilateral abusive conduct.

based on cultural or environmental policy even where they are in conflict with Community competition law.

Following the introduction of Regulation 1/2003, NCAs may be required to apply either or both national and Community competition law. Nonetheless, the difficulties envisaged under the *Walt Wilhelm* rule are insignificant now, mainly due to the distinct trend in recent years towards harmonisation of substantive national competition rules with Community law and convergence of procedural rules. This has not stemmed from any form of 'hard' harmonisation or legislative intervention by the Community authorities, but has been based on four principal developments. First, expansion of the European Union has been on the basis that accession countries are required to adopt market-based competition laws framed, at least loosely, on the Community competition rules model. A clear example of this exists in relation to the four Visegrad countries: Poland, Hungary and the Czech and Slovak Republics, each of which introduced competition laws in 1990–91, modelled on the Community rules. Secondly, certain Member States (for example, Italy and the Netherlands), which previously had little or no national competition law provision, have adopted legislation based on the Community model. Thirdly, other Community Member States have amended their existing competition law systems to be modelled on or complement the Community rules. The UK Competition Act 1998 is a classic example of this trend, introducing new competition prohibitions modelled on Arts 81 and 82, with a general requirement to interpret the prohibitions consistently with Community law. Finally, co-operation and dialogue between NCAs within the ECN has led to procedural convergence with NCAs assimilating the investigative and fining powers accorded to the Commission under Regulation 1/2003.

The European Commission

The Commission's main task under Art 211 of the Treaty is to 'ensure the proper functioning and development of the Common Market' and it has been described as the 'guardian of the Treaty'. It represents the Community's interests and seeks to ensure that the provisions of Community law are applied. Accordingly, the Commission was granted general supervisory powers under the Treaty, for dealing with competition law enforcement, and more specific powers, under Regulation 1/2003, in relation to enforcement of Arts 81 and 82. Diagram 1 provides an outline illustration of the enforcement framework where the Commission enforces Arts 81 and 82. The Commission has a number of members, presently one from each Member State with 27 in total, called Commissioners, one of whom is allocated responsibility for competition policy. Currently the Commissioner for competition policy is Neelie Kroes. The staff of the Commission is divided into a number of departments, each with a specialist portfolio of responsibilities. These departments are known as 'Directorates General', shortened to DG for ease

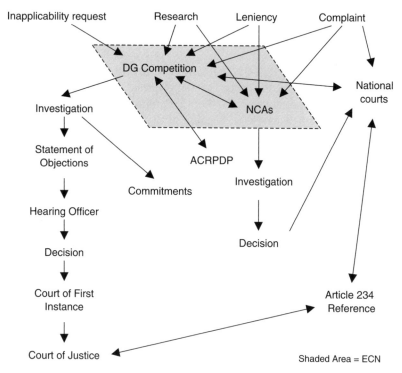

Diagram 1: The Community system.

of reference, each headed by a Director General. There are a number of DGs, which cover the full range of Community policies from Agriculture to Taxation and Customs Union. Competition policy and enforcement is allocated to the DG for Competition and the current Director General is Philip Lowe, who follows two German Director Generals, Alexander Schaub and Claus-Dieter Ehlermann. The Commission also has a separate Legal Service.

Community competition law enforcement is complex and the Commission has to be careful how it allocates its limited resources. Therefore, the number of formal decisions taken has been relatively small, and those have generally concerned important points of principle in the development of Community competition policy or particularly serious transgressions of the rules. For many years the Commission has been keen to encourage the enforcement of Community competition law before the national courts and through the NCAs. This push towards the decentralisation of competition enforcement has been a priority of the Commission for some time,[39] and has come to fruition through the adoption of Regulation 1/2003. Community competition

39 The Commission's early attempts can be seen in the Commission Co-operation Notices, OJ 1993, C39/6 and OJ 1997, C313/3.

law can now be enforced at either the Community level or the national level. At whatever level 'day-to-day' enforcement takes place the Commission is still required to supervise and enforce Community competition law under its general duty, by virtue of Art 211, to apply the Treaty. Following the coming into force of Regulation 1/2003, the Commission will focus its efforts on its overall supervisory role, ensuring that enforcement within the network of NCAs is consistent and follows broader Community policies.[40] The Commission will also handle cases which, because of their nature, are better suited to direct enforcement by the Commission. As the Commission has been released from the responsibility for Art 81(3) notifications that it bore under Regulation 17, it should have more resources available to investigate serious competition problems, such as secret pan-European cartels.

The Commission, alongside the NCAs, has wide powers to carry out investigations into possible infringements of the competition rules and it also has the power to impose fines or, in some cases, a structural remedy. Some of the Commission's powers have been criticised as being unfair as the Commission is involved in all stages of investigation, effectively acting as police, prosecutor and judge. In order to deflect some of that criticism the Commission has taken a number of procedural steps to protect the rights of the defence during Commission proceedings. The enforcement process by the Commission can be divided into three broad phases:

1   initiation of proceedings and investigation;
2   decision-making; and
3   judicial review.

Initiation

This refers to the fact finding stage of the enforcement process and there are three main ways in which the Commission can gather initial information about potential competition problems:

1   its own research, for example, sectoral surveys of particular markets;[41]
2   complaints; and
3   information from those who may be involved in infringing behaviour.

---

40 See Brammer, S, 'Concurrent Jurisdiction under Regulation 1/2003 and the issue of case allocation' (2005) 42(5) CMLRev 1383; and Dekeyser, K, and Jaspers, M, 'A New Era of ECN Cooperation, Achievements and Challenges with Special Focus on Work in the Leniency Field' (2007) 30(1) World Competition 3.

41 See, for example, Communication from the Commission – Inquiry pursuant to Article 17 of Regulation (EC) No 1/2003 into the European gas and electricity sectors (Final Report), COM(2006) 851 final and the Sector Inquiry into pharmaceuticals, Commission Press Release IP/08/49 'Antitrust: Commission launches sector inquiry into pharmaceuticals with unannounced inspections', 16 January 2008.

The latter two methods raise certain issues which need to be addressed before analysing the Commission's investigative powers.

Complaints

The Commission receives numerous complaints that Community competition rules have been infringed, most frequently from competitors or customers of the company that is the subject of the complaint. There is a specific form, Form C, which is provided by the Commission and upon which complaints can be made, although its use is not obligatory. Any natural or legal person who can show a legitimate interest is entitled to lodge a complaint.[42] Any communications to the Commission are privileged for defamation purposes.[43] The Commission has no obligation to act positively on a complaint. The Court has made it clear that the Commission can reject complaints on the basis that there is no 'Community interest' in pursuing the matter.[44] The Commission may also reject a complaint on the basis that an NCA is already dealing with the matter.[45] The ability to reject a complaint on this latter ground is designed to avoid the duplication of investigations across the enforcement network. The judgment in *Guerin* held that when a complaint is rejected by the Commission, complainants can have that decision reviewed.[46] It is intended that the NCAs will deal with most of the day-to-day enforcement activity and the majority of complaints, with the Commission only becoming involved in important cases or those that span a number of Member States. In 2004, the OFT referred a complaint by Which? to the Commission relating to alleged price discrimination in Apple's iTunes service as the latter operated in more than three Member States and the Commission would be in a better position to consider the online exploitation of music across Europe.[47] The Commission gives guidance on the appropriate body to approach with a complaint in its Notice on the handling of complaints by the Commission.[48]

Information from those who may be infringing

Although Regulation 1/2003 has brought to an end the need, for those who wish to gain an exemption under Art 81(3), to notify their agreements, there

---

42 Regulation 1/2003/EC, Art 7(2).
43 See *Hasselblad (GB) Ltd v Orbinson* [1985] QB 475.
44 See Case T-24/90 *Automec v Commission II* [1992] ECR II-2223; [1992] 5 CMLR 431.
45 Regulation 1/2003/EC, Art 13(1).
46 Case C-282/95P *Guerin Automobiles v Commission* [1997] ECR I-1503; [1997] 5 CMLR 447.
47 OFT Press Release, 'OFT refers iTunes complaint to EC', 3 December 2004.
48 Commission Notice on the handling of complaints by the Commission under Arts 81 and 82 of the EC Treaty, OJ 2004, C101/65.

are still a number of situations in which companies may wish to bring their potentially anti-competitive agreements or practices to the attention of the Commission.

The first situation in which a company might approach the Commission is where it is seeking a 'finding of inapplicability'. The Commission can, under Art 10 of Regulation 1/2003, adopt a decision that an agreement or practice does not breach the prohibition in Art 81(1); fulfils the conditions within Art 81(3); or does not fall within the prohibition in Art 82. Such a decision would be of obvious benefit to the parties concerned as it would ensure that they could proceed with such a course of conduct without fear of inter-ference from the Commission or the NCAs, and they would also be able to defend any competition challenge in the national courts. It is, however, unlikely that the Commission will adopt a large number of such decisions and in most cases is much more likely to proceed informally. The Commission has published a Notice on informal guidance relating to novel questions,[49] which makes it clear that it will only issue such guidance in limited circum-stances. The status of informal Commission communications has proven to be controversial in the past, particularly in relation to Commission 'com-fort letters' under Art 81(3).[50] Informal clearance is not formally binding on the Commission, but it will not normally act inconsistently with its own advice. Nor is informal guidance binding on the NCAs or national courts, although they should bear any such guidance in mind when taking their own decisions.[51]

The other, increasingly important, instance when companies may approach the Commission with evidence of infringing behaviour is where a cartel member brings evidence of the existence of the cartel to the Commission in order to seek leniency. Leniency programmes are becoming an important part of a competition authority's enforcement armoury. The idea behind the emergence of leniency programmes is that cartels are inherently unstable, with each member of the cartel constantly balancing the benefits of solidarity with the other cartel members against the benefits of withdrawing co-operation. By offering leniency to cartel members, who inform the authority of the existence of a cartel, the authority hopes to significantly increase the benefits of withdrawing from the cartel, and therefore increase the likelihood that a cartel will break up. If the offer of leniency also encourages the breakaway cartel member to provide useful information to the authority it also means that the authority can take enforcement action against the other cartel

---

49 Commission Notice on informal guidance relating to novel questions concerning Arts 81 and 82 of the EC Treaty that arise in individual cases (guidance letters), OJ 2004, C101/78.

50 See Case 71/74 *FRUBO v Commission* [1975] ECR 563; [1975] 2 CMLR 123.

51 See the 'Perfumes' cases, for example, Case 99/79 *Lancome v Etos* [1980] ECR 2511; [1981] 2 CMLR 164, and *Inntrepreneur Estates Ltd v Mason* [1993] 2 CMLR 293.

participants.[52] In the US system this is known as the 'race to the courtroom door'.[53] The Commission adopted a leniency programme in 1996,[54] but the most recent version of that policy was adopted in 2006.[55] Under the Commission programme a 'whistle-blower' who seeks leniency can be granted immunity from Commission fines if it is the first to provide sufficient evidence to allow the Commission to carry out a targeted inspection or find an infringement.[56] Any undertaking that comes forward after an investigation has begun and co-operates with the investigation may be granted a reduction in any fines subsequently imposed by the Commission.[57]

Investigatory powers

During the course of an investigation, the Commission has wide powers to collect information, even from third parties. The full extent of those powers can be witnessed when a 'dawn raid' is carried out simultaneously on multiple businesses across the Community in relation to alleged infringements of Art 81. The information gathering powers are contained in Arts 17–22 of Regulation 1/2003.[58] The principal powers are contained in Arts 18, 19 and 20. Article 17 provides for inquiries where there may be a competition problem in a sector of the economy. Article 22 allows the Commission to request authorities of Member States to carry out investigations into alleged breaches of the competition rules.

Article 18: requests for information

Article 18 sets out two separate procedures by which the Commission can make requests for information. The first procedure, in para 2, provides for the Commission to make a 'simple request' for information. This is the less invasive of the two procedures. There is no penalty for a failure to provide information, but there are penalties, under Art 23, for supplying incorrect or misleading information. This procedure is often used where

---

52 For fuller discussion of leniency programmes at the EC and UK levels, respectively, see Chapter 5.
53 For a useful discussion of the US leniency programme, see Harding, C and Joshua, J, *Regulating Cartels in Europe – A Study of Legal Control of Corporate Delinquency*, 2000, Oxford: OUP, Chapter VIII.
54 OJ 1996, C207/4.
55 Commission Notice on immunity from fines and reduction of fines in cartel cases, OJ 2006, C298/17. See, generally, Wils, W, 'Leniency in antitrust enforcement: theory and practice' (2007) 30(1) World Competition 25, and Sandhu, JS, 'The European Commission's Leniency Policy: a success?' [2007] ECLR 148.
56 Paragraphs 8–13.
57 Paragraphs 23–26.
58 The Commission's powers of investigation under the Merger Regulation are contained in Regulation 139/2004/EC, OJ 2004, L24/1, Arts 11–13.

information is sought from undertakings that are not the subject of a competition investigation. The request itself will set out the information that is requested, the legal basis for the request, the deadline for the provision of the information, and an indication of the possible penalties that could be imposed. The procedure for a mandatory request for information is set out in Art 18(3). In respect of a mandatory request, the Commission uses the vehicle of a Decision to require the undertaking to produce the information. The Decision resembles the format of a simple request under Art 18(2), but will also set out the penalty that will be imposed if the undertaking fails to provide the information within the time limit set. Article 24 allows the Commission to impose a periodic penalty of up to 5% of daily turnover on a continuing basis for each day of failure to provide the information. The Art 23 penalties for supplying incorrect or misleading information also apply.

Article 19: taking of statements

This power was introduced by Regulation 1/2003. Under the Regulation 17 regime the Commission could not take oral statements and could only formally deal with documentary evidence. Article 19 of Regulation 1/2003 allows the Commission to interview persons, who consent to be interviewed, in order to gather information. While this power will not be used in contested investigations, as there is no provision for compulsion, it will be useful in non-contested investigations where information can be gathered orally from the competitors or customers of an undertaking that is alleged to have infringed the competition rules or, in leniency cases, where a member of a cartel co-operates with a Commission investigation. The Commission's Leniency Notice includes provision for corporate statements to be made orally.[59] This is done to prevent leniency statements being the subject of legal discovery for use in litigation in the United States.

Article 20: inspections

Article 20 empowers the Commission to carry out inspections, which are more commonly known as 'dawn raids'. To authorise an inspection, the Commission must adopt a Decision, after consulting the relevant NCAs, setting out the subject matter of the inspection, the nature of the inspection, the date of the inspection, and the possible penalties under Arts 23 and 24 of Regulation 1/2003. Officials who undertake the inspection are required to produce written authorisation, setting out the above information, at the beginning of the inspection. The Commission co-operates closely with the

---

59 Commission Notice on Immunity from fines and reduction of fines in cartel cases, OJ 2006, C298/1, paras 31–35.

NCAs in the exercise of its powers, and in many cases the initial information that has led to the need for an inspection may have come to the Commission via the NCAs. Article 20(6) requires the officials of the NCA to assist the Commission within their territory, including acquiring judicial authority if that is required. During an inspection the Commission has a wide range of powers, including:

a   entering any premises, land, and means of transport;
b   examining the books and other records related to the business, irrespective of the medium on which they are stored;
c   taking, or obtaining in any form, copies of, or extracts from, such books or records;
d   sealing any business premises and books or records for the period and to the extent necessary for the inspection; and
e   asking any representative or member of staff of the undertaking for explanations of facts or for documents relating to the subject matter and purpose of the inspection and thereafter recording the answers.

In addition to the power in Art 20 to inspect business premises, Art 21 gives the Commission the power to inspect other premises, if a reasonable suspicion exists that books or other records related to a serious violation of Art 81 or 82 EC are being kept in those premises. This includes the homes of the directors or managers of the undertakings concerned. An order for such an inspection must also be made by Decision, which must set out the reasons such a suspicion exists. Before an Art 21 inspection takes place an application must be made for the appropriate judicial authority, for instance, a search warrant, within the relevant Member State.

In cases such as *Hoechst*,[60] the Court has shown that it is concerned with the rights of the undertaking which is the subject of an inspection, but it also indicated that such undertakings receive relatively limited protection. The judgments of the European Court of Human Rights in *Colas Est*[61] and the Court of Justice in *Roquette Freres*[62] indicate that the matter is still controversial. The lesser extent of protection afforded to business premises by Art 8 of the European Convention on Human Rights explains the stricter test which must be met for an inspection of premises other than business premises in Art 21 of Regulation 1/2003.

---

60 Cases 46/87 and 227/88 *Hoechst v Commission* [1989] ECR 2859; [1991] 4 CMLR 410.
61 *Ste Colas Est v France* (37971/97) (2002) unreported, 16 April, ECHR.
62 Case C-94/00 *Roquette Freres SA v Director General de la Concurrence, de la Consommation et de la Repression des Fraudes* [2002] ECR I-9001; [2003] 4 CMLR 1.

Special types of information

In most mature legal systems there exists some form of protection for certain kinds of documents, or information, and those documents, or information, are granted privileged status. This means that they need not be disclosed and cannot be relied upon by the other party in a dispute. The two main types of information which need not be divulged by companies to the Commission are that covered by professional legal privilege and that covered by the privilege against self-incrimination.

Professional legal privilege

The existence of this doctrine under competition law enforcement was confirmed in *A, M & S Europe Ltd v Commission*.[63] In that case, which was undertaken under the investigation powers of Regulation 17, the Commission sought to carry out an inspection but documentation was withheld by the company. The Commission had demanded disclosure of certain documents in an inquiry into an alleged zinc suppliers' cartel. A, M & S Europe Ltd had withheld the documents on the basis of the professional legal privilege, which was attached to certain documents and correspondence between the company and its legal advisers. The Commission fined A, M & S for its failure to produce the documents. A, M & S sought a review of the Commission Decision before the European Court. The Court confirmed the existence of the doctrine of professional legal privilege, subject to three limitations:

1   it only covers documents between lawyer and client and related to the purpose of the defence;
2   it only applies to communications between a client and an independent lawyer. Advice and documents prepared by in-house lawyers are not covered; and
3   it extends only to independent lawyers based in the Community.

The latter two limitations have been criticised. The exclusion of in-house lawyers makes little sense in legal systems where such lawyers have the same status as independent lawyers, and this exclusion may also prejudice the ability of companies to organise an effective competition law compliance programme. The exclusion of in-house lawyers from the privilege was confirmed by the CFI in *Akzo Nobel Chemicals v Commission*.[64] The restriction to Community-based lawyers is discriminatory, but the restriction still

---

63 Case 155/79 [1982] ECR 1575; [1982] 2 CMLR 264.
64 Cases T-125/03 and T-253/03 *Akzo Nobel Chemicals v Commission*, judgment of 17 September 2007. On appeal, Case C-550/07 P *Akzo Nobel Chemicals & Akcros Chemicals v Commission and others*, pending. Interestingly the Law Society of England & Wales, *inter alia*, have sought to intervene in the appeal.

applies. Nonetheless, the CFI in *Akzo Nobel* relaxed the first limitation by extending the potential scope of the privilege to company documents or memoranda drawn up exclusively for the purpose of seeking legal advice from an external lawyer in exercise of the rights of the defence. In practice, should the Commission demand information for which privilege is claimed, the recourse available is to seek review of that demand by the CFI.[65] These principles apply equally to information required under Art 18 or 20 of Regulation 1/2003.

Self-incrimination

The increasing impact of 'human rights' on competition investigations is exemplified by the growing importance of the privilege against self-incrimination in competition proceedings. The privilege was initially developed in the criminal law field but its use has now spread, through the operation of Art 6 of the ECHR, to other fields including competition law.[66] In *Orkem*,[67] *Solvay*[68] and *Société Générale*[69] the Court set out that the Commission is entitled to compel, under Art 18 of Regulation 1/2003, an undertaking to provide all necessary information and to disclose to the Commission such documents in its possession, even if they may be used to establish the existence of anti-competitive conduct. An undertaking required to produce information can rely on the privilege only where the undertaking would be compelled to provide answers that might involve an admission of an infringement. The Court's judgments in these cases were thrown into doubt by a number of important decisions by the European Court of Human Rights (ECtHR), most notably *Funke v France*,[70] but the ECJ confirmed the position it adopted in *Orkem* in *Mannesmannröhren-Werke AG v Commission*.[71] There has been an interesting debate whether the ECJ's position on this matter is sustainable.[72] There is also the wider issue of whether

---

65 The detailed procedure for sealing documents in dispute for review by the CFI was set out in Cases T-125/03 and T-253/03 *Akzo Nobel*.
66 Even though Art 23(5) of Regulation 1/2003 states that fines imposed under that Regulation 'shall not be of a criminal law nature'.
67 Case 374/87 *Orkem v Commission* [1989] ECR 3283; [1991] 4 CMLR 502.
68 Case 27/88 *Solvay v Commission* [1989] ECR 3355.
69 Case T-34/93 *Société Générale v Commission* [1995] ECR II-545; [1996] 4 CMLR 665.
70 [1993] 1 CMLR 897; (1993) 16 EHRR 297. See, also, *Saunders v UK* (1997) 23 EHRR 313.
71 Case T-112/98 [2001] ECR II-729; [2001] 5 CMLR 1.
72 See, for example, Lasok, KPE, 'The privilege against self-incrimination in competition cases' [1990] 2 ECLR 90; Van Overbeek, WBJ, 'The right to remain silent in competition investigations: the *Funke* decision of the Court of Human Rights makes revision of the ECJ's case law necessary' [1994] 3 ECLR 127; Riley, A, 'Saunders and the power to obtain information in Community and United Kingdom competition law' [2000] ECLR 264; Riley, A, 'The ECHR implications of the investigation provisions of the draft competition regulation' (2002) 51 ICLQ 55; Wils, W, 'Self-incrimination in EC antitrust enforcement: a legal and economic

companies that are the subject of competition investigations can benefit from 'human rights', such as the privilege against self-incrimination, or whether they should have different rights to represent their different status.[73]

Decision-making

Once the Commission has gathered sufficient information, using any of the methods mentioned, it will then decide which decision-making process is most appropriate. If the competition rules have not been breached, the Commission will take no further action. If a finding of inapplicability has been sought, and it is considered that there is a Community interest, the Commission will proceed to adopt the appropriate decision. Should the Commission consider that the competition rules have been breached, the Commission will initiate infringement proceedings. At an earlier stage, most commonly upon receipt of a serious complaint, the Commission may exercise its powers to take interim measures.

Interim measures

Article 8 of Regulation 1/2003 provides the Commission with power to take interim measures where necessary. The power to take interim measures is subject to certain limitations, the most important of which is that the measures must be necessary due to the urgency of the situation. The urgency must arise 'due to the risk of serious and irreparable damage to competition'.[74] For the Commission to act there must be a reasonably strong *prima facie* case, though it is not necessary to establish an infringement with certainty.[75] Another significant limitation is that the Commission must adhere to the essential procedural requirements within the Regulation. Accordingly, unlike certain interlocutory court orders, interim measures will not be awarded *ex parte* and interested undertakings will be given the opportunity to be heard. The Commission has rarely granted interim measures; the most noteworthy example in the UK context is *BBI/Boosey and Hawkes: Interim Measures*,[76] in which the Commission took action in respect of a refusal, by a

    analysis' (2003) 26 W Comp 567; and, MacCulloch, A, 'The Privilege against Self-Incrimination in Competition Investigations: Theoretical Foundations and Practical Implications' (2006) 26(2) Legal Studies 211.

73 See Harding, C and Joshua, J, *Regulating Cartels in Europe: A Study in the Legal Control of Corporate Delinquency*, 2003, Oxford: OUP, Chapter 7, and MacCulloch, A, 'The Privilege against Self-Incrimination in Competition Investigations: Theoretical Foundations and Practical Implications' (2006) 26(2) Legal Studies 211.

74 For the Court's view on the interim measures under Regulation 17, see Case 792/79R *Camera Care v Commission* [1980] ECR 119; [1980] 1 CMLR 334.

75 Case T-44/90 *La Cinq v Commission* [1992] ECR II-1; [1992] 4 CMLR 449.

76 OJ 1987, L286/36; [1988] 4 CMLR 67.

company, to supply brass band instruments to an existing customer who was also going to produce similar instruments in competition with it. A Commission Decision to adopt interim measures is subject to review by the CFI.

Infringement proceedings

Infringement proceedings are brought under Art 7 of Regulation 1/2003 and commence with the Commission issuing a document called the 'Statement of Objections' to the undertakings involved in the alleged breaches. The Statement of Objections must contain a statement of the facts, a legal assessment of the position and, if the Commission intends to impose a fine, state the alleged period of infringement. When adopting its final decision the Commission cannot rely on matters not included in the Statement of Objections or matters which are discovered after it has been issued. The parties involved, and any interested third parties, must be given a hearing,[77] although representations are also made to the Commission in writing. The Hearing Officer conducts the hearing[78] and their remit is to ensure that the parties receive a fair hearing and that the rights of the defence are respected.[79] After the hearing, in consultation with the Advisory Committee on Restrictive Practices and Dominant Positions,[80] the Commission may adopt a formal Decision.[81] Article 7 of Regulation 1/2003 sets out that an infringement decision can require the undertakings concerned to bring any breach of the competition rules to an end. The Commission may also impose any proportionate behavioural or structural remedies that are necessary to bring the infringement to an end. Structural remedies will only be adopted, under Art 7, where there is 'no equally effective behavioural remedy or where any equally effective behavioural remedy would be more burdensome for the undertaking concerned than the structural remedy'. Regulation 1/2003 also contains a new power, in Article 9, for the Commission to accept binding commitments from a party to address the Commission's competition concerns instead of proceeding to a formal decision requiring the infringement to be brought to an end.

---

77 See Regulation 1/2003, Art 27. See, also, Commission Regulation 773/2004/EC relating to the conduct of proceedings by the Commission pursuant to Articles 81 and 82 of the EC Treaty, OJ 2004, L123/18.

78 Commission Regulation 773/2004/EC, OJ 2004, L123/18, Art 14.

79 See, more generally, Commission Decision (2001/462/EC, ECSC) on the terms of reference of hearing officers in certain competition procedures, OJ 2001, L162/21, replacing Commission Decision (94/810/ECSC, EEC), OJ 1994, L330/67. See, also, House of Lords Select Committee on the European Union, Session 1999–2000, 19th Report, *Strengthening the Role of the Hearing Officer in EC Competition Cases*, HL Paper 125, HMSO, 21 November 2000.

80 Regulation 1/2003, Art 14. A body staffed by officials from each of the Member States' NCAs whose task is to advise the Commission on competition law and policy issues.

81 It is assisted in this process by the Legal Service of the Commission.

Fines

The most common type of behavioural remedy imposed is a fine. Article 23 of Regulation 1/2003 allows the Commission to impose fines of up to 10% of the undertaking's total turnover in the preceding year. Periodic penalty payments can also be imposed under Art 24 for continued infringements. The largest fines imposed have tended to be for price-fixing agreements and agreements which divide up the internal market in the Community.[82] The Commission enjoys a wide discretion in imposing fines and generally takes into account such factors as the gravity of the behaviour, its duration, the size of the market in question and the likely deterrent effect of a fine. To improve transparency in this area the Commission published a Notice in 1998 on the setting of fines.[83] According to that Notice the basic amount of the fine was to be set according to the gravity and duration of the infringement, with infringements categorised into several levels of gravity. Minor infringements, usually vertical in nature and affecting a limited market, would receive fines of up to €1m. Serious infringements, usually horizontal or vertical infringements or abuses with more effect over a larger area, could receive fines of up to €20m. Very serious infringements, usually horizontal price-fixing or market-sharing or serious abuses of near monopoly positions, could be fined in excess of €20m. The duration of the infringement was also important, with infringements of a medium duration, of more than one year, receiving a 50% uplift on the fine. In relation to infringements of long duration, of more than five years, an uplift of 10% would be applied for each year the infringement continued. On top of this 'basic' amount there are certain aggravating factors which, if present, may result in a fine being increased further. Aggravating circumstances include, for example, refusals to co-operate or being the 'leader' of the infringement. In contrast with the aggravating circumstances just described, there may alternatively be attenuating circumstances that may result in the reduction of the basic fine. These include, for example, a passive role in the infringement or the speedy termination of the infringement. Since the case of *Re Pioneer*,[84] in which the Court was asked to review the Commission's Decision on fines, fines issued by the Commission have increased markedly.[85] The highest total fine imposed for an infringement, to date, on a group of undertakings under the 1998 Notice was

---

82 Although the largest single fine was for a breach of Art 82 EC.
83 Guidelines on Method of Setting Fines, OJ 1998, C9/3; [1998] 4 CMLR 472. See, also, Spink, PM, 'Enforcing EC competition law: fixing the quantum of fines' [1999] JBL 219.
84 Cases 100–03/80 *Musique Diffusion Francaise SA, C Melchers and Pioneer Electronic (Europe) and Pioneer High Fidelity (GB) Ltd v Commission* [1983] ECR 1825; [1983] 3 CMLR 221.
85 The CFI continues to exercise strict control over the Commission's fining practice; see, for example, Cases T-236, 239, 244–246, 251 and 252/01 *Tokai Carbon v Commission* [2004] ECR II-1181.

€855.2m[86] and the highest fine imposed on a single undertaking for an infringement remains €497m.[87]

The 1998 Notice was revised in 2006 in three principal ways to further enhance deterrence.[88] First, the fine will be based on a percentage, of up to 30%, of the yearly sales in the relevant sector for each company participating in the infringement, multiplied by the years of participation. Secondly, the Commission may impose an additional 'entry fee' of 15% to 25% of yearly relevant sales for seriously illegal conduct, including cartels. Thirdly, the most significant change to the detailed guidance on what constitutes aggravating factors concerns repeat offenders, and provides for increases in fines of up to 100% for each prior infringement. There has been a dramatic increase in the overall fines imposed by the Commission, particularly in relation to cartels, in 2006 and especially 2007, during which the Commission fined participants in the Gas Insulated Switchgear cartel a total of over €750m and also set a current record total fine of over €990m in relation to the Elevators and Escalators cartel.[89]

Another, increasingly important, factor in the setting of the level of fines is the operation of the Commission's cartel leniency programme. 'Whistle-blowers' who have participated in secret cartels can secure either partial or total immunity from fines by disclosing the existence of the cartel to the Commission.[90] The first undertaking that brings sufficient information to the Commission to allow it to carry out a targeted inspection or find an infringement, will normally receive complete immunity from any subsequent Commission fines. Any other undertakings that go on to provide the Commission with information and continue to co-operate may receive a reduction in any subsequent fines.[91]

The Commission has amended Reg 773/2004 to provide for, and published a Notice to explain, a direct settlement process whereby infringing parties may be granted a fine rebate of 10% conditional upon acceptance, within a set deadline, of the commission of the infringement, admission of liability, and the level of fine. The faster and simplified procedure envisaged will, it is hoped, lead to a more efficient use of enforcement resources.[92] The

---

86 See Commission Press Release, IP/01/1625 and Commission Decision 2003/2/EC *Vitamins*, OJ 2003, L6/1.
87 Commission Decision 2007/53/EC, *Microsoft*, OJ 2007, L32/23, on appeal Case T-201/04 *Microsoft v Commission*, judgment of 17 September 2007.
88 Guideline on the Method of setting fines imposed pursuant to Article 23(2) of Regulation 1/2003, OJ 2006 C 210/2.
89 Commission Press Release IP/07/209, 21 February 2007. See Chapter 5 for fuller discussion.
90 Commission Notice on immunity from fines and reduction of fines in cartel cases, OJ 2006, C298/17. See, also, the discussion of the leniency programme above.
91 For fuller discussion of leniency programmes at the EC and UK levels respectively, see Chapter 5.
92 Commission Regulation 622/2008/EC, OJ 2008, L171/3, Commission Notice on settlement procedures, OJ 2008, C167/1.

expedited procedure will operate only in relation to cartel cases, although there are clearly implications in such a system for third party rights, due process and 'fair trial' objections, and for follow-on private enforcement actions.

Rights of the defence

The development of the rights of the defence in Community competition law enforcement has been a feature of the Court's jurisprudence. An important starting point would be to note the decision of the European Human Rights Commission (EHRC) in *Stenuit*.[93] In that case, the EHRC considered that competition law proceedings, which may lead to the imposition of a fine, are of such a nature that Art 6 of the European Convention for the Protection of Human Rights and Fundamental Freedoms is applicable to them. The Community is not a signatory to the European Convention; however, it is clear from the Treaty and Court jurisprudence that the principle in Art 6, providing for a fair and public hearing within a reasonable time by an independent and impartial tribunal, is to be respected. In the Community context, administrative decisions by the Commission are not contrary to this general right because of the existence of a full and independent review, involving due process, before an independent tribunal, the CFI or European Court.[94] Nonetheless, the Court has continually insisted that the Commission is obliged to give a fair hearing in terms of its procedure and administration. In response to this, the Commission has taken several steps, including the introduction of the Hearing Officer,[95] to clarify and enhance the Commission's hearings procedure with a view to improving the rights of the defence. Even the role of the Hearing Officer has been criticised as hearing officers may become entrenched in proceedings where the proceedings have been running for a lengthy period of time.[96] While some useful steps have been taken, it is clear that further developments will still be necessary.[97] In addition to the issues of legal professional privilege and self-incrimination, the greatest focus has been on the issue of access to the Commission file by parties involved in the decision-making process.

93 (1992) 14 EHRR 509.
94 For a discussion on this, see the House of Lords Select Committee on the European Union, 19th Report, *Strengthening the Role of the Hearing Officer in EC Competition Cases*, 21 November 2000, HL Paper 125, paras 55–56 and 75–78.
95 Commission Regulation 773/2004/EC, OJ 2004, L123/18, Art 14.
96 House of Lords Select Committee on the European Union, 19th Report, *Strengthening the Role of the Hearing Officer in EC Competition Cases*, 21 November 2000, HL Paper 125, and also Levitt, M, 'Commission hearings and the role of the hearing officers: suggestions for reform' [1998] ECLR 404.
97 Andreangeli, A, 'Toward an EU Competition Court: "Article-6-proofing" Antitrust proceedings before the Commission?' (2007) 30(4) World Competition 595.

Access to the file

The Commission, under Art 27(2) of Regulation 1/2003, is bound to disclose all documents upon which it relies to substantiate its allegations to the undertakings accused of infringing the competition rules. In addition, according to the case law in *Hercules*[98] and *Hoechst*,[99] this requirement of disclosure extends equally to exculpatory documents held by the Commission. These are documents that tend to clear the undertaking under investigation of the allegations made by the Commission. In the first instance, the Commission decides which documents must be disclosed and will then forward them to the undertakings concerned. Deciding which documents must be disclosed is not straightforward, and the Commission has produced guidance in a Notice.[100] Deciding which documents to disclose is a difficult task to combine with the Commission's duty of confidentiality to those who provide it with information. No access will be given to confidential information or the internal documents of the Commission. There exists a general duty of confidentiality under the Treaty, although the extent of the duty is unclear where there is a conflict with the principle of access to the file. More specifically, Art 28 of Regulation 1/2003 places a duty on the Commission not to disclose information which falls within the heading of professional secrecy,[101] and the Notice sets out that 'business secrets' are also non-communicable. The breadth of the concept of professional secrecy is unclear, but in practice the protection of business secrets is more crucial. It has been established by the Court, in *AKZO v Commission*,[102] that business secrets may never be divulged by the Commission. If there is a dispute as to whether information or documentation falls within this category the Commission will take a decision subject to review by the Court.

There have been a significant number of legal challenges to Commission Decisions on access to the file issues. For instance, judgments in the *Soda Ash*[103] cases annulled, on procedural grounds, Commission Decisions in five related cases. Two of the cases involved a failure by the Commission to respect the rights of the defence in relation to access to the file. These cases were a major setback for the Commission, and the most significant judicial pronouncement on the exercise of the right of access to the file and the rights

98 Case T-7/89 *SA Hercules Chemicals NV v Commission* [1991] ECR 1171; [1992] 4 CMLR 84.
99 Cases 46/87 and 227/88 *Hoechst AG v Commission* [1989] ECR 2859; [1991] 4 CMLR 410.
100 Commission Notice on the rules for access to the Commission file in cases pursuant to Articles 81 and 82 of the EC Treaty, Articles 53, 54 and 57 of the EEA Agreement and Council Regulation (EC) No 139/2004, OJ 2005, C235/7.
101 See, also, Art 287 EC.
102 Case 53/85 *AKZO Chemie BV v Commission* [1986] ECR 1965; [1987] 1 CMLR 231.
103 Cases T-30–32/91 *Solvay SA v Commission* [1995] ECR II-1775, II-1821, II-1825, and T-36 and 37/91 *Imperial Chemical Industries plc v Commission* [1995] ECR II-1847 and II-1901.

of the defence generally. Importantly, the CFI confirmed that the right of access to the file is a fundamental right of the defence and not a self-imposed requirement by the Commission. Parties are entitled to see all documents relating to the case. The three protected categories of information are retained: professional secrets, business secrets and other confidential information. The third category would protect information which would breach the requested anonymity of an informant, and also sensitive commercial information that is not technically a business secret. Determination of what constitutes a business secret will be made on a case-by-case basis and will cover information relating to the commercial interests of its owner, such as internal price calculations, market strategy plans and know-how. Access to the file helps to ensure that the right to be heard is protected, but the *Soda Ash* cases demonstrated the difficulties involved when access to documentation, relating to competitors, held by the Commission is requested. The Commission has to carry out a sensitive balancing act in conducting the procedure due to the conflict between the rights of the defence and the duty of confidentiality.

Review of Commission decision-making

The appellate bodies involved in Community competition law are the CFI and the Court of Justice.

Court of First Instance (CFI)

The CFI was established in 1989[104] in order to reduce the increasing workload of the Court of Justice. The remit of the CFI is currently limited,[105] but as it includes the review of the Commission's competition Decisions its workload is substantial and significant. The CFI reviews Commission Decisions, under Art 230 EC, on points of fact and law. The broad scope that the CFI has adopted in its review role equates, in effect, to a near appeal; however, it is in reality a form of judicial review. This scope is apparent from the recent judgments of the CFI which can be lengthy and highly detailed, explaining the arguments of the parties on every point raised, before the CFI sets out its own judgment. In the majority of cases where large fines are imposed there will be, in practice, automatic recourse to the 'appeal' process. Thereafter, a further appeal may be made to the Court of Justice on a point of law. A party may apply for an expedited procedure before the CFI, where there exists special urgency.

---

104 As provided for by the Single European Act 1986.
105 While it currently has a limited remit, the Treaty of Nice provided that the powers of the CFI may be substantially increased by the Council.

European Court of Justice (the Court)

The task of the Court under Art 220 EC is to 'ensure that in the interpretation and application of the Treaty the law is observed'. The Court is the ultimate authority on Community law issues, including competition law. The Court is renowned for its creative techniques of interpretation, partly due to the need to 'fill the gaps' in the Treaty. It has been criticised for this judicial activism, which has been obvious in the development of competition law principles from the limited text of the Treaty. In addition to the Court's judgments, there are the opinions of the Advocates General. An Advocate General is an official with the same status as a Court judge, but their task is to prepare a review of the facts and legal analysis of the issues, together with recommendations for the Court. The Advocate General's opinion is delivered in advance of the Court's final deliberations and is important because it is of persuasive effect in both the instant case and later cases, and also because it gives a wider picture of Community competition law development. The opinions tend to look more fully at the background of the case and related developments, and make a comparative assessment of national laws. This contrasts with the shorter and more precise judgments of the Court, which can give little indication of their rationale or the developments leading to the particular legal analysis. The trend has changed in recent years with longer judgments in competition law cases, particularly where the ECJ is dealing with a technical appeal from the CFI.

Article 230 EC

Article 230 provides for review of the legality of any act by a Community institution. Accordingly, the legality of a Commission Decision taken in competition proceedings may be reviewed under this procedure, which allows for annulment of the act. There are three requirements which need to be satisfied for an act to be annulled:

1   Who may seek review?
    Article 230(2) states that the act must be of 'direct and individual concern' to the party seeking its annulment. This would obviously apply to a party that is the subject of a Commission Decision. It has also been held to apply to a complainant who was unhappy with a Commission's Decision[106] and, in appropriate circumstances, a non-complainant may also qualify under this head.[107]

---

106 Case 26/76 *Metro v Commission* [1977] ECR 1875; [1978] 2 CMLR 1.
107 For fuller analysis of the issue of 'direct and individual concern' see Nordberg, C, 'Judicial remedies for private parties under the state aid procedure' [1997] LIEI 35, pp 54–59, which is of general interest regarding *locus standi* for competitors. See, also, Case C-70/97 *Kruidvat BVBA v Commission* [1998] ECR I-7183; [1999] 4 CMLR 68.

2   What constitutes an 'act'?

This term covers more than the formal decisions, such as infringement decisions, taken by the Commission. A wide view was taken in the *IBM* case,[108] which held that an act capable of affecting the interests of an applicant, by bringing about a change in their legal position, could be challenged. On the particular facts of that case the action was unsuccessful as an 'act' did not include issuing a Statement of Objections, as this was held to constitute merely a procedural step in the process. In subsequent case law,[109] letters rejecting complaints have been held to constitute 'acts' and it is also possible that informal guidance could be construed as an act. The Court of First Instance held in *Alrosa v Commission* that although commitments under Art 9 of Regulation 1/2003 were proposed by an undertaking, the decision by the Commission to make those commitments binding was subject to review by the Court.[110] However, an act does not extend to decisions taken by the Commission on whether, and to what extent, it will allow access to its files by undertakings under investigation.

3   Grounds for review?

The following are the grounds for review available when seeking annulment of a Commission act: lack of competence/authority; infringement of an essential procedural requirement; infringement of the Treaty or any rule of law relating to its application; or misuse of powers. These grounds are alternatives, although they overlap to a certain extent. Annulment may be sought for, for instance: failure to give a party a hearing; inadequate reasoning in a decision; a decision based on inadequate evidence; or erroneous application of the competition rules. An action for annulment is often combined with an action seeking review of a decision by the Commission to fine. Article 229 of the Treaty provides the Court with unlimited powers to annul, vary or increase the fine imposed by the Commission.

Article 232 EC

This provides for an appeal against a failure by a Community institution to act. In competition law proceedings, this may be appropriate for a complainant that considers that the Commission has not dealt with its complaint properly, for instance, by taking action against the alleged infringements. There are limitations on the availability of this review mechanism.[111]

---

108 Case 60/81 [1983] ECR 3283; [1981] 3 CMLR 635. See also Cases T-125/03 and T-253/03 *Akzo Nobel Chemicals v Commission*, judgment of 17 September 2007.
109 Case 142/84 *BAT v Commission* [1986] ECR 1899; [1988] 4 CMLR 24.
110 Case T-170/06, judgment of 11 July 2007, [2007] 5 CMLR 7.
111 Case 15/71 *Mackprang v Commission* [1971] ECR 997; [1972] CMLR 52.

Article 234 EC

Article 234 provides for a system of 'preliminary rulings' to be given by the Court. This means that the Court has final interpretative jurisdiction over references from national courts concerning the application and meaning of Community law. This seeks to ensure the uniform application of Community law throughout the legal systems of the various Member States. A national court may refer an issue to the Court where a ruling is necessary to enable the national court to give judgment, and must do so where there is no right of further appeal. The Court does not decide the dispute between the parties, but provides an interpretative 'preliminary ruling' which provides guidance on the interpretation of the point of Community law which is at issue. This will become increasingly important for the development of Community competition law given the role of enforcement at the national level in the 'modernised' enforcement system under Regulation 1/2003. The review of infringement actions instigated by the NCAs will occur before the domestic courts, which may then use Art 234 rulings to ensure there is a consistent application of Community law. Recourse may also be made to the Art 234 procedure when a domestic court is dealing with a private dispute between parties which involves Community competition law.[112]

Ancillary enforcement issues

Articles 83–85 EC

Article 83 of the Treaty enables implementing Regulations, such as Regulation 1/2003, to be introduced. Article 84 provides that national authorities retain the power to apply the rules in Arts 81 and 82 until appropriate provisions have been adopted under Art 83 and are in force. Article 85 allows the Commission to act and to authorise Member States to act on its behalf where the appropriate implementing Regulations have not been introduced under Article 83.

Exclusions from Regulation 1/2003

Regulation 1/2003 does not apply to merger control which has its own separate Regulation, Regulation 139/2004, containing both the substantive and procedural rules for reviewing merger activity.[113] There is also specific

---

112 See for a comprehensive analysis of all competition law-related preliminary rulings, Rodger, B (ed), *Article 234 and Competition Law: An Analysis*, 2008, The Hague: Kluwer Law International.

113 Regulation 139/2004/EC on the control of concentrations between undertakings, OJ 2004, L24/1.

provision under Art 89, which regulates the procedure in respect of State aid.[114] Regulation 1/2003 has limited application to various market sectors, such as transport, agriculture, telecommunications and various energy markets, in relation to which particular Treaty provisions exist with specialised enforcement regimes.[115]

Administrative enforcement in the UK

Introduction

This section is concerned with the principal bodies involved in the same general stages of administrative enforcement – initiation, decision and review – of UK and Community competition law within the UK. Several introductory comments are necessary nonetheless. The UK framework is particularly interesting given the remarkable changes introduced within the last 10 years by the Competition Act 1998, Enterprise Act 2002 and Regulation 1/2003. The 1998 Act introduced new enforcement authorities and abolished other bodies, such as the Restrictive Practices Court. It also varied the functions performed by the competition authorities and the powers available to them. Although the Competition Act prohibitions can also be enforced by consumers or other interested parties through normal court processes, it is important to note that an essentially administrative enforcement framework has been retained. The Enterprise Act 2002, largely replacing the Fair Trading Act 1973, continues an administrative enforcement scheme in respect of UK market and merger investigations. It also made other important changes in respect of UK enforcement: transfer of functions from the Director General of Fair Trading (DGFT) to the OFT;[116] provision of a role for the CAT in private damages claims; introduction of a fast-track super-complaints procedure for consumer organisations;[117] and creation of a criminal offence for involvement in cartel activity.[118] Finally, the OFT, as the NCA for the UK, now has a duty to apply both domestic prohibitions and the Community rules in Articles 81 and 82, often simultaneously. Following implementation of the Community Modernisation Regulation, and in order to ensure harmony between the enforcement of Arts 81 and 82 EC and the domestic prohibitions under the 1998 Act, a number of amendments were

---

114 Regulation 659/1999/EC lays down detailed rules for the application of Art 88 of the EC Treaty, OJ 1999, L83/1. See Chapter 7.
115 See Whish, R, *Competition Law*, 5th edn, 2003, London: LexisNexis, Chapter 23 for further detail on these issues, which are outside the scope of this book.
116 Section 2.
117 Section 11.
118 Section 188.

made to that statute and OFT practice;[119] for instance, the extension of the appeals process to the appeal tribunal, CAT, in relation to OFT decisions on Articles 81 and 82, and the alignment of calculation of fines with Community practice at that stage.[120] The OFT has, therefore, the same processes, powers and decision-making competences in relation to the domestic and Community prohibitions, and accordingly OFT enforcement under both will be examined together.

The Competition Act 1998

The Competition Act 1998 repealed the 1976 Acts and the competition-related provisions of the Competition Act 1980. Accordingly, the enforcement structure under those provisions will not be considered here, although brief discussion of the role of the legislation will be considered in later chapters as appropriate. The Competition Act 1998 introduced a new prohibition approach, based on the Community provisions Arts 81 and 82 to both anti-competitive agreements and the abuse of a dominant position.

Diagram 2 illustrates the enforcement mechanism in relation to the domestic and Community prohibitions. It should be noted that s 2 of the Enterprise Act 2002 transferred the functions of the DGFT to the OFT. The OFT will derive information, at the outset of any investigation, from specific complaints, leniency applications and general market research. Crucially, the 1998 Act provided the OFT with extensive new investigative powers based on those available to the European Commission.

Office of Fair Trading (OFT)

The most important change in terms of enforcement, when the 1998 Act was introduced, was the increased role, and enhanced powers, afforded to the DGFT, carried out on his behalf by the OFT. Section 1 of the Enterprise Act 2002 established the OFT as a body corporate to which all of the powers and functions of the DGFT were transferred. The OFT Board consists of a chairman, currently Philip Collins, and no fewer than four members appointed by the Secretary of State. The Board is entrusted with the strategic direction of the OFT, including the publication of its annual plan. In order to undertake the OFT's competition law tasks, the OFT staff are split into the

---

119 See the Competition Act 1998 and Other Enactments (Amendment) Regulations 2004, SI 2004/1261; the Competition Act 1998 (Determination of Turnover for Penalties) (Amendment) Order 2004, SI 2004/1259; the Competition Act 1998 (Land Agreements Exclusion and Revocation) Order 2004, SI 2004/1260; the Competition Act 1998 (Office of Fair Trading's Rules) Order 2004, SI 2004/2751.

120 'OFT's guidance as to the appropriate amount of a penalty', OFT 423. It should be noted that the Commission subsequently revised their equivalent Notice and practice in 2006 as discussed above.

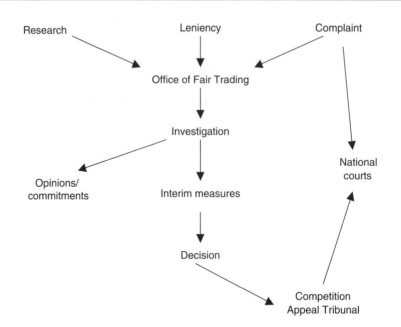

Diagram 2: Competition Act 1998 and the Chapter I and II prohibitions.

Policy and Strategy Division and the Markets and Projects Division. The former devises OFT strategies and policies and ensures their consistent implementation, whereas the latter is split into three groups responsible for goods, services and infrastructure. These groups review markets and consider remedies using the range of enforcement tools available to the OFT. There are also two specialist teams within this Division focusing on mergers and cartels. The OFT has the crucial role, charged with investigating and taking decisions on whether the prohibitions have been breached. The OFT has the central investigative and decision-making role in the process, as opposed to involvement only at the initiation and enforcement stages, as was the case prior to the introduction of the 1998 Act. In addition to the statutory provisions, information and guidance on the OFT enforcement mechanism can be sought from the OFT Rules[121] and Guidelines on enforcement.[122] The OFT has also published criteria which it uses to prioritise its casework, to allow the OFT to concentrate resources on high impact cases and enhance transparency for complainants.

It is evident, from the enforcement practice under the 1998 Act to date, that complaints by rival competitors or customers have played a key role in the detection of anti-competitive behaviour. In addition, when the 1998 Act was

---

121 Competition Act 1998 (Office of Fair Trading's Rules) Order 2004, SI 2004/2751.
122 OFT 407, *Enforcement*, December 2004. See, also, *Powers of Investigation*, OFT 404.

introduced, parties could notify the OFT in order to seek negative clearance or an exemption from the prohibitions, as was demonstrated by the OFT Decision to exempt an agreement primarily between British motor insurers in April 2004.[123] Nonetheless, the Government decided to withdraw the notification and individual exemption scheme from the Act.[124] Prior to May 2004, the OFT could issue informal guidance, but this has been replaced by a system of non-binding opinions in cases raising novel or unresolved questions of law. The power for the OFT to accept binding commitments in Chapter I and II cases has also been introduced for the 1998 Act and Arts 81 and 82 EC cases.[125] The OFT can also make a formal decision that the rules have been infringed and impose penalties. The OFT has considerable powers to enable officials to enforce the domestic and Community prohibitions,[126] including: entering premises to inspect and copy documents; using force to enter premises upon authority of a warrant; and allowing OFT officials to be accompanied on raids by other professional support personnel, such as IT experts. To support these powers the Act also creates a criminal offence of obstructing the OFT's right of entry or deliberately or recklessly supplying false or misleading information. The OFT has the power to make decisions on an interim basis to protect the public interest or to prevent serious damage from occurring. The European Commission's practice, under Community law, gives some guidance as to when such decisions can be made. Where the OFT proposes to decide that there has been an infringement of either prohibition it is required to issue a Rule 7 Notice[127] to persons likely to be affected and give them the opportunity to make representations. This is the equivalent of the Commission's statement of objections under Community law.[128] The OFT can also impose civil financial penalties for infringement of the prohibitions. In addition, the OFT can order the parties in breach to stop the infringement. Appeals from decisions of the OFT may be made to the Competition Appeal Tribunal.

Section 52 of the 1998 Act required publication of advice and information on the Act. Accordingly, the OFT has published a wide range of guidelines

---

123 See OFT Press Release, 'Association of British Insurers' general terms of agreement exempt from Competition Act', 22 April 2004.
124 See paras 2 and 9 of Sched 1 to the Competition Act 1998 and Other Enactments (Amendment) Regulations 2004, SI 2004/1261.
125 See para 18 of Sched 1 to the Competition Act 1998 and Other Enactments (Amendment) Regulations 2004, SI 2004/1261 and Sched 6A to the Competition Act 1998. See, also, 'Enforcement, incorporating the Office of Fair Trading's guidance as to the circumstances in which it may be appropriate to accept commitments', OFT 407. See, for instance, 'OFT consults on horseracing commitments notice', OFT Press Release, PN 101/04, 28 June 2004.
126 See ss 25–29 generally as amended by paras 10–14 of Sched 1 to the Competition Act 1998 and Other Enactments (Amendment) Regulations 2004, SI 2004/1261.
127 Formerly known as a Rule 14 notice.
128 See, for instance, OFT press release 52/08, 17 April 2008, where the OFT had issued a statement of objections against 112 construction companies.

on various aspects of the legislation. In relation to enforcement, the guidance on the appropriate level for penalties, issued in accordance with s 36 of the Act, was particularly notable,[129] although the guidance has been revised following EC modernisation.[130] When the 1998 Act was enacted, the OFT also established the Compliance and Education Unit with the aim of increasing awareness of the implications of the Act and encouraging the introduction of effective compliance programmes in industry.[131] The introduction of a leniency programme for whistle-blowers has also sought to enhance the deterrent effect of the legislation.[132] It is clear that the OFT is seeking to ensure the effectiveness of the Act's provisions, particularly in relation to dealing with cartels.[133]

Penalties

The most important sanction, in practice, is the power to impose penalties under s 36 of the 1998 Act. Section 36(8) provides that no penalty may be imposed which exceeds 10% of the turnover of an undertaking, calculated in accordance with the Competition Act 1998 (Determination of Turnover for Penalties) Order 2000.[134] The OFT Guidance on the Appropriate Amount of a Penalty sets out a five-step approach for the OFT to use when calculating financial penalties:

1   Prior to the revised Guidance introduced in 2004, the OFT calculated the starting point by applying a percentage, determined by the nature of the infringement, to the relevant turnover of the undertaking. The relevant turnover was that in the relevant market affected by the infringement in the last financial year. The maximum starting point was 10% of this figure, and the percentage was determined according to the gravity of the infringement. In order to bring UK fines into line with Commission practice, the guidance was revised in 2004 to ensure that the starting point for fines in relation to the domestic and Community prohibitions is a lump sum calculated with reference to the seriousness of the infringement and the relevant turnover (as calculated previously). Ironically, as outlined above, the Commission's revised guidance in 2006 means that Commission fining practice now utilises a percentage of the relevant sales turnover as the starting point.

---

129 OFT 423.
130 OFT 423.
131 See Rodger, BJ, 'Compliance with competition law: a view from industry' [2000] Commercial Liability Law Review 249.
132 See Guidance as to the appropriate amount of a penalty, OFT 423, Pt III.
133 See Chapter 5 for a fuller discussion.
134 SI 2000/309, as amended by the Competition Act 1998 (Determination of Turnover for Penalties) (Amendment) Order 2004, SI 2004/1259.

2   Thereafter, the OFT can make an adjustment, which will be related to the duration of the infringement. This allows the starting figure to be multiplied by the number of years during which the infringement has continued.

3   The OFT can also adjust the figure, taking into consideration other factors. The penalty may be adjusted at this stage to enhance deterrence, an important policy objective under the Act.

4   The OFT can also adjust the figure in light of other further aggravating or mitigating factors. This stage allows a range of factors to be considered, such as the role of the undertaking, the involvement of senior managers, continued or repeated infringements, genuine uncertainty as to the existence of an infringement, adequate steps taken to ensure compliance and co-operation with the OFT.

5   The OFT can make a final adjustment to the figure to prevent the maximum penalty being exceeded and to avoid double jeopardy. The s 36(8) turnover was revised in 2004 to allow a maximum penalty of 10% of the worldwide turnover of an undertaking, as opposed to the UK turnover of the undertaking, for the previous business year. The OFT is also required to take into account any fine imposed by the European Commission, other NCA, or national court.

In addition, the OFT Guidance contains a leniency programme, which provides for immunity from, or reduction in, financial penalties for undertakings coming forward with information in cartel cases.

There are already a number of cases in which fines based on the OFT's five-stage approach have been imposed for breach of one of the prohibitions, although some of the examples arose before the revised guidance was introduced in 2004. The first financial penalty to be imposed by the Director General concerned a breach of the Chapter II prohibition by Napp Pharmaceuticals, which charged both excessive and predatory prices for sustained-release morphine. The Competition Commission Appeal Tribunal (CCAT), now the Competition Appeal Tribunal (CAT), upheld the DGFT's decision as to the infringement itself, but reduced the penalty imposed from £3.21m to £2.2m.[135] This case demonstrated that the appeal tribunal is not bound by the OFT Guidance on determining the appropriate amount of a penalty. In July 2001 the DGFT adopted a Decision, finding that Aberdeen Journals had abused a dominant position in the market for the supply of advertising space in local newspapers in the Aberdeen area.[136] The Director imposed a penalty of £1,328,040. Subsequently, the CAT upheld the decision against Aberdeen

---

135 CCAT Case No 1001/1/1/01 *Napp Pharmaceutical Holdings Ltd v DGFT*, 15 January 2002, paras 497–541.

136 DGFT Decision CA98/5/2001, Case CF/99/1200/E *Predation by Aberdeen Journals Ltd*, 16 July 2001. See, also, subsequent DGFT Decision CA98/14/2002, 16 September 2002.

Journals, and confirmed the alleged conduct of predatory pricing. The CAT did, however, reduce the penalty imposed from the original £1,328,040 to £1,000,000.[137] In November 2003 the OFT decided that Argos, Littlewoods and Hasbro had been involved in price-fixing agreements, in relation to games and toys, in breach of the Chapter I prohibition.[138] Argos was accordingly fined £17.28m, Littlewoods £5.37m, and Hasbro's fine of £15.59m was reduced to zero on the basis of its co-operation under the OFT leniency programme. In August 2003 the OFT fined 10 businesses that had engaged in resale price maintenance in the market for replica football kits manufactured by Umbro, thereby infringing the Chapter I prohibition.[139] The OFT imposed a total of £18.6m in fines, the size of the fines varying between the businesses according to the OFT guidance, with some qualifying for reductions under the terms of the leniency programme. The fines included the following: JJB Sports – £8.373m; Umbro – £6.641m; Manchester United – £1.652m; the FA – £198,000 (reduced to £158,000); and Sports Connection – £27,000 (reduced to £20,000). In 2006, in one of a number of cases in recent years involving the construction industry, and the roofing trade in particular, the OFT fined 13 roofing contractors a total of £2.3m, reduced to £1.6m by leniency, for collusive tendering processes ('bid-rigging') to fix prices in relation to flat roofing and car park surfacing contracts.[140] In 2007, the OFT imposed a record fine of £121.5m on British Airways for colluding with Virgin Atlantic in increasing prices payable for long-haul passenger fuel surcharges.[141] These cases, together with a number of other decisions,[142] highlight the important role played by the new fining powers under the 1998 Act and that deterrence is a

---

137   *Aberdeen Journals v The Office of Fair Trading (formerly the Director General of Fair Trading)*, [2002] CAT 6; [2003] CAT 11, paras 476–500.

138   OFT Decision CA98/8/2003, Case CP/0480–01 *Agreements between Hasbro UK Ltd, Argos Ltd and Littlewoods Ltd Fixing the Price of Hasbro Toys and Games*, 21 November 2003. On appeal, the CAT, in *Argos Ltd & Littlewoods Ltd v OFT*, upheld the OFT decision on liability ([2004] CAT 24) but reduced the fines to Argos to £15m, and to Littlewoods to £4.5m respectively ([2005] CAT 13). See also *Argos Ltd /Littlewoods Ltd/JJB v OFT* [2006] EWCA Civ. 1318, where the Court of Appeal upheld the CAT.

139   DGFT Decision CA98/06/2003, Case CP/0871/01 *Price-fixing of Replica Football Kit*, 1 August 2003. On appeal, the CAT reduced JJB's fine to £6.7m, Manchester United's fine to £1.5m, and Umbro's fine to £5.3m ([2005] CAT 22). See also *Argos Ltd /Littlewoods Ltd/JJB v OFT* [2006] EWCA Civ. 1318, where the Court of Appeal upheld the CAT.

140   *Collusive Tendering for flat roof and car park surfacing contracts in England and Scotland*, OFT Decision No. CA98/01/2006 (Joined Cases CE/3123–03 and CE/3645–03); OFT press release 34/06, 23 February 2006.

141   Virgin Atlantic qualified in principle for full immunity under the OFT's leniency programme. See OFT press release 113/07, 1 August 2007. Publication of a formal OFT decision in this case is awaited.

142   Including, for instance, the early resolution of the tobacco price fixing case where six agreed to pay total penalties, after leniency and early resolution discounts, of £132.3m. See OFT press release 82/08, 11 July 2008.

key aspect of the imposition of penalties. Like Community law, fines can only be imposed if the infringement is intentional or negligent. Furthermore, the Government has amended the 2000 Order to ensure that the maximum penalty for infringing Chapter I or II is aligned with that for Arts 81 and 82 EC, that is, based on 10% of an undertaking's worldwide turnover for the previous business year.[143]

Like the European Commission, the OFT has been developing its policy on remedies to enhance compliance and effective case management by considering the swift conclusion of enforcement proceedings by administrative settlements, loosely akin to plea-bargaining processes in criminal law. For example, the OFT imposed a reduced fine of £10,000 on each participant in the systematic exchange of information on future fees by a group of 50 independent fee-paying schools, in return for a voluntary admission by those parties and an ex gratia payment to fund a £3m educational trust.[144] The OFT considers that this type of resolution may benefit parties by reducing the financial penalties and would lead to a faster outcome and a more efficient use of resources as the lengthy and costly administrative procedure could be avoided.[145] Following a provisional finding of collusion between certain large supermarkets and dairy processors, in September 2007, a number of the parties admitted their participation in anti-competitive prices and agreed to pay fines of over £116m in total.[146]

Concurrent powers

It should be noted that s 54 of the 1998 Act provides for the OFT to exercise its powers concurrently with the utility regulators, Office of Gas and Electricity Markets (OFGEM), Office of Communications (OFCOM), Office of Water Services (OFWAT), Office of Rail Regulation (ORR), and the Northern Irish Office for the Regulation of Electricity and Gas (OFREG).[147] The general principle is that a 'case will be dealt with by whichever of the OFT or the relevant regulators is better, or best, placed to do so'.[148] Section 54(4) provides for the Secretary of State to make regulations for the purpose

---

143 DTI 'Government response to the consultations on giving effect to Regulation 1/2003 and aligning the Competition Act 1998 including exclusions and exemptions' 16 January 2004. See the Competition Act 1998 (Determination of Turnover for Penalties) (Amendment) Order 2004, SI 2004/1259.

144 See OFT press release 166/06, 23 November 2006.

145 See also, for instance, OFT press release 49/07, 22 March 2007, 'OFT makes "fast track" offer in biggest ever UK cartel investigation' involving bid-rigging by construction companies in England, where 57 companies were raided and 37 applied for leniency.

146 See OFT Press Releases 170/07, 7 December 2007 and 82/08, 11 July 2008.

147 See, for a detailed consideration of this issue, Prosser, T, 'Competition, regulators and public service', in Rodger, BJ and MacCulloch, A, *The UK Competition Act: A New Era for UK Competition Law*, 2000, Oxford: Hart.

148 Concurrent application to regulated industries, OFT 405, para 3.13.

of co-ordinating functions under the Act and s 54(5) makes provision for joint decision-making. The Competition Act 1998 (Concurrency) Regulations 2004 provide for appropriate allocation of competence in enforcing the domestic and Community prohibitions.[149] The OFT's Guideline, 'Concurrent application to regulated industries',[150] outlines the practical aspects of case handling, both in relation to the 1998 Act prohibitions and Arts 81 and 82, and there have also been other guidelines published in relation to particular sectors.[151]

Competition Appeal Tribunal (CAT)

The Enterprise Act 2002 established the CAT[152] to replace the CCAT. The CAT is independent from the Competition Commission (CC), and is administered by the Competition Service, which was created at the same time.[153] The CAT hears appeals against the OFT's decisions. Appeals are available against the substance of any decision taken by the OFT, as detailed in s 46(1), including the level of any penalties imposed. In the case of *Bettercare v DGFT*,[154] one case in a line of judgments on the topic, the CAT made clear that whether an appealable decision has been taken by the OFT is a matter of substance, based on the position adopted by the OFT on the complaint and the stage the investigation has reached.[155] Accordingly, an appeal may be made to the CAT where the OFT has not formally issued a decision, but, for instance, advised a complainant informally that it will not proceed with a complaint because it does not appear that either prohibition has been infringed. The main party or parties against whom the OFT has made decisions can appeal, as can 'qualifying third parties' with a sufficient interest in the issue. The qualifying test is wider than the Community law test under Art 230 EC, and includes interested consumers and organisations representing such consumers. Section 47 originally provided for the DGFT to grant leave to a third party to appeal, but this requirement has been repealed by the Enterprise Act 2002 and third parties can now appeal directly to the CAT. Section 12, and Sched 2, of the 2002 Act make provision for the constitution of the CAT, including the appointment of a President of the Competition Appeal Tribunal who presides over the Tribunal. As set out in s 14 of the 2002 Act, a Tribunal dealing with

---

149 SI 2004/1077.
150 Concurrent application to regulated industries, OFT 405, para 3.13.
151 For example, 'Application of the Competition Act in the Telecommunications Sector', OFT 417.
152 Enterprise Act 2002, Pt 2, particularly s 12.
153 Ibid, s 13.
154 *Bettercare v DGFT* [2002] CAT 6; [2002] Comp AR 226. See, also, *Freeserve.com v DGFT* [2002] CAT 8; [2003] Comp AR 1; *Claymore/Express Dairies v DGFT* [2003] CAT 3; and *Pernod Ricard SA and Campbell Distillers Ltd v OFT* [2004] CAT 10.
155 See the fuller discussion in Alese, F, 'The office burden: making a decision without a decision for a third party' [2003] ECLR 616.

an appeal consists of a Chairman, who is either the President or a member of the panel of Tribunal Chairmen, and two other appeal panel members. The CAT may confirm, set aside, or vary the OFT's decision, or remit the matter to the OFT, or make any other decision that the OFT could have made. Detailed rules concerning the CAT procedure have been adopted as required under the legislation.[156] There is a right to an oral hearing, although oral hearings have tended to be short and structured, being conducted on the basis of the detailed skeleton arguments submitted to the CAT by counsel. There is a further right of appeal, under s 49 of the 1998 Act, on a point of law to the Court of Appeal in England and Wales, the Court of Session in Scotland and the High Court in Northern Ireland.[157] Accordingly, the CAT must determine in which jurisdiction it is sitting for the purposes of an appeal from the OFT, and this determines in which jurisdiction a subsequent appeal will be heard.[158] Rule 60 of the 2003 CAT Rules allows for the possibility of a reference to the European Court for a preliminary ruling under Art 234 EC.[159] There have already been a number of judgments by the CAT in which they have resorted to the range of powers available to them under the Act.[160] For instance: in *Napp Pharmaceuticals v DGFT*,[161] *Toys*, and *Replica Kits*,[162] the fine was reduced; in *Aberdeen Journals v DGFT*,[163] the case was remitted to the DGFT after the first appeal hearing; and, in *Bettercare v DGFT*, the decision was set aside and the issue remitted for reconsideration;[164] and the decision of the OFT was simply set aside in *The Racecourse Association and others v OFT*.[165]

In addition to its appellate role, ss 47A and 47B of the Competition Act, introduced by ss 18 and 19 of the Enterprise Act, provide for the CAT to hear claims for monetary awards in respect of established infringements of the Chapter I and II prohibitions and Arts 81 and 82 EC,[166] and for aggregated

156 The Competition Appeal Tribunal Rules 2003, SI 2003/1372, applicable to proceedings commenced after 20 June 2003, replacing the 2000 Rules (SI 2000/261).

157 Note that the requirement for resolution of a point of law limits the potential availability of appeal. See, for instance, *Napp Pharmaceutical Holdings Ltd v DGFT (No 5)* [2002] 4 All ER 376; [2002] UKCLR 726.

158 See Rodger, B, 'Competition law in a Scottish forum' (2003) Juridical Review 247.

159 See Middleton, K, 'Harmonisation with Community law: the Euro-clause', in Rodger and MacCulloch, above, fn 147.

160 Under para 3(2) of Sched 8 to the 1998 Act. See CAT judgments on the CAT website at www.catribunal.org.uk.

161 [2001] CAT 1.

162 *Umbro and Others v OFT*, [2005] CAT 22 and *Argos Ltd & Littlewoods Ltd v OFT* [2005] CAT 13, respectively.

163 [2002] CAT 6.

164 [2002] CAT 7.

165 The appeals were allowed and the OFT Decision that the sale of certain rights infringed the Chapter I prohibition was set aside, [2005] CAT 29.

166 See, for instance, *HealthCare at Home Ltd v Genzyme Ltd* [2006] CAT 29, and a number of cases before the CAT in relation to the *Vitamins* cartel.

claims by consumer representative bodies.[167] Furthermore, the CAT is responsible for reviewing decisions by the CC, the Secretary of State and the OFT in relation to merger and market investigation inquiries under the Enterprise Act.[168] It also sits as an appellate body in relation to penalties imposed by the CC during merger and market investigation inquiries.

The Enterprise Act 2002

During the late 1980s and 1990s there was considerable debate on reform of UK competition law, as outlined in Chapter 1.[169] Ultimately, when the Competition Act 1998 was introduced, the Restrictive Trade Practices Act 1976 was repealed, but the Fair Trading Act 1973, with its investigative system for mergers and 'monopoly' was retained. However, these investigative systems were replaced by the provisions in Pts 3 and 4 of the Enterprise Act 2002, for merger and market investigations, respectively. A similar administrative enforcement framework as under the 1973 Act has been retained for these purposes, although the DGFT's functions have been transferred to the OFT, and the role of the Secretary of State considerably limited, while the role of the CC is enhanced.

Diagrams 3 and 4 depict, in relation to market and merger investigations respectively, the bodies and processes established under the Enterprise Act 2002. The enforcement framework outlined in each diagram will be discussed in the following sections, and in more detail in Chapters 3 and 6, respectively.

Initiation

Office of Fair Trading (OFT)

Information is gathered by the staff of the OFT using a variety of research methods. For market investigations, initial information may come from complaints by aggrieved competitors or as a result of inquiries by parliamentary committees. The OFT may undertake a study of a particular market to ascertain whether it is working well for consumers, and recently utilised its powers

167 For instance, *The Consumers' Association v JJB Sports plc* (Case No 1078/7/9/07), a follow-on consumer representative action under these provisions before the CAT in relation to Replica Kit, although this case was settled out of court in January 2008 following an agreement by JJB to pay consumers who were unlawfully overcharged £20 each (see CAT Order of 14 January 2008).

168 In relation to the former, see *IBA Health Ltd v OFT* [2003] CAT 28, discussed more fully in Chapter 6.

169 See, for instance, Whish, R, 'The Competition Act 1998 and the prior debate on reform', in Rodger, BJ and MacCulloch, A, *The UK Competition Act: A New Era for UK Competition Law*, 2000, Oxford: Hart.

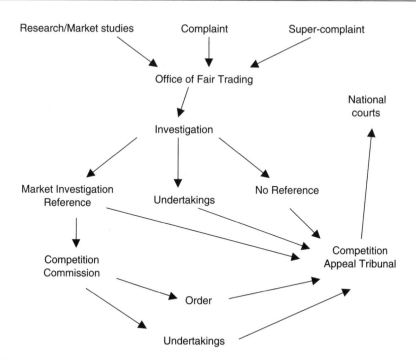

Diagram 3: Enterprise Act 2002 and market investigations.

in s 5 of the Enterprise Act 2002 to gather information by undertaking a study into store card services, which led to a referral to the CC and an investigation and very critical report by the CC.[170] In addition, s 11(1) of the 2002 Act introduced a fast-track complaints procedure for 'super-complaints' submitted by designated consumer bodies about market factors which may be significantly harming consumers' interests; this has already proved to be a valuable source of information in initiating proceedings.[171] Under the 1973 Act the DGFT's primary function was to decide whether or not to initiate, or recommend initiation of, proceedings under the appropriate legislation. With monopolies, the DGFT could refer matters to the CC for further consideration, or advise the Secretary of State upon a possible reference. Regarding mergers, the DGFT's function was merely to give advice to the Secretary of State. The latter was the only person with power to refer a merger situation to the CC. Following the coming into force of the Enterprise Act 2002, the OFT

---

170 See OFT news release, 47/04, 18 March 2004, 'OFT refers store cards to Competition Commission'. See further in Chapter 3.

171 See OFT, *Super-Complaints: Guidance for Designated Consumer Bodies*, OFT 504. See OFT website, and note for instance the inquiries commenced following a super-complaint, in Northern Irish Banking, Payment Protection Insurance, and the Scottish Legal Profession. See further in Chapter 3.

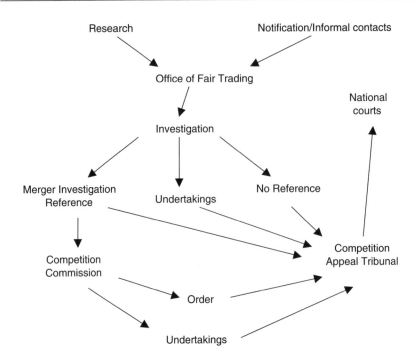

Diagram 4: Enterprise Act 2002 and merger investigations.

has the task of deciding whether to refer markets or mergers for investigation to the CC, and the Secretary of State now has only a minor residual role in this area.

Secretary of State for Trade and Industry

Under the 1973 Act, the Secretary of State had an exclusive power to refer mergers to the CC. The DGFT gave advice, but the decision remained ultimately a political decision. However, since 1973 there has been a gradual shift in prominence in UK competition law matters from the Secretary of State to the DGFT, and now to the OFT. This process was continued by the Competition Act 1998, although the Secretary of State's crucial role under the 1973 Act remained. Following DTI proposals to reduce ministerial influence and involvement in merger control[172] the Enterprise Act 2002 confines the Secretary of State's role to cases involving an exceptional public interest.

---

172 *Productivity and Enterprise: A World Class Competition Regime*, Cm 5233, 31 July 2001.

Investigation and reporting

Competition Commission (CC)

As of 1 April 1999 the CC replaced the Monopolies and Mergers Commission (MMC). The CC cannot initiate competition law proceedings but can investigate and report on references made to it under the market or merger provisions of the Enterprise Act 2002.

The CC is composed of a Chairman, deputy chairmen and members.[173] The Commission has a council, the strategic management board, which includes the Chairman, the deputy chairmen, the chief executive and two non-executive Commission members. Members are appointed by the Secretary of State for Trade and Industry following an open competition and serve for an eight-year term. Members are selected according to their 'individual experience, ability and diversity of background, not as representatives of particular organisations, interests or political parties'. The Commission conducts in-depth inquiries into mergers, markets and the major regulated industries, but cannot institute inquiries on its own initiative. The Commission has specialist panels for the utilities and newspaper markets. Upon receiving a reference, four or five members, but a minimum of three, are appointed by the Chairman to form an inquiry group, one of whom is selected as Chairman of that inquiry. Each inquiry group has the ability to decide upon its own procedures; however, decisions must be made and published within statutory time limits. The main stages of inquiries are as follows:

a   gathering information, including the issue of questionnaires;
b   hearing witnesses;
c   verifying information;
d   providing a statement of issues;
e   considering responses to the statement of issues;[174]
f   notifying parties of and publishing provisional findings;
g   notifying and considering possible remedies;
h   considering exclusions from disclosure; and
i   publishing reports.

The Enterprise Act 2002 gave the Commission the authority to make and implement decisions with regard to most competition questions arising out of merger and market inquiries in the UK – the Commission no longer merely makes recommendations to the Secretary of State. Commission

173 For further information, see www.competition-commission.org.uk.
174 In market investigations, the CC will inform parties at this stage of their 'emerging thinking'.

reports are located in the government publications section of libraries and are available at the Commission's website.[175]

Enforcement

Prior to the Enterprise Act 2002, the CC could only make non-binding recommendations in its reports. The Secretary of State would take action on the basis of a report, although subsequent enforcement was normally delegated to the DGFT. There were two methods of enforcement available under the legislation. Usually, if there was an adverse report that considered a practice to be against the public interest, the DGFT would negotiate and seek to obtain appropriate undertakings from the companies involved as to their future market conduct. This practice demonstrated the administrative and non-legalistic enforcement framework under the pre-Enterprise Act 2002 provisions. The undertakings could be reviewed if circumstances changed and it was the DGFT's duty to keep such undertakings under review. Alternatively, the 1973 Act provided for order-making powers by the Secretary of State.[176] This more drastic action could be taken if undertakings were not agreed, if they were broken, or if the conduct was particularly serious. The powers provided were fairly exhaustive and included, for instance, publication or notification of prices, regulation of prices, prohibition of the acquisition of undertakings or assets, and division of a business. Significant and controversial 'structural' orders were made by the Secretary of State following upon the Commission's recommendations in its Report, *The Supply of Beer*, in 1989.[177] The Commission was critical of, in particular, the tied-house system, which resulted in a lack of competition and a virtual monopoly over beer sales of the 'big six' brewers. The Secretary of State made two orders, with the most important and controversial orders forcing the major brewers to shed a number of licensed premises, to allow a guest beer to be sold in their tied houses, and to end all ties relating to non-alcohol beers, low alcohol beers and non-beer drinks.[178]

---

175 See fn 173.
176 See the Fair Trading Act 1973, ss 56 and 73. The scope of the orders was defined in s 90 and Sched 8. Section 91 and Sched 9 laid down the appropriate procedures, and enforcement was regulated by ss 88 and 93.
177 *The Supply of Beer: A Report on the Supply of Beer for Retail Sale in the United Kingdom*, Cm 651, 1989.
178 Supply of Beer (Tied Estate) Order 1989, SI 1989/2390 and the Supply of Beer (Loan Ties, Licensed Premises and Wholesale Prices) Order 1989, SI 1989/2258. These have been reviewed and revoked. See The Supply of Beer (Tied Estate) (Revocation) Order 2002, SI 2002/3204. See, also, Monopolies and Mergers – the Restriction on Agreements and Conduct (Specified Electrical Goods) Order 1998, SI 1998/1271, introduced in order to increase price competition in respect of televisions, washing machines and other electrical goods. See DTI Press Release, P/98/397, 20 May 1998. See, also, *Foreign Package Holidays: A Report on the Supply of Tour Operators' Services and Travel Agents' Services in Relation to Foreign*

The Enterprise Act 2002, in addition to reducing the significance of the Secretary of State's role, enhanced the role and range of tasks to be performed by the CC. The CC has been afforded the power to receive undertakings from parties and to impose orders, as appropriate, following a report, although the OFT has a duty to monitor, review and enforce undertakings and orders.[179] There is also provision in the 2002 Act for judicial review of the CC in relation to its functions under the merger and market investigation provisions by the CAT.[180]

Cartel offence investigations and director disqualification

Section 188 of the Enterprise Act 2002 introduced criminal penalties for individuals who dishonestly participate in cartels involved in such practices as horizontal price-fixing, market-sharing or bid-rigging. The OFT will investigate and the Serious Fraud Office[181] will prosecute. Section 190 provides for a maximum of five years imprisonment and an unlimited fine.[182] The idea is to enhance the deterrent effect by increasing personal incentives to comply, and to increase the destabilising impact on cartels by the possibility of immunity from prosecution for individuals who 'whistleblow' on a cartel.[183] In addition, s 204 of the Enterprise Act empowers the OFT to seek a competition disqualification order, which will disqualify a director of a company that breaches any of the competition law prohibitions.[184] Both these measures should enhance the likelihood that many organisations will institute and maintain effective competition law compliance programmes.

There has only been one successful prosecution under the cartel offence. Three men plead guilty, in 2008, to charges in relation to international bid-rigging in the marine hoses cartel and were sentenced to two and a half to three years imprisonment.[185] The adoption of criminal penalties for

---

Package Holidays, Cm 3813, 1997. Following the report, concerns over the transparency of ownership links between tour operators and travel agents were remedied by the Foreign Package Holidays (Tour Operators and Travel Agents) Order 2000, SI 2000/2110.

179 On enforcement generally in relation to merger and market investigations, see Chapter 4 of Pt 3 and Chapter 3 of Pt 4 respectively. Developments in enforcement practice under the market and merger investigations provisions of the 2002 Act will be considered in Chapters 3 and 6, respectively.

180 Sections 120 and 179, respectively.

181 The Lord Advocate in Scotland.

182 See OFT guidance, Powers for Investigating Criminal Cartels, OFT 505. See, also, MacNeil, I, 'Criminal investigations in competition law' [2003] ECLR 151; Joshua, MJ, 'The UK's new cartel offence and its implications for EC competition law: a tangled web' (2003) 28 EL Rev 620; Azevedo, JP, 'Crime and punishment in the fight against cartels: the gathering storm' [2003] ECLR 399.

183 'The cartel offence: guidance on the issue of no-action letters to individuals', OFT 513.

184 Competition Disqualification Orders, OFT 500.

185 See OFT Press Release 72/08, 11 June 2008.

involvement in cartel activities in the UK is part of a wider move towards criminalising certain 'hard core' cartel activity across Europe. Several Member States now have criminalised certain elements of competition law.[186] The main reason for the adoption of individual criminal penalties is to bolster the deterrent effect of the administrative sanction available under Art 81 EC and the equivalent national prohibitions. There is a fear that administrative fines alone will not act as a sufficient deterrent to discourage cartel behaviour.[187] Criminal penalties can improve the deterrent effect by affecting the individuals who decide that an undertaking should participate in a cartel. While fines imposed on an undertaking will simply affect its profit and loss account, the real threat of the imprisonment of company decision-makers is expected to have a more immediate impact. If a number of Member States adopt such penalties, the existence of complementary criminal sanctions, which are specifically approved in Regulation 1/2003,[188] could benefit the Community as a whole. The existence of criminal law sanctions for competition violations in a number of Member States raises questions regarding the relationship between domestic criminal prosecutions and the enforcement of the Community prohibitions. The cartel offence within the UK's Enterprise Act 2002, as an example, is illustrative of some of the potential problems.[189] A prosecution may be brought by the Office of Fair Trading (OFT), under s 188 of the Enterprise Act 2002, with regard to cartel activity which may also be the subject of an investigation under Art 81 EC by either the OFT, another NCA, or the Commission. While the ECN has systems to ensure that only one NCA deals with an Art 81 investigation, there is no similar procedure to decide whether an Art 81 investigation should be suspended to allow a domestic criminal investigation to go ahead. It is relatively clear that a criminal prosecution must precede an Art 81 infringement decision, in order to avoid prejudicing the criminal trial, but the matter is less clear at the investigation stage.[190] It is possible that both procedures could operate in parallel, using two different sets of investigatory powers, but with, perhaps, only one set of officials involved. The potential for procedural conflicts and appeals against conviction on the basis of procedural irregularities makes this area an obvious minefield for the investigating authorities. It has been suggested that the

---

186 Including Austria, France, Ireland and the UK.

187 See Wils, W, 'Does the effective enforcement of Articles 81 and 82 EC require not only fines on undertakings but also individual penalties, in particular imprisonment?', in Wils, W, *The Optimal Enforcement of EC Antitrust Law: Essays in Law and Economics*, 2002, Hague: Kluwer Law International.

188 See Article 3 and Recital 8 of Regulation 1/2003, OJ 2003, L1/1.

189 For detailed discussion of the cartel offence, see Chapter 5.

190 While it has always been presumed that a criminal prosecution must come first it should be noted that in the investigation into BA's fuel surcharge the Art 81 case was settled while the criminal investigation was still ongoing, see OFT Press Release, 'British Airways to pay record £121.5m penalty in price fixing investigation', 113/07, 1 August 2007.

Commission may find itself increasingly sidelined if the NCAs use their criminal powers regularly, and effectively suspend the application of Art 81 EC in important cartel cases.[191]

Private enforcement of EC and UK competition law

EC law

This became a core Commission competition policy during the 1990s. Enforcement in the national courts by individuals, as opposed to the traditional method of administrative centralised enforcement, is facilitated by the applicability of the direct effect doctrine to the basic Community competition prohibitions.[192] Through direct effect, Community law gives rise to rights and obligations that may be enforced by individuals before their national courts. Community competition law can therefore be resorted to in domestic litigation. It can be used as a 'shield' in defence to an action, for example, as a defence to a breach of contract claim. More contentiously, the competition provisions may be used as a 'sword' to claim damages, in the national court, based on an infringement of the prohibitions.

The possibility of individual enforcement in the national courts had existed for a number of years. However, as part of its decentralisation policy developed in the 1990s, the Commission recognised the need to stimulate interest and increase awareness of the possibilities of national court action. Historical support for decentralisation by the Commission stemmed from the practical problems the Commission faced under Regulation 17, together with the greater focus in the political arena on the role of subsidiarity as a Community principle. The judgment in *Automec (No 2)*[193] was a very significant development in the Commission's decentralisation policy. In that case, the CFI held that the Commission may prioritise its resources and, accordingly, it may refuse to investigate a complaint fully if it cannot offer the remedy the person seeks or, most importantly, if there is a lack of Community interest in pursuing the investigation, for instance, if the complainant can seek appropriate remedies in a domestic court. This judgment confirmed that the duty of the Commission to investigate is dependent on the Commission's priorities in enforcement. As a result, in 1993 the Commission issued the Notice on co-operation between the Commission and the national courts.[194] The Notice referred to the perceived benefits that would be gained by a complainant raising a court action based on breach of the competition rules

---

191   See Riley, A, 'EC antitrust modernisation: the Commission does very nicely thank you!' Pt 1 [2003] ECLR 604; Pt 2 [2003] ECLR 657.
192   See Case 127/73 *BRT v SABAM* [1974] ECR 51.
193   Case T-24/90 *Automec Srl v Commission* [1992] ECR II-2223; [1992] 5 CMLR 431.
194   OJ 1993, C39/6.

at domestic level as opposed to, or in addition to, making a complaint to the Commission. The stated benefits included the availability of damages, the use of interim measures and the award of costs, together with the likelihood of a speedier resolution of the dispute. However, the Notice also highlighted the formidable nature of the Commission's fact-finding powers and the fact that a complaint to the Commission was cheap and anonymous. The Notice provided an informal procedure for national courts to use to seek guidance directly from the Commission when faced with a Community competition law issue. It was hoped that this procedure would assist national courts to deal effectively with Community competition law claims and thereby encourage further domestic litigation. The Notice was criticised as it failed to provide for judicial training and was too timid in that it did not bring about more detailed harmonisation. In the absence of common rules of procedure or set levels of damages across the domestic courts in different Member States it was feared there could be divergent national approaches and a lack of uniformity. This problem was partially addressed as the Court, in a series of judgments, placed emphasis on the requirement that national courts should develop remedies to support the rights created by Community law.[195]

Despite an increase in litigation in the national courts involving Community competition law, there has, as yet, been only one reported court decision awarding damages in the UK, in *Crehan*, although ultimately even this award was overturned by the House of Lords.[196] In the early case of *Garden Cottage Foods v The Milk Marketing Board*[197] the House of Lords considered private litigation for breaches of competition law. Their Lordships confirmed the possibility of direct action before the national courts on the basis of infringement of Art 81 and/or Art 82 EC. The Milk Marketing Board sold bulk butter to distributors for resale but reduced their number of distributors

---

195 See Cases C-6 and 9/90 *Francovich v Italian Republic* [1991] ECR I-5357; [1993] 2 CMLR 66; Cases C-46–49/93 *Brasserie du Pêcheur v Germany (Factortame III)* [1996] ECR I-1029; [1996] 1 CMLR 889; Case 23/67 *Brasserie de Haecht SA v Wilkin (No 1)* [1967] ECR 407; [1968] CMLR 26; Case 48/72 *Brasserie de Haecht SA v Wilkin (No 2)* [1973] ECR 77; [1973] CMLR 287. For an example of the problems experienced in pursuance of these aims, from a UK perspective, see MacCulloch, A and Rodger, BJ, 'Wielding the blunt sword: interim relief for breaches of EC competition law before the UK courts' [1996] ECLR 393. See, more generally, Kon, S and Maxwell, A, 'Enforcement in national courts of the EC and new UK competition rules: obstacles to effective enforcement' [1998] ECLR 443.

196 See *Crehan v Inntrepreneur Pub Co (CPC)* [2004] EWCA Civ 637, [2004] 2 Eu LR 693, CA. See Andreangeli, A, '*Courage Ltd v Crehan* and the Enforcement of Article 81 before National Courts' [2004] ECLR 758; *Crehan v Inntrepreneur Pub Co (CPC)* [2006] UKHL 38, [2007] 1 AC 333, HL, see Hanley, C, 'The abandonment of deference' (2007) 44(3) CMLRev 817. For general discussion of private litigation in the UK courts, see Rodger, B, 'Competition Law Litigation in the UK Courts: A Study of All Cases to 2004', Pt 1 [2006] ECLR 241, Pt II [2006] ECLR 279, Pt III [2006] ECLR 341.

197 [1984] AC 130. See, also, the Scottish cases of *Argyll v Distillers* 1987 SLT 514, and *Millar & Bryce v Keeper of the Registers of Scotland* 1997 SLT 1000 (OH).

from 20 to four. Garden Cottage Foods was not on the new list. It raised an action, primarily seeking an injunction to stop the Milk Marketing Board from revoking its contract with Garden Cottage Foods, claiming the revocation to be an infringement of Art 82. The House of Lords overturned the Court of Appeal decision and held that the claimant was not entitled to injunctive relief. However, the majority of the House of Lords suggested that it would be possible to bring a claim alleging infringement of the Community competition rules.[198] It is now self-evident that, given the right conditions, a remedy would be available. There were concerns about how the courts should frame the appropriate remedy, although it now seems clear that 'breach of a statutory duty' is the most appropriate form of claim.[199] As suggested above, there has been pressure applied by the Community courts, in recent years, to seek to ensure that appropriate remedies are available in the national courts. Indeed, there were statements in *Francovich v The Italian Republic*[200] that suggested that there may be an obligation under Community law for Member States to provide a remedy in damages. Rather surprisingly, in a number of English cases in the 1990s, parties to contracts which were caught by Art 81 EC were denied remedies.[201] In particular, in a case where a publican sued for unjust enrichment or restitution in respect of a beer-tying arrangement between himself and a brewer, the Court of Appeal held that, as a party to an illegal agreement prohibited by Art 81, the publican was not entitled to a remedy in damages.[202] That position has now been reversed following the Court's ruling in *Crehan v Courage*.[203] In that ruling the Court made it clear that there could be no absolute bar to parties to a contract, found to infringe Art 81, bringing an action for damages. It also stressed that:

> . . . it is for the domestic legal system of each Member State to designate the courts and tribunals having jurisdiction and to lay down the detailed procedural rules governing actions for safeguarding rights which individuals derive directly from Community law, provided that such rules are not less favourable than those governing similar domestic actions (principle of equivalence) and that they do not render practically impossible

---

198   See above, MacCulloch and Rodger, fn 195.

199   Especially as that is the form of claim used in relation to claims framed under the Competition Act 1998.

200   Cases C-6 and 9/90 [1991] ECR I-5357; [1993] 2 CMLR 66. See, also, Case C-224/01 *Kobler v Austria* [2003] 3 CMLR 28.

201   See Maitland-Walker, J, 'Have English courts gone too far in challenging the effectiveness of EC competition law?' [1999] ECLR 1.

202   See *Gibbs Mew v Gemmell* [1998] EuLR 588.

203   Case C-453/99 *Courage Ltd v Bernard Crehan* [2001] ECR I-6297; [2001] 5 CMLR 28. See, also, Komninos, AP, 'New prospects for private enforcement of EC competition law: *Courage v Crehan* and the Community right to damages' (2002) 39 CML Rev 447.

or excessively difficult the exercise of rights conferred by Community law (principle of effectiveness).[204]

According to the Court in *Crehan*, Community law does not generally preclude the availability of damages to parties to an unlawful agreement, where the parties do not bear significant responsibility for the breach of Art 81 EC. It also indicated that where one of the parties to the agreement was in a considerably weaker position than the other, such as in the case of an individual publican in a relationship with a brewery, that weaker party may be entitled to claim damages under national law.[205]

The Commission has sought to encourage and develop private enforcement in order to enhance the effectiveness and deterrence of Community competition law. Regulation 1/2003 and the 2004 Notice on Co-operation with the national courts[206] seek to further develop the role of national courts, as there is very limited jurisprudence across the Community to date. Nonetheless, the dearth of reported cases gives an understated impression of the number of competition-related actions due to the frequency with which actions are settled prior to a final hearing.[207] The European Court has also sought to ensure the effectiveness of national remedies, although this is a slow process.[208] Litigants have a number of obstacles to overcome in order to succeed in damages actions for breach of competition law,[209] including: gathering evidence and court discovery procedures; quantification of loss; causation; and establishing the jurisdiction of the court.[210] This was confirmed by the *Ashurst Report*,[211] which reported to the Commission that private damages actions were completely underdeveloped throughout the

---

204 At para 29.
205 For the disposition of the case, see *Crehan v Inntrepreneur Pub Co (CPC)* [2003] EWHC 1510 (Ch), [2003] UKCLR 834, overturned on appeal by the Court of Appeal [2004] EWCA Civ 637, [2004] Eu LR 693. The Court of Appeal noted, in particular, at para 167, that 'the effect of the ECJ decision was to put its imprimatur on the particular claim of Mr Crehan, holding that a right to the type of damages he claimed was conferred on him by Community law'. Nonetheless, the Court of Appeal's ruling was also subsequently overturned by the House of Lords: *Crehan v Inntrepreneur Pub Co (CPC)* [2006] UKHL 38, [2007] 1 AC 333, HL, see Hanley, C, 'The abandonment of deference' (2007) 44(3) CMLRev 817.
206 OJ 2004, C101/54.
207 See Rodger, B, 'Private Enforcement of Competition Law, The Hidden Story: Competition Litigation Settlements in the UK 2000–2005' [2007] ECLR 96.
208 See for instance Case C-295/04 *Manfredi v Lloyd Adriatico Assicurazioni SpA* [2006] ECR I-6619.
209 Kon, S and Maxwell, A, 'Enforcement in national courts of the EC and new UK competition rules: obstacles to effective enforcement' [1998] ECLR 443.
210 See *Provimi Ltd v Aventis Animal Nutrition SA* [2003] EWHC 961 (Comm), [2003] 2 All ER (Comm) 683.
211 'Study on the Conditions of claims for damages in case of infringement of EC competition rules', available at http://ec.europa.eu/comm/competition/antitrust/others/actions_for_damages/study.html.

Community, and emphasised the considerable disparities between court procedures and remedies in different national courts. It is not inconceivable that the Commission may seek to propose some form of measure to harmonise elements of national court procedures and/or remedies for private actions involving Community competition law. Following the *Ashurst Report*, the Commission published a Green Paper on damages actions for breach of the EC antitrust rules,[212] assessing a range of potential options to facilitate private competition law litigation in the national courts.[213] There has been no Community legislation introduced, as yet, to lay down procedural rules for national courts to follow in such actions, although, following the entry into force of the Treaty of Amsterdam, the adoption of legal measures in the field of judicial co-operation in civil matters is now within Community competence.[214] A White Paper was published in April 2008 and makes a number of interesting suggestions which would require co-ordination between Community activity and reform of civil procedure within the Member States.[215] The proposals are based on the principle that all Community citizens who suffer damage through antitrust violations should be able to claim full compensation, enhanced deterrence through private actions being incidental to the compensation principle. The proposals include: guaranteed standing for all indirect purchasers, potentially through representative and opt-in collective actions; a minimum level of disclosure *inter partes*; the binding effect of NCA Decisions, when enforcing the Community prohibitions, across the Community; the limitation of the requirement of fault within a private action; a non-binding framework to facilitate the calculation of damages; the availability of the passing-on defence to defendants, but a rebuttable presumption that damage has been passed on to indirect purchasers; the

212 COM (2005) 672, 19 December 2005, and associated staff working document, SEC (2005) 1732, both available at http://ec.europa.eu/comm/competition/antitrust/actionsdamages/documents.htmlpeenpaper.
213 Pheasant, J, 'Damages Actions for Breach of the EC Antitrust Rules – The European Commission's Green Paper' [2006] ECLR 365; Brkan, M, 'Procedural Aspects of Private Enforcement of EC Antitrust law: Heading Toward New Reforms?' (2005) 28(4) World Competition 479; Hodges, C, 'Competition Enforcement, Regulation and Civil Justice: What is the Case?' (2006) 43(5) CMLRev 1381.
214 Article 65 provides that measures in the field of judicial co-operation in civil matters having cross-border implications are to be taken in accordance with Art 67 and, in so far as is necessary for the proper functioning of the internal market, shall include eliminating obstacles to the good functioning of civil proceedings, if necessary by promoting the compatibility of the rules on civil procedure applicable in the Member States. See Eilmansberger, T, 'The Green Paper on Damages for Breach of the EC Antitrust Rules and Beyond: Reflections on the Utility and Feasibility of Stimulating Private Enforcement through Legislative Action' (2007) 44(2) CMLRev 431.
215 White Paper on Damages actions for breach of the EC antitrust rules, COM(2008) 165 final. See, also, Commission Staff Working Paper accompanying the White Paper on Damages actions for breach of the EC antitrust rules, SEC(2008) 404.

extension of limitation periods to account for administrative enforcement procedures; cost allocations rules; and, protection for leniency applicants.

This section has concentrated on Arts 81 and 82 EC, although actions can also be brought by third parties in respect of a breach of the State aid rules. National court enforcement is not available for mergers that are within the scope of the Merger Regulation. It is clear that the process of decentralisation to the national courts, being partly dependent on the willingness of claimants to raise actions, still has considerable difficulties to overcome. In any event, court enforcement by national judges is merely part of a wider strategy aimed at the most efficient enforcement of Community law.[216]

UK law

It was clearly intended that the prohibitions introduced by the Competition Act 1998 should be enforceable by means of private law actions through normal court processes.[217] This was a dramatic change in the enforcement regime for UK competition law. Previously, the only provision that could have been enforced by individuals was s 35(2) of the Restrictive Trade Practices Act 1976, although no damages were awarded under this provision. The 1998 Act facilitates claims by providing, in s 58, that those findings of fact by the OFT, which are relevant to an issue arising in a court action, are binding on the parties, if that decision in which the findings of fact were made is no longer subject to appeal. Also, s 55 enables the OFT to disclose information to third parties, subject to the limitations under s 56 relating to, *inter alia*, the public interest and certain confidential information. The Act contains no express provision stating that the prohibitions can be enforced by private civil law action. Where statutes do not state specifically that private law remedies are available, it is a matter of construction of the particular statute as to whether Parliament intended to create such remedies.[218] In any event, in the first case on the substance of the Chapter II prohibition, *Claritas (UK) Ltd v the Post Office and Postal Preference Service Ltd*,[219] the matter was not raised and the case proceeded on the assumption that the new prohibitions could be enforced in private litigation. There have been a number of more recent

216 Cf Wils, WPJ, 'Should private enforcement be encouraged in Europe?' (2003) 26(3) World Competition 473, for a heretical view, suggesting that there is, and should be, little scope for the private enforcement of Community competition law. See, also, Jones, CA, 'Private antitrust enforcement in Europe: a policy analysis and reality check' (2004) 27(1) World Competition 13.

217 See A Prohibition Approach to Anti-Competitive Agreements and Abuse of a Dominant Position: Draft Bill, DTI, August 1997.

218 See MacCulloch, A, 'Private enforcement of the Competition Act prohibitions', in Rodger, BJ and MacCulloch, A, above, fn 169, Chapter 5. See, also, Rodger and MacCulloch, above, fn 195.

219 [2001] UKCLR 2.

examples of private litigation in which claims have been made on the basis of infringement of the prohibitions, notably *Provimi Ltd v Aventis Animal Nutrition SA and Others*.[220]

The Enterprise Act 2002 has made further provision for encouraging private actions in relation to breaches of the 1998 Act prohibitions. Under s 47A of the 1998 Act, as introduced by s 18 of the 2002 Act, the CAT, in addition to its role as an appeal tribunal, will be able to award damages and other monetary awards where there has already been a finding by the relevant authorities of an infringement of the Chapters I and II prohibitions, or Arts 81 and 82 EC.[221] Section 19 of the 2002 Act added s 47B to the 1998 Act, which allows damages actions to be brought before the CAT by a consumer representative body – a form of 'class action'.[222] The greatest impact may result from s 58A of the 1998 Act, added by s 20 of the 2002 Act. It provides that, in any action for damages for infringement of the prohibitions under UK or EC law, prior decisions on the infringement by the OFT or CAT will be binding.[223] It is anticipated that measures will be introduced to facilitate private enforcement in the UK, following the publication in November 2007 by the OFT of recommendations to enhance private means of redress in relation to competition law.[224]

Co-operation between courts and authorities

As with enforcement by the NCAs, there is the potential for court actions to run in parallel with other proceedings before the Commission or an NCA. Articles 15 and 16 of Regulation 1/2003 and the Commission Notice on the

---

220 This is a post-Vitamins cartel dispute, [2003] EWHC 961 (Comm), [2003] 2 All ER (Comm) 683, QBD. See, also, *Devenish Nutrition Ltd and others v Sanofi-Aventis SA and others* [2007] EWHC 2394 (Ch).

221 See, for instance, *HealthCare at Home Ltd v Genzyme Ltd* [2006] CAT 29. There are also a number of cases before the CAT in relation to the *Vitamins* cartel.

222 For instance, *The Consumers' Association v JJB Sports plc* (CAT Case 1078/7/9/07), a follow-on consumer representative action under these provisions before the CAT in relation to Replica Kits, although this case was settled out of court in January 2008 following an agreement by JJB to pay consumers who were unlawfully overcharged £20 each (see CAT Order of 14 January 2008).

223 Generally, for the potential impact of these provisions, see Rodger, B, 'Private enforcement and the Enterprise Act: an exemplary system of awarding damages' [2003] ECLR 103. A number of actions, pending before the CAT, have already been raised under the 2002 Act provisions. See, for instance, *Emerson Electric Co and others v Morgan Crucible Company plc*, [2007] CAT 28, following fines imposed on a number of companies including the defendants by the Commission for involvement in a carbon and graphite products cartel. The CAT held that the time limit for bringing a damages claim only started to run when appeal proceedings before the European Court were finalised, even where the specific defendant before the CAT had not appealed the earlier Commission decision.

224 'Private Actions in Competition Law: effective redress for consumers and business' OFT 916resp, see OFT Press Release 162/07, 26 November 2007.

co-operation between the Commission and the courts[225] set out the co-operation process between the national courts and other authorities. Under Art 15 the national courts may ask for the Commission to provide them with information and the Commission or the NCAs may submit observations on particular cases. Article 15(3) also sets out a more controversial procedure where, with the permission of the national court concerned, the Commission may appear in order to make oral observations, effectively appearing as *amicus curiae*.[226] In the English courts, this process has been facilitated by a Practice Direction requiring any claim relating to Art 81 or 82 EC to be raised in the High Court and assigned to the Chancery Division, and a copy of the statement of case served on the OFT. Article 16 sets out the position where a national court is asked to rule on a situation that is being, or already has been, considered by the Commission. The court is required to ensure it does not act inconsistently with the Commission, if necessary staying its proceedings. The relationship between the domestic courts and Commission decisions was considered fully in *Masterfoods v HB Ice Cream*.[227] The Irish Supreme Court was dealing with a private action relating to Arts 81 and 82 of the Treaty at the same time as one of the parties was appealing a Commission decision on the same issue to the CFI. It was held by the CFI that when the national courts rule on an agreement or practice, which is already the subject of a Commission decision, the national court cannot make a decision running counter to that of the Commission. Legal measures adopted by Community institutions are, in principle, presumed to be lawful until such time as they are annulled or withdrawn. If a national court has doubts as to the validity or interpretation of an act of Community institution it may, or must, refer the question to the Court of Justice for a preliminary ruling. Accordingly, the only options that appear to be open to a national court are to stay proceedings, and await the finalisation of the Community proceedings, or to make a reference to the Court under Art 234. Both options may be unsatisfactory in many cases because of the inherent delay. Given the attempts to decentralise enforcement the *Masterfoods* judgment appears to be very 'centralist' in nature.

Globalisation and extraterritoriality

Extraterritoriality

Extraterritoriality concerns the extent to which competition laws can be applied and enforced outside the specific territory of their competence. For

---

225 Commission Notice on the co-operation between the Commission and the courts of the EU Member States in the application of Arts 81 and 82 EC, OJ 2004, C101/54.

226 Fuller explanation of the amicus procedure appears in the Notice, paras 17–35.

227 Case C-344/98 [2001] 4 CMLR 14. See, also, more recently, *Crehan v Inntrepreneur Pub Co (CPC)* [2006] UKHL 38, [2007] 1 AC 333, HL; discussed in Hanley, C, 'The abandonment of deference' (2007) 44(3) CMLRev 817.

instance, can UK competition law be applied to an agreement between companies based in America, or can Community law be applied in respect of a merger between a Japanese company and an American company? The reason for the significance of extraterritoriality in competition law is the potential for effects on international trade, or another economic area, as a result of competition violations. This potential has increased in recent years, due to enhanced globalisation of markets. For instance, there may be a production cartel based in State A which artificially increases the supply price of the product to State or economic area B, thereby affecting the latter state's economic interests. As a result, State B may decide to apply its competition laws to the participating companies and impose fines. This issue is controversial as it implies a breach of territorial sovereignty of State A. On the other hand, many systems of competition law that are applicable to anti-competitive action, which is harmful within a State or which affects the economy of a State, make no provision for conduct which produces effects only outside the State's territory. An example of this would be the grant of a competition law exemption to an export cartel. The potential impact of extraterritorial enforcement of US antitrust law can be seen in the UK's intervention in *Hoffmann-La Roche v Empagran*[228] before the US Supreme Court. In that case a number of organisations which had suffered losses through the activities of the Vitamins cartel in Australia, Ecuador, Panama and Ukraine, were seeking damages before the US courts. The UK Government intervened, as *amicus curiae*, to argue that an extension of the US's jurisdiction to this extent would be damaging to global competition enforcement.[229]

Subject matter jurisdiction

The basic problem that faces the enforcement of competition law outwith the territory of a State arises from the commonly accepted principle of public international law that there are limits to a State's jurisdictional competence. The starting point is to differentiate between subject matter jurisdiction and enforcement jurisdiction. A State may consider that it has subject matter jurisdiction to apply its rules to conduct, or more often to the economic effects of conduct, irrespective of the precise locus of the conduct. The principal reason this issue has arisen in competition law is because the economic effects of market conduct are often easily separable from the conduct itself. Accordingly, it is perhaps understandable that difficulties arise and that States may consider their competition laws applicable to economic effects produced within their State, which derive from conduct or activity that

228 *F Hoffmann-La Roche Ltd, Hoffmann-La Roche Inc, Roche Vitamins Inc, BASF AG, BASF Corp, Rhône-Poulenc Animal Nutrition Inc, Rhône-Poulenc Inc v Empagran SA* 124 S Ct 2359 (2004).

229 See the UK's *amicus* brief at: http://www.berr.gov.uk/bbf/competition/international/ukbriefs/page33060.html.

originated elsewhere. However, this becomes particularly contentious if the State seeks to go further and exercise enforcement jurisdiction, enforcing its competition rules by normal means, such as serving court papers or demanding evidence from a company. Enforcement of competition laws abroad may cause conflict with the State in which enforcement is sought.

Under international law, subject matter jurisdiction may be based on nationality or territorial grounds. Under the territoriality principle, jurisdiction may exist if the act originated abroad but was completed within the jurisdiction. A straightforward example would be the refusal to supply goods or services. However, it is less clear whether the territoriality principle can be applied where there are only economic effects produced within the territory. Often, the anti-competitive behaviour, such as predatory or excessive pricing, will be within the jurisdiction, or at least one party to an agreement will be based within the territory. Should this not be the case, one possibility for competition authorities would be to invoke the 'economic entity' doctrine. Using this approach, enforcement may be sought against a parent company outwith the jurisdiction on the basis of the actions of a subsidiary company within the jurisdiction, where the conduct or activity was controlled or directed by the parent company. The main controversy arises where the actions take place outside the jurisdiction but produce economic effects in a market within the jurisdiction. A clear example of this would be a price-fixing cartel based in another jurisdiction. One possible solution to this controversial problem is to adopt the effects doctrine derived from the famous *Alcoa*[230] decision in the US, which confirmed that liability can exist for breach of the antitrust rules for conduct outside the borders of the US that produces consequences within it. Regarding the UK, there is little or no mention of extraterritorial enforcement within the competition law provisions. The main reason has been a strict adherence to traditional international law principles which are opposed to concepts such as the effects doctrine. The Competition Act makes no reference to extraterritorial application and the prohibition of anti-competitive agreements only applies to those 'implemented within the United Kingdom'.[231]

Community competition law and extraterritoriality

Community law applies if there is an effect on interstate trade. Beyond this basic rule, it is unclear whether an effects doctrine may be applied by the Commission. The economic entity doctrine was approved by the Court in early case law.[232] The *Dyestuffs* case involved illegal price-fixing within the

230 *United States v Aluminium Co of America (Alcoa)* 148 F 2d 416 (1945), 2 Circ. Cf *Hoffmann-La Roche Ltd v Empagram SA* 124 S Ct 2359 (2004).
231 For the limits of the new Chapter I and II prohibitions, see ss 2 and 18, respectively.
232 Case 48/69 *ICI v Commission (Dyestuffs)* [1972] ECR 619; [1972] CMLR 557.

Community, where the price-fixing was principally carried out by non-Community-based undertakings through Community-based subsidiaries. The anti-competitive conduct was attributed to the parent company as the subsidiaries were effectively under its control. The application of the economic entity doctrine has been criticised as ignoring the separate legal personality of the companies, but it has been relied on by the Commission.[233]

Application of the doctrine is dependent on the existence and exercise of control by the parent company, such as its representation on the subsidiary board. Although the doctrine allows Community competition law to be enforced against companies beyond the Community, enforcement is ensured, practically, by serving documentation on the subsidiary. An alternative approach would be the adoption by the Commission of the effects doctrine. However, its application is still unclear as a result of the Court's judgment in *Wood Pulp*.[234] The *Wood Pulp* case involved allegations of price-fixing between wood pulp producers throughout the world, including various non-Community based producers. The Commission claimed that Community competition law applied where the conduct produced effects within the Community. The Court avoided the controversial issue of the applicability of the economic effects doctrine by stating that, based on the facts, the agreement had indeed been implemented within the Community. It remains unclear what constitutes implementation and also whether purely economic effects within the Community would be considered sufficient. A possible scenario could, for instance, involve a refusal to supply within the Community by a cartel boycotting the Community market. As far as enforcement is concerned, the Court has considered that the Commission is competent to serve documents, and indeed necessary for enforcement to be pursued, on a non-Community company.[235] On a practical level, the main difficulty in enforcing any Commission decision and/or penalty may be overcome by seizing that company's assets in the Community.

Extraterritorial application of Community law has been a particularly high profile issue in recent years, given the Commission's involvement in the mergers between US companies, for example, McDonnell Douglas and Boeing, and GE and Honeywell, and the controversial CFI ruling in *Gencor Ltd v Commission*.[236] In that case, parent companies Gencor and Lonrho agreed to merge the activities of their platinum mining subsidiary companies in South Africa. The South African authorities did not object to the merger,

---

233 For example, Case 7/73 *Commercial Solvents v Commission* [1974] ECR 223; [1974] 1 CMLR 309.
234 Cases C-89, 104, 114, 116, 117 and 125–29/85 *A Ahlstrom Oy v Commission* [1988] ECR 5193; [1988] 4 CMLR 901.
235 Case 52/69 *Geigy v Commission* [1972] ECR 787; [1972] CMLR 557. However, see Feibig, A, 'International law limits on the extra-territorial application of the European merger control regulation and suggestions for reform' [1998] 6 ECLR 323.
236 Case T-102/96 [1999] ECR II-753; [1999] 4 CMLR 971.

but the Commission blocked the merger on the basis of the collective dominance theory.[237] A key issue concerned the territorial reach of the Merger
Regulation.[238] The starting point was that the Regulation applies to all
mergers with a Community dimension, and there was a Community dimension in the case in this instance. Sales within the Community constituted
substantial operations in the Community,[239] and were deemed to satisfy the
implementation test set out in *Wood Pulp*. The most controversial aspect of
the case was the CFI's view that the 'application of the Merger Regulation is
justified under public international law when it is foreseeable that a proposed
concentration will have an immediate and substantial effect in the Community'.[240] This appears to endorse the widely criticised effects doctrine,
although the impact of the judgment may be restricted to merger control.
The Commission Decision to prohibit the proposed acquisition by General
Electric Co of Honeywell Inc, two American undertakings involved in aero-
engines, avionics and other aircraft components and systems, resulted in tension between the US and Community competition authorities, as the former
had earlier approved the merger.[241]

Resistance to extraterritorial application

Disputes can arise between different legal systems due to the controversial
nature of the extraterritorial application and enforcement of competition
laws. For example, in the mid-1980s, Laker Airways sued certain UK-based
airline companies for breach of US antitrust law, and that litigation involved
sensitive considerations of the possibility of UK courts preventing the US
courts from enforcing US antitrust laws against the UK-based companies.[242]
A number of countries have passed blocking statutes to prevent the extraterritorial application of US antitrust law, in some instances as a direct response
to the *Alcoa* decision. This demonstrates how the extraterritoriality issue

---

237 For further discussion of collective dominance, see Chapters 3 and 6.
238 See Fox, E, 'The merger regulation and its territorial reach: *Gencor Ltd v Commission*' [1999]
ECLR 334; Porter Elliott, G, 'The Gencor judgment: collective dominance, remedies and
extraterritoriality under the merger regulation' (1999) 24 EL Rev 639.
239 *Per* the 11th recital to the Merger Regulation.
240 [1988] ECR 5193; [1988] 4 CMLR 901, para 90.
241 Commission Decision 2004/134/EC *General Electric/Honeywell*, OJ 2004, L48/1. See
Zanettin, B, *Cooperation between Antitrust Agencies at the International Level*, 2000,
Oxford: Hart, for discussion on the impact of the Commission prohibition on US/EU
antitrust relations. See, also, Burnside, A, 'GE, honey, I sunk the merger' [2002] ECLR 107.
The Commission's decision was upheld by the CFI in Case T-209/01 *Honeywell International Inc v Commission* [2005] ECR I-5527 and Case T-210/01 *General Electric Co
v Commission* [2005] ECLR I-5575. See Howarth, D, 'The Court of First Instance in
GE/Honeywell' [2006] ECLR 485.
242 See *Midland Bank plc v Laker Airways plc* [1986] 1 All ER 526; and *British Airways v Laker
Airlines* [1984] 3 All ER 39.

clearly relates to political and nationalistic considerations and is evidenced by the introduction of the Protection of Trading Interests Act 1980 in the UK. This legislation is not limited to the possible extraterritorial enforcement of US antitrust laws, but may be more broadly applicable in relation to possible harm to commercial interests in the UK. The Act gives the Secretary of State powers to prohibit UK firms from complying with foreign laws and/or complying with any requirement to submit information to any foreign authority beyond the territorial jurisdiction of the foreign authority.[243] Sections 5 and 6 of the Protection of Trading Interests Act 1980 provide that multiple damages awards are not enforceable in the UK and that an action may be brought in the UK to 'claw back' the excess awarded in a foreign multiple damages action when compared to a domestic single damage action.

International co-operation and global competition rules

Enforcement jurisdiction, as noted, may lead to possible conflicts where authorities seek to serve court papers or order the production of documents. However, as markets become more global and the larger companies operate on a worldwide scale, information regarding a company's operations beyond the particular territory of the enforcement authority is becoming even more important. Partly as a result of globalisation, and in an attempt to ensure more effective enforcement of competition law generally, there have been various developments to seek to ensure some form of co-operation between national and supranational agencies. Efforts to improve co-operation have developed on both a multilateral and a bilateral basis. The United Nations Conference on Trade and Development (UNCTAD) and the Organisation for Economic Cooperation and Development (OECD) are active in this area and there are suggestions that competition enforcement should be brought within the auspices of the World Trade Organization (WTO). Bilaterally, there has been increased international co-operation in competition law enforcement between a number of States.[244] There have also been important developments involving the Community. The Community entered a co-operation Agreement with the US in 1991. The Agreement was successfully challenged before the Court by the French Government on the basis that the Commission was acting *ultra vires*. In April 1995 this was remedied with retroactive effect by a Decision of the Council and Commission.[245] The

---

243 Protection of Trading Interests Act 1980, ss 1–3.
244 See, for instance, Galloway, J, 'Moving towards a template for bilateral antitrust agreements' (2005) 28(4) World Competition 589.
245 Agreement Between the Government of the United States of America and the European Communities Regarding the Application of their Competition Laws, OJ 1995, L95/47, as corrected by OJ 1995, L131/38.

Agreement is significant and provides for notification, consultation, information sharing, and co-operation and co-ordination in enforcement, although the Agreement makes clear that it should be interpreted in conformity with the respective substantive rules of the US and European Union and that the competition authorities remain bound by their own internal rules on confidentiality.[246] There has been a substantial body of practice developed under the Agreement and the Commission publishes an annual report on its operation. In 1999 the Community and Canada also finalised a co-operation agreement due to the increase in the number of cases being investigated by the authorities of both jurisdictions.[247] In a European context, the European Economic Area (EEA) Agreement provides a clear system of collaboration between the Commission and the European Free Trade Association (EFTA) Surveillance Authority in the enforcement of Community and EEA competition rules. Furthermore, the European Competition Network is probably the best example of co-operation and co-working involving a number of competition authorities, albeit in the application of the same set of substantive rules.[248]

Finally, there have been developments within the WTO framework with a view to establishing, in the longer term, an international antitrust code.[249] At present, a global code or competition authority seems unlikely. Nonetheless, there was an important report, in 2001, by the International Competition Policy Advisory Committee (ICPAC) of the antitrust division of the US Department of Justice.[250] It focused on the issues of multi-jurisdictional mergers and international co-operation, particularly in relation to cartels, and the interface between trade and competition rules. The report considered that the WTO was not the appropriate forum for advancing global competition issues and it proposed a global competition initiative as a new venue for the exchange of ideas and progress towards common solutions for competition

---

246 The Community and the US entered into an agreement on the application of 'positive comity' principles to further strengthen existing co-operation under the 1995 Agreement. The main objective, further to Art V of the 1995 Agreement, is to provide that either party, whose interests are adversely affected by anti-competitive activities occurring in whole or in substantial part in the territory of one of the parties, may request the other party to take action in the form of investigating and remedying the anti-competitive activities. See, in particular, Arts I and III, OJ 1998, L173/28. More recently there has been increased focus on best practices, on the basis that these achieve a greater degree of procedural convergence, thus lessening the risk of conflicting decisions.

247 OJ 1999, L175/50. See, also, Agreement between the EC and the Government of Japan concerning co-operation on Anti-Competitive Activities, 05 2003, L183/12.

248 See, for instance, Canebley, C, and Rosenthal, M, 'Co-operation between Antitrust Authorities In- and Outside The EU: What does it mean for multinational corporations?' Part I [2005] ECLR 106; Part II [2005] ECLR 178.

249 See Koczarowska, A, 'International competition law in the context of global capitalism' [2000] 2 ECLR 117.

250 At www.usdoj.gov/atr/icpac/finalreport.htm, 20 April 2001.

law and policy problems. The search for a worldwide competition culture has been developed through the International Competition Network (ICN), launched in 2001 as a project-orientated, consensus-based informal network of antitrust agencies from developed and developing countries. The ICN does not seek to introduce any form of global competition law but, instead, gradual convergence through understanding of best practice in the area of competition law enforcement.

Further reading

Regulation 1/2003, The Network Notice and the ECN

Brammer, S, 'Concurrent Jurisdiction under Regulation 1/2003 and the issue of case allocation' (2005) 42(5) CML Rev 1383.

Dekeyser, K, and Jaspers, M, 'A New Era of ECN Co-operation' (2007) 30(1) World Competition 3.

Gilliams, HM, 'Modernisation: from policy to practice' (2003) 28 EL Rev 451.

Riley, A, 'EC antitrust modernisation: the Commission does very nicely – thank you! Part one: Regulation 1 and the notification burden' [2003] ECLR 604; 'Part two: between the idea and the reality; decentralisation under Regulation 1' [2003] ECLR 687.

Venit, J, 'Brave new world: the modernization and decentralization of enforcement under Articles 81 and 82 of the EC Treaty' (2003) 40 CML Rev 545.

Wesseling, R, 'The Commission White Paper on modernisation of EC antitrust law: unspoken consequences and incomplete treatment of alternative options' [1999] ECLR 420.

UK competition law reform, the Competition Act 1998 and the Enterprise Act 2002

Goodman, S, 'Steady as she goes: the Enterprise Act 2002 charts a familiar course for UK merger control' [2003] ECLR 331.

Lawrence, J and Moffat, J, 'A dangerous new world – practical implications of the Enterprise Act 2002' [2004] ECLR 1.

Rodger, B, 'The Competition Act and the Enterprise Act 2002 Reforms: Sanctions and Deterrence in UK Competition Law, in Dannecker, G, and Jansen, O, (eds), *Competition Law Sanctioning in the European Union, The EU Influence on the National System of Sanctions in the European Area*, 2003, The Hague: Kluwer Law International.

Rodger, BJ and MacCulloch, A, *The UK Competition Act: A New Era for UK Competition Law*, 2000, Oxford: Hart.

Wilks, S, *In the Public Interest: Competition Policy and the Monopolies and Mergers Commission*, 1999, Manchester: MUP.

Private enforcement

Brkan, M, 'Procedural Aspects of Private Enforcement of EC Antitrust Law: Heading Toward New Reforms?' (2005) 28(4) World Competition 479.

Eilmansberger, T, 'The Green Paper on Damages for Breach of the EC Antitrust Rules and Beyond: Reflections on the Utility and Feasibility of Stimulating Private Enforcement through Legislative Action' (2007) 44(2) CMLRev 431.

Hodges, C, 'Competition Enforcement, Regulation and Civil Justice: What is the Case?' (2006) 43(5) CMLRev 1381.

Jones, CA, 'Private antitrust enforcement in Europe: a policy analysis and reality check' (2004) 27(1) World Competition 13.

Komninos, A, 'New prospects for private enforcement of EC competition law: *Courage v Crehan* and the Community right to damages' (2002) 39 CML Rev 447–87.

Kon, S, and Maxwell, A, 'Enforcement in national courts of the EC and new UK competition rules: obstacles to effective enforcement' [1998] ECLR 443.

Rodger, BJ, 'Private enforcement and the Enterprise Act: an exemplary system of awarding damages?' [2003] ECLR 103.

Singla, T, 'The Remedies (Not) Available for Breaches of Article 81 EC' [2008] ECLR 201.

Wils, W, 'Should private antitrust enforcement be encouraged in Europe?' (2003) 26 World Competition 473.

Globalisation

Amato, F, 'International Antitrust: What Future?' (2001) 24(4) World Competition 451.

Canenbley, C, and Rosenthal, M, 'Co-operation between Antitrust Authorities In- and Outside the EU: What does it mean for multinational corporations?' Part 1 [2005] ECLR 106; Part 2 [2005] ECLR 178.

Maher, I, 'Competition law in the international domain: networks as a new form of governance' [2002] Journal of Law and Society 111.

Von Meibom, W, and Geiger, A, 'A world competition law as an ultima ratio' [2002] ECLR 445.

Discussion

1   What changes did Regulation 1/2003 introduce to the enforcement of EC competition law?

2   What mechanisms exist for case allocation within the ECN and how is EC law applied by the OFT?

3   How has UK competition law been transformed by the Competition Act 1998 and Enterprise Act 2002?

4   To what extent does the Enterprise Act enhance the deterrent impact of UK competition law?

5   To what extent has private enforcement played a significant role in enhancing the deterrent effect of EC and UK competition law? What are

the primary obstacles and how are the Commission/OFT seeking to develop this area?

6   Why is globalisation a problem for competition law? How has international co-operation been facilitated and to what extent are global competition initiatives likely to be successful?

Chapter 3

The control of dominance

In the introductory chapter of this book it was clear that one of the central concerns of the economics of competition was the control of market power. It is therefore unsurprising that all competition law regimes have measures which seek to control the exercise and maintenance of such power. In this chapter we shall discuss the ways in which the EC, through Art 82 EC, and the UK, through the Chapter II prohibition, seek to deal with market power or dominance, as it is known in the prohibitions, and also the provisions in the Enterprise Act 2002 on market investigations.

Introduction to Art 82 of the EC Treaty

The essence of the single market within the European Community is the freedom of movement of goods, services, labour and capital. Competition law is vital as the four freedoms will only be fully attained if businesses within the Community can compete freely. A principal objective of Community competition law is to prevent businesses from distorting or dividing up markets within the Community. The objective of the Community's competition provisions is set out in Art 3(1)(g) of the EC Treaty.[1] The Community is to set up 'a system ensuring that competition in the internal market is not distorted'. The first substantive provision in the EC Treaty that we shall discuss is Art 82 EC. It is designed to deal with the activities of businesses, 'undertakings' in European terminology, which have a powerful market position similar to the economists' concept of monopoly. The actions of a business that has market power can have serious effects on the operation of a market. Article 82 is directed at the activities of a powerful single business which is not subject to effective competition. An undertaking in a dominant position may use its market power in several ways: to exploit consumers by restricting

---

1 It is very interesting to note that, following intervention by the French Government, the EU Reform Treaty will, if ratified by the Member States, remove the reference to 'free and undistorted competition' from the objectives of the Treaty and relegate it to a legally binding protocol annexed to the Treaty. The main competition prohibitions remain unchanged.

output and increasing prices; to perpetuate its own position, perhaps through unfair discounting; or, to extend its position into another market, perhaps by tying the sale of one product to another. For that reason, Art 82 prohibits the 'abuse' of a 'dominant position' within the Community so far as it may affect trade between Member States.

The European Commission, beginning in December 2005, has been undertaking a large scale review of the operation of a number of aspects of Art 82.[2] This review can seen as the end of wide reform of much of EC competition law that has resulted in reform of the way the EC handles vertical restraints under Reg 2790/99,[3] the modernisation of the enforcement system under Reg 1/2003,[4] and the merger control provisions under Reg 139/2004.[5] The Art 82 review focuses on the handling of exclusionary abuses within the prohibition. This review is expected to be completed in 2008 and may result in a major reform of the Commission's practice in relation to Art 82, if not the wording of the prohibition itself. The key features of the reform discussion will be introduced below. It is clear, however, that the reform process has resulted in a lengthy debate about the correct way forward in determining what Art 82 should seek to achieve.

When examining the application of Art 82 in practice, it is better to consider the interpretation of the constituent parts of the prohibition in reverse order: 'effect on trade between Member States', 'dominant position' and, finally, 'abuse'.

Undertakings and the effect on trade between Member States

Only 'undertakings', within the terms of EC law, are controlled by the competition provisions of the Treaty. The definition used is the same for both Arts 81 and 82 EC.[6] The Court and the Commission have interpreted the term very broadly, maximising the scope of the competition rules. All natural or legal persons carrying on some form of commercial activity in the goods or services sectors will be included.[7] Commercial activity includes those activities which are not designed to be profit-making.[8] For instance, it was held, in proceedings before a Scottish court, that a statutory body, the Keeper of the Registers of

---

2 DG Competition discussion paper on the application of Article 82 of the Treaty to exclusionary abuses, Brussels, December 2005.
3 OJ 1999, L336/21.
4 OJ 2003, L1/1.
5 OJ 2004, L24/1.
6 See, also, the discussion of the concept of 'undertaking', within Art 81 EC, in Chapter 4.
7 Eg, opera singers in Commission Decision 78/516/EEC *RAI/UNITEL*, OJ 1978, L157/39; [1978] 3 CMLR 306.
8 Commission Decision 82/1283/EEC *ANSEAU-NAVENA*, OJ 1982, L167/39; [1982] 1 CMLR 221.

Scotland, which is also an officer of the Crown, constituted an undertaking for the purposes of Art 82.[9] The interaction between the State and the competition rules, as seen in *FENIN*[10] and *AOK Bundesverband*,[11] is a very sensitive, and highly politicised, issue.[12] Both these cases involved the State's provision of health services, and the question of whether the bodies managing that health service provision were undertakings within the competition rules. The Court has consistently held that where a body entrusted with the management of statutory health provision pursues an exclusively social objective it does not engage in economic activity and is therefore not considered to be an 'undertaking'. Legally distinct companies, when they are not independent from each other, may be considered as one undertaking for the purposes of Community competition law. This is the case in a parent/subsidiary situation. Although legally separate, the subsidiary may be controlled by the parent company. This is known as the 'economic entity' doctrine.[13] Accordingly, when dealing with connected companies it is important to examine the economic and managerial independence of the companies in question.[14]

The prerequisite that there should be an effect on trade between Member States acts as a jurisdictional test to demarcate the boundary between the application of Community and national competition law. The interpretation of this concept, therefore, is politically important. The relationship between EC and national competition law is now governed by Art 3 of Reg 1/2003.[15] Article 3(1) provides that, where there is an effect on interstate trade, national courts and authorities shall, in applying domestic competition law rules, also apply Arts 81 and 82. Article 3(2) provides that domestic competition law may apply stricter standards to that which constitutes unilateral abusive conduct. These rules seek to ensure a clearer substantive rule of precedence in the application of Community law and national law. Not surprisingly, the Community Courts have given the inter-State trade concept a broad interpretation. The general test, which applies to cases under Arts 82 and 81 EC, was laid down in *Société Technique Minière*:[16]

9 *Miller & Bryce v Keeper of the Registers of Scotland* 1997 SLT 1000 (OH).

10 Case T-319/99 *FENIN v Commission* [2003] ECR II-357; [2003] 5 CMLR 1.

11 Cases C-264, 306/01, 354 and 355/01 *AOK Bundesverband v Ichthyol-Gesellschaft Cordes, Hermani & Co* [2004] 4 CMLR 22.

12 This will be discussed more fully in Chapter 7. See, also, Montana, L and Jellis, J, 'The concept of undertaking in EC competition law and its application to public bodies: can you buy your way into Article 82?' (2003) 2 Comp LJ 110.

13 Case 22/71 *Beguelin Import v GL Import Export* [1971] ECR 949; [1972] CMLR 81. See, also, the recent discussion in the English courts in *Provimi Limited v Aventis Animal Nutrition SA* [2003] ECC 29.

14 Case T-102/92 *Viho v Commission* [1995] ECR II-17; [1997] 4 CMLR 469. On appeal Case C-73/95P [1996] ECR I-5457; [1997] 4 CMLR 419.

15 Regulation 1/2003/EC, OJ 2003, L1/1.

16 Case 56/65 *Société Technique Minière v Maschinenbau Ulm GmbH* [1966] ECR 235; [1966] CMLR 357.

... it must be possible to foresee with a sufficient degree of probability on the basis of a set of objective factors of law or fact that the agreement in question may have an influence, direct or indirect, actual or potential, on the pattern of trade between Member States.

The effect on trade test, therefore, covers any conduct which could affect the way in which trade patterns operate across the Community.[17] In addition to this general test, because of the importance of market structure, there is a structural test peculiar to Art 82. Where market power is concentrated in one undertaking, it can have damaging effects on competition. An undertaking's economic power can discourage other undertakings from entering the market. The economic models of competition require new market entrants to control the power of existing undertakings. The ability of a dominant undertaking to use market power to exclude competitors, or potential competitors, is therefore of particular concern. The structural test operates where there is an alteration in the structure of competition within the market.[18] The test will usually be fulfilled even where the dominant undertaking only operates in one national market, as the strength of that undertaking will tend to reinforce the division of markets along national lines. The strengthening of such a division will have an effect on trade between Member States.[19]

Dominant position

The use of economic analysis in the application of Art 82 is very important. A finding of dominance will be based on economic factors, although there are legal guidelines laid down by the Court and the Commission. In practice, three main areas have to be examined before dominance[20] can be established. These are: the definition of the relevant market; the establishment of market strength; and, the consideration of possible barriers to entry. Only once all three of these areas have been examined will any finding be reliable.

The relevant market

The first, and potentially most vital, step is to define exactly which market the undertaking is competing in. That market is known as the relevant market. Without delineating the products or services that are in competition it is impossible to gauge how much power an undertaking has over its competitors and consumers. The relevant market is itself divided into three parts: product market, geographical market, and temporal market.

---

17 See, also, Case C-359/01P *British Sugar v Commission* [2004] ECR I-4933.
18 Cases 6 and 7/73 *Commercial Solvents v Commission* [1974] ECR 223; [1974] 1 CMLR 309.
19 See Case T-30/91 *Solvay v Commission (Soda Ash)* [1995] ECR II-1775.
20 In more general terms, it is sometimes known as 'market power'.

The Commission has produced a Notice on the definition of the relevant market. In that Notice it sets out the methods it employs in market definition. The Commission's aim is to increase the transparency of its decision-making process. It is particularly interesting in that the Notice explains the practical steps the Commission takes when it examines a market.[21]

The relevant product market

Before it is possible to say that an undertaking is dominant in a market, it has to be ascertained what constitutes that market and that is done by defining the range of products in competition with those of the undertaking in question. Only an undertaking's position in relation to actual or potential competitors will give a true indication of its dominance. The importance of market definition was emphasised in *Continental Can v Commission*,[22] where the Commission's decision was annulled by the Court because of the Commission's failure to properly demarcate the relevant market. The definition of a market can be very controversial. If the product market is drawn narrowly, with relatively few competing products, it is much more likely that the undertaking will be found to be dominant. The legal test, as set out by the Court, is that of interchangeability,[23] while the Commission, in its Notice, relies on SSNIP tests otherwise known as the 'hypothetical monopolist' test. It is worth looking at both tests in turn as they are different in methodology, although they may produce similar results.

The Commission's practice is based on discovering the level of demand substitution in a market; that is, the ease with which customers will switch their allegiance to other products when faced with price increases. SSNIP is an acronym for a 'Small, but Significant, Non-transitory Increase in Price'. The test operates by applying a hypothetical permanent increase in price to a product; usually the price increase will be in the range of 5–10%. Initially this hypothetical increase is applied to the products produced by the undertaking in question. If there is evidence that customers would switch to purchasing other products when faced with such a price increase the original product and the substitute products are considered to be in the same market. This calculus is undertaken until there are no further products which would be considered as substitutes. If one undertaking produced all such products it could be said that the undertaking would not be subject to competition from other products and would, therefore, be a 'hypothetical monopolist'.[24] Although this is

---

21 Commission Notice on the definition of the relevant market for the purposes of Community competition law, OJ 1997, C372/3. See Baker, S and Wu, L, 'Applying the market definition guidelines of the European Commission' [1998] 5 ECLR 273.
22 Case 6/72 *Continental Can v Commission* [1973] ECR 215; [1978] 1 CMLR 199.
23 Sometimes referred to as 'substitutability'.
24 See Crocioni, P, 'The hypothetical monopolist test' [2002] ECLR 354.

a hypothetical test the Commission must still gather hard evidence to support its arguments that substitution would occur in this way. It therefore gathers evidence from a great many sources, and that evidence includes evidence of substitution in the recent past, econometric studies, views of customers and competitors, customer preference, and marketing studies. The use of this test gives Commission practice a solid economic grounding, but it is not free of potential difficulties. One problem is the application of such a test where there is a paucity of economic evidence, particularly in very small or new markets. In that case it is very difficult to gather sufficient evidence to make useful findings. Another problem is known as the 'cellophane fallacy'. This is not directly related to cellophane as a product, but to the US case in which the fallacy was discussed.[25] It relates to the situation in which a dominant undertaking has already been able to increase prices to a monopolistic level. In most markets there will be some level of competition in the market and a rational dominant undertaking will only raise its prices above the competitive level until the point where the existence of remaining competitors would make any further rises unprofitable. At that point any increase in price might result in demand substitution for products which would not have been considered as substitutes at the lower hypothetical 'competitive' price. Application of the SSNIP test to this elevated price may lead to the assumption that the products were effective substitutes, whereas they would not have been at the 'competitive' price. Accordingly, in markets where competition is already severely limited, the SSNIP test may give erroneous results. It is, therefore, vital that the Commission handles the available economic data sensitively.

While Commission practice is important, it is not the authoritative legal test; for that we must look to the judgments of the Community Courts.[26] However, while it has not adopted the terminology of the Notice, it is clear that the Court is generally supportive of the practice adopted by the Commission. The Court's traditional test is also based on substitution, or interchangeability. In *Continental Can* the Court considered that an examination must be made of products which are '. . . particularly apt to satisfy an inelastic need and are only to a limited extent interchangeable with other products'.[27] At its simplest level the test requires an examination of the products which a consumer will regard as interchangeable with the product in question; demand side interchangeability or substitution. This raises very similar questions to those posed by the Commission under the SSNIP test. To help to define the market the Court has set out a number of areas to be considered.

---

25 *United States v EI du Pont de Nemours & Co* 118 F Supp 41 (D Del 1953); aff'd 351 US 377 (US Sup Ct 1956).

26 While the Court's tests may be legally authoritative, they have been economically criticised: see Azevedo, JP and Walker, M, 'Dominance: meaning and measurement' [2002] ECLR 363.

27 [1973] ECR 215, para 14. 'Inelastic' is an economic term describing a type of demand. For a simple explanation of cross-elasticity, and other economic terms, see Glossary.

Cross-elasticity of demand

The economic test of cross-elasticity of demand is, in effect, the same test as applied by the Commission under its Notice. Where cross-elasticity is high any increase in the price of a product will cause significant shifts by consumers to other products. If demand is 'elastic' it means that customers switch readily, whereas if demand is 'inelastic' they will not shift to other products until there is a relatively high price increase. Cross-elasticity may be valuable in that it gives an objective determination of the actual operation of the market. Such economic analysis has been found to be of value[28] but, as with all statistical analysis, great care must be taken to ensure that the results are a true reflection of the market.

Physical characteristics

The physical characteristics of a product will obviously be vital to a decision as to whether products are interchangeable. If products are physically similar and have similar functions the consumer is more likely to see them as being interchangeable. Even where products have broadly similar characteristics, it may be possible to find ways in which particular characteristics place them in separate markets. A classic example of such a distinction was seen in *United Brands*.[29] The Commission argued that the market for bananas was separate from the market for fresh fruit generally. The Commission concentrated on the year-round availability of bananas, their appearance, softness and seedlessness, which meant that they satisfied the particular needs of the very young, the old and the sick. On the basis of this and other arguments the Court accepted that bananas should be differentiated from other fresh fruit. The Court's reasoning on this point has been challenged but it illustrates the way in which minor differences between products can affect the consideration of the market in which they are competing with other similar goods.

Price

The price of a product can affect the relevant market. Take, for example, the market for domestic vehicles. It is unlikely that a Ferrari 430 and a Mazda MX-5 would be considered to be competing in the same market. Even though they fulfil the same function, 2-seater sports cars, they do not compete. It is unlikely that a consumer would consider them interchangeable.

---

28 See, for example, Case 27/76 *United Brands Continental BV v Commission* [1978] ECR 207; [1978] 1 CMLR 429.
29 See Case 27/76 *United Brands Continental BV v Commission* [1978] ECR 207; [1978] 1 CMLR 429.

Intended use

The intended use of the product is a very important consideration. A product may have a number of different uses, each of which may form a different market. In *Michelin*,[30] the Court examined the market for car tyres. Because of the differing nature of demand, the Court found that the original-equipment tyres, to be fitted to new vehicles during manufacture, and replacement tyres, to be fitted during repairs, were in separate markets. Manufacturers ordered original-equipment tyres in bulk while replacement tyres were ordered as and when required.

Another way in which the intended use criterion can narrow a market was seen in *Commercial Solvents*.[31] A subsidiary of Commercial Solvents supplied Zoja with nitropropane, which Zoja processed into an anti-TB drug. When Commercial Solvents ceased supplies of the raw material, Zoja claimed Commercial Solvents was in a dominant position. Commercial Solvents argued that other chemicals could be used to produce the drug, and that those chemicals should be considered as part of the overall market of materials for producing the drug. The Court disagreed and focused on the fact that the process in Zoja's plant relied on supplies of nitropropane; no other raw material could be used. Therefore, the way in which Zoja utilised the product limited the market.

Supply side interchangeability

So far, we have considered a number of demand-based factors, concentrating on consumer perception, but the supply side can also affect the relevant product market. A product may not be directly interchangeable with any others but this may not mean that it is the only product to be considered. The Commission Notice on market definition indicates this calculation is also an important part of its practice, but only in situations where supply-side substitutability is equivalent to demand substitution in terms of effectiveness and immediacy. If other suppliers, currently manufacturing other products, can 'switch production to the relevant products and market them in the short term without incurring significant additional costs',[32] they should also be considered as part of the market. This possible alternative supply, known as potential competition, is likely to exert a competitive pressure on the current supplier. In the Notice, the example of paper production is used. While different grades of paper may not be substitutable by the consumer, it may be relatively easy for a paper manufacturer to alter production to produce

---

30 Case 322/81 *Nederlandsche Banden-Industrie Michelin NV v Commission* [1983] ECR 3461; [1985] 1 CMLR 282.
31 See Cases 6 and 7/73 *Commercial Solvents v Commission* [1974] ECR 223; [1974] 1 CMLR 309.
32 Commission Notice on market definition, OJ 1997, C372/5, para 20.

different grades. In *Continental Can*,[33] the Court annulled the Commission's decision on the basis that it had not properly considered whether the producers of other types of can, largely cylindrical cans, could enter the market for meat and fish cans.

The relevant geographical market

It is also important to determine the geographical extent of the relevant market. Before evaluating dominance it is important to ensure that the same conditions of competition exist across the whole market.[34] There may be legal, technical or practical reasons why a product only competes within a limited area of the Community. Accordingly, the assessment of market power can only take place in the geographical area where competition can be realistically expected. The general test was laid down in *United Brands* where the Court limited the geographical market to '. . . an area where the objective conditions of competition applying to the product in question must be the same for all traders'. In the market for bananas, the UK, France and Italy were excluded from consideration, as the conditions of competition were different in those States because of their long-term relationships with former colonies which produce bananas.

Geographical markets may also be limited by transport restrictions on the product. If the unit transport cost of the product is high it is less likely that the product will have a Community-wide market. This is particularly important for products which are difficult to transport over long distances, for instance, dangerous chemicals, or for some types of fresh food, such as bread.

The temporal market

A market may vary over time. This can be due to seasonal variations in production. The seasonal nature of fruit production was raised in *United Brands*.[35] External factors may also affect the market, altering the conditions of competition. If those factors are temporary in nature the period in which they affected the nature of competition will be considered separately.[36]

---

33 See Case 6/72 *Continental Can v Commission* [1973] ECR 215; [1978] 1 CMLR 199.
34 In Commission practice, the geographical market is addressed alongside the product market using the SSNIP test.
35 See Case 27/76 *United Brands Continental BV v Commission* [1978] ECR 207; [1978] 1 CMLR 429. As the Court defined the market narrowly it did not rely on the seasonal nature of the market in its judgment.
36 This was the case during the 1970s oil crisis. See Commission Decision 77/327/EEC *ABG*, OJ 1977, L117/1; [1977] 2 CMLR D1. On appeal Case 77/77 *Benzine Petroleum Handelmaatschappij BV v Commission* [1978] ECR 1513.

Dominance

Once the relevant market has been determined it is then possible to calculate if an undertaking is dominant. The traditional definition of dominance was laid down by the Court in *United Brands*:

> The dominant position thus referred to [by Art 82] relates to a position of economic strength enjoyed by an undertaking which enables it to prevent effective competition being maintained on the relevant market by affording it the power to behave to an appreciable extent independently of its competitors, customers and ultimately of its consumers.[37]

The dominance test has two main elements. First, the allusion to the ability to act independently refers to an economic view of market power: the fact that the undertaking's actions are not constrained by effective competition. The dominant undertaking is no longer a 'price-taker'.[38] Secondly, the reference to the prevention of effective competition refers to a dominant undertaking's ability to prevent potential competitors from entering the market. This is referred to as exclusionary conduct and it enables an undertaking to protect its dominant position. The difference between these two elements is more important in the discussion of types of abusive conduct. The tools used to investigate whether an undertaking is dominant are the same in both situations.

For the purposes of this text we shall split that investigation into two separate sections, market strength and barriers to entry, although in practice both are usually considered together. There is an ongoing policy debate as to what should properly be termed as a barrier to entry, and for that reason it warrants separate discussion. The debate over the importance of barriers to entry has largely been conducted in the US and its impact has been limited in the Community. In Community cases there has been very little reference to the conceptual problems but, in practice, problems concerning barriers to entry are being addressed in an increasing number of cases. Before we go on to deal with that debate, the somewhat less controversial area of market strength will be discussed.

Market strength

One of the first steps in investigating dominance is to establish the market share held by the undertaking in question. The market share will not in itself

---

37 Case 27/76 *United Brands Continental BV v Commission* [1978] ECR 207; [1978] 1 CMLR 429, para 38.

38 For an argument that the concept of dominance should rely exclusively on the constraining effect of competitors, see Azevedo, JP and Walker, M, 'Dominance: meaning and measurement' [2002] ECLR 363.

establish an undertaking's dominance but it will be evidence of that organisation's strength on the market. It is only the ability to maintain that strength over time which will constitute dominance. That is why barriers to entry, which give an insight into potential long-term strength, are very important. A market share percentage only gives a snapshot of the relative strengths of undertakings at a particular moment. If market shares have changed considerably over a period of time it suggests that there may be effective competition on the market.

The Court has relied heavily – some would say too heavily – on market shares. By analysing the Court's judgments and statements by the Commission it is possible to suggest some rules of thumb. Market shares nearing 100% are very rare in practice, although some undertakings have come close to that mark.[39] Although it may be tempting to think so, very high market shares will not always indicate the existence of a dominant position; however, the higher the market share, the easier it will be to find good evidence of restricted competition within a market. The existence of market shares approaching 75% may lead to an undertaking being deemed so powerful as to have the special responsibilities of 'super-dominance' placed upon them.[40] Although the Community Courts have not used the term 'super-dominance' it has been adopted by the Commission,[41] and the Courts have approved the Commission's thinking.[42] It is now clear that undertakings with such high market shares have an increased responsibility not to adopt behaviour that will further disrupt the already weak competitive process in their markets. This issue was discussed in the CFI in *Microsoft*, where it found that:

> the Commission was correct to find . . . that when Microsoft had responded to the letter of 15 September 1998 it had not taken sufficiently into account its special responsibility not to hinder effective and undistorted competition in the common market. The Commission was also correct to state . . . that that particular responsibility derived from Microsoft's 'quasi-monopoly' on the client PC operating systems market.[43]

---

39 In Case T-6/89 *BPB and British Gypsum v Commission* [1993] ECR II-389; [1993] 5 CMLR 32, it was established that the undertakings had a 96–98% market share of the plasterboard market in the UK, and a 92–100% share in Ireland.

40 The figure of 75% is used by the Commission in its DG Competition discussion paper on the application of Article 82 of the Treaty to exclusionary abuses, Brussels, December 2005, at para 92.

41 See the comments of the Competition Commissioner with regard to the *Microsoft* decision and judgment in Commission Press Release, IP/04/382, and SPEECH/07/539 respectively.

42 See Case T-228/97 *Irish Sugar plc v Commission* [1999] ECR II-2969; [1999] 5 CMLR 1300; Case C-396/96 *Compagnie Maritime Belge Transports SA v Commission* [2000] ECR I-1365; [2000] 4 CMLR 1076; and, Case T-201/04 *Microsoft v Commission* [2007] 5 CMLR 11.

43 Case T-201/04 *Microsoft v Commission* [2007] 5 CMLR 11, at para 775.

Where market shares are slightly lower, perhaps below 70%, there is no question of super-dominance, but a finding of dominance is still a distinct possibility. In *Hoffmann-La Roche*, the Court took the view that very large market shares will give rise to a presumption of dominance, unless there are exceptional circumstances.[44] The reference to 'exceptional circumstances' takes account of potential competition from outside the existing market. Large market shares held for a period of time will give rise to a stronger presumption. A market share of 50% was considered to be very large in *AKZO*.[45]

Market shares below 50% can still be indicators of market strength. When shares are between 35 and 50%, it is important to compare the undertaking's market share with the share of its nearest rivals. If an undertaking has a 40% share and its rivals all have small shares of the remaining market, that undertaking will still have considerable strength in the market. In *United Brands*, the undertaking in question, UBC, had a market share between 41 and 45%, but its closest rival held only 16% of the market. It was, therefore, apparent that UBC had a position of considerable strength. If UBC had a competitor with a 35% market share, the findings in that case might have been very different. An undertaking with similar market strength would have been in a position to exert competitive pressure on UBC. The lowest market share which the CFI has confirmed as supporting a dominant position was 39.7% in *British Airways v Commission*.[46]

As an undertaking enjoys a larger market share it is more likely that it will be found to have a dominant position in a market. When an undertaking has a smaller market share an increasing number of other factors will need to be used as evidence to support a finding of dominance. Temporary strength on a market does not become dominance until there is an element of permanence. A strong undertaking must be in a position to effectively protect its market share before it will be truly dominant.

Barriers to entry

There is great debate over what should be included within the term 'barrier to entry'. The debate occurs in both law and economics. For the purposes of this text we will concentrate on the legal implications of the debate, but the economic arguments will be noted where relevant. A commonly accepted view is that a barrier to entry is any cost which is higher for a new entrant to the

---

44 Case 85/76 *Hoffmann-La Roche v Commission* [1979] ECR 461, p 463; [1979] 3 CMLR 211.
45 Case C-62/86 *AKZO Chemie BV v Commission* [1991] ECR I-3359; [1993] 5 CMLR 215, para 60.
46 Case T-219/99, [2003] ECR II-5917. The finding of dominance was not raised on appeal in Case C-95/04 P *British Airways v Commission* [2007] 4 CMLR 22.

market than for an existing market player.[47] Any such cost is important because where there are few barriers to entry an undertaking with market strength cannot easily protect itself from new entrants to a market should it act inefficiently, either through charging a supra-competitive price or by stifling innovation. Accordingly, potential entrants to markets with few entry barriers will exert competitive pressures on existing market players, and there will be little need for competition law to intervene and control undertakings with market strength. Such a market is sometimes described as being 'contestable'. Where barriers to entry exist, undertakings with market strength are, on the other hand, more likely to be considered to hold a dominant position, and will be in a better position to exert an anti-competitive influence on the market.

Barriers to entry play an important role in the indication of the existence of dominance of an undertaking in a market; therefore, any decision as to what is included in the term, barriers to entry, is vital to the way in which Art 82 works in practice. The debate over what is included in the definition centres around two schools of thought. One school perceives many purported barriers to entry as entirely natural, being related to efficiency. That school of thought would argue that a true barrier to entry is a cost to new entrants which was not applicable to the existing market operators when they entered the market.[48] This strict view of barriers to entry discounts many potentially massive costs that face new entrants, as those costs were also faced by the operators who currently hold positions of market strength. Under this type of analysis, the only real barriers to entry are legal provisions that restrict entry to the market. The narrow view of barriers concentrates on the perceived ability of the market to rectify any inefficiency without intervention by the law.

The other school of thought that is linked, for instance, with the Commission approach views barriers to entry as being much wider, and including any factor which would tend to discourage new entrants from entering the market. This is a more practical view which focuses on the actual difficulties faced by potential entrants. This view has been challenged on the basis that it penalises, through the increased likeliness of a finding of dominance, those undertakings which entered a market early and made large investments to become efficient. They paid the costs of entry and through that investment reached a position of strength. The position is often referred to as a 'first mover' or 'strategic' advantage. Should potential entrants not be forced to do the same? In any jurisdiction the decision to prefer a particular school will largely depend on policy or political views as to the need for intervention in

---

47 See Stigler, GJ, *The Organization of Industry*, 1968, Chicago: Chicago UP.

48 See the work of the Chicago school of antitrust economics and, in particular, Bork, R, *The Antitrust Paradox: A Policy at War with Itself*, 1978, NY: Basic Books, and Posner, RA, *Antitrust Law: An Economic Perspective*, 1976, Chicago: Chicago UP.

markets. Another important factor in determining what constitutes a barrier to entry is the timescale which is used for reference purposes. The Commission uses short to medium timescales for its calculations and, therefore, might intervene more readily than a regulator that utilises a long-term reference period. For these reasons, distinctions can be seen amongst the practices in the Community, the UK and the US, partly reflecting the Community's caution and conservatism and the US's optimism about how real markets operate and their contestability.

In the Community, the Court and the Commission have followed a policy closer to the broader definition of barriers to entry, as set out above. In their reasoning they have suggested many factors as being potential barriers to entry or, as they are sometimes referred to, factors indicating dominance.

Legal provisions

Statutory or regulatory powers granted by national legislation can act as barriers to entry. One example is intellectual property rights that protect the exclusivity of the right holder. Such rights can effectively grant a monopoly which can be protected through the national courts.[49] Dominance can also arise through government licensing restrictions which impede entry to a market.[50]

Technological advantage

The possession of existing technology, and potential access to future technology, is also relevant.[51] This is one of the areas in which the divergence between the two schools of thought is clearly seen. Advocates of the narrow view of barriers to entry would argue that a new entrant would face the same research costs as the existing market operators faced and, therefore, that any purported technological advantage is not a true barrier to entry but merely evidence of the efficiency of the incumbent undertaking. As the Court has indicated that it may accept technological advantage as a potential barrier, it has indicated its support for the broader view.

Financial resources

A leading undertaking that has easy access to large amounts of capital, often termed as having 'deep pockets', will be able to utilise its capital to protect itself from new entrants. Access to capital is one of the major difficulties for

---

49 See Case T-30/89 *Hilti AG v Commission* [1991] ECR II-1439; [1992] 4 CMLR 16; and Case T51/89 *Tetra Pak v Commission* [1990] ECR II-309; [1991] 4 CMLR 334.
50 Case 311/84 *Tele-Marketing v CLT* [1985] ECR 3261; [1986] 2 CMLR 558.
51 See Case 85/76 *Hoffmann-La Roche v Commission* [1979] ECR 461; [1979] 3 CMLR 211.

all small- and medium-sized enterprises (SMEs). The sheer size of the leading undertakings, and their international links, were considered by the Court in *Continental Can*[52] and *United Brands*.[53]

Economies of scale

Some markets, particularly those which demand complex manufacturing processes, require an operation to be on a large scale before high levels of efficiency are reached. Where there are economies of scale it can be very difficult for new entrants; to be as efficient as existing undertakings they must enter the market with a high level of output. If there was a market with one major supplier, but the efficient scale of operation was 60% of that market, it would be very difficult for a new entrant to compete. If the new entrant operates below the 60% scale, they would be less efficient. If they operate at the 60% scale, there would be overcapacity in the market.[54]

Vertical integration

An undertaking is vertically integrated when it controls upstream and down-stream production facilities. Integration allows an undertaking a much higher level of control over the way in which a product reaches the market. A good example of vertical integration was seen in *United Brands*.[55] For bananas to reach the European market there are many stages in the production process: growing, picking, shipping, ripening and distribution. United Brands (UBC) was highly vertically integrated, controlling its own research and development, plantations, refrigerated ships, ripening stores and distribution system. As UBC had complete control over the product, it had the advantage of commercial stability. A new entrant would be forced to invest heavily or rely on others to provide those services.

Product differentiation

Product differentiation can be a barrier to entry. It occurs when consumers perceive, due to advertising or brand loyalty, homogeneous products as being different. Consequently, the consumer will not consider the new entrant's product as interchangeable, making it difficult for the entrant to break into the market. Again, this phenomenon could be observed in *United Brands*.

---

52 See Case 6/72 *Continental Can v Commission* [1973] ECR 215; [1978] 1 CMLR 199.
53 See Case 27/76 *United Brands Continental BV v Commission* [1978] ECR 207; [1978] 1 CMLR 429.
54 Similar problems were discussed in Case T-6/89 *BPB and British Gypsum v Commission* [1993] ECR II-389; [1993] 5 CMLR 32.
55 See Case 27/76 *United Brands Continental BV v Commission* [1978] ECR 207; [1978] 1 CMLR 429.

Some of UBC's bananas were marketed under the 'Chiquita' brand, the bananas having a small blue sticker attached to them. The branded bananas sold at a premium of around 10%. Despite this, the Court found that there was no real difference in quality between the unbranded and branded product. The consumer was willing to pay 10% more for the branded product as they perceived it as being of a higher quality. A new entrant would not only be competing against the product but also the consumers', sometimes erroneous, perceptions. The increasing importance and value of branding emphasises the increasing level of product differentiation in many markets. Nonetheless, it has been argued that the increasing importance of brands can facilitate entry by allowing new entrants to adopt a 'niche marketing' strategy, whereby they do not directly compete with the incumbent, but rather differentiate their products into separate 'niche' markets.[56]

Conduct

One of the most controversial barriers to entry adopted by the Court has been the conduct of the undertaking in question. The Court adopted this reasoning in *AKZO*.[57] Conduct is normally considered when the alleged abuse is examined, but in *AKZO* an exclusionary abuse, one designed to discourage new entrants, was seen as a barrier to entry that indicated dominance. This approach can be seen as somewhat circular. Conduct will not normally be considered abusive until an undertaking is in a position of dominance. However, if conduct can indicate dominance, through being a barrier to entry, it could greatly increase the likelihood of such a finding. Such an argument has logical flaws but the reasons for its adoption are straightforward. If an undertaking has a history of reacting to new entrants with exclusionary conduct, it will discourage potential entrants from attempting entry. They will be well aware of the likely response of that undertaking.

Criticism

The Court and the Commission have reacted to criticism about their broad definition of dominance by emphasising that a finding of dominance is not, in itself, a finding of wrongdoing.[58] There are no penalties for simply being dominant. As long as the dominant undertaking does not abuse its position, it will not come under the scrutiny of the competition authorities.

Such an assertion is of little comfort to undertakings that have achieved a position of market strength, particularly if they have market shares of around 40% or more. Undertakings will have to be very careful to ensure that

56 See Paterson, L, 'The power of the puppy – does advertising deter entry?' [1997] ECLR 337.
57 Case C-62/86 *AKZO Chemie BV v Commission* [1991] ECR I-3359; [1993] 5 CMLR 215.
58 Case 322/81 *Michelin v Commission* [1983] ECR 3461; [1985] 1 CMLR 282.

their actions do not attract an accusation of abuse, particularly where their market shares are very high. The cost of compliance programmes and the potential cost of defending such an accusation may lead to undertakings acting in a manner which may be less efficient, but less likely to fall foul of the competition provisions. In addition, the Court has often reiterated that what is acceptable competitive behaviour, for instance in terms of pricing, by a non-dominant undertaking may be abusive when engaged in by a dominant undertaking; accordingly, the assessment of dominance can have an important impact on an undertaking's overall competitive strategy. It is questionable whether the broad definition of dominance used in the Community truly encourages efficient competition within the Single Market. Nonetheless, the different context in which barriers to entry are considered under US antitrust law means that we should not be over-reliant on the criticisms levelled at the broader definition by some commentators.[59] It appears, from an examination of recent enforcement trends, that there is a greater enforcement focus on undertakings with a position of super-dominance in a market and that such undertakings should be aware of, and particularly sensitive to, the potential application of the competition rules.[60]

Abuse

Article 82 of the Treaty gives several examples of abusive conduct. The list is purely indicative, leaving the Court a wide discretion when interpreting the basic prohibition. The list includes:

a   directly or indirectly imposing unfair purchase or selling prices or other unfair trading conditions;
b   limiting production, market or technical development, to the prejudice of consumers;
c   applying dissimilar conditions to equivalent transactions with other trading parties, thereby placing them at a competitive disadvantage; and
d   making the conclusion of contracts subject to acceptance by the other parties of supplementary obligations which, by their nature or according to commercial usage, have no connection with the subject of such contracts.

59 For an insightful examination of the contextual differences between the EC and US systems see Amato, G, *Antitrust and the Bounds of Power*, 1997, Oxford: Hart.
60 As Neelie Kroes, the Competition Commissioner, said in September 2007, following the CFI's confirmation of the Microsoft decision, 'That 2004 Decision set an important precedent in terms of the obligations of dominant companies to allow competition, in particular in high tech industries. The Decision upheld by the Court is particularly important because so many people use computers, be they individual consumers, schools, businesses or governments, and because 95% of the world's personal computers run Microsoft's Windows PC operating system.'; see Commission SPEECH/07/539, 17 September 2004.

The Court, using teleological interpretation of Arts 2, 3(1)(g) and 82 of the Treaty, has given the concept of abuse a very wide scope. The test used is objective, although intent may be a factor in the determination of the level of fine, and there is no requirement that there be a causal link between the existence of dominance and the abuse itself.

There are two main forms of abusive behaviour, although some types of behaviour contain elements of both. First, exploitative abuse, which most closely follows the neoclassical economic models concerned with monopolies. The concern is that a monopolist will be in a position to maximise profits by reducing output and increasing the price of its product above a competitive level. By ensuring such a price increase, the monopolist will exploit its customers. Sometimes this form of exploitative behaviour is, rather confusingly, known as pro-competitive. This is because, without the existence of barriers to entry, it would encourage new entrants to enter and compete on the market. If there are barriers to entry the dominant undertaking will not be constrained effectively and may be in a position to charge a supra-competitive price.

The second form of abusive conduct is exclusionary abuse, sometimes referred to as abuse which forecloses a market. Exclusionary abuse is where a dominant undertaking adopts behaviour which would be considered perfectly legitimate if the undertaking had no market power, but may cause serious concerns when a position of market dominance is held. The Court has held that an undertaking in a dominant position has 'a special responsibility not to allow its conduct to impair undistorted competition on the Common Market'.[61] As an undertaking's level of dominance increases, its responsibility to the rest of the market becomes more onerous, and it is more likely that its behaviour will be considered abusive.[62] Therefore, any form of conduct by a dominant undertaking which threatens the competitive structure of the market might be considered abusive. Exclusionary abuses, that actually or potentially foreclose the market to existing competitors or new entrants, have been the subject of Community action more frequently than exploitative abuses. This may be because exclusionary abuses are often easier to prove and can also be seen as more likely to damage the competitive process. Exclusionary abuses tend to bolster the undertaking's dominant position, making it more difficult for entrants to challenge the undertaking's market strength. An undertaking that indulges in exclusionary abuses may also find it easier to engage in exploitative abuses as there is less chance that competition will be encouraged by potentially high returns.

Not all types of abuse can be easily categorised into these two forms. Some abuses can fall into both categories. An example is discriminatory pricing; by way of illustration, consider the scenario of a dominant undertaking offering

---

61 Case 322/81 *Michelin v Commission* [1983] ECR 3461; [1985] 1 CMLR 282, para 10.
62 See the discussion of super-dominance above.

different prices to different consumers. This strategy may be adopted in order to exploit some of those consumers who would find it difficult to get supplies elsewhere, but it could also be charging lower prices to customers who may be tempted to obtain supplies from another undertaking. While the Court has never found it necessary to explicitly state whether a particular abuse falls into either category it is easier to discuss the different forms of abuse separately.

Exploitative abuses

Excessive prices

The classic form of exploitative abuse is the charging of a monopoly price or 'monopoly rent'. An undertaking which is unconstrained by competitive pressures no longer takes a price from the market but can maximise profits by reducing output and charging a higher monopolistic price. The difficulty is deciding exactly what price is excessive or unfair.

In *General Motors v Commission*,[63] the Court confirmed that it is an abuse to charge an excessive price. It suggested that prices would be excessive where they do not reflect the 'economic value' of the goods. In that case the Court decided that the prices were not excessive. No real indication was given as to exactly how the 'economic value' of a product could be calculated other than by reference to a hypothetical competitive market. In *United Brands*,[64] the Commission used various factors to support its finding of excessive pricing in continental Europe. It compared prices between Member States of branded and unbranded bananas, and between different brands of banana. After these comparisons were made, the prices charged on the relevant market appeared to be unjustifiably high. The Court quashed the Commission's findings as it had failed to examine UBC's costs before coming to its Decision.

In subsequent cases there have been two main approaches taken to excessive prices. The first is to examine prices in markets across Europe to determine if one price is *prima facie* excessive. This approach has its limitations in that different markets have very different cost structures. The variations in taxation, marketing strategy and consumer behaviour may result in different price levels without there being any hint of exploitation. The Court has recognised this by treating evidence pointing to excessive prices as raising a presumption of abuse that can be rebutted by evidence of differences among the markets on which the comparison was based.[65] The second approach has a 'cost plus' basis. The Court's assertion about the need to examine costs in

---

63 Case 26/75 [1975] ECR 1367; [1976] 1 CMLR 95.
64 See Case 27/76 *United Brands Continental BV v Commission* [1978] ECR 207; [1978] 1 CMLR 429.
65 Case 110/88 *Lucazeau v SACEM* [1989] ECR 2811; [1991] 4 CMLR 248.

United Brands suggests that a certain level of profit may be excessive. So far, the Court has made no statement about what level above cost constitutes a reasonable profit.

Many commentators consider direct intervention in market pricing decisions as a step too far for competition law, and that the operation of the market alone should control prices. If high prices are charged, new entrants will be encouraged, and intervention is an inefficient tool ill-suited to control market prices. The difficulties in proving excessive pricing are reflected in Commission policy. It has not made a decision based on excessive pricing since *United Brands*, and all subsequent cases have been considered by the Court under the Art 234 EC reference procedure. The amount of information that would need to be gathered before an excessive price could be proved constitutes a major hurdle. Nonetheless, it should be noted that the first case under the Chapter II prohibition of the UK's Competition Act 1998, discussed later in this chapter, involved excessive pricing by a dominant undertaking, Napp Pharmaceuticals Ltd, as an infringement of that prohibition.[66] While the OFT was successful in showing excessive pricing in *Napp*, the difficult nature of establishing what is excessive was illustrated in *Attheraces Ltd v The British Horse Racing Board Ltd*.[67] The Court of Appeal, considering an appeal against a finding of excessive pricing, rejected the High Court's use of a 'cost +' approach. Two of the reasons given for allowing the appeal were the difficulty in establishing which costs to take into account in a cost + calculation and, more importantly, the fact that 'economic value' of the product to the purchaser was not only related to the costs of the producer, but also the value that the purchaser could expect to gain from exploiting the product on downstream markets.

Unfair conditions

One of the only cases in which unfair conditions have been considered as an abuse in themselves is *BRT v SABAM*.[68] SABAM, a performing rights society, was found to have abused its dominant position by imposing on its members obligations which were not absolutely necessary for the attainment of its object. This unfairly restricted the members' freedom to exercise their copyright as they wished. Many other abuses, where additional unfair conditions are imposed by a dominant undertaking, are considered to be exclusionary rather than exploitative.

---

66 DGFT Decision CA98/2/2001 *Napp Pharmaceutical Holdings*, 30 March 2001. On appeal *Napp Pharmaceutical Holdings v DGFT* [2002] CAT 1.
67 *Attheraces Ltd v The British Horseracing Board Ltd* [2007] EWCA Civ 38, [2007] UKCLR 309.
68 Case 127/73 [1974] ECR 313; [1974] 2 CMLR 238.

The quiet life

The final type of exploitative abuse is predicted by the neoclassical economic models. Accordingly, a monopolist will not be subject to competitive pressure forcing it to innovate and it can enjoy a 'quiet life'. It is sometimes also known as 'x-inefficiency'. The Court has adopted this form of reasoning in its judgments. In *Porto di Genova*,[69] the Court held that a port operator's refusal to utilise modern technology in its unloading operations constituted an abuse. The use of older methods meant that the unloading of vessels took much longer and was consequently more expensive.

As can be observed from the cases mentioned above, the difficulty in proving exploitative abuse stems from the subjective decisions involved. How excessive, unfair or inefficient must a practice be before an abuse is proved? The inherent uncertainty in such a question discourages both the Commission and individual claimants or pursuers from bringing actions. This may be one of the reasons why most of the cases coming before the Commission and the Court have concentrated on exclusionary abuses in recent years.

Exclusionary abuses

The majority of abuses dealt with under Art 82 are exclusionary. While this type of abuse is not expressly predicted by the neoclassical economic model of monopoly, discussed in Chapter 1, it is very important in practice. Exclusionary, or anti-competitive, abuses are harmful to competition in that they allow dominant undertakings to protect their market power, usually by discouraging or making it more difficult for new entrants to challenge them on the market. Such abuses are harmful in that they distort the process of competition itself by actually or potentially foreclosing a market to competitors. As we have already discussed, easy entry and exit from markets are important. By discouraging or stopping entry, a dominant undertaking will be able to perpetuate its market power. Furthermore, it will be in a better position to exploit its customers. It is also important that a dominant undertaking should not be able to drive out existing weaker competitors by using methods other than normal competition.

The Court has shown willingness to consider many forms of conduct as exclusionary, even when they are economically beneficial to the undertaking itself. The concept of abuse in such situations is an objective one. The Court concentrates on the effect of a practice on the structure of the market itself, not necessarily on the benefits to the dominant undertaking. The Court explained its approach in *Michelin*:[70]

---

69 Case C-179/90 *Merci Convenzionali Porto di Genova SpA v Siderurgica Gabrielli* [1991] ECR I-5889; [1994] 4 CMLR 422.
70 Case 322/81 [1983] ECR 3461; [1988] 1 CMLR 282, para 70.

Article 82 covers practices which are likely to affect the structure of the market where, as a direct result of the presence of the undertaking in question, competition has already been weakened and which, through recourse to methods different from those governing normal competition in products or services based on traders' performance, have the effect of hindering the maintenance or development of the level of competition still existing on the market.

How far the methods of the dominant undertaking have to differ 'from those governing normal competition' is a controversial question. What is normal in competitive situations is a perplexing question in itself. The Court has taken a broad pro-competitive approach, condemning methods of competition which in practice could be exclusionary but which many critics would argue were 'normal' in competitive situations. A controversial example of this broad approach was seen in the Commission's decision in *British Midland v Aer Lingus*.[71] British Midland was attempting to enter the market for the Dublin to Heathrow air route. The Commission required Aer Lingus, the dominant operator, to allow British Midland to 'interline' with it. This meant that British Midland was allowed to use the Aer Lingus computer system to sell its tickets for the same route. The effect was that Aer Lingus was to assist a competitor in entering the market. Although interlining is common on established air routes, arguably it is unusual to interline with a new competitor. The broad approach can partially be explained by examining the objectives of the EC Treaty. Article 3(1)(g) sets out, as one of the Community's goals, that 'competition in the internal market should not be distorted'. Thus, the structure of competition itself is one of the main planks upon which the whole Community system is built. A recent example of the way in which Art 82 focuses on the structure of the market can be seen in *Microsoft v Commission*.[72] The CFI confirmed the Commission's Decision, which required Microsoft to provide interoperability information, which allows network clients and servers to communicate with each other, to allow competitors to develop products that would compete with its own work group server operating system. The absence of proper interoperability reinforced Microsoft's position and risked the elimination of competition on the market.

The divergent nature of exclusionary abuses can best be noted by examining the types of behaviour that have been found to be abusive. Although the situations examined below are by no means an exhaustive list, they do give a good indication of the types of behaviour that the Court and the Commission are likely to consider as distorting competition, and therefore condemn.

The Commission's ongoing review of Art 82 focuses on exclusionary abuses. The review is at a relatively early phase, with a Commission Discussion Paper

---

71 Commission Decision 92/213/EEC, OJ 1992, L96/34.
72 Case T-201/04 *Microsoft v Commission* [2007] 5 CMLR 11.

beginning the process.[73] Some of the issues raised in the Discussion Paper will be introduced below, in the context of the particular abuses, but the general thrust of the process to date appears to suggest that the handling of abuses under Art 82 will become increasingly economically sophisticated. The focus is moving towards the identification of particular behaviour or conduct which has actual and demonstrable anti-competitive effects on particular markets, and away from rules that are based on the form of the behaviour or conduct.[74] It will be interesting to observe the result of the review process; a balance must be struck between economic sophistication and workable legal rules.

Export bans

Any attempt by a dominant undertaking to impose export bans on its purchasers will be considered abusive. Obviously, this forms part of the Community's attempt to stop undertakings re-erecting trade barriers which have been dismantled at State level. Export bans distort both trade flows across the Community and intra-brand competition (competition between same brand products). If such bans were put in place, a dominant undertaking would be able to segregate national markets. In *United Brands*, a clause prohibiting the resale of green bananas[75] was considered to be an export ban and was condemned because it would grant national distributors protection from parallel imports. Export bans may also be dealt with under Art 81, even when they appear to be unilaterally imposed.[76]

Pricing strategies

Article 82 limits the pricing strategies of undertakings where those undertakings are considered to be dominant.[77] The most important cases in this area have considered discounting, rebates and predatory pricing. While many of these practices will lower prices for the customer in the short term, it may be

---

73 DG Competition discussion paper on the application of Article 82 of the Treaty to exclusionary abuses, Brussels, December 2005.
74 For more detailed discussion see, Mertikopoulou, V, 'DG Competition's Discussion Paper on the Application of Article 82 EC to Exclusionary Abuses: the Proposed Economic Reform from a Legal Point of View' [2007] ECLR 241 and Dreher, M, and Adam, M, 'Abuse of Dominance Under Reform – Sound Economics and Established Case Law' [2007] ECLR 278.
75 Unripe 'green' bananas are much easier to transport long distances.
76 See Commission Decision 96/478/EEC *Adalat,* OJ 1996, L201/1. On appeal, see Case T-41/96 *Bayer v Commission* [2000] ECR II-3383, and Cases C-2 and 3/01 P *BAI and Commission v Bayer* [2004] ECR I-23.
77 For a critique of this area of law, see Ridyard, D, 'Exclusionary pricing and price discrimination abuses under Article 82 – an economic analysis' [2002] ECLR 286.

possible for the seller to benefit by reducing the level of competition they face on the market in the longer term. These pricing strategies can therefore be exclusionary as they tend to foreclose markets. New entrants may be discouraged by the dominant undertaking's pricing policy. Prices may be lowered to drive out an existing competitor or make it difficult for the new entrant to obtain a foothold in the market.

Discounts and rebates

The use of discounts and rebates can be problematic when an undertaking is in a dominant position. Discounts can be used to tie a customer to a particular supplier. The customer may be aware that if they were to take supplies from a competitor they would lose their discount with the dominant supplier. A new supplier would have to charge prices low enough to compensate their new customers for the loss of those discounts. The impact of such discounts is sometimes known as a 'suction' or 'loyalty-inducing' effect. One particularly damaging form of discount is known as a 'loyalty rebate'. These rebates are given to a customer who takes a certain percentage of their total requirements from a supplier. For example, they may receive a 10% discount if they buy 75% of their requirements from the supplier and a 15% discount if they purchase 90% of their requirements. Such a discounting structure may be useful for an entrant firm but as dominant undertakings are the major supplier on a market they can act anti-competitively. The discount tends to tie customers to the dominant undertaking and makes it very difficult for other undertakings to increase their market share.

Hoffmann-La Roche[78] concerned the adoption of loyalty rebates alongside some other abusive discounts. The loyalty rebate was connected to a so-called English clause, which allowed customers to obtain supplies from other undertakings where they were charging a lower price if the customers informed La Roche of the lower price. While this may appear to be pro-competitive, it meant that La Roche was given full information about its competitors' pricing policies by its customers, allowing La Roche to react and maintain its market share. This was also found to be abusive. It did not matter that the use of loyalty rebates was at the request of customers; the effects on potential competitors were obvious. Hoffmann-La Roche also used 'across the board' rebates. These rebates awarded a discount where a customer purchased all of the supplier's range of products. This type of rebate would tend to foreclose the market in that it would discourage customers from dealing with different suppliers for different products.

Another abusive discounting practice was considered in *Michelin*.[79] The

78 See Case 85/76 *Hoffmann-La Roche v Commission* [1979] ECR 461; [1979] 3 CMLR 211.
79 Case 322/81 *Michelin v Commission* [1983] ECR 3461; [1985] 1 CMLR 282.

Court found that annual discounts awarded by Michelin, on the basis of sales targets set for dealers, amounted to an abuse, as the dealers could not deal with another supplier without fear of heavy economic loss. The discounts were awarded on an informal basis, for short time periods, and the rates varied enormously between dealerships. It was considered that the ad hoc nature of the rebates, and the lack of certainty faced by dealers, tended to increase the tying effect.

In *Irish Sugar* the Commission appeared to take a stronger view, which was supported by the Court, on targeted discounts suggesting that such discounts will always be unlawful as they are 'clearly aimed at tying customers closely to the dominant company'.[80] In *British Airways v Commission*,[81] the Commission's fine of €6.8 m, imposed on British Airways for offering commission bonuses to travel agents who exceeded BA sales targets, was confirmed. BA's 'performance reward scheme' was found to be 'fidelity building' because of its progressive nature, with the potential for exponential changes in the levels of bonus payable based on marginal changes in sales.[82]

Although the Court has challenged a number of different types of discount, not all such discounts or rebates are abusive. If the discounts are objectively based on savings made by the producer, they will be justifiable.[83] If, for example, a manufacturer can reduce costs by making volume sales, enabling larger manufacturing runs, those savings can be reflected in discounted pricing. However, any such discounts must be fixed objectively and be open to all customers. The *Irish Sugar* case suggests there may be an overlap between the case law on discounts and the abuse of predatory pricing, in that prices could be considered as predatory where they discriminate between different customers without any objective justification. The controversy surrounding the Commission's *Michelin II* Decision[84] indicates a number of the diverging views in this area. The Commission's Decision found that Michelin had abused its dominant position through the operation of a complex discount system. Following the publication of that Decision, a number of commentators challenged the Commission's findings on the basis that insufficient economic analysis had been undertaken and that the Commission's approach did not take account of the complex economic reality of

---

80 Commission Decision 1997/624/EC, OJ 1997, L258/1, para 152. On appeal Case T-228/97 *Irish Sugar plc v Commission* [1999] ECR II-2969; [1999] 5 CMLR 1300, para 191.
81 Case T-219/99, [2003] ECR II-5917, on appeal, C-95/04 P, [2007] ECR I-2331.
82 See, in particular, paras 271–75.
83 Case 102/77 *Hoffmann-La Roche v Centrafarm* [1978] ECR 1139; [1978] 3 CMLR 217; and Case 85/76 *Hoffmann-La Roche v Commission* [1979] ECR 461; [1979] 3 CMLR 211.
84 Commission Decision 2002/405/EC *Michelin*, OJ 2002, L143/1, on appeal, Case T-203/01 *Michelin v Commission* [2003] ECR II-4071.

pricing strategy in modern economies.[85] On appeal, before the Court of First Instance (CFI), Michelin argued that the Commission had not undertaken sufficient economic analysis of the actual effects of the complex discount system, but its argument was rejected by the Court. The Court stressed that once it was established that the discounting practice adopted by the dominant undertaking was 'loyalty-inducing' it was not necessary to show that the discounting practice actually had anti-competitive effects on the market. All the Commission was required to establish was that 'the purpose of the discount systems was to tie the dealers to [Michelin]' as this tended to make it 'more difficult for . . . competitors to enter the relevant market'.[86] The rebates in *Michelin* were particularly damaging as they were: non-transparent, many of the factors afforded Michelin a degree of discretion; covered a lengthy period of up to 13 months, where a vendor would be required to sell at loss for a long period before it was able to claim the rebate that would bring it into profit; and, that they covered all sales during the reference period, not only those sales that were beyond the targets set.[87] The DG Comp Discussion Paper describes exclusionary rebates as being, 'in general conditional rebates which may differentiate the price for each customer, depending on its purchasing behaviour, in order to obtain more purchases from these customers', and focuses on the foreclosing effects of such rebates. The Commission suggests various methodologies that may be used to calculate the foreclosing effects of certain rebates systems, whether they make it difficult, or impossible, for efficient competitors to compete with the dominant undertaking.[88]

Predatory pricing

This type of abuse is characterised by a selective price reduction which is intended to harm a competitor. The reduction will usually be to levels at or below cost. Because of its economic strength, the dominant undertaking will be able to sustain its losses for a limited time but its weaker competitor, with access to fewer resources, will be driven from the market.

The Court of Justice first upheld the proposition that not all such price competition is legitimate in *AKZO*.[89] The Court set out a formula with which it is possible to calculate whether pricing is 'predatory'. If prices are below average variable costs (costs which vary according to the quantities produced) predatory pricing is presumed. If prices are between average variable costs

---

85 See Ridyard, D, 'Exclusionary pricing and price discrimination abuses under Article 82 – an economic analysis' [2002] ECLR 286, and the less-tempered Sher, B, 'Price discounts and Michelin 2: what goes around, comes around' [2002] ECLR 482.

86 Case T-203/01 *Michelin v Commission* [2004] 4 CMLR 18, particularly paras 235–46.

87 For a fuller discussion see, Roques, C, 'CFI Judgment, Case T-203/01, *Manufacture Francaise des Pneumatiques Michelin v Commission*' [2004] ECLR 688.

88 DG Comp Discussion Paper, see fn 73, paras 151–169.

89 Case C-62/86 *AKZO Chemie BV v Commission* [1991] ECR I-3359; [1993] 5 CMLR 215.

and average total costs (variable costs plus fixed costs), pricing will be predatory where it is part of a plan to eliminate competition. This test is very difficult to apply for two main reasons. First, the assessment of what costs should be considered in either category is very controversial. Even if it is possible to categorise costs, the information will be difficult to gather and may change rapidly. Secondly, it will be very difficult to prove the intentions of the dominant undertaking in the grey area between average variable costs and average total costs. In a competitive situation, most firms will be trying to 'eliminate' their competitors. That is the nature of competition. The guidelines set out by the Court in *AKZO* are inherently difficult to apply and may be of little use in practice.

Predatory pricing policy was developed in a novel way in *Tetra Pak II*.[90] In the Court's consideration of liquid food packaging, it decided that Tetra Pak was dominant in the aseptic packaging market and had been involved in abusive predatory pricing in the non-aseptic packaging market, in which it was not dominant. This was a novel extension of the doctrine, but only appears possible where there are associative links between the dominant market and the market in which the predatory behaviour took place. In the *Tetra Pak II* case, the markets were separate but closely related.

In *Irish Sugar*,[91] the Commission appeared to take a rather different approach to predation. It concentrated on the selectivity of Irish Sugar's price cuts rather than on the relation of prices to costs. Irish Sugar was cutting prices, in the border region, to protect the sugar market in the Republic of Ireland from competition from imports from Northern Ireland. Although this point was not directly addressed by the CFI, the Decision indicates that where price cuts are targeted at customers who might seek supplies from a competitor this may be enough to found a finding of predatory pricing unless all customers are offered the favourable terms.[92] Similarly, in *Compagnie Maritime Belge*,[93] the practice of scheduling low-cost 'fighting ships' against competitors' vessels was considered predatory even where prices were above cost. It should be noted that in these cases the dominant undertakings were both in arguably 'super-dominant' positions.

The Commission's policy has been criticised as being confusing for undertakings that will have to decide what type of price competition is legitimate. Case law had suggested that meeting, but not beating, competition would be

90 Case C-333/94P *Tetra Pak International SA v Commission* [1996] ECR I-5951; [1997] 4 CMLR 662.
91 Commission Decision 1997/624/EC, OJ 1997, L258/1. On appeal Case T-228/97 *Irish Sugar plc v Commission* [1999] ECR II-2969; [1999] 5 CMLR 1300.
92 See Andrews, P, 'Is meeting competition a defence to predatory pricing? – the *Irish Sugar* decision suggests a new approach' [1998] ECLR 49.
93 Case C-395/96 *Compagnie Maritime Belge Transports SA v Commission of the European Communities* [2000] ECR I-1365; [2000] 4 CMLR 1076.

acceptable. Nonetheless, in *France Télécom v Commission*[94] the CFI made it clear that dominant undertakings had no 'absolute right' to align their prices with those of a competitor, especially where they are potentially abusive, being below cost. It also rejected the argument that a price below cost would not be predatory unless it was possible for the dominant undertaking to recoup its losses. Accordingly, it is potentially difficult to establish when an undertaking's behaviour crosses the line. This uncertainty arguably chills potential competition. However, it is clear that there are no abuses per se in this context, and in assessing the foreclosing effect of pricing strategies the Commission, when prioritising its enforcement resources, had predominantly focused on the activities of super-dominant undertakings where the exclusionary impact is more self-evident. The DG Comp Discussion paper suggests a new approach to predatory pricing replacing the *AKZO* test. Rather than using prices below AVC as being predatory, the Discussion Paper suggests using 'Average Avoidable Cost' in the majority of situations.[95] This will often be the same as AVC, but will include fixed costs when investments were made to expand capacity in order to predate.

Tying and leverage

As discussed above, an undertaking can be dominant in one market and abuse its dominance in another. With tie-ins, a dominant undertaking attempts to extend, or leverage, its market power from the market in which it is dominant to another market. This usually involves a requirement for customers to obtain supplies of the tied product when purchasing the tying product in relation to which the supplying undertaking has a dominant position. In this way, dominance over the market of the tying product is extended into another market. If a customer wants to buy the dominant product, it must also purchase the tied product. The customer may have been able to obtain that product on better terms elsewhere, or it may not want the product at all. In that sense, the abuse is exploitative, but it is also exclusionary in that it forecloses the tied market. Other suppliers of the tied product will struggle to find outlets for their versions of the product as most customers will have been forced to obtain tied supplies from the dominant undertaking.

A simple example of a tying arrangement was evident in *Napier Brown/ British Sugar*.[96] A sugar processor forced customers to buy bulk sugar at delivered prices, that is, the price including delivery costs. The purchase of

94   Case T-340/03 *France Télécom v Commission* [2007] 4 CMLR 21. On appeal Case C-202/07 P, pending. See, also, Gal, MS, 'Below-cost Price Alignment: Meeting or Beating Competition? The France Telecom case' [2007] ECLR 382.

95   DG Comp Discussion Paper, see fn 73, paras 93–133.

96   Commission Decision 88/518/EEC, OJ 1988, L284/41; [1990] 4 CMLR 196. See, also, Case C359/01P *British Sugar v Commission* [2004] ECR I-4933.

haulage services was, therefore, tied to the purchase of the sugar. Other haulage undertakings would have found it very difficult to break into the market.

The Court's approach to tying arrangements was further explained in *Hilti*.[97] A manufacturer of nail guns refused to supply cartridge strips containing the charge which fired the nails, and over which it had intellectual property (IP) rights, without customers also purchasing the corresponding nails. Suppliers of Hilti-compatible nails complained about the tie. In its Decision, the Commission concentrated on two particular consequences of the abuse: the extension of monopoly power into a new market and the foreclosure of competitors. Hilti was protected from competition in the market for Hilti-compatible cartridge strips as it had registered design rights. It was attempting to extend its power over that market into the market for Hilti-compatible nails where it was much more vulnerable to competition. By extending that power Hilti was, in effect, seeking to exclude potential competitors from the secondary market in Hilti-compatible nails. All purchasers of Hilti-compatible nails would have already been required to obtain supplies with the cartridge strips and would not need to buy nails from any other competing source. Therefore, no viable competition would be able to develop on the market. Hilti's attempts to justify the tie were dismissed. The controversy surrounding tying arrangements was rekindled by the Commission's Decision in the *Microsoft* case, which was confirmed by the CFI.[98] In that Decision the Commission required that Microsoft, which was found to be dominant in the PC client operating systems market, offer an unbundled version of its operating system without Windows Media Player to PC manufacturers. Microsoft was also challenged with regard to similar practices in the US.[99]

Mergers

Article 82 has, in the past, been used to control mergers. In *Continental Can*,[100] the Court held that it was an abuse for a dominant undertaking to strengthen its position in a market by merging with a competitor. Now, mergers are controlled by a more sophisticated system, under Regulation 139/ 2004,[101] but the judgment in the *Continental Can* case does show the Court's concern to maintain a competitive structure within a market.

97 Case C-53/92P *Hilti AG v Commission* [1994] ECR I-666; [1994] 1 CMLR 590.
98 Commission Decision 2007/53/EC *Microsoft* OJ 2007, L32/23, Case T-201/04, *Microsoft v Commission* [2007] 5 CMLR 11.
99 For further discussion see, Ridyard, D, 'Tying and Bundling – Cause for Complaint?' [2005] ECLR 316.
100 See Case 6/72 *Continental Can v Commission* [1973] ECR 215; [1978] 1 CMLR 199.
101 OJ 2004, L24/1.

Refusal to supply

The treatment of refusals to supply is a particularly controversial area; due, in no small part, to competition law's interaction with other long-standing legal principles in the law of contract and intellectual property. Most legal systems have shied away from insisting that an undertaking be forced to contract when it does not see it to be in its best interests to do so. However, under Community law the basic rule is that a refusal to supply by a dominant undertaking must be objectively justified. The justification must not be based solely on the undertaking's commercial interests but on more general concerns.[102] In *ABG*,[103] a refusal to supply was justified on the basis of a global shortage of the goods in question, and in *Leyland DAF v Automotive Products*[104] the English Court of Appeal considered that an undertaking's failure to pay for previous contract goods constituted sufficient justification.

There are three broad categories in which Art 82 has intervened, although it is sometimes difficult in practice to place a particular set of facts clearly in one class to the exclusion of others. The broad categories are as follows:

i   where a refusal to supply a customer, on an existing market, is used to damage or deter a competitor (usually known as a refusal to deal);
ii   where there is a refusal to allow a customer access to an 'essential facility'; or
iii   where there is a refusal to grant a licence of IP rights.

Refusal to deal

The first category covers the most obvious threat to competition raised by a refusal to supply: a direct refusal to supply an existing customer where that refusal can be linked to an attempt to eliminate an actual or potential competitor. The central issue within the refusal to deal cases is, arguably, the general principle under Art 82 that a dominant undertaking has a special responsibility not to 'impair undistorted competition', as outlined in *Michelin*.[105] When a dominant undertaking has embarked on a commercial relationship with an actual or potential competitor, it must ensure that it acts in such a way as not to further damage the, already weak, competitive process by refusing to deal without objective justification. A clear

---

102   Commission Decision 87/500/EEC *BBI/Boosey & Hawkes (Interim Measures)*, OJ 1987, L286/36; [1988] 4 CMLR 67.
103   Commission Decision 77/327/EEC *ABG*, OJ 1977, L117/1. On appeal Case 77/77 *Benzine Petroleum Handelmaatschappij BV v Commission* [1978] ECR 1513.
104   [1994] 1 BCLC 245.
105   Case 322/81, [1983] ECR 3461, para 10.

example of an attempt to eliminate a competitor was seen in *Commercial Solvents*.[106] Commercial Solvents was the dominant supplier of a bulk chemical used in the production of pharmaceuticals. Another undertaking had purchased supplies of the chemical for manufacturing purposes but was refused further supplies when Commercial Solvents decided to expand into the market for the finished product. The Court held the refusal to be an abuse. By refusing to supply the raw material, Commercial Solvents had, in effect, removed its main competitor. In subsequent cases, such as *United Brands*,[107] refusals to supply which did not seek to eliminate, but which were likely to adversely affect competitors, have fallen foul of Art 82. In *United Brands*, the mere fact that a distributor had been involved in a competitor's promotional campaign did not justify the refusal to supply that distributor.

An overzealous reaction to a new competitor may also be seen as abusive. In *BBI/Boosey & Hawkes*,[108] an established manufacturer of brass band instruments refused to supply one of its existing distributors after that distributor started producing competing instruments. The Commission was of the opinion that a dominant undertaking can take steps to defend itself when faced by new competition, but those steps must be proportionate to the threat. In this case, the new competitor's level of production was such that an outright refusal to supply was disproportionate. Obviously, it will be difficult for a dominant undertaking to decide how to react to new competition in these circumstances. The interpretation of the proportionality doctrine can be very difficult. Two distinct types of refusal to deal can be indentified from the cases. The first, described as 'primary line injury', is where the competitor who would be damaged or deterred is on the same level of the market as the undertaking refusing to deal, as in *United Brands* and *BBI*. The second, described as 'secondary line injury', is where the competitor is at a different level of the market from the undertaking refusing to deal, as in the secondary, finished product, market in *Commercial Solvents*.

A refusal to supply an entirely new customer may also be classified as a refusal to deal. This would be the case when a supplier already provides such supplies or services to other customers but refused to extend supplies to a potential new customer. Once the dominant supplier has created a market in the product, an unjustified refusal to deal with a new customer may be abusive where it could damage or deter an actual or potential competitor. An example of such circumstances can be seen in *Sea Containers v Stena Sealink – interim measures*,[109] where Sea Containers sought access to

106 See Cases 6 and 7/73 *Commercial Solvents v Commission* [1974] ECR 223; [1974] 1 CMLR 309.

107 See Case 27/76 *United Brands Continental BV v Commission* [1978] ECR 207; [1978] 1 CMLR 429.

108 Commission Decision 87/500/EEC, OJ 1987, L286/36; [1988] 4 CMLR 67.

109 Commission Decision 94/19/EC *Sea Containers v Stena Sealink – interim measures*, OJ 1994, L15/8.

Holyhead Port, which was owned and used by Sealink, but also by other ferry operators.

New markets and essential facilities

The next controversial area is the refusal to supply a new customer where supply would open up a new market where there has been no previous competition. This is particularly problematic when the supply of the goods or service would allow the new customer to compete with the dominant under-taking in a secondary market where there is no existing competition. The development of the law in this area has been complex and confusing. Many of the early cases, which developed some of the key concepts, may now be better understood as unique decisions, falling on their own facts, or as 'refusal to deal' cases, as discussed above. In light of their developmental importance, however, we shall discuss them in this section. It was only after more recent cases, such as *Oscar Bronner*,[110] that it became possible to more clearly draw distinctions between the different situations.

Most of the cases in this area have dealt with the refusal to supply a service. In a number of early cases the Court went some way towards holding that a dominant undertaking acts abusively if it fails to help a new competitor enter the market, but did little to indicate in which circumstances this would be required. An example is *London-European/Sabena*,[111] where Sabena was held to be abusing its position by refusing London-European access to its com-puterised reservation system. London-European wished to introduce an air service, in competition with Sabena, between London and Brussels. To compete effectively, London-European needed access to Sabena's reservation system. The Commission decided that access to the system was essential for any competition to develop and, therefore, refusal of access to the service was an abuse. A similar decision was seen in *British Midland/Aer Lingus*.[112] This was the starting point for a number of cases where competitors have been granted access to what has become known as an 'essential facility', particularly where competition would not be possible without access. The inception of the 'essential facility' concept can be traced back to a number of US antitrust cases, notably *Terminal Railroad*[113] and *Associated Press*;[114] however, its place in US antitrust is still highly controversial, there being little agreement on its proper meaning.[115] Nevertheless, it became clear that

---

110 Case C-7/97 *Oscar Bronner GmbH and Co KG v Mediaprint Zeitschriftenverlag GmbH and Co KG* [1998] ECR I-7791; [1999] 4 CMLR 112.
111 Commission Decision 88/589/EEC, OJ 1988, L317/47; [1989] 4 CMLR 662.
112 Commission Decision 92/213/EEC *British Midland/Aer Lingus*, OJ 1992, L96/34.
113 *United States v Terminal RR Ass'n*, 224 U.S. 383 (1912).
114 *Associated Press v United States*, 326 U.S. 1 (1945).
115 The classic discussion of the early US cases can be found in Areeda, P, 'Essential Facilities: An Epithet in Need of Limiting Principles' (1989) 58 Antitrust LJ 841.

the Commission, under Art 82, was keen to develop a European version of the doctrine.

In *Sealink/B & I – Holyhead: Interim Measures*,[116] the nature of an essential facility was demonstrated. Sealink owned the port of Holyhead and operated ferry services from it. The port was deemed to be an essential facility and Sealink was forced to grant B & I, a competing ferry operator, access on a non-discriminatory basis. Ports, such as the one at Holyhead, are good examples of the kind of facility to which access is vital to allow competition to develop, but the case itself is not a very good example of the doctrine in operation. Sealink had already granted B & I access to the facility; the dispute was focused on discriminatory access rather than refusal to grant access at all. It is, therefore, possible to read this decision as falling within the 'refusal to deal' category above, where Sealink had failed to fulfil its 'special responsibility' to an existing customer by discriminating without objective justification. While there is still debate over the proper understanding of the decision in *Sealink/B & I*, it was clearly the first step in the process, which led to a fuller exposition of an essential facility doctrine in Art 82.[117]

The Court clarified its position on a new competitor's access to an essential facility in *Oscar Bronner*.[118] The publisher of an Austrian daily newspaper, Bronner, sought access to a dominant rival's newspaper home-delivery system. The Court set out the conditions upon which the essential facilities doctrine could be invoked as follows:

i the facility must be indispensable to carrying on the entrant's business, in that there are no potential substitutes;
ii there must be technical, legal, or economic obstacles which make it impossible or unreasonably difficult to replicate the facility; and
iii the refusal must not be objectively justified.

The Court was of the view that there were no such obstacles to Bronner, alone or in co-operation with other publishers, in setting up an alternative distribution system. It was also made clear that it was not enough to argue that the alternative service would not be economically viable given the low circulation of Bronner's newspaper.[119] The Court's clarification in *Bronner* has, in effect, significantly reduced the potential scope of the essential facilities doctrine to situations in which it would be very difficult to replicate

---

116 [1992] 5 CMLR 255.
117 See, for example, Ridyard, D, 'Essential Facilities and the Obligation to Supply Competitors under the UK and EC Competition Law' [1996] ECLR 438. See also Müller, U, and Rodenhausen, A, 'The Rise and Fall of the Essential Facility Doctrine' [2008] ECLR 310.
118 Case C-7/97 *Oscar Bronner GmbH and Co KG v Mediaprint Zeitungs und Zeitschriftenverlag GmbH and Co KG* [1998] ECR I-7791; [1999] 4 CMLR 112.
119 See Bergman, MA, 'The *Bronner* case – a turning point for the essential facilities doctrine' [2000] ECLR 59.

the indispensable facility. By bringing the relevant cases together it is now possible to set out a three-stage test for the use of the essential facility doctrine:

i   the facility must be indispensable to carrying on the entrant's business; there must be no potential substitutes and it must be impossible or unreasonably difficult to replicate;
ii the refusal would exclude any effective competition on a neighbouring market; and
iii the refusal must not be objectively justified.

These cases can be distinguished from 'refusal to deal' cases in that the owner/creator of the facility has not already allowed other competitors access, and therefore has not already allowed a market for the facility to develop; arguably, they are not now required to create such a market through their 'special responsibility' as a dominant undertaking.[120]

This judgment in *Bronner* was a significant restriction compared to some of the more hysterical predictions which followed the Court's judgment in the *Magill* case,[121] which itself was further complicated by the introduction of intellectual property issues. There was also academic argument that the essential facilities doctrine in *Bronner* was very different from the IP doctrine developed in *Magill*, but following the *IMS* case[122] it is clear that *Bronner* and *Magill* are closely related, and that the existence of an IP right simply adds a further complication to the essential facility problem.

Intellectual property rights

The coexistence of IP rights and competition law has always been problematic. Intellectual property rights encourage innovation by rewarding the innovator with exclusivity, but that may in turn become statutory dominance which may be abused. Article 82 makes an attempt to balance the various goals. It has always been held that the ownership of an IP right was not, in itself, an abuse but that the use of such a right may amount to one.[123] One area where abuses have been found is in relation to the refusal to grant licences of IP rights. One of the most important cases concerned the licensing of copyright in TV listings. Magill, an Irish company, wished to publish a weekly TV guide listing all the programmes which could be viewed in

---

120 This is difficult to reconcile with cases like Commission Decision 92/213/EEC *British Midland/Aer Lingus*, OJ 1992, L96/34, but perhaps if the Commission revisited them in light of *Bronner* they would be decided differently.
121 Commission Decision 89/205/EEC *Magill TV Guide/ITP, BBC & RTE*, OJ 1989, L78/43, and Cases C-241 & 242/91P *RTE and Others v Commission* [1995] ECR I-743.
122 Case C-418/01 *IMS Health GmbH v NDC Health GmbH* [2004] 4 CMLR 28.
123 Case 24/67 *Parke, Davis & Co v Probel* [1968] ECR 55; [1968] CMLR 47.

the Republic of Ireland. Those programmes included those broadcast by RTE, the national Irish station, BBC and ITV. All three broadcasters published weekly guides of their own programmes and licensed newspapers to publish daily listings. The broadcasters all refused to grant Magill a licence to publish a weekly listing. This refusal meant that no comprehensive guide existed and consumers were forced to purchase three separate weekly guides. The Commission held that the broadcasters had abused their dominant positions by preventing a new product, the comprehensive guide, from reaching the market[124] and using their copyright in the listings beyond the purpose for which the right was granted. On appeal, the Court concentrated on the fact that the broadcasters were denying consumers a product for which there was demand.[125] In addition, they were attempting to reserve a secondary market – TV guides being a secondary market to broadcasting – for themselves by denying others the basic information required.

Two recent disputes, *IMS*[126] and *Microsoft*,[127] indicate the potential conflicts between Art 82 and IP law. The *IMS* and *Microsoft* cases both involve IP licensing, albeit in different ways. In *IMS*, a dispute before the German courts which was the subject of a preliminary ruling, an undertaking which had developed a system of 1,860 geographical areas, known as 'bricks', which segmented the German market for pharmaceuticals and enabled the undertaking to produce usage statistics, challenged the argument that its failure to license potential competitors to use the 'brick' system was abusive. In the *Microsoft* Decision, the Commission, confirmed on appeal by the CFI, required the dominant work group server operating system supplier, Microsoft, to disclose complete and accurate interface documentation to allow non-Microsoft work group servers to be fully interoperable with Windows PCs and servers. To the extent that such a disclosure requires the licensing of IP rights, Microsoft should receive reasonable remuneration. Both the decisions of the Court of Justice, in *IMS*, and the Court of First Instance, in *Microsoft*, are heavily dependent on the reasoning in *Bronner*. It appears, therefore, that cases involving refusal to license IP will be treated as similar to essential facility cases. This is presumably because the existence of the IP right means that right holder always has the right to refuse to supply, as that right is implicit

---

124 Commission Decision 89/205/EEC *Magill TV Guide/ITP, BBC & RTE*, OJ 1989, L78/43; [1989] 4 CMLR 757.

125 Cases C-241 and 242/91P *RTE and Others v Commission* [1995] ECR I-743; [1995] 4 CMLR 718. For further consideration of the area, see Case T-504/93 *Tierce Ladbroke v Commission* [1997] ECR II-923.

126 Commission Decision 2002/165/EC *NDC Health/IMS Health: Interim Measures*, OJ 2002, L59/18, subsequently withdrawn; Commission Decision 2003/174/EC, OJ 2003, L268/69; and Case C-418/01 *IMS Health GmbH v NDC Health GmbH* [2004] ECR I-5039, [2004] 4 CMLR 28.

127 Commission Decision 2007/53/EC *Microsoft*, OJ 2007, L32/23. On appeal, Case T-201/04 *Microsoft v Commission*, judgment of 17 September 2007.

within the grant of an IP right, unless there are very strong competition reasons for requiring the license. As the right holder has an implicit justification for refusing to licence these cases cannot fall into the 'refusal to deal' category discussed above, and are treated differently to other essential facility cases. The Courts have effectively combined the three elements of the essential facility test in *Bronner*, with the 'new product' requirement, which is unique to IP, from *Magill*. The test, as set out in Microsoft,[128] is as follows:

i   the refusal relates to a product or service indispensable to the exercise of a particular activity on a neighbouring market;
ii   the refusal is of such a kind as to exclude any effective competition on that neighbouring market;
iii the refusal prevents the appearance of a new product for which there is potential consumer demand; and
iv   the refusal is not objectively justified.

The *Micosoft* judgment also went some way to explaining how a number of the controversial elements of the test should be applied.[129] It made it clear that in relation to the second criteria it is only necessary to show that the refusal is 'is liable to, or is likely to, eliminate all effective competition on the market'.[130] The most controversial element of the *Magill/IMS* test has always been the 'new product' criteria. This essentially delimits the protection an IP right receives. The holder can refuse to license the IP right where the competitor will simply replicate the right holder's provision; but, how new does a new product need to be? The CFI in *Microsoft* made it clear that problems may arise, 'where there is a limitation not only of production or markets, but also of technical development'.[131] It is now clear that those seeking supply must show that the refusal denies them the opportunity to supply a new product or market, or to innovate in the way they provide products or services.

Collective dominance

One of the most hotly debated issues in the 1990s was the attempt by the Commission to control oligopolistic markets using Art 82. An oligopolistic market is one that has few suppliers, none of which have market dominance, but all of which are relatively large. A small number of undertakings exercise

---

128 At paras 331–334.
129 The *IMS* and *Microsoft* cases have generated an enormous amount of literature. A few of the more balanced examples are: Killick, J, '*IMS* and *Microsoft* Judged in the Cold Light of *IMS*' (2004) 1(2) CompLRev 23; Ong, B, 'Building Brick barricades and other Barriers to Entry: Abusing a Dominant Position by Refusing to Licence Intellectual Property Rights' [2005] ECLR 213; and, Vezzoso, S, 'The Incentives Balance Test in the EU Microsoft Case: A Pro-Innovation "Economics Based" Approach' [2006] ECLR 382.
130 At para 563.
131 At para 647.

collective market power. Although all oligopolistic markets will be different, they will tend to have similar features. There will usually be a small number of sizeable undertakings operating in a market with homogeneous products. The market may also be characterised by limited price competition and parallel behaviour. It is because of this tendency toward limited competition and parallelism that the competition authorities are interested in finding ways to regulate such markets. An example of an oligopolistic market is the groceries market in which a small number of supermarket companies sell nearly all the UK's groceries. It is now very common to see markets becoming oligopolistic in Europe as competition drives out weaker competitors, and mergers lead to increased market concentration.

Although oligopolistic markets do not raise the same problems as monopolies, they can have similar effects. Often, oligopolists do not compete strongly on price, and there is little incentive to compete in other ways. This is because of what is known as 'oligopolistic interdependence'. For example, in a market with three equally strong undertakings, known as a tight oligopoly, no one undertaking would be dominant. In a truly competitive situation, a price cut by one undertaking should result in an increase in profit. Customers would switch to the lower priced good. However, in a tight oligopoly, such a cut would result in a swift response from the other undertakings. They would quickly be aware of the price change and would be forced to respond with a similar cut. As there are few competitors, it is easy to keep track of the actions of rivals. The reaction of the competitors would quickly negate any rise in market share. As all the undertakings would be charging at the same level, market shares would remain at similar levels as before the price cut. The end result of a price cut would be a similar market share, but much lower levels of income as the unit price would have dropped. A unilateral price cut, therefore, would bring little benefit.

Similarly, there will be little benefit from a unilateral price increase. If one undertaking were to increase its prices its customers would soon switch to purchase from the undertaking's rivals whose prices remain at the original level. Such an increase would simply result in a loss of custom. As unilateral price changes appear to have little merit, it follows that price competition tends to stagnate. Although the undertakings may try to compete in other ways, through service or product differentiation, the competitive process is very limited, with no benefits passing on to the customer or the economy.

When oligopolists become aware of this situation they become very sensitive to each other's actions, and are aware that they have limited opportunities to increase their profit levels. At this stage 'game theory' and practice suggest that an even more worrying development may occur. When the oligopolists become sensitive to the situation they are in, it becomes apparent that they can maximise their profits by gradually increasing their prices. If they do this simultaneously, they will not lose any market share, but will receive a higher unit price. They can act, in effect, as a single 'monopolistic' entity. At this stage, they realise that they are interdependent and can work together to maximise profits. The difficulty competition law has with this type of market is that there is little need for formal organisation of such a scheme; it can occur through 'tacit co-ordination' – a natural operation of such a market. Most of the regulatory tools used in competition law are aimed at dealing with market behaviour rather than market structure itself.

While the theory of oligopolistic interdependence can help to explain apparent parallelism in oligopolistic markets, it does not satisfactorily explain how the simultaneous action comes about. Traditional theory suggests that a price rise will result in customer desertion and, therefore, it is unlikely that an undertaking would be willing to risk such desertion without some form of guarantee that its competitors would follow. There are several possible explanations. First, a branch of economics known as 'game theory' has attempted to explain business behaviour by examining the way in which business decisions are taken as part of a game of strategy. This theory is interesting in that it helps to explain why such interdependent behaviour might come about, but not how it occurs in practice. The second possible explanation relies on the existence of a 'price leader'. The price leader is an undertaking in the market that traditionally signals price rises to other under-takings, which then habitually follow the signalling undertaking because it has a good eye for changes on the market. If that price leader becomes aware of its position, it will be able to gradually increase prices in the knowledge that the others will follow and that, hence, profits will be maximised. The other undertakings will be aware that a failure to follow could result in a destructive price war, which would be harmful for all. As oligopolistic markets differ greatly, no single theory can hope to explain all the potential scenarios, but the explanations above may help to describe some of the problems that are likely to be encountered.

To control the competitive problems in oligopolistic markets, the Commis-sion was keen to extend its ability to regulate under Art 82 by using the concept of collective dominance. It argued that such a concept was envisaged by the drafters of the Treaty, wherein it states, in Art 82, that 'Any abuse by *one or more undertakings* of a dominant position' will be prohibited. Some view this as a reference to the possibility of more than one undertaking being collectively dominant. The Commission tried to raise the possibility of collective dominance in *Hoffmann-La Roche*,[132] but the Court rejected it on the basis that dominance requires unilateral action. The Court relaxed its position in *Ahmed Saeed*,[133] where it held that Arts 81 and 82 could be applied to the same situation.

---

132 See Case 85/76 *Hoffmann-La Roche v Commission* [1979] ECR 461; [1979] 3 CMLR 211.
133 Case 66/86 *Ahmed Saeed Flugreisen v Zentrale zur Bekämpfung Unlauteren Wettbewerbs* [1989] ECR 803; [1990] 4 CMLR 102.

It was not until the CFI dealt with *Italian Flat Glass*[134] that the position of collective dominance was clarified. Three Italian undertakings, in the automotive and non-automotive flat glass markets, had aggregate market shares of 79% and 95%, respectively. The Commission found that the three undertakings had formed a cartel contrary to Art 81, but also found that there was a collective dominant position as the undertakings 'present themselves on the market as a single entity and not as individuals'.[135] The Commission based this Decision on the existence of a tight oligopoly, the long-term stability of market shares, the interdependence of the three undertakings, and the structural links between them. When the case reached the CFI, the findings on Art 81 were struck down as the Commission had failed to prove the case to the necessary standard. When it came to consider collective dominance, the CFI adopted the interpretation of Art 82 suggested above, allowing for collective dominance, and stated:

> There is nothing, in principle, to prevent two or more independent economic entities from being, on a specific market, united by such economic links that, by virtue of that fact, together they hold a dominant position vis à vis the other operators on the same market.[136]

The actual Decision of the Commission was overturned as it had 'recycled' the facts found under Art 81 and had not detailed the necessary findings on the nature of the market. However, the concept of collective dominance as set out by the CFI in *Italian Flat Glass* was approved by the Court of Justice in *Almelo*.[137]

The Commission went on to use the CFI's findings in *Flat Glass* in its *Cewal* Decision.[138] The Commission decided that the shipping conference, Cewal, had abused its collective dominant position. Shipping conferences are organisations of shipping companies that plan schedules and pricing levels for particular shipping routes. Shipping conferences were exempted from the prohibition in Art 81 by Council Regulation 4056/86.[139] Cewal controlled 90% of the market and had abused its position by using 'fighting ships' against its main competitor.

On appeal before the Court of Justice,[140] the nature of the 'economic links'

---

134 Cases T-68, 77 and 78/89 *Società Italiana Vetro v Commission* [1992] ECR II-1403; [1992] 5 CMLR 302.
135 Commission Decision 89/93/EEC, OJ 1989, L33/44; [1990] 4 CMLR 535.
136 [1992] ECR II-1403; [1992] 5 CMLR 302, para 358.
137 Case C-393/92 *Municipality of Almelo v Energiebedrijf Ijsselmij NV* [1994] ECR I-1477, an Art 234 reference.
138 Commission Decision 93/82/EEC, OJ 1993, L34/20; [1995] 5 CMLR 198.
139 OJ 1986, L378/4.
140 Case C-395/96 *Compagnie Maritime Belge Transports SA v Commission of the European Communities* [2000] ECR I-1365; [2000] 4 CMLR 1076.

required for a finding of collective dominance was clarified. Although there was strong evidence of linkage through the conference agreement, the Court did not find it necessary to limit its discussion to such formal arrangements. It noted that:

> The existence of a collective dominant position may therefore flow from the nature and terms of an agreement, from the way in which it is implemented and, consequently, from the links or factors which give rise to a connection between undertakings which result from it. Nevertheless, the existence of an agreement or of other links in law is not indispensable to a finding of a collective dominant position; such a finding may be based on other connecting factors and would depend on an economic assessment and, in particular, on an assessment of the structure of the market in question.[141]

This suggested that it may be possible to show that there are 'links' between undertakings and that those links stem entirely from the structure of the market. Links stemming from market structure would obviously be useful in dealing with undertakings in oligopolistic markets. The CFI elaborated on this issue in *Gencor*,[142] stating that 'there is no reason whatsoever in legal or economic terms to exclude from the notion of economic links the relationship of interdependence existing between the parties to a tight oligopoly'.[143] Nonetheless, the Court, in *Airtours*,[144] clarified that the Commission must satisfy the following three issues in order to establish collective dominance:

i   each member of the dominant oligopoly must have the ability to know how the other members are behaving, in order to monitor whether or not the oligopolists are adopting the common policy;
ii   there must be an incentive for oligopolists not to depart from the common policy on the market; and
iii the foreseeable reaction of current and future competitors, as well as of consumers, would not jeopardise the results expected from the common policy.[145]

It must be noted that both *Gencor* and *Airtours* discussed the creation of a collective dominant position within the terms of the Merger Regulation. The same 'dominance'-based terminology is used in Art 82 and the Merger Regulation; although its importance has been reduced in the latter since its

---

141 Ibid, para 45.
142 Case T-102/96 *Gencor Ltd v Commission* [1999] ECR II-753; [1999] 4 CMLR 971.
143 Ibid, para 276.
144 Case T-342/99 *Airtours v Commission* [2002] ECR II-2585; [2002] 5 CMLR 7.
145 Ibid, para 62.

reform in 2004, the control of mergers does raise a somewhat different set of issues.[146] Nonetheless, the developments in these cases should bring the control of oligopolistic markets more securely within the terms of Art 82, subject to the requirement of presenting convincing economic evidence.

Control of dominance in the UK

Introduction

The remainder of this chapter shall look at the anti-monopoly laws in the UK, providing a review of the key sets of current legislative provisions: the Competition Act 1998 Chapter II prohibition, and Pt 4 of the Enterprise Act 2002 on market investigations. However, to understand the current legislative framework, one has to gain an outline appreciation of the nature of the Fair Trading Act (FTA) 1973 and the reform proposals which led first to the 1998 Act, including the Chapter II prohibition, and thereafter the 2002 Act. Accordingly, in the UK, there exist two parallel systems for dealing with 'monopoly' markets – the 'abuse of dominance' approach in the Chapter II prohibition under the 1998 Act and the 'market investigation' approach under the 2002 Act.

Reform of UK anti-monopoly laws

Abuse of Market Power

Prior to 1998, the FTA 1973 was the most important provision in UK anti-monopoly laws, although there was continued debate regarding its reform and/or replacement by new rules. Broadly speaking, the 1973 Act established an investigative system to look at 'monopolies' and at markets where there was some form of 'market failure', but there was no provision for deterrent effect, no prohibition of conduct as such, and no effective sanctions, as the 1973 Act merely required a consideration of the public interest impact of the 'monopoly' market. A Green Paper,[147] published in 1992, considered the case for reform of the UK antimonopoly laws for dealing with situations of market power. It assessed the advantages and disadvantages of the FTA 1973 and the Competition Act 1980 in comparison with Community experience under the model of Art 82 EC. The advantages identified under the 1973

---

146 Under the Merger Regulation the issue concerns whether a concentrated market may, in the future, be oligopolistic, whereas under Art 82 the Commission or an NCA must establish collective dominance in existing markets. For the discussion of collective dominance under the Merger Regulation, see Chapter 6. See, also, Haupt, H, 'Collective dominance under Article 82 EC and EC merger control in the light of the *Airtours* judgment' [2003] ECLR 434.

147 *Abuse of Market Power*, Cm 2100, 1992.

Act were its flexibility, the wide range of remedies available and its particular suitability for dealing with market structure issues, notably oligopolistic markets. On the other hand, it lacked deterrent effect, there were no penalties, the powers of investigation were limited, and its provisions were not enforceable in the courts. The Art 82 model would remedy each of these disadvantages but it concentrated on behavioural issues and lacked the flexibility to deal with certain problems, particularly market structural issues and oligopoly.

Trade and Industry Committee report on UK policy on monopolies

In this report, produced in 1995,[148] the Committee considered that there were a variety of flaws in the UK approach to monopoly control. The report considered the criticism that the public interest criteria were too broad and vague, resulting in inconsistency and unpredictability. The Committee was also concerned that Department of Trade and Industry (DTI) policy was not clear as to the objectives of UK competition policy and the report advocated that consumer policy interests should be at the heart of UK competition policy. Four main shortcomings of the 1973 Act were highlighted:

1   the lack of deterrence provisions;
2   the limited investigation powers;
3   the existence of no provisions for interim measures; and
4   the absence of rights for private parties to take action for damages or other relief.[149]

The Committee reviewed earlier reform proposals and confirmed that a prohibition approach, based substantially on Art 82, should be adopted. The Committee considered that a prohibition approach would provide greater deterrence and had the potential to provide greater clarity, consistency and predictability. This report is notable because of the remarkable similarities with the ultimate reform proposals introduced in the Competition Act 1998.

Legislative developments

The Conservative Government finally decided, in 1996, to introduce legislation to reform UK competition law and published a DTI consultation document followed by an explanatory document and draft Bill.[150] In 1997, the new

---

148 Fifth Report, HC 249-I, 1995.
149 Ibid, para 94.
150 Department of Trade and Industry, *Tackling Cartels and the Abuse of Market Power: Implementing the Government's Policy for Competition Law Reform, a Consultation Document,* March 1996, London: DTI; and *Tackling Cartels and the Abuse of Market Power: A Draft Bill, an Explanatory Document,* August 1996, London: DTI.

Labour Government, almost immediately upon election, published a new explanatory document and draft Bill, which formed the basis of the Competition Act 1998.[151] The Competition Act 1980 provisions on anti-competitive practices were repealed by the 1998 Act and are no longer considered in any detail in this chapter. However, at this stage, the FTA 1973 was retained due to the perceived advantages of flexibility and pragmatism under its provisions for control of structural and complex monopolies. One of the principal reasons was its suitability for dealing with problems in oligopolistic markets. The Competition Act 1998 provided a new prohibition on the abuse of a dominant position based on Art 82. Accordingly, as at 1 March 2000 when the new prohibition came into force, there were two sets of controls in parallel, under the 1973 and 1998 Acts respectively, each with a different focus.

Nonetheless, in 2001, the DTI proposed further radical reform of UK competition law.[152] Subsequently, the Enterprise Act 2002 was enacted and it replaced the monopoly investigation provisions of the 1973 Act with new provisions for market investigations, set out in Pt 4 of the 2002 Act. These new provisions will be outlined in this chapter and any pertinent differences from the 1973 Act highlighted where appropriate. In addition, given that the main provisions entered into force in June 2003,[153] we will look at the practice to date under the 2002 Act provisions and also key aspects of the prior practice under the FTA 1973 as the latter will illustrate some issues that are likely to remain a concern under Pt 4 of the 2002 Act. It should be noted that, for reasons of space, the particular problems involved in the regulation of utilities will not be dealt with in this book.[154]

The Competition Act 1998 – the Chapter II prohibition

Part I of the Act introduces two new prohibitions based on Arts 81 and 82. These are known respectively as the Chapter I and Chapter II prohibitions. The Chapter II prohibition is in respect of abuse, by an undertaking or undertakings, of a dominant position in the UK. The Chapter II prohibition is contained in s 18 of the Act, which contains virtually identical provisions to those contained in Art 82. Section 18(1) provides that 'any conduct on the

---

151 Department of Trade and Industry, *A Prohibition Approach to Anti-Competitive Agreements and Abuse of a Dominant Position: Draft Bill*, August 1997, London: DTI. The subsequent Bill, which had its first reading in the House of Lords on 15 October 1997, was amended in certain respects from the original draft Bill.

152 White Paper, *Productivity and Enterprise: A World Class Competition Regime*, Cm 5233, 31 July 2001.

153 The Enterprise Act 2002 (Commencement No 3, Transitional and Transitory Provisions and Savings) Order 2003, SI 2003/1397, brought the main powers and offences of the Enterprise Act 2002 into force on 20 June 2003.

154 See, for instance, Robinson, C, *Utility Regulation in Competitive Markets: Problems and Progress*, 2007, London: Edward Elgar.

part of one or more undertakings which amounts to the abuse of a dominant position in a market is prohibited if it may affect trade within the United Kingdom'. The only difference is that s 18 refers to a dominant position and the effect on trade within the UK. Consistency of interpretation with Community law, Art 82 in this context, is ensured by s 60 of the Act. Section 60 provides that the determination of any questions in relation to the prohibitions should be consistent with the treatment of corresponding questions arising under Community law. This provision clearly ensures that Community case law on what constitutes an abuse of a dominant position will be followed to the extent that it is relevant in a national context. It is also clear from Office of Fair Trading (OFT) decisions and, crucially, from judgments by the Competition Appeal Tribunal, that Community case law is relied on as underpinning the interpretation of the domestic prohibition.

Enforcement and ancillary issues

Chapter III makes provision for the investigation and enforcement of the Chapter I and II prohibitions, and the Community prohibitions in Articles 81 and 82. As noted in Chapter 2, the DGFT's key role of enforcing and applying the new regime is undertaken by the OFT. Section 25 of the 2002 Act provides that the OFT may conduct an investigation upon reasonable suspicion that any of those prohibitions has been infringed. The powers of investigation provided under ss 26–29 are similar to those powers afforded to the Commission under Arts 18–21 of Regulation 1/2003.[155] Similarly, the OFT is required under s 31 to give persons affected by a proposed decision on whether the prohibition has been infringed an opportunity to make representations; this opportunity is effected by a Notice issued under Rule 7 of the OFT's rules.[156] The OFT may make interim measures under s 35, and is empowered to require conduct in breach of the prohibition to be modified or terminated.[157] Section 36 provides for the imposition of a fine of up to 10% of the worldwide turnover of an undertaking whose conduct infringes the Chapter II prohibition. Fines are imposed in accordance with the Guidance, published as required under s 38 of the 1998 Act, on the determination of the appropriate level of fines.[158] There is a detailed discussion in Chapter 2 on

---

155 Sections 42–44 of the 1998 Act create certain offences in relation to the obstruction of the OFT's information gathering tasks under these provisions.

156 The Competition Act 1998 (Office of Fair Trading's Rules) Order, SI 2004/2751, previously Rule 14 under the Competition Act 1998 (Director's Rules) Order 2000, SI 2000/293.

157 Under s 33. Section 34 provides that this may be enforced by a court order.

158 See Guidance as to the appropriate level of a penalty (OFT 423) and discussion in Chapter 2. Section 52 required publication of general information and advice about enforcement of the prohibition and there are a number of guidelines available on the OFT website at www.oft.gov.uk. A number of these guidelines were revised during 2004 to include reference to the new relationship between Arts 81 and 82 and domestic competition law, and to the

the fining policy and practice under the 1998 Act to date. Where conduct infringing the prohibition is of 'minor significance' there is immunity from the imposition of any fines under s 40. Chapter V of Pt I of the Act contains a variety of provisions, for instance, enabling rules to be made about procedural matters under Pt I of the Act (the 'OFT's rules'), restricting the disclosure of information obtained under the Act by ss 55 and 56,[159] and providing, under ss 58 and 58A, for findings of fact by the OFT to be binding and findings of infringements to be relied upon in subsequent actions for damages.

The Competition Appeal Tribunal (CAT), established by s 12 and Sched 2 to the Enterprise Act 2002, acts as an appeals tribunal in relation to decisions made, primarily by the OFT, in respect of the Chapter II prohibition, the mechanism for appeals being regulated by Sched 8 to the 1998 Act. Third parties with a sufficient interest may also appeal. The CAT (and the Competition Commission Appeals Tribunal (CCAT), prior to the Enterprise Act) has already made a significant contribution to the interpretation and application of the Chapter II prohibition, and its judgments are available on the CAT website.[160] Appeals against CAT judgments may be made, on a point of law, to the Court of Appeal, Court of Session or Court of Appeal in Northern Ireland in respect of England and Wales, Scotland and Northern Ireland, respectively.

Consistency with Community law

Section 60(1) of the 1998 Act provides that:

> The purpose of this section is to ensure that so far as is possible (having regard to any relevant differences between the provisions concerned), questions arising under this Part in relation to competition within the United Kingdom are dealt with in a manner which is consistent with the treatment of corresponding questions arising in Community law in relation to competition within the Community.

The basic rule, stemming from the overall objective of introducing a set of rules harmonised with Community law and minimising the risk of a double burden on UK business, is that the Chapter II prohibition should be

---

requirement on the OFT to apply the former Community prohibitions, following the introduction of Regulation 1/2003, and to reflect changes introduced to domestic law to ensure greater harmony between the application of the domestic prohibitions and Arts 81 and 82. In addition, the OFT issued a Guideline on the Modernisation Regulation and the application of Arts 81 and 82 by the OFT, 'Modernisation', OFT 442.

159 Competition Act 1998; s 56 restricts the disclosure of types of confidential information.
160 At www.catribunal.org.uk/judgments/default.asp.

interpreted consistently with the interpretation of Art 82 utilised by the Community authorities.[161] Section 60(2) provides that a court (which includes any court or tribunal for these purposes) must act with a view to ensuring that its decisions are consistent with the jurisprudence of the European Court. Furthermore, courts are to have regard to any relevant decision or statement of the Commission.[162] The requirement of consistency applies equally to decisions by the OFT in relation to the prohibitions. Section 60 contains the important proviso that consistency should be achieved, 'in so far as is possible (having regard to any relevant differences between the provisions concerned)'. This permits departure from Community law principles, but the scope of the proviso is uncertain. It was introduced primarily to avoid the application of Community principles designed to further individual Community objectives which would be irrelevant for domestic purposes, primarily the attainment of the single market. It should be noted, in the context of the Chapter II prohibition, that the application of Art 82 has not been greatly influenced by the integration imperative although there has been case law in relation to abuses, such as prohibiting imports[163] and discriminatory refusals to supply on the basis of nationality.[164] A particular difficulty in the application of the basic rule, and the proviso, is that the Art 82 case law is often complicated and involves different types of abusive conduct; therefore, the selection of particular aspects of the case law to apply in a UK context will not always be straightforward.[165] Nonetheless, the CAT's treatment and application of Community jurisprudence in appeals under the Chapter II prohibition has generally been thorough and impressive. In its judgments on key issues, such as relevant market, dominance and abuse, following submissions from the parties, the Tribunal sets out its findings commencing with an outline of the relevant law, derived primarily from European Court pronouncements. These outlines provide readers with an excellent summarised account of the development of Community jurisprudence.[166]

Guidelines on the prohibition

Section 52(1) of the Act required publication of general advice and information about:

161 See Middleton, K, 'Harmonisation with Community law: the Euro clause', Chapter 2 in Rodger, BJ and MacCulloch, A (eds), *The UK Competition Act: A New Era for UK Competition Law*, 2000, Oxford: Hart.

162 Competition Act 1998, s 60(3). This will extend to Commission Decisions and Notices published indicating Commission practice.

163 See Case 226/84 *British Leyland v Commission* [1986] ECR 3263; [1987] 1 CMLR 185.

164 See, generally, Sufrin, B, 'The Chapter II prohibition', Chapter 6 in Rodger and MacCulloch, above, fn 161.

165 See Case 7/82 *GVL v Commission* [1983] ECR 483; [1983] 3 CMLR 465.

166 *Napp Pharmaceutical Holdings Ltd v DGFT* [2002] CAT 1, [2002] ECC 13.

a the application of the Chapter I prohibition and the Chapter II prohibition; and

b the enforcement of those prohibitions.

With the exception of debates on the introduction of a predatory pricing provision for the newspaper industry, there was little technical debate in Parliament during progress of the Competition Bill. The key statutory provision, s 18, like Art 82, is fairly succinct and the absence of any definition of key concepts is notable.[167] This absence was remedied to a certain extent by the publication, after consultation, of a wide range of guidelines on the application of the prohibition. Following the introduction of Regulation 1/2003, s 52 of the Act was amended to require the OFT to publish, as soon as practicable after 1 May 2004, advice and information about the application and enforcement of Arts 81(1) and 82 EC. Accordingly, a number of the Guidelines were revised during 2004 to include reference to the new relationship between Arts 81 and 82 and domestic competition law, the requirement on the national authorities to apply Arts 81 and 82, and to reflect changes introduced to ensure greater harmony between the application of the domestic prohibitions and Arts 81 and 82. In addition, the OFT issued a new general Guideline on the modernisation regulation and the application, by the OFT, of Arts 81 and 82.[168] These Guidelines can be found on the OFT's website and include a range of guidance of direct relevance to the Chapter II prohibition, such as the Guidelines on 'Article 82 and the Chapter II prohibition', 'Assessment of Market Power' and the 'Assessment of Conduct'.[169] The publication of the series of guidelines on the Act formed an integral part of the OFT's compliance programme aimed at encouraging companies to comply with the new prohibitions, by educating companies and informing them of the potential sanctions involved for any breach. These Guidelines provide a helpful guide to the relevant Art 82 case law, notwithstanding its inherent uncertainty and unpredictability. Subsequent tribunal judgments, in particular, provide examples of the interpretation and application of the Chapter II prohibition in the light of the s 60 requirement for consistency with Community law and its development.

Practice and case-law to date

Tribunal judgments

To date, there have been numerous decisions taken under the Chapter II prohibition, including several by the Director General of Telecommunications.

---

167 See interpretation section, s 59 of the Competition Act 1998.
168 'Modernisation', OFT 442.
169 OFT 402, 415 and 414 respectively.

Decisions by the DGFT, and now the OFT, are available on the public register of decisions available on the OFT website.[170] This includes decisions by other regulators and also decisions, following an investigation, finding that there has been no infringement of the prohibition.[171] This decision-making transparency facilitates understanding of OFT practice under the prohibition. In this section, we will focus on key examples of the emerging jurisprudence of the CAT.[172] Nonetheless, it should be stressed that not all OFT or regulator decisions are appealed and those decisions, which are not appealed, may also raise important legal issues.[173] It should also be noted that there have been no subsequent appeal court judgments as yet in relation to the Chapter II prohibition, although the Court of Appeal refused Napp permission to appeal.[174] The Tribunal has dealt with a number of issues pertaining to the application of the Chapter II prohibition, including the general role of Community jurisprudence: identifying what constitutes an undertaking; the determination of the relevant market; the establishment of dominance; and, also, what constitutes an abuse, as illustrated in the following cases.

Napp Pharmaceuticals Ltd v DGFT

The first infringement decision was taken against *Napp*;[175] the DGFT imposed a fine of £3.21m. Napp had a persistently high market share, well in excess of 90% in the market for sustained release morphine tablets and capsules in the UK. The abusive behaviour adopted by Napp included predatory discounting of drugs sold to hospitals. Discounts in excess of 90% were made available in some circumstances, particularly where there was a potential competitor. The DGFT followed the case law of the European Court, in particular *AKZO*, when discussing predation.[176] Napp was also found to be

---

170 At http://www.oft.gov.uk/advice_and_resources/resource_base/ca98/decisions/

171 See, for instance, Rodger, B, 'Early steps to a mature competition law system: case law developments in the first eighteen months of the Competition Act 1998' [2002] ECLR 52.

172 See, also, Rodger, B, 'The impact of the Competition Act 1998: a new competition culture emerges' (2002) SLPQ 97.

173 See, for instance, OFT Decision CA98/07/2003; Case CP/1761/02 *EI Du Pont de Nemours & Company and Op Graphics (Holography) Ltd*, 9 September 2003, in which the OFT did not consider there was an abuse in relation to a complaint concerning a refusal to supply by a dominant company. See also OFT Decision CA98/05/2004; Case CP/0361–01, *First Edinburgh/Lothian*, 29 April 2004 where fare reductions did not constitute abusive predatory pricing.

174 *Napp Pharmaceutical Holdings Ltd v DGFT* [2002] EWCA Civ 796, [2002] 4 All ER 376.

175 *Napp Pharmaceutical Holdings Ltd and Subsidiaries (Napp)*, Decision CA98/2/2001, 30 March 2001. On appeal *Napp Pharmaceutical Holdings Ltd v DGFT* [2002] CAT 1. See, also, OFT Decision CA98/05/2004; Case CP/0361–01 *First Edinburgh/Lothian*, 29 April 2004 in relation to alleged predatory pricing in commercial bus services in Greater Edinburgh.

176 Case C-62/86 *Commission v AKZO* [1991] ECR I-3359; [1993] 5 CMLR 215, although it was interesting that the DGFT did not rely on the more recent decision in Case T-228/97 *Irish Sugar plc v Commission* [1999] ECR II-2969; [1999] 5 CMLR 1300.

charging excessive prices to community customers where Napp charged a 40% premium above its nearest rival while still maintaining a 90% plus market share. The price to community customers was 10 times that charged to hospitals. It was considered that this price was well in excess of that which would be expected in normal competitive conditions. It is interesting that there was a finding of excessive pricing in this first infringement Decision under the Act, as the European Commission has struggled to support findings of excessive pricing since the 1970s.[177] The Tribunal confirmed the finding of abuse, based on excessive prices, but paid greater attention to the predatory pricing abuse, setting out the principles established in *AKZO, Tetra Pak II*,[178] *Compagnie Maritime Belge*[179] and *Irish Sugar*.[180] The Tribunal stressed that the 'special responsibility' of a dominant undertaking was particularly onerous where, as with Napp's high and persistent market shares, the company enjoyed a position of 'dominance approaching monopoly' or 'super-dominance'. In line with *Tetra Pak II* and *AKZO*, Napp's pricing at below cost was presumed to be an abuse. Moreover, the principles set out in *Compagnie Maritime Belge* and *Irish Sugar* demonstrate that selective discounting by a super-dominant undertaking, without any objective justification which tends to eliminate competition, is an abuse. This judgment clearly applied very recent Community jurisprudence widening the net of predatory pricing beyond below cost pricing, at least where super-dominance is involved, in accordance with s 60 of the Act.[181] Nonetheless, the CAT reduced the fine payable by Napp to £2.2m.

Aberdeen Journals Ltd v DGFT

In the second formal Decision that the Chapter II prohibition had been infringed, a penalty of over £1.3m was imposed on Aberdeen Journals Ltd for breach of the Chapter II prohibition in respect of predation, by incurring losses for selling advertising space in an attempt to expel its only local rival.[182] Following its first hearing in Scotland, the Tribunal set aside the original Decision on the basis that the treatment of the relevant product market was inadequate, and remitted the matter to the DGFT. A second Decision against

---

177 See, for example, Case 26/75 *General Motors Continental NV v Commission* [1975] ECR 1367.
178 Case T-83/91 *Tetra Pak International v Commission* [1994] ECR II-755; [1997] 4 CMLR 726; and Case C-333/94P *Tetra Pak International v Commission* [1996] ECR I-5951; [1997] 4 CMLR 662.
179 Case T-24–26, 28/93 *Compagnie Maritime Belge Transport NV v Commission* [1996] ECR II-1201; [1997] 4 CMLR 273.
180 Case T-228/97 *Irish Sugar plc v Commission* [1999] ECR II-2969; [1999] 5 CMLR 1300.
181 See Kon, S and Turnbull, S, 'Pricing and the dominant firm: implications of the Competition Commission Appeal Tribunal's judgment in the *Napp* case' [2003] ECLR 70.
182 [2003] CAT 11.

Aberdeen Journals, on an almost identical basis to the first Decision, was also appealed to the Tribunal. The relevant market issue was particularly complicated as in essence the allegation was that Aberdeen Journals was using its free weekly journal as a fighting title to protect its sister paper, the daily paid-for *Evening Express*, from the new entrant, *The Independent*, by reducing its advertising prices. In order for Aberdeen Journals to be considered as dominant, its two titles would have to be deemed to be in the same relevant market. This was the focus of considerable debate between the parties, particularly on the issue of whether the two titles were complementary or substitutes for the purposes of advertisers. Ultimately, the Tribunal determined, on the basis of, *inter alia*, Aberdeen Journals' commercial strategy and the characteristics of the products, that the products were in potential competition for the business of local advertisers. The abuse issue was complicated even though the Tribunal relied on the Community jurisprudence on predatory pricing. The Tribunal considered that pricing below average variable cost by Aberdeen Journals was prohibited as predatory pricing. However, the Tribunal recognised that there were difficulties, both on the facts of the case and in guidance from the Community case law, in determining the precise approach to quantifying costs for the purpose of ascertaining the existence of predatory pricing. In any event, the Tribunal stressed that the cost-based predatory pricing rules were not to be applied mechanistically and that, as the Act sought to prevent dominant companies from strengthening their position by ways that were different from those under normal competitive conditions, the Chapter II prohibition applied to Aberdeen Journals' predatory pricing strategy. Despite confirming the infringement finding, the CAT reduced the fine imposed on Aberdeen Journals to £1m.

BetterCare II

In this case[183] the Tribunal decided that a Northern Irish health and social services trust (N & W) was engaged in economic activities, and, therefore, constituted an undertaking for the purposes of the Chapter II prohibition, in running its statutory residential homes and engaging in the contracting out of social care to independent providers. BetterCare had appealed against an OFT Decision that the prohibition had not been infringed following BetterCare's complaint that N & W was abusing its dominant position as the sole purchaser of residential and nursing care home services from BetterCare by offering unreasonably low contract prices. The Tribunal considered a wide range of recent Community jurisprudence[184] on the controversial issue of when a public body constitutes an undertaking and for these purposes. The Tribunal concluded that N & W's purchasing activities satisfied the test of

---

183 Case 1006/2/1/01 *BetterCare Group Ltd v DGFT* [2002] CAT 7.
184 See discussion earlier in this chapter regarding the issue of 'undertakings' under Art 82.

whether the body was 'engaging in economic activities'. Subsequently, the OFT has decided that N & W's conduct was not abusive as it did not set the prices in any event.[185] More generally, the OFT has issued a policy note advising that it is unlikely to take enforcement action against public bodies engaged in the purchasing and provision of goods and services for non-economic purposes. This approach was largely justified by the European Court's subsequent judgment in *AOK Bundesverband*, which provides further clarification of when a public body constitutes an undertaking for the purposes of competition law enforcement.[186]

Genzyme Ltd v OFT

In *Genzyme*, the DGFT, in March 2003, decided that Genzyme had abused its dominant position in the market for the supply of drugs in the UK for the treatment of Gaucher disease, a rare inherited disorder, and that Genzyme had breached the Chapter II prohibition.[187] Genzyme had a dominant position in the supply of the drug, Cerezyme, which it supplied to the NHS. Genzyme had abused its position by making the NHS pay a price for the drug where the price included home delivery of the drug and homecare service. This practice resulted in a margin squeeze for other potential homecare service providers, thereby preventing competition and reducing choice for consumers and the NHS. This was considered to be a serious infringement of the prohibition and Genzyme was fined £6.8m. Genzyme appealed to the CAT, which upheld the earlier finding that without any objective justification Genzyme had adopted a pricing policy which effectively resulted in a margin squeeze and foreclosed competition in the downstream market for provision of healthcare services.[188] Nonetheless, the CAT reduced the fine imposed on Genzyme to £3m.

Burgess v OFT

This case involved an alleged abuse of a dominant position by the refusal by Austins, a firm of funeral directors in Hertfordshire, which also owned and

---

185 OFT Decision CA98/09/2003, Case CE/1836–02 *Bettercare Group Ltd/North & West Belfast Health & Social Services Trust*, 18 December 2003.
186 Policy note 1/2004, 'The Competition Act 1998 and public bodies', January 2004, OFT 443. See Case T-319/99 *FENIN v Commission* [2003] 5 CMLR 1; on appeal OJ 2003, C184/19. See Cases C-264/01, C306/01, C-354/01 and C-355/01 *AOK Bundesverband* [2004] ECR I-2493, [2004] 4 CMLR 22.
187 DGFT Decision CA98/3/03, Case CP/0488–01 *Exclusionary Behaviour by Genzyme Ltd*, 27 March 2003.
188 *Genzyme Ltd v OFT* [2004] CAT 4. The CAT delivered a subsequent judgment in relation to the appropriate remedy, including a draft direction, [2005] CAT 32. As noted below, a follow-on claim was subsequently raised against Genzyme Ltd again before the CAT in relation to this infringement.

ran the Harwood Park crematorium in Stevenage, to allow access to Burgess, another firm of funeral directors in Hertfordshire, to Harwood Park crematorium. Burgess complained to the OFT in January 2002, and a long procedure ensued, including three failed applications by Burgess for interim measures, before the OFT finally adopted its Decision to reject the substance of the complaint on 29 June 2004. Burgess appealed to the CAT, which delivered its judgment on 6 July 2005.[189] The Tribunal set aside the OFT's Decision on a number of grounds including its analysis of the relevant geographic market and abuse issues. Furthermore, the Tribunal adopted its own decision on the issues of dominance and abuse, first considering that Austins/Harwood Park had a dominant position in at least the Stevenage/Knebworth area in the supply of crematoria and funeral directing services. In relation to abuse, the Tribunal referred to *Genzyme* and reiterated the previous jurisprudence of the European Court in relation to refusal to supply, notably *Hoffmann-La Roche, Michelin, Commercial Solvents* and, in particular, *Oscar Bronner*,[190] to distil the key propositions to be applied in this area.[191] The Tribunal was clearly satisfied that the refusal to allow access constituted 'recourse to methods different from those which condition normal competition', and that the protection or strengthening of Austins' dominant position for funeral directing services which resulted from the elimination, or serious weakening of, Burgess was not the result of competition on the merits. Furthermore, even if Harwood Park was not dominant in relation to crematoria services, the Tribunal applied the *Tetra Pak II* 'associative links' doctrine[192] to hold that Austins' actions would also constitute an abuse of its dominant position in the related funeral directing services market. It is instructive to quote the Tribunal's discussion of the scope of the abuse concept and the justifications for competition law intervention in the competitive process:

> We accept therefore that the OFT is correct, up to a point, in submitting that the aim of the Chapter II prohibition is not to protect competitors, but to protect competition. On the other hand, where effective competition is already weak through the presence of a dominant firm, there are circumstances in which competition can be protected and fostered only by imposing on the dominant firm a special responsibility under the Chapter II prohibition not to behave in certain ways vis-à-vis its remaining competitors, particularly where barriers to entry are high. In such

---

189 *Burgess and Sons v OFT* [2005] CAT 25.

190 Case 85/76 *Hoffmann-La Roche v Commission* [1979] ECR 461, Case 322/81 *Michelin v Commission* [1983] ECR 3461, Cases 6 and 7/73 *Commercial Solvents v Commission* [1974] ECR 223, and Case C-7/97 *Oscar Bronner v Mediaprint* [1998] ECR I-7791.

191 *Burgess and Sons v OFT* [2005] CAT 25, at para 311.

192 Case T-83/91 *Tetra Pak v Commission* [1994] ECR II-755, and Case C-333/94 P *Tetra Pak v Commission* [1996] ECR I-5951.

circumstances the enforcement of the Chapter II prohibition may in a sense 'protect' a competitor, by shielding the competitor from the otherwise abusive conduct of the dominant firm. However, that is the necessary consequence of taking action in order to protect effective competition. In a case such as the present, intervention under the Chapter II prohibition should not therefore be seen, as the OFT seemed to suggest, as merely 'protecting a competitor', but from the point of view of the wider interest of preserving effective competition for the ultimate benefit of consumers. While Burgess is not entitled to be protected against normal market forces, it is in our view entitled under the Act not to be eliminated as an efficient operator in the market by the abusive practices of a dominant firm.[193]

Court case law

There have been a number of private court disputes in which the prohibition has been raised by one of the parties, and there is a database of court judgments available on the OFT website.[194] The first judgment on the substance of the Chapter II prohibition was delivered eight months after its introduction, on 2 November 2000, by Lawrence Collins J in the High Court of Justice, Chancery Division, in *Claritas (UK) Ltd v The Post Office and Postal Preference Service Ltd*.[195] This judgment was in the context of an action for an interim injunction to restrain the despatch of consumer preference questionnaires using the Royal Mail brand and logo throughout the UK by the Royal Mail. The Post Office owned 30% of Postal Preference Service Ltd (PPS), and Claritas, a company involved in procuring, supplying and analysing consumer information for a fee for businesses, claimed that this amounted to an abuse of the Royal Mail's dominant position. The key question was whether, at this interim stage, there was a serious issue to be tried. Different strands of European jurisprudence were analysed. First, the possibility of an abuse based on refusal to license IP rights was rejected as Claritas would not be excluded from the market because it could not use the Royal Mail logo.[196]

---

193 *Burgess and Sons v OFT* [2005] CAT 25, at para 312. It should be noted that Burgess has raised a claim for damages against Austins before the CAT under section 47A of the 1998 Act.

194 At www.oft.gov.uk/business/uk+competition+court+cases+database/default.htm, but this database does not appear to be up-to-date. See Robertson, A, 'Litigating under the Competition Act 1998: the early case law' [2002] Comp Law 335; and, Rodger, B, 'Competition Law Litigation in the UK Courts – A Study of All Cases to 2004' [2006] ECLR Parts I, II and III at 241, 279 and 341 respectively.

195 [2001] UKCLR 2. This was followed by the DGFT Decision in relation to the same dispute, *Consignia plc and Post Preference Service Ltd*, Decision CS 98/4/2001, 15 June 2001.

196 See Case T-68/89 *Radio Telefis Eireann v Commission* [1991] ECR II-485; [1991] 4 CMLR 586.

Secondly, the application of the essential facilities doctrine was deemed inappropriate as Claritas retained full access to the postal facilities. Finally, in any event, given that the alleged abuse was not in a market in which the Post Office was dominant, Claritas had failed to demonstrate that this situation fell within the scope of the *Tetra Pak II* requirement for close links between the dominant market and abuse market.[197] Although the application was dismissed, this early resort to the prohibition in private litigation demonstrated an awareness of the possibilities under the Act for aggrieved competitors, subsequently demonstrated by the emergence of a body of case law on the OFT database. It is interesting to note the way that Lawrence Collins J applied the s 60 'consistency with Community law' requirement and seamlessly applied European jurisprudence to the Chapter II prohibition as the Act intended.

In *Attheraces Ltd v British Horseracing Board*, the claimant, which supplied websites, TV channels, and other media relating to British horse racing, alleged that the defendant, which had a central role in the organisation and promoting of British horse racing and which kept a computerised database of pre-race data, including the date and place of the race meeting, name of the race, list of horses entered, etc., had abused a dominant position and thereby infringed both Article 82 and the Chapter 2 prohibition. BHB effectively held a monopoly in the provision of the pre-race data and it was held in the High Court that it had abused its dominant position by excessive, unfair and discriminatory pricing.[198] It was held, following the Court's jurisprudence on refusal to supply, that the pre-race date constituted an 'essential facility', essential to ATR's business, and that a constructive refusal to supply was caught by the prohibitions. Referring to court case-law on excessive and discriminatory pricing, the price was excessive in comparison to the cost to BHB plus a reasonable return, and discriminatory in being markedly higher than the sum normally charged to other broadcasters. On appeal, this ruling was overturned by the Court of Appeal, which was sceptical about Article 82/ Chapter II becoming a general provision for the regulation of prices.[199] The Court stated that exceeding cost was a necessary but not a sufficient test for abuse of dominance, there was little evidence that competition on the market was being distorted by BHB's demands and that the value to ATR of the pre-race data was relevant in determining whether the price was excessive. Furthermore, differential pricing was not necessarily abusive, and prices essentially were dependent on market forces. Accordingly, BHB's pricing strategy was not abusive and the Court of Appeal clearly advocated a restrained approach to court involvement in claims of excessive or discriminatory pricing. There have been no final awards of damages under the Chapter

---

197 Case C-333/94P [1996] ECR I-5951; [1997] 4 CMLR 662.
198 [2005] EWHC 3015 (Ch) Ch D.
199 [2007] EWCA Civ 38, CA.

II prohibition and we await resolution of the range of difficult issues pertaining to a successful competition law damages claim, such as who may sue, how to determine causation, and the quantification of damages. Nonetheless, in *Healthcare at Home Ltd v Genzyme Ltd*,[200] in an interim application, the CAT awarded £2m in damages to be paid to the claimant, in a follow-on action brought under section 47A of the Competition Act 1998.[201] Healthcare at Home Ltd were seeking exemplary damages, based on an account of the profits of Genzyme in relation to the infringement, but the case settled out of court before this issue was considered by the CAT.

The Enterprise Act 2002

The structure imposed by the Act is that the OFT may make a market investigation reference to the Competition Commission (CC).[202] After a period of investigation, the CC will compile a report and has a duty to take action to remedy any adverse effects on competition identified in its report. There are a number of changes from the enforcement mechanism under the FTA 1973, notably the transfer of functions from the DGFT to the OFT and the enhanced role of the CC at the remedies stage. Nonetheless, despite considerable change in the statutory language adopted, the basic purpose of market investigations under the 2002 Act is broadly similar to 'monopoly investigations' under the 1973 Act. Accordingly, although there are now a number of reports under the Enterprise Act provisions, many references in this chapter will be to reports completed by the Monopolies and Mergers Commission (MMC) (pre-1 April 1999) and CC under the 1973 Act. The Secretary of State for Trade and Industry formerly had an important role under the 1973 Act, being able to make monopoly references, receive CC reports and to take any formal action on the basis of those reports. Following the 2002 Act, the Secretary of State's role has been removed, subject to possible involvement in public interest cases. A list of public interest cases is set out in Chapter 2 of Pt 4 of the Act, and the cases are restricted to matters involving national security. For reasons of space, this complicated set of provisions will not be considered in this chapter.

Investigation and information gathering

Under s 5 of the 2002 Act the OFT has the function of acquiring information necessary for it to undertake its tasks, and this includes commissioning research. The OFT will undertake market studies where there is a concern

---

200 [2006] CAT 29.

201 The original action, and basis of the claim, was *Genzyme Ltd v OFT* [2004] CAT 4.

202 The reporting panel of the Competition Commission assumed the functions of the Monopolies and Mergers Commission under the FTA 1973 from 1 April 1999.

that a particular market is not working well and this study may lead to a reference of the market to the CC. There have been a considerable number of market studies undertaken by the OFT, for instance in relation to *UK airports, Personal current accounts in the UK,* and *Home Building in the UK.*[203] In addition to normal complaints, the OFT may also receive super-complaints from a designated consumer body when such a body thinks that a market, or market feature, is significantly harming the interests of consumers.[204] The OFT has only 90 days from the date of the complaint to state what action it proposes to take in response. Super-complaints have undoubtedly been an invaluable source of preliminary information; the OFT has already referred a number of markets to the CC following a super-complaint, for example, in *Payment Protection Insurance* and *Northern Ireland Banking.*[205] The OFT has been given investigatory powers, identical to those of the CC, by s 174 of the Act, where the OFT believes it has the power to make a reference, including the following: to require the attendance of parties to give evidence; to require the production of specified documents; and to require the supply of specified information, including estimates and forecasts.

Market investigation references

Under s 131 of the 2002 Act a market investigation reference may be made by the OFT where it has reasonable grounds for suspecting that any feature, or combination of features, of a UK market prevents, restricts or distorts competition. It is clear that the OFT has a discretion, rather than a duty, to make a reference.[206] Section 131(2) states that a market feature includes reference to market structure and any conduct of one or more parties supplying or acquiring goods or services in that market. In addition, the OFT will consider whether it would be more appropriate to deal with the competition issues under the 1998 Act. Most references under the monopoly provisions of the 1973 Act concerned specified practices in a market and were not confined to one company. A notable instance of specified practices in a market resulted in the report on *Electrical Goods.*[207] Similarly, market investigations

---

203 See, for information on all market studies, http://www.oft.gov.uk/advice_and_resources/ resource_base/market-studies/.

204 Section 11 of the Enterprise Act 2002.

205 See, for information on all super-complaints, http://www.oft.gov.uk/advice_and_resources/ resource_base/super-complaints/. Clearly not all super-complaints lead to a referral to the CC, even where the OFT findings are adverse, as in *Scottish Legal Profession,* Response to Which's Super-complaint, July 2007.

206 See OFT Guideline, 'Market investigation references', OFT 501.

207 Monopolies and Mergers Commission, *Electrical Goods: A Report on the Supply in the UK of Washing Machines, Tumble Driers, Dishwashers and Cold Food Storage Equipment,* Cm 3676-I and II, 1997.

have focused on industry-wide problems where the market is not working effectively, as opposed to the Chapter II prohibition which concentrates on the abuse of a dominant position. The OFT first utilised its powers in s 5 of the Enterprise Act 2002 to gather information by undertaking a study into store card services which led to a reference to the CC,[208] and there have been a number of subsequent references, for instance in relation to the *Grocery Market* and *UK Airports*.[209] A reference may be avoided where an undertaking has been accepted in lieu of a reference under s 154 of the Act.[210] This is unlikely to be a regular practice because the requirement to negotiate as comprehensive a solution as is reasonable and practicable with a range of undertakings involved in an industry-wide problem is likely to be problematic. However, a reference will only be made where the OFT suspects that the adverse effects on competition are significant, taking into account any potential detriment to consumers in the form of higher prices, lower quality, less choice or less innovation. Factors indicating significance include the size of the market, the proportion of the market affected and the persistence of the anti-competitive feature. The OFT is required to consult any person on whose interests the reference is likely to have a substantial impact. Finally, it should be noted that the OFT's functions may also be exercised by sectoral regulators with concurrent powers to make references under the Act.

The reference test: prevention, restriction or distortion of competition

Under the 1973 Act, the OFT, or Secretary of State for Trade and Industry, could refer a 'monopoly situation' to the CC for investigation. Scale or structural monopoly situations could be referred where at least 25% of the goods of any description were supplied in the UK by the same person. Complex or behavioural monopoly situations could be referred where at least 25% of the goods of any description were supplied to, or by, two or more persons who 'whether voluntarily or not, and whether by agreement or not' so conducted their respective affairs in any way to prevent, restrict or distort competition in the production or supply of those goods.[211]

The complex monopoly provisions under the FTA 1973 were useful in providing the possibility of oligopolistic markets to be referred to the CC,

---

208 See OFT news release, 47/04, 18 March 2004, 'OFT refers store cards to Competition Commission'.

209 See OFT 845, May 2006 and OFT 912, April 2007 respectively. See, for information on all market investigation references, http://www.oft.gov.uk/advice_and_resources/resource_base/references/.

210 The term 'undertaking' used in this context is very different from the usage of the term in Community law or the 1998 Act. In the 2002 Act it is used to refer to commitments given by those on the market with regard to future conduct.

211 Section 6(2) of the 1973 Act.

and any problems or market failure in the oligopolistic markets to be considered. Indeed, a key factor in retaining the FTA 1973 monopoly provisions, alongside the 1998 Act prohibitions, was the 1973 Act's effectiveness and adaptability when dealing with oligopoly issues. These provisions in the 1973 Act have been repealed but leave a lasting legacy both in the terminology of the new reference test and the intended application of market investigations to industry-wide problems.

The new reference test requires a 'prevention, restriction or distortion of competition' to be identified. The OFT must specify the goods or services in relation to which competition is adversely affected and this will require the relevant market to be defined. Thereafter, the OFT will consider a range of issues pertaining to market structure. Concentration is the obvious starting point, although in oligopolistic industries the OFT will look for a range of structural market features which are conducive to co-ordination, such as firm symmetries, market transparency and stable demand conditions. Other relevant market structure factors include entry conditions and barriers to entry, countervailing buyer power, and the existence of any regulations or government policies which impact upon competition. The OFT, as required under s 131(2), will also consider firms' conduct and, again with reference to oligopolistic markets, examine practices which facilitate or co-ordinate market activity, such as any history of pre-announcing prices. Other general industry custom and practice may be relevant, as will the existence of networks of vertical agreements. Nonetheless, it should be stressed that the OFT merely identifies competition concerns that warrant a fuller investigation of the market by the CC, as evidenced by its references in relation to the grocery market in 2006, and the payment protection insurance (PPI) market in 2007. In relation to the latter there were 'reasonable grounds to suspect that there are features of this market which restrict competition to the detriment of consumers', notably the excessive prices for PPI.

The reporting stage

The CC has responsibility for reporting on market investigation references under the Act.[212] One aspect of the monopoly controls under the FTA 1973, which was criticised in the past, was the apparent duplication of effort by the Commission and the DGFT. Nonetheless, the existing system of reference and report by two separate authorities, OFT and CC, remains intact under the 2002 Act.

The CC is required to conduct its investigation and publish its report within two years of a reference.[213] Upon receipt of a reference, the Commission

---

212 See, for fuller detail on its role under the Act, Competition Commission, 'Market Investigation References: Competition Commission Guidelines' CC3.
213 Section 137 of the Enterprise Act 2002.

will carry out detailed investigations of the market under reference. The Chairman will select members to serve on a group, which will conduct the inquiry, consisting of a minimum of three and normally four to five members. The Commission invites evidence from all interested parties including the main parties to the inquiry and third parties, such as competitors and consumer organisations. The Commission will gain information by a variety of means including letters and questionnaires, press notices, and advertisements, surveys and visits to the principal parties. At an early stage, the Commission will publish an issues statement, which identifies the key questions being addressed during the investigation.[214] Its purpose is to inform interested parties and afford them an opportunity to raise further issues with the Commission, before an 'Emerging Thinking' document is published. A series of oral hearings with the parties in attendance, normally in private, may be held in order to confirm factual evidence obtained and clarify issues arising in relation to the inquiry. The Commission consults with all interested parties when publishing its provisional decisions. For instance, in relation to *Groceries*, the Commission identified disadvantages to consumers by a lack of competition in local markets due to an absence of effective competing retailers in some areas, and suggested various remedies including requiring grocery retailers to divest land-holdings and proposed changes to the planning system.[215] In order to take any form of remedial action, the group must agree on an adverse finding by a two-thirds majority, and may consult separately on its package of finalised remedies. The Commission's final report, containing its decisions on competition issues and remedies, is published on the Commission website[216] and is available in hard copy.

The competition test

One of the key reforms in the 2002 Act was the replacement of the substantive test for assessing 'monopolies' under the 1973 Act. The public interest test under the 1973 Act was recognised as the cornerstone of UK competition law, at least until the Competition Act 1998. The public interest test was set out in s 84 of the 1973 Act. It is instructive to read the section in full to

---

214 See for example, Competition Commission Press Release 57/07, *BAA Airports* Market Investigation – Issues statement, 9 August 2007, where the Commission indicates that it was considering, *inter alia*, 'how common ownership could affect BAA's incentives both to invest in and develop its airports, and operate them.' See also, for example, *Groceries* – issues statement, Press Release 33/06, 15 June 2006.

215 *Groceries Market* – Provisional Findings, Competition Commission Press Release 61/07, 31 October 2007. See also, for example, Competition Commission Press Release 18/08, *PPI* – *Provisional Findings*, 5 June 2008.

216 At www.competition-commission.org.uk/rep_pub/reports/index.htm. See, for instance, *Store Card Credit Services; Store Cards Market Investigation*, 7 March 2006; *Home Credit*, 30 November 2006; *Northern Irish Personal Banking*, 15 May 2006.

acquire the 'flavour' of the goals of this once key component of UK competition law. It required the CC to:

> ... take into account all matters which appear in the particular circumstances to be relevant, and among other things, shall have regard to the desirability:
>
> (a) of maintaining and promoting effective competition between persons supplying goods and services in the UK;
> (b) of promoting the interests of consumers, purchasers and other users of goods and services in the UK in respect of the prices charged for them and in respect of their quality and the variety of goods and services supplied;
> (c) of promoting, through competition, the reduction of costs and the development and use of new techniques and new products, and of facilitating the entry of new competitors into existing markets;
> (d) of maintaining and promoting the balanced distribution of industry and employment in the UK;
> (e) of maintaining and promoting competitive activity in markets outside the UK on the part of producers of goods, and of suppliers of goods and services, in the UK.

This section was notable for the breadth of interests which it provided within the public interest remit. It contained no presumption in favour of competition and no weighting of the conflicting criteria that could be considered. This section was an important example of the principal characteristics enshrined in the 1973 Act: pragmatism, discretion, and the role of politics. Over the years there were repeated demands for reform of the public interest test as the basis for Commission reports. Nonetheless, reform to a competition-focused test was clearly less controversial in this area than in relation to merger control. The Commission practice in relation to monopoly investigations concentrated on competition-related problems in certain markets and this has continued, although the precise statutory requirements under the new test are a novelty.

Under s 134(1) of the 2002 Act, the Commission is required to decide:

> ... whether any feature, or combination of features, of each relevant market prevents, restricts or distorts competition in connection with the supply or acquisition of goods or services in the United Kingdom or in a part of the United Kingdom.

This would constitute an 'adverse effect on competition' under s 134(2) and would require the Commission to decide what action should be taken to remedy, prevent or mitigate that effect or any detrimental effect on consumers which results. A detrimental effect on consumers may be constituted by higher prices, lower quality, less choice or less innovation in relation to the goods or services considered under s 134(1).[217] For instance, in *Store Cards*, the Commission confirmed that there was an adverse effect in relation to the supply of consumer credit through store cards in the UK, indicating that annual percentage rates (APRs) were on average too high and that consumer detriment was estimated as at least £55m a year. The CC approaches the competition test in two stages – identifying the relevant market, and then assessing competition in that market and whether any market features adversely affect competition. The Commission's consideration of the relevant market issue follows the generally accepted approach, outlined in relation to Art 82 earlier in this chapter, of the SSNIP or hypothetical monopolist test.

Of greater interest in the new framework is the second stage of the investigation and the CC's assessment of competition. To a great extent, many of the pertinent issues are already broadly familiar to competition lawyers and may previously have been considered by the CC in reports under the 1973 Act. The CC's Guidance on how it makes its competition assessment mirrors the OFT Guidance on the situations in which the OFT will make a reference; the tests at OFT reference and CC assessment are identical. Accordingly, the Commission will focus first on market structure issues and how these affect intra-market rivalry between businesses. Thereafter the Commission will consider to what extent the conduct of players in a market might adversely affect competition. The Commission in its Guidance highlights the problem of co-ordinated pricing or 'conscious parallelism' and the conditions which facilitate such co-ordinated effects. Nonetheless, consideration of market structure and conduct alone may be insufficient to allow a determination of the effectiveness of competition. Therefore, the Commission has indicated that it may also examine the outcome of the competitive process as indicated by prices and the pattern of price changes over time, persistently high profits and international price comparisons.

In addition to examining emerging practice under the Enterprise Act 2002, it remains instructive to review the practice of the CC under the 1973 Act as, despite the different statutory framework, it gives an idea of the likely approach to structural and conduct issues in industry-wide investigations. However, it should be noted that certain issues, such as predatory pricing and refusal to supply, the subject of various reports under the 1973 Act, would generally now be considered under the 1998 Act.[218]

217 Section 134(5).
218 See, for example, Wilks, S, *In the Public Interest: Competition Policy and the Monopolies and Mergers Commission*, 1999, Manchester: Manchester UP.

Market structure

Relatively few reports under the 1973 Act found that the market conditions themselves operated against the public interest.[219] A major problem when criticising the structure of the market is the difficulty of devising the appropriate remedy. The only logical solution would appear to be divestiture, but this is beset by a variety of practical and political difficulties. Divestiture has been criticised in political debate as too gross an interference in market processes. Nonetheless, at one stage there was a greater willingness to consider this remedy, most notably in 1989 in *The Supply of Beer* report[220] which made recommendations on the maximum number of retail outlets each of the six big brewers could own.[221] More dramatically, in its 1999 report on the supply of raw milk in the UK, the Commission noted that Milk Marque had a scale monopoly with 49.6% market share. With a view to eliminating the market power of Milk Marque, the Commission recommended that Milk Marque should be divided into a number of independent quota holding bodies.[222]

Oligopolistic pricing

The theory of oligopolistic interdependence suggests that, where there are few firms in a market, they may act collectively and in parallel without the necessity of collusion between or amongst them. The investigative and non-doctrinaire approach under the 1973 Act was particularly suitable for dealing with competitive problems associated with oligopoly. Anti-competitive activity was not punishable as such but the Commission would seek ways to improve competition and the Commission recognised that many factors might contribute to oligopolistic market failure. In its general report on *Parallel Pricing*,[223] the Commission considered parallel pricing in the absence of parallel costs to be generally detrimental to consumer welfare. After years of speculation concerning similar price movements in the UK petrol retail

---

219 See, for example, *Roadside Advertising Services* (1980–81) HCP 365; *Contraceptive Sheaths* (1974–75) HCP 394.
220 Cm 651, 1989.
221 The Secretary of State subsequently made two orders, although these did not replicate the recommendations: Supply of Beer (Tied Estate) Order 1989, SI 1989/2390 and Supply of Beer (Loan Ties, Licensed Premises and Wholesale Prices) Order 1989, SI 1989/2258. The Beer Orders were reviewed in 2000, following which, the Supply of Beer (Tied Estate) (Revocation) Order 2002, SI 2002/3204 repealed the 1989 Order and the Supply of Beer (Tied Estate) (Amendment) Order 1997. See, also, MMC report, *Domestic Gas Appliances* (1979–80) HCP 703, and the subsequent report, *Gas and British Gas plc*, Cm 2317, 1993, which also recommended divestiture as a possible remedy.
222 *Supply of Raw Milk: A Report on the Supply in Great Britain of Raw Cows' Milk*, Cm 4286, 1999.
223 Cmnd 5330, 1973.

market, the Commission produced its report, *Supply of Petrol*.[224] To the surprise of many, the Commission did not find the parallel prices and price movements to be against the public interest, as they could be accounted for by the same international cost factors. On the other hand, in *White Salt*,[225] the Commission had earlier produced a classic example of a report on parallel pricing in an oligopoly. In fact, the market was a duopoly involving British Salt and ICI. The report demonstrated how parallel pricing could also lead to excessive pricing, at least for one producer. The Commission recommended that British Salt's prices should be regulated and ICI could, therefore, only charge parallel prices in the future if its efficiency improved. More recently, in its *Banking* report,[226] the Commission noted that the similarity of pricing structure between the main clearing banks restricted competition. It is clear, from the respective guidance issued by the OFT and the CC, that oligopolistic markets and associated competition problems are likely to remain a major concern under the market investigation provisions of the Enterprise Act 2002.

Conduct

The Commission has accepted that in certain markets competitive pressures are likely to be muted between 'rival' firms. There are various types of conduct that the Commission has, in the past, been required to report upon, including pricing policies within certain industries.

Excess or unfair prices or profits

The Commission has never sought to define excessive pricing; this was not necessary in a system, similar to Pt 4 of the 2002 Act, which did not seek to punish and apportion blame. Nonetheless, the Commission has over the years frequently criticised profit levels. For instance, in its report on *Valium and Librium*,[227] it recommended reduction in the prices of the two drugs to 25% and 40% of their existing level. In its report on *Ready Cooked Breakfast Cereal Foods*,[228] the Commission concluded that the prices charged were excessive and, as a result, Kelloggs gave an undertaking not to increase prices without government approval. In *White Salt*,[229] the Commission recommended that British Salt's prices should be controlled directly and any increases were to be related to rises in costs.

224 Cm 972, 1990.
225 Cmnd 9778, 1986.
226 *The Supply of Banking Services by Clearing Banks to Small and Medium-Sized Enterprises*, Cm 5319, 2002.
227 *Chlordiazepoxide and Diazepam* (1972–73) HCP 197.
228 (1972–73) HCP 2.
229 Cmnd 9778, 1986.

Thus, it is evident that the form of price regulation recommended by the Commission has varied, according to the circumstances, from a price reduction to direct control of prices and monitoring or requiring the provision of more information to consumers. The three reports mentioned above reflected an attitude, more prevalent in the 1970s, that direct regulation of prices was appropriate for the competition authorities. The suitability of this approach was doubted in the 1980s and early 1990s when there were fewer reports directly criticising pricing levels, and little evidence of the direct approach to price regulation in enforcement. Two reports by the Commission in the mid-1990s nonetheless indicated a willingness to consider and criticise prices that were unfair on consumers. These reports again demonstrate how market failure, excessive prices in these instances, may result from a variety of factors. In its report, *Video Games*,[230] the Commission concluded that Sega and Nintendo used their control over IP rights to set excessive prices for their games, while setting low prices for consoles to lock customers into their systems. In *Domestic Electrical Goods*,[231] the Commission was critical of high prices maintained by a system of recommended retail prices, and suggested various ways to increase competition in order to reduce prices of electrical goods for the consumer. In the late 1990s we also witnessed the campaign by the Labour Government after the 1997 election concerning 'Rip-Off Britain' with its focus on the effect of excessive pricing on UK consumers. This resulted in the reports on *Supermarkets*[232] and *New Cars*.[233] The supermarket report was largely uncritical, but the direct impact of competition law on the consumer was evidenced by the reduction of UK prices by a number of car manufacturers after the introduction of an Order following the *New Cars* report.[234] Similarly in the *Banking* report in 2002, the CC was highly critical of the excessive prices charged to small- and medium-sized enterprises by major banks.[235]

Interestingly, there has been a considerable focus on financial services in the market investigations undertaken under the Enterprise Act 2002, with an emphasis on consumer protection and remedies aimed generally at reducing prices/interest rates by enhancing transparency and increasing consumer awareness. The first report under the Act was *Store Cards*, in 2006, and three

230 Monopolies and Mergers Commission, *Video Games: A Report on the Supply of Video Games in the UK*, Cm 2781, 1995.
231 Cm 3676, 1997. The Restriction on Agreements and Conduct (Specified Domestic Electrical Goods) Order 1998, SI 1998/1271, came into force on 1 September 1998.
232 *Supermarkets: A Report on the Supply of Groceries from Multiple Stores in the United Kingdom*, Cm 4842, 2000.
233 *New Cars: A Report on the Supply of New Motor Cars Within the UK*, Cm 4660, 2000.
234 See DTI Press Release, P/2000/549, 1 August 2000. The Supply of New Cars Order 2000, SI 2000/2088.
235 *The Supply of Banking Services by Clearing Banks to Small and Medium-Sized Enterprises*, Cm 5319, 2002.

of the first reports published under the Act related to financial services: *Store Cards*;[236] *Home Credit*;[237] and *Northern Irish Banking*.[238] In *Store Cards*, the Commission was critical of the excessive APRs on store cards and its remedies included warnings that cheaper credit may be available elsewhere, to provide fuller information on monthly statements, and a requirement to offer an option to pay by direct debit. In *Home Credit*, the Commission identified obstacles that restricted competition and raised prices, notably the advantageous position of existing lenders in knowing customer creditworthiness. Remedial measures in this context include a requirement to share customer information, and, importantly, a requirement to provide clearer information on the cost of loans to allow consumers to shop around and compare offers. In *Northern Irish Banking*, the Commission found that competition in relation to personal current accounts (PCAs) in Northern Ireland was limited by banks' complicated charging structures, their failure to explain them adequately, and by customers' reluctance to switch banks; as a result banks will have to provide better and clearer information about their PCA services, charges and interest rates, and facilitate the switching process.

Consumer protection

The OFT has a role in both competition and consumer protection. These roles are obviously linked, as is clear from s 134 of the Enterprise Act 2002, and previously under s 84 of the 1973 Act. In the early 1990s the Commission was criticised for reports in which the Commission was not considered to be as protective of the consumer interest as in earlier years, and the view was taken that the Commission had, in its outlook, become too favourable toward big business. However, it was possible to identify a reinvigorated and pro-consumer oriented Commission during the late 1990s, particularly evidenced by its investigations into video games, domestic electrical goods, supermarkets, and new cars. In the early part of this decade, this reorientation was exemplified by the lengthy and high-profile investigation into extended warranties on domestic electrical goods.[239] Extended warranties are contracts which extend the manufacturer's guarantee on domestic electrical goods. The Commission found that the practices of extended warranty providers restricted or distorted competition by limiting the choice of product and relevant information, and resulted in lack of choice, excessive prices, insufficient information and lack of competition. Interestingly, although the investigation was undertaken under the 1973 Act, that type of market failure is also ideally suited to investigation under Pt 4 of the Enterprise Act. The

236 7 March 2006.
237 30 November 2006.
238 15 May 2007.
239 18 December 2003, Cm 6089 (I–III).

emphasis on the impact on consumers and the requirement to consider customer benefits in designing appropriate remedies, together with the innovation of the consumer super-complaints procedure, which has kick-started a number of inquiries already, demonstrate that consumer protection has been a key focus of the Commission's assessment under the market investigation provisions of the Enterprise Act. For instance, as discussed above, its reports in *Store Cards, Home Credit* and *Northern Irish Banking* each focused on the direct financial impact on consumers resulting from the absence of effective competition and the remedies were designed to enhance transparency and facilitate more informed consumer decision-making. The Commission's investigation in relation to *Payment Protection Insurance* is considering similar issues in that market.[240]

Remedial action

If the Commission decides that there is an adverse effect on competition, it has to decide what action should be taken. The Commission may exercise its order-making powers or accept undertakings from parties under ss 159 and 162 of the 2002 Act, respectively. These powers are broadly similar to the twin remedies available under the 1973 Act although, clearly, the Commission's role is enhanced by the new set of provisions.

Under the 1973 Act the Secretary of State had power[241] to make a wide range of orders. The exercise of these powers was demonstrated by the Orders following the report, *The Supply of Beer*. The Orders had a significant effect on the brewing industry in the UK. More recently, the Order introduced following the report into new car pricing had a dramatic impact on the price of many new cars in the UK.[242] Nonetheless, the preferred method of enforcement was through a process of negotiation between businesses, which were the subject of an adverse report, and the OFT, leading to businesses giving undertakings as to their future conduct with those undertakings based on the findings and recommendations in the report. For example, following the *Ice Cream* report[243] undertakings were subsequently accepted from BEW, Mars and Nestlé on outlet exclusivity, and from BEW on, *inter alia*, freezer exclusivity.[244] Reflecting the pragmatic, political and ultimately discretionary approach of the 1973 Act, the Secretary of State was not bound by the advice

---

240 See, *Payment Protection Insurance Market Investigation – Emerging Thinking*, 6 November 2007; Provisional Findings, 5 June 2008.

241 1973 Act, ss 56 and 90.

242 The Supply of New Cars Order 2000, SI 2000/2088.

243 *The Supply of Impulse Ice Cream: A Report on the Supply in the UK of Ice Cream Purchased for Immediate Consumption*, Cm 4510, 2000.

244 DTI Press Release, P2000/509, 20 July 2000.

of the DGFT or the findings of a CC report which he could choose to ignore.[245]

Under the 2002 Act, the Commission has assumed the primary role in taking remedial action following a market investigation and has a duty, under s 138, to remedy any adverse effects on competition. In doing so, it is required to:

> have regard to the need to achieve as comprehensive a solution as is reasonable and practicable to the adverse effect on competition and any detrimental effects on customers so far as resulting from the adverse effect on competition.[246]

Schedule 8 to the Act specifies what may be included in an order, although there are no such limits on the Commission's power to obtain undertakings. The types of remedies which may generally be available include: the divestiture of a business or assets; the removal of entry barriers by requiring know-how licensing; the requirement for specific behaviour to be either discontinued or adopted; the imposition of a price cap; and the monitoring of prices and profits. The Act allows the Commission to take into account, in deciding on appropriate remedial action, any customer benefits derived from the anti-competitive market feature, such as lower prices, higher quality or choice of goods and greater innovation.[247] The Commission will also consider the effectiveness of remedies, in particular whether they are likely to be implemented and complied with. As remedies are likely to be market-wide, in order to avoid delays in negotiating undertakings it may be more effective to impose a remedy by order. For instance, in *Store Cards*, the Commission's report addressed the necessary remedies, which included the requirement to provide full information on statements, to provide APR warnings on statements, and to prominently display a facility to pay outstanding balances by direct debit. Following a period of consultation after publication of a notice of intention to make an order, the Store Cards Market Investigation Order was introduced and came into force on 1 May 2007 to implement the remedies set out in the Commission's report.[248] The Competition Commission's Final Report on remedies in relation to its Groceries Markets

---

245 This power was demonstrated when the Secretary of State rejected the Commission's recommended structural remedy following the Commission's report into the *Supply of Raw Milk: A Report on the Supply in Great Britain of Raw Cows' Milk*, Cm 4286, 1999.

246 Section 134(6).

247 Section 134(7)–(8).

248 Store Cards Market Investigation Order, 26 July 2006. Similarly, the Home Credit Market Investigation Order 2007, 13 September 2007, came into force on 4 October 2007, and implements the remedies set out in the earlier Commission Report. See also, The Northern Ireland PCA Banking Market Investigation Order 2008, 19 February 2008, which came into force on 22 February 2008.

Investigation contains a number of remedial measures, including a recommendation to include a 'competition test' for planning authority decisions in relation to large grocery stores.[249] It should be noted that before any remedial action can follow a Commission report, the decision, that there is an adverse effect on competition, must be supported by at least two-thirds of the members of the Commission group. This is the same requirement as existed under the Fair Trading Act 1973.[250]

The OFT is required to monitor undertakings and orders following a market investigation report.[251] Any decision by the OFT or CC under Pt 4 of the Act is subject to judicial review by the CAT and, thereafter, is subject to an appeal to the Court of Appeal in England and Wales or the Court of Session in Scotland.

Further reading

Article 82

General

Azevedo, JP, and Walker, M, 'Dominance: meaning and measurement' [2002] ECLR 363.

Eilmansberger, T, 'How to Distinguish Good from Bad Competition under Article 82 EC: In Search of Clearer and More Coherent Standards for Anti-competitive Abuses' (2005) 42(1) CMLRev 129.

Gormsen, L, 'Article 82 EC, where are we coming from and where are we going?' (2005) 2(2) CompLRev 5.

Jebson, D, and Stephens, R, 'Assumptions, goals and dominant undertakings: the regulation of competition under Art 86 of the European Union' (1996) 64 Antitrust LJ 443.

Pricing strategies

Gal, MS, 'Below-Cost Price Alignment: Meeting or Beating Competition? The France Telecom Case' [2007] ECLR 382.

Hamann, H-G, and Bergmann, E, 'The Granting of Rebates by Dominant Undertakings under Article 82 of the EC Treaty' [2005] ECLR 83.

---

249 Competition Commission, *Groceries Market: Final Report*, 30 April 2008. Tesco has applied to the CAT to challenge, under s 179, certain findings in the CC Report.

250 *Scottish Milk: A Report on the Supply of Fresh Processed Milk to Middle Ground Retailers in Scotland*, Cm 5002, 2000. DTI Press Release, P/2000/863, 22 December 2000.

251 For instance, the Competition Commission accepted the advice of the OFT to release undertakings given by a company in relation to condom distribution, where these were given to address concerns raised in a 1994 Report by the MMC, where retailer buyer power had subsequently led to increased consumer choice and lower wholesale prices for condoms.

Ridyard, D, 'Exclusionary Pricing and Price Discrimination Abuses under Article 82 – An Economic Analysis' [2002] ECLR 286.

Roques, C, 'CFI Judgment, Case T-203/01, Manufacture Francaise des Pneumatiques Michelin v Commission' [2004] ECLR 688.

Refusal to supply/essential facilities

Bergman, M, 'The Bronner Case – A turning point for the essential facilities doctrine' [2000] ECLR 59.

Killick, J, 'IMS and Microsoft judged in the cold light of IMS' (2004) 1(2) Comp LRev 23.

Müller, U, and Rodenhausen, A, 'The Rise and Fall of the Essential Facility Doctrine' [2008] ECLR 310.

Ong, B, 'Building Brick Barricades and other Barriers to Entry: Abusing a Dominant Position by Refusing to Licence Intellectual Property Rights' [2005] ECLR 213.

Vezzoso, S, 'The Incentives Balance Test in the EU Microsoft Case: A pro-Innovation "Economics based" Approach' [2006] ECLR 382.

Chapter II prohibition

Kon, S, and Turnbull, S, 'Pricing and the dominant firm: implications of the Competition Commission Appeal Tribunal's judgment in the Napp case' [2003] ECLR 70.

Rodger, B, 'Early steps to a mature competition law system: case law developments in the first eighteen months of the Competition Act 1998' [2002] ECLR 52.

Sufrin, B, 'The Chapter II prohibition', in Rodger, BJ, and MacCulloch, A, (eds), *The UK Competition Act: A New Era for UK Competition Law*, 2000, Oxford: Hart.

The Enterprise Act 2002, Pt 4

Morris, D, 'The Enterprise Act 2002: aspects of the new regime' [2002] Comp Law 318.

Sufrin, B and Furse, M, 'Market investigations' [2002] Comp Law 244.

Discussion

1   Why is the identification of what constitute barriers to entry crucial for anti-monopoly laws?

2   If an undertaking is considered 'dominant' under Community or UK law, is it really in the position of a monopolist with the power to influence the market? When does the concept of super-dominance apply and what difference, if any, does it make?

3   To what extent do Art 82 EC and the Chapter II prohibition restrict the ability of companies to compete effectively, in particular in relation to their competitive pricing strategies? Can and should dominant companies be allowed to meet and beat competitors' prices?

4   To what extent do you agree with the proposition that the development of the law in relation to refusals to supply/essential facilities, particularly in the CFI *Microsoft* judgment, stifles incentives to innovate?

5   Explain the different focus of the Chapter II prohibition and market investigations under the Enterprise Act 2002, and why there is little scope for overlap between the two sets of provisions.

Chapter 4

Control of anti-competitive agreements

In the previous chapter, abuse of market power was considered. In this chapter we examine situations where undertakings can alter competition on a market in another way, by entering into anti-competitive agreements with other undertakings. In this chapter we shall discuss the ways in which the EC, through Art 81 EC, and the UK, through the Chapter I prohibition, seek to deal with anti-competitive agreements.

Introduction to Art 81 of the EC Treaty

The Community rules surrounding the control of agreements[1] have been influenced to a much greater extent by the general goals of the Community than have the rules on control of dominant undertakings. The neoclassical model of competition, discussed in Chapter 1, highlighted the problems which a monopoly can create. It is also possible for undertakings to reach that monopoly position by agreeing with their competitors that they should not compete. In effect, the parties to the agreement, forming what is known as a cartel, will have a monopoly position on what was previously a competitive market. Historically, the existence of cartels was common in European markets and, therefore, their removal was one of the central goals of the Community.[2] The competition rules in relation to anti-competitive agreements were also very important in relation to securing the four freedoms of the Community. The achievement of free movement of goods would have been hampered were undertakings in a position to erect barriers to free trade after the Community had removed barriers put in place by Member States. Undertakings which had previously been protected from competition by those State barriers might have been tempted to try to maintain their privileged

---

1 In this context, the term 'agreement' should be used loosely; its more technical meaning will be introduced later.
2 For an historical examination of cartels in Europe, and their regulation, see Harding, C and Joshua, J, *Regulating Cartels in Europe – A Study of Legal Control of Corporate Delinquency*, 2003, Oxford: OUP.

position by entering into agreements with their potential competitors in other Member States.

Throughout the development of case law under Art 81, there have been observable tensions between the desire to promote market integration on the one hand and to improve economic efficiency on the other. In some cases, market integration has been preferred over economic reasoning. Article 81 is designed to prohibit agreements that restrict competition. This is self-evident in blatant breaches of competition law involving horizontal price-fixing and market-sharing; however, beyond those examples there are a great many types of agreement which are less obviously problematic. The important distinction between the treatment of horizontal agreements, which are between businesses operating at the same level of the market[3] and are much more likely to restrict competition, and vertical agreements, which are between businesses operating on different levels of the market[4] and are less likely to restrict competition, gives an indication of the problems which the law faces.[5] Awareness of these problems, and the balancing of different goals, are key to understanding the development of competition policy in relation to anti-competitive agreements. It is also necessary to consider the debate surrounding the modernisation of Community competition law enforcement, discussed in Chapter 2. The introduction of Regulation 1/2003 significantly altered the way in which Art 81 is enforced and this chapter will focus on the new system, although reference will be made to the practice under Regulation 17 where it illustrates the reasons for the adoption of Regulation 1/2003. Article 81 consists of three discrete paragraphs. The first paragraph lays down the prohibition, the second the consequences of infringement, and the third declares the prohibition in Art 81(1) to be inapplicable if certain criteria are met. Each of these paragraphs will be dealt with in turn.

Article 81(1)

Article 81(1) EC prohibits agreements, decisions of associations and concerted practices that may affect trade between Member States and which have as their object the prevention, restriction or distortion of competition. It also includes an indicative list of types of agreement which may be covered. The Court and the Commission have given the Article a very wide interpretation, encapsulating many types of collusive behaviour. The simplest way to approach the detailed analysis of the prohibition is to break it down into its constituent parts.

3 For example, between two manufacturers of the same product.
4 For example, between a manufacturer and a distributor or retailer. Vertical agreements are dealt with in detail in the following chapter.
5 See Lugard, HHP, 'Vertical restraints under EC competition law: a horizontal approach' [1996] ECLR 166, p 166, which suggests that 'One of the most intricate aspects of EC competition law is the notion of restriction of competition'.

Agreements, decisions of associations and concerted practices

Each of the terms used in Art 81 has a separate emphasis but there is considerable overlap amongst them. It is, therefore, not crucial that a particular 'agreement' is identifiable, so long as it is demonstrable that some form of collusion, falling within the concept of 'agreement' or 'concerted practice', has occurred.

Agreements

The concept of agreement is not restricted to legally binding and enforceable agreements, as this would make evasion of the prohibition very simple. In one of its early judgments in this area, *ACF Chemifarma v Commission (Quinine)*,[6] the Court found that an unsigned 'gentlemen's agreement' fell within the prohibition. The modern definition was more fully developed in *Polypropylene*.[7] Here, the Commission investigation centred on a complex cartel involving 15 undertakings. The agreement took the form of several oral, non-binding, arrangements for which there were no enforceable sanctions. It was held that the various arrangements formed a single agreement infringing Art 81(1). Some of the undertakings concerned had not attended all of the meetings or had deviated from the terms of the agreement but they were still considered to be party to it. The concept of a single ongoing 'agreement' has proved to be very important in recent Commission practice,[8] which illustrates that the concept does not focus on a one-off event whereby an agreement is reached but rather an ongoing and developing process where undertakings agree on a continuing course of conduct. It is also clear that any participation in the process may lead to a finding that an undertaking is part of the ongoing agreement, no matter how minor a role it may have played. The extent of an undertaking's involvement is only taken into account when deciding the level of fine to be imposed.

In one of the first competition cases to come before the Court, the parties tried to draw a distinction between horizontal and vertical agreements. A horizontal agreement exists between undertakings at the same level of the market, for example, an agreement between two manufacturers of a product. Vertical agreements exist between undertakings that operate at different levels of the market, for example, an agreement between a manufacturer and a

---

6 Cases 41, 44 and 45/69 [1970] ECR 661; [1970] CMLR 8083.
7 Commission Decision 86/398/EEC, OJ 1986, L230/1; [1988] 4 CMLR 347. Upheld, on appeal, in Case T-7/89 *Hercules NV v Commission* [1991] ECR II-1711; [1992] 4 CMLR 84 and Case C-49/92P *Commission v Anic Partecipazioni SpA* [1999] ECR I-4125.
8 See, for example, Commission Decision 89/191/EEC *LdPE*, OJ 1989, L74/21; Commission Decision 94/599/EC *PVC*, OJ 1994, L239/14; Commission Decision 94/601/EC *Cartonboard*, OJ 1994, L243; and Commission Decision 2001/418/EC *Amino Acids*, OJ 2001, L152/24.

distributor or retailer. In *Consten and Grundig*, the Commission found that an exclusive distribution agreement between Grundig, a German electronics manufacturer, and Consten, a French distributor, infringed Art 81(1).[9] On appeal, the undertakings argued that vertical agreements such as this did not fall within the terms of the prohibition. The Court was not convinced by the argument and came to the conclusion that Art 81 protected both inter-brand competition (between different brands of the same product) and intra-brand competition (between the same branded product sold by different retailers).[10] Under the terms of the vertical agreement in question, intra-brand competition would have been almost eliminated; however, inter-brand competition may have been increased. Without the guarantee of exclusivity, Consten may not have been willing to invest as much time and as many resources into the promotion of Grundig's products. By investing in promotion, Consten would have increased competition between Grundig products and other brands. Without exclusivity, other retailers selling Grundig profits would benefit from Consten's promotional efforts; these retailers are known as 'free-riders'.

Another interesting interpretation of the concept of an agreement concerns situations where there is apparently unilateral behaviour. The Court has been willing to infer the existence of an agreement where behaviour confers a benefit on another undertaking. In *Ford Werke v Commission*,[11] the refusal of Ford in Germany to supply right-hand drive cars to its German distributors was challenged on the basis that the refusal was designed to protect Ford's UK distributors from competition from distributors selling right-hand cars in Germany. Although the refusal appeared to be unilateral, it was held to be part of an agreement. The extent of this ability to impute apparently unilateral behaviour to an agreement was further discussed by the Court in *BAI and Commission v Bayer*.[12] The Court stated that for an agreement to be concluded by 'tacit acceptance' it is necessary that 'the manifestation of the wish of one of the contracting parties to achieve an anti-competitive goal constitute an invitation to the other party, to fulfil that goal jointly'.[13]

Concerted practices

The term 'concerted practice' in Art 81(1) has been given a particularly broad definition. In many cases, the Commission will merely state that co-operation

9   Commission Decision 64/556/EEC, OJ 1964, 2545; [1964] CMLR 489.
10 Cases 56 and 58/64 *Consten and Grundig v Commission* [1966] ECR 299; [1966] CMLR 418.
11 Cases 25 and 26/84 [1985] ECR 2725; [1985] 3 CMLR 528.
12 Cases C-2 and 3/01 [2004] ECR I-23, [2004] 4 CMLR 13.
13 Cases C-2 and 3/01 *BAI and Commission v Bayer* [2004] ECR I-23, [2004] 4 CMLR 13, at para 102. The Court also made it clear, at para 141, that 'the mere fact that a measure adopted by a manufacturer, which has the object or effect of restricting competition, falls within the context of continuous business relations between the manufacturer and its wholesalers is not sufficient for a finding that such an agreement exists'.

between undertakings amounts to an agreement 'and/or' a concerted practice. The important point, when dealing with concerted practices, is the existence of some form of collusion between undertakings. There is no easy way to define exactly where an agreement stops and a concerted practice begins, although it is evidently a looser form of 'agreement', which involves some form of understanding or collaboration. The seminal definition was given by the Court in *ICI v Commission (Dyestuffs)*[14] as follows:

> . . . a form of co-ordination between undertakings which, without having reached a stage where agreement properly so called has been concluded, knowingly substitutes practical co-operation between them for the risks of competition.[15]

The forms of practical co-operation that were alluded to in *Dyestuffs* were more fully explained by the Court in *Suiker Unie v Commission (Sugar)*.[16] The emphasis was placed upon mental consensus[17] between the co-operating undertakings. The Court stated that Art 81 precluded:

> . . . any direct or indirect contact between such operators, the object or effect whereof is either to influence the conduct on the market of an actual or potential competitor or to disclose to such a competitor the course of conduct which they themselves have decided to adopt or contemplate adopting on the market.[18]

It should be noted that the term, concerted practice, has been left broadly defined. This is a necessity due to the lengths to which undertakings go to disguise their activities. Moreover, the form of the agreement or practice is less important than the economic effect it has on the market. A formalistic approach would not help the law attain its objectives. Despite this broad definition, the concept of a 'concerted practice' is not suited to dealing with oligopolistic behaviour.

One of the reasons for avoiding formalism when dealing with concerted practices is the difficulty in proving the existence of collusion. There may be a suspicion that some form of collusion exists when there are parallel price rises

---

14 Case 48/69 *ICI v Commission* [1972] ECR 619; [1972] CMLR 557.
15 Ibid, para 64.
16 Cases 40–48, 50, 54–56, 111 and 113–14/73 [1975] ECR 1663; [1976] 1 CMLR 295.
17 It is interesting to note the increasing focus on mental consensus in the Commission's and Court's jurisprudence surrounding both 'concerted practices' and 'agreements'. It is arguable that there is in practice no real distinction between the two terms.
18 [1975] ECR 1663, at para 174; [1976] 1 CMLR 295. See also the recent UK cases of *Argos, Littlewoods and JJB v OFT* [2006] EWCA Civ 1318 on appeal from [2004] CAT 24, [2005] CAT 13, [2004] CAT 17, [2005] CAT 22 and *Apex Asphalt and Paving Co Limited v OFT* [2005] CAT 4.

or similar forms of behaviour. However, the Commission must be able to prove the existence of a concerted practice before it makes a decision against the relevant undertakings. To prove the existence of a concerted practice, or an overall agreement, the Commission will usually seek to rely on so-called 'plus' evidence. This is evidence that indicates that the parallel behaviour has occurred as a result of some form of collusion rather than other market factors. An example of the sort of 'plus' evidence that might be sought is illustrated by the *Dyestuffs* case. An investigation was carried out into similar price rises for aniline dyes across the Common Market. In total, 10 undertakings were investigated. It was discovered that there were identical percentage increases within two or three days across the industry on a number of occasions. On one occasion, instructions were telexed by different undertakings to subsidiary companies on the same evening at the following times: 5.05 pm, 5.09 pm, 5.38 pm, 5.57 pm, 6.55 pm and 7.45 pm. On another occasion the telexes of 'competitors' used the same wording. On the basis of this evidence, the Commission had little difficulty showing that there must have been collusion between the undertakings. Unfortunately, in many cases, such clear proof will not always be available.

Decisions of associations of undertakings

This section of Art 81 deals with the organisation of undertakings through a trade or professional association. Such associations have the aim of representing and promoting the interests of their members. It is easy to understand how the decision of such an association may affect competition in a market. An obvious example of how an association's rules may affect the market was the subject of investigation in *COAPI*.[19] The Colegio de Agentes de la Propiedad is an association of all the industrial property agents practising in Spain. Any property agent breaching the set scale of fees could be punished by fines, suspension or expulsion from the association. It was argued that the association was a body set up by statute, with special regulatory functions, but the Commission concentrated on the fact that it was an association of independent undertakings attempting to fix prices across a market. Even non-binding recommendations by an association may be caught by Art 81, as those recommendations are likely to affect the behaviour of association members.[20]

Parallelism and oligopoly

Where there is evidence of parallel behaviour there is often the temptation immediately to categorise the behaviour as a concerted practice. While

19 Commission Decision 95/188/EC, OJ 1995, L122/37; [1995] 5 CMLR 468.
20 See Case 8/72 *Cementhandelaren v Commission* [1972] ECR 977; [1973] CMLR 7.

parallelism may be an indicator that undertakings are colluding, it would be premature for the Commission to conclude that a concerted practice exists. The burden is on the Commission to prove the existence of the concerted practice. This may be difficult as parallelism may occur through the natural operation of an oligopolistic market. In such circumstances proof may be very difficult.

As discussed in the previous chapter, oligopolists become interdependent and tend to follow each other's behaviour very closely. In the *Dyestuffs* case, the 'oligopoly' defence was raised by the parties, claiming that their parallel behaviour was a natural result of the oligopolistic market structure, but the Commission was able to show evidence of collusion. In other cases, the oligopoly defence has proved more successful. In relation to the oligopoly defence, economic evidence is vital. The Court has accepted that in oligopolistic markets undertakings must take into account the behaviour of their competitors, and in so doing they may appear to act in parallel with their competitors. However, the Court has added that parallel behaviour may constitute strong evidence of collusion where parallelism would not result from the normal operation of the market. The Court considered the difficulties faced in such situations in the *Wood Pulp* case.[21] In his opinion, Advocate General Darmon explained the potential for parallelism as follows:

> ... parallel conduct is not necessarily the result of prior concentration. It can be explained or even dictated by the very structure of certain markets ... The first situation involves a concentrated oligopoly, in which undertakings are independent: each undertaking must take into account in its decisions the conduct of its rivals. Alignment on others' conduct constitutes a rational response, independently of any concentration. 'Price leadership' constitutes the second situation: undertakings align themselves on a 'price leader' on account of the latter's power on the market. Mention may also be made of the spontaneous alignment on a price leader which acts as barometer, either its decisions reflecting changes in market conditions or for reasons linked, for instance, to previous knowledge of that market.[22]

The Court instructed two independent economic experts to investigate the market for wood pulp to aid it in its judgment. The experts' analysis explained in some detail the workings of the market and the external pressures that had effects on pricing within the period of the alleged infringement. In its judgment the Court accepted the findings of the experts and concluded that concerted practices were not the only plausible explanation

---

21 Cases C-89, 104, 114, 116, 117 and 125–29/85 *A Ahlstrom Oy v Commission* [1993] ECR I-1307; [1993] 4 CMLR 407.
22 Ibid, at para 177.

for the parallel price announcements on the wood pulp market. The experts had identified that the long-term nature of purchasing requirements, the limited number of customers for each producer and the transparency of price information, particularly through a dynamic trade press, could account for parallel behaviour in the market. As the parallel behaviour could be explained by the operation of the market, and the Commission had produced no evidence of actual collusion, the Court annulled the majority of the Commission's Decision.

Much of the literature on oligopolistic markets refers to the phenomenon of parallel behaviour as 'tacit collusion'. This terminology might suggest that Art 81 may be an appropriate tool to control this form of 'collusion' alongside other concerted practices, but it has become clear, in cases such as *Wood Pulp*, that Art 81 should only be used in situations where 'active' collusion has been proved. It may still be possible to use Art 81 where there is no other plausible explanation for the parallelism. However, regarding proof, the Court has confirmed the use of economic analysis where other means of proof may be impracticable or impossible. The Commission has to overcome a difficult burden in terms of the economic evidence required. The problem with dealing with 'tacit collusion' under Art 81 is that the problem is structural, in that the structure of the market creates the conditions where tacit collusion may occur, rather than behavioural, where there is active collusion between undertakings. The main remedy under Art 81, the imposition of a fine, is behavioural in nature and therefore not well suited to dealing with a structural problem. It will be interesting to note whether the availability of structural remedies under Regulation 1/2003 may lead to Commission attempts to extend the use of Art 81 to future oligopoly cases.[23]

Undertakings

The definition of an undertaking in Art 81 is very similar to that under Art 82, that being any legal or natural person involved in a commercial enterprise. In the context of Art 81 the 'economic entity' doctrine is of importance. If legally separate bodies are linked, through ownership or management agreements, any form of 'agreement' between them will not be considered under Art 81 as the separate bodies will be deemed to be within the same undertaking.[24] The Court's jurisprudence on groups of companies is illustrated by *Viho Europe v Commission*.[25] Viho had challenged the restrictions imposed by Parker Pen on its national distributors which prohibited the distributors from supplying customers outside their respective national

---

23 Article 7, Regulation 1/2003/EC on the implementation of the rules on competition laid down in Arts 81 and 82 of the Treaty, OJ 2003, L1/1.
24 See Case 22/71 *Beguelin Import v GL Import Export* [1971] ECR 949; [1972] CMLR 81.
25 Case C-73/95P [1996] ECR I-5457; [1997] 4 CMLR 419.

territories. The Court confirmed that the arrangements between Parker and its national distributors, which were also its subsidiaries, fell outside Art 81(1). The reason for this finding was that Parker owned 100% of the shares in the subsidiary companies and their sales and marketing activities were directed by an area management team appointed by the parent company. It would appear that both ownership and management are important when deciding if intra-group agreements are caught by Art 81. This use of the economic entity doctrine has been criticised as it encourages undertakings to vertically integrate their distribution systems to avoid the prohibition. If an undertaking owns or manages its own distributors it can impose whatever restrictions it considers necessary without the threat of sanction under Art 81. A good example of the sort of finance and management links between parent and subsidiary companies which can lead to them being considered a single undertaking under the UK's Chapter I prohibition, was considered by the CAT in *Sepia Logistics Ltd & Precision Control Ltd v OFT*.[26] One man, Mr Sander, was on the board of both the parent and subsidiary companies and had personally guaranteed debts of both companies. All the shares of the parent company were in the ownership of Mr Sander's family, and the parent owned 80% of the shares in the subsidiary.

Effect on interstate trade

The requirement of an effect on interstate trade concerns the jurisdictional scope of the provision. The Court and the Commission have given the phrase a broad interpretation. Many agreements which at first sight appear to only affect one Member State have been held to come within the ambit of the Community rules. Article 3 of Regulation 1/2003 sets out the relationship between Community law and national law in the area of interstate trade.[27]

The Court laid out the basic test for the effect on interstate trade in *Société Technique Minière v Maschinenbau Ulm* as follows:[28]

> ... it must be possible to foresee with a sufficient degree of probability on the basis of an objective set of factors of law or fact that the agreement in question may have an influence, direct or indirect, actual or potential, on the pattern of trade between Member States.

This broad test has also been given a wide interpretation in the Commission

26 [2007] CAT 13.
27 Regulation 1/2003/EC on the implementation of the rules on competition laid down in Arts 81 and 82 of the Treaty, OJ 2003, L1/1. National law may be applied alongside Community law where there is an effect on interstate trade but must not lead to the prohibition of agreements which are not prohibited by Art 81 EC.
28 Case 56/65 [1966] ECR 235; [1966] CMLR 357.

Notice, Guidelines on the effect on trade concept contained in Arts 81 and 82 of the Treaty.[29] Where an agreement is between undertakings based in the same Member State, it may still be deemed to affect interstate trade. Agreements in one State may have the effect of compartmentalising the market and thus discouraging undertakings from other States from entering the market.[30] Very minor agreements may also affect interstate trade if the agreements are part of a larger network of agreements.[31] The importance of such networks can be seen when one considers complex distribution systems used in industries such as brewing. A brewer may have thousands of agreements with pubs, relating to the supply of beer. Each one of those agreements would have little impact on interstate trade but, taken as a network, the economic impact of the agreements may be significant.

Prevention, restriction or distortion of competition

The next section of the prohibition in Art 81(1) concerns the competitive impact of an agreement or concerted practice. Unless the Commission or the Court is satisfied that an agreement has as its 'object or effect the prevention, restriction or distortion of competition', it will not infringe Art 81. There has been great difficulty in discerning clearly what types of agreement should be of concern to competition law; in other words, when does an agreement distort, restrict or limit competition?[32] This area, the distortion, restriction or limitation of competition, has proved to be one of the most controversial in Community competition law. It is an area that highlights the conflict between the economic and political goals that exist within Community competition policy, particularly in relation to vertical restraints.[33] For that reason, this chapter will concentrate on the basic application of Art 81, giving examples of some of the common types of restrictive agreements. In the following chapter, there will be a more detailed discussion on the difficulties faced by the competition authorities in dealing with secret cartels.

Article 81 includes an indicative list of the types of agreement that will prevent, restrict or distort competition, though, as with Art 82, this list is not exhaustive. The Commission and the Court have given the terminology a wide interpretation. Some commentators have argued that the interpretation

---

29 OJ 2004, C101/81.

30 Case 8/72 *Cementhandelaren v Commission* [1972] ECR 977; [1973] CMLR 7. See, also, Cases T-202, 204 and 207/98 *Tate & Lyle and Others v Commission* [2001] ECR II-2035. Cf Cases C-215/96 and C-216/96 *Carlo Bagnasco and Others v Banco Polare di Navara and Others* [1999] ECR I-135.

31 Case C-234/89 *Delimitis v Henniger Bräu* [1991] ECR I-935; [1992] 5 CMLR 210.

32 See Lugard, HHP, 'Vertical restraints under EC competition law: a horizontal approach' [1996] ECLR 166.

33 See Hawk, B, 'System failure: vertical restraints and EC competition law' (1995) 32 CML Rev 973.

adopted is so wide that it bears little relation to competitive reality. One possible reason for this broad interpretation is the existence of Art 81(3) which allows for the prohibition to be inapplicable. The US antitrust regime, to which the Community rules are usually compared, has no corresponding provision. As a result, in the US the consideration of any economic benefits stemming from an agreement is made within the prohibition itself; such a process is usually known as a 'rule of reason', and therefore requires a more flexible definition. Another reason may be historic as, in the early years of Community competition law's development, a broad interpretation of Art 81(1) meant that most potentially restrictive agreements required notification for exemption under Regulation 17. As the power to grant an exemption, at that time, rested solely with the Commission, the Commission was in the position to shape the development of the rules through its use of the Art 81(3) exemption procedure. If more flexibility had been built into Art 81(1) the national courts would have had a far greater role to play in the evolution of the rules. The Commission used its position to develop the rules and prevent the development of conflicting interpretations. Whatever the reason behind the broad interpretation of Art 81(1), as the Community system became more mature its continued use caused many problems.[34]

The 'object' of restricting competition

A distinction has been made between agreements which have the object of restricting competition and those which have the effect of doing so. In *STM*,[35] the Court stated that the words should be read disjunctively and thus consideration should first be given to whether an agreement has the object of restricting competition. Only when it does not is it necessary to consider, in detail, the effects of the agreement. In *Polypropylene*,[36] there was considerable evidence of the cartel members' intention of co-operating across the market but there was little evidence of any anti-competitive effects. Nonetheless, the Commission imposed a large fine that was upheld on appeal.[37]

The simplification of the Commission's task, when there is no need to consider an agreement's effects, is limited by a number of factors. Shortly after the Decision in *Polypropylene* the Court of First Instance (CFI) appeared to question the paucity of economic evidence in 'object' cases. In *Flat Glass*,[38]

---

34 A number of those problems, and the prospective solutions, were discussed in Chapter 2 and will be examined in detail later in this chapter.
35 Case 56/65 *STM v Maschinenbau Ulm* [1966] ECR 235; [1966] CMLR 357.
36 Commission Decision 86/398/EEC, OJ 1986, L230/1; [1988] 4 CMLR 347.
37 Commission Decision 86/398/EEC, OJ 1986, L230/1; [1988] 4 CMLR 347. Upheld on appeal in, for example, Case C-49/920 *Hercules NV v Commission* [1991] ECR II-1711; [1992] 4 CMLR 84 and *Commission v Anic Partecipazioni SpA* [1999] ECR I-4125.
38 Commission Decision 89/93/EEC *Industria Vetrana Alfonso Cobelli v Società Italiana Vetro*, OJ 1989, L33/44; [1990] 4 CMLR 535.

the Commission viewed the object of the agreement as obviously restrictive and did not analyse it further. The CFI considered that there was a need for some form of delineation of the market in all competition cases to ensure there is an accurate determination if an agreement has an 'appreciable' effect on competition.[39] This requirement for some form of analysis to ensure that the effect on competition is appreciable is even more important since the reformulation of the notice on agreements of minor importance.[40] As market share tests have been adopted by the Commission, market analysis will obviously be required to establish if the undertakings involved have a market share above the necessary threshold. Other issues, such as the effect on interstate trade, will also require evidence as to the effects of the agreement. Despite the apparently conflicting judicial pronouncements, certain types of agreements are deemed to be 'object' or '*per se*' infringements of Art 81(1),[41] whereas other possible infringements require a fuller examination of the economic context in which the possible infringements take place.[42]

Many of the types of agreement which have been considered to have the object of restricting competition are well-known cartel activities, such as price-fixing[43] or market-sharing.[44] However, other forms of behaviour, such as collective boycotts[45] and information exchanges,[46] have also been challenged.

---

39 Cases T-77–78/89 *Società Italiana Vetro v Commission* [1992] ECR II-1403; [1992] 5 CMLR 302.

40 Commission Notice on agreements of minor importance which do not appreciably restrict competition under Art 81(1) of the Treaty establishing the European Community (*de minimis*), OJ 2001, C368/07. The Notice is discussed in more detail below in this chapter.

41 See Case T-14/89 *Montedipe SpA v Commission* [1992] ECR II-1155 where the Court noted, at para 265, that if the infringement is a clear one, this 'precludes the application of a rule of reason'. See, also, Case T-148/89 *Trefilunion SA v Commission* [1995] ECR II-1063, at para 109: 'Moreover, the fact that the infringement of Article 85(1) of the Treaty . . . is a clear one necessarily precludes the application of a rule of reason, assuming such a rule to be applicable in Community competition law, since in that case it must be regarded as an infringement *per se* of the competition rules' and Case T-112/99 *Métropole Télévision (M6) v Commission* [2001] ECR II-2459; [2001] 5 CMLR 1236, at para 72: 'in various judgments the Court of Justice and the Court of First Instance have been at pains to indicate that the existence of a rule of reason in Community competition law is doubtful.' Finally, see, also, Case C-235/92P *Montecatini v Commission* [1999] ECR I-4539, at para 74.

42 See Cases T-374, 375, 384 and 388/94 *European Night Services Ltd v Commission* [1998] ECR II-3141, at para 136: '. . . account should be taken of the actual conditions in which it functions, in particular the economic context in which the undertakings operate, the products or services covered by the agreement and the actual structure of the market concerned . . . unless it is an agreement containing obvious restrictions of competition, such as price-fixing, market-sharing or the control of outlets.'

43 Cases 48, 49 and 51–57/69 *ICI v Commission (Dyestuffs)* [1972] ECR 619; [1972] CMLR 557.

44 Case 41/69 *Quinine, ACF Chemifarma v Commission* [1970] ECR 661; [1970] CMLR 8083.

45 Case 71/74 *FRUBO v Commission* [1975] ECR 563; [1975] 2 CMLR 123.

46 Commission Decision 80/1334/EEC, OJ 1980, L383/19; *Italian Cast Glass* [1982] 2 CMLR 61. See, also, Cases T-202/98, T-204/98 and T-207/98 *Tate & Lyle etc* regarding meetings where parties revealed future price intentions, particularly para 73.

Due to the importance of market integration in Community competition law, many forms of export restriction, in both vertical and horizontal agreements, have been taken to have the object of restriction of competition.[47] An excellent example of such a situation can be seen in the *Nintendo* Decision.[48] Prices for Nintendo games cartridges were lower in the UK than other Member States, and Nintendo and their UK distributor, THE Games, had taken steps to reduce the potential for parallel trade from the UK into continental Europe. First, THE Games would only supply cartridges to retailers who sold directly to end-consumers. Secondly, any approaches from retailers outside the UK would initially be referred to the local distributor, as selling to retailers outside the UK was 'not a desirable practice'. Thirdly, THE Games would not sell to wholesalers in the UK, as they could sell on to UK retailers or retailers outside the UK, and lead to violations of one of the first two principles.[49] Even with these policies Nintendo was still concerned that UK stocks were reaching the continental market, but THE Games assured it that 'we will try at all costs, to prevent product arriving in Europe'.[50] Because of this, and other practices designed to reduce parallel exports, Nintendo and its distributors were found to be in breach of Art 81.

The *Polypropylene* case, mentioned above, is a good example of the way that a horizontal cartel can operate.[51] After its investigation, the Commission found strong evidence that 15 undertakings working in the polypropylene market had formed an agreement to restrict competition. It was discovered that there had been regular contact between the suppliers of polypropylene since 1977. These meetings were held on a Community-wide basis between senior management, referred to as the 'bosses' meetings, and technical managers, referred to as the 'experts' meetings. The bimonthly Community-wide meetings were supplemented by occasional national meetings.

In its legal assessment of the cartel, the Commission decided that the complex scheme of arrangements between the 15 suppliers formed a single continuing agreement. There was no need for the agreement to contain sanctions or to be in writing. There was also no need, when considering the cartel, to differentiate between the aspects which constituted an agreement and those which were merely concerted practices. Even where particular undertakings were not present at all the meetings, they were held to be involved

---

47 See Cases 56 and 58/64 *Consten and Grundig v Commission* [1966] ECR 299; [1966] CMLR 418.

48 Commission Decision 2003/675/EC *Video Games/Nintendo*, OJ 2003, L255/33.

49 Recital 102.

50 Recital 118.

51 Cartel control is discussed in more detail in Chapter 5. For an excellent account of the operation of cartels in Europe and their legal regulation, see Harding, C and Joshua, J, *Regulating Cartels in Europe – A Study of Legal Control of Corporate Delinquency*, 2003, Oxford: OUP.

via a reporting system whereby all the undertakings knew what was being proposed by the others. The important point was the consensus that was reached between the producers and the steps that were taken over a period of time to implement that consensus. The Commission did not consider it necessary to address in any detail the effects of the agreement as its object was obviously anti-competitive, but the Commission did outline a number of ways in which it believed the effects were manifested.

On appeal, the CFI upheld the Commission's findings.[52] It agreed that there was effectively a single 'agreement' operated over a period of time. It added that where some parts of the 'agreement' could be described as an agreement proper, others could be better categorised as concerted practices. Despite this, there was no need to distinguish between them, especially where the various schemes formed a single infringement of a complex nature. The argument that the cartel's activities did not affect competition was also dismissed by the CFI on the basis that the effects of the agreement were not relevant as its object was clear. The relevant question was whether the agreement could have affected the market, and as the undertakings concerned represented nearly the whole market that question must be answered in the affirmative. The CFI's findings were upheld by the Court of Justice.[53]

The 'effect' of restricting competition

Where an agreement does not have the object of restricting competition, it is necessary to consider its effects. Even horizontal agreements between competitors may not have the object of restricting competition. In innovative or high technology industries it is common for undertakings to co-operate in the development of new technology or products. That co-operation will be designed to improve competition by bringing new products on to the market or to improve the technology used in existing production, thereby allowing for greater efficiency. Without spreading the risks involved in research and development the project may not be viable. Even if the research would have gone ahead, the co-operation may result in the development reaching the market more quickly. While the agreements in such situations may result in advantages, they may also have disadvantages. When the research work is complete should there also be co-operation in production and marketing of the new technology? At what stage should the co-operation cease? By allowing competitors to work together on the development programme, will co-operation blunt their desire to compete in other areas? These concerns

---

52 See Case T-7/89 *Hercules NV v Commission* [1991] ECR II-1711; [1992] 4 CMLR 84. The appeal to the Court of Justice did not directly address this issue: Case C-51/92P [1999] ECR I-4235; [1999] 5 CMLR 976.

53 See, for example, Case C-49/92P *Commission v Anic Partecipazioni SpA* [1999] ECR I-4125.

mean that the particular agreement must be carefully considered to establish its potential effects on the market.[54]

When the effect of an agreement is considered, it is important to examine the market in its economic context. Without a full analysis of the market in question it will be impossible to discover if the agreement has prevented, restricted or distorted competition, or has the potential to do so. This was emphasised by the Court in *Brasserie de Haecht v Wilkin*:[55]

> It would be pointless to consider an agreement, decision or concerted practice by reason of its effect if those effects were to be taken distinct from the market in which they are seen to operate.[56]

The Court adopted similar reasoning in *Delimitis*.[57] In both these cases the agreements were between brewers and cafes. The agreements tied the cafe owners to purchase beer supplies from the brewer. A single agreement would be of limited impact; however, a network of similar agreements across a national market could have the effect of foreclosing competition. If large numbers of outlets were tied to brewers, potential competitors might find it difficult to enter the market and compete against existing brewers. Although the definition of the relevant market is more traditionally associated with Art 82, in this type of Art 81 case it is vital. Before deciding whether a network of agreements can foreclose a market it is important to define exactly which type of outlets are competing. For example, do cafes compete with off licences and supermarkets? It is also apparent from the reasoning in *Delimitis* that not only must consideration be given to the effects of the agreement on the existing market, but also to the agreement's potential effects on the development of the market. The Court emphasised that the effects of the agreement, taken together with other contracts of the same type, may have an impact on the opportunities for other organisations to gain access to the market. This would in turn have an effect on the products offered to consumers. The Court decided that the demand structure for beer to be consumed on the premises, in particular in public houses and restaurants, was very different from the retail sector in that there was also a provision of services where beer was consumed on the premises. The differing nature of different sectors of the trade was also indicated by the different distribution

---

54 For the Commission's treatment of such agreements, see Commission Regulation 2659/2000/ EC on the application of Art 81(3) of the Treaty to categories of research and development agreements, OJ 2000, L304/7, and Commission Notice, Guidelines on the applicability of Art 81 of the EC Treaty to horizontal co-operation agreements, OJ 2001, C3/2.

55 Case 23/67 [1967] ECR 407; [1968] CMLR 26.

56 Ibid, at para 40.

57 See Case C-234/89 *Delimitis v Henniger Bräu* [1991] ECR I-935; [1992] 5 CMLR 210. For an application of these principles by the CFI, see Case T-25/99 *Roberts v Commission* [2001] ECR II-1881.

systems. As this was a preliminary ruling under the Art 234 procedure, the Court indicated a number of factors which should be taken into account when examining the potential to foreclose the market through a network of agreements:[58]

a the possibilities for a new competitor to penetrate the bundle of contracts by acquisition of an established operator or the establishment of new outlets;
b the conditions of competition on the market, including the level of product saturation and customer loyalty.

When a market is difficult to enter, the national court should also examine the effects of the bundle of agreements in question to decide the extent to which the bundle of agreements contributes towards that effect. If the effect is insignificant, the agreements will not fall within the Art 81(1) prohibition.

The legality of exclusive purchasing commitments was considered by the CFI in *Van Den Bergh v Commission*.[59] This dispute concerned single-wrapped ice creams intended for immediate consumption, referred to as 'impulse ice cream'.[60] In the late 1980s and early 1990s, HB supplied its retailers with freezer cabinets free or at nominal rent. The freezer agreements could be terminated at any time with two months' notice on either side. HB owned and maintained the cabinets and they were to be used exclusively for products supplied by HB. At least 40% of all outlets in the relevant market only had freezer cabinets supplied by HB with its freezer exclusivity requirements. The CFI stressed that 'the contractual restrictions on retailers must be examined not just in a purely formal manner from the legal point of view, but also by taking into account the specific economic context in which the agreements in question operate'.[61] The CFI supported the view that the HB network had a 'considerably dissuasive effect on retailers' and 'operate *de facto* as a tie on sales outlets' such that 'the effect of the exclusivity clause in practice is to restrict the commercial freedom of retailers to choose the products they wish to sell in their sales outlets'.[62] Accordingly, the CFI rejected a

---

58 Case C-234/89 *Delimitis v Henniger Bräu* [1991] ECR I-935; [1992] 5 CMLR 210, paras 20–26. See, also, Case T-25/99 *Roberts v Commission* [2001] ECR II-1881, for consideration of the network of brewers and potential foreclosures in a UK context. See, also, more recently, the application of the *Delimitis* principles in *Crehan v Inntrepreneur Pub Co (CPC)* [2004] EWCA Civ 637.
59 Case T-7/93 *Langnese-Iglo GmbH v Commission* [1995] ECR II-1533; Case C-279/95P *Langnese-Iglo GmbH v Commission* [1998] ECR I-5609; Case T-65/98 *Van den Bergh Foods v Commission* [2004] 4 CMLR 1. See also *IMS v Ofcom* [2008] CAT 13.
60 The Commission found, at para 28, that HB's value share of the impulse ice cream market in Ireland was about 85% from June to September 1986.
61 At para 84.
62 At para 98.

purely formalistic approach which would rely on formal contractual periods of notice.

Market analysis is now very important in the consideration of the effect of an agreement, though in the early years of the Community competition system the Commission and the Court gave the 'effect' requirement a very broad interpretation, catching many agreements which appeared to be restrictions on conduct rather than on competition. The Commission subsequently used Regulation 17's exemption procedure to allow agreements, which had positive benefits, to proceed. This approach came under strain as the workload of the Directorate General for Competition increased. The Commission was no longer capable of giving each potentially restrictive agreement individual attention. Partly in order to relieve this problem, a number of block exemptions[63] were adopted to exempt classes of agreements from the prohibition. The block exemptions adopted to date have covered a number of common types of agreement, including vertical agreements[64] and technology transfer agreements.[65]

The Court also became involved in developing jurisprudence, which has gone some way to reducing the scope of Art 81(1). When considering a number of vertical agreements, the Court appeared to be willing not to prohibit agreements that contained restrictive clauses, if the clauses were pro-competitive when considered in context.[66] More particularly, in a series of cases, the Court has shown that it will analyse restrictions in agreements to examine whether they are 'necessary' for the agreement to be of commercial value. One of the earliest examples was in *Remia*.[67] This case involved an agreement, for the sale of a business, which included a restrictive covenant. It is common for the sale price of a business to include an amount for the goodwill that the business has built up over time. The purchaser would not wish to pay for this goodwill if the vendor were able to open a competing business in the vicinity and entice customers away from the original business. A restriction is often placed in such contracts prohibiting the vendor from

---

63 While the term block exemption is somewhat erroneous in light of the abolition of the exemption process under Regulation 1/2003 it still forms a useful shorthand reference for the Regulations.

64 See Regulation 2790/99/EC on the application of Art 81(3) of the Treaty to categories of vertical agreements and concerted practices, OJ 1999, L336/21, and Commission Notice, Guidelines on vertical restraints, OJ 2000, C291/01.

65 See Regulation 772/2004/EC on the application of Art 81(3) of the Treaty to categories of technology transfer agreements, OJ 2004, L123/11, and Commission Notice, Guidelines on the application of Art 81 of the EC Treaty to technology transfer agreements, OJ 2004, C101/2. See, also, Korah, V, 'Draft block exemption for technology transfer' [2004] ECLR 247.

66 See Case C-234/89 *Delimitis v Henniger Bräu* [1991] ECR I-935; [1992] 5 CMLR 210. For an implementation of the *Delimitis* principles in the UK, see *Passmore v Moreland and Others* [1999] 3 All ER 1005; [1999] 1 CMLR 1129 where the English Court of Appeal ruled that the validity of an agreement may change as the market conditions alter.

67 Case 42/84 *Remia and Nutricia v Commission* [1985] ECR 2545; [1987] 1 CMLR 1.

trading in the same type of business in that vicinity for a period of time. A restrictive covenant was examined in this case. Looking at the term, it is clear to see how competition might be affected. One potential competitor is barred from entering the market for a stipulated period, but, on the other hand, the whole agreement is pro-competitive, as without such a term a potential purchaser would be deterred from investing in the business. They would not want to pay for the goodwill. It would, therefore, be considerably more difficult to enter, or exit, the market. The Court found that the restrictive covenant was necessary as an ancillary restraint.[68] Without the restrictive term, the pro-competitive agreement would not go ahead. It did not, therefore, fall within Art 81(1).

On a number of occasions, the Court has used similar reasoning to find that agreements, which are pro-competitive but which contain potentially restrictive terms, do not fall within the prohibition so long as the restrictions are necessary for the agreement to work. Examples can be found in a variety of areas: the licensing of intellectual property rights, as in *Nungesser*;[69] the qualitative membership criteria in selective distribution systems, as in *Metro I*;[70] and the prescribed sales methods and limited territorial restrictions in franchising systems, as in *Pronuptia*.[71]

The conception of the 'ancillary restraints' doctrine within Art 81(1) is not universally supported, and is difficult to reconcile with some of the case law. In some cases it would appear that the Court is effectively balancing the pro-competitive and anti-competitive elements of a particular agreement. One of the leading cases that supports this reading is *Wouters*,[72] an Art 234 reference regarding the compatibility of Dutch rules that prevented members of the Bar operating in multidisciplinary partnerships with accountants. The Court initially stated that the rules, which were a decision of an association of undertakings, were restrictive of competition; but it also stressed that account must be taken of the 'overall context' in which the decision was taken and its effects.[73] After completing its analysis the Court came to the view that the rules did not go beyond, 'what is necessary in order to ensure the proper practice of the legal profession'.[74] The manner in which the Court undertook its analysis seemed much closer to a balancing approach than in many other

---

68 The CFI has gone some way to define what constitutes an ancillary restraint in Case T-112/99 *Métropole Télévision and Others v Commission* [2001] ECR II-2459; [2001] 5 CMLR 1236. See, also, Commission Notice, Guidelines on the application of Art 81(3) of the Treaty, OJ 2004, C101/97, paras 28–31.

69 Case 258/78 *Nungesser v Commission* [1982] ECR 2015; [1983] 1 CMLR 278.

70 Case 26/76 *Metro v Commission* [1977] ECR 1875; [1978] 2 CMLR 1.

71 Case 161/84 *Pronuptia v Schillgalis* [1986] ECR 353; [1986] 1 CMLR 414.

72 Case C-309/99 *Wouters v Algemene Raad van de Nederlandse Orde van Advocaten* [2002] ECR I-1577, [2002] 4 CMLR 913.

73 At para 97.

74 At para 109.

cases.[75] The arguments surrounding the Court's approach to restrictions within vertical agreements, which have their own specific Regulation, are discussed in more detail later in this chapter.

Agreements of minor importance

A very important limit on the application of Art 81 is the *de minimis* principle. The *de minimis* principle covers agreements which, due to their limited significance, may not be caught by the prohibition. Such agreements do not fall within the prohibition as either they do not have an appreciable effect on competition or they do not affect interstate trade. This principle was first expounded by the Court in *Völk*[76] and has been formalised by the Commission in a series of Notices. The latest Notice on agreements of minor importance was published in 2001.[77] The Notice is based on a market share test and differentiates between horizontal and vertical agreements. Paragraph 7 of the Notice states that an agreement will not appreciably restrict competition if the aggregate market share of the participating undertakings does not exceed 10% of the relevant market for a horizontal agreement, or 15% of the relevant market for a vertical agreement.[78] For mixed agreements, the 10% threshold is applicable. The market share threshold is reduced to 5% where a market is affected by networks of similar agreements.[79] In addition to the market share test, the Commission states that agreements between small- and medium-sized undertakings will rarely be capable of affecting trade between Member States.[80] Even where an agreement falls below the thresholds in the Notice it may still be considered to be appreciable if it contains one of the 'hard core' restrictions set out in para 11, such as price-fixing, limitation of output, or allocation of markets.

---

75 For a discussion of many of these issues in the UK context see, *The Racecourse Assoc v OFT* [2005] CAT 29, discussed further below.
76 Case 5/69 *Völk v Ets Vervaecke Sprl* [1969] ECR 295; [1969] CMLR 273.
77 Commission Notice on agreements of minor importance which do not appreciably restrict competition under Art 81(1) of the Treaty establishing the European Community (*de minimis*), OJ 2001, C368/07. See, also, Commission Notice, Guidelines on the effect on trade concept contained in Arts 81 and 82 of the Treaty, OJ 2004, C101/81. The original *de minimis* Notice was based on turnover thresholds rather than market shares. The shift to a market share test, as in other areas of competition law, is closer to the economic rationale behind appreciability but may reduce legal certainty for those who have to apply the notice in practice.
78 The importance of this figure has been reduced following the adoption of the Vertical Agreements Regulation, Regulation 2790/1999/EC, OJ 1999, L336/21.
79 At para 8 of the Notice.
80 At para 3 of the Notice. Medium-sized undertakings are defined, in Commission Recommendation 2003/361/EC concerning the definition of micro-, small- and medium-sized enterprises, OJ 2003, L124/36, as undertakings with fewer than 250 employees and either an annual turnover of no more than €50m or a balance sheet not exceeding €43m.

Within the Common Market

The final part of the prohibition focuses on its territorial extent. Only agreements which restrict competition within the Common Market are prohibited. Questions have been raised as to the application of the Community rules to agreements between undertakings established outside the Community. The Commission has always been of the opinion that such application is possible under the Treaty. In *Dyestuffs*,[81] the Commission found against ICI on the basis that, even though it was at that time established outside the Community, it had put the concerted practice into effect through its subsidiaries in Europe.

The same question was considered in *Wood Pulp*.[82] The majority of wood pulp suppliers investigated by the Commission were based outside the Community in North America and Scandinavia. Sales were made directly into the Community via subsidiaries, branches or agents. The Court's judgment concentrated on the 'implementation' of the agreement, decision or concerted practice within the Common Market, but the Court added that it was immaterial that the implementation was carried out through persons operating within the Common Market. The exact meaning of implementation within the judgment is unclear, though it appeared that the Court was willing to uphold the application of Community competition law against undertakings which had no physical presence in the Community.

Although *Wood Pulp* is still the leading judgment in this area the CFI adopted a different approach in *Gencor*.[83] Rather than discussing the 'implementation' of the agreement the CFI concentrated on whether there was an 'immediate and substantial effect in the Community'.[84] The concentration on 'effect' rather than 'implementation' leads to a wider and much more flexible test.

Article 81(2)

Article 81(2) describes the consequence of breaching the prohibition contained in Art 81(1). The agreement is automatically void. The sanction of nullity is not significant for agreements which involve market sharing or price-fixing, as it would be incredibly unusual if the parties to such an agreement were to seek its enforcement. In those circumstances, the parties would seek to deny the agreement and hope that they could avoid a fine or the civil consequences of being found in breach.

---

81 Cases 48, 49, 51–57/69 *ICI v Commission* [1972] ECR 619; [1972] CMLR 557.
82 See Cases C-89, 104, 114, 116, 117 and 125–27/85 *A Ahlstrom Oy v Commission* [1993] ECR I-1307; [1993] 4 CMLR 407.
83 Case T-102/96 *Gencor v Commission* [1999] II-ECR 753; [1999] 4 CMLR 971. Although this is a merger case, the principles are similar.
84 Ibid, at para 90.

The sanction of nullity is more important when Art 81 is used as a 'Euro-defence' by a party that is already in breach of the contested agreement or wishes to escape its terms. The use of Art 81 as a defence is quite common in respect of agreements for the licensing of intellectual property rights or for other vertical restraints, such as distribution agreements. One of the first competition cases to come before the UK courts involved, *inter alia*, an Art 81 Euro-defence, although the defendant in that case was not party to the relevant agreement. *Application des Gaz v Falks Veritas*[85] was a preliminary hearing in a copyright dispute. A French company, Application des Gaz, claimed copyright in a metal gas canister and sought to prevent an English company, Falks Veritas, from producing an identical can. The French company had already granted an exclusive right to production to another English company. After the coming into effect of the UK's accession to the Community, Falks Veritas sought to amend its defence to include an alleged breach of Art 81. It claimed that there was a concerted practice between the French company and its English licensees to discourage retailers from stocking the Falks Veritas product. The Court of Appeal did not consider the merits of the case in detail but accepted that the defence based on Art 81 appeared to be valid.

Another example of an Art 81 Euro-defence was considered by the English High Court in *Inntrepreneur Estates v Mason*.[86] Inntrepreneur, the landlord of a chain of pubs, sought to forfeit the lease granted to Mason after Mason fell into arrears with his rent. The landlord sought rent arrears and other sums due, a total of £38,000. The tenant claimed in his defence that because of the 'tie' in the lease requiring the tenant to purchase beers and other drinks directly from the landlord the lease was an agreement falling within the prohibition under Art 81(1) and therefore null and void under Art 81(2). In the interlocutory appeal it was not contested that the argument based on Art 81 had a real prospect of success. The contentious issue concerned the effects of nullity. If the whole lease became void the claim would fail, but if Art 81(2) only affected the clause of the agreement which restricted competition, the 'tie', the rest of the lease would stand and the back rent would still be due. This question of severance was also considered by the European Court of Justice in *STM*.[87] The Court stated that the sanction of nullity only applied to those parts of the agreement that were subject to the prohibition. If it is possible to sever the offending parts, the rest of the agreement may stand. This coincides with the English case law on severance. In an earlier English intellectual property case involving Art 81, *Chemidus Wavin*,[88] the Court of

85 [1974] 1 Ch 381.
86 [1993] 2 CMLR 293.
87 Case 56/65 *STM v Maschinenbau Ulm* [1966] ECR 235; [1966] CMLR 357.
88 *Chemidus Wavin v Société pour la Transformation et L'Exploitation des Resines Industrielles SA* [1978] 3 CMLR 514.

Appeal decided that the offending term should be severed unless the contract would be so altered in character as not to be the contract into which the parties entered. Such an alteration would occur if a major term of the contract was removed and the removal dramatically changed the nature of the contract.

In *Passmore v Moreland and Others*,[89] the English Court of Appeal addressed the question of when an agreement becomes void. Mr Passmore was, at the time of the dispute, the tenant of a pub which was tied to a small brewery. Because of the brewery's size the beer tie did not have an appreciable effect on competition. When the lease was originally granted the pub was owned by a much larger brewer that had transferred the lease to the current owner. It was argued that the lease was void when it was granted and was, therefore, still unenforceable. The Court of Appeal decided that the sanction of nullity is 'temporaneous or transient'[90] in effect, as is the prohibition. Even if the lease might have been void when it was granted it was not to be considered as still being void following the change in circumstances. It must, however, be noted that the Court of Justice has not expressed a view on this issue and the Court of Appeal did not consider it necessary to make a preliminary reference under Art 234 EC.[91]

Article 81(3)

Article 81(3) allows for the prohibition in Art 81(1) to be declared inapplicable if certain criteria are met. The importance of Art 81(3) stemmed from the wide interpretation adopted under Art 81(1). As a result, a large range of common agreements which fell within the prohibition could not be enforced without benefiting from the terms of Art 81(3). Under the Regulation 17 regime, the Commission had the sole power to grant exemption under Art 81(3). This gave the Commission extensive and exclusive powers which it used to mould the shape of the competition system in the Community. It also gave the Commission the opportunity to promote other goals, such as market integration, within the competition sphere. The broad interpretation of Art 81(1) worked well for the Commission in the early years of competition enforcement as it allowed the Commission to gather a large amount of information about the way in which agreements operated across the Community. As undertakings became more aware of the provisions, and the Common Market became more integrated, the number of exemptions which

---

89 [1999] 3 All ER 1005; [1999] 1 CMLR 1129.
90 *Per* Chadwick LJ, at p 1014.
91 See Maitland-Walker, J, 'Have English courts gone too far in challenging the effectiveness of EC competition law?' [1999] 1 ECLR 1. See, also, the discussion of *Gibbs Mew v Gemmell* [1998] EuLR 588 and Case C-453/99 *Courage Ltd v Bernard Crehan* [2001] ECR I-6297; [2001] 5 CMLR 28, in Chapter 2.

were sought increased to such levels that the Commission had difficulty handling the workload.

The Commission took several steps to reduce the number of agreements notified for exemption. A number of block exemptions, which automatically exempted certain classes of agreement, were adopted. These allowed many common agreements, such as exclusive distribution agreements, to go ahead without Commission involvement. The Commission also sought to adopt more efficient procedures, including informal methods of closing cases. Even with these efforts the Commission's workload was still overwhelming and led to the more radical steps in the 1999 White Paper and ultimately the reforms introduced in Regulation 1/2003;[92] primarily the abolition of the notification requirement and the Commission's exclusive power to grant exemptions, with Art 81(3) becoming directly effective.

The exception rule

Under the Regulation 17 regime, if the parties to an agreement sought to benefit from the terms of Art 81(3) they needed to notify their agreement to the Commission. The Commission would then investigate the agreement, using information supplied by the parties, and decide whether it was appropriate to grant an exemption. An exemption was granted through a formal Commission decision. Because of the complexity of the procedure required, the Commission granted very few formal exemptions every year and a great many cases were closed informally. Because of the level of informality in the process the detailed processes which led to exemption decisions were often somewhat opaque. In practice, the Commission tended to favour the exemption of particular classes of agreement, particularly those between parties without market power. The Commission also took into account a broad range of factors, including wider Community policies, when making a decision. For that reason the Court was not willing to interfere with the Commission's discretion, even where the Commission's reasoning was remarkably brief.[93]

Under Regulation 1/2003 there is no longer any notification procedure and the criteria for inapplicability in Art 81(3) can be applied directly by the National Competition Authorities (NCAs) and national courts, as well as by the Commission. However, the Commission's previous practice is still important as guidance on how these other authorities should approach their role under Art 81. The Commission also retains a pivotal position within the new enforcement system, being consulted by NCAs before decisions are taken and having the ability to appear before national courts as an *amicus*. The Community Courts also have an increased role under Art 81(3) through the Art 234 EC preliminary ruling procedure.

92 The reform process is outlined more fully in Chapter 2.
93 See Case 8/72 *Consten and Grundig v Commission* [1972] ECR 977; [1973] CMLR 7.

The four conditions for inapplicability

To benefit from the exception the agreement must satisfy the four conditions in Art 81(3). An agreement must:

a   improve the production or distribution of goods or promote technical or economic progress;
b   ensure that consumers receive a fair share of the resulting benefits;
c   not contain indispensable restrictions; and
d   must not substantially eliminate competition.

To assist the NCAs and the courts in discharging their role under Regulation 1/2003 the Commission has produced Guidance on the application of Art 81(3).[94] The Guidelines follow, and expand on, the analytical framework developed by the Commission in its block exemption Regulations. The Guidelines state that once an agreement has been found to infringe Art 81(1) the role of Art 81(3) is to determine the pro-competitive benefits produced by that agreement and to assess whether these pro-competitive effects outweigh the agreement's anti-competitive effects.[95] In *Van Den Bergh*, the Commission and the CFI rejected HB's arguments for an exemption on the grounds that, *inter alia*, 'those arrangements did not present appreciable objective advantages of such a character as to compensate for the disadvantages caused to competition'.[96] Each of the criteria will be examined in turn.

Benefit – efficiency gains

The benefit, usually through some form of efficiency gain, must be for the Community as a whole, not just the parties to the agreement. All efficiency claims must be substantiated in several ways: the nature of the efficiencies; the link between the agreement and the efficiency; the likelihood of and magnitude of the efficiency; and how and when the efficiency will be achieved.[97] In its practice under Regulation 17 the Commission was creative in using the other goals of the Community to demonstrate benefit where the beneficial effects, defined strictly, for competition, were limited. In *Metro*,[98] the Court accepted that the stabilisation of employment might improve production, and may therefore fall under Art 81(3). In *CECED* the Commission took into account environmental benefits that would be achieved through an agreement

---

94 Commission Notice, Guidelines on the application of Art 81(3) of the Treaty, OJ 2004, C101/97.
95 At para 11.
96 Case T-65/98 *Van den Bergh Foods Ltd v Commission* [2003] ECR II-4653, [2004] 4 CMLR 1, para 140.
97 Guidelines, at para 52.
98 See Case 26/76 *Metro v Commission* [1977] ECR 1875; [1978] 2 CMLR 1.

to restrict the manufacture or import of the least energy-efficient washing machines.[99] The Commission's approach to 'crisis cartels' is also instructive in this area.[100] Crisis cartels are cartels which may be permitted within an industry to allow for reorganisation during periods of economic difficulty. It will be interesting to note whether the NCAs or national courts will use this type of approach in their decision-making. There is little reference to wider Community goals in the Commission Guidelines.

No indispensable restrictions

This condition can be regarded as the Art 81(3) version of the proportionality test. An exemption will not be granted unless the restriction of competition is no less than is necessary to allow the agreement to go ahead. The Commission does not apply this test as rigorously as it does in other areas of Community law. The test has two elements: (i) the restrictive agreement must be reasonably necessary in order to achieve the efficiencies; and (ii) the individual restrictions of competition must also be reasonably necessary for the attainment of the efficiencies. The decisive factor is 'whether or not the restrictive agreement and individual restrictions make it possible to perform the activity in question more efficiently than would likely have been the case in the absence of the agreement or the restriction concerned'.[101] However, there are some forms of restriction which are very unlikely to be accepted, even if the restrictions make commercial sense in the particular agreement. This is especially the case with price-fixing, absolute territorial protection, and the other 'hard core' restraints identified in block exemptions and the Commission Notices. Under the Regulation 17 regime the Commission often took the opportunity, post-notification, to suggest possible amendments which would have made the agreement more likely to be exempted. This will not be necessary under Regulation 1/2003 and the parties to the agreement have a much more central role.

Fair share to consumers

The parties are unlikely to proceed with an agreement unless they benefit in some way from it. This criterion seeks to ensure that the benefits received by the parties to the agreement are ultimately passed on to the consumer. The reference to the consumer refers to 'the customers of the parties to the agreement and subsequent purchasers'.[102] The consumers who may receive a share of the benefit therefore range from manufacturers to high street

---

99 Commission Decision 2000/475/EC, OJ 2000, L187/47.
100 For example, Commission Decision 84/380/EEC *Synthetic Fibres*, OJ 1984, L207/17.
101 Guidelines, at paras 73–74.
102 Guidelines, at para 84.

shoppers. The main benefit is likely to be improved quality or a reduction in price. The Guidelines explain that:

> ... the pass-on of benefits must at least compensate consumers for any actual or likely negative impact caused to them by the restriction of competition ... If such consumers are worse off following the agreement, the second condition of Article 81(3) is not fulfilled.[103]

No substantial elimination of competition

The final condition is a catch-all provision which may stop agreements that would remove competition from a market. As the Guidelines put it, 'the protection of rivalry and the competitive process is given priority over potentially pro-competitive efficiency gains which could result from restrictive agreements'.[104] It is likely that agreements which substantially eliminate competition would have fallen at an earlier stage of the deliberations under Art 81(3), though, in some circumstances, this condition posed problems for the Commission under Regulation 17. This was the case where the Commission was inclined to grant an exemption but where it was difficult to show that some competition would remain on the market. The Commission considered this issue in *Synthetic Fibres*.[105] A crisis cartel was organised to reduce production levels in the fibres market. The cartel involved most of the market operators but it was argued that competition from other types of fibre would retain a level of competition. Many considered the Commission arguments not to be particularly convincing in this case. Under the modernised system it is unlikely that other national authorities will be given this type of latitude.

Block exemptions

The main Commission weapon, under Regulation 17, in the struggle to control its exemption workload was the adoption of Block Exemption Regulations. Block exemptions differed from individual exemptions in that they exempted a class of agreements automatically without formal intervention by and approval from the Commission. Even though the Commission's notification burden has been removed by Regulation 1/2003, the role of block exemptions remains vital. The Regulations create 'safe harbours' for the parties to common types of agreement. The parties know that if they bring their agreement within the terms of the block exemption it will be safe from challenge under Art 81. Before the Commission may adopt a Block

---

103 Guidelines, at para 85.
104 Guidelines, at para 105.
105 Commission Decision 84/380/EEC, OJ 1984, L207/17.

Exemption Regulation it must be given authority by Council.[106] Once a block exemption is in place a large number of common business agreements can be assured of validity without the parties having to individually assess their agreements under Art 81(1) and (3).

Block exemptions have been adopted for the following types of agreement: vertical agreements,[107] specialisation,[108] research and development,[109] motor vehicle distribution,[110] technology transfer,[111] and insurance agreements.[112] The way in which the block exemptions operate has been largely overhauled since the mid-1990s. The details of the block exemptions are quite technical and therefore will not be discussed fully here. A more detailed discussion of the Vertical Agreements Regulation is contained later in this chapter. The format of all 'new-style' Regulations is basically similar. Although many of the Regulations are quite long the central provisions are relatively short. The bulk of each Regulation deals with specialist areas which require more detailed consideration.

The format of a 'traditional style' block exemption regulation has now been largely replaced, but it is useful to briefly outline the format in order to understand the move towards the new style Regulations. The first section of a traditional block exemption outlined which agreements fell within the Regulation. That section was phrased in a general manner, describing the type of agreement intended to benefit from the exemption. The second section contained what was known as the 'white list'. This was a list of terms common in agreements which did not fall within the prohibition in Art 81(1). The list was included for the purpose of certainty as, in some circumstances, it may have been possible that those terms could have fallen within the prohibition.

106 For example, Regulation 19/65/EEC on application of Art 85 (3) of the Treaty to certain categories of agreements and concerted practices, OJ 1965, Spec Ed 35.
107 Regulation 2790/1999/EC on the application of Art 81(3) of the Treaty to categories of vertical agreements and concerted practices, OJ 1999, L336/21; [2000] 4 CMLR 398. See, also, Commission Notice, Guidelines on vertical restraints, OJ 2000, C291/1; [2000] 5 CMLR 1074.
108 Regulation 2658/2000/EC on the application of Art 81(3) of the Treaty to categories of specialisation agreements, OJ 2000, L304/3. See, also, Commission Notice, Guidelines on the applicability of Art 81 of the EC Treaty to horizontal co-operation agreements, OJ 2001, C3/2.
109 Regulation 2659/2000/EC on the application of Art 81(3) of the Treaty to categories of research and development agreements, OJ 2000, L304/7. See, also, Commission Notice, Guidelines on the applicability of Art 81 of the EC Treaty to horizontal co-operation agreements, OJ 2001, C3/2.
110 Regulation 1400/2002/EC on the application of Art 81(3) of the Treaty to categories of vertical agreements and concerted practices in the motor vehicle sector, OJ 2002, L203/30.
111 Regulation 772/2004/EC on the application of Art 81(3) of the Treaty to categories of technology transfer agreements, OJ 2004, L123/11.
112 Regulation 358/2003/EC on the application of Art 81(3) of the Treaty to certain categories of agreements, decisions and concerted practices in the insurance sector, OJ 2003, L53/8.

The third section contained the 'grey list'.[113] These were terms which normally fell within the Art 81(1) prohibition but which were exempted under the Regulation. These were the typical terms which one would expect to see in an agreement of the type covered by the Regulation. One of the most important sections of a traditional block exemption was the 'black list'. This contained the terms which, if included in an agreement, would result in that agreement losing the benefit of the block exemption. Due to the restrictive nature of the terms, their inclusion in exempted agreements was prohibited. If such a term was to be included in an agreement, an individual exemption should have been sought, but was unlikely to have been granted. A common criticism of the traditional block exemptions was that they forced parties into very narrow forms of agreement, the block exemption, in effect, providing a standard form agreement.

An important development in block exemptions was the introduction of the first 'new-style' Regulation in 1999 when the Commission adopted the Vertical Agreements Regulation.[114] The Vertical Agreements Regulation is discussed in detail below and epitomises the new approach. Rather than a white and grey list, the Regulation creates an 'umbrella' exemption for all vertical agreements that are not covered by other block exemptions and where the lead party[115] has a market share of less than 30%. A form of black list is retained in that the benefit of the exemption will be removed if the agreement contains any of the 'hard core' restraints, such as maximum price-fixing or certain territorial restrictions. A more flexible exemption system, which does not concentrate on a clause by clause examination of each agreement, has been created. Following the adoption of the Vertical Agreements Regulation, a process of reform was undertaken in which the other block exemptions were transformed to reflect the new style, for instance the revised Technology Transfer Regulation in 2004.[116]

The introduction of the new-style Regulations indicates the extent to which the Commission has recognised industry's concerns about the lack of flexibility in traditional block exemptions. The problems of formalism and flexibility were discussed at length in the consultation process which led to the adoption of the Vertical Agreements Regulation.[117] The use of market share thresholds to allow for increased flexibility has always been controversial. The calculation of market share is a potentially complex problem, which creates

---

113 In some of the oldest Regulations the white and grey lists were combined into a single white list. Latter regulations introduced the grey list to differentiate between those terms exempted and those which were not normally prohibited.

114 Regulation 2790/99/EC, OJ 1999, L336/21; [2000] 4 CMLR 398.

115 It may be the seller or buyer, depending on the nature of the agreement.

116 Regulation 772/2004/EC on the application of Art 81(3) of the Treaty to categories of technology transfer agreements, OJ 2004, L123/11.

117 See, for example, the Green Paper on vertical restraints in EC competition policy C(96) 721 final, and the follow-up Commission communication, OJ 1998, C365/3.

uncertainty in many areas, but it would appear that a consensus has been reached and that it is one of the most practicable ways to move forward. A similar approach has now been adopted in all the other block exemptions and the *de minimis* notice.[118]

The Commission's radical reforms in Regulation 1/2003,[119] as discussed in Chapter 2, also move forward the discussion of block exemptions. The exception in Art 81(3) is now directly applicable and any agreement that falls within its terms is excepted from the prohibition without the need for notification. The position of block exemptions under such a system is interesting. The Commission intends to continue to utilise 'new-style' wider block exemptions under the directly applicable system to ensure that the legal certainty offered by block exemptions is retained. While the block exemptions will be useful for organisations planning agreements it is clear that block exemptions will not be the only way that parties could seek clearance. Even if an agreement falls outside a block exemption it will still be possible to benefit from the exception in Art 81(3) as a matter of course. It will be interesting to see whether the national courts are willing to clear agreements that fall outside the block exemptions but where the parties argue that the agreement falls within the terms of Art 81(3); however, it is questionable whether the courts will be quick to approve agreements containing a block exemption's black list terms.

Article 81 and the national courts

As Art 81 is directly effective it has an important impact on national courts. Under Regulation 17 the concurrent jurisdiction of the national courts and the Commission resulted in several problems, especially where a dispute over an agreement came before the national courts and the agreement had been notified to the Commission. As the national courts could not apply Art 81(3) they had difficulty dealing with such cases. The majority of those problems have been resolved by the introduction of Regulation 1/2003 and the direct applicability of Art 81(3). However, some problems may still occur where the Commission or an NCA is investigating a potential breach of the prohibition and the matter also comes before the courts in a domestic dispute. The Commission has issued guidance to the national courts as part of the 'modernisation package'.[120] The guidance states that where the Commission is dealing with a matter that comes before a national court the court should ensure that

---

118 Commission Notice on agreements of minor importance which do not appreciably restrict competition under Art 81(1) of the Treaty establishing the European Community (*de minimis*), OJ 2001, C368/13.

119 Proposal for a Council Regulation on the implementation of the rules on competition laid down in Arts 81 and 82 of the Treaty, C(2000) 582, OJ 2000, C365/284.

120 Commission Notice on the co-operation between the Commission and the courts of the EU Member States in the application of Arts 81 and 82 EC, OJ 2004, C101/54.

it does not adopt a decision that would conflict with the decision contemplated by the Commission. The national court may, therefore, wish to stay its proceedings until the Commission has reached its decision.[121] If a Commission decision has been adopted the courts cannot make a decision contrary to the Commission decision without referring a question to the Court under Art 234 EC.[122] While it is hoped that domestic litigation will now be less problematic, the *Crehan* litigation indicates the number of problems which may be encountered.[123] As many of the questions concerning the uniform application of the law are common between Art 81 and 82 EC these issues are dealt with more fully in Chapter 2.

Introduction to UK controls on anti-competitive agreements

This section will focus on the Competition Act 1998 which repealed the restrictive trade practices legislation of 1976 and set out a new prohibition on anti-competitive agreements, the 'Chapter I prohibition', modelled largely on Art 81. However, it is instructive to consider the structure and nature of the legislation it replaced in order to understand the rationale for reform and basis for introducing the new rules.

The 1976 Restrictive Trade Practices legislation

The principal, pre-1998, legislation was the Restrictive Trade Practices Act (RTPA) 1976 which, together with the Resale Prices Act 1976, consolidated earlier UK legislation. After the enactment of the Fair Trading Act 1973, the Director General of Fair Trading (DGFT) was given the functions of the Registrar under the existing restrictive trade practices legislation, and those functions were continued when the RTPA 1976 was introduced. The formalistic style of the RTPA 1976 was one of the most significant aspects of the legislation, as the Act's provisions relied on the technical form of an agreement in order for an agreement to be registrable. This aspect was criticised and often led to very technical arguments as to which types of restrictions in agreements were covered by the legislation. If parties failed to register a registrable agreement it was rendered void.

The purpose of the restrictive practices legislation was to prevent agreements that were anti-competitive and against the public interest. The basic

---

121 Ibid, at para 12.
122 Although the issue is potentially more problematic where it is not the same agreement and parties under scrutiny. See *Masterfoods Ltd v HB Ice Cream* [2001] 4 CMLR 14; cf *Crehan v Inntrepreneur Pub Co (CPC)* [2004] EWCA Civ 637, [2004] EuLR 693.
123 For the culmination of the lengthy saga see, *Crehan v Inntrepreneur Pub Co (CPC)* [2006] UKHL 38, [2007] 1 AC 333, [2006] 4 All ER 465.

problem was to clarify what constituted an agreement, or looser form of collaboration, which would be caught by the legislation. There was also difficulty regarding the gathering of evidence to prove any informal anti-competitive collaboration. If firms engage in conspiracy it is most likely that they will seek to destroy or hide direct evidence of any meetings or plans. It was the duty of the DGFT to register registrable agreements and, in most cases,[124] to take proceedings before the Restrictive Practices Court (RPC) to determine if the agreement was in the public interest. If the RPC found the relevant restrictions to be contrary to the public interest it would make an appropriate declaration and those restrictions would be void. The RPC also had power to make orders prohibiting parties from giving effect to the void restrictions or from making an 'agreement to the like effect'. Usually the RPC would accept undertakings from parties, though if the parties breached either an order or an undertaking such a breach constituted contempt of court and the parties were liable to heavy fines. This was clearly demonstrated in the ruling of the House of Lords in the *Pioneer Concrete* case, a case which involved a cartel in the market for ready-mixed concrete.[125] The House of Lords held that a company would find itself in contempt of an existing injunction if one of its employees entered into an agreement in the course of their employment, even if higher management knew nothing about the employee's actions. The *Pioneer Concrete* case clearly increased the deterrent effect of the 1976 Act. Accordingly, corporate compliance schemes were required to be even more vigilant. The House of Lords also confirmed the possibility of the ultimate sanction – imprisonment – for contempt of court. The possibility of imprisonment was expected to act as a greater deterrent against both the employees and the directors who constituted the directing mind or will of the company.

The 1976 Act was partially successful in dealing with restrictive trade practices. In the 1990s the DGFT stepped up the campaign to remove cartels, and their pernicious effects on the economy, by establishing a cartels task force within the Office for Fair Trading (OFT) in 1994. Nonetheless, the evidence that many cartels still operated without detection was one of the reasons for reform proposals which addressed the lack of sanctions under the legislation. There was also criticism of the limited investigation powers afforded to the DGFT. However, an examination of the DGFT's record demonstrated that the 1976 Act did catch a number of cartels operating in the UK. Nonetheless, the DGFT remained adamant that new powers of investigation and power to

---

124 Subject to s 21 of the RTPA 1976.
125 *Re Supply of Ready Mixed Concrete (No 2); DGFT v Pioneer Concrete (UK) Ltd and Another* [1995] 1 All ER 135, in which the House of Lords overruled earlier case law of the Court of Appeal in *Re Supply of Ready Mixed Concrete (No 1); DGFT v Smiths Concrete Ltd* [1991] 4 All ER 150. See Robertson, A, 'Corporate liability for contempt of court under the Restrictive Trade Practices Act 1976' [1995] ECLR 196.

penalise companies for involvement in cartels were necessary to enhance the OFT's ability to deal effectively with cartels.

Reform of UK restrictive trade practice laws

A Green Paper, *Review of Restrictive Trade Practices Policy*,[126] assessed the operation of the RTPA 1976 and highlighted a number of weaknesses and disadvantages resulting from the system under that legislation. In particular, it identified major criticisms, such as the lack of sufficient investigative powers, the absence of effective sanctions, the failure to catch certain significant agreements, particularly vertical restraints, and the complexity and over-technical nature of the legislation. The Green Paper recommended the adoption of a prohibition system modelled on Art 81, and based on the effects of anti-competitive agreements rather than on the form of anti-competitive agreement. The main proposal in the subsequent White Paper, *Opening Markets: New Policy on Restrictive Trade Practices*,[127] was to replace the existing legislation with a prohibition similar to the provisions of Art 81. Following the publication of the White Paper, the Government declared itself to be committed to implementing the proposed reforms and it reaffirmed this commitment on a number of subsequent occasions although there were no further significant developments until 1996.[128] The Conservative Government decided, in 1996, to finally introduce legislation to reform UK competition law and published a Department of Trade and Industry (DTI) consultation document followed by an explanatory document and draft Bill[129] which also proposed the replacement of the 1976 Acts with a prohibition on anti-competitive agreements, based on Art 81. Following the 1997 election the new Labour Government almost immediately published a new explanatory document and draft Bill, the latter forming the basis of the Competition Act 1998.[130]

---

126 Cm 331, 1988.
127 Cm 727, 1989.
128 See Robertson, A, 'Recent developments in UK law' [1997] JBL 358.
129 Department of Trade and Industry, *Tackling Cartels and the Abuse of Market Power: Implementing the Government's Policy for Competition Law Reform, a Consultation Document*, March 1996, London: DTI and *Tackling Cartels and the Abuse of Market Power: A Draft Bill, an Explanatory Document*, August 1996, London: DTI. See, also, Robertson, A, 'The reform of UK competition law – again?' [1996] ECLR 210; and Rose, S, 'Tackling cartels: the Green Paper proposal for implementing the Government's policy on restrictive trade practices' [1996] ECLR 384.
130 Department of Trade and Industry, *A Prohibition Approach to Anti-Competitive Agreements and Abuse of a Dominant Position: Draft Bill*, August 1997, London: DTI. The subsequent Bill, which had its first reading in the House of Lords on 15 October 1997, was amended in certain respects from the original draft Bill. See Peretz, G, 'Detection and deterrence of secret cartels under the UK Competition Bill' [1998] ECLR 145.

The Competition Act 1998

The Chapter I prohibition – an outline

Part I of the Act introduces two new prohibitions based on Arts 81 and 82 EC. These are known as the Chapter I and Chapter II prohibitions. The Chapter I prohibition is in respect of agreements, decisions and concerted practices, between or by undertakings or associations of undertakings, which are implemented in the UK and the object or effect of which is the prevention, restriction or distortion of competition in the UK. The Chapter I prohibition is in s 2 of the Act, which sets out virtually identical provisions to those in Art 81. The principal difference is that s 2 refers to agreements, etc, which are implemented and affect trade in the UK. Consistency of interpretation with Community law, Art 81 in this context, is ensured by s 60 of the Act. This provides that the determination of any questions under the prohibitions should be consistent with the treatment of corresponding questions arising under Community law. Section 60 ensures that Community case law, as to what types of agreement are caught by the Chapter I prohibition, will be followed to the extent that it is relevant in a national context. It is also clear, from DGFT and OFT decisions and in judgments of the Competition Appeal Tribunal (CAT), that Community case law underpins the interpretation of the domestic prohibition.

Chapter III of the 1998 Act makes provision for the investigation and enforcement of the Chapter I and II prohibitions. As noted in Chapter 2, the OFT's key role of enforcing and applying the new regime has been transferred to the newly constituted OFT by s 2 of the Enterprise Act 2002. Section 25 of the 1998 Act provides that the OFT may conduct an investigation upon reasonable suspicion that the prohibition has been infringed. The powers of investigation provided under ss 26–29 are similar to those powers afforded to the Commission under Arts 18–21 of Regulation 1/2003.[131] Similarly, the OFT is required under s 31 to give persons affected by a proposed decision on whether the prohibition has been infringed an opportunity to make representations; this is effected by a notice issued under Rule 7 of the OFT's rules.[132] The OFT may make interim measures under s 35, and is empowered to require conduct in breach of the prohibition to be modified or terminated.[133] Section 36 allows the imposition of a fine of up to 10% of the worldwide turnover of an undertaking whose conduct infringes the Chapter I prohibition. Fines are imposed in accordance with the Guidance, published as required under s 38 of the 1998 Act, on the determination of the appropriate level of

---

131 Sections 42–44 of the 1998 Act create certain offences in relation to the obstruction of the OFT's information gathering tasks under these provisions.

132 The Competition Act 1998 (Office of Fair Trading's Rules) Order 2004, SI 2004/2751 previously Rule 14 under The Competition Act 1998 (Director's Rules) Order 2000, SI 2000/293.

133 Under s 33. Section 34 provides that this may be enforced by a court order.

fines.[134] There is a detailed discussion, in Chapter 2, on the fining policy and practice under the 1998 Act. 'Small agreements' are immune from the imposition of penalties for breach of the prohibition.[135] Chapter V of Pt I of the Act contains a variety of provisions, for instance, enabling rules to be made about procedural matters under Pt I of the Act (the 'OFT's rules'), restricting the disclosure of information obtained under the Act by ss 55–56,[136] providing, under ss 58 and 58A, for findings of fact by the OFT to be binding, and findings of infringements to be relied upon in subsequent actions for damages.

The CAT, established by s 12 and Sched 2 to the Enterprise Act 2002, acts as an appeals tribunal in relation to decisions taken in respect of the prohibition. The mechanism for appeals is regulated by Sched 8 to the 1998 Act. Third parties with a sufficient interest may also appeal. CAT judgments are available on its website.[137]

Further appeals against CAT judgments may be made on a point of law to the Court of Appeal, Court of Session in Scotland or Court of Appeal in Northern Ireland in respect of England and Wales, Scotland and Northern Ireland, respectively.

The operation of the prohibition

Harmonisation and the Guidelines

Section 60(1) of the 1998 Act provides that:

> The purpose of this section is to ensure that so far as is possible (having regard to any relevant differences between the provisions concerned), questions arising under this Part in relation to competition within the United Kingdom are dealt with in a manner which is consistent with the treatment of corresponding questions arising in Community law in relation to competition within the Community.

---

134 See Guidance as to the appropriate level of a penalty, OFT 423, and discussion in Chapter 2. Section 52 requires publication of general information and advice about enforcement of the prohibition and there are a number of guidelines available on the OFT website. A number of these Guidelines were revised during 2004 to include reference to the new relationship between Arts 81 and 82 and domestic competition law, the requirement on the OFT to apply the former following the introduction of Regulation 1/2003, and to reflect changes introduced to domestic law to ensure greater harmony between the application of the domestic prohibitions and Arts 81 and 82. In addition, the OFT has issued a Guideline on the modernisation regulation and the application of Arts 81 and 82 by the OFT, 'Modernisation', OFT 442.

135 Competition Act 1998 (Small Agreements and Conduct of Minor Significance) Regulations 2000, SI 2000/262.

136 Section 56 of the Competition Act 1998 restricts the disclosure of types of confidential information.

137 At www.catribunal.org.uk.

The introduction of the new Chapter I prohibition was intended to harmonise domestic law with Community law. Thus, s 2 replicated the Art 81 model and was reinforced by the requirement, under s 60, to interpret the prohibition consistently with Community law. The difficulties in translating the Community provision into UK law were clear. Indeed, s 60 explicitly notes that interpretation under the Act is to have 'regard to any relevant differences' between the national and Community provision.[138] In addition, the Act was based on the Community model that was in use at the time when the Community was considering reform which has now been implemented abolishing the system of notification and exemption. The notification and exemption system introduced by the 1998 Act was novel for the UK, but was short-lived; the OFT's involvement in the grant of individual exemptions has been removed in order to align UK law with Community law post-Regulation 1/2003.[139] The substantive treatment of cartels has changed little through the introduction of the 1998 Act. The crucial changes were in terms of the enhanced investigatory and enforcement powers. Cartels, accepted as the most heinous form of competition law 'crime', will not be treated substantively differently than prior to the Act, but their detection will be facilitated through the enhanced powers, including the leniency programme available to the OFT, as evidenced, for instance, by the cartel finding in *Arriva plc/FirstGroup plc*. However, certain horizontal agreements may enjoy new status following the introduction of the Act, either by falling outside the Art 81 prohibition[140] or by being eligible for exemption. For instance, indirectly, through the parallel exemption system in s 10, certain forms of horizontal agreement, such as research & development and specialisation agreements, may be exempted. The OFT produced some helpful Guidelines on the application of the prohibition, for instance, 'Article 81 and the Chapter I Prohibition'.[141] The Guidelines provide an overview of Community jurisprudence as it stands to be applied by the UK authorities. Following the introduction of Regulation 1/2003, s 52 of the Act was amended to require the OFT to publish, as soon as practicable after 1 May 2004, advice and information about the application and enforcement of Arts 81(1) and 82. Accordingly, a number of the Guidelines were revised during 2004 to include reference to the new relationship between Arts 81 and 82 and domestic competition law, the requirement on the national authorities to apply Arts 81 and 82, and to reflect changes introduced to ensure greater harmony between

---

138 As discussed more fully by Middleton, K, Chapter 2, 'Harmonisation with Community law – the Euro clause', in Rodger, BJ and MacCulloch, A (eds), *The UK Competition Act: A New Era for UK Competition Law*, 2000, Oxford: Hart.

139 See, in particular, paras 2 and 9 of Sched 1 to the Competition Act 1998 and Other Enactments (Amendment) Regulations 2004, SI 2004/1261.

140 See, for instance, Commission Notice, Guidelines on the applicability of Art 81 of the EC Treaty to horizontal co-operation agreements, OJ 2001, C3/2.

141 OFT 401.

the application of the domestic prohibitions and Arts 81 and 82. In addition, the OFT issued a general Guideline on the modernisation Regulation and the application of Arts 81 and 82 by the OFT.[142]

In relation to vertical agreements the justification for harmonising domestic law with Community rules on anti-competitive agreements was initially ignored and a different approach altogether was adopted; except for the prohibition on resale price maintenance which has been a high-profile feature of recent OFT enforcement activity. More generally, it was apparent that Community rules surrounding the control of agreements were influenced to a greater extent by the Community's market integration goal than the rules on control of dominant undertakings. The distinctive approach to vertical restraints adopted under the Act was illustrated in the OFT's Guideline, 'Vertical agreements and restraints',[143] which outlined the initial treatment of vertical restraints under the Competition Act 1998 (Land and Vertical Agreements Exclusion) Order 2000.[144] Following the Community law's modernisation programme, as discussed more fully below, the DTI decided to modify the UK's original approach to vertical restraints by repealing the exclusion order to ensure closer alignment with Community law.[145]

Agreements and concerted practices

Like Art 81(1), s 2 prohibits certain agreements, decisions of associations and concerted practices; it also includes an indicative list of types of agreement which may be covered. Each of the terms used in Art 81 – agreements, decisions of associations and concerted practices – has a separate definition, but there is considerable overlap between them. It is, therefore, not crucial that an 'agreement' is identifiable, so long as it is demonstrable that some form of collusion, falling within the concept of 'concerted practice', has occurred.[146] The concept of agreement is not restricted to legally binding and enforceable agreements as this would make evasion of the prohibition very simple. Article 81 also deals with the grouping of organisations through trade or professional associations. The term 'concerted practice' has been given a particularly broad definition. There is no simple way to define exactly where an agreement stops and a concerted practice begins, although a concerted

---

142 Modernisation, OFT 442.
143 OFT 419.
144 SI 2000/310.
145 DTI, 'Public consultation on the Government's proposals for exclusions and exemptions from the Competition Act 1998 in light of Regulation 1/2003 EC', 17 June 2003. See the Competition Act 1998 (Land Agreements Exclusion and Revocation) Order 2004, SI 2004/1260, and the Guideline, 'Vertical agreements', OFT 419.
146 The European Court discussed the overlap between 'concerted practices' and 'agreements' in Case C-49/92P *Commission v Anic Partecipazioni SpA* [1999] ECR I-4125.

practice is evidently a looser form of 'agreement' which involves some form of understanding or collaboration.[147]

Effect on competition and appreciability

Section 2 mirrors Art 81(1) by prohibiting agreements, etc, which 'have as their object or effect the prevention, restriction or distortion of competition'. What constitutes such an effect on competition has been at the core of the prolonged Community debate on vertical agreements, which are discussed in more detail below. Market analysis is now crucial when considering the effect of an agreement;[148] certain restrictions will be allowed as they are 'necessary' for the commercial agreement to proceed, although, in the early years of the Community competition system, the Commission and the Court gave the 'effect' requirement a very broad interpretation, catching many agreements that appeared to be restrictions on conduct rather than of competition.

The concept of the appreciability of the effect on competition is crucial in delimiting the scope of the prohibition, although no express criterion of appreciability was included in s 2. The 'Article 81 and the Chapter I prohibition'[149] Guideline confirms that the concept of appreciability follows established Community jurisprudence.[150] When applying the principle of appreciability the OFT reserves the power to find that an agreement does not have an appreciable effect on competition even where Community thresholds are exceeded.[151] However, appreciability is irrelevant where the agreement involves price-fixing or market sharing, imposes minimum resale prices, or forms part of a network of agreements with cumulative effects.

Extra-territoriality

Section 2(3) states that the prohibition only applies 'if the agreement, decision or practice is, or is intended to be, implemented, in the United Kingdom'. There is no equivalent explicit provision setting out a territorial limitation on the effect of the prohibition in Art 81. The form of words adopted in the

---

147 See 'Article 81 and Chapter I prohibition', OFT 401, paras 2.12–2.14. See, for instance, *Apex Asphalt and Paving Co Limited v OFT* [2005] CAT 4, and *Argos, Littlewoods and JJB v OFT* [2006] EWCA Civ 1318 on appeal from [2004] CAT 24, [2005] CAT 13, [2004] CAT 17 [2005] CAT 22, as considered in further detail in Chapter 5.

148 See Case 234/89 *Delimitis v Henniger Bräu* [1991] ECR I-935; [1992] 5 CMLR 210. See now, also, Commission Notice, Guidelines on vertical restraints, OJ 2000, C291/1; [2000] 5 CMLR 1074.

149 OFT 401.

150 See Commission Notice on agreements of minor importance which do not appreciably restrict competition under Art 81(1) of the Treaty establishing the European Community (*de minimis*), OJ 2001, C368/7.

151 OFT 401, at para 2.28. Cf the OFT's original version of the Guidance, 'The Chapter I prohibition', which had a higher threshold than the Community.

provision replicates the European Court's test of 'implementation' as set out in *Wood Pulp* and maintains this test for the future.[152] However, the line between implementation and effects is not particularly clear and the adoption of the term specifically from Community jurisprudence suggests that UK competition authorities will be required by s 60 to follow the line of authorities about implementation.[153]

Voidness and private litigation

Section 2(4) provides that '[a]ny agreement or decision which is prohibited by subsection (1) is void'. The European Court has confirmed that it is only those elements of an agreement that are prohibited under Art 81 that are void.[154] Ultimately, it is a matter of the general law of contract applicable in England and Wales, Scotland and Northern Ireland as to whether or not the offending provisions are severable from the agreement and the remaining agreement is enforceable. In recent years there has been a noticeable increase in case law, before the English courts, involving Art 81 and the question of remedies, particularly in relation to unjust enrichment arising out of void and illegal contracts.[155] The Court has considered, to an extent, in *Courage v Crehan*, whether Community law requires appropriate remedies for breach of competition law to be made available by the courts; this issue is discussed more fully in Chapter 2. The development of remedies under Community law is important for the 1998 Act, given that the s 60 consistency requirement also applies to decisions as to 'the civil liability of an undertaking for harm caused by its infringement of Community law'.[156]

Notification, exemption and harmonisation

When the 1998 Act was introduced, ss 12–16 of Chapter I made provision for a person to make notification, in accordance with the procedure provided in Sched 5, in respect of conduct which may infringe the prohibition. Section 14 provided for notification of a decision as to whether the prohibition had been infringed and whether or not the agreement was likely to be exempt. Where an agreement had been notified, the OFT had the power, under s 4, to grant individual exemptions to agreements which met the appropriate criteria specified in s 9. Accordingly, parties could notify agreements for negative clearance or exemption as under Community law prior to Regulation 1/2003.

---

152 Cases C-89, 104, 114, 116, 117 and 125–29/85 *A Ahlstrom Oy v Commission* [1988] ECR 5193; [1988] 4 CMLR 901.

153 Community law appears to developing in a different direction. See, for instance, Case T-102/96 *Gencor v Commission* [1999] II-ECR 753.

154 Case 56/65 *STM v Maschinenbau Ulm* [1966] ECR 235; [1966] CMLR 357.

155 See *Gibbs Mew plc v Gemmell* [1998] EuLR 588, CA.

156 Competition Act 1998, s 60(6)(b).

However, in light of the adoption of Regulation 1/2003, the Government decided, as it was empowered to do by s 209 of the Enterprise Act 2002, to remove the notification and individual exemption system which existed under the Competition Act.[157] The OFT could issue informal guidance but this has been replaced by a system of nonbinding opinions in cases raising novel or unresolved questions of law.[158] The OFT now has the power to accept binding commitments in Chapter I and II cases, and Art 81 and 82 cases.[159] As in the Community system, block exemption orders may be introduced under s 6 of the 1998 Act. Only one block exemption order has been introduced to date, the Competition Act (Public Transport Ticketing Scheme Block Exemption) Order 2001, which exempts public transport ticketing schemes which meet the Order's requirements.[160] Agreements are also exempted from the Chapter I prohibition, under s 10 of the 1998 Act, where they fall within a block exemption Regulation or an Art 10 Decision by the Commission, or would do so if they had an effect on interstate trade.

The Chapter I prohibition and vertical agreements

This is a complex issue which was the subject of considerable debate as the Competition Bill was proceeding through Parliament. Under Community law, the European Court established in its first substantive judgment on the competition rules, that Art 81 was capable of applying to both horizontal and vertical agreements, and, furthermore, that Art 81 could apply to restrictions of intra-brand competition as well as to restrictions of inter-brand competition.[161] As a consequence, a very large number of vertical agreements were brought within the scope of Art 81(1), although they could then be eligible for exemption under Art 81(3). Given the aim of harmonisation with Community law, how would the UK deal with vertical agreements under the 1998 Act? This issue will be considered in fuller detail below.

Other exclusions from the prohibition

The 1998 Act excludes the application of the Chapter I prohibition from a number of other areas, some of which will be outlined here. For further

---

157 See, in particular, paras 2 and 9 of Sched 1 to the Competition Act 1998 and Other Enactments (Amendment) Regulations 2004, SI 2004/1261.
158 See Art 81 and the 'Chapter I prohibition', OFT 401, paras 8.1–8.6.
159 See in particular para 18 of Sched 1 to the Competition Act 1998 and Other Enactments (Amendment) Regulations 2004, SI 2004/1261 and Sched 6A to the Competition Act 1998. See, also, Enforcement, incorporating the Office of Fair Trading's guidance as to the circumstances in which it may be appropriate to accept commitments, OFT 407, Pt 4.
160 As amended by the Competition Act 1998 (Public Transport Ticketing Schemes Block Exemption) (Amendment) Order 2005, SI 2005/3347.
161 Cases 56 and 58/64 *Consten and Grundig v Commission* [1966] ECR 299; [1966] CMLR 418.

detail, reference should be made to Scheds 1–3 to the Act. Schedule 4 to the Act originally excluded a range of designated professional rules from the application of the prohibition, but this exclusion was subsequently repealed by the Enterprise Act 2002.

Land agreements

The Competition Act 1998 (Land and Vertical Agreements Exclusion) Order 2000 excluded any agreement from the scope of the Chapter I prohibition to the extent that it constituted a 'land agreement'. This exclusion is now effected by the Competition Act 1998 (Land Agreements Exclusion and Revocation) Order 2004.[162] An interest in land is defined, in Art 3, as:

> ... any estate, interest, easement, servitude or right in or over land (including any interest or right created by a licence), and in Scotland also includes any interest under a lease and other heritable right in or over land including a heritable security.

It should be noted that there is no analogous exclusion from the Art 81 prohibition and, therefore, land agreements could still be challenged directly if it were possible to show that they had an effect on trade between Member States.

Mergers

Agreements are excluded, under Sched 1, from the Chapter I prohibition to the extent that they give rise to a merger situation within the terms of Pt 3 of the Enterprise Act 2002.[163] The exclusion is automatic and no notification need be made. Thus, where a merger falls within the jurisdiction of the 2002 Act merger system the merger will not usually be subject to dual control under the 1998 Act. Any ancillary restriction that facilitates a merger is also excluded where it is 'directly related and necessary to the implementation of the merger'.[164]

Enforcement: deterrence and compliance

The enhanced investigatory and enforcement powers introduced in Chapter III of the Act make a marked difference to the impact of the new anti-cartel

---

162 The Competition Act 1998 (Land Agreements Exclusion and Revocation) Order 2004, SI 2004/1260, Art 4 replacing the equivalent provision in SI 2000/310, Art 5.
163 This exclusion also applies to the Chapter II prohibition.
164 Competition Act 1998, Sched 1, para 1(2).

law, compared to the previous legislation. On various occasions it has been emphasised that dealing with cartels will be the top priority of the OFT's work. This was highlighted when the OFT organised a conference of international 'cartel busters' from a number of competition authorities from throughout the world.[165] The OFT set up a compliance and education unit in order to drive home the message of the need for compliance with the new prohibition. The unit established a programme of education about the various guidelines published in relation to the Act, together with a number of simple business guides and a video focusing on compliance. OFT officials toured the UK delivering seminars on the significance of the Act in an effort to enhance awareness of the prohibitions.[166] Underlying the compliance initiative is the enhanced deterrent effect of the greater powers of investigation under ss 26–28 of the Act and the ultimate sanction of a fine for companies breaching the prohibitions. The OFT has clearly sought to increase the deterrent power of the legislation by instilling a fear of being caught out under the Act. Copying US and Community enforcement initiatives, the fear factor has been extended to existing and ongoing cartels by the introduction of a leniency programme for whistle-blowers in cartel cases.[167] The leniency programme openly encourages companies to confess to participation in a cartel with a view to being granted immunity from fines or receiving reduced fines. The extent of the reduction is dependent on a range of factors, primarily whether the company is first to come forward to the OFT and the extent of its involvement in the cartel. In its fight against cartels, in the early stages of enforcement of the new prohibition, the OFT emphasised its three-pronged strategy for companies to 'complain, comply or confess'. Cartel enforcement and the application of the OFT leniency policy will be considered in greater detail in Chapter 5.

Practice and case law to date

There is already a considerable body of decisions by the OFT in relation to what is generally regarded as the most heinous type of competition law infringement, the secret cartel, notably in relation to price-fixing and bid-rigging. This will be considered in detail in Chapter 5, together with the application of the UK leniency programme. The following sections will look briefly at developments in assessing whether agreements qualify for exemption and the case-law relating to resale price maintenance.

---

165 OFT Press Release, PN 46/00, 21 November 2000.
166 See OFT Press Release, PN 12/99, 'Low awareness of new Competition Act to be addressed', 19 April 1999.
167 See 'OFT's guidance as to the appropriate amount of a penalty', OFT 423.

Notification/Exemption

When the Act was introduced, OFT officials stressed 'don't notify, complain'; the OFT did not really want to deal with notified agreements under the Act. However, clearly, the two options are not alternatives and there were numerous notifications for exemption under the Act. The OFT maintains a public register of its decisions, although it should be noted that the provisions for notification and exemption by the OFT have now been removed from the Act. Under s 6 of the Act a block exemption was introduced to allow bus and train companies to continue to offer travel cards and through-tickets. The block exemption was introduced with a view to balancing convenience to consumers with the benefits of competition between operators.[168] The first Decision by the DGFT and judgment by the Competition Commission Appeal Tribunal (CCAT) (now the CAT) dealt with a notification in relation to the Chapter I prohibition.

The first Decision was in *General Insurance Standards Council*. On 26 January 2001 the DGFT informed the General Insurance Standards Council (GISC) that the rules notified by the GISC did not infringe the Chapter I prohibition.[169] Members of GISC agree to abide by its rules, which aim to ensure members are competent to carry on general insurance activities and the Members put in place safeguards to protect consumers. The DGFT accepted that the rules were protective of consumers and were unlikely to restrict competition and drive up prices. The rules did not impose considerable entry barriers nor would they appreciably reduce or distort the overall level of competition.[170] This Decision was appealed to the CCAT by a third party. The CCAT judgment extends to 272 paragraphs and is a thorough and convincing analysis of the application of the Chapter I prohibition to the GISC rules, with extensive reference to Community authority where appropriate.[171] The Tribunal looked at s 2(1)(b) of the Act, in combination with s 60, and reviewed the economic and legal background to the case. The concept of appreciability was explored and reference was also made to the 'rule of reason' line of cases in Community law. Accordingly, an appreciable restriction would not fall outside the prohibition merely because it pursues some public interest objective. Given this background, the Tribunal carried out a preliminary analysis of Rule F42 of the GISC rules. In effect, Rule F42 prevented the carrying on of insurance business with intermediaries who

---

168 Competition Act 1998 (Public Transport Ticketing Schemes Block Exemption) Order 2001, SI 2001/319, as amended by the Competition Act 1998 (Public Transport Ticketing Schemes Block Exemption) (Amendment) Order 2005, SI 2005/3347.

169 Notification by the General Insurance Standards Council (GISC), CA 98/1/2001, 24 January 2001.

170 See OFT Press Release, PN 03/01, 26 January 2001.

171 *IRB v DGFT* (1002/2/1/01(IR), *IRB v DGFT* (1003/2/1/01), *ABTA v DGFT* (1004/2/1/01), 17 September 2001.

were not members of the GISC. The effect, therefore, was that it was manda-tory to be a member or an appointed agent of a member; the rule was, therefore, *prima facie* caught by the prohibition as it limited the freedom of the insurer members of GISC to deal with whom they wished. In addition, an important aspect of the freedom for intermediaries is to decide how and in what manner insurance is to be arranged, and mandatory rules on member-ship constitute a significant fetter in this context. The rules applied to more than 85% of insurers active in the UK and such a collective boycott or refusal to supply was an appreciable restriction on freedom. Rule F42 was a hori-zontal agreement among competing undertakings, denying their freedom to deal in an unrestricted manner. The compulsion to join or go out of business appeared, where imposed by the majority of a £27bn industry, to be an appre-ciable restriction. Whether it could be justified was for consideration under s 4 of the Act. Parliament had not taken the GISC rules outside the ambit of the Act and the conclusion was that Rule F42 was within the ambit of the prohibition. The Tribunal withdrew the GISC Decision and remitted for fur-ther investigation the issues of exit levels from the industry and the role of GISC as sole regulator. Nonetheless, GISC subsequently removed Rule F42 and the OFT concluded that, in the absence of this provision, the GISC rules did not infringe the Chapter I prohibition.[172]

The Racecourse Association and BHRB and others v OFT[173] involved two appeals against an OFT decision in April 2004 that the sale of certain media rights infringed the Chapter I prohibition and did not qualify for an individual exemption under s 9. At the time of the dispute the RCA repre-sented the interests of all 59 racecourses in the UK, undertaking marketing, administrative and representational functions for the courses. Each course owner owns the media rights for events at its course or courses, although historically the RCA has negotiated agreements for the exploitation of cer-tain of those rights on behalf of its members, including those for broadcasts to off-course licensed betting offices (LBOs). The BHRB is the governing body of British racing and has a duty to ensure the proper financing of the indus-try. In 2001, a 'Media Rights Agreement' (the MRA), was made between var-ious parties including Attheraces Holdings Limited (Holdings), Attheraces (ATR), the RCA and 49 of the 59 racecourses (the Courses). ATR was a wholly owned subsidiary of Holdings, a joint venture company formed by various broadcasting organisations, and was used to acquire various media rights from the Courses under the MRA, in particular 'the Non-LBO book-making rights', and it was their sale that the OFT held to infringe the prohib-ition. These were picture rights which, in combination with betting rights and data, could be used to allow interactive betting using television or the inter-net. ATR exploited these rights through broadcasting a basic pay-TV channel

172 DGFT Decision CA98/16/2002 *General Insurance Standards Council*, 13 November 2002.
173 [2005] CAT 29.

and running a website, which together allowed the provision of fixed-odds betting services and the placing of pool bets. By ATR's purported termination of the MRA, live British horseracing was no longer available on the channel or website under the arrangements set out by that agreement. The OFT decided that the MRA involved a collective sale of the Non-LBO bookmaking rights by the courses that infringed the prohibition and did not qualify for exemption as it had the effect of appreciably preventing, restricting, or distorting competition in the supply in the UK by increasing the price for these rights. On appeal, the CAT considered the extent to which the collective negotiating or selling of the rights was necessary, taking into account earlier European Court jurisprudence, notably in *Wouters*,[174] and held that arrangements that are necessary 'to achieve a proper commercial objective will not, or may not, constitute an anti-competitive infringement at all'.[175] The CAT concluded that 'the central negotiation in which the Courses engaged was necessary for the achievement both by them and by ATR of the legitimate commercial objective of creating the new product that ATR proposed to exploit for the benefit of itself, the punters, the racecourses and racing generally'.[176] Further, in any event, the OFT had not proved that the MRA resulted in an appreciable increase in the price that would have been paid by ATR.

Resale price maintenance

Probably the greatest publicity has been attracted by enforcement under the Chapter I prohibition in relation to resale price maintenance schemes. It is generally accepted in the European Community that resale price maintenance agreements, where minimum prices are set in vertical relationships, for instance between manufacturer and retailer, are prohibited. However, the *Leegin* judgment of the US Supreme Court, outlined below, advocated a more lenient approach to RPM, which is also reflected in recent academic debate on the issue on the basis that the practice can be pro-competitive by ensuring the provision of pre-sale promotional services and an increase in the number of retail outlets.[177]

Nonetheless, the OFT has frequently condemned RPM mechanisms. In the early case of *John Bruce (UK) Ltd, Fleet Parts Ltd and Truck and Trailer Components*, commercial-vehicle component companies were fined a total of £33,737 for price-fixing, which was in the form of resale price maintenance (RPM) agreements in respect of automatic slack-adjusters, which are

---

174 Case C-309/99 *Wouters v Algemene Raad van de Nederlandse Orde van Advocaten* [2002] ECR I-1577, [2002] 4 CMLR 913.
175 Para 167.
176 Para 175.
177 See Kneepens, M, 'Resale Price Maintenance: Economics Call for a More Balanced Approach' [2007] ECLR 656.

devices for buses, trailers and trucks, sometimes known as 'automatic brake-adjusters'.[178] Evidence of the agreement was partly derived from a private and confidential internal memo dated 2 March 2000, one day after the entry into force of the Chapter I prohibition. The immunity for small agreements under s 39(1) of the Act was inapplicable as price-fixing agreements are excluded from its ambit. Although price-fixing was recognised as a very serious infringement that would normally attract the 10% starting point, special circumstances in this case were recognised – a new product, difficulties in penetrating the market and a small new entrant was involved – which reduced that figure to 5%. This was only a minor case and resulted in an insubstantial fine, but it did send out the message that vertical RPM arrangements were caught by the Chapter I prohibition. That message proved to be important in other, more high-profile, cases; notably *Toys and Games* and *Replica Kits* both outlined below and discussed in Chapter 5.

In March 2003, the DGFT concluded that Lladró Comercial SA, a producer of luxury porcelain and stoneware figurines, and 155 UK retailers had infringed the Chapter I prohibition by entering into bilateral price-fixing agreements.[179] Lladró Comercial SA and the retailers concerned were required to remove the price-fixing clauses from each agreement as appropriate. No financial penalty was imposed in this case because Lladró Comercial had mistakenly relied on a comfort letter issued by DG Competition to the effect that there was no infringement of Article 81(1) as trade between Member States was not substantially affected.

In the *Toys and Games* case, the DGFT adopted a Decision finding that Argos, Littlewoods and Hasbro had been involved in price-fixing agreements in relation to games and toys and in breach of the Chapter I prohibition.[180] Argos was fined £17.28m and Littlewoods £5.37m. Hasbro's fine of £15.59m was reduced to zero under the leniency scheme.[181] It should be noted that following a successful appeal by Argos and Littlewoods, the OFT issued a new Decision to the same effect, replacing its earlier Decision.[182] Prior to this case the DGFT had also imposed a fine of £4.95m on Hasbro in November 2002 for participating in price-fixing agreements with a range of distributors.

178 DGFT Decision CA98/12/2002, Case CP/0717/01, 13 May 2002.
179 Decision of Director General of Fair Trading No. CA98/04/2003, Case CP/0809-01 *Agreements between Lladró Comercial SA and UK retailers fixing the price of porcelain and stoneware figurines*, 31 March 2003.
180 DGFT Decision CA98/2/2003, Case CP/0480-01 *Agreements between Hasbro UK Ltd, Argos Ltd and Littlewoods Ltd Fixing the Price of Hasbro Toys and Games*, 19 February 2003. See, also, OFT Decision CA98/04/2003, Case CP/0809-01 *Agreements between Lladró Comercial SA and UK Retailers Fixing the Price of Porcelain and Stonework Figurines*, 31 March 2003.
181 See Young, G, 'Punishment for toys and games' [2003] Comp LJ 5.
182 OFT Decision CA98/8/2003, Case CP/0480-01 *Agreements between Hasbro UK Ltd, Argos Ltd and Littlewoods Ltd Fixing the Price of Hasbro Toys and Games*, 21 November 2003.

In the *Replica Kits* case, on 1 August 2003, the OFT issued a finding that 10 businesses had been engaging in a practice of price-fixing in the market for replica football kits, specifically those manufactured by Umbro.[183] The businesses were found to be infringing the Chapter I prohibition of the Competition Act 1998. The OFT imposed a total of £18.6m in fines, varying in size among the businesses according to the OFT Guidance, with some businesses qualifying for reductions under the leniency programme. The fines imposed included the following: JJB Sports – £8.373m; Umbro – £6.641m; Manchester United – £1.652m; Allsports – £1.35m; the Football Association – £198,000, reduced to £158,000 under the leniency programme; Blacks – £197,000; Sports Soccer – £123,000; JD Sports – £73,000.

Appeals were lodged by various parties to the CAT in both *Toys and Games* and *Replica Kits*, and although fines were reduced by the CAT in some cases, both the CAT, and ultimately the Court of Appeal, hearing joined appeals by Argos, Littlewoods and JJB Sports, upheld the OFT's findings in liability.[184] Both these cases involved the application of the leniency programme, and although *prima facie* they are RPM infringements, they were held as constituting a concerted practice involving at least three parties. Accordingly, for these reasons, although neither *Toys and Games* nor *Replica Kits* are traditional horizontal cartel price-fixing cases, they will be considered in Chapter 5.

Case law

There have been a number of private disputes in which the prohibitions has been raised by one of the parties. There is a database of court judgments available on the OFT website.[185] For example, in *Suretrack Rail Services Ltd v Infraco JNP Ltd*,[186] it was alleged that the Chapter I prohibition was breached by an anti-competitive agreement stopping the applicant providing railway safety services. The application was dismissed by Laddie J on the basis that the three companies involved were all subsidiaries of the same parent and were not individual undertakings. Accordingly, no 'agreement between undertakings' existed. There have also been a number of follow-on court actions in the UK, in the CAT and the High Court, in relation to the *Vitamins* cartel.

---

183 OFT Decision CA98/06/2003, Case CP/0871/01 *Price-fixing of Replica Football Kit*, 1 August 2003.
184 *Argos, Littlewoods and JJB v OFT* [2006] EWCA Civ 1318 on appeal from [2004] CAT 24, [2005] CAT 13, [2004] CAT 17, [2005] CAT 22.
185 At www.oft.gov.uk/business/uk+competition+court+cases+database/default.htm although it is not comprehensive. See, also, Robertson, A, 'Litigating under the Competition Act 1998: the early case law' [2002] Comp LJ 335.
186 [2002] All ER (D) 261.

Vertical restraints

Vertical agreements are agreements made between undertakings operating at different levels of the same market. A typical example is an agreement between the producer of a product and a distributor. The contractual restrictions employed in vertical agreements, known as vertical restraints, are used, *inter alia*, to facilitate the distribution of goods and services. This part of the chapter will focus on the impact of the competition rules on distribution agreements, in particular on exclusive distribution agreements. We will also look more briefly at exclusive purchasing agreements, referred to recently by the Commission as 'single-branding' agreements. However, it should be noted that there are a variety of types of vertical agreement, including franchising and selective distribution systems, and often a particular vertical agreement may contain a complex mix of different vertical restraints.

The efficient distribution of goods is crucial to the success of a business and the vibrancy of the economy. It is, therefore, important that the legal framework which applies to distribution agreements is clear so that firms may operate their distribution systems efficiently. The Community's treatment, particularly by the Commission, of vertical agreements was criticised for failing to create such a framework. The Commission, aware of the criticisms of its approach, published a Green Paper, *Vertical Restraints*,[187] as part of a consultation process that considered reform in this area and which culminated in the adoption of the Vertical Agreements Regulation[188] (which will be referred to, interchangeably, as 'Regulation 2790' and 'the Vertical Agreements Regulation').

The effects of vertical restraints

There are various potential positive and negative effects of vertical restraints and, although much depends on the format, content and context of the specific restraint, those effects may result from all forms of vertical restraints. The following are the principal considerations which require balancing in any set of competition rules dealing with vertical restraints.[189]

Restriction of intra-brand competition

The difference between inter-brand and intra-brand competition was outlined previously. The former involves competition between the varying brands of different producers, for example, Nike and Adidas sports shoes, and the latter

---

187 C(96) 721 final.
188 Regulation 2790/99/EC on the application of Art 81(3) of the EC Treaty to categories of vertical agreements and concerted practices, OJ 1999, L336/21.
189 The Commission Guidelines on vertical restraints, OJ 2000, C291/1, should be referred to for a fuller discussion of these issues.

concerns competition by retailers or distributors in the sale of a producer's particular brand, for example, between two competing retailers selling Nike sports shoes. Exclusive distribution is a good example of the potential restriction of intra-brand competition. A distributor will be appointed as the sole distributor within a particular territory. The extent of the restriction will depend upon the terms of the agreement. If absolute territorial protection is provided then intra-brand competition will be virtually eliminated, as supplies of the product will only be available to customers from that one distributor. However, if it is possible for another distributor to make passive sales into the territory, that is, without an active marketing campaign, the restriction in intra-brand competition will be reduced. In either case, the main objection to any restriction on intra-brand competition is that it may lead to reduced consumer choice, due to the excessive concentration on brand image, and ultimately higher prices for the consumer of the particular branded product.

Foreclosure of competition

Single-branding commitments imposed upon a distributor, restricting the distributor to the supply of that particular brand, can cause foreclosure of markets by making it more difficult for other producers of competing brand products to find outlets for their particular products. Distribution agreements often contain single-branding obligations and may also, therefore, cause foreclosure of markets.

Compartmentalisation of markets

Exclusive distribution systems directly impose some form of restraint on the free flow of trade. For instance, in the most extreme case of an agreement creating an absolute territorial protection in favour of a distributor of a branded product, no possibility exists for any trade in that product, from other countries, into the restricted territory. This is particularly objectionable in the Community context given the overriding goal of market integration in the application of Community competition law. Indeed, the Community has attempted to strike a balance between the pro-competitive effects of vertical restraints and limitations on cross-border trade necessitated by distribution agreements.

Efficiency gains

Distribution agreements allow a producer to manage the number of outlets that are to be supplied, which enables greater efficiency to be achieved in the overall distribution system. There may be economies of scale in particular forms of distribution, and efficiencies may be gained by the imposition of single-branding commitments.

Increase in inter-brand competition

A distributor may be unwilling to promote a producer's product unless it is granted some form of territorial exclusivity. For a product to compete effectively with other products on the market it will usually require promotion, particularly if it is a new product. Accordingly, exclusive distribution agreements may stimulate inter-brand competition by facilitating the entry of new products on to the market. This will increase inter-brand competition with existing branded products to the ultimate benefit of the consumer.

Free-rider problems

Exclusive distribution may help to prevent one distributor from free-riding on the promotion efforts of another, particularly with new or complex products. An extension of this argument is the 'certification free-rider issue' whereby the supplier seeks to ensure a positive introduction of a new product by restricting its sale to quality retailers; this is common in selective distribution systems. A related factor is known as the 'hold-up problem' whereby exclusivity is required to induce a party to invest in special equipment or training where the investment is relationship specific.

Given these potential pros and cons, there has been a vigorous debate on the merits of vertical restraints, particularly in the US. Proponents of the Chicago school have based their favourable approach to distribution restraints on the free-rider rationale. This rationale suggests that intra-brand protection is necessary to allow a distributor to promote a brand effectively and thereby enhance inter-brand competition.[190] Vertical restraints would only be considered harmful under this broad approach where the parties had market power and, accordingly, inter-brand competition was weak. Bork has even argued that every restraint should be completely lawful on the basis that the only reason for any form of vertical restraint is that it creates efficiencies.[191] Bork has argued that a producer will impose restraints only where it can derive higher profits by increasing sales, and consumers will increase purchases only when the value of any additional services exceeds the additional charge imposed by the distributor. His conclusion is that vertical restraints will only lead to higher profits when customers receive a net benefit. This argument has been challenged on the basis that it fails to discriminate between existing or new consumers and established or new products. For the latter, vertical restraints may have net benefits, but, otherwise, a more hostile

190 See Telser, LG, 'Why should manufacturers want fair trade?' (1960) 3 JL & Econ 86. See, also, Marvel, HP, 'The resale price maintenance controversy: beyond conventional wisdom' (1994) 63 Antitrust LJ 59, pp 69–71.
191 See Bork, R, *The Antitrust Paradox: A Policy at War with Itself*, 1993, Oxford: Maxwell Macmillan, Chapters 14 and 15.

treatment is required.[192] In the Community context the Commission has been criticised in the past for its hostile treatment of vertical restraints and its failure to consider the free-rider rationale.[193] The Commission reviewed the position in its Green Paper on vertical restraints,[194] which led to the 1999 Vertical Agreements Regulation which, in turn, introduced a new more favourable approach to vertical restraints under Community law; the more favourable approach focused on market power and inter-brand competition. Interestingly, some US commentators have suggested that we should be concerned with downstream market power of distributors, and that intra-brand competition remains important.[195] Nonetheless, in 2007, the US Supreme Court overturned the long-established rule, set out in *Dr Miles Medical Co v John D Park & Son co*[196] that RPM was *per se* illegal, and it is now to be assessed according to the rule of reason.[197]

General Commission approach to vertical restraints under Art 81(1)

The crucial issue under Art 81(1) is the determination of what constitutes a 'prevention, restriction or distortion of competition'. Many commentators considered that the Commission interpreted this requirement as being satisfied by a restriction of the economic freedom, or the freedom of action, of the contracting parties to an agreement.[198] This interpretation attracted widespread criticism as such an approach could lead to a variety of undesirable consequences.[199] The Commission approach resulted in a wide interpretation of Art 81(1), subject to the application of the *de minimis* doctrine,[200] leaving

192 Comanor, WS, 'Vertical price-fixing, vertical market restrictions and the new antitrust policy' (1984–85) 98 Harv L Rev 983.

193 See Gyselen, L, 'Vertical restraints in the distribution process: strength and weakness of the free rider rationale under EEC competition law' (1984) 21 CML Rev 647; Hawk, B, 'System failure: vertical restraints and EC competition law' (1995) 32 CML Rev 973; Korah, V, 'EEC competition policy – legal form or economic efficiency?' (1986) 39 CLP 85; and Carlin, F, 'Vertical restraints: time for change?' [1996] ECLR 283.

194 C(96) 721 final.

195 See, for example, Grimes, WS, 'Brand marketing, intrabrand competition, and the multi-brand retailer: the antitrust law of vertical restraints' (1995) 64 Antitrust LJ 83; and Comanor, WS, 'The two economics of vertical restraints' (1992) 21 Sw UL Rev 1265.

196 220 U.S. 373 (1911).

197 *Leegin Creative Leather Products Inc v PSKS Inc.* 127 S.CT. 2705 US (2007).

198 See, for example, Hawk, B, 'System failure: vertical restraints and EC competition law' (1995) 32 CML Rev 973.

199 See, also, Hawk, B, 'The American (antitrust) revolution: lessons for the EEC?' [1988] ECLR 53; Bodoff, J, 'Competition policies of the US and EEC: an overview' [1984] ECLR 51; and Whish, R and Sufrin, B, 'Article 85 and the rule of reason' (1987) 7 Ox YEL 1.

200 Commission Notice on agreements of minor importance which do not appreciably restrict competition under Art 81(1) of the Treaty establishing the European Community, OJ 2001, C368/13.

fuller analysis to the Commission under Art 81(3). Accordingly, under Regulation 17, a considerable number of vertical agreements required notification and exemption under Art 81(3). This formalistic approach, coupled with the Commission's resources problem, meant that very few formal decisions were taken each year, leading to delays and uncertainty for businesses. As the Commission had sole power to grant exemptions, the delays hampered the ability of national courts to deal with disputes involving the purported validity of restrictions in vertical agreements. Finally, the formalistic approach may also have impeded innovative and efficient forms of distribution, as well as other forms of investment, for example, investment through technology licensing arrangements. The Commission's policy in the past of issuing block exemptions for certain types of restraints, such as exclusive distribution, alleviated the situation, although the policy also led to criticisms of 'straitjacketing' companies' commercial strategies. The Vertical Agreements Regulation, discussed further below, has sought to provide a more general solution, under Art 81(3), to vertical agreements. In addition, the Commission has clearly indicated, in its Guidelines on vertical restraints,[201] that its future approach under Art 81(1) will be based on the economic effects of vertical agreements and will focus on agreements where market power is involved or where there is a network of similar agreements potentially foreclosing market access.

Particular types of restriction

The view of the Commission's traditional approach under Art 81(1), outlined in the previous section, is perhaps an oversimplification and it is of more interest to note the attitude of the Community authorities to particular types of restriction. In particular, export bans, both direct and indirect, are considered by both the Commission and Court as being clear infringements of Art 81(1).[202] Similarly, resale price maintenance provisions in vertical agreements are routinely prohibited under Art 81(1).[203] Otherwise, the Court has taken a more flexible approach to the consideration of when there is a 'restriction of competition' under Art 81(1). However, before considering other case law it is necessary to look at the treatment of territorial restrictions in vertical restraints, as these territorial restrictions are very important in a wide range of vertical agreements, particularly exclusive distribution agreements.

---

201 OJ 2000, C291/1; [2000] 5 CMLR 1074.
202 For direct export bans, see Case 19/77 *Miller International Schallplatten GmbH v Commission* [1978] ECR 131; [1978] 2 CMLR 334. Cf Case 262/81 *Coditel II* [1982] ECR 3381; [1983] 1 CMLR 49. For an example of a prohibition of an indirect export ban, see Case 31/85 *ETA Fabriques d'Ebauches v DK Investments SA* [1985] ECR 3933; [1986] 2 CMLR 674.
203 See Case 27/87 *Louis Erauw-Jacquery v La Hesbignonne* [1988] ECR 1919; [1988] 4 CMLR 576. See, also, Case 161/84 *Pronuptia de Paris GmbH v Pronuptia de Paris Irmgard Schillgalis* [1986] ECR 353; [1986] 1 CMLR 414 in which resale price maintenance in a franchise network infringed Art 81(1) and was not capable of exemption.

Territorial restrictions

The starting point is the *Consten and Grundig* case.[204] It involved an agreement between Grundig, a major West German (as then was) manufacturer of electrical and electronic equipment, and Consten, a French distributor. The agreement was a sole or exclusive distributorship for France, and it included three main features:

a   it imposed an obligation on Consten, similar to that imposed on Grundig distributors in other Member States, not to export the contract goods from France;
b   Grundig undertook not to sell directly to anyone in France; and
c   Grundig assigned the rights under the trademark attached to each piece of equipment for sale in France to Consten.

Later, a French company obtained Grundig's products in another Member State and sought to import them to and sell them in France. Consten brought an action to stop the resale of those goods. A complaint was made by the French company to the Commission, which ruled that the contracts intended that Consten be free from competition in the distribution of Grundig products in France and, therefore, the contracts restricted competition within Art 81(1). Furthermore, an exemption would not be granted under Art 81(3) as the absolute territorial protection granted was not indispensable.

On appeal to the Court, it was argued that Art 81 did not apply to vertical agreements. This was rejected by the Court, which stated that competition can also be limited by agreements which restrict competition between one of the parties and any third party. It was also argued by the parties that Art 81 should only apply to restrictions of inter-brand as opposed to intra-brand competition. This argument was also rejected by the Court, although the Court did state that unless the object of the agreement was to restrict competition, an analysis of the effects of the agreement was required. In this case, the Court considered that the object was to restrict competition and further analysis was not required. The Court also confirmed that absolute territorial protection is prohibited under Art 81(1) and that an exemption would not be justified. However, the Court stressed that the Commission should not have prohibited the whole agreement but merely the clauses which created the absolute territorial protection. The clauses providing for exclusive distribution were not necessarily an infringement, although the third aspect, the assignation of the trademark, created absolute territorial protection and was, therefore, prohibited.

Consten and Grundig was a decisive case and the Court sought to achieve a

204 Cases 56 and 58/64 *Etablissement Consten SA and Grundig Verkaufs-GmbH v Commission* [1966] ECR 299; [1966] CMLR 418.

balance by prohibiting absolute territorial protection, which sought to stop any parallel imports of the contract goods, while providing that the provision of territorial exclusivity did not in itself infringe Art 81(1). Nevertheless, the line between legal territorial restrictions and illegal absolute territorial protection has become clouded in subsequent Commission decisions and Court judgments. For instance, in *Van Vliet*[205] an undertaking, given by a producer to its Dutch distributor to prohibit its other distributors from exporting to Holland, was held to be unlawful as the undertaking could result in a partitioning of the market contrary to the fundamental principles of Community law. This judgment apparently signified a shift away from the more lenient approach adopted by the Court in *Consten and Grundig*. Subsequent case law confirmed a more restrictive approach to exclusive distribution agreements; the subsequent cases took the view that the existence of export bans on the distributor constituted the infringement of Art 81(1).[206] The wide ambit of the Art 81(1) prohibition, as construed by the Commission, and also by the Court, after *Consten and Grundig*, has led to repeated calls for reform of the approach to that of a model based on a US style 'rule of reason'. Nonetheless, it should be noted that, even following the recent reform process, the Commission's approach to territorial restrictions appears to have altered little.

US rule of reason

In the US there is a dual approach to the consideration, under s 1 of the Sherman Act, of restrictions in vertical agreements.[207] Some restraints of trade are considered to be illegal *per se* and others are subject to the 'rule of reason' in order to determine whether they are reasonable or unreasonable. The major development in US antitrust law has been the dramatic reduction in restrictions which are subject to the *per se* test, which is now limited, for instance, to horizontal market division and price-fixing; as of 2007 the *per se* test no longer applies to vertical resale price maintenance. Under the *per se* rule, no further inquiry is made into the existence of anti-competitive effects, market power or intent. The rule of reason test, which requires consideration of the impact of the restraint on competitive conditions, is more complex. It now applies to all of vertical restraints and requires a detailed economic analysis of the restraint, market structure and market conditions to assess the restraint's likely pro- and anti-competitive effects. The rule of reason test, inevitably, has increased the complexity of antitrust litigation and reduced its

---

205 Case 25/75 *Van Vliet Kwasten & Ladderfabrieke v Fratelli Dalle Crode* [1975] ECR 1103; [1975] 2 CMLR 549.

206 See, for example, Cases 100–03/80 *SA Musique Diffusion Francaise and Others v Commission (Pioneer)* [1983] ECR 1825; [1983] 3 CMLR 221.

207 See Hawk; Bodoff; and Whish and Sufrin, above fn 199.

certainty and predictability. Nonetheless, a particularly important development in this context was the US Supreme Court decision in *Continental TV Inc v GTE Sylvania*,[208] which confirmed that the rule of reason test should be applied to non-price vertical restraints to assess their legality. Sylvania had decided to limit the number of retail franchises granted, and to restrict each of its brand dealers to sales only at the particular point where it held its franchise. These territorial and customer restrictions were held to be subject to the rule of reason test. The adoption of the rule of reason acts as a significant point of comparison for Community law and since that case, in line with general academic opinion in the US,[209] US authorities have adopted a particularly tolerant approach based primarily on the free-rider rationale to vertical restraints.[210] The *Sylvania* rule of reason test was extended to vertical resale price maintenance by the majority of the Supreme Court in 2007 in *Leegin Creative Leather Products Inc v PSKS Inc*.[211]

The Court and the rule of reason

There has been continued criticism of the Community authorities' treatment of vertical restraints, and calls for the adoption of a US-style rule of reason approach. Although US antitrust law has attempted to provide a more refined formulation of what actually constitutes a restraint of trade, the rule of reason approach can be criticised for its complexity and lack of certainty. In addition, Community law should not necessarily follow US antitrust law because Community law objectives, particularly the creation of the integrated market, are different to US antitrust objectives. Finally, and most importantly, there are significant textual differences between the two sets of laws. The existence of Art 81(3) and the possibility of the prohibition being inapplicable to beneficial agreements means that there is not the same pressure under Art 81(1), compared to the Sherman Act, to delimit what constitutes a 'restriction of competition' within the prohibition alone. Nonetheless, there have been certain important developments, including the introduction of various block exemptions, particularly the recent Vertical Agreements Regulation.[212] In any event, Art 81(1) refers both to agreements which have as their object the restriction of competition and agreements which have the

---

208 433 US 36 (1977).

209 Although see Grimes and Comanor, above fn 195, for alternative perspectives.

210 See, for example, 'Vertical restraints guidelines of the National Association of Attorneys General' (1995) 68 Antitrust & Trade Regulation Report 1706. For an analysis of the complexity of the rule of reason approach in the US context, see Calvani, T, 'Some thoughts on the rule of reason' [2001] 6 ECLR 201.

211 127 S.Ct. 2705 US (2007).

212 See Whish and Sufrin, above fn 199, and Forrester, I and Norall, C, 'The laicisation of Community law, self-help and the rule of reason: how competition law is and could be applied' (1984) 21 CML Rev 11.

effect of restricting competition. Accordingly, the Court has distinguished between types of vertical restraints which are *per se* prohibited by Art 81(1), such as export bans, and other vertical restraints which require an economic analysis of the effects of an agreement, although this is not characterised as a rule of reason approach as such.[213]

In addition to the broader developments in the Court's approach towards ascertaining the market effects of potentially anti-competitive agreements, there has been more specific recognition of the need to adopt a flexible attitude towards vertical restraints. For instance, there is now a body of case law that indicates that selective distribution agreements may escape the prohibition under Art 81(1) on qualitative grounds in order to allow for the maintenance of the brand names. The Court has also decided, in a series of judgments, that restrictions, often known as 'ancillary restraints', which are necessary for the agreement to proceed may not infringe Art 81(1). For instance, in *Remia*[214] the Court ruled that a restriction on a seller not to compete with a business sold with its goodwill does not infringe Art 81(1), provided the restriction is reasonably limited in time and space. Similarly, the result of the judgment in *Pronuptia*[215] is that many provisions in franchises fall outside the Art 81(1) prohibition, where those provisions are necessary to protect intellectual property rights and the common identity of the franchise. Finally, there has been a move, led by the Court, towards a limited rule of reason approach, particularly in relation to licensing arrangements involving intellectual property rights (IPRs) and certain exclusive distribution agreements. The premise acknowledged by the Court is that the parties would not have invested in the promotion of new technology without some form of protection. For example, in *Nungesser*,[216] the Commission's finding that an exclusive licence of plant breeders' rights infringed Art 81(1) was quashed by the Court, as the Commission had failed to consider whether 'open exclusivity' was justifiable on the basis that investment was necessary to develop the product and the German market for it. Nevertheless, absolute territorial protection, or 'closed exclusivity', remains prohibited and the Commission's application of the *Nungesser* principle has been restrictive, emphasising, and thereby limiting, its applicability to the novelty of the product.[217] There has also been limited acceptance of certain territorial restrictions in exclusive distribution agreements.

---

213 See Lasok, KPE, 'Assessing the economic consequences of restrictive agreements: a comment on the *Delimitis* case' [1991] ECLR 194.
214 Case 42/84 *Remia BV and Others v Commission* [1985] ECR 2545; [1987] 1 CMLR 1.
215 Case 161/84 *Pronuptia de Paris GmbH v Pronuptia de Paris Irmgard Schillgalis* [1986] ECR 353; [1986] 1 CMLR 414.
216 Case 258/78 *Nungesser (LC) KG and Kurt Eisele v Commission* [1982] ECR 2015; [1983] 1 CMLR 278.
217 There is, in addition, a Technology Transfer Regulation, Regulation 772/2004/EC, OJ 2004, L123/11.

Article 81(3) – the old Block Exemption Regulation 1983/83

It is instructive to be aware of the weaknesses in Regulation 1983/83, which dealt with exclusive distribution agreements, even though the Regulation has been replaced by the Vertical Agreements Regulation. Regulation 1983/83 was criticised on a number of grounds. It only applied to purely bilateral agreements covering goods for resale, and agreements for services were excluded. It was also criticised for its straitjacketing effect and its concentration on the form of an agreement rather than on its effect. The straitjacketing effect may have discouraged industry from developing innovative forms of distribution, as parties to agreements were required to tailor their agreements to fit within the terms of the Regulation, even though the Regulation did not necessarily reflect commercial reality.

The reform of vertical restraints policy

The Commission published a Green Paper[218] in January 1997 in order to review Community policy on vertical restraints. The Green Paper set out the framework of rules and procedures for dealing with vertical restraints and their strengths and weaknesses, and suggested four possible options for reform, which were to form the focus of a consultation process. One of the principal reasons for undertaking a review of Community policy on vertical restraints was the expiry, on 31 December 1999, of the block exemption Regulations governing exclusive distribution, purchasing agreements and franchising. In the Green Paper the Commission acknowledged the dilemma of vertical restraints. Exclusive arrangements may enhance efficiency and result in cost savings for the consumer, yet they could also lead to weakened competition in relation to the product, which could drive up prices. The risk of entry into a market may be diminished by the protection offered by an exclusive arrangement. Vertical restraints policy also indirectly affects employment which would be bolstered by efficient forms of distribution. These advantages may be outweighed if the distributor was able to exploit its position. The Commission, in the Green Paper, considered that its vertical restraints policy had been 'largely successful' and, although it was clear, for instance, that the Commission would not permit absolute territorial protection to be employed, the Green Paper acknowledged that reform was required, partly to ensure that it was easier to enforce contractual provisions necessary to protect those who must be induced to invest. The Green Paper stressed the importance of market structure and the role of inter-brand competition and suggested a shift in emphasis from intra-brand competition to an analysis focused on inter-brand competition, in which the anti-competitive effects of vertical restraints would only be considered where inter-brand

218 C(96) 721 final.

competition is weak and there were barriers to entry at either producer or distributor level.

Following the Commission's subsequent Communication on the Application of the Community Competition Rules on Vertical Restraints,[219] the existing law was reformed when the Vertical Agreements Regulation was introduced in 1999. In particular, it should be noted that the reform has been introduced in relation to Art 81(3). Nonetheless, the Commission has indicated, in its *Guidelines on Vertical Restraints*, that its future policy under Art 81(1) will also focus on vertical restraints associated with market power.

The Vertical Agreements Regulation

Introduction

Regulation 2790 is a radical change from previous Commission block exemption practice. The black list approach adopted ensures that every type of restraint is permitted unless it is strictly prohibited. Using only a black list increases the flexibility of parties allowing them to adopt agreements which are appropriate for their commercial setting. Flexibility is also ensured by having one umbrella block exemption for all forms of vertical agreements as defined in the Regulation. The belief that the anti-competitive nature of vertical restraints is dependent on a degree of market power is reflected in the safe haven which is created by the Regulation, which sets the market share threshold at 30%. As the Commission noted in Recital 6 of the Regulation:

> Vertical agreements of the category defined in this Regulation can improve economic efficiency within a chain of production or distribution . . . in particular they can lead to a reduction in the transaction and distribution costs of the parties and to an optimisation of their sales and investments levels.

The Regulation entered into force on 1 January 2000 and will expire on 31 May 2010. Regulation 2790 does not apply to vertical agreements falling within the scope of other block exemptions.[220] The following section will provide a brief overview of the key provisions of the Regulation.

---

219 OJ 1998, C365/3; [1999] 4 CMLR 281.

220 This, currently, excludes motor vehicle distribution, Regulation 1400/2002/EC on the application of Art 81(3) of the Treaty to categories of vertical agreements and concerted practices in the motor vehicle sector, OJ 2002, L203/30, and technology transfer agreements, Regulation 772/2004/EC on the application of Art 81(3) of the Treaty to categories of technology transfer agreements, OJ 2004, L123/11.

Vertical agreements

Article 2(1) defines vertical agreements for the purposes of the Regulation as:

> ... agreements or concerted practices entered into between two or more undertakings, each of which operates, for the purposes of the agreement, at a different level of the production or distribution chain, and relating to the conditions under which the parties may purchase, sell or resell certain goods or services.

Many vertical agreements will not infringe Art 81(1) in the first place and will not require exemption under the Regulation; for instance, agreements satisfying the *Delimitis* principle outlined above. For a wide range of other vertical agreements the above definition is certainly more expansive than under previous practice as the definition extends to agreements in relation to intermediate goods and services. However, agreements containing provisions relating to the assignment or use, by the buyer, of IPRs are not to be exempted under Art 2(3) unless those provisions do not constitute the primary object of such agreements. Accordingly, where the agreement is, for instance, a licence of know-how it would fall beyond the scope of the Regulation, although the agreement may be exempted under the Technology Transfer Regulation.[221] Distribution agreements containing the assignment of an IPR, such as a trademark right, would potentially be subject to exemption, where the assignation of the IPR was ancillary to the main object of the agreement; for instance, setting up an efficient distribution system. A further limitation is contained in Art 2(4) which provides that vertical agreements between competing undertakings are not exempted unless they satisfy certain conditions.

Market share threshold

Following the Commission Communication's focus on market power, Art 3 of the Regulation creates a safe haven for all vertical agreements, subject to Art 4, where 'the market share held by the supplier does not exceed 30% of the relevant market on which it sells the contract goods or services'. The use of market shares as a key element of the Regulation's coverage has been criticised as being likely to lead to uncertainty and unpredictability given the difficulties in defining the relevant market and, thereafter, market share. The Commission and Court's jurisprudence over the years should act as a guide and the Commission's 1997 Notice on market definition, considered in Chapter 3, will also provide assistance. Articles 9–11 provide the detailed rules on the calculation of market shares. It should also be noted that, in agreements involving

---

221 Regulation 772/2004/EC on the application of Art 81(3) of the Treaty to categories of technology transfer agreements, OJ 2004, L123/11.

exclusive supply obligations, the relevant market share is that of the buyer in the market in which the buyer purchases the contract goods or services.

Hard core restraints

The 'black list' is provided in Art 4 of the regulation. Article 4 sets out the list of provisions which are prohibited and which will render an agreement not capable of exemption under the Regulation. The following are the two most significant types of hard core restraint in Art 4: resale price maintenance and excessive territorial protection.

Resale price maintenance

Article 4(a) provides that resale price maintenance is considered to be a hard core restriction, whether it is imposed directly by fixing a resale price or indirectly, by fixing discount levels or linking threats of delayed supplies or penalties to the observance of a given price level. This hard core restriction is unobjectionable and most competition law systems prohibit vertical forms of resale price maintenance.

Territorial restrictions

Article 4(b) excludes from the scope of the exemption any 'restriction of the territory into which, or the customers to whom, the buyer may sell the contract goods or services'. This exclusion is predicated upon the Community market-integration goal and the concern over the creation of compartmentalised markets within the Community. Nonetheless, even in *Consten and Grundig*, and in a number of developments since then, notably the exclusive distribution Regulation 1983/83, it has been recognised that some form of territorial exclusivity may be required as an incentive for a distributor to promote a product effectively, even if absolute territorial protection is not allowed. Accordingly, there are exceptions to this exclusion and the key exception allows for the restriction of 'active sales to the exclusive territory or exclusive customer group'. This may allay some of the criticisms of the Community's past approach to territorial restrictions. The Commission's Guidelines on vertical restraints highlight the distinction between active and passive sales.[222] The Commission is obviously wary of deterring the growth of e-commerce and, in general, the Commission has confirmed that the use of the internet is not considered a form of active sales as it is a reasonable way of reaching customers. As long as the website is not specifically targeted at specific customers or customers primarily inside another territory it will not constitute active sales; the language used on the

---

222 Commission Notice, Guidelines on vertical restraints, OJ 2000, C291/1; [2000] 5 CMLR 1074, paras 50–51.

website is not a crucial factor. The Commission's view of passive selling, aside from e-commerce, appears to be limited to catalogue selling and responding to unsolicited emails. This restrictive view means that the exclusion of territorial restrictions from the exemption will be wide and may exclude from the Regulation many distributorship agreements which limit web-selling across territories. The uncertainty as to what constitutes an active sale may need to be resolved by the European Court, but in the meantime, the uncertainty may lead to difficulties for national courts attempting to interpret the Regulation.

Other excluded obligations

There are certain other obligations contained in vertical agreements which are not exempt. Article 5 details three types of obligations:

a   non-compete obligations;
b   post-term non-compete obligations; and
c   obligations regarding competing products in a selective distribution network.

The key difference from the hard core restraints is that, provided these non-exempted obligations are severable, the remainder of the agreement can benefit from exemption under the Regulation.

Withdrawal of the Block Exemption Regulation

There are two ways in which the benefit of the block exemption may be withdrawn from a particular agreement. The first is set out in Art 6, which provides that the Commission may so act where the agreement has effects which are incompatible with Art 81(3). In particular, incompatible effects may arise where there are parallel networks of similar vertical restraints imposed by competing customers and access to the market is foreclosed. This possibility for withdrawal is based on the rationale underlying the *Delimitis* judgment. In addition, Art 7 provides that the competent authorities of a Member State may, where an agreement produces effects incompatible with Art 81(3) on a distinct geographic market within a Member State, withdraw the benefit of the exemption in respect of that territory.

The Guidelines

Following adoption of Regulation 2790/1999 the Commission published its Guidelines on vertical restraints.[223] The Guidelines seek to give assistance on

223 Commission Notice, Guidelines on vertical restraints, OJ 2000, C291/1; [2000] 5 CMLR 1074.

the interpretation of the Regulation, and to outline the Commission's new policy, with a view to encouraging self-assessment of agreements. The starting point is that there is no presumption of illegality outside Regulation 2790.[224] The Commission has set out a four-stage approach for the analysis of vertical restraints. First, parties should define their relevant market and ascertain their market share. Secondly, if market share does not exceed 30%, the agreement is covered by the Regulation, subject to the existence of hard core restrictions. The third and fourth stages, where the agreement has a higher than 30% market share, involve an assessment of whether the agreement is caught by Art 81(1) and, thereafter, falls within the terms of Art 81(3).[225] In formulating general rules for assessing vertical restraints, the key to the new approach is that agreements only raise competition concerns if there is insufficient inter-brand competition[226] and that a reduction of inter-brand competition is generally more harmful than a reduction in intra-brand competition. This is the new market-power based economic approach which the Commission claims will inform its approach to individual restraints. This approach is supported by ancillary factors, for example, a combination of restraints aggravates their negative effects, and restraints linked to relationship-specific investments are easier to justify, as are restraints in relation to opening up new product or geographic markets. The Commission notes that particular factors in the assessment of the position under Art 81(1) will be the market position of competitors, the existence of entry barriers and the maturity of the market, in that negative effects are more likely in mature markets, rather than in dynamic markets.

Impact of the reform package

Exclusive distribution

Exclusive distribution is a form of distribution whereby a producer agrees with a distributor to supply only to that distributor within a particular territory. The crucial elements in such an agreement are the allocation of a particular sales territory to the distributor and the undertaking by the producer not to appoint another distributor within that territory. It will also normally involve an undertaking by the producer not to sell directly within the territory. The producer's obligations are the key elements of the relationship, but certain obligations will also normally be imposed upon the distributor, for example:

---

224 Ibid, at para 62.
225 As the Guidance was published under the Regulation 17 regime it refers to the old notification procedure.
226 Ibid, at para 119.

a   to stock the complete range of a producer's goods;
b   to stock certain spare parts; and
c   to promote the producer's goods.

Reasons for adopting exclusive distribution

A producer may distribute its own goods either by in-house means or by setting up a subsidiary company. However, it may be more efficient for a producer to appoint a third party to distribute the goods. If the producer is supplying goods to a new market it would be sensible to appoint a distributor who is familiar with that market, thereby avoiding difficulties resulting from a lack of knowledge of the market or because of linguistic and legal differences. In addition, a smaller producer may lack the necessary resources for the distribution of its own goods.

Exclusive distribution may also avoid the additional cost of supplying a large number of distributors. One of the primary reasons for adopting the exclusive distribution format is to encourage a distributor to advertise the producer's goods and to provide any necessary after-sales customer service, as this would be prohibitively expensive for most distributors unless they are provided with the protection of exclusivity. Without exclusivity, other potential distributors, within the contract territory or beyond, may be able to 'free-ride' on the distributor's promotional efforts and undercut the distributor's selling price. Exclusive distribution may be particularly important for new products entering the market, as a distributor may be required to expend a considerable sum on advertisement and promotion of the product and will not want to risk such an outlay if other potential sellers of the product could free-ride on his efforts, that is, if they sought to market the product without incurring the same promotional expenditure.

Treatment of exclusive distribution agreements under Art 81

The discussion of the pros and cons of vertical restraints outlined above is particularly relevant in this section. The problem for Community law has been how to achieve the appropriate balance between the necessary restrictions on intra-brand competition through territorial exclusivity, which may enhance inter-brand competition, and the avoidance of the restrictions on parallel trade which are contrary to the Community goal of market integration. The most important restrictions in this context are those which create territorial restrictions.

Territorial restrictions

A distributor may only be prepared to enter into an exclusive distribution agreement which confers absolute territorial protection in order to ensure protection from 'free-riders' and safeguard investment in the promotion of the product. This will particularly be the case in respect of a new product, which will require more promotional effort than an established product, entering the market. Without adequate protection the distributor may not be prepared to distribute the product and it therefore may never reach the market. The Community authorities have recognised that territorial protection is necessary in order for certain distribution agreements to be established. For instance, in *Société La Technique Minière*,[227] the Court found that a term conferring territorial exclusivity on a distributor might not infringe Art 81(1) where the term is a vital element for the distributor to market a producer's product. Although the Commission is aware of the commercial necessity for territorial protection, it has never accepted the principle that all territorial restrictions should be permitted to facilitate pro-competitive agreements. The Commission will accept limited territorial exclusivity but will not tolerate the obstruction of parallel imports, even where agreements conferring absolute territorial protection may increase inter-brand competition, and therefore indirectly aid the integration of markets within the Community. *Consten and Grundig*[228] established the prohibition on the creation of an absolute territorial protection. The reason for the strict approach is that such restrictions may impede the development of the internal market by isolating national markets. The Community authorities are keen to ensure that some form of parallel trade is maintained by passive sales from outside the contract territory. Despite the recent criticisms of the Community approach and subsequent reform introduced in the Vertical Agreements Regulation, absolute territorial protection is still not permitted. Although absolute territorial protection remains prohibited, the Court has adopted a more lenient approach to less restrictive territorial limitations, but the line between absolute and less restrictive limitations is not always clear. Indeed, even the Vertical Agreements Regulation fails to draw a clear boundary between active sales into another territory, which can be restricted, and passive sales, which must not be prohibited.

Post-Regulation 2790

Regulation 2790 is more accommodating than Regulation 1983/83 in many respects. The restrictions on the form of the agreement under Regulation 1983/83, for instance, that the goods supplied must be for resale, or that the distributor must be granted exclusivity within the whole, or a defined area, of the Community,[229] are no longer applicable. However, on the key issue of what territorial restrictions are permitted in an exclusive distribution agreement, it

---

227 Case 56/65 [1996] ECR 235; [1966] CMLR 357.
228 Cases 56 and 58/64 [1966] ECR 299; [1966] CMLR 418.
229 Regulation 1983/83/EEC, OJ 1983, L173/1, as corrected by OJ 1983, L281/24, Art 1.

appears that the Regulation, and certainly the Commission's interpretation of Art 4(b), is, if anything, even more restrictive. Regulation 1983/83 permitted qualified exclusivity and, accordingly, a producer was permitted to agree not to supply the contract goods directly in the contract territory,[230] and the distributor could be obliged to obtain the contract goods only from the producer[231] and to refrain from seeking customers outside the contract territory. However, the benefit of Regulation 1983/83 was lost where users could obtain the contract goods only from the exclusive distributor in its territory and had no alternative source of supply from outside that territory,[232] or where it was more difficult for users to obtain the contract goods from other distributors.[233] As discussed above, Regulation 2790 places considerable restrictions on the types of territorial exclusivity which can be granted, particularly notable in the context of e-commerce and methods of attracting trade via the internet, and the new rules appear to be even stricter than under Regulation 1983/83.

If an exclusive distribution agreement infringes Art 81(1) and falls outside the terms of the Regulation the parties to the agreement can either seek a finding of inapplicability from the Commission under Regulation 1/2003, or seek to defend the agreement's validity, under Art 81(3) in any court proceedings before a national court. However, it is extremely unlikely that Art 81(3) would be applicable in respect of an agreement conferring absolute territorial protection or providing for resale price maintenance.[234]

Exclusive purchasing or single-branding agreements

In addition to the more detailed consideration of exclusive distribution agreements, we will also briefly review the impact of the Regulation on exclusive purchasing agreements, now referred to by the Commission as single-branding agreements. The Guidelines note that single-branding agreements involve noncompete obligations 'which make the buyer purchase practically all his requirements on a particular market from only one supplier'.[235] The primary competition risk concerns foreclosure of the market to competing and potential suppliers. The traditional approach to Art 81 is reversed by considering first if an agreement falls within the block exemption 'safe harbour', where the supplier has less than 30% market share; if this is not the case, one proceeds to consider the possible application of Art 81(1) and (3). Accordingly, single-branding agreements will gain an automatic exemption

---

230 Ibid, Art 2(1).
231 Ibid, Art 2(2)(b).
232 Ibid, Art 3(c).
233 Ibid, Art 3(d).
234 In Case 161/84 *Pronuptia* [1986] ECR 353; [1986] 1 CMLR 414, the Court held that resale price maintenance infringed Art 81(1) and was not entitled to exemption under Art 81(3).
235 Guidelines, at para 138.

where the supplier's market share does not exceed 30%[236] and the noncompete obligation[237] is limited to five years.[238] It should be noted that Art 5(a) of the Regulation applies to any 'direct or indirect non-compete obligation'. This would cover indirect exclusive purchasing commitments imposed, for example, through the freezer exclusivity provisions in the Irish ice cream dispute.[239] Nonetheless, the Commission has power under the Regulation to withdraw the benefit of the Regulation where an agreement falls within Art 81(1) and does not fulfil the conditions in Art 81(3). In particular, the Guidelines indicate that withdrawal may result where competition is significantly restricted 'by the cumulative effect of parallel networks of similar vertical agreements practised by competing suppliers or buyers'.[240] Similarly, Art 8 allows the Commission to exclude from the scope of the Regulation parallel networks of similar vertical agreements where the networks cover more than 50% of a relevant market.[241] Where the block exemption does not apply, the Guidelines outline, at paras 140–52, a range of factors for assessing whether a single-branding agreement may be caught by Art 81(1); those factors include the supplier's market position, the duration of the non-compete obligations, the likelihood of 'significant foreclosure' of the market,[242] and the existence of entry barriers. Of particular relevance is the Commission's concern that with reduction in inter-brand competition 'for final products at the retail level, significant anti-competitive effects may start to arise, taking into account all other relevant factors, if a non-dominant supplier ties 30 per cent or more of the relevant market'.[243] The impact of a cumulative foreclosure effect is also outlined in the Guidelines.[244] In *Calor Gas Ltd v Express Fuels (Scotland) Ltd*[245] gas suppliers and distributors, Calor Gas Ltd, raised an action of damages against a dealer following their termination of a principal dealer agreement and their subsequent dealership with a rival supplier. The defence that the exclusivity arrangement for a minimum of five years rendered the agreement void under Article 81(1) was successful, relying, *inter alia*, on the principles set out in *Delimitis*. The Scottish court stressed the importance of market power and the duration of the single branding obligation in

236 Article 3. See in particular paras 21–22 and 88–89 of the Guidelines. See, also, Griffiths, M, 'A glorification of *de minimis* – the Regulation on vertical agreements' [2000] ECLR 241.
237 See Art 1(a) and (b) of the Regulation. Article 1(a) provides that a non-compete obligation means an obligation not to manufacture, purchase, sell or resell goods or services which compete with the contract goods or services.
238 Article 5(a).
239 Case T-65/98 *Van den Bergh Foods v Commission* [2004] 4 CMLR 1.
240 At para 73.
241 Guidelines, at paras 80–87.
242 At para 141.
243 At para 148.
244 At para 149.
245 [2008] CSOH 13. Cf *IMS v Ofcom* [2008] CAT 13.

holding that there was a sufficient contribution to a competition restriction and an actual or potential effect on inter-State trade where a nationwide network of principal dealers is tied to the brand leader for a period of five years, especially in a mature market.

Conclusion

Regulation 2790 is an important, although limited, revolution in the Community treatment of vertical restraints. The format of the Regulation, a general Regulation for vertical agreements incorporating a black list approach, is welcome, although there may be some problems in applying the market share threshold with the ensuing difficulties regarding uncertainty and legal security certainty. This development, in relation to vertical restraints, is clearly linked to the earlier revision of the *de minimis* Notice and the modernisation in Regulation 1/2003, in particular the abolition of the notification requirement under Art 81(3). The Regulation and Guidelines demonstrate a new emphasis on market power but much also depends on the new role for national courts and authorities in interpreting and applying Art 81 post-Regulation 1/2003. One important issue, which may raise important questions about the degree of territorial protection permitted within the Regulation, is the interplay between competition law and e-commerce, and the issues surrounding what constitutes a restriction on active sales in the context of the internet.

UK competition law and vertical restraints

Introduction

There has never been the same level of debate in the UK as in the Community as to the relative merits of vertical restraints. This is partly due to the particular format of Art 81 and the special status accorded to market integration in the application of Community competition law. Unsurprisingly, UK law has never adopted a unified and consistent approach towards varying forms of vertical restraints. Indeed, UK law has been characterised by the consideration of vertical restraints under the full range of different competition law provisions, including the common law doctrine of restraint of trade.[246] UK law has also generally adopted a fairly lenient approach, typified by the initial exclusion of vertical agreements from the Competition Act 1998 Chapter I prohibition. Nonetheless, more recently the emphasis has been on ensuring an approach to vertical restraints which is consistent with Community law, by emphasising the scope for parallel exemption from the UK Chapter I prohibition by virtue of the application of Regulation 2790/99.

---

246 See Chapter 1, particularly in relation to exclusive purchasing agreements, and *Esso Petroleum Co Ltd v Harper's Garage (Stourport) Ltd* [1968] AC 269; [1967] 1 All ER 699.

Section 50 and the 2000 Order

Section 50(1) of the 1998 Act states that the Secretary of State may, by order, provide for any provision of Pt I of the Act to apply to vertical agreements with such modifications as may be prescribed. The Competition Act 1998 (Land and Vertical Agreements Exclusion) Order 2000[247] came into force on 1 March 2000 and excluded vertical agreements from the Chapter I prohibition. It is clear that the purpose of excluding vertical agreements was to reduce the number of precautionary notifications of benign agreements, and thereby help to ensure that the competition authorities could concentrate their resources on matters of significant competition concern. The exclusion of vertical agreements would also avoid the unnecessary burden on business of notifying very large numbers of essentially benign agreements and of scrutinising agreements to determine whether or not notification should be made. It followed that there was a good case for disapplying the Chapter I prohibition from a broad range of vertical agreements.

Reform and the 2004 Order

In the White Paper, *Productivity and Enterprise: A World Class Competition Regime*,[248] the Government indicated its intention to repeal the exclusion of vertical restraints and rely on parallel exemptions stemming from the EC Vertical Agreements Regulation. In a subsequent consultation document, in June 2003,[249] the DTI noted that under Regulation 1/2003 the OFT would be required to apply the UK prohibition and Art 81 in tandem. The application of two different regimes, the Vertical Agreements Regulation and the Order, to the same agreement would be burdensome and confusing for business. Accordingly, the Government proposed the removal of the Order for vertical agreements.[250] This was effected by the Competition Act 1998 (Land Agreements Exclusion and Revocation) Order 2004,[251] which ensures the application of the Vertical Agreements Regulation to all vertical agreements, either directly, or by parallel application where, in fact, there is no effect on inter-State trade. In addition to the non-applicability of the Regulation to hard core restraints such as price-fixing, vertical agreements that give rise to

247 SI 2000/310.
248 Cm 5233, 31 July 2001, paras 8.14–8.16.
249 See DTI consultation, 'Modernisation – a consultation on the Government's proposals for giving effect to Regulation 1/2003 EC and for re-alignment of the Competition Act 1998', 1 April 2003.
250 See DTI 'Government response to the consultations on giving effect to Regulation 1/2003 and aligning the Competition Act 1998 including exclusions and exemptions', 16 January 2004.
251 As of 1 May 2005. See the Competition Act 1998 (Land Agreements Exclusion and Revocation) Order 2004, SI 2004/1260, and the Guideline, 'Vertical agreements', OFT 419.

concern could be dealt with in one of three ways. First, the OFT has the power, under Art 29(2) of Regulation 1/2003, to withdraw the benefit of the block exemption in the UK or in a part of it. Secondly, vertical agreements do not enjoy any exclusion from the Chapter II prohibition, and, consistent with the view that market power is the core concern, a vertical agreement entered into by undertakings with market power could be scrutinised under s 18 of the 1998 Act. Thirdly, where there is a competition problem in a particular sector because of the cumulative effect of the vertical agreements in operation, the OFT may refer the matter to the Competition Commission for investigation.

In the past, under the complex monopoly provisions of the Fair Trading Act 1973, the Competition Commission has frequently commented adversely on the contractual restrictions imposed upon distributors,[252] most recently in relation to new cars and ice cream,[253] although there has been minimal consideration of exclusive distribution, a particular concern of the Community authorities. Subject to the application of the Vertical Agreements Regulation, the 2002 Act provisions on market investigations maintain a role for the Competition Commission in considering vertical agreements where there is concern over industry-wide use of certain vertical restraints.[254]

Further reading

Article 81

Bouterse, RB, *Competition and Integration – What Goals Count? EEC Competition Law and Goals of Industrial, Monetary and Cultural Policy*, 1994, The Hague: Kluwer Law International.

Ehlermann, CD, 'The modernisation of EC antitrust policy: a legal and cultural revolution' (2000) 37 CML Rev 537.

Odudu, O, *The Boundaries of EC Competition Law: The Scope of Article 81*, 2006, Oxford: OUP.

The Competition Act 1998: Chapter I prohibition

Rodger, BJ and MacCulloch, A (eds), *The UK Competition Act: A New Era for UK Competition Law*, 2000, Oxford: Hart; in particular Chapter 1, Whish, R, 'The Competition Act 1998 and the prior debate on reform'; Chapter 4, MacNeil, I, 'Investigations under the Competition Act 1998'; and Chapter 8, Rodger, BJ and

---

252 For example, in *Carbonated Soft Drinks*, Cm 1625, 1991; *New Motor Cars*, Cm 1808, 1992; and *Films*, Cm 2763, 1994.

253 *New Cars: A Report on the Supply of New Motor Cars Within the UK*, Cm 4660, 2000 and *The Supply of Impulse Ice-cream*, Cm 4510, 2000, respectively.

254 See Competition Commission, 'Market investigation references: Competition Commission guidelines', CC3, June 2003, at www.competition-commission.org.uk.

MacCulloch, A, 'The Chapter I prohibition: prohibiting cartels? Or permitting vertical? Or both?'

Vertical restraints, the US rule of reason and the Vertical Agreements Regulation

Bork, R, *The Antitrust Paradox: A Policy at War with Itself*, 1993, Oxford: Maxwell Macmillan, Chapters 14 and 15.

Comanor, WS, 'Vertical price fixing, vertical market restrictions and the new antitrust policy' (1985) 98 Harv L Rev 983.

Gyselen, L, 'Vertical restraints in the distribution process: strength and weakness of the free rider rationale under EEC competition law' (1984) 21 CML Rev 647.

Hawk, B, 'System failure: vertical restraints and EC competition law' (1995) 32 CML Rev 973.

Rodger, B, 'The big chill for national courts: reflections on market foreclosure and freezer exclusivity under Article 81 EC' (2004) 11(1) Irish Journal of European Law 77.

Whish, R, 'Regulation 2790/99: the Commission's "new style" block exemption for vertical restraints' (2000) 37 CML Rev 887.

Discussion

1 Does Art 81(1) cover all forms of understanding between competitors?
2 Is the US rule of reason debate appropriate in the context of the Community approach to contractual restraints?
3 To what extent should competition law focus on market power or market share and the effect on inter-brand competition when dealing with vertical restraints?
4 Are national courts an appropriate forum for dealing with the issues raised in Art 81(3)?
5 To what extent is the Chapter I prohibition in the Competition Act 1998 a dramatic reform in UK competition law on anti-competitive agreements?
6 Do you agree that UK policy on vertical restraints should be aligned with the Community approach?

Chapter 5

Cartels: deterrence, leniency and criminalisation

Introduction

The cartel is generally recognised as the most serious violation of competition law. A classic cartel is an agreement between horizontally related producers of a particular product across an industry. By being members of the cartel the producers no longer compete against each other and, effectively, gain the power of a monopolist through agreement. They will normally exploit that market power by fixing prices, reducing output, or sharing customers or markets. All of those activities will increase costs for customers, compared to the costs that would have been faced in a competitive market, and increase the profit levels for the cartel members. One of the reasons that cartels are seen as being so damaging is that there is very little economic justification for their existence; they are always detrimental and offer little or no redeeming benefit.

Not all horizontal agreements between competitors are cartels. There are some circumstances in which some horizontal agreements may be allowed to go ahead; usually through Art 81(3) EC. One such example would be a research and development (R&D) agreement. Under such an agreement two competing undertakings would agree to co-operate in a research project with a view to creating a new hi-tech product. That agreement would be beneficial as it would encourage the parties to invest in expensive, and potentially risky, research activities. The new products developed would be of benefit to their customers who would get access to new technology much more quickly than would have been possible without the agreement. But the competition authorities must be alert to the possibility that the undertakings who jointly undertook the research would have decreased incentives to compete with each other on the market created by the joint activity. In the EC Block Exemption, which deals with R&D agreements,[1] there is tension between the desire to encourage research and the concern that horizontal co-operation could lead to cartel

---

1 Commission Regulation 2659/2000/EC on the application of Article 81(3) of the Treaty to categories of research and development agreements, OJ 2000, L304/7.

activity. Art 5 of the Regulation sets out the agreements that are not covered by the block exemption; these include the limitation of output or sales or the fixing of prices when selling the contract product to third parties.

The contemporary definition of a cartel, as used within the EC, is as follows:

> What is a cartel?
>
> It is an illegal secret agreement concluded between competitors to fix prices, restrict supply and/or divide up markets. The agreement may take a wide variety of forms but often relates to sales prices or increases in such prices, restrictions on sales or production capacities, sharing out of product or geographic markets or customers, and collusion on the other commercial conditions for the sale of products or services.[2]

It is therefore clear that the type of horizontal agreement that generally falls within the definition of a cartel is one that seeks to: set prices, either directly or by manipulating output; share customers by allocating them between suppliers directly or by allocating each supplier control over customers in a specific geographical area; or agree to co-ordinate other terms and conditions of sale over which customers might expect sellers to compete. One practice, which would clearly fall within the concept of a cartel, but is usually known by a more specific name, is bid-rigging. This is where a contract is to be allocated through a bidding or tendering process, which is specifically designed to ensure competing suppliers go head to head to win a contract, and that process is subverted by the potential suppliers getting together in advance of making their bids to decide upon a collective strategy and thereby 'rig' the bidding process. Essentially, this is simply a strategy of co-operation in order to share customers among the bidding cartel members.

The history of European cartels

The history of the European cartel in the twentieth century is a particularly interesting one.[3] At the beginning of the century the cartel was a normal feature of industry. They were so prevalent in Germany that it became known as the 'Land of Cartels'[4] with 400 operating in 1905.[5] The reasons for this high level of cartelisation are complex, but in many regards it mirrors the

---

2 Commission, 'Competition: Commission action against cartels – Questions and answers' MEMO/08/154, 11 March 2008.

3 For a full historical account see, Harding, C and Joshua, J, *Regulating Cartels in Europe: A Study of Legal Control of Corporate Delinquency*, 2003, Oxford: OUP, and Gerber, D, *Law and Competition in Twentieth Century Europe: Protecting Prometheus*, 1998, Oxford: Clarendon Press.

4 Gerber, ibid, pp 74–75.

5 Henderson, WO, *The Industrial Revolution on the Continent 1800–1914*, 1961, London: Frank Cass, p 60.

reasons that cartels form in contemporary industries. The impact of the industrial revolution, alongside the political impact of the building of the German State, had resulted in volatile markets. Many of the cartels were originally defensive in nature, in that smaller businesses grouped together for protection, but as they grew in size, and industry coverage, they became more powerful and were able to exert greater influence. The growth of cartels was generally positively received as they were perceived as bringing stability and order to markets. It was also more closely aligned with the corporatist trad-ition within German society.[6] The ability of customers to access lower prices was seen as being less important than the stability of the State economy, as reflected in the health of its industrial base. Cartel-type arrangements were found in other European economies in the early part of the century, but in economies like Britain they were less formal and businesses tended to be more independent and entrepreneurial. This began to change in the inter-war period when multinational cartels began to form, often in industries where a national cartel had been successful. The wary toleration of cartels can be seen in the 1927 Geneva Declaration on Cartels:

> The Conference has recognized that the phenomenon of such agree-ments, arising from economic necessities, does not constitute a matter upon which any conclusion of principle be reached, but a development considered as good or bad according to the spirit which rules the consti-tution and the operation of the agreements, and in particular according to the measure in which those directing them are actuated by a sense of the general interest.[7]

The political turmoil in Europe which led to the 1939–45 war brought this period of development to an end. The tentative control methods first seen in the mid-1920s were overtaken by events.

The immediate post-war period saw a change in attitude towards the cartel. Part of that attitude shift probably relates back to the use of cartels by the totalitarian governments in Germany, Italy and Japan in the lead up to the 1939–45 war. That association, and the influence of the United States in European politics,[8] led to increased suspicion of previously accepted organ-isations. Notwithstanding that change in attitude there was no rush to follow

---

6 This can seen, in part, as a reaction to, and rejection of, the 'Manchester School' economic model; the highly unregulated laissez-faire economic development characterised by the earlier industrial expansion in the North of England. See Harding and Joshua, above, fn 3, pp 69–70. It is also interesting to note that the socialist parties that sought to represent the 'worker', the closest to the contemporary conception of the consumer, supported cartels as being a step towards State control and ensuring the stability of employment (p 72).

7 Adopted 24 May 1927, by the Economic Conference.

8 The decartelisation of German industry ran alongside the deNazification process in occupied Germany; see Harding and Joshua, above, fn 3, p 85.

the US prohibition model. The first European level control was seen in the European Coal and Steel Community (ECSC) in 1951. It is interesting to note that the ECSC regime did not challenge cartels per se – it promoted the public use of cartel-like organisations in industry, but certainly challenged the operation of private cartels. It did have a prohibition, in Art 65, of anti-competitive cartel practices, but also had a system of exemptions decided by the High Authority. The new model was a blend of European and American experience.

Before going on to examine the EC prohibitions, which will be the focus of much of this chapter, it is interesting to spend a few moments looking at the UK's relationship with cartels before the UK joined the EEC in 1973. The changing relationship is indicative of the wider European view. The common law always had a tolerant attitude towards cartel arrangements.[9] In *Jones v North* in 1875 a, no-doubt secret, bid-rigging arrangement was described as 'perfectly lawful'.[10] In later cases, such as *North Western Salt Co v Electrolytic Alkali Co Ltd*[11] and *Rawlings v General Trading Co*,[12] attitudes had hardened somewhat, but cartel agreements were still not unlawful, unless there were aggravating features such as fraud, misrepresentation, or intimidation, although they may have been considered to be a restraint on trade and held to be void and unenforceable. The first statutory controls in the UK, The Restrictive Practices (Inquiry and Control) Act 1948, allowed the Secretary of State to refer cartels to the Monopolies Commission to establish whether they operated contrary to the public interest. The next legislative attempt to control cartel activity was the Restrictive Trade Practices Act 1956. It introduced compulsory registration of cartel agreements on the basis of a rebuttable presumption that such agreements were contrary to the public interest. Parties could seek to justify their agreements before the Restrictive Practices Court. It therefore appeared that the UK had a relatively strong control regime; however, studies of the registration requirements indicated that while formal legal agreements had been abandoned, with some increase in competition, there was a move towards less formal restrictions which could have had a similar result.[13]

The early history of the EC provisions

The introduction of the competition law provisions in the EC Treaty was a significant step forward in European cartel control. The prohibition-based

---

9 In *Norris v Govt of the United States* [2008] UKHL 16 the House of Lords set out an interesting history of the common law in relation to cartels.
10 *Jones v North* (1875) LR 19 Eq 426, at 430.
11 [1913] 3 KB 422.
12 [1921] 1 KB 635.
13 See, Allen, GC, *Monopoly and Restrictive Practices*, 1968, London: George Allen & Unwin.

administrative enforcement model, that retained the possibility of notification for the purpose of approval, followed the developing European norm, but the move to supranational control was a decisive step away from political interference by national governments. One of the key features of the prohibition was its place within the common market programme set out in the Treaty: such agreements are deemed 'incompatible with the common market'. There was relatively little enforcement of the new EC rules in the early stages of the Community's development, certainly before the Commission was granted its enforcement powers in Regulation 17/62. But even after the Commission was empowered to enforce the rules there was a significant gap before those powers were exercised against cartels. Early Art 81 cases seemed to focus on certain types of vertical agreements, typified by *Consten & Grundig*,[14] which contained explicit, Member State-centred, territorial market-sharing clauses. It was not until the early 1970s that the Commission brought its enforcement resources to bear on cartels. The first Decisions, in the late 1960s and early 1970s, were in relation to the Noorwijks Cement Accord,[15] but as this was an 'old' agreement which pre-dated the Treaty there was immunity from the imposition of a fine. The first examples of the Commission challenging 'underground' cartels, of the type more likely to be encountered in the current climate, were in *Quinine*[16] and *Dyestuffs*.[17] These were particularly significant cases in that they highlighted industry's attempts to adapt to the changing regulatory climate and the Commission's new willingness to challenge less formal, better concealed, arrangements. Co-operation in the quinine industry dated back to 1913 with a defensive cartel being formed in the late 1950s. The existence of this cartel was not notified to the Commission, unlike the *Cement* cases. The cartel was formally discontinued – due to changing market conditions – in 1965, but investigations in both the EC and US were launched in 1967, leading to the Decision adopted in 1969. At the same time the Commission was investigating the Dyestuffs cartel, which proved to be a much more complicated case, based largely on economic and circumstantial evidence. It also heralded the beginning of a long battle between the Commission and the chemicals industry in Europe.

Cartel wars: the cartel strikes back

Emboldened by its early successes, the Commission increased its activity against cartels leading to an increasing number of cartel prosecutions

14 Cases 56 and 58/64 *Consten & Grundig v Commission* [1966] ECR 299; [1966] CMLR 418.
15 See Cases 8–11/66 *Cimenteries v Commission* [1967] ECR 75 and Case 8/72 *Vereeninging van Cementhandelaren v Commission* [1972] ECR 977.
16 Cases 41, 44–45/69 *ACF Chemiefarma v Commission* [1970] ECR 661, [1970] CMLR 8083.
17 See, for example, Case 48/69 *ICI v Commission* [1972] ECR 704.

through the 1970s into the 1980s. In the first half of this period a number of cases came from traditional arrangements in the Low Countries, but towards the end of the period the most significant cases came from large pan-European cartels supplying bulk industrial commodities.[18] By the late 1980s it became apparent that those accused of being involved in cartel activity were more willing to challenge the Commission's imposition of, increasingly sizable, fines. The Commission was embroiled in a number of complex legal challenges before the European Courts in relation to, for instance, *Wood Pulp*,[19] *Polypropylene*,[20] and *PVC*.[21] The Commission's decisions were upheld in the majority of cases, but they also suffered some major defeats. It became abundantly clear that the Commission would have to invest significant resources in order to find good evidence to support their cartel findings, and then support those decisions against the judicial review that would inevitably follow. It is interesting to note that the challenges to the Commission's decisions were largely on procedural and due process grounds, rather than on the basis of the substantive findings. Another growing complexity stemmed from the increasingly broad scope of large cartel cases. An increasing number of cases were not only pan-European, but global in nature. This necessitated greater co-operation with other enforcement agencies, particularly the Department of Justice in the United States, who were running parallel investigations within their jurisdictions. As the fight against cartels moved into the 1990s, it was clear that the Commission was keen to focus its efforts on fighting international cartels, and that it would need to develop new tools and make better use of its resources to be more effective. It is the development of those tools that the rest of this chapter will focus upon.

The contemporary view of cartels

It is a truism to suggest that cartels are generally seen as being the most heinous and damaging form of competition law violation. They are the only form of anti-competitive conduct that is almost universally condemned. A great many forms of anti-competitive behaviour are treated differently, for cultural and political reasons, in different jurisdictions, but in the majority of industrial economies cartels are seen as being highly damaging and are therefore treated harshly. The high level of co-ordination in cartel control is

---

18 While the Commission's attitude had definitely hardened, it was still willing to occasionally sanction 'crisis cartels' when an industry was in significant difficulties. See, for example, Commission Decision 84/380/EEC *Synthetic Fibres*, OJ 1984, L207/17.

19 Cases C-89/85 etc *Ahlström Oy & Others v Commission* [1993] ECR I-1307.

20 Cases T-1/89 etc *Rhône-Poulenc v Commission* [1991] ECR II-867, on appeal Case C-51/92P *Hercules Chemicals v Commission* [1999] ECR I-4235.

21 Cases T-79/89 etc *BASF & Others v Commission* [1992] ECR II-315.

demonstrated by the depth of international co-operation into best practice published by bodies such as the OECD[22] or ICN.[23]

The problem facing the competition authorities is somewhat different in cartel control compared to other areas of competition law and merger control. The problem is not identifying which conduct is anti-competitive and inefficient, and therefore should be prohibited. All cartel behaviour is clearly damaging and should therefore be unlawful. The 'cartel problem' is identifying when such behaviour occurs, and gathering enough evidence of the unlawful behaviour to bring the behaviour to an end and successfully prosecute cartel members. Much of the debate is therefore about designing an enforcement regime that will be successful at catching cartelists and dissuading undertakings from entering cartel arrangements. It is clearly better that cartels are not formed, and therefore the economy does not suffer the economic harm that would follow. Accordingly, the contemporary focus is on the regulatory successes and failures of the key competition regimes, largely in the US, Europe and Australia. The key issues in the debate are not always clearly stated but, in essence, the driving force behind much of the contemporary thinking is the concept of deterrence. This is the idea that the regulatory regime should seek to deter potential cartelists from entering into cartel arrangements. The usual method of deterring such behaviour is through some form of punishment or consequence should an undertaking violate the rules. The basic concept of deterrence is very simple, but the difficulty stems from attempts to design a system of deterrence that works to produce the right level of deterrence, optimal deterrence, which discourages unlawful behaviour, but does not discourage any lawful, and therefore legitimate, business activity.

Optimal deterrence

When a regulator seeks to design a regulatory system to deter violations of a set of legal rules they have to balance various elements within that system in order to try and create the appropriate level of deterrence.[24] If the system fails to sufficiently deter, producing underdeterrence, it will not discourage potential violators from embarking on unlawful behaviour. If the system deters too

22 See OECD, 'Recommendation of the Council concerning effective action against hard core cartels', 1998; OECD, 'Hard Core Cartels', 2000; and, OECD, 'Hard Core Cartels: Third Report on the Implementation of the 1998 Recommendation', 2005.

23 See the work of the ICN Cartel Working Group as set out in its 'Work Plan 2007–2008', available at: www.internationalcompetitionnetwork.org.

24 For discussion of deterrence see, for example: Motta, M, 'On Cartel Deterrence and Fines in the European Union' [2008] ECLR 209; Wils, WPJ, 'Optimal Antitrust Fines: Theory and Practice' (2006) 29(2) World Comp 183; Landes, WM, 'Optimal Sanctions for Antitrust Violations' (1983) 50 Uni Chicago LRev 652; and, Becker, GS, 'Crime and Punishment: An Economic Approach' (1968) 76 J of Political Economy 169.

much, producing overdeterrence, the system will discourage businesses from adopting legitimate business models near the edge of legitimate conduct. Businesses will be discouraged as they will be concerned about the potentially high levels of punishment which they may face if they have misread the rules as to what is permissible; the rules may therefore have a 'chilling' effect on legitimate competition. The process of finding the right level of deterrence follows a utilitarian calculus. To effectively discourage the behaviour the system must ensure that there is no incentive for the potential violator to embark on the unlawful conduct. One clear way to ensure there is no benefit is to ensure that the punishment imposed removes all the benefit the potential violator would expect to gain from the unlawful acts. In the context of cartels this would mean that the increased profit that a cartelist would expect to gain from the operation of the cartel is removed when the cartelist is caught. If that were the case, there would be no incentive for them to enter into a cartel. That is only one side of the calculus; the expected gain/punishment equation alone is not sufficient to devise a policy. No matter how effective the enforcement system is, it is unrealistic to expect the regulators to catch all violations of the rules. If the regulator only catches one in every three violations there will still be an incentive to act unlawfully. The cartelist will expect to keep the gain from two cartels, even if the gain from the third cartel is stripped away. The chances of being caught and punished must therefore be factored into the equation. As one of the key punishments in competition law is an administrative fine, Wils explains the optimal deterrent punishment in the following way:

> The minimum fine for deterrence to work thus equals the expected gain from the violation multiplied by the inverse of the probability of a fine being effectively imposed.[25]

An example of this approach would be the following. A cartelist expects to gain an increase in profits of approximately £200,000 by being a member of a cartel. They also have reason to believe that there is only a one in four chance of being caught and a fine being imposed. In such a situation the optimal fine to deter that behaviour would be:

$$gain \times \left(\frac{inverse}{probability} \right) = fine \qquad £200,000 \times \left(\frac{4}{1} \right) = £800,000$$

It is obviously impossible to try and calculate accurately what a potential cartelist's expected gain may be: the calculation will have been made at a

---

25 Wils, WPJ, 'Optimal Antitrust Fines: Theory and Practice' (2006) 29(2) World Comp 183, at p 191.

point in time when they considered the course of action, and it is possible that they decided to act without making proper calculation or one based on limited information.[26] Deterrence theory may not offer a perfect model but it does form a useful structure in which to consider the likely success of a particular enforcement regime and gives a useful methodology to assess any attempt to improve the regulation of hard core cartels. Deterrence is a model used in many areas of law,[27] but it is particularly suited to cartel regulation as it might be expected that business people, whose main aim is profit maximisation, can be expected to act as 'amoral calculators' in that they will calculate the expected costs and benefits of any behaviour before acting.

It is clear that in many recent reforms the aim of increasing the deterrent effect of the law has been an important factor. While the competition authorities can do little to reduce the profit that can be gained from being a member of a successful cartel, they can use enforcement tools to try and put in place effective and deterrent punishments to strip away the expected gains and increase the chances of the cartelist being caught and punished.

Punishment

One of the key features of any attempt to regulate hard core cartels is effective punishment or sanctions. Most regimes use fines as their main sanction, but there is increasing resort to other forms of sanction to bolster the effect of traditional fines. Before going on to look at the range of new sanctions being used to control cartels, and other anti-competitive behaviour, we shall first examine the way in which corporate fines are calculated in the EC and the UK.

Administrative corporate fines in the EC

The level of fines imposed for cartel infringement under EC competition law has increased dramatically since the 1990s.[28] The largest fine for a single competition law infringement, of €992.3m, was imposed against the *Elevators and Escalators* cartel in 2007. The level of fines imposed in cartel cases in the last few years was as follows:[29]

---

26 The limited ability of a cartelist to calculate the real gains or chance of being caught is often described as 'bounded rationality'.

27 Criminal law is an obvious example, but regulatory theory is employed in many areas. Notable examples, as they share many commonalities with competition law, are consumer law and environmental law.

28 For an analysis of fines across this period see, Motta, M, 'On Cartel Deterrence and Fines in the European Union' [2008] ECLR 209.

29 All figures from, 'Competition: Commission action against cartels – Questions and answers' MEMO/08/30, 23 January 2008.

Year	Fines imposed	No of undertakings	Average fine
2003	€40,791,000	26	€15,415,038
2004	€390,209,100	30	€13,006,970
2005	€683,029,000	41	€16,659,244
2006	€1,846,385,500	47	€39,284,798
2007	€3,333,802,700	45	€74,084,504

The increase in fines in 2006 can largely be ascribed to a combination of the severity of the cartel conduct, the size of the markets affected, and the Commission's hardening attitude. The level of fines subsequent to 2006 will rise even further as the Commission begins to operate on the basis of the policy set out in the 2006 'Guidelines on the method of setting fines'.[30] It will take some time for cases dealt with under the previous 1998 Notice to work through the system.[31]

The Guidelines explain the process that the Commission uses to calculate fines. It is important that the Commission is able to justify the fines it imposes as they will invariably be subject to review by the CFI.[32] In many cases the CFI has been critical of the fines imposed by the Commission. While the Guidelines set out the process, the Commission still retains a significant amount of discretion, which can make it incredibly difficult to predict, in advance, what fine might be imposed. The Commission's approach has a two-step methodology: first, it sets the basic amount of the fine; and, second, it may adjust that amount either upwards or downwards.

The basic amount

The first step in calculating the fine for a single undertaking is to calculate the value of the goods or services that relate, directly or indirectly, to the infringement within the EEA within the last business year.[33] Adjustment may be made to the figures if, because the cartel extends beyond the EEA, the

30 Commission Guidelines on the method of setting fines imposed pursuant to Article 23(2)(a) of Regulation No 1/2003, OJ 2006, C210/02. For discussion of the Guidelines see, Volcker, SB, 'Rough justice? An analysis of the European Commission's new fining guidelines' (2007) 44(5) CMLRev 1285.

31 Commission Guidelines on the method of setting fines imposed pursuant to Article 15(2) of Regulation No 17 and Article 65(5) of the ECSC Treaty, OJ 1998, C9/3. It is interesting to note that the largest fine imposed, in *Elevators and Escalators*, was set under the, arguably weaker, 1998 Guidelines in 2007.

32 All the Commission's cartel decisions in 2005 and 2006 were subject to review. See, also, Motta, M, 'On Cartel Deterrence and Fines in the European Union' [2008] ECLR 209.

33 Commission Guidelines on the method of setting fines imposed pursuant to Article 23(2)(a) of Regulation No 1/2003, OJ 2006, C210/02, para 13.

EEA value does not properly represent the relevant weight of each undertaking within the infringement.[34] The basic amount is a proportion of the value of sales multiplied by the duration of the infringement. The proportion of the value of sales will be set at a level up to 30%. Because of the nature of secret hard core cartels, fines will generally be at the top end of that scale. The duration, in years, acts as a multiplier, with the multiplier being calculated in six-month increments.[35] To reflect the damage caused by mere entry into a cartel the Commission will also impose an additional 'entry penalty' of between 15 and 25% of the value of sales.[36] While the basic amount is calculated from actual figures it will always be rounded out to produce a final amount.

Adjustment to the basic amount

Once the basic amount has been calculated the Commission can then take into account a number of other factors that may then increase or decrease the applicable fine. A number of aggravating circumstances may result in an increase in the level of fine. These include: continuation of the infringement; refusal to co-operate; or, being a leader or instigator of the infringement or coercing others to participate.[37] Mitigating factors that may result in a decrease of the fine include: evidence of limited involvement or the adoption of competitive behaviour during the infringement; co-operation with the Commission; or, where the anti-competitive conduct has been authorised or encouraged by public authorities or legislation.[38] Provision is also made for a specific increase for deterrence purposes.[39] This would be applied where a fine is being imposed against an undertaking that has a large turnover outside the market affected. In that situation the fine may look relatively small compared to the overall financial resources of the undertaking. The Commission may also increase the fine, to ensure its deterrent effect, when the gains made by the cartelists are large compared to the value of relevant sales.

Once this calculation has been made there are two final caveats that the Commission must consider. The power of the Commission to impose fines under Regulation 1/2003 is limited. It cannot impose a fine that exceeds 10% of an undertaking's total turnover in the preceding business year.[40] In the majority of cases this has not proved to be a practical limitation, as the

---

34 Ibid, para 18.
35 Cartel duration of two years would result in a multiplier of 2. Duration of two years and three months would result in a multiplier of 2.5. Duration of two years and nine months would result in a multiplier of 3.
36 Commission Guidelines on the method of setting fines imposed pursuant to Article 23(2)(a) of Regulation No 1/2003, OJ 2006, C210/02, para 25.
37 Ibid, para 28.
38 Ibid, para 29.
39 Ibid, paras 30–31.
40 Regulation 1/2003, OJ 2003, L1/1, Art 23(2).

fine is calculated based on a percentage of sales affected by the infringement rather than total sales, but it may prove to be an issue if a single product undertaking is involved in a cartel, given that the basic amount in cartel cases is likely to start at 20–30% of sales value. Finally, upon application by an undertaking, the Commission may consider reducing a fine on account of an undertaking's inability to pay.[41] Such reductions are rare, but SGL's fines in *Speciality Graphite* and *Carbon & Graphite* were reduced, due to financial constraints.[42]

Administrative corporate fines in the UK

The methodology through which the OFT calculates administrative fines in cartel cases is set out in the 'OFT's guidance as to the appropriate amount of a penalty'.[43] The two main objectives of the policy are to impose penalties that reflect the serious nature of the infringement and to deter undertakings from engaging in anti-competitive practices. The Guidance stresses that cartels are one of the most serious infringements of competition law.[44] The OFT's approach mirrors that of the Commission in many respects, but pre-dates the Commission's 2006 Guideline.

The starting point

The level of the starting point for the fine is calculated on the basis of the seriousness of the infringement and the relevant turnover of the undertaking.[45] The seriousness of the infringement will be based on consideration, *inter alia*, of the following: the product, the nature of the market, the market shares of the undertakings involved, and the effect on third parties and consumers. The relevant turnover is the turnover of the undertaking in the relevant product market in the preceding business year. The OFT may take into account turnover outside the UK, in another EC Member State, if the market is wider than the UK. The level of fine imposed may not exceed 10% of the relevant turnover of the undertaking.

Adjustment for duration and other factors

The starting point may be increased to take into account the duration of the infringement. Infringements that last for more than one year may be

---

41   Commission Guidelines on the method of setting fines imposed pursuant to Article 23(2)(a) of Regulation No 1/2003, OJ 2006, C210/02, para 35.

42   Commission Decision 2006/460/EC *Specialty Graphite*, OJ 2006, L180/20, and Commission Decision 2004/420/EC *Carbon & Graphite*, OJ 2004, L125/45, para 360. See Stephan, A, 'The Bankruptcy Wildcard in Cartel Cases' [2006] JBL 511.

43   OFT's guidance as to the appropriate amount of a penalty, OFT 423, December 2004.

44   Ibid, para 1.4.

45   Ibid, paras 2.3–2.9.

multiplied by the number of years of the infringement.[46] Part years may be treated as full years. Other adjustments may be made to the fine imposed during the third step. At this stage explicit adjustments may be made to ensure the deterrent effect of a penalty, because of the financial benefit made from the infringement or the size and financial position of the undertaking.[47] Step four allows the OFT to adjust for aggravating or mitigating factors,[48] and step five ensures that the final penalty imposed does not exceed the maximum penalty of 10% of the worldwide turnover of the undertaking in the preceding business year.[49]

The problem with corporate fines

The clear problem with deterring cartelists through corporate fines, in both the EC and UK, is that the current fining levels are simply too low. While, in absolute terms, the amounts of money involved may appear to be large, they are unlikely to strip away all the benefits of being involved in a cartel. That is particularly true if one considers that it is highly unlikely that the competition authorities are able to discover and successfully fine all the participants in all cartel arrangements. It is obviously difficult to estimate the gains that a cartelist can expect from taking part in an infringement, but a number of academic studies have sought to calculate the overcharge caused by discovered cartels.[50] By looking at those figures it is estimated that the median overcharge from a cartel is about 25%. There appears to be some variation depending on the type of cartel and its geographic extent. A cartel within a single European country has a median overcharge of 17%, but a Europe-wide cartel has a median overcharge of 43%. These figures tend to suggest that cartel fines in Europe tend towards underdeterrence. Policy within the UK is based on a starting point of 10% of turnover in the affected market, whereas the overcharge is likely to be nearer 20% of sales. EC fines, under the 2006 Guidelines, are larger and it would therefore appear that fines at the top end of the basic amount, 25–30%, are close to the overcharge which cartels may be able to impose; however, the figures indicate that, historically at least, pan-European cartels are among the most profitable for the participants. If the authorities wish to impose fines with real deterrent effect it therefore appears that they should not be discouraged from using the full extent of their powers.

Even if the EC and UK authorities impose fines at the top end of their

---

46 Ibid, para 2.10.
47 Ibid, para 2.11.
48 Ibid, paras 2.14–2.16.
49 Ibid, para 2.17.
50 See, in particular, Connor, JM and Lande, RH, 'The size of cartel overcharges: Implications for US and EU fining policies' (2006) 51(4) Antitrust Bulletin 983.

Guidance there are still two issues that mean that fines alone are unlikely to be of deterrent effect. Both EC and UK fining powers are limited by a 10% global turnover cap. While this has not proved to be an issue in too many cases it does not sit well with a policy aimed at deterrence. This limitation, combined with the limitation based on ability to pay, is usually justified on the basis that a corporate fine should not result in the social costs associated with corporate insolvency.[51] The fines imposed must punish, but should not in effect be a 'corporate death sentence', which substantially damages share-holders, employees and suppliers who had no part to play in the infringement itself. The second, and probably most important, issue is the cartels that 'get away'. As it is unlikely that the authorities will be able to impose fines on all infringements, we would expect to see some form of multiplier to ensure that optimal deterrence is achieved. At present it appears that corporate fines in the EC and UK do not strip away the full benefits of being a member of a cartel; they will therefore not deter when there is always a chance to escape detection and retain all the profit. One way of enhancing deterrence would be to dramatically increase the level of fines, but as noted above, the existence of the 10% global turnover cap means that such a policy is impossible in the current European legislative context. It has therefore become import-ant to find ways of increasing deterrence by means other than ever-larger corporate fines.

Increasing financial penalties: damages

One area that offers the potential for increasing deterrence in cartel cases is compensation claims. These would be private claims for compensation brought by those who have suffered loss at the hands of the cartel. If cartelists were required to pay large sums in compensation this would con-stitute an additional 'penalty' faced by them for acting unlawfully. Private enforcement of competition law is, at the time of writing, a topical issue and is likely to remain so in the future. There is little history of suc-cessful private actions in Europe, but this can be contrasted with a strong plaintiff-led history of compensation claims in the US. The reasons for this disparity are both legal and cultural, but the European authorities are seeking to learn from the US experience and encourage a more active role for compensation claims in Europe. In developing this area there are a number of difficulties that need to be addressed. One issue is the bal-ance between EC law and national procedure. The other is the balance between the, sometimes competing, goals of compensating loss and increas-ing deterrence.

---

51 For discussion of the insolvency concern see Stephan, A, 'The Bankruptcy Wildcard in Cartel Cases' [2006] JBL 511, and Motta, M, 'On Cartel Deterrence and Fines in the European Union' [2008] ECLR 209.

The seminal ruling in *Courage v Crehan*,[52] and the Court's subsequent judgment in *Manfredi*,[53] set out the position of compensation claims in relation to EC competition law. It is now clear that, as a matter of law, 'any individual' who has suffered loss through a breach of EC competition law can bring a claim. Domestic procedure is also restricted through EC law in that it cannot make such a claim 'excessively difficult'. While Mr Crehan's claim was eventually unsuccessful,[54] it was crucial in setting the scene for future developments in the area. What became clear in the *Crehan* and *Manfredi* litigation was that the procedural rules in place in the Member States can make it very difficult to bring compensation claims in competition cases. The particular problems in cartel cases were highlighted by the circumstances in *Manfredi*, where hundreds of small claims were brought by Italian consumers who had been affected by an insurance cartel. This means that in competition cases there is a mix of EC and domestic law operating together. As the number of cases increase it is likely that the Court of Justice, through the Art 234 EC procedure, will be involved in an increasing number of disputes, and may begin to develop a body of procedural rules that apply across Europe. This would be relatively novel as the Court has always been at pains to respect the 'procedural autonomy' of Member States' domestic legal systems.

When one looks at the substantive problems in bringing claims it is clear why the use of private actions across Europe was described as being in a state of 'astonishing diversity and total underdevelopment' in 2004.[55] The main problem with bringing such claims in cartel cases can be explained by looking at the nature of the loss suffered. The cartelist will charge an inflated price to its customers and therefore they will apparently suffer a loss. But in a great many cartel cases the direct purchaser is a manufacturer, as many cartelised industries are in bulk products used as industrial inputs, and therefore may be in a position to pass on the cartel overcharge, in whole or in part, to its customers when it places its product into the retail chain. The eventual harm may well be suffered by the final consumer who cannot pass the loss any further down the supply chain. The direct purchaser is probably in the best position to claim against the cartel, but in reality they may have not suffered much, or any, loss. The final consumer will definitely have suffered loss, but their loss is very remote from the unlawful act and may, in each individual case, be relatively small; will they be able to effectively bring a claim and be incentivised to undertake the cost, and risk, associated with legal action?

52 Case C-453/99 *Courage v Crehan* [2001] ECR I-6297.
53 Cases C-295-298/04 *Manfredi* [2006] ECR I-6619.
54 *Inntrepreneur Pub Company (CPC) and others v Crehan* [2006] UKHL 38.
55 Ashurst, 'Study on the conditions of claims for damages in case of infringement of EC competition rules', August 2004.

Standing and procedure

All jurisdictions that allow individuals to make compensation claims in relation to cartel activity must decide on who should be allowed to claim. The decision as to who can claim, and how, will impact on whether the system is designed to encourage compensation or designed to encourage deterrence. All compensation claims will obviously further both goals, but a balance must be struck between them. In the EC it seems likely that the indirect purchaser will be given standing to claim. This stems from the Court's ruling in *Crehan v Courage*, where it held that 'any individual' can make a compensation claim under EC law. Domestic procedure that makes such claims 'excessively difficult' must be disapplied. That choice means that the EC focus will necessarily be on compensation, but that has consequences for the deterrent effect of private actions. The main problem that follows from allowing indirect purchaser standing is that, in a compensation-focused system, you cannot allow both indirect and direct purchasers to claim for the same loss; if both were able to claim for the whole sum one would make a 'windfall' recovery greater than their actual loss. Either only one class is given standing, or a potentially complex apportionment task must be undertaken. If the indirect purchaser only is given standing the problem is that the indirect purchaser has limited incentive to bring a claim. They are comparatively distant from the unlawful activity and their individual loss is usually quite small. If they are unlikely to receive a significant sum of compensation they are unlikely to begin the costly process of litigation. Under Federal law in the US only the direct purchaser is given standing.[56] As the direct purchaser is closer to the unlawful activity they will find it easier to calculate their loss. They are also more likely to have suffered a significant individual loss which would incentivise them to bring a claim.

When indirect purchasers have been given standing the direct purchaser's ability to claim is limited as they will face the passing-on defence, that they have passed on their loss to their customers. The indirect purchaser will be less incentivised to sue. The question then becomes: How do we make it easier for them to bring a claim, and therefore more likely that they will? Much of the current debate focuses on this issue. The European Commission began a consultation in 2005 with its Green Paper.[57] That was followed, in the UK, in

---

56 See, *Hanover Shoe v United States Shoe Machinery Corp* 392 US 481 (1968) and *Illinois Brick Co v Illinois* 431 US 720 (1977). It is interesting that while this is the position in federal law many State legislatures have overturned the federal position to give back standing to indirect purchasers.

57 Green Paper on damage actions for breach of the EC antitrust rules, COM(2005) 672 final. For discussion see, Pheasant, J, 'Damages Actions for Breach of the EC Antitrust Rules: the European Commission's Green Paper' [2006] ECLR 365; and, Eilmansberger, T, 'The Green Paper on Damages Actions for Breach of the EC Antitrust Rules and Beyond: Reflections on the Utility and Feasibility of Stimulating Private Enforcement through Legislation' (2007) 44(2) CMLRev 431.

2007, by the OFT's Discussion Paper and Recommendations.[58] In 2008, the Commission then furthered the debate when it published its White Paper.[59] Many of the issues in this debate concern procedural mechanisms to make it easier for the final consumer, who will have clearly suffered loss, to bring a successful claim. One of the most popular options is the encouragement of representative actions, where a representative body brings an action on behalf of a wide class of purchasers.[60] Such an action would spread the cost, and the risk, within a wide class. The representative body would also be incentivised to bring an action as it would enhance its standing and legitimacy with the consumers it represents. Such actions are already available under s 47B of the 1998 Act, but have so far been of limited use. The only major representative action was *The Consumers Association v JJB Sports PLC*, which settled in January 2008.[61] While the action did recover compensation, and the Consumers Association recovered its costs, the action highlighted the limitations of representative actions in their current form. Further procedural modifications will be needed to facilitate other actions in the future. Some of the suggestions in the OFT's Recommendations indicate areas of possible reform: the further encouragement of representative actions, which could be based on opt-in procedures, with a named class, or opt-out procedures, representing claimants at large, depending on the circumstances of the case; increased conditional fees; and cost-capping and cost-protection to encourage claimants. The Commission White Paper is somewhat more conservative but proposes similar mechanisms.

In the ongoing debate it will be important for DG Comp and the national authorities to balance the needs of compensation – ensuring that those who have suffered loss can seek compensation – with the needs of deterrence, maximising the number and value of claims to increase the 'penalty' faced by cartelists.[62] Those who are best placed to bring a claim may not be those who suffered a loss, and those who have suffered the clearest loss may be the least able to bring a claim. Any increase in private actions from the current low base will improve the current situation and the risks of a US-style 'litigation culture' are probably overstated.[63] Even if there is individual overcompensation,

---

58 OFT Discussion Paper, Private actions in competition law: effective redress for consumers and business, OFT 916, April 2007, and OFT Recommendations, Private actions in competition law: effective redress for consumers and business, OFT 916resp, November 2007.

59 White Paper on Damages actions for breach of the EC antitrust rules, COM(2008) 165 final.

60 On representative actions see, Dayagi-Epstein, O, 'Representation of Consumer Interests by Consumer Associations – Salvation for the Masses' (2006) 3(2) CompLRev 209.

61 CAT Case 1078/7/9/07. For information on the settlement see, Consumers Association, 'JJB to pay fans over football shirt rip-off', 9 January 2008.

62 See, Nebbia, P, 'Damages actions for the Infringement of EC Competition Law: compensation or deterrence?' (2008) 33(1) ELRev 23.

63 See Martin, JS, 'Private Antitrust Litigation in Europe: What Fence is High Enough to Keep out the US Litigation Cowboy?' [2007] ECLR 2.

in that the total amount of compensation exceeds the losses suffered by that claimant, it is unlikely that the compensation awarded will, in reality, exceed the amount of gain made by the cartelist. This is because, even in opt-out actions, some of those who have suffered loss will not be in the class making the claim and the gains made by a cartel do not always equate to direct losses attributable to their customers.[64]

Individual penalties: criminalisation and disqualification

The penalties discussed so far have been imposed on undertakings, usually against companies. One of the reasons that it is not possible to simply increase corporate fines to a deterrent level is that it may result in insolvency for the company, thereby causing undesirable social costs. The cost of insolvency would fall upon the shareholders, employees and suppliers of the company. The shareholders may have benefited from the cartel, via increased profitability, but they would not have been aware of, or responsible for, the unlawful behaviour. The company's suppliers and the majority of the employees, barring those directly involved,[65] would also suffer when they were not responsible for the harm caused. Accordingly, we should seek to direct penalties to those directly responsible. If the only penalties are imposed on the undertaking there is a risk that individual decision-makers will decide to risk a future penalty being imposed on the undertaking as its impact will be diffused across the company, whereas they would be more circumspect if a penalty would be directly imposed upon them. On the basis of this rationale the UK introduced a number of individual penalties in relation to competition law. The most severe penalty, the cartel offence, is only available in cartel cases.

The cartel offence

When the cartel offence was introduced in ss 188 and 189 of the Enterprise Act 2002 the rationale put forward was largely based on the deterrence of cartel conduct.[66] The offence itself criminalises an individual who 'dishonestly agrees' to 'make or implement' a horizontal cartel arrangement within the UK.[67] The scope of the offence is limited to the most serious,

---

64 It is interesting that the award of restitutionary damages – those based on the gain made through the unlawful conduct – were rejected in the *Vitamins* litigation; see, *Devenish Nutrition Ltd v Sanofi-Aventis SA* [2007] EWHC 2394 (Ch).

65 It is often the case that by the time a corporate fine is imposed those individuals who were directly responsible may have left the company and will not be directly affected by the penalty. This can be justified as it is the company who must take responsibility for ensuring that its officers and employees comply with the law.

66 See MacCulloch, A, 'The Cartel Offence and the Criminalisation of UK Competition Law' [2003] JBL 615.

67 Enterprise Act 2002, s 188(1).

so-called 'hard core', cartel restrictions, namely, price fixing, preventing supply or production, dividing supply or customers, or bid-rigging.[68] The sanctions available under the cartel offence are important. It is generally believed that individual financial penalties are of limited effectiveness. There is nothing to stop the undertaking concerned from compensating an executive who has been held personally liable and, in effect, paying the fine. This would simply increase the corporate fine imposed to a minimal extent. For that reason it is believed that the possibility of a real chance of imprisonment is an important aspect of deterrence. Under the cartel offence the maximum sanction is one of up to five years imprisonment.[69] While a fine can be paid by a company, it cannot go to jail on behalf of an offender. The likelihood of spending time in jail should focus the mind of those company representatives who are actively involved in a cartel. Even if the company is willing to risk the chances of being caught, and having a corporate fine imposed, an individual may not be willing to risk their liberty in order that the company may inflate its profits.[70] This seeks to drive a wedge between the incentives for the company to involve itself in a cartel and the individual incentives of those who have to implement the day-to-day cartel activity. The first successful prosecutions, in the Marine Hose cartel, resulted in three cartelists being sentenced to jail time between two and a half and three years.[71] If there was no real prospect of jail time the cartel offence would have limited deterrent effect.

The introduction of the concept of dishonesty into the cartel offence raises a number of interesting issues. The dishonesty test is that developed under the Theft Act 1968 as set out in *Ghosh*:[72] is the behaviour dishonest according to the 'ordinary standards of reasonable and honest people'? It is arguable that there was no need to introduce the, potentially difficult, concept into the cartel offence at all.[73] The challenge for the OFT to prove the dishonesty of cartel behaviour was highlighted by the House of Lords in *Norris*, which held that, in the period before the adoption of the cartel offence, the collusive fixing of prices was not, in itself, dishonest under English law.[74] While the

68 Enterprise Act 2002, s 188(2).
69 Enterprise Act 2002, s 190. An unlimited fine is also available, but, for the reasons given, even large fines would have limited impact.
70 In US cases there is some evidence that some individuals are willing to risk imprisonment for a personal gain through promotion and financial reward. They are sometimes dubbed the 'Vice President in Charge of Going to Jail'.
71 OFT Press Release 72/08, 'Three imprisoned in first OFT criminal prosecution for bid rigging', 11 June 2008. This case was a result of guilty pleas based on a US plea bargain.
72 *R v Ghosh* [1982] 2 All ER 689.
73 See, in particular, Fisse, B, 'The Australian Cartel Criminalisation Proposals: An Overview and Critique' (2007) 4(1) CompLRev 51. The US has brought a large number of criminal prosecutions without having such a mechanism.
74 *Norris v Government of the United States of America* [2008] UKHL 16.

dishonesty test may in practice pose a significant challenge for the prosecution it forces competition lawyers to address an interesting set of questions regarding the morality of cartel conduct.[75] As the dishonesty test is essentially a question of morality for the jury to decide, according to their 'ordinary' standards of honesty, it poses questions as to whether the public at large consider cartel activity to be dishonest or immoral. The best evidence in relation to the UK suggests that while the public see price-fixing as wrong, and deserving of punishment, they do not, as yet, equate it with serious crimes where one would necessarily expect imprisonment as a sanction.[76] If the existence of the cartel offence, and publicity surrounding prosecutions, creates a general environment in which such behaviour is considered intrinsically 'wrong', and therefore deserving of moral sanction, it is far more likely that individuals will be deterred from entering into such arrangements. The reason most people do not breach the law is that they see themselves as decent law-abiding people, not just because they fear being caught and sanctioned. It would therefore be useful if the competition authorities used publicity surrounding cases to clearly set out why such conduct is wrong and develop increased stigma associated with hard-core cartels.[77]

Competition Disqualification Orders

The Enterprise Act also introduced another form of individual penalty, the Competition Disqualification Order. The Company Directors Disqualification Act 1986 was amended – adding s 9A – to allow for a court to disqualify an individual from being a Director as 'unfit' where they were a Director of a company that has breached competition law.[78] This would include any breach of Arts 81 or 82 EC, or the 1998 Act. The Director's conduct must have contributed to the breach, they should have suspected the breach, or they ought to have known of the breach. A disqualification under this provision can be for up to 15 years. This gives the OFT the opportunity to seek an individual sanction against a company director in relation to their involvement in anti-competitive conduct. It is possible to seek such an order where a prosecution under the cartel offence would be unlikely to succeed.

---

75 See MacCulloch, A, 'Honesty, Morality and the Cartel Offence' [2007] ECLR 355, and Stucke, ME, 'Morality and Antitrust' [2006] Colum Bus LRev 443.

76 See Stephan, A, 'Survey of Public Attitudes to Price-Fixing and Cartel Enforcement in Britain' CCP Working Paper 07–12, May 2007.

77 It is clear that OFT is stepping up its publicity efforts in cartel cases, although there are risks associated with increased publicity, OFT Press Release 54/08 'Wm Morrison Supermarkets plc: an apology', 23 April 2008. See also, Yeung, K, 'Does the Australian Competition and Consumer Commission Engage in "Trial by Media"?' (2006) 27 Law & Policy 549.

78 See OFT Guidance, 'Competition Disqualification Orders', OFT 510, May 2003.

Increasing punishment

The level of punishment associated with cartels has increased dramatically as the attitude towards cartels has hardened. That trend will continue as the authorities appear to be more willing to adopt ever-larger fines and more legal systems consider the imposition of individual penalties to bolster the 'standard' corporate penalties. This inexorable increase is not without costs. As penalties increase the likelihood that undertakings will challenge infringement decisions also increases. A legal challenge to the imposition of a fine is now the norm under EC law. The cost and complexity of bringing both a criminal prosecution and an administrative infringement procedure in relation to the same conduct will be considerable. Nonetheless, an examination of the deterrent effect of the current regimes in the EC and UK indicates that underdeterrence is a distinct possibility. While penalties are now increasing it is unlikely that an increase in penalties alone will sufficiently deter cartels.

Increasing the likelihood of catching cartels

European competition authorities have a number of tools at their disposal to investigate possible cartel activity in European markets, but those investigative powers are only really useful when the enforcer has a clear indication that something is amiss within a particular industry. As the authorities have limited resources, they have to focus their regulatory efforts on situations where there is a realistic chance of discovering an infringement. One potential source of information for the authorities is complaints from customers of a cartel; however, there are many reasons why customers are unlikely to have a good indication that their supplier's behaviour is a result of a cartel agreement, or they may simply be wary of complaining about an important trading partner. Given the clearly unlawful nature of cartels, they can only be truly effective if they are organised in secret. A cartel that acted openly would face challenge very quickly. It is therefore likely that cartelists will take steps to disguise their activity from both the authorities and their customers. Even if a customer had suspicions that something was going on it is unlikely they have much in the way of useful evidence that they could pass on to an enforcement agency. When a customer is suspicious about their suppliers there are reasons they may not want to press the issue and make a formal complaint. A successful cartel is likely to include the vast majority of suppliers in a market. If that is the case a potential complainant may be wary of harming its relationship with all the potential suppliers of an important input product. It is not unheard of for cartels to protect themselves by disciplining customers who act against the cartel's interests.

It is vital that enforcement authorities develop tools to break open secretive cartel arrangements and gather enough evidence to initiate a formal investigation. There are a number of ways that information from inside a cartel has found its way to the attention of the authorities. Information may leak from the cartel and find its way into the media.[79] Information may come from disgruntled former employees of cartelists. In recent years an interesting new route for the discovery of cartels has emerged: due diligence in mergers and takeovers. When companies are in merger discussions there will be a process of diligence whereby the parties will attempt to ensure all potential legal liabilities are taken into account. If one party discovers the other may have been involved in a cartel in the past they will require that that liability be minimised before the deal can go ahead. The cartel will often then come out into the open.

The problem with relying on these sources of information is that they will occur relatively rarely. The authorities need to find a way to get good information out of the cartel itself, as the participants will obviously be able to provide the best evidence of what has gone on and be able to point the authorities in the right direction when they want to undertake an investigation. The most viable option for the authorities to facilitate the break-up of cartels is by encouraging some of the participants to inform the authorities of what has gone on. Accordingly, the main tool that is used to put pressure on cartels and encourage parties to 'whistle-blow' is a leniency policy, which offers some form of immunity in return for information.

Leniency policies

Leniency policies have proved to be the most significant feature in the ongoing battle between competition law enforcers and cartels. The potential reward of immunity for information to assist in the investigation of an infringement is not a new feature of enforcement regimes, but the way in which leniency policies operate has now been fine-tuned, through a greater understanding of cartels, to make them increasingly effective. To understand how a leniency policy works it is important to understand the pressures that a cartel faces and the mechanisms that are used to keep cartels together.

Cartelisation is not the natural state of an industry. In order for a cartel to operate successfully there must be some form of structure and management to maintain it. If one accepts that the natural state is competition, in the sense that it serves self-interest and profit maximisation, in order for a cartel to form there must be a concerted effort to reshape a market. Even in situations where an industry can get together and come to some form of arrangement as to future conduct there will still be strong individual incentives to 'cheat' on that arrangement. The best way for a cartel member to maximise its short-term profits is to agree the cartel price with other cartel members and then cheat by selling larger quantities at a slightly lower price.

---

79 See, for instance, OFT Decision CA98/05/2006 Exchange of information on future fees by certain independent fee-paying schools, 20 November 2006.

This is sometimes known as 'chiselling' and is beneficial in the short term as the cheat will gain extra customers, as it has undercut the cartel, but will make a supra-competitive profit on each sale, as the price will be above the 'competitive' price, even though it is below the inflated cartel price. This incentive to cheat suggests that cartels may be inherently unstable and are only likely to succeed if the cartel is able to hold its members together. Although there are short-term benefits in cheating, it does jeopardise the future prospects of the cartel as a price war may break out, which would return the market to competitive pricing levels. The long-term benefit of a cartel comes from all cartel members keeping to the deal and staying true to the commonly adopted policy.

For a cartel to be successful there must be some mechanism to ensure that all the members of the cartel are keeping to the agreement. The most obvious way of doing so is through a formal, and legally enforceable, cartel agreement; the cartelists would all know that if any member stepped out of line there would a legal sanction for noncompliance. The first step in the early days of cartel control was to deny the enforceability of such agreements and other legal mechanisms, such as Trust Companies in the US, which were used to support cartels. As cartels are driven underground, with increasing levels of secrecy, it becomes more difficult for them to successfully build and maintain long-term cartel organisations. The secret of a cartel's success is building trust within the group.[80] The problem for cartelists is that most of the trust-building mechanisms which they might employ would increase the risk that the cartel's activities will be noticed by the authorities, thereby increasing the risk of prosecution. Many such mechanisms, such as direct communication, information sharing or auditing, leave a paper trail, which, if discovered, would provide good evidence of the cartel's activity. By reducing the ability to use such trust-building mechanisms, competition law decreases the chance of cartels successfully forming and increases the likelihood that a cartel will collapse through chiselling and the reprisals which would no doubt follow.

Leniency policy has been particularly effective as a regulatory tool when deployed against contemporary cartels, as it accentuates the inherent instability and distrust within them. A leniency policy is designed to give members of an ongoing cartel further reason to distrust their co-conspirators. If there is an active leniency policy, they not only have to worry about cheating, but also that a member of the cartel who wishes to exit and resume competition, may seek to protect its future position by going to the authorities and blowing the whistle on the cartel in return for immunity. By gaining immunity they protect themselves, but by informing on the cartel they also place their former friends, but future competitors, at a competitive disadvantage. When a cartel does not have strong trust relationships within it the existence of such

---

80 The important nature of trust in the formation and maintenance of cartels is comprehensively discussed in Leslie, CR, 'Trust, Distrust, and Antitrust' (2004) 82(3) Texas LRev 515.

a policy can generate a level of fear and distrust, that someone might conceivably go to the authorities, such that it might encourage one member to 'get their retaliation in first'. For a leniency policy to be successful it only needs to encourage one cartelist to leave and inform. This is sometimes known as the 'race to the courthouse door', where former cartelists compete to be the first to inform and get the benefit of immunity. A successful leniency policy will play on these fears to maximise the chances of two things happening: (i) the cartel breaking up, and (ii) one of the cartel members providing good evidence, in return for immunity, which will allow the authorities to begin infringement proceedings.

Leniency in the EC

The leniency policy operational within the Community is set out in the Commission's 2006 'Notice on Immunity from fines and reduction of fines in cartel cases'.[81] This Notice follows on from the earlier 2002 and 1996 Notices.[82] The 2002 Notice was generally perceived as being a success, particularly as a great many cartelists sought immunity or fine reductions under the Notice, but the 2006 Notice seeks to refine the earlier practice and make the leniency option more enticing by increasing the transparency and predictability of the scheme. Some form of leniency has been seen in the majority of recent cartel cases. In *Elevators and Escalators*,[83] KONE received immunity in relation to the cartel's activity in Belgium and Luxembourg (€74.5m) and Otis received immunity in relation to its activities in the Netherlands (€108m). The 2006 Notice offers immunity to the first undertaking to come forward disclosing its participation in a cartel and offering information and evidence to allow the Commission to: (a) carry out a targeted inspection, or (b) find an infringement of Article 81 EC.[84] In order to be able to carry out a targeted inspection the Commission will need a corporate statement, which includes: a detailed description of the alleged cartel arrangement; the names and addresses of all the other undertakings that participated in the alleged cartel; the names, positions and locations of all individuals who, to

---

81 Commission Notice on Immunity from fines and reduction of fines in cartel cases, OJ 2006, C298/17. On the operation of the 2006 Notice see, Sandhu, JS, 'The European Commission's Leniency Policy: a success?' [2007] ECLR 148.

82 OJ 2002, C45/3 and OJ 1996, C207/4. The offer of immunity was introduced by the 2002 Notice, with only fine reductions being available under the 1996 Notice. For discussion of the earlier Notices see, Riley, A, 'Cartel Whistle-Blowing: Towards an American Model?' (2002) 9 Maastricht J 67, and Arp, DJ and Swaak, RAA, 'A Tempting Offer: Immunity from Fines for Cartel Conduct under the European Commission's Leniency Notice' [2003] ECLR 9.

83 Commission Press Release IP/07/209, 'Commission fines members of lifts and escalators cartels over €990 million', 21 February 2007, and Commission Decision, *Elevators and Escalators*, C(2005) 512 final.

84 2006 Notice, OJ 2006, C298/17, para 8.

the applicant's knowledge, are or have been involved in the alleged cartel; information on which other competition authorities have been approached in relation to the alleged cartel; and other evidence relating to the alleged cartel in the possession of the applicant or available to it.[85] The applicant must also continue to co-operate with the Commission's investigation.[86] The introduction of a 'marker' system in the 2006 Notice was designed to enhance confidence in the system. An applicant may now go to the Commission and provide information concerning its name and address, the parties to the alleged cartel, the affected products and territory, the estimated duration of the alleged cartel and the nature of the alleged cartel conduct.[87] On the basis of that limited information the Commission will grant a marker, essentially holding a place in the leniency queue, and allow the applicant to provide the rest of the information, and 'perfect' its marker, within a particular time frame. Only the first undertaking to provide such information can be granted immunity. To benefit from the leniency policy undertakings must provide information the Commission is not already aware of through its own efforts,[88] or immunity may be denied if the undertaking concerned took steps to coerce other undertakings to join the cartel or to remain in it.[89] If an undertaking is not the first to come forward it will not be able to seek immunity, but it may still be able to be rewarded for information it provides through a reduction in fine. In order to be eligible for a fine reduction it must provide evidence of the alleged infringement which represents significant added value with respect to the evidence already in the Commission's possession, and co-operate fully.[90] Information of added value does not need to be completely new, as long as it strengthens the Commission's ability to prove its allegations. An undertaking that provides the first information of added value can expect a reduction in fine of between 30 and 50%; the second between 20 and 30%; and, subsequent applicants up to 20%.[91] The availability of fine reductions is somewhat controversial. There are no such reductions formally available under the Department of Justice's (DoJ) Corporate Leniency Policy (CLP) in the US.[92] It only offers immunity to the first applicant; there is no prize for second place. The DoJ's CLP is generally regarded as being highly effective and therefore the starkness of the incentive to be first could be one of the reasons for its success. In practice the difference between the EC policy and its

---

85 Ibid, para 9.
86 Ibid, para 12.
87 Ibid, para 15.
88 Ibid, para 10.
89 Ibid, para 13.
90 Ibid, paras 24–25.
91 Ibid, para 26.
92 Department of Justice, Corporate Leniency Policy, August 1993. For a discussion of the CLP see, Harding, C, and Joshua, J, *Regulating Cartels in Europe – A Study of Legal Control of Corporate Delinquency*, 2000, Oxford: OUP, Chapter VIII.

counterpart in the US is less stark. Although there is no leniency for second place set out in the policy the DoJ is often willing to enter into a plea bargain if a cartelist is willing to admit involvement and co-operate with its investigation; a fine reduction will usually be the reward for accepting a plea bargain.

The EC's leniency policy, particularly since 2002, has proved to be very successful. The increasing decentralisation of competition law enforcement does, however, create some problems for a centralised approach to leniency. An undertaking that is granted leniency by the Commission, protecting it in relation to the application of Art 81 EC, is not necessarily protected from the application of domestic competition law within one or more Member States. The Commission has sought to address this by adopting an EC Model Leniency Programme.[93] The model sets out the treatment that a leniency applicant should expect from any NCA within the ECN. This creates a minimum leniency standard across the Community, although each Member State can operate a more generous policy if it desires. It is hoped this will reduce the chance that an undertaking will decide not to seek leniency because of the fear that it will be subject to fines in one Member State.

Leniency in the UK

The OFT has adopted a full leniency policy. As there are a wider range of sanctions for cartel conduct in the UK, there are a range of leniency policies which give protection against all those sanctions. Immunity is available from administrative fines under the Art 81 EC and the Chapter I prohibition under the 1998 Act, the Cartel Office under the Enterprise Act 2002, and Competition Disqualification Orders under the Company Directors Disqualification Act 1986.[94]

Leniency from Art 81 and the Chapter I prohibition

The OFT's leniency policy is set out in the same document as its guidance on the calculation of fines, clearly indicating the linkage between the two policies.[95] In order to be guaranteed immunity an undertaking must: be the first to come forward with information, before the OFT has commenced an investigation; provide all the information available to it; maintain co-operation; refrain from further activity; and, not have taken steps to coerce others to take part in the activity.[96] A second level of protection is available in

---

93 DG Comp, ECN Model Leniency Programme, 29 September 2006.
94 General guidance about all forms of OFT leniency can be found in, Leniency in Cartel Cases, OFT 436, March 2005 and Leniency and no-action – OFT's draft final guidance note on the handling of applications, OFT 803a, November 2006.
95 OFT's guidance as to the appropriate amount of a penalty, OFT 423, December 2004.
96 Ibid, para 3.9.

situations where an undertaking is the first to come forward but the OFT has already begun an investigation, but has not yet issued a Statement of Objections. In such circumstances, on receiving the same level of co-operation as required for immunity, the OFT may grant a discretionary reduction in fine of up to 100%. The OFT will only grant a full reduction if it takes the view that such a reduction is deserved, given the stage of the investigation and the value of the information provided.[97] While such discretion may be seen as 'fair' it may be counterproductive. The key factor in encouraging a leniency applicant to come forward is, as discussed above, a balance between the fear of betrayal, and its associated costs, against the rewards of leniency. If the rewards of the leniency policy are not clear to a potential applicant, because they cannot predict whether they will get immunity or a much lower reduction, it may discourage them from coming forward. In this area there is much to be said for offering potentially 'unfair' rewards in order to ensure that cartels are much more likely to break down. If another undertaking comes forward with information to the OFT before the Statement of Objections is issued, they can be rewarded with a fine reduction of up to 50%. The grant of such a reduction is, again, discretionary. Nonetheless, in the case of a subsequent applicant, the discretionary nature of the reduction is less problematic. The OFT has operated its leniency policy on many occasions. One of the most notable cases was *Long-Haul Passenger Fuel Surcharges*[98] where Virgin Atlantic was awarded full immunity for bringing the cartel to the OFT's attention.

The OFT has adopted a number of innovative reforms to bolster its leniency policy. The first is known as 'Amnesty Plus' after its US counterpart. If an undertaking is not able to be awarded immunity in relation to a cartel, perhaps because it was not the first applicant, it may be awarded an increased fine reduction in that case if it can provide information on another, separate, cartel of which the OFT is not aware.[99] Of course, by being the first to come forward in relation to the second cartel, the undertaking may also be entitled to immunity in regard to that case. They can therefore be described as getting 'amnesty' in the second cartel 'plus' an additional fine reduction in the first. Such a policy is potentially very powerful as practice tells us that if an undertaking has been a member of a successful cartel in one market it is more likely to be involved in cartels in related markets.[100] The second innovation adopted

---

97 Ibid, paras 3.11–3.12.
98 See OFT Press Release 113/07, 'British Airways to pay record £121.5m penalty in price fixing investigation', 1 August 2007.
99 Ibid, paras 3.16–3.17.
100 The complex series of cartels across the chemicals industry is a clear example of this sort of behaviour. The US also operates a 'Penalty Plus' policy, whereby a company or individual under investigation for cartel activity, which decides not to take 'Amnesty Plus', and inform the DoJ of another ongoing offence, will be treated very harshly should a second offence be discovered later.

by the OFT is the offer of direct financial incentives for information about cartels. In February 2008 the OFT introduced a policy, which sits alongside its leniency policy, which offers a financial reward to anyone who can provide useful information about cartel activity.[101] The discretionary financial reward offered can be up to £100,000, depending on the nature and usefulness of the information. This will not usually be available to anyone directly involved in the cartel, who will be expected to seek leniency, but will be for others, of a more peripheral nature, who have 'inside' information on a cartel's activity.

Leniency from the Cartel Offence and CDOs

The OFT also offers a leniency scheme in relation to the cartel offence. Where an individual comes forward with information the OFT can grant immunity from prosecution through a no-action letter issued under s 190(4) of the Enterprise Act 2002.[102] Such a letter is effective in England, Wales, and Northern Ireland. The position in Scotland is somewhat different, in that the OFT will inform the Lord Advocate of the individual's co-operation and the Lord Advocate will take that into account in deciding whether or not a prosecution should be brought in Scotland. The information that should be provided for individual leniency is similar to that required for Chap I/Art 81 leniency.[103] If an individual has sought leniency from the cartel offence, or is the director of a company that has sought Chap I/Art 81 leniency, they will be reassured that the OFT will not seek a Competition Disqualification Order against them.[104]

The individual leniency policies offer the same incentives as the corporate policies, discussed above, but they also offer another dimension to the effectiveness of leniency as a whole. Corporate leniency seeks to heighten distrust between the corporate members of a cartel, to encourage undertakings to defect and inform. An individual leniency programme not only heightens inter-corporate distrust, but also encourages distrust within an undertaking. Not all the individuals within an undertaking will be as willing to risk their liberty or career to generate an increased corporate profit. For a leniency policy to be successful it does not need to encourage the undertaking as a corporate entity to seek leniency, although that would be beneficial in terms of gathering evidence. All that is required is that one individual, who has limited personal incentive to stay in the cartel, informs the OFT about the cartel activity. An undertaking that is involved in a cartel will therefore have to be very careful about which personnel become involved as

101 OFT, Rewards for information about cartels, 29 February 2008.
102 The Cartel Offence – Guidance on the issue of no-action letters for individuals, OFT 513, April 2003.
103 Ibid, para 3.3.
104 Ibid, para 3.15.

they are all potential leniency applicants. This further level of distrust makes it more likely that the cartel will collapse.

Direct settlement

The most recent development in the fight to increase the Commission's effectiveness against cartels is the adoption of a Regulation implementing 'settlement procedure' in cartel cases in the Community. Such a procedure allows the Commission to negotiate a settlement with the members of a cartel and bring the case to a successful conclusion more quickly. If the Commission has to devote less resources to a case that settles, it will be in a position to handle more cases and take action against a greater number of cartels. If the Commission is seen as being more active, and is seen as catching more cartels, this will obviously have a positive impact on deterrence.

The availability of direct settlement in the US, through its plea bargaining system, is an acclaimed feature of its regime, with the majority of cases settling in this way following leniency applications. A settlement procedure is attractive to cartelists as, after a leniency application has triggered an investigation, their continued co-operation in an investigation is rewarded through a fine reduction. The model envisaged by the Commission is not as flexible, or as attractive to cartelists, as a US plea bargain.[105] The settlement discussions between DG Comp and the members of the cartel would take place before the Statement of Objections is issued. Discussions would seek to reach a 'common understanding' on the following: the facts alleged, the gravity and duration of the infringement, and an estimation of the range of the fines. At the end of the discussions the parties should formally request to settle in a settlement submission acknowledging their liability, indicating a maximum amount of fine they foresee being imposed, confirming they have had the opportunity to make their views known, and that they do not envisage requesting access to the file or requesting an oral hearing. The last of these elements indicates the benefit for the Commission of settling such a case. It will be able to proceed to adopt an infringement decision, on the basis of the settlement submission, without having to give full access to the file or conducting a hearing. To avoid going through these steps it is vital that all the parties settle. It is unlikely that the Commission will seek a settlement where one of the parties is unable to come to a 'common understanding'. The reward for the parties will be a fine reduction of 10%. It is questionable whether this will be enough to offer sufficient encouragement to settle.

---

105 Commission Regulation 622/2008/EC amending Regulation (EC) No 773/2004, as regards the conduct of settlement procedures in cartel cases, OJ 2008, L171/3. See also Commission Notice on the conduct of settlement procedures in cartel cases, OJ 2008, C167/1.

One key difference between a US plea bargain and the form of settlement envisaged in the Community is the ability of the parties to appeal following a settlement. In the US there is a fuller form of negotiation, resulting in a full agreement over the fine levied and the information that becomes public. As a result the party who 'pleas out' will generally waive its right to appeal. The Commission does not foresee such a broad negotiation. The Commission has stated that it 'would neither negotiate nor bargain the use of evidence or the appropriate sanction, but could reward the parties' co-operation'.[106] The final fine will still be set by the Commission and a relatively full Statement of Objections will still be published. The parties will also retain their right to seek a review of the Commission decision before the CFI. It is hoped that as the parties have accepted their liability the chances of a legal challenge are reduced. However, most challenges do not concern liability, but the calculation of the fine. Accordingly, the potential for challenge would still exist in a great many cases. As the costs, and delay, surrounding review before the courts are potentially extensive, the savings involved in settlement may be minor.

The OFT has operated a flexible settlement process in appropriate cases. One of the most striking examples was the innovative settlement in the *Independent Schools* case.[107] As the schools involved in the price-fixing arrangement were charitable institutions it was not seen as appropriate to set anything more than a nominal fine of £10,000 on each institution. The OFT reached a settlement with the schools that they should make an 'ex-gratia' payment of £3m into an educational charitable trust to benefit the pupils who attended the schools during the affected period. More typical settlements can be seen in cases like *Long-Haul Passenger Fuel Surcharges*,[108] in which British Airways agreed to pay a penalty of £121.5m, thereby allowing the OFT to close its case, and *Dairy Products*,[109] in which Asda, Dairy Crest, Safeway, Sainsbury's, The Cheese Company and Wiseman admitted liability in relation to certain activities in an 'early resolution agreement' and agreed to pay reduced penalties of £116m.

106 Commission Press Release IP/07/1608, Antitrust: Commission calls for comments on a draft legislative package to introduce settlement procedure for cartels, 26 October 2007.

107 See OFT Press Release 88/06, 'Independent schools agree settlement. Competition investigation resolved', 19 May 2006, and OFT Decision CA98/05/2006 Exchange of information on future fees by certain independent fee–paying schools, 20 November 2006.

108 See OFT Press Release 113/07, 'British Airways to pay record £121.5m penalty in price fixing investigation', 1 August 2007.

109 OFT Press Release 170/07, 'OFT welcomes early resolution agreements and agrees over £116m penalties', 7 December 2007. See also OFT Press Release 82/08, 11 July 2008, on the tobacco cartel.

The future of cartel regulation

The fight against cartels, the 'supreme evil of antitrust',[110] has been stepped up remarkably in the early years of the twenty-first century. It is also notable that there appears to be a broad consensus within the global competition law enforcement community that cartels pose a serious threat that must be addressed through co-ordinated action. The 'spiritual' leader of competition policy in this sphere is the United States, as its long history of criminal enforcement is seen as a useful model for other jurisdictions. Other competition regimes are now learning from that experience and moving to increase the effectiveness of their regulatory efforts. The rapid development of cartel control mechanisms, typified by the increase in penalties and the development of leniency, which went in hand-in-hand with the European Commission's modernisation, through Reg 1/2003, highlights the renewed ambition in Brussels to take real steps to seek out and deal with cartels in Europe. The number of cases dealt with by the Commission indicates two things. First, the policy is having some success. The possibility of immunity from sanctions following the introduction of a leniency policy appears to have been successful in bringing cartels to the attention of the Commission. There is, however, evidence that the policy does not disrupt successful cartels; rather, it encourages members of a failing cartel to seek protection from potential liability.[111] Secondly, it appears that while we may have had some success, there are a significant number of cartels still operating. That indicates that still more needs to be done.

The introduction of individual criminal offences in relation to cartel activity in the UK and Australia also indicates the increasing seriousness with which the cartel problem is being treated. It is interesting that the debate surrounding the criminalisation of cartels is not about whether the use of criminal law is appropriate, but rather that the form of offence used is suitable to ensure that successful prosecutions can be brought.[112]

While there is a consensus that strenuous efforts must be taken to control cartels, there are also potential areas of concern that should be addressed. There are fears that while the competition law enforcement community share a consensus that cartels are highly damaging and deserve serious punishment, that feeling is not necessarily shared by the wider public,[113] politicians, or the

---

110 *Verizon Communications v Law Offices of Curtis V Trinko*, 540 U.S. 398, 408 (2004).
111 See, for example, Stephan, A, 'An Empirical Assessment of the 1996 Leniency Notice' CCP Working Paper 05–10, September 2005.
112 See, for example, MacCulloch, A, 'The Cartel Offence and the Criminalisation of UK Competition Law' [2003] JBL 615; Fisse, B, 'The Australian Cartel Criminalisation Proposals: An Overview and Critique' (2007) 4(1) CompLRev 51; and, Beaton-Wells, C, 'The politics of cartel criminalisation: a pessimistic view from Australia' [2008] ECLR 185.
113 See, Stephan, A, 'Survey of Public Attitudes to Price-Fixing and Cartel Enforcement in Britain' CCP Working Paper 07–12, May 2007.

business community.[114] It is important that the authorities take steps to ensure that the public are educated as to the problems that cartels cause in markets. Another important issue for competition enforcement agencies is to seek a balance between the various elements of any successful anti-cartel regime. In this chapter we have outlined a number of policies that operate to increase the regulatory pressure on cartels. While they all have a role to play, it is also true that some of the individual elements 'pull' in opposing directions. For example, increasing compensation awards in private actions increase the effective 'penalty' for involvement in a cartel and therefore overall deterrence; however, an increase in compensation claims can reduce the impact of leniency policy, by limiting the reward for leniency, as a leniency applicant can only be given immunity from administrative fines and will continue to face potentially large compensation payments. Similarly, a move towards direct settlement will mean that a competition authority is able to better utilise its resources against other cartels, but it will also mean that the overall level of fines is reduced and the limited information published by an authority in a case that settles may hinder 'follow-on' compensation claims. If the EC and UK competition authorities want to use all these enforcement tools fully, they must be aware of these overlaps and seek to ensure that they are coordinated, where possible, to ensure that overall policy is as effective as it can be. The debate on the future of private compensation actions in Europe gives a clear indication that the effective coexistence of compensation actions and leniency policy is one of the key issues being considered.[115]

The control of cartels has seen rapid development in Europe since the 1980s. The change of legal attitude is even more remarkable when you consider that the 'cartel problem' is almost as old as European industry itself. Many changes in the EC and UK have been put in place to increase the deterrent effect of the law. As these policies develop it will be interesting to see how effective they are at breaking up existing cartels and deterring others from coming together.

Further reading

General

Harding, C and Joshua, J, *Regulating Cartels in Europe: A Study of Legal Control of Corporate Delinquency*, 2003, Oxford: OUP.
Leslie, CR, 'Trust, Distrust, and Antitrust' (2004) 82(3) Texas LRev 515.

---

114 See, Yeung, K, 'Does the Australian Competition and Consumer Commission Engage in "Trial by Media"?' (2006) 27 Law & Policy 549.
115 See White Paper on Damages actions for breach of the EC antitrust rules, COM(2008) 165 final. See, also, Commission Staff Working Paper accompanying the White Paper on Damages actions for breach of the EC antitrust rules, SEC(2008) 404.

Fines

Connor, JM and Lande, RH, 'The Size of Cartel Overcharges: Implications for US and EU fining policies' (2006) 51(4) Antitrust Bulletin 983.

Motta, M, 'On Cartel Deterrence and Fines in the European Union' [2008] ECLR 209.

Wils, WPJ, 'Optimal Antitrust Fines: Theory and Practice' (2006) 29(2) World Comp 183.

Private actions

Dayagi-Epstein, O, 'Representation of Consumer Interests by Consumer Associations – Salvation for the Masses' (2006) 3(2) CompLRev 209.

Nebbia, P, 'Damages Actions for the Infringement of EC Competition Law: compensation or deterrence?' (2008) 33(1) ELRev 23.

Criminalisation

MacCulloch, A, 'Honesty, Morality and the Cartel Offence' [2007] ECLR 355.

Leniency

Sandhu, JS, 'The European Commission's Leniency Policy: a success?' [2007] ECLR 148.

Discussion

1   Are the financial penalties imposed on cartels sufficient to discourage cartelists from entering into potentially lucrative arrangements? Would there be negative implications if financial penalties were increased ever higher?

2   What do individual penalties, particularly criminal penalties, add to competition law enforcement which cannot be provided by corporate penalties alone?

3   An effective leniency policy is one of the key tools in the fight against cartels, but is it appropriate to waive sanctions, and reward an undertaking, which has entered into a clearly unlawful agreement and profited from it?

Chapter 6

Control of mergers

Introduction

Merger control is a particularly political area, principally due to divergent beliefs as to the merits of mergers and the contrasting analysis of the likely outcomes of proposed individual merger arrangements. In this context the term merger connotes a welcome, uncontested, union but it applies equally to a hostile takeover. The intricacies of both Community and UK merger controls ensure that the respective controls also apply to wider situations than the commonly understood full legal merger. The principal focus of merger control concerns the potential competitive consequences that may arise as a result of the increased concentration in a market caused by a merger. However, other policies and interests may also have a role to play, such as industrial and employment policy or national ownership of industry.

The general consensus in a free-market economy is that shareholders of a company are entitled to act as they wish in the pursuit of a more profitable return on their property. This right can be viewed as an incentive, or threat, to the management of the company to maintain a high degree of efficiency and profitability. The interests of the shareholders can consequently be viewed as a stimulant for a vibrant economy and, hence, any takeovers or mergers acceptable to shareholders should be welcomed. However, it is also generally recognised that mergers may have implications which extend beyond the shareholders' interests, requiring some form of control due to their possible wide-ranging effects on the economy. There are two general schools of thought concerning the appropriate degree of control of merger activity. The first would advocate intervention only if the proposed merger is likely to have an adverse effect on competition in a market, otherwise merger decisions should be left in the capable hands of entrepreneurs and, ultimately, shareholders. The second approach believes that a more interventionist stance is required because mergers have generally not yielded the anticipated benefits and have wide-ranging potential repercussions.

The primary benefit which a merger can bring is to improve the efficiency of the companies involved, particularly when there are economies of scale which can only be achieved by a merger. Efficiency can also be enhanced by better management or easier access to capital, both of which can result from a merger. Other benefits include the possibility of the takeover of a firm facing closure, thereby extending its life and reducing concerns regarding unemployment.

Of all the arguments raised against mergers, the most significant argument concerns the potential reduction in competition which may result. However, there are also wider concerns raised by mergers which may justify intervention by national and supra-national competition authorities. These concerns include objections as to the size and power of the merged firm, the possible detrimental effect of the merger on the balance of payments, and the transfer of control of a company into 'foreign' ownership. It may, in appropriate circumstances, be considered that these disadvantages reduce or negate any purported economic advantages which are raised in justification of a particular merger. There is also empirical evidence which suggests that merger objectives are not always achieved.[1]

The three generic types of merger which may be affected are horizontal mergers, vertical mergers and conglomerate mergers. One can identify different objections to each type of merger based on the outline of the purported benefits and detriments of each type of merger. Horizontal mergers are generally of greatest concern for competition law. They are effected by parties at the same level of the market, such as a merger between two producers, and the concern is that the increased concentration in the market may result in a reduction in inter-brand competition. This will particularly be the case where there are already few market participants, competition is limited, and the merged entity will have significant market share and market power, all of which is seen as being contrary to the pure competition policy objective outlined in Chapter 1. A vertical merger may result between a producer and a distributor of its products. Such mergers may have competitive consequences if they foreclose competitive opportunities to other market participants at either level of the market; for instance, if another producer can no longer find an outlet for its products as a result of the merger. On the other hand, as with vertical restraints, and as considered in Chapter 4, a vertical merger may enhance inter-brand competition by increasing the efficiency of that particular brand. Finally, although conglomerate mergers may not be directly associated with any competition gains or losses, it has been suggested, according to the 'deep-pocket theory', that conglomerates may cross-subsidise across products, thereby facilitating predatory pricing to defeat competition illegitimately, and that their wide 'portfolio' of products across a whole range

---

1 Cowling, K et al, Mergers and Economic Performance, 1980, Cambridge: CUP. See, also, Schenk, H, 'The performance of banking mergers: propositions and policy implications', in The Impact of Mergers and Acquisitions in France on Workers, Consumers and Shareholders, 2000, Uni Europa.

may give them other advantages.[2] However, the most interesting issue concerns the extent to which conglomerate mergers, and indeed also vertical and horizontal mergers, may be controlled on the basis of policies unconnected with the pure competition policy objective. This has been of particular interest in the UK context, although there has also been some discussion of this issue at the Community level. Finally, the trend towards 'global' mergers has an impact on merger control, requiring closer international co-operation between competition authorities.

This chapter will look at the approach to merger control undertaken by the Community and UK authorities, respectively. In the Community context, the Merger Regulation will be addressed.[3] Thereafter, we will focus on the UK merger control system contained within Pt 3 of the Enterprise Act 2002.

Historical background to the Community controls

There was no explicit provision for the control of mergers in the Treaty of Rome,[4] but the lack of a regulatory mechanism was recognised as being a problem. In a report in 1966 the Commission suggested that Art 82 would cover mergers where the merger amounted to an abuse of a dominant position.[5] This view was controversial although it was supported by the European Court of Justice in *Continental Can*.[6] Continental Can, a US company with a dominant position in the market for metal containers, attempted to obtain control of a Dutch undertaking operating in the same market. The Commission argued that the acquisition of the target company would constitute an abuse of Continental Can's dominant position as it would eliminate future competition between the two undertakings. On appeal, the Court overturned the Commission's Decision but upheld its reasoning in relation to the possibility of Art 82 applying to the extension of a dominant position through a merger.

The control of mergers by the use of Art 82 raised a number of problems. Article 82 would only apply to the extension of an existing dominant position, not to the creation of a dominant position through a merger. Article 82 would, therefore, not be useful in the regulation of a hostile takeover of a

---

2 See Scherer, FM and Ross, D, *Industrial Market Structure and Economic Performance*, 3rd edn, 1990, Boston: Houghton Mifflin. See, also, Bork, R, *The Antitrust Paradox: A Policy at War with Itself*, 1993, Oxford: Maxwell Macmillan.

3 Regulation 139/2004/EC on the control of concentrations between undertakings (the EC Merger Regulation), OJ 2004, L24/1.

4 There were merger provisions in the European Coal and Steel Community Treaty (the Treaty of Paris). See Newton, C, 'Do predators need to be dominant?' [1999] ECLR 127.

5 'Le problème de la concentration dans le marché commun' (1966) 3 Etudes CEE, série concurrence.

6 Case 6/72 *Continental Can v Commission* [1973] ECR 215; [1973] CMLR 199.

dominant undertaking by a non-dominant undertaking, a conglomerate merger,[7] or a vertical merger. Article 82 would also be limited in that there is no provision for defences or exemptions where a merger may prove to be beneficial. Beneficial mergers would only be permitted if they could be objectively justified and, therefore, not considered to be abusive within the terms of Art 82 itself. Furthermore, a major procedural difficulty in the use of Art 82 is that it would only be possible to control mergers after they had been completed. Once a merger is complete, and the appeal process is exhausted, a number of years may have passed and it would then be difficult to return the market to its original position.

The use of Art 81 to control mergers was not envisaged in the 1966 report; however, in the *Philip Morris* case,[8] Art 81 was held to be applicable to some mergers. Philip Morris was to purchase a 50% share of Rothmans Holdings, another cigarette manufacturer. After receiving complaints from competitors, the Commission intervened and Philip Morris agreed to change the nature of the purchase to lessen its competition concerns. Philip Morris reduced the size of its holding to 30.8% of the shares, with only 24.9% of the voting rights, and gave the Commission undertakings as to its influence on the Rothmans board. The Commission was happy with this arrangement but the original complainants challenged the Commission's Decision before the Court. The Court stated that Art 81 was applicable to the acquisition of shares in a competitor where the acquisition leads to an ability to influence the conduct of the target undertaking. The Court was careful to emphasise that it was discussing the acquisition of a minority shareholding in undertakings which remained independent after the purchase, but the Commission took a much wider view of the judgment, arguing that the judgment also meant that Art 81 would be applicable where a majority interest was acquired.[9] Nonetheless, the use of Art 81 to control acquisitions has a number of problems. The sanction of nullity under Art 81(2) is not suitable to the purchase of a controlling interest in an undertaking, and an Art 81(3) exemption can only be granted on the basis of the narrow grounds set out in the Treaty. The concerns raised by mergers are much broader than those mentioned in Art 81(3). There would appear to be limited scope for important social and political concerns to be taken into account. Exemptions granted must also be of limited duration. It is very difficult to undo a merger after a period of time, and it would be better practice to give the parties a firm decision after the initial consideration.

Alongside the development of potential merger controls under Arts 81 and 82 of the EC Treaty, the Commission attempted to persuade the Council

---

7 As there would be no extension of market power in any one market.

8 Cases 142 and 156/84 *BAT v Commission* [1987] ECR 4487; [1988] 4 CMLR 24.

9 A wide interpretation of the applicability of Art 81 appeared to be used in *Smalbach-Lubeca v Carnaud*, IP/88/14; [1988] 4 CMLR 262.

to adopt a separate system for the control of mergers within the Community. The Commission put forward its first proposal for a Merger Regulation in 1973 but the Council did not give the introduction of specific merger controls a high priority. The low political priority accorded to merger control meant that the Commission proposals were not acted on for 15 years. Several of the larger Member States wished to maintain their own controls over mergers while the smaller Member States, who did not have their own controls, wanted the Community to assume responsibility. One of the major impediments to reaching agreement was the setting of an appropriate demarcation between Community- and nationally-controlled mergers. The change in the Council's priorities resulted from two factors. First, the increasing number of large-scale and cross-border Community mergers, which resulted from preparation for the 1992 Single Market programme, raised awareness of the need for a unitary Community control system. A Community system was viewed as being better placed to deal with large multi-State mergers, as there would be one set of controls applicable rather than a number of separate national regimes. In addition, Community-based criteria could be used rather than criteria which focused on national interests. Secondly, the Commission argued that a specific merger control system would be more satisfactory than increasing resort to the existing, and deficient, set of rules under Arts 81 and 82 of the Treaty. Finally, the Regulation may have been advocated as a means of promoting Community-scale mergers which would make European industry more competitive in the global market, particularly in relation to industry in Japan and the US.

The original Merger Regulation was adopted by Council in December 1989 and came into force in September 1990.[10] The new system operated well in practice; however, the debate continued over the thresholds which brought a merger within the Community system. In 1996 the Commission issued a Green Paper outlining the issues which would be addressed in the review of the Merger Regulation.[11] The main concern was the level of the thresholds. They were initially fixed at a very high level in order to obtain support from Member States that wished to retain control over 'national' mergers. The Commission proposed that the thresholds be lowered. Political agreement was reached on the reform of the merger control system along the lines of a 'multiple filing' proposal, whereby a merger which would otherwise have to be filed in several Member States would go to the Commission, and an amending Regulation was adopted by Council in June 1997.[12] The Commission

10 Regulation 4064/89/EEC on the control of concentrations between undertakings, OJ 1990, L257/13.
11 Community Merger Control Green Paper on the review of the Merger Regulation, C(96) 19 final.
12 Regulation 1310/97/EEC amending Regulation 4064/89 on the control of concentrations between undertakings, OJ 1997, L180/1.

process of review continued and a Commission report on the application of the Merger Regulation thresholds was published in 2000.[13] Following that report, the Commission proceeded to investigate a number of issues and published a Green Paper on the review of the Merger Regulation in 2001.[14] Following consultation a draft proposal was published in late 2002[15] but was not adopted immediately and was subject to some important revisions, outlined below. The new Regulation was eventually approved in early 2004 and came into force on 1 May 2004.[16]

The Merger Regulation

The Merger Regulation was originally designed to reduce the confusion and bureaucracy arising from large-scale mergers in the Community. Cross-border mergers and mergers affecting different national markets often required notification under several different systems, each with different filing requirements. This duplication was costly and time consuming. A single system at the Community level would reduce the administrative burden, the single system being a 'one stop shop'. Control at a Community level was also seen to be important to allow Community undertakings to compete with US and Japanese competitors. Mergers between successful European undertakings were perceived as being one way in which Community-based industries could compete effectively in global markets. National controls were considered to be more likely to prevent important mergers on national, rather than competition, grounds. In addition, national merger controls were more likely to consider the competitive effects on the national market alone, even if the merger made competitive sense in a global industry. The adoption of the Regulation also led to a reorganisation of the Directorate General for Competition. A special unit, the Mergers Task Force, was set up to deal with all the cases stemming from the new system.[17]

The scope of the Regulation

Although the Regulation is known as the Merger Regulation, it does not use the term 'merger' but refers rather to the 'control of concentrations'. The Regulation covers not only full mergers, as used in the normal commercial

---

13 Report from the Commission to the Council on the application of the Merger Regulation thresholds, C(2000) 399 final.

14 Green Paper on the review of Council Regulation 4064/89, C(2001) 745/6 final.

15 Proposal for a Council Regulation on the control of concentrations between undertakings, C(2002) 711 final, OJ 2003, C20/06.

16 Regulation 139/2004/EC on the control of concentrations between undertakings (the EC Merger Regulation), OJ 2004, L24/1.

17 See Krause, H, 'EC merger control: an outside view from inside the merger task force' [1995] JBL 627.

sense, but all concentrations, whether through the acquisition of shares or assets, where an undertaking acquires control over another undertaking. Some joint ventures are also considered to be concentrations. Article 3 of the Regulation defines concentrations as:

(a) the merger of two or more previously independent undertakings or parts of undertakings; or
(b) the acquisition, by one or more persons already controlling at least one undertaking, or by one or more undertakings, whether by purchase of securities or assets, by contract or by any other means, of direct or indirect control of the whole or parts of one or more other undertakings.[18]

Article 3 of the Regulation gives a fairly detailed definition of the term 'concentration' and the Commission has published a Notice giving more detailed guidance as to how it will be applied.[19]

An obvious form of concentration is where previously independent undertakings merge and where one or both original undertakings cease to exist. Less obvious concentrations occur where a transaction results in a change of control over an undertaking. In these cases the central concern is whether the rights gained by one undertaking in another confer on the undertaking that gains the rights 'the possibility of exercising decisive influence'.[20] It is possible to gain such influence over another undertaking by acquiring a majority of voting shares in that undertaking, or by having the right to appoint half of the members of the controlling board. In *St Gobain/Poliet*, a 4.7% interest in Poliet was enough to give sole control when the majority shareholder agreed that St Gobain would appoint the majority of the supervisory board.[21] It is possible to be seen as having 'decisive influence' even where the undertaking concerned has a minority holding in the target. In *Arjomari/Wiggins Teape Appleton*,[22] Arjomari acquired a 39% share of Wiggins Teape and this was seen as being capable of giving sole control. No other shareholder had more than a 4% holding and only three shareholders owned over 3% of the issued share capital. As Arjomari had such a comparatively large holding, Arjomari was considered to be, in effect, gaining control of Wiggins Teape. When examining whether the acquisition of a minority holding establishes decisive influence, it is important to explore the practical implications of such a level of control. It may be the case that shareholder participation is historically

18 Regulation 139/2004/EC, OJ 2004, L24/1, Art 3(1).
19 Commission Consolidated Notice under Council Regulation (EC) No 139/2004 on the control of concentrations between undertakings, 10 July 2007.
20 Regulation 139/2004/EC, OJ 2004, L24/1, Art 3(2).
21 Case IV/M764, OJ 1996, C225/08.
22 Case IV/M025, OJ 1990, C321/16; [1991] 4 CMLR 854.

low in that undertaking. If it is, a relatively low shareholding may give de facto control over its decision-making.

The discussion above concerns sole control of an undertaking but it is also possible for two or more undertakings to acquire joint control of another. The utilisation of such joint ventures or strategic alliances is becoming increasingly common. This situation normally occurs where two undertakings transfer part of their respective businesses to a joint venture. Both the parent undertakings will have joint control over the joint venture. Even where one of the parents has a majority shareholding, for example, 60% of the voting shares, the minority party may well be in a position to cast a blocking vote over certain strategic decisions. Where the undertakings are forced to co-operate to avoid a minority veto, they are considered to have joint control.[23] Where one of the parent undertakings has a much smaller shareholding, for example, 20%, it will not normally have a blocking veto; however, there may still be joint control where a shareholders' agreement provides for co-operation.[24] There is a distinction between concentrative and co-operative joint ventures in Community law. The distinction between the two types of joint venture and the difficulties surrounding them will be discussed in more detail in a later section.

The 'Community dimension' and case allocation

The concept of the Community dimension is crucial to the creation of what is known as the 'one stop shop' in Community merger control. Once the existence of a concentration has been established the next step is to decide whether a concentration will be considered at the Community level or by the relevant national authorities. One of the key benefits of the Community system is the creation of a 'one stop shop', whereby the parties to a concentration are only subject to one set of administrative controls. This avoids potential conflicts between different administrative systems. The Regulation sets out the thresholds for the application of the Community system, where the thresholds are based on the concept of 'concentrations with a Community dimension'.[25] Furthermore, Art 21(1) of the Regulation provides that only the Commission shall take action in respect of Community dimension mergers. This provision is supported by Art 21(3), which provides that no national law will apply to such mergers. Due to the importance of the thresholds, they have proved to be one of the most controversial, and most revised, elements of the Regulation.

The main threshold for the existence of a Community dimension in a concentration is where:

23 Case IV/M010 *Conagra/Idea*, OJ 1991, C175/18; [1991] 4 CMLR 580.
24 Case IV/M229 *Thomas Cook/LTU/West LB*, OJ 1992, C199/16.
25 Regulation 139/2004/EC, OJ 2004, L24/1, Art 1.

a   the combined aggregate worldwide turnover of the undertakings concerned is more than €5,000m; and

b   the aggregate Community-wide turnover of at least two of the undertakings concerned is €250m, *unless* each of the undertakings concerned
achieves more than two-thirds of its aggregate Community-wide turnover within one Member State.[26]

The main threshold test for identifying a Community dimension merger is,
therefore, based entirely on the turnover of the undertakings concerned.
There is no qualitative assessment at this stage. For those involved, this
approach has the benefit of certainty, which will only be apparent where the
figures on worldwide, Community and Member State turnover are available.
As undertakings may not keep accounts in this fashion, the certainty may be
more apparent than real. Other difficulties arise in relation to the calculation
of the relevant figures for turnover. To aid the undertakings involved, there
is more detailed guidance in Art 5 of the Regulation, as well as in the
Commission Consolidated Jurisdictional Notice.[27]

The 1997 amendment of the regime introduced a second way in which
concentrations are deemed to have a Community dimension. A concentration
will also have a Community dimension where:

a   the combined aggregate worldwide turnover of all the undertakings
concerned is more than €2,500m;

b   in each of at least three Member States the combined aggregate turnover
of all the undertakings concerned is more than €100m;

c   in each of at least three Member States included for the purpose of point
(b), the aggregate turnover of at least two of the undertakings concerned
is more than €25m; and

d   the aggregate Community-wide turnover of each of at least two of
the undertakings concerned is more than €100m, *unless* each of the
undertakings concerned achieves more than two-thirds of its aggregate
Community-wide turnover within one Member State.[28]

It is important to note that if this final proviso applies, the concentration will
not have a Community dimension even if the other four criteria are satisfied.

The Art 1(3) criteria are designed to catch concentrations which fall below
the original, and principal, threshold test but which would normally qualify
for consideration under more than one Member State's national controls.
Following the 1996 review, the addition of Art 1(5) was preferred to a simple
reduction of the thresholds contained in Art 1(2). The outcome is probably

26 Regulation 139/2004/EC, OJ 2004, L24/1, Art 1(2) (emphasis added).
27 10 July 2007.
28 Regulation 139/2004/EC, OJ 2004, L24/1, Art 1(3) (emphasis added).

best understood in the context of subsidiarity. The Member States were unwilling to extend further power to the Commission unless it was in circumstances where the duplication of national merger controls was imminent. That was likely to be the case where the concentration was significant in several Member States and, therefore, the Commission would be best placed to consider the concentration. The retention of the two-thirds rule, and the requirement that the turnover of the relevant undertakings reaches €25m in at least three Member States, will exclude from the Commission's competence concentrations which are likely to have their principal effects in one Member State.

This option made sense as a political compromise but has several practical difficulties. One of the original benefits of the Community regime was the 'one stop shop' principle, and the certainty produced by this may have been reduced by the introduction of the alternative threshold criteria, although the recent changes in Arts 4(4), 4(5), 9 and 22 suggest that, increasingly, flexibility is preferred to certainty. The question whether a concentration between undertakings with a combined turnover of between €2,500m and €5,000m falls under the Community regime will depend on a complex breakdown of the turnover spread between Member States. Each undertaking will need to examine its turnover in each Member State to assess whether the various thresholds have been reached. In the 2000 review of the Merger Regulation, the Commission noted that 9% of notifications came through the Art 1(3) route and most of those notifications had a clear Community dimension.[29] In the Commission's view the new threshold had been successful. Notwithstanding that success, the Commission report suggested that a large number of mergers still do not fall within Art 1(3) and require notification in several Member States. To resolve that concern the 2004 reforms added a further 'multiple filing' route through the procedure for pre-notification referral in Art 4(5) of Regulation 139/2004. Under that provision, undertakings whose concentration may be reviewed under the national competition laws of at least three Member States may, before notifying those Member States, inform the Commission, by reasoned submission, that the concentration should be reviewed by the Commission. The Member States are then informed of such a submission, but if there is no disagreement by any Member State within 15 days of being referred the concentration will be deemed to have a Community dimension.[30] This procedure should minimise the potential for wasteful multiple filings in cases where the normal thresholds have not been met, without extending the scope of the Merger Regulation to a large number of smaller concentrations which do not have a significant multi-State dimension. While the intention behind the procedure has been welcomed, there

29 Report from the Commission to the Council on the application of the Merger Regulation thresholds, C(2000) 399 final.
30 See Commission Notice on case referral in respect of concentrations.

are concerns that the administrative requirements that go with making a reasoned submission, in Form RS, are very burdensome for the parties, and that the process could be improved.[31]

Case allocation and referral

As can be seen from the reference to the 'multiple filing' procedure under Art 4(5) of the Regulation, there is a move away from a simple reliance on the 'Community dimension' thresholds in Art 1. There are various case allocation mechanisms, in Arts 4, 9 and 22 of the Regulation, which allow cases to be referred to authorities other than those suggested by the normal thresholds. These case allocation mechanisms work to fine-tune case allocation between the Commission and the National Competition Authorities (NCAs). The Commission has also produced a Commission Notice on case referral.[32] The Notice states that the intention of the system is to create a 'jurisdictional mechanism which is flexible, but which at the same time ensures effective protection of competition'.[33] Cases should be allocated to the authority most appropriate for dealing with the merger, bearing in mind the characteristics of the case and the tools and expertise available to the agency.[34] In the following paragraphs the various case allocation mechanisms will be examined; first, where concentrations without a Community dimension are brought within the Regulation, and secondly, where concentrations which would normally fall within the standard thresholds can be referred back to the Member States.

Article 22 of the Regulation allows a Member State or Member States to seek to refer a concentration which does not have a Community dimension, according to the thresholds, to the Commission.[35] The NCAs can only make such a request where the concentration 'affects trade between Member States and threatens to significantly affect competition within the territory of the Member State or States making the request'. The request can only be made within 15 days of the concentration being notified or made known to the Member States concerned. The Commission then has 10 working days to decide if the criteria have been fulfilled and if it will take on the case. The

---

31 See, J Connolly *et al*, 'Pre-notification Referral under the EC Merger Regulation: simplifying the route to the one-stop shop' [2007] ECLR 167. The same administrative burden applies to the procedure under Art 4(4) of the Regulation.

32 Ibid. See also, Krajewska, T, 'Referrals under the New EC Merger Regulation Regime: a UK perspective' [2008] ECLR 279.

33 Commission Notice on case referral, para 7. See, also, Regulation 139/2004/EC, OJ 2004, L24/1, Recital 11.

34 Commission Notice on case referral, para 9.

35 This Article is sometimes know as the 'Dutch clause' as it was originally included at the behest of the Dutch authorities who did not, at the time, have a system of domestic merger control.

referral test in Regulation 139/2004 is less strict than the previous test under Regulation 4064/89. The increased co-operation of NCAs under the European Competition Network (ECN) should also facilitate such referrals. The case referral Notice foresees the use of Art 22 only where there are serious concerns in markets which are wider than national, or where there are a series of concerns in a number of sub-national markets across the Community.[36]

The 'back referral' procedure in Art 9 of the Regulation is designed to allow concentrations with a Community dimension to be referred back to the NCAs for consideration under domestic merger control.[37] Article 9 allows a Member State to request that consideration of a concentration be referred back to its competent authority if:

a a concentration threatens to affect significantly competition in a market within that Member State, which presents all the characteristics of a distinct market; or
b a concentration affects competition in a market within that Member State, which presents all the characteristics of a distinct market and which does not constitute a substantial part of the Common Market.[38]

The Member State must seek a referral within 15 working days of it receiving the copy notification from the Commission. The Commission may invite a Member State to seek a back referral but the Member State is not required to act following such an invitation. The Commission should, as a general rule, make a decision whether to refer all or part of the concentration to the competent authority within the 25 working day period set out in Art 10(1) of the Regulation, where proceedings are not initiated, or within 65 working days, where proceedings have been initiated, but no preparatory steps to adopt measures under Art 8 have been taken.[39] If the Commission does not take a decision within the relevant time period, or has not taken the preparatory steps towards a decision, the concentration is deemed to have been referred back to the competent national authority.[40] Once the concentration is referred back, the competent authority should report on its findings under national law within 45 working days after referral.[41] The Member State may only take measures which are strictly necessary to safeguard or restore effective competition on the market.[42]

---

36 Commission Notice on case referral in respect of contributions, at para 45. See also OFT press release 29/05, 16 February 2005, confirming the OFT's decision not to request the Commission to examine the proposed bids for the Stock Exchange.
37 The exception is sometimes known as the 'German clause' as it was inserted at the behest of the German authorities.
38 Regulation 139/2004/EC, OJ 2004, L24/1, Art 9(2).
39 Regulation 139/2004/EC, OJ 2004, L24/1, Art 9(4).
40 Under Art 9(5).
41 Under Art 9(6).
42 Under Art 9(8).

While the NCAs may seek a 'back referral' under the now extended scope of Art 9, the parties to a concentration may seek to initiate the newly introduced procedure of back referral, pre-notification, via Art 4(4). The parties may submit a reasoned request to the Commission setting out why they consider the concentration to significantly affect competition in a market which presents all the characteristics of a distinct market and should, therefore, be considered by that Member State. After receiving such a submission the Commission must transmit it to the Member State without delay. The Member State then has 15 working days to agree or disagree with the referral. If there is no disagreement from the Member State the Commission then has 25 working days to decide whether it will refer the case back to an NCA to be considered under its domestic merger control, if the criteria have been fulfilled and the NCA is the most appropriate authority.[43]

Another exception to the 'one stop shop' principle is provided for in Art 21(4) of the Regulation which allows for the protection of legitimate interests. This exception is designed to allow Member States to protect three named interests: public security, plurality of the media, and prudential rules. If the Member State wants to invoke a 'legitimate interest' it must notify the Commission of its intention prior to the adoption of the measure, and the Commission will consider its applicability with the general principles of Community law before the adoption of the measure. The Commission has 25 working days to undertake this task. The exception in Art 21(4) allows a Member State to adopt measures based on existing national law on the basis of non-competition grounds. Those measures must comply with general Community law principles, such as non-discrimination and proportionality. The exception does not allow a Member State to permit a prohibited concentration to go ahead, but it does allow a Member State to impose restrictions on a concentration which has been cleared by the Commission.

In addition to the exceptions provided for in the Merger Regulation, there are additional challenges to the concept of the 'one stop shop' within the EC Treaty. Article 296 provides that Member States are not precluded from taking measures necessary to protect national security. This is most likely to arise in the context of takeovers and mergers related to the defence industry. Also, the Merger Regulation, as secondary Community legislation, does not prevent the continued applicability, as discussed above, of Arts 81 and 82 EC. Accordingly, for mergers without a Community dimension, as defined in Art 1 of the Regulation, Arts 81 and 82 may have continued effect. While it is unlikely that the Commission would take any such action, Arts 81 and, particularly, 82 are directly enforceable in the national courts which might seek to provide remedies, for instance, interim relief, in the context of merger.

All of the above provisions, and the co-operation mechanisms in the ECN,

---

43 See the Commission Notice on case referral in respect of concentrations, paras 19–23.

are designed to avoid jurisdictional conflict between the Commission and the NCAs in merger cases, but a number of high-profile disputes have shown the sensitivity of these issues. In the *Gas Natural/Endesa*[44] and *E.ON/Endesa*[45] dispute the Commission took action under Art 21 of the Merger Regulation regarding several conditions imposed by the Spanish Energy Regulator (CNE) following E.ON's successful bid for Endesa. The Commission had previously cleared the merger without remedies. The conditions were eventually modified. In *Abertis/Autostrade*[46] the Commission cleared the merger but it was blocked by ANAS, the Italian body responsible for granting motorway concessions, as they were concerned that the merged entity might not be able to properly carry out the investment required to maintain and improve the motorway network. The Commission opened proceedings and the Italian measure was withdrawn.[47]

Mandatory notification and suspension

Concentrations which have a Community dimension must be notified, under Art 4(1), to the Commission 'prior to their implementation and following the conclusion of the agreement, the announcement of the public bid, or the acquisition of a controlling interest'. The 2004 reforms introduced into Art 4(1) the possibility of undertakings notifying a merger where they can demonstrate 'a good faith intention to conclude an agreement'.[48] It is obviously important that the Commission is informed of a proposed concentration as soon as possible, but it is also vital that sufficient finalised detail is available in order that there can be a full consideration of the relevant facts. As a quick resolution of the procedure is vital in commercial situations, a timely notification is beneficial to the parties involved. If the undertakings fail to notify the Commission of a concentration, a fine not exceeding 10% of aggregate turnover may be imposed.[49] On receipt of a notification the Commission publishes the fact of the notification, along with the names of the parties and the nature of the concentration.[50] The publication of the notification is designed to elicit third party observations. These will have to

---

44 Case COMP/M.3986, 15 November 2005. In this case it was decided that there was no Community dimension.
45 Case COMP/M.4110, 25 April 2006, and Case COMP/M.4197, 20 December 2006.
46 Case COMP/M.4249, 22 September 2006, and Commission Press Release IP/06/1418, 18 October 2006.
47 The balance between merger control and national industrial policy is discussed in Galloway, J, 'The Pursuit of National Champions: the intersection of competition law and industrial policy' [2007] ECLR 172.
48 See Berg, W and Ostendorf, P, 'The reform of EC merger control: substance and impact of the proposed new procedural rules' [2003] ECLR 594.
49 Regulation 139/2004/EC, OJ 2004, L24/1, Art 14(2)(a).
50 Regulation 139/2004/EC, OJ 2004, L24/1, Art 4(3).

reach the Commission within a tight time limit, which is specified in the published Notice. The notification must contain a considerable amount of detailed information about the relevant undertakings and the market concerned. The Commission must be in a position to decide whether the concentration has a Community dimension and to make an initial appraisal based on the facts provided. Due to the complexity of the information required it is often advisable for parties to approach the Commission informally before the official notification is made.[51] Consultation will assist the undertakings concerned in compiling the relevant information.

According to Art 7, a concentration cannot be put into effect until the concentration has been declared compatible with the Common Market by the Commission. Suspension of a concentration is the key to the success of the merger control system; as concentrations are very difficult to undo once they have gone ahead it is important that the appraisal of any concentration takes place during the period of suspension. The Commission can, if it considers it necessary, waive the suspension period and allow the concentration to be implemented.[52] Before granting a derogation the Commission must take into account the potential effects of implementation on other parties and competition.

Appraisal procedure

Once notification has taken place the Commission will begin the examination of the concentration. Because of the sensitive commercial nature of most concentrations, it is considered vital that the Commission examination is completed without delay. To that end very strict time limits are imposed by the Regulation. The timetable was reformed in 2004 to introduce increased flexibility, but it remains highly focused. The initial decision must be taken within 25 working days, that period starting on the day following receipt of the notification.[53] The Commission has been very successful in adhering to the Regulation's time limits. Increasing merger activity and the strict deadlines have placed great pressure on the Mergers Task Force. The Commission has sought relief from that pressure from two sources. First, the Commission has been given increased resources[54] and, secondly, a simplified procedure for

---

51 In October 2006, OJ 2006, C251/2, the submission rules were altered to require one signed original, five paper copies, and 30 copies on CD or DVD-ROM format. This will facilitate electronic transmission of files.

52 Regulation 139/2004/EC, OJ 2004, L24/1, Art 7(3).

53 Regulation 139/2004/EC, OJ 2004, L24/1, Art 10(1). If the information supplied with the notification is incomplete the period does not start running until the necessary information is provided. The period may be extended to 35 working days if the Commission receives a 'German' clause request from a Member State under Art 9. Under Regulation 4064/89 the period was one calendar month.

54 *XXXth Report on Competition Policy*, 2000, Point 238.

the treatment of certain concentrations[55] has been introduced. The detail of the simplified procedure will be discussed shortly.

The Commission has been given various investigative powers to assist in its appraisal. Article 11(1) gives the Commission the power to request information from undertakings. Information will usually be sought from the undertakings involved in the merger and the Commission is required to detail the information requested, to set a time limit for the provision of the information and to set out the penalties for noncompliance. It must also provide the relevant competent authority with a copy of the request. The Commission may, alternatively, make a formal decision requiring the provision of information.[56] Fines for failing to provide information or for providing incomplete information have been revised dramatically in the revised Regulation to a figure not exceeding 1% of aggregate turnover and a periodic penalty payment not exceeding 5% of average aggregate daily turnover is possible for each day of delay.[57] The Commission may also, under Art 11(7), interview, with the purpose of collecting information, any person who consents to be interviewed. These powers are not restricted to the undertakings who are the subjects of the investigation.

The Commission may also conduct on the spot investigations[58] or ask the competent authorities of the Member States to conduct investigations on its behalf.[59] The Commission can enter the undertaking's premises to examine books and business records, take copies and ask for explanations. The Commission may also seal premises or records, if necessary. The Commission is required to co-operate closely with the competent authorities of the relevant Member States while planning and conducting investigations. Requests for information and investigations will often take a considerable amount of time. This will cause the Commission difficulties in meeting the strict time limits imposed by the Regulation. Consequently, in situations where one of the relevant undertakings is responsible for the circumstances leading to the request or investigation, the time periods will be suspended.[60] Details of the procedure followed by the Commission during an investigation are set out in the implementing Regulation[61] and the Commission's guidance on 'best practices'.[62]

---

55 Commission Notice on a simplified procedure for the treatment of certain concentrations under Council Regulation 4064/89, OJ 2000, C217/32.
56 Regulation 139/2004/EC, OJ 2004, L24/1, Art 11(3).
57 Regulation 139/2004/EC, OJ 2004, L24/1, Arts 14(1) and 15(1).
58 Regulation 139/2004/EC, OJ 2004, L24/1, Art 13.
59 Regulation 139/2004/EC, OJ 2004, L24/1, Art 12.
60 Regulation 139/2004/EC, OJ 2004, L24/1, Art 10(4).
61 Regulation 802/2004/EC implementing Council Regulation (EC) No 139/2004 on the control of concentrations between undertakings, OJ 2004, L133/1.
62 Directorate General for Competition, 'Best Practices on the conduct of EC merger control proceedings', Directorate General for Competition website: http://europa.int/comm/competition/index_en.html.

A simplified procedure for dealing with certain concentrations was introduced in 2000 and reformed in 2004. It allows uncontroversial concentrations to be declared, with minimal investigation, as compatible with the Common Market. The Commission Notice[63] sets out a number of categories of concentration which will benefit from this procedure:

1 where undertakings acquire joint control over a joint venture and where that joint venture has no, or negligible, activities in the European Economic Area (EEA); or
2 where none of the parties are engaged in business activities in the same product and geographic market (horizontal relationships), or in a product market which is upstream or downstream of a product market in which any other party is engaged; or
3 where two or more of the parties are engaged in the same product and geographic market or upstream or downstream market, provided that their combined market share is not 15% or more for horizontal relationships or 25% or more for vertical relationships; or
4 where a party is to acquire sole control of an undertaking over which it already has joint control.

Commission practice has shown that these types of concentration rarely give rise to competition concerns. If a concentration falls within any of these categories, a short form decision will be published within one month of the notification. The Commission may intervene at any point before the publication of the decision and revert back to the normal procedure. The simplified procedure should reduce the administrative burden for both the parties and the Commission.

After the initial examination the Commission may deal with the case in a number of ways. It may conclude that the concentration does not fall within the scope of the Regulation,[64] and will close the case. If the concentration does fall within the Regulation the Commission may declare, under Art 6(1)(b), that the concentration does not raise serious doubts as to its compatibility with the Common Market, and allow it to go ahead. In 2006 there was an interesting development, in *Impala v Commission*, as the CFI upheld an appeal against a clearance Decision in a merger case.[65] The CFI made clear that when the Commission is adopting a clearance Decision it must provide the same level of clarity and completeness as it would in a prohibition

---

63 Commission Notice on a simplified procedure for the treatment of certain concentrations under Council Regulation (EC) No 139/2004.
64 Regulation 139/2004/EC, OJ 2004, L24/1, Art 6(1)(a).
65 Case T-464/04 *Impala v Commission* [2006] ECR II-2289. On appeal, Case C-413/06P *Bertelsmann and Sony v Impala*, judgment of 10 July 2008, the ECJ allowed the appeal on various grounds and referred the case back to the CFI. It did, however, confirm that the same standards apply to approval and prohibition Decisions.

Decision. The Commission went on to reassess the merger and it was approved again in October 2007.[66]

During the initial investigation the Commission may be concerned that a concentration may raise serious concerns for the Common Market, but, through negotiation with the parties, may be able to agree changes to the proposed concentration which would alleviate those concerns. If the undertakings concerned agree to modify the proposed concentration, the modified concentration can be declared compatible, under Art 6(2). The Commission can also attach conditions and obligations to the decision that a modified concentration is compatible with the Common Market in order to ensure that the undertakings concerned comply with the commitments they have entered into. Negotiated modifications of this nature are known as 'remedies' in the Commission's parlance. In order to assist parties who are planning a merger, and to encourage them to consider potential remedies and bring them to the Commission as soon as possible, the Commission published a Notice on Remedies and, at the time of writing, is consulting on a new Notice.[67] In *Vodafone/Airtouch*,[68] a merger between UK and US mobile communications operators, the Commission was concerned as the merged company would have control over two of the four major mobile communication operators in Germany. In order to allay its concerns, a divestment remedy in which Vodafone agreed to sell its stake in one of those operators was submitted to the Commission by Vodafone. The sale eliminated the overlap in the German market for mobile telecommunications between Vodafone and Airtouch. If the conditions attached to a decision are not fulfilled the Commission may revoke its decision and initiate the second stage. Where an undertaking offers remedies the time limit for the initial stage of the investigation is extended to 35 working days.[69] Another example of an Art 6(2) decision was seen in *Air France/KLM* where the Commission approved the creation of Europe's largest airline group.[70]

The Commission's final option is to decide to initiate proceedings – the second phase of the examination – if it believes the concentration raises serious doubts as to its compatibility with the Common Market. The second phase investigation is more detailed and operates in accordance with longer

66 See Commission Press Release IP/07/1437, 'Mergers: Commission confirms approval of recorded music joint venture between Sony and Bertelsmann after re-assessment subsequent to Court decision', 3 October 2007.

67 Commission Notice on remedies acceptable under Council Regulation (EEC) No 4064/89 and under Commission Regulation (EC) No 447/98, OJ 2001, C68/3, and Draft revised Commission Notice on remedies acceptable under the Merger Regulation, 24 April 2007. See, also, Went, D, 'The Acceptability of Remedies under the EC Merger Regulation: structural versus behavioural' [2006] ECLR 455.

68 Case IV/M1430, OJ 1999, C295/2.

69 Regulation 139/2004/EC, OJ 2004, L24/1, Art 10(1).

70 Case IV/M3280, OJ 2004, C60/5, Commission Press Release, IP/04/194.

time limits. After the decision has been made to go into the second stage the Commission must notify the undertakings concerned and the relevant Member States. Where the Commission fails to make a decision within the time period the concentration will automatically be deemed to be compatible with the Common Market under Art 10(6).

The second stage proceedings involve a more detailed investigation and have a time limit of 90 working days from the initiation of second stage proceedings.[71] An example of the rationale behind a second stage investigation can be seen in the *Sony/Bertelsmann* case.[72] The Commission was concerned that the concentration might create a dominant position in the market for recorded music, but also that it might have an impact on other vertically integrated markets, such as television, downloadable music, and portable music players.[73] At the end of the investigation the Commission may declare the concentration to be compatible, under Art 8(1), or incompatible, under Art 8(3), with the Common Market. Where a concentration has been implemented and is then declared to be incompatible with the Common Market, the Commission can order the separation of the assets and/or the cessation of joint control.[74] The Commission may impose a fine on the undertakings concerned. The fine can be up to 10% of aggregate turnover and, in addition, a periodic penalty (increased in 2004) of up to 5% of average aggregate daily turnover per day until the assets are separated or control is relinquished.[75] The final options for the Commission are therefore very simple, but in practice the procedure can be quite complex. When making a Decision the Commission must provide sufficient justification. Following the CFI's judgment in *Schneider II*[76] it is clear that if the Commission makes a 'manifest error', it will be liable to pay compensation to the parties to the merger, under Art 288(2) EC; however, the Commission retains a margin of discretion in complex economic analysis. During the investigation it may well become apparent that the concentration is unlikely to be compatible with the Common Market, and if that is the case a process of negotiation may begin in an attempt to find some form of compromise with a view to allowing a modified concentration to proceed. The Commission has the power to clear a concentration, under Art 8(2), if the concentration has been modified in such a way that it is compatible with the Common Market. The use of remedies is the norm if a clearance is granted after an investigation advances into the second stage. Where the parties involved offer commitments after day 54

---

71 The time period under Regulation 4064/89 was four calendar months.
72 Case IV/M3333 (4064).
73 See Commission Press Release, IP/04/200.
74 Under Art 8(4).
75 Regulation 139/2004/EC, OJ 2004, L24/1, Arts 14(2) and 15(2).
76 Case T-351/03 *Schneider Electric SA v Commission* [2008] 4 CMLR 22. On appeal Case C-440/07 *Commission v Schneider Electric*, pending.

of the proceedings the time limit for the investigation is extended to 105 working days. The extension of the time limits, where remedies are offered late, should encourage the parties to offer commitments within the first 54 days. In order to assist the transparency of negotiations, the Commission's Remedies Notice, which is likely to be replaced in 2008, sets out the underlying principles upon which Commission practice is based, but it must be noted that each case is very different and the Commission retains a large degree of flexibility.[77] It is for the parties to show that the commitments they suggest remove the competition concerns highlighted by the Commission. The Commission prefers structural solutions, as opposed to behavioural remedies, to competition concerns as they are more likely to solve the problem and do not require medium- to long-term monitoring.[78] It is also clear that an authorisation cannot be granted where suggested remedies are so complex that the Commission cannot determine whether competition will be effectively restored.[79] An incompatibility decision under Art 8(3) is required to avoid automatic clearance under Art 10 at the end of the investigation period. As the Commission must consult the Member States and the Advisory Committee on Concentrations before granting a clearance, the Commission needs to finalise the modifications in advance of the deadline. In a number of cases, late commitments have been rejected as it would have been impossible for the Commission to undertake sufficient 'market testing'.[80] The automatic extension of the time limit for late commitments should mitigate this problem to some extent. If the parties do not fulfil the conditions contained within a clearance, the Commission may impose a fine of up to 10% of aggregate turnover and, in addition, impose a period penalty payment of up to 5% of average aggregate daily turnover per day until the situation is rectified.[81]

An example of a negotiated clearance was *Kimberly-Clark/Scott Paper*.[82] The deal would have combined the Andrex, owned by Scott Paper, and the Kleenex, owned by Kimberly-Clark, brands of paper products in the UK and Ireland. The post-merger undertaking would have had a combined market share of 20–45% of branded products, that is, Kleenex and Andrex, and 40–60% of branded and private label products, products made by the companies for others. The Commission discovered that the concentration raised particular concerns as the vast majority of relevant retailers stocked the branded products, and that the merger would result in the creation of the

---

77 Commission Notice on remedies acceptable under Council Regulation 4064/89/EEC and under Commission Regulation 447/98/EC, OJ 2001, C68/3, and Draft revised Commission Notice on remedies acceptable under the Merger Regulation, 24 April 2007.

78 At para 9.

79 At para 32.

80 See, for example, Case IV/M1524, Commission Decision 2000/276/EC *Airtours/First Choice*, OJ 2000, L93/1.

81 Regulation 139/2004/EC, OJ 2004, L24/1, Arts 14(2) and 15(2).

82 Case IV/M623, Commission Decision 96/435/EC, OJ 1996, L183/01.

leading supplier of private branded products. Before the Commission cleared the concentration, the Commission required the divestiture of a major UK production facility and the licence of the use of the Kleenex brand for 10 years to a third party. In other geographical markets the competition concerns were different. To address those concerns, other conditions were attached by the Commission in relation to those markets: the continued use of the Kleenex brand was allowed, while the Andrex brand was not to be used for an indefinite period. It is interesting to note that the merger was also the subject of investigation, and eventual approval, in the US.

In *AOL/Time Warner*,[83] another large-scale international merger, the Commission approved the merger after the parties agreed to sever all links with the German media group Bertelsmann. The merger between AOL, the leading internet access provider in the US and the only access provider across Europe, and Time Warner, one of the world's biggest publishing and media companies, created the first vertically integrated internet content provider with access to Time Warner's content library. AOL operated in Europe through several joint ventures with Bertelsmann whose operations include a large music publishing interest and, therefore, a large musical library. The Commission was concerned that AOL would have had a dominant position on the market for online delivery of music as it could utilise both Time Warner's and Bertelsmann's content. There was also concern that AOL would have been in a position to format its music libraries to work only with their own music player, Winamp, allowing that player to become dominant. By severing all links between AOL and Bertelsmann the concerns were removed.

Basis of the appraisal

The Commission's decisions under Arts 6 and 8 are based on the concept of 'compatibility with the Common Market', and that concept is explained in Art 2 of the Regulation. The basic prohibition is against concentrations that:

> ... would significantly impede effective competition, in the common market or in a substantial part of it, in particular as a result of the creation or strengthening of a dominant position.[84]

This test was introduced by Regulation 139/2004 and replaced the test in Regulation 4064/89. The original substantive test focused on concentrations that created or strengthened a dominant position as a result of which competition would be significantly impeded in the Common Market.[85] Although

---

83 Case IV/M1845, Commission Decision 2001/718/EC, OJ 2001, L268/28.
84 Regulation 139/2004/EC, OJ 2004, L24/1, Art 2(3).
85 Regulation 4064/89/EEC, OJ 1990, L257/13, Art 2(3).

similar words are used in the Regulation 139/2004 test and in Regulation 4064/89, the change in emphasis of the new test, emphasising the impediment of competition rather than dominance, focuses the Merger Regulation on wider competition concerns rather than a narrow focus on 'dominance', as in Art 82 EC. The impact of the change in focus, and one of the main reasons for it, is set out in Recitals 24–26 of the Regulation which centre on the consequences of concentrations in 'oligopolistic market structures'. The particular problems of oligopolistic markets will be discussed more fully below. The retention of the dominance criteria within the new 'significant impediment' ('SIEC') test means that previous Commission practice under Regulation 4064 is still, however, of relevance.[86] The Commission is also required to take into account the need to maintain and develop competition within the Common Market, the market position of the undertakings, and the development of technical and economic progress that is to the consumers' advantage.[87] Practice since the coming into force of the new Regulation has indicated that the Commission has refocused its decision-making, and the language used concentrates on 'unilateral effects' or 'coordinated effects' on competition rather than dominance or collective dominance.

The appraisal of a particular concentration will, therefore, require detailed market analysis to establish if there is a significant impediment to competition. The Commission Notice on the definition of the market[88] is largely based on the Commission's practice in merger control. In the context of some joint ventures the Regulation provides, in Art 2(4), that any co-ordination between the competitive behaviour of independent undertakings is to be appraised within the merger investigation and in accordance with the criteria in Art 81 EC.

To enhance transparency in the appraisal of horizontal concentrations under the Regulation the Commission has published an important Guideline.[89] The Guideline stresses that while it sets out the analytical approach of the Commission, the Guideline cannot detail all possible applications, and each case will be handled according to its own particular facts.[90] The Guideline also makes clear that most prohibition decisions will still be based on a finding of dominance;[91] although its subsequent decisional practice indicates that it does not rely heavily on the dominance concept in its

---

86 Regulation 139/2004/EC, OJ 2004, L24/1, Recital 26.
87 Regulation 139/2004/EC, OJ 2004, L24/1, Art 2(1).
88 OJ 1997, C372/03. See the discussion in Chapter 3.
89 Commission Notice, Guidelines on the assessment of horizontal mergers under the Council regulation on the control of concentrations between undertakings, OJ 2004, C31/3. On the draft Notice, see Bishop, S and Ridyard, D, 'Prometheus unbound: increasing the scope for intervention in EC merger control' [2003] ECLR 357.
90 At para 5.
91 At para 4.

Decisions, preferring to rely directly on the SIEC test.[92] Following the perceived success of the Horizontal Guideline the Commission went on to publish a Guideline on Non-Horizontal Mergers, which gives similar guidance on
the assessment of vertical and conglomerate mergers.[93] The Commission's
assessment is split into two main elements: the definition of the market and
the competitive assessment of the merger. Market definition follows the
same process as under Art 82 EC, as discussed in Chapter 3. Once the market
is defined the Commission uses a number of tools to appraise the impact
of the concentration. Market shares can be used to calculate the overall level
of concentration in the market. A combined market share of less than
25% rarely leads to the creation of a dominant position and is unlikely to
significantly impede competition.[94] Another useful tool is the Herfindahl-
Hirschman Index (HHI). The HHI is calculated by adding the squares of the
individual market shares of all the firms in the market.[95] The difference
between the pre-merger HHI and post-merger HHI, the 'delta', is useful to
show the impact of the merger.[96] If the post-merger HHI is less than 1,000 the
merger is unlikely to raise concerns. Mergers with a post-merger HHI of
between 1,000 and 2,000 and with a 'delta' of less than 250 are also unlikely
to raise concerns[97] unless there are special factors present; for example, if one
of the merging parties is an important market innovator or a maverick firm
with a likelihood of disrupting co-ordinated conduct.[98]

If a concentration is above the 'safe harbour' outlined in the Horizontal
Notice there are two main competitive concerns which the Commission will
examine: the merger may eliminate important competitive constraints on
one or more firms which would have increased market power; or the merger
may change the nature of competition in such a way that firms would be
significantly more likely to co-ordinate and raise prices or otherwise harm
effective competition.[99] The first concern corresponds more closely with the

92 See, for example, Case COMP/M.3916 *T-Mobile Austria/Tele.ring*, C (2006) 1695 final,
    26 April 2006, where there were unilateral effects, but it would have been difficult to conceive
    of the Decision being made in the context of a single dominant position.
93 Commission Notice, Guidelines on the assessment of non-horizontal mergers under the Coun-
    cil Regulation on the control of concentrations between undertakings, 28 November 2007.
94 At para 18.
95 The Commission Notice uses, as an example, a market containing five firms with market
    shares of 40%, 20%, 15%, 15% and 10%, respectively, which has an HHI of 2,550 ($40^2 + 20^2 +$
    $15^2 + 15^2 + 10^2 = 2,550$). The HHI ranges from close to zero (in an atomistic market) to
    10,000 (in the case of a pure monopoly).
96 The increase in concentration can be calculated independently of the overall market concen-
    tration by doubling the product of the market shares of the merging firms. For example, a
    merger of two firms with market shares of 30% and 15%, respectively, would increase the
    HHI by 900 ($30 \times 15 \times 2 = 900$).
97 Or mergers with a post-merger HHI above 2,000 with a delta below 150.
98 Commission Notice, at paras 19–21.
99 Commission Notice, at paras 22–23 et seq.

Commission's previous practice under the dominance test in Regulation 4064. In the Horizontal Guideline the Commission set out a number of factors which might be taken into account, if they are appropriate for the individual concentration: the merging firms have large market shares; the merging firms are close competitors; the customers have limited possibilities of switching supplier; the competitors are unlikely to increase supply if prices increase; the merged entity is able to hinder expansion by competitors; and/or the merger eliminates an important competitive force.[100] The Guideline also sets out several distinct issues that the Commission will examine: whether the merger might involve a potential competitor; whether the merger might create or strengthen buyer power in upstream markets; whether there is countervailing buyer power on the market which could control the post-merger undertaking; or whether entry into the market is sufficiently easy to ensure sufficient competitive constraint on the post-merger undertaking. The concern regarding co-ordinated effects is more likely to be of importance in cases where there is not a clear problem with the creation or strengthening of single firm dominance. The problem arises where the concentration of the market makes future tacit collusion or co-ordination more likely in an oligopolistic market. Mergers in oligopolistic markets are considered in more detail below.

A number of 'defences' are also discussed by the Commission in the Guideline. These are factors which tend to reduce the impediment to competition which may be threatened by the concentration. One of the most important 'defences' available to merging undertakings is to indicate that the merger would result in a level of efficiency which would outweigh the competition concerns.[101] The possibility of an efficiency defence was partially recognised under Regulation 4064/89 in *Mercedes Benz/Kassbohrer*[102] where the improvements in research and development, and savings in production and administration, were recognised. The existence of efficiencies giving rise to consumer benefit was also considered in *St Gobain/Wacker-Chemie/NOM*.[103] The proposed joint venture was prohibited even though the concentration would have improved efficiencies in Wacker-Chemie's troubled operations. The Commission was of the opinion that consumers would receive more benefit through the cessation of Wacker-Chemie's operation than through the concentration.[104] The Guideline sets out that '[i]t is possible that efficiencies brought about by a

---

100 Commission Notice, at paras 24–38.
101 See, for example, Luescher, C, 'Efficiency considerations in European merger control – just another battle ground for the European Commission, economists and competition lawyers?' [2004] ECLR 72.
102 Case IV/M477, Commission Decision 95/354/EC, OJ 1995, L211/1.
103 Case IV/M774, Commission Decision 97/610/EC, OJ 1996, L247/1.
104 See Camesasca, PD, 'The explicit efficiency defence in merger control: does it make the difference?' [1999] ECLR 14, and Halliday, J, 'The recognition, status and form of the efficiency defence to a merger' (1999) 22 World Comp 91.

merger counteract the effects on competition and in particular the potential harm to consumers that it might otherwise have'.[105] For an efficiency defence to be successful, 'the efficiencies have to benefit consumers, be merger-specific and be verifiable'.[106] All of these conditions must be met. As only the merging undertakings will have sufficient evidence to verify the efficiencies created by their merger the responsibility is on the parties to the merger to provide all the necessary information to the Commission. The other major defence discussed in the Guideline is the 'failing firm' defence.[107] To qualify for the merging, undertakings must show that one of the undertakings is a failing firm and that, therefore, the merger itself does not bring about any anti-competitive effects. The logic in the defence is that the deterioration in the competitive structure of the market would have occurred even in the absence of the merger through the exit of the failing firm. There are three criteria for the defence:

a   the allegedly failing firm would, in the near future, be forced out of the market;
b   there is no less anti-competitive alternative purchase than the merger; and
c   in the absence of a merger, the assets of the failing firm would inevitably exit the market.[108]

Other broader goals within the Community may also have an impact on merger control. Recital 19 of the Regulation states that consideration should be given to the objectives set out in Art 2 of the EC and EU Treaties.[109] The Court of First Instance (CFI) was asked to rule on non-competition factors under Regulation 4064/89 in *Comité Central d'Entreprise de la Société Anonyme Vittel v Commission*.[110] The CFI was of the opinion that the primary considerations should be competition related, though in some circumstances social goals could be taken into account where the concentration was likely to have adverse effects on the objectives set out in Art 2 of the EC Treaty. The extent to which the Merger Regulation can be used as a tool of Community industrial policy by the promotion of 'European champions' is also of interest. As noted earlier, one of the considerations in introducing the Regulation was the intention to ease the formation of European alliances which could

105 Commission Notice, Guidelines on the assessment of horizontal mergers under the Council regulation on the control of concentrations between undertakings, OJ 2004, C31/3, para 76.
106 At para 78.
107 See, for example, Baccaro, V, 'Failing firm defence and lack of causality: doctrine and practice in Europe of two closely related concepts' [2004] ECLR 11.
108 At para 90.
109 It is interesting to note that Regulation 139/2004 removes the reference to Art 158 EC on economic and social cohesion in Regulation 4064/89, but replaces it with reference to Art 2 EU, which has a somewhat broader ambit.
110 Case T-12/93 [1995] ECR II-1247.

go on to compete on the global market. Nonetheless, the Commission pro-hibited a merger in *Aerospatiale/Alenia/de Havilland*,[111] where the objective was to create such a 'European champion' in the aircraft manufacturing industry. The role of Community industrial policy in merger control remains doubtful.[112]

Concentrations in oligopolistic markets

The substantive appraisal test in Regulation 4064/89 referred only to the 'creation or strengthening of a dominant position' and made no direct refer-ence to the control of 'collective' or 'joint' dominance in oligopolistic mar-kets. As the definition of dominance under Art 82 EC was extended to cover collective dominance the Commission also sought to extend the scope of Regulation 4064/89 to similar situations. In *Nestlé/Perrier*,[113] the Commission attached conditions to its clearance that certain parts of the business were to be sold to third parties to avoid the strengthening of a collective dominant position. In *Kali and Salz/MdK/Treuhand*,[114] the Commission again cleared a concentration on the basis of conditions attached to the Decision to avoid the creation of a duopolistic dominant position. The Commission was of the opinion that the concentration would create a duopoly controlling 60% of the market for potash. As outside operators were fragmented they would provide little competition, and competition between the duopolists would probably be limited because of the structure of the potash market and close economic links between the duopolists. The Decision was challenged before the Court in *France v Commission*[115] on the basis that Regulation 4064/89 had no appli-cation to the creation or strengthening of collective dominance. The Court rejected that argument, confirming that collective dominance did come within the terms of the Regulation. Although the Court upheld the principle, it annulled the Commission Decision on the basis that the Decision had not established, to the necessary legal standard, that the concentration would give rise to a collective dominant position.

The most comprehensive examination of the handling of collective domin-ance under Regulation 4064/89 was seen in the litigation which followed the Commission Decision in *Airtours/First Choice*.[116] The Commission was of the view that a merger between Airtours and First Choice would result in a

111 Case IV/M53, Commission Decision 91/619/EEC, OJ 1991, L334/42; [1992] 4 CMLR M2.
112 See Banks, D, 'Non-competition factors and their future relevance under European merger law' [1997] 3 ECLR 182 and Galloway, J, 'The Pursuit of National Champions: the intersec-tion of competition law and industrial policy' [2007] ECLR 172. See, also, Case IV/M315, Commission Decision 94/208/EC *Mannesmann/Valourec/Ilva*, OJ 1994, L102/15.
113 Case IV/M190, Commission Decision 92/553/EEC, OJ 1992, L356/1; [1993] 4 CMLR M17.
114 Case IV/M308, Commission Decision 94/449/EC, OJ 1994, L186/38.
115 Cases C-68/94 and C-30/95 [1998] 4 CMLR 829.
116 Case IV/M1524, Commission Decision 2000/276/EC *Airtours/First Choice*, OJ 2000, L93/1.

collective dominant position between the post-merger undertaking and the two remaining leading tour operators, Thomson and Thomas Cook, on the short-haul package holiday market in the UK. The Commission therefore prohibited the merger. The Commission's Decision was eventually overturned on appeal but the CFI set out important guidance on the standard and type of proof that was required under Regulation 4064/89 to support a finding of the creation of or strengthening of a collective dominant position.[117] The quashing of the Commission's Decision was seen as being a serious setback and the evidential requirements set out by the CFI seemed to be a very difficult hurdle for the Commission to cross. The CFI made it clear that if the Commission wanted to support a finding of collective dominance it must be able to show that the post-merger undertaking and the other undertakings remaining on the market would be able to adopt a common policy without having to enter into an agreement or a concerted practice.[118] The CFI set out three conditions which must be met before a potentially dominant oligopoly would be shown to be possible. First, the dominant oligopoly must be transparent in order that each of the members is aware of the others' market conduct. Secondly, the co-ordination must be sustainable with the members of oligopoly able to deter others from departing from the common policy. Thirdly, the reactions of current and future competitors and customers should not be able to end the benefits of the common policy.

The new test, in *Airtours*, for a finding of collective dominance was, arguably, one of the reasons for the Commission's volte-face with regard to the substantive test in Regulation 139/2004.[119] Recitals 24–26 of the Regulation make it clear that to improve 'legal certainty' it was necessary to bring oligopolistic markets clearly within the Merger Regulation. The shift away from dominance, and therefore collective dominance, as the only test, towards the consideration of collective dominance as an aspect of what significantly impedes effective competition, may mean that the dicta in *Airtours* will be less crucial in future decisions. Recital 25 makes it clear that the new test extends:

> ... beyond the concept of dominance, only to the anti-competitive effects of a concentration resulting from the non-coordinated behaviour of undertakings which would not have a dominant position on the market concerned.

---

117 Case T-342/99 *Airtours v Commission* [2002] ECR II-2585; [2002] 5 CMLR 7. See, also, Haupt, H, 'Collective dominance under Article 82 EC and EC merger control in the light of the *Airtours* judgment' [2002] ECLR 434, and Stroux, S, 'Collective dominance under the merger regulation: a serious evidentiary reprimand for the Commission' (2002) 27 EL Rev 736.

118 At para 61.

119 The Commission strongly rejected the 'substantial lessening of competition' test in early reform discussions and the new substantive test was not introduced until after the final draft Regulation was published in December 2002.

In the horizontal merger Guideline the Commission relies heavily on the judgment in *Airtours* but does seem to depart from it in some instances.[120] The section of the Guideline that examines the 'co-ordinated effects' of a merger sets out that it may be possible, post-merger, for undertakings to co-ordinate their behaviour, 'even without entering into an agreement or resorting to a concerted practice within the meaning of Article 81 of the Treaty'.[121] Paragraph 41 of the Guideline, in effect, replicates the three conditions in *Airtours*. It would, therefore, appear that while the substantive test has been widened by Regulation 139/2004 the Commission still foresees the need to utilise the conditions in *Airtours*, even though the conditions are no longer the only issues which may be taken into account. The Commission decided not to oppose the Sony/BMG merger after a Phase II investigation which resulted in four major record companies[122] holding 80% of the recording market.[123]

Vertical and conglomerate mergers

Three years after publishing its Guideline on Horizontal Mergers the Commission began consultation on Guidelines setting out its approach to non-horizontal cases.[124] A vertical merger is a merger between a manufacturer of a product and a supplier, an upstream firm, or a customer, a downstream firm. In a conglomerate merger the relationship is neither vertical nor horizontal, but the firms supply products that can be described as complementary. The consultation and subsequent Notice must also be viewed in light of the criticism of the Commission's approach to such mergers by the Community courts in cases such as *Tetra Laval/Sidel* and *GE/Honeywell*.[125] As vertical and conglomerate mergers do not result in the direct elimination of a competitor they are less likely to result in a significant impediment to effective competition. There are, however, some situations in which such a merger may allow the post-merger entity to damage future competition by using power in one market to foreclose competition in the related market.[126] It is this foreclosure

---

120 See Black, O, 'Collusion and co-ordination in EC merger control' [2003] ECLR 408.

121 Commission Notice, Guidelines on the assessment of horizontal mergers under the Council Regulation on the control of concentrations between undertakings, OJ 2004, C31/3, para 39.

122 Universal, SonyBMG, Warner and EMI.

123 Case IV/M3333 (4064), OJ 2004, C13/15, Commission Press Release, IP/04/200 and IP/04/959; there were also concerns about Sony and BMG's vertically integrated structure.

124 Draft Commission Notice, Guidelines on the assessment of non-horizontal mergers under the Council Regulation on the control of concentrations between undertakings, 13 February 2007.

125 Case T-5/02 *Tetra Laval v Commission* [2002] ECR II-4381, Case C-12/03P *Commission v Tetra Laval* [2005] ECR I-987, and Case T-210/01 *GE v Commission* [2005] ECR II-5575. See Killick, J, 'The GE/Honeywell Judgment – in reality another merger defeat for the Commission' [2007] ECLR 52.

126 See Bishop, S, et al, 'Turning the Tables: why vertical and conglomerate mergers are different' [2006] ECLR 403.

question that the Guidelines seek to address.[127] The Guidelines first stress the generally benign nature of such mergers and that they may lead to enhanced efficiencies.[128] It also notes that a vertical or conglomerate merger may be able to 'change the ability and incentive to compete on the part of the merging companies and their competitors in ways that cause harm to consumers'.[129] Foreclosure is only likely to occur when the merged entity has significant market power, but not necessarily dominance. It is therefore unlikely that the Commission will find concern in mergers where the post-merger market share is below 30% and the post-merger HHI is below 2,000.[130]

In vertical mergers two potential harms are foreseen: input and customer foreclosure. In input foreclosure the post-merger entity can make it more difficult for a downstream rival (who was merely a customer in the pre-merger situation) by supplying at less advantageous prices or conditions, allowing the post-merger entity to raise prices. In order to do this the vertically integrated firm must have market power in the upstream market.[131] Customer fore-closure occurs when a supplier merges with a downstream customer holding market power. Such a merger may make it difficult for upstream rivals to find outlets for their output, effectively reducing competition in the upstream market.[132] The Guideline also indicates the Commission's concern that a vertical merger may make it more likely that co-ordinated effects, tacit collusion within an oligopolistic market, would be sustainable, as the market becomes easier to monitor, increasing the effectiveness of punishment mechanisms, or reducing the scope for external destabilisation by removing a 'maverick' firm.[133]

The main concern with conglomerate mergers is the ability of the post-merger entity to leverage market power from one market and foreclose another, largely through the tying and bundling of products. Pure bundling occurs when the products are only sold jointly, in a fixed proportion, whereas mixed bundling occurs when the products are available separately but at a higher price than the bundled product. Tying occurs when the sale of the tying product is linked to the sale of the tied product. The tie can be

---

127 Commission Notice, Guidelines on the assessment of non-horizontal mergers under the Council Regulation on the control of concentrations between undertakings, November 2007. For a critique of the Guidelines see, Bishop, S, '(Fore)closing the Gap: the Commission's draft non-horizontal merger guidelines' [2008] ECLR 1, and Alese, F, '(Fore)closing the Gap: the Commission's draft non-horizontal merger guidelines – a "response" to Simon Bishop' [2008] ECLR 196.
128 Ibid, paras 11–14.
129 Ibid, para 15.
130 Ibid, paras 23–27. The introduction of the HHI test is criticised by Simon Bishop as being more relevant in horizontal mergers, Bishop, above fn 127.
131 Ibid, paras 31 et seq.
132 Ibid, paras 58 et seq.
133 Ibid, paras 79–90.

'technical', when the tying product only functions when used with the tied product,[134] or 'contractual', when the products are tied through a contractual agreement between the parties.

Joint ventures

The control of joint ventures, sometimes also known as strategic alliances, has presented challenges to Community competition law for many years. Joint ventures involve the setting up of a company by two or more parent companies. The main difficulty for merger control when dealing with joint ventures is that in practice the formation of the joint venture, and the roles undertaken by the various parties, can vary to such a great extent that a unified approach is difficult. Under the original form of the Merger Regulation, if two independent undertakings transferred their activities in one area to a joint venture and then withdrew permanently from that area the joint venture would be considered to be a concentration, a concentrative joint venture, falling within the Merger Regulation and its procedures. If, on the other hand, two independent undertakings set up a joint venture to control their sales, for instance, through a joint sales agency, this would have been seen as part of a strategy to operate a cartel and would have fallen under Art 81(1) as a co-operative joint venture. These are fairly polarised examples of what are termed concentrative and co-operative joint ventures, respectively. It was often difficult to decide whether a proposed joint venture would be concentrative or co-operative and, consequently, under which procedure it should be considered. In most circumstances, joint ventures are encouraged by the Community authorities on policy grounds. It is considered that European industry will enhance its competitiveness on the global market by the formation of alliances between companies which are able to pool their resources and respective specialisations. The Merger Regulation's speedy procedures allow such beneficial concentrative joint ventures to proceed with minimal disruption to the parties' competitive strategy. However, many businesses complained that co-operative joint ventures – those that fell under the Art 81 procedure but were not anti-competitive – were disadvantaged because of the uncertainty and delays in the then Art 81(3) exemption procedure. Many advisers suggested that undertakings should structure their joint ventures so that the joint ventures fell within the definition of a concentrative joint venture and, as such, would be considered within the Merger Regulations time limits. In an attempt to deal with many of these criticisms the Commission sought to both clarify the distinction between concentrative and co-operative joint ventures and reduce the scope of co-operative joint ventures to situations where there was likely to be co-operation between the parents.

---

134 An example would be a laser printer, which will only function when using the 'tied' proprietary toner cartridges.

The distinction between concentrative and co-operative joint ventures still exists but the balance has shifted with many more joint ventures now being considered as concentrative.

Every 'full function' joint venture, that is, a 'joint venture performing on a lasting basis all the functions of an autonomous economic entity',[135] will be considered to be a concentrative or a structural joint venture to be dealt with under the Merger Regulation. A joint venture which is not full function will be considered under Art 81 of the Treaty. Before a joint venture is considered to be full function it must have all the characteristics of an independent, self-contained, business unit. It must not be reliant on its parents for survival. It should, therefore, have its own human and material resources to allow it to carry on business, and not rely on others' staff or assets. The Commission has also considered the research and development capacity, ownership of intellectual property rights, and access to distribution networks as being relevant to the status of a joint venture.[136] Even if it has limited staff and financial resources, a joint venture may not be considered full function if those resources would not enable it to operate on a lasting basis.[137] In many cases the joint venture will continue to deal, in some capacity, with its parent companies. This will obviously bring into question the joint venture's status of independence on the market.[138] The Commission must be sure that the joint venture is not simply a disguised sales agency.[139] An example of the way in which the Commission determines the existence of a joint venture was in *Texaco/Norsk Hydro*.[140] The joint venture was established to distribute refined oil products to consumers in Denmark, Norway and Iceland. The parent oil companies withdrew from the market but would still be active in the upstream market, supplying products to the joint venture. Although the parent companies would have supplied the joint venture with up to 50% of its requirements in some areas the Commission ensured that the sales by the parent company would be at arm's length and the joint venture would be able to purchase substantial supplies from the parents' competitors. The Commission was, therefore, of the opinion that the joint venture was sufficiently independent to be concentrative. In *BT/AT&T*,[141] the parties gave various divesture undertakings to allay Commission fears over parental co-ordination.

---

135 Regulation 139/2004, OJ 2004, L24/1, Art 3(4). See, also, relating to the position under Reg 4064/89, the Commission Notice on the concept of full function joint ventures, OJ 1998, C66/1. For criticism of the Commission's handling of the 'full function' test see Radicati di Brozolo, LG and Gustafsson, M, 'Full-function joint ventures under the merger regulation: the need for clarification' [2003] ECLR 574.
136 See Case IV/M160 *Elf Atochem/Rohm and Haas*, OJ 1992, C201/27.
137 See, for example, Case IV/M722 *Téneo/Merrill Lynch/Bankers Trust*, OJ 1996, C159/4.
138 See Case IV/M3003 *Electrabel/Energia Italiana/Interpower*, OJ 2003, C25/2.
139 See Commission Notice, OJ 1998, C66/1, para 14.
140 Case IV/M511, OJ 1995, C23/3.
141 Case IV/JV15, Commission Decision 30 March 1999; Commission Press Release, IP/99/209.

There are still, however, concerns that full function concentrations may give rise to the threat of co-ordination of competitive behaviour between the parties forming the joint venture, or between them and the joint venture. This might be the case where both parents retained significant activities in the same market as the joint venture. The concern is primarily about the co-ordination of competition between the parents rather than co-ordination between one or both of the parents and the joint venture.[142]

These situations are considered in the same way as other concentrative joint ventures; however, where the Commission believes that the concentration has 'as its object or effect the co-ordination of the competitive behaviour of undertakings that remain independent', that co-ordination shall be appraised 'in accordance with the criteria of Article 81(1) and (3) of the Treaty, with a view to establishing whether or not the operation is compatible with the common market'.[143] This means that the Commission will carry out its normal appraisal alongside an assessment based on Art 81. The dual appraisal must take place within the time limits set out in the Regulation. The Commission is required to take two factors into account:

a   whether two or more parent companies retain, to a significant extent, activities in the same market as the joint venture, or in a market which is downstream or upstream from that of the joint venture, or in a neighbouring market closely related to this market; and

b   whether the co-ordination which is the direct consequence of the creation of the joint venture affords the undertakings concerned the possibility of eliminating competition in respect of a substantial part of the products or services in question.

These two factors give the Commission an opportunity, within the merger system, to examine the potential for co-ordination following the creation of a joint venture, while giving the parties to a concentration the benefits of the time limits contained in the Regulation.

International mergers

The increasing globalisation of markets demands a response from the competition authorities and this is most evident in relation to merger control, given the spate of high-profile worldwide mergers which has taken place in recent years. The most dramatic solution would be to institute some form of global authority to deal with mergers which affect a range of markets and territories. The introduction of a global authority is unlikely to occur, at least

---

142   The guidance for the old system was found in the Commission Notice on the distinction between concentrative and co-operative joint ventures, OJ 1994, C385/1.
143   Regulation 139/2004/EC, OJ 2004, L24/1, Art 2(4).

in the foreseeable future, and any developments are likely to be procedural, such as ensuring similar filing requirements under different merger control systems. In the meantime the Community has entered a number of bilateral enforcement co-operation agreements, most notably with the US, as discussed in Chapter 2. It is clear that the co-operation practice under the agreement has focused on merger activity, as exemplified by the mergers involving *Boeing/McDonnell Douglas*[144] and *AOL/Time Warner*[145] which were dealt with under both Community and US competition law systems. Notwithstanding these examples of co-operation it is clear that disputes between the Commission and the US authorities will still arise. A clear example of such a conflict was seen in *GE/Honeywell*.[146] GE and Honeywell are both very large US-based companies with large Community turnovers; therefore, their proposed merger fell to be considered under both the US and Community merger regimes. The US authorities cleared the merger shortly after the Commission went into its Phase II investigation. The Commission eventually prohibited this high-profile 'US' merger when remedies could not be agreed, as the Commission was concerned with, *inter alia*, potential links between GE's aircraft engines, Honeywell's avionics, and GE's aircraft leasing businesses. More generally, the possibility for surveillance of international mergers is linked to the issue of extra-territoriality (discussed in Chapter 2) evidenced by the dispute regarding the Commission's intervention in the *Gencor/Lonrho*[147] merger, which involved two mining companies based in South Africa.[148]

Background to UK merger control

It was only in 1948, through the Monopolies and Restrictive Practices (Inquiry and Control) Act 1948, that any form of merger control was introduced into the UK. However, that legislation merely enabled the Monopolies and Restrictive Practices Commission (MRPC) to investigate mergers on an *ex post facto* basis when a merger resulted in a concentrated market. Investigations by the MRPC under the 1948 Act often condemned merger activity.[149] However, the procedures were sterile because the authorities could not prevent a merger from taking place, nor was there the possibility of remedial action through divestiture. Partly due to the inadequacy of the procedures available under these provisions and also partly due to the impact of the

---

144 Case IV/M877, Commission Decision 97/816/EC, OJ 1997, L336/16.
145 Case IV/M1845, OJ 2000, C73/4; Commission Press Release, IP/00/1145.
146 Case IV/M2220, Commission Decision 2004/134/EC, OJ 2004, L48/1, and Case T-210/01 *GE v Commission* [2005] ECR II-5575. See, also, Burnside, A, 'GE, Honey, I sunk the merger' [2002] ECLR 107.
147 Case IV/M619, Commission Decision 97/26/EC, OJ 1997, L11/30.
148 See Fox, EM, 'The Merger Regulation and its territorial reach' [1999] ECLR 334.
149 See, for example, *Matches* (1952–53) HCP 61.

Restrictive Trade Practices Act 1956, the Monopolies and Mergers Act was introduced in 1965 in order to provide effective merger controls in the UK. The 1956 Act had led to a 'merger boom' as companies sought alternatives to collusive activities which were caught by the Act's provisions. The form of control instituted in 1965 was a benign investigative system, applicable to monopoly references since 1948, reflecting the predisposition on the part of the authorities to favour mergers taking place.[150] The merger control provisions were subsequently contained in Pt V of the Fair Trading Act 1973, which maintained the same basic format as under the previous legislation.[151] The major change the 1973 Act introduced was the creation of the post of the Director General of Fair Trading (DGFT) who, assisted by the Office of Fair Trading, played a key role in the shaping and enforcement of UK competition policy, including merger control.[152] In 2001 the Department of Trade and Industry (DTI) proposed radical reform of UK competition law.[153] Subsequently the Enterprise Act 2002 was enacted and it replaced the main merger control provisions of the 1973 Act with new provisions for merger investigations, set out in Pt 3 of the 2002 Act.

The Fair Trading Act 1973 and reform

Over the years there were a number of criticisms of the Fair Trading Act 1973 and its merger control system. The system of referral, based on the exclusive power of the Secretary of State to refer mergers, was criticised as being political. The broad scope of the public interest test, under s 84, was also criticised together with the length of time taken by and the inconvenience of Commission public interest inquiries. There were a number of reports which considered possible reforms of the merger control provisions. The *Liesner Report*, in 1978, recommended the retention of the case by case basis of merger control, but also recommended that a more critical stance should be adopted towards mergers, in contrast with the presumption that mergers were beneficial.[154] No alterations were made to the 1973 Act as a result of the report. The Trade and Industry Committee report in 1991[155] followed upon the earlier government publication, in 1988, of a Blue Paper on mergers policy, which stressed that most mergers would be left to the market to decide if they proceeded and competition issues were to be accorded primacy under

---

150 Exemplified by a speech by the then President of the Board of Trade, Anthony Crosland, at a launch of the British Association of the Chambers of Commerce on 25 June 1969.

151 The market share criterion for referral was reduced from a figure of 33% to 25%.

152 See Bankes, C and Hadden, M, *UK Merger Law and Practice*, 2006, London: LexisNexis Butterworths.

153 White Paper, *Productivity and Enterprise: A World Class Competition Regime*, Cm 5233, 31 July 2001.

154 *A Review of Monopolies and Mergers Policy*, Cmnd 7198, 1978, para 2.1.

155 Trade and Industry Committee, *Takeovers and Mergers*, First Report (1991–92) HCP 90.

the system.[156] Important modifications were subsequently introduced by the Companies Act 1989 and the Deregulation and Contracting Out Act 1994. The introduction of undertakings in lieu and a statutory notification procedure were significant procedural changes.[157] The Competition Act 1998 contained no provisions directly relating to merger control, the traditional public interest investigation system being retained under the 1973 Act. However, the DTI issued a consultation document on proposals for reform, in August 1999,[158] and this was followed by the DTI's October 2000 document, *The Response to the Consultation on Proposals for Reform*, which endorsed the main proposals in the earlier document.[159] The 1999 document noted the key objectives of reform as being threefold:

a   to enhance clarity, transparency and consistency;
b   to be more responsive to the needs of business and impose only the minimum necessary burdens; and
c   to ensure effective and proportionate control of mergers with harmful effects.

The October 2000 document noted that response had been favourable on the two fundamental proposals in the 1999 consultation document: '. . . that Ministerial involvement in mergers decisions should be minimised and that the current public interest test should be replaced by a competition-based test.'[160]

In July 2001 the Government set out its legislative plans in its White Paper, *Productivity and Enterprise: A World Class Competition Regime*.[161] One of the key objectives of the White Paper was based on the populist support for 'politicians to be taken out of merger decisions'.[162] The Government favoured the retention of a system involving a fuller investigation of a merger by the Competition Commission (CC), and a clearer role for the Office of Fair Trading (OFT) to make an initial assessment of mergers and to refer mergers, in appropriate cases, to the CC. Following the barrage of criticism the public interest test received over the years, the key proposal in August 1999 was to

---

156 Blue Paper on *Mergers Policy*, 1988.
157 It should be noted that these have been retained under the Enterprise Act regime.
158 DTI, *Mergers: A Consultation Document on Proposals for Reform*, URN 99/1028, 6 August 1999.
159 DTI, *Mergers: The Response to the Consultation on Proposals for Reform*, URN 00/805, 26 October 2000. These proposals were subsequently confirmed in the Government's strategy document for the next Parliament; HM Treasury Document, 'Productivity in the UK: enterprise and the productivity challenge', June 2001 and *Productivity and Enterprise: A World Class Competition Regime*, Cm 5233, 31 July 2001.
160 Executive Summary, p 3.
161 Cm 5233, 31 July 2001.
162 DTI Press Release, P/99/690, 6 August 1999.

replace the public interest test with a competition-based test with a view to increasing certainty and predictability. The DTI proposed that the controls should deal with mergers resulting in a significant loss of competition and take into account efficiency arguments, but the DTI sought views on the exact formulation of the test, bearing in mind the 'dominance' test then adopted under the Community Merger Regulation. The October 2000 document confirmed a competition-based test as appropriate and proposed a test based on the 'substantial lessening of competition' (SLC). The experience of the Merger Regulation dominance test when dealing with problems of collective dominance suggested that this more flexible test was suitable. In addition, it was noted that the competition analysis would consider efficiency gains and consumer benefits. The 2001 White Paper confirmed the SLC test but added that mergers may be allowed where the merger brings overall benefits to UK consumers. It was recognised that there may be exceptional circumstances where the competition test will not be appropriate and where mergers should be determined on exceptional public interest grounds, which would be determined by the Secretary of State.[163] The 2000 document confirmed, uncontroversially, that criteria based on national security, covering defence interests and other public security concerns, would be introduced and defined in the legislation. In addition, the White Paper considered a number of ancillary issues, including the retention of the voluntary notification scheme and the important extension of the CC's powers to allow it to decide on remedies following a critical report. These were based largely on the drive for greater certainty and predictability in the law and the desire to take politics out of the merger control process.[164] The new approach reflects the shift to a pure competition objective, also identified with the introduction of the Competition Act 1998. These proposals were enacted by Pt 3 of the Enterprise Act 2002. These provisions will be outlined in this chapter and any pertinent differences from the 1973 Act will be highlighted where appropriate. The main provisions of the 2002 Act entered into force in June 2003[165] and there has been considerable practice to date, but we will also review practice under the 1973 Act to illustrate the types of issue that remain a concern under Pt 3 of the 2002 Act. It should be stressed that while the 2002 Act has made crucial alterations to the referral stage, institutionally and substantively, and reformed the merger assessment test, in practice the Competition Commission will be considering similar issues in relation to the potential anti-competitive outcomes of proposed and completed mergers under the 2002 Act as under the 1973 Act.

163 *Mergers: A Consultation Document on Proposals for Reform*, URN 99/1028, fn 167, para 4.12.
164 For a fuller critique, see Rodger, BJ, 'UK merger control: politics, the public interest and reform' [2000] ECLR 24.
165 The Enterprise Act 2002 (Commencement No 3, Transitional and Transitory Provisions and Savings) Order 2003, SI 2003/1397, brought the main powers and offences of the Enterprise Act 2002 into force on 20 June 2003.

Miscellaneous issues

There are specific provisions under UK legislation in relation to media mergers which will not be considered in detail in this book. The Fair Trading Act 1973 contained a distinctive set of provisions for newspaper mergers, which ensured that mergers qualifying as 'newspaper mergers' could only be effected with the approval of the Secretary of State, normally after the case was referred to and considered by the CC. In the past the Commission has, for instance, been asked to take into account, in its public interest assessment, the need for accurate presentation of news and the free expression of opinion.[166] Chapter 2 of the Communications Act 2003 repealed the 1973 Act newspaper merger regime and adapted the main merger regime introduced in the 2002 Act to apply to media mergers generally, including newspaper mergers. The provisions in ss 375–88 of the 2003 Act include media mergers within the special public interest category in which the Secretary of State still has a key role, and these provisions place emphasis on the need for a plurality of media within the UK, 'the media public interest considerations' as specified in section 582A of the 2002 Act. An example of the application of these provisions is the inquiry, during 2007, into the acquisition of a 17.9% shareholding by BSkyB in ITV, referred by the Secretary of State. The Commission concluded that the acquisition would not be expected to adversely affect the plurality of media public interest consideration. Nonetheless, the Commission's finding was that the acquisition will result in a substantial lessening of competition, with a consequent reduction in quality and innovation and increase in prices, due to the loss of rivalry in the all-TV market.[167] The Secretary of State for Business, Enterprise and Regulatory Reform subsequently ordered BSkyB to reduce its stake in ITV to below 7.5%.[168] It should also be noted that, for reasons of space, the particular issues involved in the regulation of utilities will not be dealt with in any detail in this book, although, for instance, by virtue of Schedule 4ZA to the Water Industry Act 1991, the Enterprise Act provisions apply to mergers involving water and sewerage undertakings, subject to certain modifications.

Agreements are excluded, under Sched 1 to the 2002 Act, from the

---

166 See MMC Press Release 183; *Newsquest Media Group Ltd/Westminster Press* [1996] 7 ECLR R-183. In *Daily Mail/General Trust and Bailey Forman Ltd*, Cm 2693, 1994, the MMC advised that some benefit would accrue to readers as a result of the takeover but this would be outweighed by the adverse consequences which would arise from the significant increase in the concentration of local newspapers in the region, including reduced choice for advertisers. The Secretary of State advised that unless satisfactory undertakings were negotiated consent would be refused: (1994) DTI Press Notice, 31 October; [1995] ECLR R-26.

167 Competition Commission, *Acquisition By British Sky Broadcasting Group plc of 17.9 per cent of the shares in ITV plc*, Report sent to Secretary of State (BERR), 14 December 2007.

168 See BERR Press Release, 'Final decision on BSkyB's stake in ITV', 29 January 2008. The Commission's Report and Secretary of State's decision have been appealed to the CAT by both BSkyB and Virgin Media.

Competition Act 1998 Chapter I prohibition to the extent that the agreements result in any two enterprises ceasing to be distinct enterprises within the terms of Pt 3 of the 2002 Act.[169] Thus, where a merger falls within the jurisdiction of the 2002 Act merger system it will not usually be subject to dual control of both the 2002 Act and the 1998 Act. Any ancillary restriction that facilitates a merger is also excluded from the 2002 Act where the restriction is 'directly related and necessary to the implementation of the merger'.[170]

Before assessing the merger controls in further detail, one should also be aware of the necessity to differentiate between competition-based merger control provisions and the protection of investors. The latter is a matter of company law and the additional protection afforded by the City Code on Takeovers if a quoted company is involved.

Part 3 of the Enterprise Act 2002

UK merger control principally involves two institutions, the OFT and the CC. There are three main stages involved under the merger control provisions of the 2002 Act. Those three stages will be considered in this section as follows:

a   referral;
b   investigation and report; and
c   remedial action.

The 1973 Act allocated the Secretary of State the formal statutory role in relation to referral and subsequent enforcement. The DGFT's duty, through the OFT, was merely to advise and support the Secretary of State in their tasks.[171] The CC was exclusively involved in reporting on the public interest implications arising out of merger situations.

The basic structure under the 2002 Act is that the OFT will make a merger investigation reference to the CC.[172] After a period of investigation the CC will compile a report and has a duty to take action to remedy any adverse effects on competition which it identified in its report. There are a number of changes from the enforcement mechanism under the 1973 Act, notably the transfer of functions from the DGFT to the OFT and the enhanced role of the CC at the remedies stage. The OFT also assumed the key role in referring mergers for further investigation as, following the 2002 Act, the Secretary of State's role has been removed subject to possible involvement in public interest cases.

---

169 Paragraph 1(1) of Sched 1.
170 Competition Act 1998, Sched 1, para 1(2).
171 Section 76 of the Fair Trading Act 1973.
172 The reporting panel of the CC assumed the functions of the Monopolies and Mergers Commission under the 1973 Act as from 1 April 1999.

Public interest cases are set out in Chapters II and III of Pt 3 of the Act and are restricted to matters involving national security, mergers involving defence contractors, and newspaper and other media mergers, the latter illustrated by the BSkyB/ITV inquiry.[173] For reasons of space, this complicated set of provisions will not be considered in this chapter. Overall, despite considerable change in the statutory language used, the basic purpose of merger investigations under the 2002 Act remains broadly similar, in most cases, to the purpose under the 1973 Act. Accordingly, despite the developing practice under the 2002 Act, many references in the following sections will be to reports completed under the earlier statute by the Monopolies and Mergers Commission (MMC) (pre-1 April 1999) and CC. Nonetheless, there are certain important differences. The first is the introduction of specific provision, in s 120, for review of decisions taken by the OFT and CC under Pt 3 of the Act; a number of important review cases will be considered later in the chapter. The second is the confirmation, by both the Competition Appeal Tribunal (CAT) and the Court of Appeal in *IBA Health Ltd v OFT*[174] that the duty to refer under the new statutory framework and the role afforded the OFT thereunder differs considerably from the discretionary 1973 Act scheme. Finally, the repeal of the public interest test removes the possibility for certain mergers potentially raising non-competition concerns, such as significant employment loss or regional policy, to be considered under the UK merger control process. In any event, the application of the Tebbit doctrine, by successive Secretaries of State, effectively precluded the referral of such mergers under the 1973 Act in any event.

The referral stage

For simplicity of reference this section has been termed the referral stage although it may be more accurate to depict it as the stage at which it will be decided whether to make a formal reference to the CC. The OFT makes references and is under a duty to refer mergers which satisfy the statutory threshold. It should be noted that there are almost identical provisions in ss 22 and 33 regarding, respectively, the duty to refer completed and anticipated mergers. The OFT's activities under merger control are co-ordinated by its specialist mergers team, which is part of the Markets and Projects Group. Decisions as to which mergers are to be referred involve a number of separate sub-stages where the following questions are to be addressed:

a   Does Community competition law preclude the exercise of UK merger control?
b   Is a 'relevant merger situation' established?

---

173 Competition Commission, Acquisition By British Sky Broadcasting Group plc of 17.9 per cent of the shares in ITV plc, Report sent to Secretary of State (BERR), 14 December 2007.
174 [2003] CAT 28; on appeal *OFT v IBA Health Ltd* [2004] EWCA Civ 142, 19 February.

c   Is the SLC test satisfied?

d   Can and should undertakings be sought in lieu of a reference?

e   Is notification possible?

The OFT has published guidance as required under s 106 of the Act on its procedures and how it will undertake the substantive assessment required to make references.[175]

Community merger control

As noted earlier in relation to Community merger control, the Merger Regulation, Regulation 139/2004, provides a set of merger controls at the Community level. The central idea is that mergers with a Community dimension are investigated only by the Commission. Article 21(1) provides that only the Commission is to deal with Community dimension mergers, and this is reaffirmed by Art 21(3), which states that no national legislation may be applied to such mergers. Accordingly, the first stage for the OFT is to assess whether the particular merger situation qualifies as a Community dimension merger and should, therefore, be considered solely under the Merger Regulation. This assessment involves consideration of the thresholds under Art 1 of the Merger Regulation, which were discussed in the Community merger control section of this chapter. There are certain limited exceptions to the exclusive competence of the Commission, under Arts 4, 9 and 21(4) of the Regulation and Art 296 of the EC Treaty. For instance, in relation to the anticipated *Boots/Unichem* merger,[176] the proposed merger was referred to the OFT by the Commission following a request from the parties under Art 4(4) of the Merger Regulation, in which case, the OFT was required, by s 34A of the 2002 Act, within 45 working days of the Commission Decision, to decide whether to make a reference to the Competition Commission. The UK authorities may also need to consider the possible application of Arts 81 and 82 to a merger situation which does not qualify for investigation under the Merger Regulation.[177]

Establishing the creation of a 'relevant merger situation'

The provisions for determining which mergers may qualify for investigation, primarily in s 23 of the Enterprise Act, are very similar to those under the

---

175 See 'Mergers – procedural guidance', OFT 526, and 'Mergers – substantive assessment guidance', OFT 516. At the time of writing the OFT and CC are working on a joint review of their Guidelines.

176 See *Celesio v OFT* [2006] CAT 9.

177 The EC Competition Law (Arts 88 and 89) Enforcement Regulations 1996, SI 1996/2199. See Kerse, C, 'Enforcing competition policy under Arts 88 and 89 of the EC Treaty – new powers for UK competition authorities' [1997] ECLR 17.

Fair Trading Act. The first requirement is that two or more enterprises have ceased to be distinct enterprises. In addition, the merger must satisfy one of two alternative tests, either that:

a   the value of the turnover in the UK of the enterprise being taken over exceeds £70m; or
b   the 25% market share supply test is satisfied.

Ceased to be distinct enterprises

Section 129(1) of the Enterprise Act defines a merger situation as arising where two or more enterprises, of which at least one was carried on in the UK or carried on by or under a body corporate incorporated in the UK, have ceased to be distinct enterprises. An enterprise is defined by s 129(1) of the Act as comprising the activities, or part of the activities, of a business. Accordingly, UK merger control under the Enterprise Act, as previously under the Fair Trading Act, applies to mergers and takeovers of companies, but it can equally apply to the purchase of particular assets which form a business, for example, where a bus company acquired a depot and some buses from a rival company.[178] The crucial issue under this provision is identifying when the enterprises have ceased to be distinct.

Section 26(1) is similar to the equivalent provision under the 1973 Act and provides that enterprises cease to be distinct when they are brought under common ownership or control. However, full mergers are relatively rare. The most common practice is for the acquisition of some extent of control in another enterprise, normally via the acquisition of shares. The Act envisages, under s 25(2)–(4), three possibilities in the consideration of whether or not common ownership or control has been brought about, namely where the same person has:

a   the actual control of the enterprise;
b   the ability, directly or indirectly, to control policy; or
c   the ability, directly or indirectly, to materially influence policy.

The first possibility is the most straightforward and would cover a situation where a parent company acquired a 100% stockholding in a subsidiary company, or any other shareholding, which conferred a majority in voting terms. However, the legislation acknowledges that control may be achieved even where the majority of shares and voting rights are not acquired, particularly in cases where the remaining shareholding is dispersed widely. The

---

178 *Stagecoach Holdings plc/Lancaster City Transport Ltd*, Cm 2423, 1993. The MMC considered that, in effect, the business had been acquired as the purchaser could provide all the services previously offered by the vendor.

relationship with other institutional investors may also be important. In one example, under the equivalent provisions of the Fair Trading Act, a 29% shareholding was considered sufficient for control and a 20% holding gave a position from which the company could materially influence policy.[179] In the *BSkyB/ITV* inquiry the CC considered that the acquisition of 17.9% of the shares in ITV was sufficient for BSkyB to materially influence policy partly by allowing it effectively to block special resolutions proposed by ITV's management.[180] The OFT has indicated that it will consider shareholdings of over 15% to determine if they allow for 'material influence', although whether the material influence threshold is satisfied is dependent on a range of other circumstances, notably the spread of shares, the voting rights attached to particular shareholdings and the board representation. A merger situation may arise where the acquisition of a further interest triggers a change in the level of control of the other enterprise. For example, in *Amalgamated Industries/Herbert Morris*,[181] a merger reference was not made at the stage when the ability to materially influence policy was acquired, but rather was made later when the ability to influence policy was extended to allow actual control. The thresholds for establishing a merger situation are not easily identifiable on an objective basis and it is difficult to ascertain exactly when any threshold has been triggered. Accordingly, if a transfer of common ownership or control takes place by a series of share transactions over a period of time there may be uncertainty as to when a merger situation is established, as the thresholds are only triggered when there is a change in the level of control from one threshold to another. In order to clarify this problem and prevent any attempted avoidance of the merger control provisions, s 29 of the Act, provides that, where a series of transactions over a two-year period has the aggregate effect of bringing two or more enterprises under common ownership or control, that series of transactions may be treated, for the purposes of referral under the Act's provisions, as having occurred simultaneously on the date on which the latest transaction occurred.

Value of turnover test

Under the 1973 Act, merger situations qualified for referral where the value of the assets taken over exceeded £70m, having been increased from past lower figures. In practice, the assets value test was resorted to most frequently by the authorities because of its relative simplicity, allowing, for instance, conglomerate mergers, which did not satisfy the alternative market share test, to be investigated. The Enterprise Act replaced the assets value test with a new

---

179 *Eurocanadian Shipholdings/Furness Withy/Manchester Liners* (1975–76) HCP 639.
180 Competition Commission, *Acquisition By British Sky Broadcasting Group plc of 17.9 per cent of the shares in ITV plc*, Report sent to Secretary of State (BERR), 14 December 2007.
181 (1975/76) HCP 434.

test which states that the turnover in the UK of the enterprise being taken over must exceed £70m in value before the takeover qualifies for referral. The primary reason for the change was that many 'new economy' businesses would not qualify for investigation under an assets value test. Also, turnover is generally considered to be a better indicator of the real size of an undertaking. The threshold of £70m was a compromise figure as the Bill passed through Parliament, and the figure is likely to be increased in the future.

Market share test

This alternative test, set out in s 23(3) and (4) of the 2002 Act, will be satisfied where, as a result of the merger in question, at least 25% of the goods or services of any description are supplied by, or to, the same person in the UK or in a substantial part of the UK. The test can be easily satisfied due to the use of the fairly flexible criterion of goods or services of any description and the possible resort to a wide range of criteria, including value, quantity, and/ or number of workers employed. The test will also be satisfied where one enterprise already supplies or consumes 25% of goods or services of the description, and this figure is increased as a result of the merger.[182] Case law has considered the extent to which the market share test is satisfied in a substantial part of the UK. In the *South Yorkshire Transport* case,[183] under the equivalent provision in the Fair Trading Act, the House of Lords considered that, although the term 'substantial part' could not be defined by arithmetical criteria based on area of coverage or population, 'the reference area must be of such size, character and importance as to make it worth consideration for the purposes of the Act'.[184] In *Stagecoach Holdings plc v Secretary of State for Trade and Industry*,[185] the market share test was applied and satisfied where the Commission had considered a designated area which represented 1.4% of the UK population and 1.8% of the UK geographical area. More recently, in *Lloyds Pharmacy/Pharmacy Care Centres*,[186] this test was considered to be satisfied by the OFT in relation to five primary care trusts, which represented around 2% of the total UK population.

Is the substantial lessening of competition (SLC) test satisfied?

The new competition-based test is one of the most important changes to UK merger control introduced under the 2002 Act. The Act places a duty on the

---

182 As a result of the provision in s 23(2)(5) that the conditions in sub-ss (3) and (4) prevail 'to a greater extent'.
183 *R v Monopolies and Mergers Commission ex p South Yorkshire Transport Ltd* [1993] 1 All ER 289. See, also, *South Yorkshire Transport Ltd Acquisitions*, Cm 1166, 1990.
184 *R v Monopolies and Mergers Commission* [1993] 1 All ER 289, p 296.
185 1997 SLT 940 (OH).
186 OFT Decision, 18 January 2007.

OFT to refer merger situations, but only where 'the creation of that situation has resulted, or may be expected to result, in a SLC within any market or markets in the United Kingdom for goods or services'.[187] The Act introduces a new SLC test, and this will determine whether a reference is to be made by the OFT, and the test will also determine the outcome of the CC inquiry. To understand the fundamental reform of the UK merger control process by the introduction of a competition test for referral purposes and the imposition of a duty, we will first consider in outline the merger referral process under the 1973 Act.

Policy on referrals under the 1973 Act

Under the 1973 Act, where a merger situation existed there were no further formal tests to determine which mergers could be referred. Only the Secretary of State could make a merger reference to the CC, and, given the small number of qualifying mergers which were referred, inevitably government trade and industry policy was reflected in the choice of mergers referred for further consideration. The exclusive merger referral power of the Secretary of State reflected the political nature of the UK merger control system. The Secretary of State was assisted by the DGFT in assessing which merger situations ought to be referred. The DGFT made recommendations to the Secretary of State, who exercised the ultimate political decision-making power over whether or not to refer and who was not bound by the DGFT's advice. Furthermore, there was nothing in the Act that required references to be made in accordance with the public interest test in s 84. The key policy development in UK merger control, under the 1973 Act, was known as the Tebbit doctrine. In July 1984, the then Secretary of State for Trade and Industry, Norman Tebbit, stated that his 'policy has been, and will continue to be to make references primarily on competition grounds'.[188] As merger policy was, to a great extent, made at the referral stage, the Tebbit doctrine ensured that other public interest issues in s 84, such as consideration of regional policy and employment issues, would have no practical impact on UK merger control. The practical limitations of the public interest test were exemplified by the decision not to refer the final takeover bid by Guinness for United Distillers in 1982, despite concerns over the likely effect of the takeover on the Scottish economy.[189] The continued application of the Tebbit doctrine at the referral stage was confirmed by subsequent Secretaries of State. Nonetheless, in addition to the focus on competition concerns, other

---

187 Section 22(1). Section 33(1), in relation to anticipated mergers, is in almost identical terms.
188 DTI Press Notice, 5 July 1984. A policy also confirmed subsequently in the Government's Blue Paper on *Mergers Policy*, 1988.
189 See Rodger, BJ, 'Reinforcing the Scottish "ring-fence": a critique of UK mergers policy vis à vis the Scottish economy' [1996] ECLR 104.

relevant policy factors were discernible at the referral stage in the past. These policy factors demonstrated the breadth of possible public interest issues and the diversity of approach adopted in different periods. For instance, employment and regional policy issues were often considered to be important prior to the introduction of the Tebbit doctrine.[190] Michael Heseltine stressed the international competitiveness of UK companies, and, in 1995, in order to encourage higher sales of UK board games abroad, he refused to make a merger reference of Hasbro UK Ltd's takeover of Waddington Games.[191] A policy operated by Peter Lilley in 1990 and 1991, subsequently known as the 'Lilley doctrine', was in conflict with the Tebbit doctrine. Peter Lilley would make references of mergers where the acquiring company was State owned or controlled even where competition issues were not otherwise concerned.

Substantial lessening of competition (SLC)

When assessing the effects of competition for the public interest test under the 1973 Act, the DGFT and Secretary of State would inevitably, although not formally, consider the relevant product and geographical market, and this would involve an assessment of demand-side and supply-side substitutability. Thereafter, the structure of the market would be analysed by ascertaining the market shares of the merging parties, the extent of existing competition, the likelihood of potential competition and any barriers to entry for potential competitors. For example, the proposed acquisition of Abbey National by Lloyds TSB was blocked on the basis of competition concerns that it would lead to the elimination from the market of one of the most significant branch-based competitors to the UK's largest banks.[192]

A duty to refer under s 22 of the 2002 Act arises where the creation of the merger situation:

> has resulted, or may be expected to result, in a substantial lessening of competition within any market or markets within the United Kingdom for goods and services.

In determining whether this test is satisfied, the OFT will undertake a process similar to that under the 1973 Act. This process involves market definition analysis which is required to provide a proper understanding of the competitive constraints faced by the merged undertaking. The SLC test focuses on the extent to which competitive rivalry is likely to be diminished as a result of

190 Ibid.
191 In this context the approval by the Secretary of State of the Post Office's acquisition of German Parcel in January 1999 is notable as representing a major step towards becoming a global communications organisation. See DTI Press Release, P/99/018, 11 January 1999.
192 *Lloyds TSB/Abbey National* Cm 5208, 2001; DTI Press Release, P/2001/362, 10 July 2001.

a merger, and to the detriment of consumers by increasing prices or reducing customer choice. The OFT is required to undertake a comparative exercise on the extent of competitive rivalry pre- and post-merger. This exercise may be required in the context of the three types of merger identified at the start of this chapter: horizontal, vertical and conglomerate mergers. Competition concerns are most likely, but not necessarily, to arise as a result of horizontal mergers due to the loss of a rival or the greater likelihood of co-ordination between remaining market rivals. Vertical mergers may be problematic where either party has market power, and conglomerate mergers may reduce competition by, for instance, the exercise of portfolio power, as considered by the European Commission in *GE/Honeywell*.[193] Generally, when ascertaining the likelihood of the SLC, the OFT will be guided by a range of possible indicators, including market shares, concentration ratios measuring the aggregate share of a small number of leading market firms, and the use of HHIs as favoured in America. The OFT will consider the likelihood of either non co-ordinated, or unilateral, anti-competitive effects arising directly from the merger or the possibility of co-ordinated effects; the OFT has indicated that it will apply the test set out by the CFI in *Airtours*[194] to determine whether tacit co-ordination in oligopolistic markets is feasible and/or likely. A number of other factors may also be relevant in the OFT's competition assessment, including entry and expansion by new or existing competitors, countervailing buyer power, efficiencies which are likely to increase rivalry and the possibility of a failing firm defence.[195] As an example, the OFT referred the proposed acquisition by FirstGroup plc of the ScotRail franchise on the basis that the acquisition might be expected to result in a SLC in the supply of passenger transport services and thereby reduce consumer choice.[196]

The duty to refer

In addition to the key changes already noted – the role of the OFT in making references and the introduction of a formal set of referral criteria – the Act placed an obligation on the OFT to refer mergers which satisfied the new SLC test. The impact of this change has already been considered by both the CAT and the Court of Appeal in review proceedings following the Decision by the OFT not to refer to the CC a proposed merger between Isoft plc and

---

193 Case IV/M2220, Commission Decision 2004/134/EC *GE/Honeywell*, OJ 2004, L48/1, and Case T-210/01 *GE v Commission* [2005] ECR II-5575.
194 Case T-342/99 *Airtours v Commission* [2002] ECR II-2585; [2002] 5 CMLR 7. See for instance, the reference by the OFT in *Weinerberger Finance Service/Baggeridge Brick*, 11 December 2006, although the Commission report concluded that the transaction would not give rise to co-ordinated effects.
195 The failing firm defence was rejected by the OFT in *Flybe Group/BA Connect*, OFT Decision of 7 February 2007. See OFT Press Release 16/07.
196 See OFT Press Release, 13 January 2004.

Torex plc, direct competitors in the supply of software applications to hospitals. A rival company, IBA Health Company Ltd, sought, under s 120 of the Act, review of that OFT Decision before the CAT,[197] which was required to construe the requirements placed upon the OFT in the new statutory framework.[198] The CAT considered, first, that the OFT faced a real question as to whether the merger might be expected to lead to a SLC. In that context, the CAT sought to construe the words of the statutory provision, which requires a reference when the OFT believes 'that it is or may be the case' that the competition test would be satisfied. The CAT concluded that these words implied a two-part test, requiring not only the OFT's belief that there was no significant prospect of a SLC, but also no significant prospect of an alternative view being taken, given the OFT's role merely as 'a first screen', after a fuller investigation by the CC. The statutory framework and respective roles of the OFT and CC reinforced the view that complex cases raising real issues as to SLC should not, in general, be dealt with by the OFT but should go to the Commission. The CAT subsequently granted leave to appeal as the case raised 'legal and constitutional issues as to the respective roles of the OFT, the Competition Commission and the Tribunal under the legislation'.[199] The OFT appealed and the Court of Appeal judgment provides another useful review of the relevant statutory framework. There were concerns, following the CAT judgment, that the merger control provisions would become a complainant's charter and that the OFT would be required to refer considerably more mergers than in the past, increasing the workload of both of the competition authorities and delaying more merger transactions to the detriment of the business community. However, the Court of Appeal did not follow the CAT's interpretation of the relevant provision, s 33, which involved a two-stage test, and considered that the use of the words 'may be the case' clearly excluded the 'purely fanciful'. Between the purely fanciful and a degree of likelihood 'less than 50%' of a significant lessening of competition the OFT would have a wide margin in which to exercise its judgment as to whether a reference was necessary.[200] Nonetheless, on the facts, the appeal failed as the OFT had failed to adequately explain or justify its conclusion in accordance with the test. The OFT has subsequently revised para 3.2 of its guidance, 'Mergers – substantive assessment',[201] to reflect the substance of the Court of Appeal's judgment. Instead of a 'significant prospect' of a merger resulting in a SLC, the revised guidance requires a 'realistic prospect' of SLC, identified

197 *IBA Health Ltd v OFT* [2003] CAT 28.
198 It should be noted that the dispute concerned a proposed merger and the construction of s 33 of the Act in relation thereto, although the same issues arise, under s 22 of the Act, in relation to completed mergers.
199 [2003] CAT 28, at para 6.
200 *IBA Health Ltd v OFT* [2004] EWCA Civ 142, V-C at para 48. See, also, *Celesio v OFT* [2006] CAT 9, discussed further below.
201 'Mergers – substantive assessment guidance', OFT 516.

as 'not only a prospect that has more than a 50 per cent chance of occurring, but also a prospect that is not fanciful but has less than a 50 per cent chance of occurring'. A considerable body of decisional practice by the OFT involving unconditional clearance decisions has now developed, even in mergers involving high market shares.[202] An excellent recent example is the proposed acquisition of Umbro plc by Nike Inc, which was cleared by the OFT. There were overlaps in relation to sports footwear and equipment where the parties' shares were low, and although their combined market shares in replica kits were over 45%, the OFT considered bidding data, which demonstrated that they had not been competing bidders, and the considerable strength of football clubs in negotiating deals, to conclude that there were no competition concerns regarding tacit or explicit collusion between rivals post-merger.[203]

Exceptions to the duty to refer

There are three exceptions to the duty to refer a merger for further investigation where the referral criteria appear to be satisfied. The first is where the merger, either in progress or in contemplation, is insufficiently advanced to warrant a reference, for instance where parties have sought informal advice or confidential guidance at an early stage from the OFT. The second is a *de minimis* provision, introduced by s 22(2)(a) of the Act, where the market in question is of insufficient importance to warrant fuller investigation by the CC. The OFT's guidance, revised as of 15 November 2007, raised the threshold for possible application of the *de minimis* exception to markets where the aggregate turnover of the parties is £10 million or less.[204] Subsequently, the OFT cleared two rail franchise mergers where the overlap markets between the bus company acquirer and the franchise were under £1 million and just over £1 million, respectively.[205] Finally, the OFT may decide not to make a reference where any 'relevant customer benefits' outweigh the adverse competitive consequences of the merger.[206] Relevant customer benefits are defined by s 30 as benefits in the form of, *inter alia*, lower prices, higher quality or greater choice of goods or services and greater innovation. These

---

202 As discussed in greater detail by Went, D, 'Recent Developments in UK Merger Control – Establishment of Solid Foundations for the New Regime' [2007] ECLR 627 at pp 634–637.
203 OFT Press Release 8/08, 16 January 2008.
204 Para 7.6 of OFT Substantive Assessment Guidance, as revised by OFT 516b, November 2007.
205 OFT Press Release 180/07, 20 December 2007, re awards of the Intercity East Coast Rail Franchise (ICEC) to National Express Group and the Cross Country Rail Franchise to Arriva plc. See, also, OFT Press Release 16/08, 4 February 2008 regarding the non-referral of the award of the East Midland Rail franchise to Stagecoach plc.
206 Section 22(2)(a). There is an identical provision in relation to anticipated mergers in s 33(2)(c).

benefits must be quantifiable and have accrued or be likely to accrue within a 'reasonable period' of the merger and be unlikely to have arisen without the merger. This will be a difficult balancing exercise for the OFT. Although efficiencies may be relevant at this stage, the OFT has indicated in its guidance that customers need to be better off as a result of the merger to satisfy this test, and, ordinarily, lower prices, higher quality and choice are more likely to result from a more competitive market.

Making a merger reference

In the vast majority of cases, where no serious competition issues are raised, the specialist Mergers team in the OFT will decide internally to clear the merger, and in public cases this decision will be published on the OFT website. In cases raising more complex issues or more serious competition issues, a more formal process will be undertaken, involving the distribution of an 'issues' letter to the parties and an issues meeting with officials, prior to a final decision which will also be published in a public case.[207] It should be noted that following the 2002 Act there has been a considerable increase in transparency with the publication by the OFT of all decisions on referral. A referral will often lead to the abandonment of an acquisition or merger due to the time-consuming and costly inquiry that will be undertaken by the CC. In that event the inquiry will be cancelled.[208] Accordingly, parties may seek to avoid a lengthy inquiry by meeting the OFT's competition concerns by offering what are known as 'undertakings in lieu of a reference'.

Undertakings in lieu of reference

Section 73 of the Enterprise Act provides for undertakings in lieu where the OFT considers that it is under a duty to refer a merger. To a great extent, despite the different statutory formulation, this continues the earlier practice under the 1973 Act. Accordingly, a merger reference can be avoided if the OFT's concerns about the merger, or proposed merger, can be alleviated in some way by the parties offering appropriate undertakings. 'Undertakings' is the technical term for legally binding commitments, offered by parties involved in the merger, to modify their behaviour and/or the structure of the combined enterprises in the future in order to meet the competition concerns identified by the OFT. The possibility of giving 'structural undertakings' was

---

207 See, for instance, the decision to refer the proposed acquisition by FirstGroup plc of the ScotRail franchise; OFT Press Release, 13 January 2004.
208 See, for example, Competition Commission Press Release 70/05, 4 November 2005, notifying the cancellation of an inquiry into the proposed acquisition by Robert Wiseman Dairies of the fresh milk business of Scottish Milk Dairies, where the acquisition had been abandoned following the OFT referral.

first provided for by the Companies Act 1989, which added ss 75G–75K to the Fair Trading Act 1973.[209] However, the undertakings in lieu of a reference introduced by the Companies Act 1989 were limited to undertakings relating to the sale or divestiture of assets or the splitting up of the merged enterprises. The power to accept undertakings was subsequently extended to provide for undertakings in lieu of a reference on any issue.[210] Accordingly, structural and behavioural undertakings could be accepted in lieu of a reference and this is also the position under the 2002 Act. For example, in relation to the takeover by Stagecoach Holdings plc of Cambus Holdings Ltd in 1996, undertakings were accepted which provided for the divestment of two other companies and a depot in Huntingdon, in addition to a number of behavioural undertakings regarding fares, service levels, tenders, responses to competition and the provision of information.[211] More recent examples of undertakings in lieu under the Enterprise Act 2002 include: divestment undertakings by William Hill plc following the acquisition of the licensed betting office business of Stanley plc, where the OFT were concerned about the significant lessening of competition in around 80 local areas, which would have led to a reduced choice for punters;[212] and undertakings to license IP rights to an upfront buyer by the Tetra Laval group, to protect the cheddar cheese-making equipment sector from reduced competition, innovation, and service levels and increased prices, in order to avoid a reference of a proposed acquisition to the CC.[213] It is clear that the OFT has adopted a stricter approach to the negotiation of remedies more recently and is less likely to accept behavioural remedies, particularly where they involve price controls, and the OFT's starting point in determining appropriate remedies is the status quo.

Section 73 of the 2002 Act permits the OFT to have regard to any relevant customer benefits when deciding whether particular undertakings in lieu are appropriate. Where undertakings in lieu are considered to be a suitable remedy, the OFT will normally make a public announcement and consult on the proposed undertakings in order to give interested third parties an opportunity to comment. The normal statutory timetable for making a reference may be extended to allow time for the negotiation process. Section 73 is supported by s 75, which provides the OFT with the power to make appropriate orders

209 For example, the first case in which an undertaking was accepted was in 1990 and concerned the commitment by the Rank Organisation to dispose of 10 of Mecca's bingo clubs in Greater London in order to alleviate concerns over the effects on competition of the proposed merger: DTI Press Release, P/90/576.

210 Section 39, Sched 11, para 2 of the Deregulation and Contracting Out Act 1994.

211 DTI Press Release, P/96/408. See, also, the undertakings received from Scottish and Newcastle plc in relation to its acquisition of the pubs, restaurants and lodges business of Greenalls plc; DTI Press Release, P/99/1054, 22 December 1999.

212 See OFT Press Release 144/05, 2 August 2005.

213 See OFT Press Release 162/06, 20 November 2006.

where undertakings in lieu have not been fulfilled. Any decisions by the OFT in this context are subject to review.[214]

Notification and confidential guidance

The provisions of the Enterprise Act, as with the Fair Trading Act 1973, allow for references after a qualifying merger has taken place. In the case of a proposed merger[215] there is no system of compulsory notification under the Act. However, parties can supply information voluntarily to the OFT in order to discuss and assess the likely application of the Act to their merger situation. In this way they can avoid the risk of a completed merger transaction later being investigated and ordered to be undone. There is a range of ways in which the OFT may give advice: informal advice, confidential guidance, pre-notification discussions, and statutory voluntary pre-notification. These possible options indicate that the procedures under the Act are generally preventative rather than curative. Moreover, in respect of completed mergers, the OFT has been provided with interim powers to ensure that an inquiry will not be prejudiced. The OFT has begun to utilise these powers, aimed at holding the parties' businesses separate, more frequently.

Informal advice or confidential guidance

Informal advice may be given in order to assist on the planning by companies and their advisers of possible mergers. This preliminary form of advice is normally given orally, is based on the assumed accuracy of the information provided and does not bind the OFT. At a slightly more advanced stage in the merger process, and where parties may seek to gauge whether undertakings in lieu may be acceptable, the parties can seek informal confidential guidance as to whether a proposed transaction was likely to be referred to the CC. Confidential guidance can be sought prior to the merger becoming public knowledge. The benefit for the parties is that the procedures are confidential and swift, although the guidance is not binding.

Statutory pre-notification or informal submission

Formal pre-notification procedures were first introduced by the Companies Act 1989, which added ss 75A–75F to the Fair Trading Act. The current statutory provisions are contained in ss 96 and 97 of the Enterprise Act 2002. Full details of the merger, including market shares, financial information, and the intended timescale of the merger, must be given in a formal merger notice. Section 97(1) provides that the period for consideration of a merger notice is

---

214 See *Co-operative Group (CWS) Limited v OFT* [2007] CAT 24 discussed below.
215 Section 33 provides for references of anticipated mergers.

20 days after receipt by the OFT and that if this period expires without a reference being made to the CC no subsequent reference can be made. The basic 20-day period may be extended by a further 10 days, and there is also scope for extension where: the OFT is seeking undertakings in lieu of notice; insufficient information has been provided; or there has been an intervention notice in relation to a public interest merger. The obvious advantage to the parties of proceeding with a merger notice under the statutory pre-notification procedure is that a final, formal decision should be guaranteed within 30 days. The procedure is only available if the merger proposals have been made public. However, the parties may consider the statutory procedures and, in particular, the required format of the merger notice to be too inflexible. In that event, parties may proceed via non-statutory informal submission, the advantage being that they can submit information and present the merger in the manner deemed most suitable to them. In recognition of business preference to advise the OFT by informal submission, the OFT has established a nonbinding time limit, currently 40 days, for a decision whether to make a reference. Neither of the alternative notification procedures are confidential, and the OFT will routinely seek the views of interested third parties. An example of the pre-notification process involved the proposed acquisition of NatWest Bank by the Royal Bank of Scotland, where the proposed acquisition was cleared by the Secretary of State in 1999[216] and the acquisition thereafter proceeded without concern over competition law intervention. A more recent alternative for parties, in order to avoid duplication of effort, is the submission of a 'common notification form', where a merger is to be examined in two or more of the UK, France and Germany; a 40-day deadline is also applicable for this type of informal submission.

The Competition Commission (CC) investigation and report

Introduction

As of 1 April 1999 the CC replaced the MMC. The CC investigates and reports on references made to it under the merger provisions of the Enterprise Act 2002. In addition, the Act gave the Commission the authority to make and implement decisions with regard to most competition questions arising out of merger inquiries in the UK, no longer limiting the Commission to merely making recommendations to the Secretary of State. Commission reports are located in the government publications section of libraries and are available on the Commission's website.[217]

---

216 See DTI Press Release, P/99/1036, 16 December 1999.
217 www.competition-commission.org.uk.

The Competition Commission inquiry

If a reference is made to the CC it is required to conduct an investigation and determine:

a   whether there is a qualifying merger situation; and
b   whether that merger situation has resulted, or may be expected to result, in a SLC.[218]

The CC is required to conduct its investigation and prepare and produce its report within 24 weeks of the reference, although this may be extended by no more than eight weeks. A merger reference may be laid aside by the CC if the merger has been abandoned following the reference.[219] Upon receiving a reference, four or five members, with a minimum of three, are appointed by the Chairman of the CC to form an inquiry group and one of the group is selected as Chairman of that inquiry. Each inquiry group has the ability to decide upon its own procedures; however, decisions must be made and published within statutory time limits. The main stages of inquiries are as follows:

a   gathering information, including the issue of questionnaires;
b   hearing witnesses;
c   verifying information;
d   providing an issues statement;
e   considering responses to the issues statement;
f   notifying parties of and publishing provisional findings, including possible remedies;
g   considering exclusions from disclosure; and
h   publishing reports.

The CC invites evidence from all interested parties including the main parties to the inquiry and third parties, such as competitors and consumer organisations. The CC will gain information by a variety of means including: letters and questionnaires; press notices; advertisements; surveys; and, visits to the principal parties. Unlike the merger laws of many countries there is no requirement for mergers to be pre-notified to the OFT and there are separate provisions in the legislation to deal with completed mergers. Pending completion of any investigation, and in order to prevent the outcome of a reference being frustrated by the parties' actions, the Commission may accept interim undertakings, under s 80, or adopt interim orders, under s 81.[220] This includes

---

218 Sections 35(1) and 36(1) in relation to completed and anticipated mergers, respectively.
219 Section 75(5). The parties are required to notify the Commission.
220 There are similar powers available to the OFT under ss 71 and 72 of the Act.

taking action to prevent pre-emptive steps that might prejudice the reference. In its Guidance, the Commission notes that it will normally consider the appointment of a Hold Separate Manager (HSM) and/or a monitoring trustee at the outset of an inquiry where a merger has already been completed in order to prevent the separate businesses being merged. A series of oral hearings, normally in private with the parties, may be held in order to confirm factual evidence obtained and to clarify issues arising in relation to the inquiry. The CC is required to consult on its provisional decisions where the decisions are likely to have a substantial impact on the interests of any person. The consultation process was demonstrated by the consultation by the Commission on its proposed remedies to address the SLC identified in its provisional findings on the transfer to Stena of P & O's Liverpool–Dublin operations.[221] After the consultation process the Commission will publish its report, which will normally include the following:

a   a summary of its conclusions and recommendations;
b   an analysis of the merger's effects, and conclusions on whether the merger qualifies for investigation and whether it results, or may be expected to result, in a SLC;
c   recommendations on remedies where there is an adverse finding;
d   a chapter providing details of the factual background and the parties involved;
e   a chapter detailing the markets or activities in the UK affected by the proposed transaction;
f   a chapter summarising the views of the parties;
g   a chapter summarising the views of interested third parties; and
h   appendices containing details of submissions by third parties, and other relevant financial and statistical information.[222]

The CC is required to verify that the merger meets the statutory criteria for referral. This was one of the main issues which arose in *Stagecoach Holdings plc v Secretary of State for Trade and Industry*.[223] In that case, it was held, following earlier case law of the House of Lords, that the Commission's assessment that the designated area constituted a substantial part of the UK was appropriate.[224] However, the most contentious issue in most cases will involve the CC's assessment of whether the merger satisfies the SLC test. Before we proceed to consider this new test, one can further appreciate the divergence from the 1973 Act by briefly considering previous Commission

---

221   CC news release, 2 December 2003.
222   See, for example, *British Sky Broadcasting Group plc and Manchester United plc: A Report on the Proposed Merger*, Cm 4305, 1999.
223   1997 SLT 940 (OH).
224   *R v MMC ex p South Yorkshire Transport Ltd* [1993] 1 All ER 289.

practice when it assessed broader public interest issues arising out of certain mergers.

The 1973 Act and public interest issues

The Fair Trading Act 1973 required the Commission to report on whether the merger situation was expected to operate against the public interest. Section 84, discussed earlier in connection with a historical view of UK monopoly controls, provided the Commission with a variety of factors which it should take into account in its evaluation of the public interest test. Notably, the promotion of competition was not the only factor to be considered and was not given pre-eminence over the other factors. Nonetheless, due to the over-riding importance of the referral stage and the Tebbit doctrine, the Commission was inevitably constrained in the public interest issues upon which it could consider and report. Indeed, the focus of the latter CC merger inquiries under the 1973 Act was on the potential anti-competitive consequences of referred mergers. Nonetheless, under the 1973 Act there was a period when considerable weight was attached to the regional policy aspect of the public interest test as provided for in s 84(d). Under that provision the Commission should have regard to the desirability 'of maintaining and promoting the balanced distribution of industry and employment in the United Kingdom'. In particular, there was a series of important Commission reports on take-overs of indigenous Scottish companies. In particular, the Commission's approach in consideration of the two bids for the Royal Bank of Scotland in 1982 was particularly interesting.[225] The Commission found the proposed mergers to be likely to operate against the public interest due to the removal of ultimate control from Edinburgh, the importance of the company and the industry in Scotland, the reduction of career opportunities in Scotland and the fears, generally, over the creation of a branch economy. Similar arguments were accepted by the majority Commission report into the proposed takeover of Anderson Strathclyde, an important Scottish engineering company, by Charter Consolidated in 1982.[226] However, it was clear that the period in which regional policy in UK merger control had assumed a degree of importance was waning. This was confirmed by the Tebbit doctrine and subsequent refusals to refer the *Guinness/Distillers* merger and other take-overs of Scottish companies.[227] Accordingly, the Commission did not, in more recent years, have the opportunity to deal with regional policy in its public interest assessment of mergers. In addition, under s 84 of the 1973 Act, the Commission could take into account a wide variety of factors in its

---

225 *The Hong Kong and Shanghai Banking Corporation Standard Chartered Bank/The Royal Bank of Scotland Group*, Cmnd 8472, 1982.
226 *Charter Consolidated/Anderson Strathclyde*, Cmnd 8771, 1982.
227 For example, in the *Guinness/Distillers* and *BP/Britoil* takeovers. See Rodger, fn 189.

assessment of the public interest. In the past the Commission has considered the possible inefficiencies resulting from a merger;[228] it has condemned mergers which may lead to a reduction in the UK's balance of payments;[229] and it has also commented on the consequences of a merger on unemployment[230] and even in relation to the environment.[231]

Competition-related inquiries under the 1973 Act

Despite the new statutory framework and the clear formulation of the new substantial lessening of competition test, it is still instructive to look at recent examples under the 1973 Act for the types of market competition problems that are likely to involve the Commission, given the prominence afforded the 'competition' aspect of the public interest test in recent years.[232]

Many reports were about the takeover of bus services, particularly involving Stagecoach Holdings plc, and the Commission has, on occasion, been concerned that Stagecoach may exercise local dominance, to the detriment of the travelling public, as a result of a proposed takeover. For instance, in one report the Commission was concerned that the company would engage in predatory conduct and that in the long term the company might raise prices or cut services.[233] The merger controls were also involved in the long running saga of the takeover of Strathclyde Buses Holdings Ltd (SB Holdings Ltd), based in Glasgow. The proposed takeover by FirstBus plc of SB Holdings Ltd was referred. The Commission noted that SB Holdings Ltd was the largest operator in Glasgow with over two-thirds of the market in certain districts. The merger was found to be contrary to the public interest because of the loss of actual and potential competition between the two bus companies. The Commission recommended that FirstBus should divest itself of another bus company, Midland Bluebird, and some of the operations of SB Holdings Ltd in order to allow the merger to proceed.[234] A proposed takeover by Robert Wiseman Dairies plc of Scottish Pride Holdings Ltd was

---

228 *Lonrho/House of Fraser* (1978–79) HCP 261.

229 For example, *Hiram Walker/Highland Distilleries* (1979–80) HCP 743.

230 *Enserch/Davy International*, Cmnd 8360, 1981.

231 In *Prosper de Mulder Ltd/Croda International plc*, Cm 1611, 1991, the environmental advantages of the merger were considered.

232 For a fuller discussion, see Goodman, S, 'Steady as she goes: the Enterprise Act 2002 charts a familiar course for UK merger control law' [2003] ECLR 331.

233 *Stagecoach/Ayrshire Bus (A1 Service)*, Cm 3032, 1995. See, also, [1996] ECLR R28; DTI P/95/772; and [1997] ECLR R104; DTI Press Release, P/97/293, confirming that undertakings had been accepted which remedied the Commission concerns. The Commission reported that, following the merger, there would be a modest loss of actual competition and a significant loss in potential competition between the two in commercial bus services and schools transport.

234 *FirstBus plc/SB Holdings Ltd*, Cm 3531, 1997. The Secretary of State granted FirstBus nine months to seek a buyer or divest its full interest in SB Holdings.

also considered as likely to operate against the public interest due to the proposed takeover's likely effect on competition in the supply of processed fresh milk to customers in Scotland, other than national supermarket group customers. The parties were found to have 80% of the wholesale market and, although national supermarket groups could prevent exploitation, other customers could not; therefore, the merger could lead to higher wholesale prices and possibly also increased retail prices.[235] Other examples include the report in connection with the *Bass/Carlsberg-Tetley* merger. In that report it was considered that the merger was likely to be anti-competitive by strengthening the companies' combined brand portfolios, and lead to a significant increase in market power, a conclusion similar to the conclusion in the high-profile *Ladbroke/Coral* merger. Ladbroke was required to divest Coral as the merger would damage competition and disadvantage punters.[236]

Probably the most high-profile merger investigation in the last twenty years involved the proposed acquisition of Manchester United by BSkyB.[237] The merger was blocked following the Commission report which concluded that the proposed merger would reduce competition for the broadcast rights of Premier League matches.[238] In addition, the merger would adversely affect football in two ways: first, by reinforcing the trend towards greater inequality between football clubs; and secondly, by giving BSkyB influence which might not be in the long-term interest of football. The merger between Interbrew, a Belgian brewer, and the UK business of Bass Brewers was also blocked under the 1973 Act. The Secretary of State accepted the Commission's conclusion that the merger would be against the public interest as it would reduce competition which would lead to higher prices and reduced consumer choice. As a result of the findings in the report the Secretary of State required the divestment of Bass Brewers to an approved buyer.[239] In July 2001 the proposed merger between Lloyds TSB and Abbey National was blocked on the basis of the CC's report which concluded that the merger would reduce competition in, for example, the markets for personal current accounts.[240]

In March 2003 four supermarket operators (Asda Group Ltd, Wm Morrison Supermarkets plc, J Sainsbury plc and Tesco plc) competed to acquire Safeway plc. The bids were referred to the CC. The CC report[241]

---

235 Cm 3504, 1996.
236 *Bass/Carlsberg-Tetley*, Cm 3662, 1997; [1997] ECLR R-132, *Ladbroke plc/Coral*, Cm 4030, 1998; DTI Press Release, P/98/713, 23 September 1998.
237 Cm 4305, 1999.
238 DTI Press Release, P/99/309, 9 April 1999.
239 See *Interbrew SA and Bass plc: A Report on the Acquisition by Interbrew SA of the Brewing Interests of Bass plc*, Cm 5014, 2001; DTI Press Release, P/2001/11, 3 January 2001.
240 *Lloyds TSB/Abbey National*, Cm 5208, 2001; DTI Press Notice, P/2001/362, 10 July 2001.
241 *Safeway plc and Asda Group Ltd (owned by Wal-Mart Stores Inc); Wm Morrison Supermarkets plc; J Sainsbury plc; and Tesco plc – A Report on the Mergers in Contemplation*, Cm 5950, 2003.

concluded that the acquisition by any of Asda, Sainsbury or Tesco would be anti-competitive and operate against the public interest, as such an acquisition would substantially reduce consumer choice. A takeover by any of those three companies was expected to operate against the public interest at both a national and local level which, it was decided, could not be remedied by divestiture. Morrisons, however, could overcome local level competition concerns provided it could successfully negotiate undertakings with the OFT relating to the divestment of 52 stores as recommended by the CC. UK merger control was once more under the media spotlight following the announcement of an agreed merger between Carlton Communications plc and Granada plc which was referred to the CC. In its report, in October 2003,[242] the CC found that without additional safeguards under negotiation amongst Carlton, Granada, other regional licensees and the Independent Television Commission with regard to ITV networking arrangements, the proposed merger might be expected to operate against the public interest. Furthermore, given the number of combined ITV licences held by the parties, the Commission found that the proposed merger would have an adverse effect on future competition for the sale of advertising airtime. Subsequently, undertakings were accepted from the parties and the merger was allowed to proceed.[243]

The substantial lessening of competition (SLC) test and CC practice

Following considerable debate over reform of the 1973 Act's public interest test an American-style SLC test was adopted in preference to the, then, Community dominance test. Although, in most cases, the application of both tests would lead to the same result, the SLC test should avoid the difficulties evidenced by the application of the collective dominance model under the 1989 Merger Regulation.[244] The CC issued Guidelines on merger references under the 2002 Act in June 2003 and these Guidelines indicate the Commission's views as to how it will approach the application of the new test, which essentially replicates the OFT's approach to the test at the referral stage; although this does not necessarily mean that a reference will inevitably lead to a negative finding by the Commission, as demonstrated below. In the

---

242 *Carlton Communications plc/Granada plc: A Report on the Proposed Merger*, Cm 5952, 2003.
243 On 7 October 2003 the Secretary of State decided to clear the proposed merger subject to appropriate undertakings being given by Carlton and Granada (DTI Press Release, P/2003/500). On 14 November 2003 the Secretary of State announced (DTI Press Release, P/2003/561) that she had accepted the following undertakings, from Carlton and Granada *inter alia*: to abide by a number of conditions to remedy the adverse finding regarding the operation of the ITV Network Centre and to offer other ITV licensees terms similar to those in effect on 1 November 2003 between the licensee and Carlton or Granada for the sale of commercial airtime and programme sponsorship.
244 See, for example, Case T-342/99 *Airtours v Commission* [2002] ECR II-2585; [2002] 5 CMLR 7; and Motta, M, 'EC merger policy and the *Airtours* case' [2000] ECLR 199.

Guidelines the Commission states that it 'will evaluate the competitive constraints on firms with the merger compared to the situation which would have been expected to prevail without the merger (sometimes referred to as the "counterfactual")'.[245] Clearly, the Commission's focus is on the effects on competition likely to be produced by the merger in question. The Commission's approach in applying the text involves two stages: identification of the relevant market, and assessment of whether the merger would increase the market power of firms in the market. The Commission will generally apply the hypothetical monopolist test to market definition. When assessing the competitive effects of a merger, the Commission will consider market shares and levels of market concentration in addition to looking at other structural factors, such as network effects. With particular reference to horizontal mergers, the Commission will concentrate on the likely impact of the merger on competitive rivalry. An example is the Commission's report in *Stena/P & O*,[246] which was its first report published under the 2002 Act provisions. The report blocked the transfer of the Liverpool–Dublin route to Stena as the transfer would lead to a substantial lessening of competition in the central Irish Sea corridor and give Stena the scope to increase prices. However, the Commission will also seek to ascertain if there are any efficiency gains resulting from a merger, although these gains will be required to: happen within a short period of time; be a direct consequence of the merger; and increase rivalry between the remaining firms. As with the OFT at the referral stage, the Commission will consider the likelihood of non-co-ordinated and co-ordinated effects of a merger, the latter being possible due to the greater interdependence between remaining competitors in an oligopolistic market. Finally, the Commission will consider a range of other potential competitive constraints, such as the possibility for entry and expansion on the market, or countervailing buyer/supplier power, which may offset the initial view that a merger will result in an SLC. In addition, the Commission may be required to examine a 'failing firm' justification for a merger, which would mean that the firm would be unable to meet its financial obligations in the near future and it would not be feasible for it to successfully restructure itself.

It is clear that not all CC inquiries lead to a finding that there is, or is likely to be a substantial lessening of competition.[247] For instance, in March 2006,

245 At para 1.22. At the time writing the OFT and CC are working on a joint review of their Guidelines.

246 *Stena AB and The Peninsular and Oriental Steam Navigation Company: A Report on the Proposed Acquisition of Certain Assets Relating to the Supply of Ferry Services on the Irish Sea between Liverpool–Dublin and Fleetwood–Larne*, 5 February 2004. See, also, the CC report on *FirstGroup plc and Scottish Rail Franchise*, 28 June 2004, which concluded that the merger might be expected to result in a SLC and adverse effects such as higher bus fares, poorer services and a loss of choice to passengers, mainly in the Glasgow and Edinburgh areas.

247 See PWC report for the OFT 'Ex Post Evaluation of Mergers' assessing ten merger clearance decisions by the CC, at www.competition-commission.org.uk/our_role/evaluation/ex_post_evaluation_of_mergers.pdf

the CC formally cleared the completed acquisition of HP Foods Group by Heinz, concluding that it was not expected to lead to a substantial lessening of competition within the markets for the supply of tomato ketchup, brown sauce, barbecue sauce, tinned baked beans, and tinned pasta products in the UK, despite the OFT's referral based on concerns about higher prices for consumers as a result of the combination of the two largest branded sauce suppliers in the UK.[248] In relation to the market for tomato ketchup, the Commission found that the Daddies brand, owned by HP, did not provide any competitive constraint on the leading Heinz brand prior to the merger, and accordingly the merger would not alter the competitive situation. Again, in March 2006, the acquisition of the Greater Western Rail franchise by FirstGroup was cleared by the Commission as there were only a few routes where buses and trains were in competition and therefore the profit incentive to shift passengers from bus to rail by raising fares or revising services was minimal.[249] In May 2006, the Commission cleared the Waterstones/Ottakars merger on the basis that it would not lead to a substantial lessening of competition in the sale of new books to consumers in any part of the UK. There had been a vociferous campaign in Scotland to protect the independence of Ottakars based on its role in supporting Scottish literature and culture, but these arguments were irrelevant in the context of the SLC test.

There have been a number of inquiries, in addition to Stena/P & O, under the Enterprise Act provisions, which have necessitated remedial action. In its September 2005 Report in relation to the acquisition by Somerfield of 115 stores from Morrison supermarkets, the fifth and fourth largest supermarkets, respectively in the UK at that time, the Commission considered that the acquisition would lead to a substantial lessening of competition in 12 local grocery markets in Great Britain, and ordered Somerfield to divest 12 of its stores to suitable retailers approved by the Commission.[250] The Commission's starting point was that Somerfield should divest itself of the disputed acquired stores or alternatives that were satisfactory to the Commission. This demonstrates that the Commission is often concerned with competitive effects in localised markets. Another example is the Commission's report in February 2006 into the acquisition of six multiplex cinemas in the UK by Vue Entertainment Holdings (Ltd) ('Vue'). The Commission concluded that Vue would be required to sell one of two cinemas in Basingstoke, one it already owned and one it had acquired, to avoid the higher prices and reduced choice for consumers in that area as a result of the merger.[251] In October 2006, the

---

248 See Competition Commission, Final Report, HJ Heinz and HP Foods, 24 March 2006.

249 See Competition Commission, Final Report, FirstGroup plc and the Greater Western Passenger Rail franchise, 8 March 2006.

250 Competition Commission, Acceptance of Final Undertakings, Somerfield plc/Wm Morrison, 9 March 2006.

251 Competition Commission, Final Report, Vue Entertainment Holdings (UK) Ltd and A3 Cinema Limited, 24 February 2006.

joint venture between Stagecoach, with its Megabus brand, and Scottish Citylink, was considered by the Commission as likely to lead to a substantial lessening of competition on the 'Saltire Cross' routes (Glasgow–Aberdeen and Edinburgh–Inverness routes, which cross at Perth). The removal of competition between Megabus and Scottish Citylink could have led to higher fares and reduced service levels, and the sale of certain services was required.[252] In April 2007, the Commission concluded that a merger between the largest two suppliers of shell eggs and processed eggs in the UK would reduce competition as it was likely that the merged company could raise prices.[253] It should be noted that the Commission is currently reviewing its merger Guidelines.

Remedial action

If the Commission decides that there is an anti-competitive outcome from a merger, the Commission has to decide what action should be taken. The Commission may exercise its order-making powers or accept undertakings from parties, under ss 82 and 84 of the 2002 Act, respectively. These possibilities are broadly similar to the twin remedies available under the 1973 Act although, clearly, the Commission's role is enhanced under the new set of provisions. Under the 1973 Act the Secretary of State had power to make a wide range of orders. The CC's role was limited to recommending a particular remedy or range of remedies to limit or prevent the adverse effects of a merger. Nonetheless, reflecting the pragmatic, political, and ultimately discretionary approach of the Fair Trading Act, the Secretary of State was not bound by the findings of a CC Report which the Secretary of State could, therefore, choose to ignore.[254] Under the 2002 Act the CC has assumed the primary role for taking remedial action following a market investigation. It has a duty, under s 41, to take such action as is reasonable and practicable under ss 82 and 84 to remedy, mitigate or prevent the substantial lessening of competition concerned and any adverse effects resulting therefrom.[255] In doing so, the Commission is required to 'have regard to the need to achieve as comprehensive a solution as is reasonable and practicable'.[256] Schedule 8 to

---

252 Competition Commission, Final Report, Stagecoach and Scottish Citylink, 23 October 2006.

253 Competition Commission, Final Report, Clifford Kent Holdings Limited and Deans Food Group Limited, 20 April 2007.

254 For instance, following the Commission's majority report on *Charter Consolidated/Anderson Strathclyde*, Cmnd 8711, 1982, the Secretary of State decided to allow the bid to go ahead. This refusal to accept the Commission's findings was challenged by judicial review. However, the challenge was rejected by the Court, which confirmed that the final decision in a merger case rested with the Minister: *R v Secretary of State for Trade and Industry ex p Anderson Strathclyde plc* [1983] 2 All ER 233, DC.

255 Section 41(2). At the time of writing the CC is consulting on new Merger Remedy Guidelines.

256 Section 41(4).

the 2002 Act specifies what may be included in an order, although there are no statutory limits on the Commission's power to obtain undertakings. The types of remedy which may generally be available include: divestiture of a business or assets; removal of entry barriers by requiring know-how licensing; either the discontinuance or the adoption of specific behaviour; or the imposition of a price cap, or monitoring of prices and profits. The Act allows the Commission to take into account, when deciding on appropriate remedial action, any customer benefits derived from the market feature, such as lower prices, higher quality or choice of goods and greater innovation.[257] All undertakings and orders under the Act will be published in the Public Register of Undertakings and Orders on the OFT website. Under the 1973 Act, the formal order-making powers were rarely resorted to and in most cases the Secretary of State requested the DGFT to consult the parties with a view to obtaining appropriate undertakings from the parties. In one case involving Stagecoach, the undertakings sought required Stagecoach to divest itself of its 20% shareholding and its seat on SB Holdings Ltd's board and to undertake not to reacquire any shares in SB Holdings Ltd. The required undertakings prevented the merger from proceeding and demonstrated that it was unnecessary for the Commission to resort to the Secretary of State's order-making powers.[258]

In the first two full inquiries under the Enterprise Act 2002 provisions, *Stena/P & O* and *FirstGroup/Scottish Rail Franchise*, the Commission exercised its new remedial powers by clearing the mergers, subject to undertakings being given to meet the competition concerns in each situation. The Commission publishes draft undertakings for consultation. Following the Vue cinema report, Vue gave undertakings to ensure the effective sale of one of the two Basingstoke cinemas it owned, including the appointment of a divestiture trustee to oversee the process. Similar undertakings were given following the Stagecoach/Scottish Citylink joint venture to divest either the 'Scottish Citylink' or 'Megabus' branded operations on the Saltire Cross route group. Like the OFT at the referral stage, the Commission is now less likely to accept behavioural remedies, particularly where they involve price controls, and the starting point in determining appropriate remedies is the status quo. A standardised divestiture process involving style undertakings from the parties to allow the merger to proceed where the Report outcome is negative has become the norm following the publication of divestiture guidelines by the CC in December 2004.

It should be noted that for any remedial action to follow, a decision that there is an anti-competitive outcome must be taken by at least two-thirds of the members of the CC inquiry group. This is the same requirement as under

257 Section 134(7)–(8).
258 DTI Press Release, 27 April 1995; [1995] 5 ECLR R-135.

the Fair Trading Act 1973.[259] The OFT is required to monitor undertakings and orders following a merger investigation report.

Review

Any decision by the OFT or CC under Pt 3 of the 2002 Act is subject to judicial review by the CAT and thereafter on appeal to the Court of Appeal in England and Wales and the Court of Session in Scotland. The possibility of review was demonstrated by the recent case of *IBA Health Ltd v OFT*,[260] outlined in the section above, on the duty of the OFT to refer. The next two challenges also involved mergers in the pharmaceutical industry. First, in *Unichem Ltd v OFT*, Unichem sought review of the OFT decision not to refer the proposed acquisition by Phoenix of East Anglian Pharmaceuticals Ltd ('EAP') to the Commission in relation to the supply of prescription-only medicines.[261] The OFT had earlier referred a proposed merger involving AAH and EAP, which led to its abandonment, and subsequently provided confidential guidance to Unichem to the effect that any acquisition by it of EAP would result in a reference. The CAT confirmed that the OFT had a margin of judgement or evaluation on the facts, but this did not imply that it had a policy discretion. Overall, the CAT could not be satisfied that all material considerations had been taken into account by the OFT and accordingly quashed the OFT decision and referred the issue back to the OFT for reconsideration.[262] In *Celesio v OFT*,[263] a third party sought review of the OFT's decision to negotiate undertakings with the parties in the proposed Boots/Unichem merger rather than make a reference to the Commission, where the OFT considered that there was a realistic prospect of a substantial lessening of competition. This application was unanimously rejected by the CAT, confirming the approach set out by the Court of Appeal in *IBA Health Ltd v OFT*. The first challenge to an OFT decision by a merging party was unsuccessful in *Co-operative Group (CWS) Limited v OFT*.[264] The OFT had earlier accepted an undertaking in lieu of reference, but refused purchaser approval on the basis that it would not satisfy the undertakings' requirement for a proposed purchaser to be independent and unconnected to the acquiring party. The CAT held that the OFT's decision was reasonable and supported

---

259 *Scottish Milk: A Report on the Supply of Fresh Processed Milk to Middle Ground Retailers in Scotland*, Cm 5002, 2000. DTI Press Release, P/2000/863, 22 December 2000.
260 [2003] CAT 27; on appeal *OFT v IBA Health Ltd* [2004] EWCA Civ 142, 19 February.
261 [2005] CAT 8.
262 The OFT reassessed the issue and subsequently decided again that the merger would not be expected to result in a SLC and that it would not be referred to the Commission; see OFT, Anticipated acquisition by Phoenix Healthcare Distribution Limited of East Anglian Pharmaceuticals Limited, 29 June 2005.
263 [2006] CAT 9.
264 [2007] CAT 24.

the OFT's approach that remedies should restore competition to the pre-merger levels. A more specific example in relation to the CC's procedures was the successful action for judicial review, albeit prior to the introduction of the 2002 Act, following the prohibition of the *Interbrew/Bass* merger. The judicial review was based on the fact that Interbrew was not given an adequate opportunity to comment on the remedies proposed.[265] The first challenge to a CC decision followed the September 2005 Report by the Commission in relation to the acquisition by Somerfield of 115 stores from Morrison supermarkets, which concluded that the acquisition would lead to a substantial lessening of competition in 12 local grocery markets in Great Britain. The Commission's starting point was that Somerfield should divest itself of the disputed acquired stores or alternatives that were satisfactory to the Commission. In *Somerfield plc v Competition Commission*,[266] the CAT considered this to be a reasonable approach and rejected the applicant's submission that they should be free to choose which stores to divest. In *Stericycle International LLC and others v Competition Commission*,[267] the applicants sought review of a Commission decision contained in an interim order. In this case, the Commission required the appointment of a hold separate manager ('HSM'), on the basis of concerns regarding the substantial integration of the two businesses and the strong incentives for management to operate the acquired business on behalf of the acquirer, and the potential ensuing difficulties if divestiture was to be required. The CAT dismissed the application as the Commission had taken its decision that an HSM was necessary in the public interest and within its margin of appreciation.

Further reading

General

Bankes, C, and Hadden, M, *UK Merger Law and Practice*, 2006, London: LexisNexis Butterworths.

Cook, J, and Kerse, C, *UK Merger Control*, 4th edn, 2005, London: Sweet & Maxwell.

Navarro, E, Font, A, Folguera, J, and Briones, J, *Merger Control in the EU: Law, Economics and Practice*, 2nd edn, 2005, Oxford: OUP.

Scott, A, Hviid, M, and Lyons, B, *Merger Control in the UK*, 2006 Oxford: OUP.

Merger regulation

Burnley, R, 'Who's afraid of Conglomerate Mergers? A Comparison of the US and EC approaches' (2005) 28(1) World Comp 43.

---

265 *Interbrew SA v Competition Commission* [2001] UKCLR 954.
266 [2006] CAT 4.
267 [2006] CAT 21.

Connolly, J, Rab, S, and McElwee, M, 'Pre-Notification Referral under the EC Merger Regulation: Simplifying the route to the one-stop shop' [2007] ECLR 167.

Fountoukakos, K, and Ryan, S, 'A New Substantive Test for EU Merger Control' [2005] ECLR 277.

Luescher, C, 'Efficiency considerations in European merger control – just another battle ground for the European Commission, economics and competition lawyers?' [2004] ECLR 72.

Maudhuit, S, and Soames, T, 'Changes in EU Merger Control' 3 parts: Part 1 [2005] ECLR 57; Part 2 [2005] ECLR 75; Part 3 [2005] ECLR 144.

Nikpay, A, and Houwen, F, 'Tour de force or a little local turbulence? A heretical view on the Airtours judgment' [2003] ECLR 193.

Schmidt, J, 'The New ECMR: "significant impediment" or "significant improvement"?' (2004) 41(6) CMLRev 1555.

UK merger control

Goodman, S, 'Steady as she goes: the Enterprise Act charts a familiar course for UK merger control' [2003] ECLR 331.

Rodger, BJ, 'UK merger control: politics, the public interest and reform' [2000] ECLR 24.

Went, D, 'Recent Developments in UK Merger Control – Establishment of Solid Foundations for the New Regime' [2007] ECLR 627.

Discussion

1   There are no grounds for interfering with the market for corporate control except where a serious risk to competition is likely to arise from any merger. Discuss.

2   How has the Merger Regulation proved to be a useful additional tool in the Commission's competition law armoury? Consider particularly the problems of joint ventures and oligopolistic markets.

3   Does the 'fine-tuning' of case allocation under Arts 4, 9 and 22 of the Merger Regulation fundamentally damage the 'one stop shop'?

4   The mantra 'removing politics from UK merger control' is unachievable. Discuss.

5   To what extent do you agree with Goodman's view that the 2002 Act 'charts a familiar course for UK merger control'?

Chapter 7

State aid and State regulation

Introduction to State aid

The rules on State aid form a crucial part of the relationship between State involvement in, or regulation of, national markets and Community competition law. The Treaty has specific provisions in Arts 87–89 regulating State aid which is granted by Member States. The basic rationale behind these rules is that the level competitive playing field for undertakings throughout the Community may be jeopardised by any grant of aid to undertakings by public authorities of Member States. The premise is that the competition rules would be futile if Member States could favour their own home-based companies by subsidising those companies' ability to compete or by using subsidies to attract investment. State aid can therefore be viewed as 'beggar my neighbour' subsidies which can distort competition and, in particular, harm the fabric of the Community by allowing richer Member States to use their economic well-being to give unfair support to national undertakings.

Although State aid is a potential danger for competition, the prohibition in the Treaty is neither absolute nor unconditional. State aid does have positive aspects in that it may be vital, and even necessary, to enable certain objectives of the Community to be attained. The general justification for State aid is that it may contribute to the correction of market failures or market imperfections. State aid often produces important externalities (for example, employment aid, environmental aid, aid for research and development, or regional aid) which may sufficiently compensate the distortion of competition. These potentially compensating factors will have to be considered in determining the compatibility of an aid with the common market. Accordingly, the control of State aid is a particularly political and sensitive issue, with great potential for conflict between the aims of the Community and the nationalistic concerns of Member States. It follows that supervision of the State aid rules is a task particularly suited to the Commission which should act in the general interests of the Community and without nationalistic prejudice. The State aid rules are particularly sensitive in the context of partially or fully State-owned industry that benefits from governmental financial assistance. The supervision of State aid is especially problematic in relation to States like France, in which there continues to be a high degree of public involvement in industry. In addition, the 10 accession States who joined the Community on 1 May 2004 were required to familiarise themselves with the application of the State aid rules.[1] Adherence to the State aid rules may be particularly problematic in some States where there is considerable reliance on the provision of services by the public sector. Historically, the Commission, principally through the Directorate General for Competition (DGComp), has been criticised for the lack of transparency in its decision-making in relation to State aid, partly due to the peculiar political sensitivities involved in its control. Accordingly, in recent years, it has attempted to provide greater transparency in the controversial area of State aid through the publication of numerous Guidelines, Notices and Regulations. Regulation 659/1999[2] details the procedural rules for the application of the State aid provisions.

All Member States give assistance to national industry to some extent and the Commission's workload in regulating this State aid has been increasing and will, no doubt, increase further following the Community's enlargement. Accordingly, there have been many moves to reform this area of law and the Commission is constantly seeking to review and update its State aid practices. First, it is necessary to look at the substantive content of the State aid rules and, thereafter, the procedures for enforcement will be discussed. In effect, State aid connotes selective support given to business which may confer a competitive advantage over other businesses. The detailed criteria for the assessment of what constitutes State aid that is incompatible with the Treaty and the possibility of gaining an exemption from the prohibition against State aid will be considered in the following section.[3] The general prohibition on State aid is in Art 87(1). The application of the prohibition was demonstrated in 2003 when the European Commission investigated the legality of the arrangements between the low-cost airline, Ryanair, and the publicly-owned Charleroi airport in Belgium. The Commission considered that the 'incentives' offered to induce Ryanair to use the airport, principally in the form of subsidised rates, were to be prohibited even though Ryanair argued that such a move could effectively destroy the low-cost airline industry.[4] The

---

1 See Hansen, M, Van Ysendyck, A and Zuhlke, S, 'The coming of age of EC state aid law: a review of the principal recent developments 2002 and 2003' [2003] ECLR 202, particularly at pp 225–29. See the Commission website generally in relation to the State aid rules at http://ec.europa.eu/comm/competition/state_aid/overview/index_en.cfm.

2 OJ 1999, L83/1.

3 See, generally, Biondi, A, Eckhout, P and Flynn, J (eds), *The Law of State Aid in the European Union*, 2004, Oxford: OUP; and Ross, M, 'State aids and national courts: definitions and other problems – a case of premature emancipation' (2000) 37 CML Rev 401.

4 See Commission Decision 2004/393/EC *Advantages granted by the Walloon Region and Brussels South Charleroi Airport to the Airline Ryanair in Connection with its Installation at Charleroi*, OJ 2004, L137/1; and Commission Press Release, IP/04/157.

Commission subsequently adopted Guidelines on Financing Airports and Start-up Aid to airlines departing from regional airports.[5] As discussed below, the State aid rules have been considered on numerous occasions in relation to rescue and restructuring aid provided by national governments to their flag-carrier airlines, such as Air France, but these guidelines were introduced to deal with the more recent phenomenon of regional airports attracting low-cost airlines to provide new air links to the region. It is interesting to note that in November 2007 the Commission opened an in-depth investigation into financial advantages to BT as a result of a UK Crown guarantee covering BT's pension liabilities, which has ensured that BT's pension fund is exempted from minimum funding requirements and the payment of a levy to the Pension Protection Fund, unlike other companies, including its competitors.[6] The application of the State aid rules in a UK context is also exemplified by the Commission's authorisation of a support package of temporary rescue measures provided to Northern Rock plc by the UK Government; a case that also illustrates the potential for exemption from the application of the State aid prohibition, in this instance to allow for rescue aid.[7] Mandatory exemptions are provided in Art 87(2) and there also exists the possibility of discretionary exemption under Art 87(3). The Commission has developed policies in relation to specific types of aid[8] and also certain industrial sectors.[9] The Commission website has a 'State aid scoreboard' which is a transparent source of information on State aid in the European Union and the Commission's current activities in State aid control. After the introduction of Regulation 659/1999 the Commission set up a State aid register. Part I of the register provides information on all cases which have been the subject of a Commission decision since 1 January 2000. Partly as a response to the challenges posed by the accession of the new Member States on 1 May 2004 for effective enforcement of the rules, the Commission undertook a review of State aid and published a State Aid Action Plan in 2005 with a view to further modernising and streamlining its processes. These recent developments will be discussed at the end of this section.

5 OJ 2005, C312/1.
6 See Commission press release IP/07/1802, 29 November 2007.
7 See Commission press release IP/07/1859, 5 December 2007.
8 For example, see Regulation 70/2001/EC on the application of Arts 87 and 88 of the EC Treaty to State aid to small- and medium-sized enterprises, OJ 2001, L10/33; Regulation 1998/2006/EC on the application of Arts 87 and 88 of the EC Treaty to *de minimis* aid, OJ 2006, L379/5; Regulation 68/2001/EC on the application of Arts 87 and 88 of the EC Treaty to training aid, OJ 2001, L10/20; and Regulation 2204/2002/EC on the application of Arts 87 and 88 of the EC Treaty to State aid for employment, OJ 2002, L337/3. These rules have been consolidated and extended by the adoption of a General Block Exemption Regulation ('GBER') [2008] OJ L214/3.
9 The Commission has also adopted specific substantive and formal rules into a range of other sectors such as the shipbuilding, synthetic fibres industry, and steel and coal industries.

Article 87(1): the Prohibition of State Aid

Article 87(1) states:

> Save as otherwise provided in this Treaty, any aid granted by a Member
> State or through State resources in any form whatsoever which distorts
> or threatens to distort competition by favouring certain undertakings or
> the production of certain goods shall, in so far as it affects trade between
> Member States, be incompatible with the common market.

In the past, State aid has been held to be constituted by assistance from State
subsidies and capital injections, exemptions from taxation, and loan guarantees by the State. Article 87(1) requires three criteria to be fulfilled in order for
the prohibition to apply.[10] The State assistance must:

a   constitute aid. In order to constitute aid, the assistance must:

   • confer an advantage;
   • be granted by a Member State or through state resources; and
   • favour certain undertakings or the production of certain goods
     ('selectivity');

b   affect trade between Member States; and
c   distort or threaten to distort competition.

What constitutes 'aid'?

An advantage

The text of Art 87(1) refers to aid granted in any form whatsoever, and aid
has been given a wider interpretation than was probably originally envisaged.
The Commission and Court have consistently held that a measure will be
regarded as State aid if it gives a firm an economic or financial advantage
which it would not otherwise have enjoyed.[11] State aid has been held to cover,
for example, loan guarantees, deferral of tax or social security payments,
differential rates of tax, debt write-offs to prepare a public company for privatisation and even free advertising on State-owned television. The concept
of aid is objective and is therefore defined by the effects of State intervention
irrespective of the aid's aims and objectives.[12] The Court has defined 'advantage' in terms of whether or not there has been a 'manifest' favouring of

---

10 See, for instance, Case C-5/01 *Belgium v Commission ('Cockerill Sambre')* [2002] ECR
   I-11991.
11 See Case 61/79 *Amministrazione delle Finanze dello Stato v Denkavit Italiana* [1980] ECR
   1205; [1981] 3 CMLR 694.
12 See Case C-241/94 *France v Commission (Kimberly-Clark)* [1996] ECR I-3203.

certain undertakings or goods, a test which is similar to the appreciability requirement under Art 81.[13] In *Altmark*,[14] discussed further below, it was held that no advantage was conferred where a state financial measure is regarded as compensation for services provided in order to discharge public service obligations, provided certain requirements are met.

State source of funding

The prohibition in Art 87(1) only applies where the aid has been granted by a Member State or through State resources.[15] The concept 'State resources' covers all levels of public authority, including local authorities. State resources have been interpreted widely, for instance, in *Italy v Commission*[16] where the assistance was derived from compulsory contributions imposed by State legislation. When a private body administers aid, some form of State control must be established before the aid falls within the prohibition.[17] According to earlier case law, funding by private bodies requiring public authority approval prior to allocation of the funding was considered to be covered by Art 87(1). In one case, the Commission challenged financial assistance granted to certain French farmers. The fund was financed by the operating surplus of Caisse Nationale de Credit Agricole, a private enterprise, but the decisions on the allocation of the fund required the approval of public authority members of the board of Caisse Nationale and therefore constituted State aid.[18] Other pronouncements by the Court have stressed the necessity for the measure to involve public funds or charges on the public account in order to constitute State aid.[19] In *Compagnie Nationale Air France*[20] the Court of First Instance (CFI) held that the financial assistance had come from the 'Caisse', a body

---

13 See Case C-256/97 *Déménagements-Manutention Transport SA (DMT)* [1999] ECR I-3913; [1999] All ER (EC) 601. See, also, Ross, fn 3.

14 Case C-280/00 *Altmark Trans GmbH v Nahverkehrsgesellschaft Altmark GmbH* [2003] ECR I-7747; [2003] 3 CMLR 12. See the discussion below under 'Services of General Economic Interest'.

15 In Case C-189/91 *Petra Kirsammer-Hack v Nurhan Sidal* [1993] ECR I-6185 and Cases C-72 and 73/91 *Sloman Neptun Schiffahrts AG v Seebetriebstrat Bodo Zeisemer der Sloman Neptun Schiffahrts AG* [1993] ECR I-887 the Court decided that no State resources were involved. See, also, Case C-83/98P *Ladbroke Racing Ltd v Commission* [2000] ECR I-3271.

16 Case 173/73 *Italy v Commission (Textiles)* [1974] ECR 709; [1974] 2 CMLR 593.

17 See *Regarding Aid No C39/93 by France to Air France*, OJ 1993, C334/7.

18 Case 290/83 *Commission v France* [1985] ECR 439; [1986] 2 CMLR 546.

19 See, for example, Cases C-72 and 73/91 *Sloman Neptun Schiffahrts AG* [1993] ECR I-887 and Case C-345/02 *Pearle BV and others v Hoofdbednifschap Ambachten* [2004] ECR I-7139. See, also, Slotboom, P, 'State aid in Community law: a broad or narrow definition?' [1998] ELR 289. This interpretation does not appear to fit easily with the applicability of the State aid rules to, for example, loan guarantees which would not necessarily involve a charge on the public account.

20 Case T-358/94 *Compagnie Nationale Air France v Commission (Air France)* [1996] ECR II-2112; [1997] 1 CMLR 492.

established under the supervision and guarantee of the legislature and governed by statutory and regulatory rules with its directors appointed by the State, and could, therefore, be characterised as belonging to the public sector. However, the Court, in *Viscido and Others v Ente Poste Italiane*,[21] confirmed that national labour law regimes are, in effect, excluded from the prohibition on the basis of the lack of any direct or indirect transfer of State resources.[22] Moreover, the general issue has been made more difficult by the Court judgment in *Stardust Marine*,[23] which required the Commission to establish positive State involvement in any decision, as opposed to simply relying on the fact that the undertaking is under State control.[24]

Selectivity

Aid measures which favour 'certain undertakings or the production of certain goods' are incompatible with the Common Market under Art 87(1). In order to satisfy the selectivity criteria one needs to distinguish between general economic policy measures and those economic policy measures which exclusively benefit, directly or indirectly, certain industries.[25] State aid would not normally extend to general measures of economic policy, such as taxation or other fiscal measures.[26] Tax exemptions have consistently been treated as State aid by the Commission[27] and reductions in the rates of taxation applicable to products defined by regional, sectoral or other criteria may constitute aid. The selectivity requirement will generally be satisfied where aid is provided for a particular economic activity, a particular sector, a branch of industrial activity, according to geographical area or to undertakings of a particular nature.[28] Case law indicates that it is becoming more difficult for a Member State to argue that a measure is general rather than selective. It has been held that measures that are universally applicable may constitute State aid where discretion exists in the means of their application.[29] The selectivity

---

21 Cases C-52–54/97 [1998] ECR I-2629.

22 See Rodger, BJ, 'State aid – a fully level playing field?' [1999] 5 ECLR 251.

23 Case C-482/99 *France v Commission ('Stardust Marine')* [2002] ECR I-4397; [2002] 2 CMLR 41. See, also, Case C-379/98 *Preussenelektra AG v Schleswag AG* [2001] 2 CMLR 36.

24 For a fuller discussion, see Lubbig, T and Von Merveldt, M, '*Stardust Marine*: introducing imputability into State aid rules – plain sailing into calm seas or rowing back into shallow waters' [2003] ECLR 629.

25 See Case C-241/94 *France v Commission (Kimberly-Clark)* [1996] ECR I-3203.

26 Ibid.

27 See Case 70/72 *Commission v Germany* [1973] ECR 813; [1973] CMLR 741.

28 See, for example, *XXVth Report on Competition Policy*, 1996, Points 167–70. For examples of measures which, although not applicable to all undertakings and thus not strictly general, have been considered to constitute 'general measures', see Case 173/73 *Italy v Commission* [1974] ECR 709; [1974] 2 CMLR 593; and *Maribel Quater*, OJ 1997, C201/6.

29 See Case C-295/97 *Industrie Aeronautiche e Meccaniche Rinaldo Piaggio v International Factors Italia SpA (IFITALIA)* [1999] ECR I-3735; [2000] 3 CMLR 825.

issue has become more problematic due to the increasing complexity of fiscal instruments introduced by Member States, in particular the controversy over whether a tax measure is justified by the nature or general scheme of the system, which was revisited by the Court in the *Adria-Wien* case.[30] The Court held that selectivity will exist and hence State aid will be constituted where similar undertakings in a comparable situation are disproportionately affected by the tax measure and there is no objective justification derived from the general tax scheme.[31] The Court has stressed that the logic of the tax scheme must be transparent, clear and coherent otherwise the scheme will fall foul of the selectivity principle; these requirements apply equally to any derogations from a general scheme.[32] Nonetheless, although the English Court of Appeal held in *Lunn Poly* that a differential level of taxation can constitute State aid,[33] the European Court made it clear in a subsequent English case, *GIL Insurance*, that the State aid rules do not preclude national tax or other legislation that seeks to promote a legitimate policy objective; where, for instance, the particular tax rate, or rebate, is justified by the general scheme of the national system of taxation.[34]

Effect on intra-Community trade

In most cases, the effect on intra-Community trade requirement poses little difficulty as any significant quantity of aid granted to particular undertakings or to the production of certain goods will strengthen the beneficiary's competitive position compared to its competitors throughout the Community and thereby the aid will have the potential to affect intra-Community trade. In the past the Commission has considered that where there is a problem of overcapacity even a small amount of State aid may be sufficient to produce harmful effects on competition within the Community and, hence, affect intra-Community trade. In *Italy v Commission*,[35] the Court held that trade was clearly affected where the lowering of social security charges reduced labour costs and strengthened the competitive position of the Italian undertakings;

---

30 Case C-143/99 *Adria-Wien Pipeline GmbH, Wietrsdorfer & Peggauer Zementwerke GmbH and Finanzlandesdirektion fur Karnten* [2002] ECR I-8365; [2002] 1 CMLR 38.

31 See, also, Commission Notice on the application of the State aid rules to measures relating to direct business taxation, OJ 1998, C/384/3.

32 See Golfinopoulos, C, 'Concept of selectivity criterion in state aid definition following the *Adria-Wien* judgment – measures justified by the "nature or general scheme of a system" ' [2003] ECLR 543.

33 See *R v Customs and Excise Commissioners ex p Lunn Poly Ltd and Another* [1999] EuLR 653. See Bacon, K, 'Differential taxes, state aids and the *Lunn Poly* case' [1999] 7 ECLR 384.

34 See Case C-308/01 *GIL Insurance v Customs & Excise* [2004] ECR I-4777, discussed in Robertson, A, 'State Aid and Reference Policy after *GIL Insurance*' [2004] ECLR 603. See also, Case T-210/02 *British Aggregates Association v Commission* [2006] ECR II-2789, on appeal Case C-487/06P, OJ 2007, C42/8.

35 Case 173/73 *Italy v Commission* [1974] ECR 709; [1974] 2 CMLR 593.

as shown by an increase in exports from Italy. For activities of a local nature, such as the provision of local services, there may be no effect on intra-Community trade. It should be stressed that measures which do not affect intra-Community trade do not constitute aid nor require notification.

Distortion or potential distortion of competition

When it has been shown that aid has been granted by a Member State or through State resources, the aid must also fulfil the third criterion – that it distorts or threatens to distort competition. The Commission adopted a specific *de minimis* policy in relation to State aid. The Commission's policy is based on the premise that limited aid does not affect trade between Member States nor distort competition in the Community and consequently parties should not be required to notify the aid under Art 88(3).[36] The *de minimis* policy has now been placed on a firmer legal footing. Article 2 of Regulation 944/98 empowered the Commission to set out in a Regulation a threshold under which aid measures are deemed not to constitute State aid under Art 87(1) that requires notification. The previous policy, set out in Regulation 68/2001, has been superseded by Regulation 1998/2006[37] and Art 2 provides that the conditions in Art 87(1) are not fulfilled in respect of aid of up to €200,000 to any one undertaking over a three-year period.

The distortion of competition criterion is easily satisfied once it has been demonstrated that aid has been granted. In *Phillip Morris*,[38] the Court considered that regardless of the degree of competition in the Community, State aids distorted competition. The test to establish a distortion focuses on the strengthened position of the assisted undertaking in relation to its competitors. For instance, in *Italy v Commission*[39] it was held that the aid had improved the competitive position of Italian textile producers within the Community by reducing the textile producers' production costs. The Commission is not required to quantify the actual economic advantage derived from the State aid.[40] The Court has drawn attention to the fact that the Commission has a wide discretion in monitoring State aid due to the necessity for both a complex economic assessment and a social assessment of the issues involved.[41] Further, even State aid which may be perceived as compensatory has been held by the Court to be prohibited as State aids do

---

36 See the original Commission Notice on the *de minimis* rules for State aid, OJ 1996, C68/06.
37 OJ 2006, L 379/5.
38 Case 730/79 *Phillip Morris Holland BV v Commission* [1980] ECR 2671; [1981] 2 CMLR 321.
39 Case 173/73 *Italy v Commission (Textiles)* [1974] ECR 709; [1974] 2 CMLR 593.
40 See Case T-358/94 *Air France v Commission* [1996] ECR II-2112; [1997] 1 CMLR 492, pp 165 and 166.
41 See Cases T-132/96 and T-143/96 *Freistaat Sachsen and Others v Commission* [1999] ECR II-3663.

not cancel each other out, but, instead, accumulate and cause further damage to the Community.[42]

The market economy investor principle

One of the difficulties with the identification of State aid concerns undertakings which are to any extent State owned or controlled. State ownership or control may involve a wide range of potential circumstances from completely nationalised industries to private companies with a minor State shareholding. This issue is particularly significant given the high degree of State shareholding, in a variety of forms, in private industries in the Community. Generally, therefore, where the 'State source of funding' criterion is satisfied,[43] the State aid rules must differentiate between assistance by the State acting in the same manner as a private person and State aid where the commercial sector would not intervene and invest.[44] Accordingly, a transaction involves State aid if it takes place in circumstances which would not be acceptable to a private investor operating under normal market conditions. Conversely, if under similar market conditions a private entrepreneur would also have made the same investment as the State, the assistance given by the State will not constitute State aid.[45] As a result, all equity injections have to be monitored, using the market economy investor principle (MEIP), to ensure that the State does not abuse its enormous financial power when it is involved in the ownership of undertakings.[46] Advocate General Slynn stated, in *Leeuwarder Papierwaren-fabriek v Commission*,[47] that the purpose behind State capital investments requires consideration in order to determine whether the capital investments constitute aid. If the motivation behind the investment is assessed to be the generation of income or capital, as with a private investor, it will not constitute aid. This does not require the most profitable investment to have been chosen, although it would generally have to be demonstrated that the benefit from the continued trading of the ailing firm would exceed the cost of investment and provide a sufficient return. The Commission cannot replace the judgment of the investor but it can assess whether the investment would have been acceptable to a long-term profit-oriented private investor.

---

42 See Case 78/86 *Steinike and Weinlig v Germany* [1977] ECR 595; [1977] 2 CMLR 688.

43 Note the restrictions following *Stardust Marine* outlined above.

44 See Abbamonte, G, 'Market economy investor principle: a legal analysis of an economic problem' [1996] 4 ECLR 258.

45 See Cases T-129/95, T-2/95 and T-97/96 *Neue Maxhutte Stahlwerke v Commission* [1999] ECR II-17; [1999] 3 CMLR 366, and Case T-296/97 *Alitalia v Commission* [2001] All ER (EC) 193.

46 For a discussion of this issue, see Hansen, M, Van Ysendyck, A and Zuhlke, S, 'The coming of age of EC State aid law: a review of the principal recent developments 2002 and 2003' [2003] ECLR 202, at pp 203–10.

47 Case 296/82 [1985] ECR 809; [1985] 3 CMLR 380.

Article 295 EC lays down the principle of neutrality regarding the system of property ownership in a Member State, and the principle of equality between public and private undertakings. However, the MEIP is utilised in order to balance the protection afforded to Member States in their systems of property ownership and the prohibition on State aid. The MEIP test ensures that any State investment that would not be acceptable to a private investor in a market economy will be held to constitute State aid. For instance, in one case it was considered that investment may constitute State aid if the amount in question could not have been obtained on the capital market.[48] Further, the MEIP test ascertains the amount of any State aid by providing a basis for calculating the different terms upon which the State has invested from those which would have been required by a private investor under similar circumstances.[49] A similar approach is involved where: the State defers debts owed to it by a company (known as the 'private creditor test');[50] the State is involved in public procurement (known as the 'private purchaser test'); the State is selling off State assets (known as the 'private vendor test'); and, where the State is operating in a commercial context in the market economy (known as the 'market economy operator test').[51] The following are examples of types of State aid and the way in which the MEIP test is utilised in relation to such aid.

Capital and equity injections

The MEIP will be satisfied where the structure and future prospects of the company are likely to yield a normal return within a reasonable period, when compared to a comparable private enterprise.[52] In order to calculate the expected rate of return the Commission will take into account the company's financial performance, its economic and technical efficiency and the general economic environment of the particular industry or sector. In particular, for loss-making industries the MEIP would require a viable restructuring plan, as would be required by a private investor in similar circumstances. Restructuring plans are likely to be viewed more favourably by the Commission when the plans are prepared by external, independent financial advisers. The Commission may instruct its own advisors to review the validity of any plan.[53]

---

48 Case 142/87 *Belgium v Commission* [1990] ECR I-959; [1991] 3 CMLR 213.
49 See above, Abbamonte, fn 44.
50 See Case T-36/99 *Lenzing AG v Commission* [2004] ECR II-3597, affirmed on appeal by the ECJ in Case C-525/04 P *Spain v Lenzing AG*, 22 November 2007.
51 See, for instance, Case T-158/99 *Thermenhotel Stoiser Franz Gesellschaft mbH & Co KG v Commission* [2004] ECR II-1.
52 For discussion, see Koenig, C, and Bartosch, A, 'EC State aid law reviewing equity capital injections and loan grants by the public sector: a comparative analysis' [2000] ECLR 377.
53 See discussion in Hansen, Van Ysendyck and Zuhlke, fn 46.

The issue of State aid has been particularly prevalent in the airline industry with Member States' governments providing financial assistance to 'flag-carrying' national airlines, whether State-owned or privatised. This has been a sensitive political area as Member States do not want their 'flag-carrier' to be forced out of business. Various cases have arisen which involve assessment of support, using the MEIP, given to national airlines. It should be noted at this stage that examples in relation to the air transport sector are intended merely to illuminate the various issues for the reader. The air transport sector represents a small proportion of all State aid cases and in relation to air transport there are often special rules, which differ from the general rules applied.

In the *Aer Lingus* case,[54] the Irish Government had proposed to inject IR£175m into its ailing national airline. The injection was to form part of Aer Lingus's final restructuring over a three-year period. Taking into account large losses over the previous three years and a long-term high debt/equity ratio, the Commission considered that, in the light of the particularly difficult position of Aer Lingus, it was unlikely that a market investor would have sought equity in the airline. In 1994 the Commission considered financial assistance to be given by one of Air France's shareholders, where the share-holder was deemed to be a public sector body. The Commission assessed Air France's financial position and, in particular, its massive debts, negative cash flows and continuous substantial losses, and concluded that the MEIP was not satisfied and, therefore, the measures proposed constituted State aid. The CFI subsequently confirmed that the Commission had discretion in applying what it termed 'the prudent private investor test', and that judicial review of the Commission's application was limited to the grounds of procedural irregularity, manifest error or misuse of powers.[55]

Loan guarantees

Guarantees, whether or not used to secure lending, potentially constitute State aid[56] as they extend a competitive advantage over other competitors. Again, the Commission will assess the borrower's financial situation in order to consider whether a private investor would grant a guarantee under similar conditions. If the State is deemed to be acting beyond the role of a private investor the aid element will be the difference between the rate which the borrower would pay on the free market without the State guarantee and the rate actually obtained with the benefit of the guarantee, net of any premium paid to the State for the guarantee. If the company's financial

54 Commission Decision 94/118/EC *Aer Lingus*, OJ 1994, L54/30.
55 Case T-358/94 *Air France v Commission* [1996] ECR II-2112; [1997] 1 CMLR 492, at para 72.
56 Guarantees on market conditions do not constitute State aid. They only constitute State aid if they are granted on preferential terms, according to the MEIP test.

position is so weak that a loan would not have been advanced by any financial institution without a guarantee, the amount of the aid will be the value of the loan advanced based on the guarantee. In 2000, the Commission issued a Notice which was designed to clarify the basis on which the Commission applies the rules to loan guarantees,[57] and in 2007 the Commission launched an in-depth investigation into an unlimited guarantee for the French Post Office, La Poste, which enables it to obtain finance on favourable terms.[58]

Loan financing

Loans provided by State-owned financial institutions will be considered as State aid where they are advanced at lower rates of interest than would otherwise be offered by a private financial institution under the same market conditions. However, even loans at commercial rates may still constitute State aid where the security terms upon which they are granted are less onerous than would be required by a private investor, or, indeed, where credit would not have been made available at all, taking into account the company's financial position. Quantification of the aid element will vary according to the type of situation involved. In the differential rate situation the aid element would be the difference between the applied rate and the market rate. Where a loan would not be available under market conditions the aid element will be the full loan. Finally, for inadequately or partially secured loans it has been suggested that the aid element should be the difference between the amount of the loan which would have been advanced upon the security offered and the amount actually advanced.[59]

Services of General Economic Interest

There has been considerable attention devoted recently to consideration of the ways, and extent to which, Member States may subsidise the provision of public services, for example, where a local authority compensates a private operator for running a bus route that would otherwise be unprofitable or for mail delivery to remote areas.[60] The State aid issue is part of a wider debate on State involvement in the provision of 'services of general economic

---

57 Commission Notice on the application of Arts 87 and 88 of the EC Treaty to State aids in the form of guarantees, OJ 2000, C71/7.
58 Commission press release IP/07/1572, 23 October 2007. In May 2008 the Commission adopted a Notice on the application of Articles 87 and 88 of the EC Treaty to State aid in the form of guarantees, OJ 2008, C155/10, to provide safe harbours and enhance transparency.
59 See Soames, T, and Ryan, A, 'State aid and air transport' [1995] ECLR 290, at p 297.
60 See Hansen, Van Ysendyck and Zuhlke, fn 46, particularly at pp 218–25.

interest', sometimes known as 'public service obligations'.[61] This includes, for instance, State funding of public service broadcasting in relation to which the Commission launched a public consultation on its future framework early in 2008.[62] SGEI are economic activities that are of particular importance to citizens which would not be supplied if there were no public intervention. In the *Altmark* case[63] the Court considered the complex application of State aid rules in the context of public service obligations and held that there is no advantage, and hence no State aid, where the financial measure by the State is regarded as compensation for the services provided by the business receiving the compensation in their discharge of their public service obligations. However, this relatively lenient treatment of subsidies to providers of services in the general economic interest applies only if four conditions are met:

a   the recipient must have clearly defined public service obligations to discharge;
b   the compensation payable must be calculated in advance in an objective and transparent manner;
c   the compensation must not exceed the costs necessary to discharge those special public service obligations, allowing for a reasonable profit margin; and
d   the compensation, unless in public procurement, must be determined by a comparison of the costs a typical profit-making company in that sector would incur.

This case clarified the position but it is fairly restrictive and there will be difficulties in applying the judgment and satisfying the four cumulative conditions in other cases. The Court implicitly indicated its preference for public procurement procedures for awarding contracts. It also preferred determining the level of aid with reference to an efficient 'typical undertaking' which is 'well run and adequately provided'. The hurdle imposed by the *Altmark* criteria has been subsequently demonstrated, for example, where the Court considered that the calculation of charges for loading and unloading of goods in Italian harbours had not been undertaken in an objective and transparent manner.[64] In light of the Court's judgments, notably *Altmark*, the Commission

---

61   See Commission Communication on services of general interest, OJ 2001, C17/4, and Communication from the Commission on Services of general interest, including social services of general interest: a new European Commitment, COM(2007) 725 final.
62   Commission press release IP/08/24, 10 January 2008. See the Communication from the Commission on the application of the State aid rules to public service broadcasting, OJ 2001, C320/5.
63   Case C-280/00 *Altmark Trans GmbH v Nahverkehrsgesellschaft Altmark GmbH* [2003] ECR I-7747; [2003] 3 CMLR 12.
64   Cases C-34–38/01 *Enirisorse SpA v Ministero delle Finanze* [2004] 1 CMLR 10.

has published a Framework and Decision on this issue.[65] The Decision specifies that compensation for the provision of SGEI is compatible with State aid rules and does not require to be notified where there is: a clearly defined public service mandate, no overcompensation, compensation of less than €30m per year per undertaking; and annual turnover of less than €100m per undertaking. There is no limit on the amount of compensation in some cases, including hospitals and social housing. The Framework deals with cases not covered by the Decision, and is designed to ensure there is no overcompensation or cross-subsidisation. In this context, it is crucial that transparency in accounting systems is maintained; a Directive has been introduced to ensure that separate accounts are kept by companies in respect of their public service and other market operations in order for any elements of overcompensation to be identifiable.[66]

Exemptions

Article 87(1) lays down the prohibition on State aid which is applicable when the criteria noted above are satisfied. However, it is possible for the grant of State aid to be exempted under Arts 87(2) and 87(3) of the Treaty which provide, respectively, for mandatory and discretionary exemptions from the operation of the prohibition.

Article 87(2): mandatory exemptions

Article 87(2) lays down the mandatory exemptions by stating that three specific forms of aid 'shall be compatible with the common market'. It is uncertain whether these types of aid are free from the duty of notification. The three forms of aid are:

a   aid of a social character,[67] granted to individual consumers and without discrimination as to the origin of the products;

---

65 Commission framework for state aid in the form of public service compensation, OJ 2005, C 297/4; Commission Decision of 13 July 2005 on the application of article 86(2) of the Treaty to State aid in the form of public service compensation granted to certain undertakings entrusted with the operation of services of general economic interest, OJ 2005, L312/67. See also Communication from the Commission on Services of general interest, including social services of general interest: a new European Commitment, COM(2007) 725 final.

66 Commission Directive 2006/111/EC on transparency of financial relations between Member States and public undertakings, as well as on financial transparency within certain undertakings, OJ 2006 L318/17. In November 2007, the Commission launched infringement proceedings against seven Member States, including the UK, for failure to implement this Financial Transparency Directive, per Commission press release IP/07/1667, 9 November 2007.

67 Article 87(2)(a) EC. See Case 52/76 *Benedeti v Munari* [1977] ECR 163.

b   aid to make good the damage caused by natural disasters or exceptional occurrences;[68] and

c   aid granted to certain areas of the Federal Republic of Germany in order to compensate for the economic disadvantages caused by the division of Germany.[69]

Article 87(3): discretionary exemptions

The Commission is required to interpret narrowly the discretionary exemptions under Art 87(3), which constitute derogations from the general rule, and exercise its discretion in such a manner as to ensure that any exemptions granted contribute to the achievement of the Community objectives identified in Art 87. Accordingly, the aid must be analysed from a Community, and not a national, perspective.

Article 87(3)(a)

The Commission has discretion under this provision to declare as compatible 'aid to promote the economic development of areas where the standard of living is abnormally low or where there is serious underemployment'. The regions that could potentially benefit from this exemption are those facing abnormally low living standards or serious underemployment and those where the Gross Domestic Product does not exceed 75% of the Community average.[70]

Article 87(3)(b)

Under this provision the Commission may consider for exemption, 'aid to promote the execution of an important project of common European interest or to remedy a serious disturbance in the economy of a Member State'. The former type of aid has included schemes for energy saving or diversifying energy resources.[71] Aid to remedy serious disturbances in the economy of a Member State was invoked successfully by Greece in relation to the privatisation of 208 undertakings in 1991 as there was economic evidence of serious disturbance within the Greek economy.

---

68 Article 87(2)(b) EC.
69 Article 87(2)(c) EC.
70 As set out originally in the Commission Communication on the method for the application of Art 92(3)(a) and (c) to regional aid, OJ 1988, C212/02. Now covered by the Commission General Block Exemption, Commission Press Release IP/08/1110, 7 July 2008.
71 See *XXIst Report on Competition Policy* (1991), Point 258.

Article 87(3)(c)

Exemption may be provided in respect of 'aid to facilitate the development of certain economic activities or of certain economic areas, where such aid does not adversely affect trading conditions to an extent contrary to the common interest'. Two categories of aid that are often exempted are regional aid and sectoral aid.

Article 87(3)(d)

This provision is in respect of aid to promote culture and heritage conservation where such aid does not affect trading conditions and competition in the Community to an extent that is contrary to the common interest.

Article 87(3)(e)

This provides a catch-all provision in that the Commission may consider for exemption 'such categories of aid as may be specified by decision of Council acting by a qualified majority on a proposal from the Commission'. This provision may allow for a variety of potential aid schemes by Member States but requires secondary Community legislation to be passed.

Frameworks and guidelines

For transparency reasons, the Commission has gradually developed a variety of frameworks and guidelines clarifying how the Commission will assess certain types of aid, and laying down the criteria for the approval of aid. Guidelines exist for what is termed 'horizontal aid' (aid to small- and medium-sized enterprises (SMEs), employment aid, environmental aid, aid for rescue and restructuring of enterprises in difficulties, regional aid, etc), as well as for particular industries (for example, motor vehicle, shipbuilding, transport, steel, etc). Indeed, the Commission has adopted a considerable number of measures in these areas in recent years and greater detail on the range of Commission State aid policies can be found on the Commission website.[72] For example, in 2006, the Commission adopted a new Framework for Research, Development and Innovation, setting out a series of guidelines for specific State aid measures within these broad categories to extend its scope to innovation projects and clarify how States can give such aid without infringing the State aid rules.[73] The following is a brief discussion of the Commission's approach to two types of horizontal aid: regional aid, and rescue and restructuring aid.

---

72 http://ec.europa.eu/comm/competition/state_aid/overview/index_en.cfm
73 OJ 2006, C323/1. This is based on the State Aid Action Plan, COM(2005) 107 final – SEC (2005) 795 and the Communication on State Aid for Innovation, COM(2005) 436 final.

Regional aid

On a practical basis, maps of regions eligible for national aid are developed by the Commission, which is constantly seeking to reduce the geographic extent of such areas. Member States draw up the maps according to economic ceilings defined by the Commission and the maps need the approval of the Commission. The Commission has ascertained appropriate aid ceilings for different regions according to the relative weaknesses of their economies. The Commission reviewed its regional aid Guidelines and the Regional Aid Maps in 2006 for the period 2007–2013.[74] The geographical specificity distinguishes regional aid from other forms of horizontal aid, such as for R&D. The Guidelines provide detailed advice on the criteria to be applied in identifying the object, form and level of any aid to be granted. The Greek Government sought to use the regional aid exemption, within the air transport sector framework, in relation to loan guarantees to ease the burden of its national airline, Olympic Airways. Greece claimed that it was the poorest country in the European Union and that Olympic Airways' air transport services were crucial to the Greek economy. However, these arguments were rejected. Although Greece was a region qualifying for regional aid, the aid at issue was not regional aid as it did not relate to all airlines and routes operating in Greece but was intended merely to keep Olympic Airways afloat.[75]

Rescue and restructuring aid

The Commission has developed a number of sectoral policies in its application of the State aid rules, with certain industries, such as shipbuilding, steel, coal, motor vehicle, synthetic fibres and transport, being subject to specific rules. There is considerable potential for conflict between Member States and the Commission in relation to rescue and restructuring aid and the Commission introduced general Guidelines on State aid for rescuing and restructuring firms; those Guidelines were revised in 1999 and again in October 2004.[76] Rescue aid must: consist of financial assistance at normal commercial interest rates; be restricted to the amount necessary to keep a firm in business and to the time in which a feasible recovery plan can be devised; be justified on the grounds of serious social difficulties; have no undue adverse effects on the same industrial sector in other Member States; be accompanied by an undertaking by the Member State to communicate a restructuring or liquidation plan or proof that loans have been reimbursed etc. within 6 months; and, should be granted on a one-off basis – the 'one time, last time' principle.

74 Guidelines on National Regional Aid 2007–2013, OJ 2006 C54/13.
75 Commission Decision 94/696/EC *Olympic Airways*, OJ 1994, L273/22.
76 Community Guidelines on State aid for rescuing and restructuring firms in difficulty, OJ 2004, C244/02.

In the context of restructuring aid a restructuring plan is required and that plan must satisfy the following conditions:

a   it must plan the restoration of the long-term viability of the firm which must occur within a reasonable timescale;
b   it must only be granted once – the 'one time, last time' principle;
c   it must avoid undue distortions of competition;
d   it must limit the level of aid to the strict minimum to enable restructuring to take place; and
e   it must be fully implemented.

The implementation progress of the plan is monitored by the submission of detailed annual reports.

The air transport industry is an interesting example of the application of the general State aid rules to a particular sector. As noted above, the air transport industry has been one of the most contentious areas of State aid practice due to the politically sensitive attitude of Member States towards their traditional flag-carrying airlines. Indeed, over the last 15 years the Commission has been extremely active in assessing State aid in the airline industry. The application of the provision of State aid to the aviation sector is laid down in Guidelines issued in 1994 and these Guidelines cover the issue of rescue and restructuring in that sector, as applied by the DG for Energy and Transport.[77] The Guidelines provide that State aid may be allowed in exceptional cases, where accompanied by a restructuring plan, although Commission approval is likely to be subject to a number of conditions. First, the aid provided must be of limited duration and be combined with a valid restructuring plan to restore the airline's financial health and enable it to operate viably within a reasonable period of time.[78] Further, the aid should be sufficient to achieve the objectives of the restructuring plan in that the airline will return to viability and no future aid will be required. Assurances that no future aid will be granted are generally required from Member States. The limitation on any future aid is known as the 'one time, last time' principle, although it has not always been strictly adhered to in the past. For example, Air France has been granted aid, approved by the Commission, on more than one occasion. Further tranches of aid were approved by the Commission, subject to a restructuring plan intended to return the failing airline to viability. Often the restructuring plan will necessitate a reduction in capacity to enable the troubled firm to return to long-term financial well-being. In particular, the Commission will take a more lenient attitude to non-expansionary restructuring plans as otherwise the difficulties may simply be transferred to the ailing

77 Commission Guidelines, Application of Arts 92 and 93 of the EC Treaty and Art 61 of the EEA agreement to State aids in the aviation sector, OJ 1994, C350/7.
78 Commission Decision 91/555/EC *SABENA*, OJ 1991, L300/48.

airline's competitors.[79] A further requirement is that the government concerned should not interfere in the airline's management which should be
run according to commercial principles. The need for the submission to the
Commission of a credible restructuring plan, particularly regarding the long-
term profitability of the aid recipient, was recently emphasised by the Court
in *France v Commission*.[80]

The Air France case in the mid-1990s is a particularly interesting example
of the application of these restructuring aid requirements to the proposed
grant of State aid in the airline industry. The French Government proposed
to inject capital in the sum of FF20bn into its ailing national carrier,
Air France. The French Government included a comprehensive restructuring
plan in its representations to the Commission. The restructuring plan was
designed to transform Air France's fortunes and turn Air France into a viable
company over three years from the start of 1994, with an anticipated 30%
increase in productivity. The plan detailed investment reduction, lower
operating costs, staff cuts, increased flexibility of services, new products and
a change in the company structure involving commercial investment techniques. The Commission ultimately approved the State aid as the restructuring programme was sufficient and necessary to return Air France to
long-term viability without further State assistance.[81] The CFI annulled the
Commission Decision of the approval of aid to Air France.[82] The CFI held
that the Commission had failed to provide adequate legal reasoning for
approving Air France's purchase of 17 new aircraft worth £1.1bn.[83] In
addition, in relation to criteria in Art 87(3)(c) that the aid should not
adversely affect trading conditions to an extent contrary to the common
interest, the Commission had failed to analyse the competitive effect that the
subsidy would have on the airline's business on routes outside the European
Economic Area.[84] The Commission's application of the rules has been
challenged, most notably by Air France and British Airways.[85] Air France
unsuccessfully challenged the State aid categorisation of certain financial
assistance given to Air France. In the context of that challenge it is interesting
to note that the Commission refuted the existence of a 'one time, last time'

---

79 For example, regarding the notified capital increase of Air France, Commission Decision
   94/653/EC, OJ 1994, L254/73, the Commission imposed a number of conditions such that
   Air France could not increase capacity or reduce tariffs in certain routes.
80 Case C-17/99 [2001] ECR I-2481.
81 Ibid.
82 Joined Cases T-371/94 and T-394/94 *British Airways and Others v Commission* [1998] ECR
   II-2405; [1998] 3 CMLR 429.
83 Ibid, paras 84–120.
84 Ibid, paras 238–80.
85 Case T-358/94 *Air France v Commission* [1996] II-ECR 2112; [1997] 1 CMLR 492; and Cases
   T-371/94 and T-394/94 *British Airways and British Midland Airways v Commission* [1998]
   ECR II-2405.

policy. Although the Commission will generally require adequate evidence of a suitable restructuring plan, decisions involving Air France indicate that approval is possible for a State aid scheme where other State aid has already been approved.

More generally, under the 1999 Guidelines, the Commission sought to restrict the amount of State aid classed as restructuring aid, and the following aspects of the 1999 Guidelines were particularly notable:

a   the 'one time, last time' rule prevents follow-up restructuring aid for 10 years after the end of the first restructuring process;
b   the rules on eligibility as 'firms in difficulty' were tightened to, for example, exclude new firms; and
c   the possibility for Member States to provide other types of aid, such as regional aid, to firms already receiving restructuring aid, was curtailed.

As part of the modernisation review the Commission revisited its general approach to rescue and restructuring aid and issued revised Guidelines in July 2004.[86] These generally demonstrated the Commission's intention to scrutinise restructuring aid more closely due to the Commission's avowed focus on facilitating State aid that enhances horizontal objectives of common interest in the Union. The exit of inefficient firms should be the norm, not that they should be rescued, and hence derogation from the application of the prohibition will be more limited in these areas. The Guidelines avoid a strict distinction between rescue aid and restructuring aid and, importantly, stress that where large undertakings, which are active throughout the Community, receive subsidies, they are to make a significant contribution to their own restructuring, using funds obtained by selling assets, although the policy is less strict on SMEs. These guidelines are, at the time of writing, being reviewed.

Procedure and remedies

In the late 1990s the Commission realised that the system of enforcement of the State aid rules required modification. The number of complaints and notified aids had increased, partly due to greater awareness of the rules and because of continuing resort to State aid measures by Member States. Enlargement of the Community would necessarily exacerbate these difficulties and lead to a greater workload for the Commission. A partial solution would lie in the greater involvement of national courts in the system of State aid enforcement and this is an issue which will be discussed in brief below. The key Commission proposal was to use the provisions of Art 89 to ease its workload problems by simplifying and enhancing the efficiency of the system.

---

86 OJ 2005 C244/2. See Commission Press Release, IP/04/856, 'New guidelines set forth Commission approach to saving companies in difficulty', 7 July 2004.

Article 89 empowers the Commission to adopt appropriate Regulations for the application of Art 87. The principal motivation for resorting to Art 89, in addition to the efficiency argument, was to increase transparency and legal certainty in the application of the State aid provisions. The first tranche of the Commission's modernisation programme was to introduce an enabling regulation, Regulation 994/98,[87] to enable the Commission to introduce exemption regulations for categories of horizontal aid and, also, to provide a legal basis for the *de minimis* rule. The Commission also proposed the introduction of a clear system of procedural rules, in the form of a Regulation, for the enforcement of the substantive State aid rules. This proposal was subsequently adopted in Regulation 659/99, which codified existing practice in relation to notification of new State aid.[88] The Regulation's objective was to consolidate the procedural rules and provide an integrated and binding set of legal provisions. The Regulation makes provision for notified aid, unlawful aid, misuse of aid and existing aid schemes, and sets out the appropriate procedures and rules for each area of aid. The Regulation will not be dealt with in any depth in this chapter but, where appropriate, reference will be made to appropriate aspects of it.[89] The main procedure concerns the requirement to notify new aid, although the Regulation merely refers to the criteria in Art 87(1) for the identification of State aid. The Regulation also gives the Commission requisite powers to monitor and supervise the rules, by requiring annual reports from all Member States on aid schemes, and, importantly, the Regulation provides, in Art 22, a new power for the Commission to undertake inspections in relation to its State aid functions.

Notification

Paragraph 3 of Art 88 is referred to as the 'standstill' clause and provides that any aid must be notified prior to being paid. Furthermore, the aid may not be implemented before a Commission decision under Art 88(2) is made as to the compatibility of the aid. Accordingly, any aid must be notified and not put into effect before the Commission has approved it. Article 2(1) of Regulation

---

87 Regulation 994/98/EC on the application of Arts 92 and 93 of the EC Treaty establishing the European Community to certain categories of State aid, OJ 1998, L142/1.

88 Regulation 659/99/EC laying down detailed rules for the application of Art 93 of the EC Treaty, OJ 1999, L83/1. See, also, Regulation 794/2004/EC implementing Council Regulation (EC) No 659/99/EC laying down detailed rules for the application of Art 93 of the EC Treaty, OJ 2004, L 140/1, which sets out detailed provisions concerning the form and content of notifications. Regulation 794/2004 has been amended by Regulation 271/2008/EC amending Regulation (EC) No 794/2004 implementing Council Regulation (EC) No 659/1999 laying down detailed rules for the application of Article 93 of the EC Treaty, OJ 2008, L82/1, which requires the compulsory use of an electronic notification system and a secured email system by 1 July 2008.

89 For a comprehensive review of the Regulation, see Sinnaeve, A, and Slot, PJ, 'The new regulation on State aid procedures' (1999) 36 CML Rev 1153.

659/99 codifies the requirement to notify new aid to the Commission, otherwise any aid granted will constitute illegal aid. In the UK the task of notification is carried out by the State Aid Branch of the Department of Business, Enterprise and Regulatory Reform (BERR). One of the difficulties for Member States is that it may not always be certain, due to the detailed criteria involved, notably the MEIP, which types of assistance constitute State aid under Art 87. This has been referred to as the 'existential uncertainty' faced by Member States as to whether their measures actually constitute State aid.[90] In this regard, the Regulation provides little assistance and merely refers back to Art 87 and the principles developed in the existing body of case law. Accordingly, it is safer for any measures to be notified and approved by the Commission as not constituting State aid or, alternatively, approved under the mandatory or discretionary exemptions. Aid does not require to be notified in two instances:

a   where it constitutes *de minimis* aid under Regulation 1998/2006;[91] or
b   where it is existing aid already authorised and the level authorised will not be exceeded by 20%.

Upon notification the Commission will undertake a preliminary investigation of the proposed aid. If the Commission has no doubts about the compatibility of that aid with the common market, the aid will be approved. Otherwise, the Commission will initiate the contentious procedure in Art 88(2) culminating in a final decision. In *Lorenz*,[92] the Court decided that the preliminary examination should not take more than two months. The Regulation codifies existing practice in that during the preliminary examination phase the Commission has to decide within two months of 'complete notification':

a   that a measure does not constitute aid;
b   not to raise objections to the notified aid; or
c   to initiate the formal investigation procedure according to Art 88(2).

The detailed rules for the formal investigation procedure are set out in Art 6. Three options are open to the Commission upon culmination of the procedure:

a   a decision that the measure does not constitute aid;
b   a positive decision of compatibility; or
c   a negative decision of incompatibility.

90 Ibid.
91 Regulation 1998/2006/EC on the application of Arts 87 and 88 of the EC Treaty to *de minimis* aid, OJ 2006, L379/5.
92 Case 120/73 *Gebr Lorenz GmbH v Germany* [1973] ECR 1471.

Article 7(6) provides a time limit of 18 months from the opening of the procedure for the Commission to make a decision.

If State aid, whether notified or not, is implemented prior to approval by the Commission the State aid is illegal, sometimes referred to as unlawful. It is important to outline the appropriate procedures in respect of illegal aid. In *Boussac*[93] the Court considered how the Commission should proceed in cases of illegal aid. The Court made it clear that the Commission is still required, despite the procedural irregularity, to examine the compatibility of the aid with the Common Market. If the aid is compatible the Commission will approve it. Only if the Commission takes a negative final decision will it require the Member State to recover the aid with interest from the beneficiary. In relation to unlawful aid the Regulation codifies existing powers available to the Commission to require information, under Art 10(3), order suspension of unlawful aid, under Art 11(1), and to issue a provisional recovery injunction, under Art 11(2). Article 14 is crucial and reinforces the Commission's power to order recovery of aid, subject to two exceptions: where recovery is contrary to a general principle of Community law, or a 10-year limitation period has expired. In 2007, the Commission adopted a Notice on the implementation of decisions ordering Member States to recover illegal and incompatible State aid due to concerns regarding the excessive duration of recovery proceedings in Member States, emphasising the shared responsibility for the enforcement of the rules between the Commission and the Member States.[94]

The competence of the Commission with regard to illegal aid is different from the competence of the courts in Member States.[95] The notification obligation and the standstill clause of Art 88(3) have direct effect. Therefore, if a Member State has not respected the State aid rules, a national court, where an action has been raised before it, will take all necessary measures in respect of the illegally granted aid, such as ordering suspension and recovery. For instance, in an English case involving Lunn Poly, an application for judicial review of a Finance Act, which imposed differential taxes, as being contrary to Community law and therefore illegal was successful at the Court of Appeal.[96] The national court does not have to wait until the Commission has taken a decision on the compatibility of the aid. If the national court faces difficulties in this process, for example, in establishing the aid character of the measure, it can seek assistance from the Court under the Art 234 EC

---

93 Case C-301/87 *France v Commission* [1990] ECR I-307.
94 Commission Notice, Towards an effective implementation of Commission decisions ordering Member States to recover unlawful and incompatible State aid, OJ 2007, C272/05; see Commission press release, IP/07/1609, 26 October 2007.
95 See Case C-354/90 *FNCE v France (Salmon)* [1991] ECR I-5505 and Case C-39/94 *Syndicat Francais de l'Express International v La Poste (La Poste)* [1996] ECR I-3547; [1996] 3 CMLR 369.
96 *R v Customs & Excise Commissioners ex p Lunn Poly* [1998] 2 CMLR 560, DC; [1999] EuLR 653, CA.

procedure. As noted above, the difficulties facing a national court in identifying State aid are manifold and the new Regulation simply refers back to the Treaty provision.

Arguments invoked by Member States before the Court in respect of their failure to ensure recovery, pursuant to a Commission decision in respect of illegally granted State aid, are rarely successful. In practice, only absolute impossibility is likely to preclude repayment or recovery. In *Belgium v Commission*,[97] it was held that the requirement to repay was absolute even if the company had gone into liquidation. The State, therefore, had to compete in the process of the division of assets with trade creditors. The Court confirmed that the only limitations on recovery are where it is absolutely impossible[98] or where repayment would contravene the beneficiary's legitimate expectations, a defence available only in exceptional circumstances.[99] The beneficiary is unlikely to be successful in invoking the legitimate expectations argument if the beneficiary has not checked whether the aid was notified and approved. According to the Court, enterprises should normally be able to verify this information.[100] The only situation in which this defence is likely to be successful is where the Commission itself was responsible for the legitimate expectations of the beneficiary. In the context of national court actions the Court has adopted a similarly restrictive approach in respect of the possibilities for beneficiaries to rely on the legitimate expectations defence.[101] If the State aid is not approved by the Commission, an appeal to the CFI is available and, thereafter, to the Court of Justice. In numerous cases the Court has confirmed that the beneficiary of State aid, which is subject to a Commission decision, is directly and individually concerned by the decision and has standing to bring an action under Art 230(2).[102]

Competitors' remedies

In addition to the possibility of judicial review of a Commission State aid decision by a recipient of the aid, competitors of a State aid recipient may also become involved in the process. However, one of the main problems, initially, for complaining competitors was the absence of a Regulation containing the procedural rules for enforcement of the State aid rules. The ability

---

97 Case 142/87 [1990] ECR I-959; [1991] 3 CMLR 213.
98 Confirmed in Case C-261/99 *France v Commission* [2001] ECR I-2537.
99 See Case 5/89 *Commission v Germany* [1990] ECR I-3437; [1992] 1 CMLR 117.
100 Ibid.
101 See Case C-24/95 *Land Rheinland Pfalz v Alcan Deutschland* [1997] ECR I-1591; [1997] 2 CMLR 103.
102 Case 332/82 *Intermills v Commission* [1984] ECR 3809; [1986] 1 CMLR 614; and Case 62/87 *Executif Regional Wallon v Commission* [1988] ECR 1573; [1989] 2 CMLR 771. For a general discussion on *locus standi*, see Soltesz, U and Bielesz, H, 'Judicial review of State aid decisions – recent developments' [2004] ECLR 133.

of competitors to lodge complaints with the Commission had become established practice and the CFI also provided for complainants to be heard during the preliminary investigation of the issues.[103] Regulation 659/99 deals with the rights of interested third parties but does not radically alter the position or give interested third parties a status similar to that of competitors in Art 81 or 82 cases. Interested third parties can submit comments, per Art 20(1), and thereafter be sent a copy of the decision concluding the formal procedure. They also have the right to complain to the Commission under Art 20(2). Competitors can also use the provisions of Arts 230 and 232 EC to take proceedings before the Court. Article 230 allows for actions against the Commission by Member States or other third parties who are directly and individually concerned by any Commission decision to approve State aid.[104] As a result of recent Court case law, in most cases it should be relatively straightforward for a competitor or potential competitor of the undertaking receiving aid to satisfy the requirements under Art 230.[105] The CFI, in *British Airways and Others v Commission*,[106] confirmed that those whose interests might be affected by the granting of aid, in particular, competing undertakings, would qualify. The Court confirmed that the applicants satisfied the Art 230 requirements given that their market position was significantly affected by the measure.[107] The same general limitations and difficulties are likely to exist in proceedings by a complainant competitor under Art 232 for failure to act in a State aid case, as exists under Arts 81 and 82, although perhaps the judgment in *Guerin*[108] provides some assistance. More directly, in relation to State aid, in *Gestevision*,[109] the CFI confirmed that an action under Art 232 is not limited to persons to whom a Commission act could potentially be addressed. Accordingly, satisfaction of the direct and individual concern criterion, for example, by companies active in the same market, would appear to be sufficient.[110] Nonetheless, the CFI has adopted a rather

---

103 Case T-95/94 *Sytraval v Commission* [1995] ECR II-2651.
104 On the grounds of lack of competence, infringement of an essential procedural requirement, infringement of the Treaty or any rule of law relating to its application, or misuse of powers.
105 See Case C-169/84 *COFAZ and Others v Commission* [1986] ECR 391; [1986] 3 CMLR 385; and, in particular, Case C-225/91 *Matra SA v Commission* [1993] ECR I-3203; and Case C-198/91 *Cook v Commission* [1993] ECR I-2486; [1993] 3 CMLR 206.
106 Cases T-371/94 and T-394/94 *British Airways and Others v Commission* [1998] ECR II-2405.
107 Ibid, at para 93.
108 Case C-282/95P *Guerin Automobiles v Commission* [1997] ECR I-1503; [1997] 5 CMLR 447. See Chapter 2.
109 Case T-95/96 *Gestevision Telecinco SA v Commission* [1998] ECR II-3407.
110 See Case C-106/98 *Comité d'Entreprise de la Société Française de Production v Commission* [2000] ECR I-3659, where a works council and trade union representing the sector in question were considered not to be individually concerned. Generally, see Soltesz, U and Bielesz, H, 'Judicial review of State aid decisions – recent developments' [2004] ECLR 133, particularly at pp 137–48.

strict approach to this issue by insisting on a direct link between the loss of profits by the competitor and the grant of the disputed aid, rather than merely generally affecting the competitor's competitive position.[111] Finally, the validity of a Commission State aid decision may be challenged in the national courts utilising the preliminary ruling procedure under Art 234.[112]

The possibility exists for further direct action by a disgruntled competitor.[113] Although Art 87 itself does not have direct effect, it may, for instance, be relied on before a national court where the Commission has taken a decision pursuant to Art 88(2) to prohibit the granting of State aid. In addition, the last sentence of Art 88(3), which provides that '[t]he Member State concerned shall not put its proposed measures into effect until this procedure has resulted in a final decision', has direct effect.[114] Accordingly, if aid is implemented prior to notification and approval and, therefore, constitutes illegally granted State aid, an individual can seek redress in the national courts. Normally, a competitor would seek some form of interim relief to prevent the implementation of the State aid. The competitor can seek an interlocutory injunction in England or interim interdict in Scotland to stop financial assistance, or a subsidy or loan guarantee being granted. Damages may also be sought from the relevant State on the basis of the non-contractual liability of Member States for breaches of Community law.[115] Finally, damages may be sought from the beneficiary in so far as there exists such a provision in the relevant national law.[116] The remedy against the recipient is more limited because the State aid rules and Commission decisions taken under the rules are directed towards the Member State concerned. In the context of national

---

111 See Case T-69/96 *Hamburger Hafen- und Lagerhaus Aktiengesellschaft and Others v Commission* [2001] ECR II-1037, particularly at paras 39–48. See also Case C-199/06 *CELF and Others v SIDE*, judgment of 12 February 2008.

112 See Case C-188/92 *TWD Textilewerke Deggendorf GmbH v Germany* [1994] ECR I-833; [1995] 2 CMLR 145, particularly regarding the time limits on the availability of this possibility of challenging the validity of a Commission decision.

113 See Abbamonte, G, 'Challenges to illegally granted aid and the problem of conflicting decisions in the field of competition' [1997] ECLR 87.

114 See Case C-354/90 *Salmon* [1991] 1 ECR 5505.

115 See Case 48/93 *Brasserie du Pêcheur-Factortame III* [1996] ECR I-1029; [1996] 1 CMLR 889; [1996] All ER (EC) 301; and Hernandez, AG, 'The principle of non-contractual State liability for breaches of EC law and its application to State aids' [1996] ECLR 355. However, the difficult issues of causation and quantification of damages need to be resolved adequately under the relevant national rules.

116 See Case C-39/94 *Syndicat Francais de l'Express International and Others v La Poste and Others (La Poste)* [1996] I-ECR 3547; [1996] All ER (EC) 685; [1996] 3 CMLR 369, pp 373–75. Although the Court does not discuss this in any detail, it is likely that this would be determined as follows: the private international law rules of the court with jurisdiction over the subject matter would determine the applicable law to govern this matter likely to be characterised as an issue of unjust enrichment. See Rodger, BJ, 'The interface between State aid, unjust enrichment and private international law', in *Unjust Enrichment and the Law of Contract*, Schrage, EJH (ed), 2001, The Hague: Kluwer Law International, pp 347–66.

court actions the Court has adopted a similarly restrictive approach in respect of the possibilities for beneficiaries to rely on the legitimate expectations defence.[117]

Article 88 has limited direct effect; only the last sentence of Art 88(3) is directly effective and the national courts cannot determine the compatibility of the aid but can only provide remedies if the aid has been illegally implemented. The Commission has introduced a Notice to assist the national courts in the application of Art 88(3) in actions brought by competitors in the context of remedies against illegal aid.[118] The Notice seeks to encourage courts to exercise their powers and for undertakings to resort to the appropriate legal remedies under their national system. In addition, in *La Poste*,[119] the Court confirmed that the national courts have an important and complementary role to that of the Commission regarding State aid. The Court, in *La Poste*, provided that national courts should co-operate with the Commission or seek a preliminary ruling under Art 234 EC in order to avoid the possibility of reaching conflicting decisions as to whether the measure constitutes State aid.

Recent and future developments

The Commission's developing policy has been that aid should be oriented towards horizontal goals where there exists a gain for the common interest. Overall, the Commission has indicated a shift away from supporting aid to individual companies or sectors, towards tackling horizontal objectives of Community interest. The Autumn 2007 State Aid Scoreboard, published in December 2007, demonstrated, in line with the State Aid Action Plan objective, that overall levels of aid are decreasing and that Member States have steadily reoriented their State aid towards horizontal objectives in the Community interest. Welfare gains include regional development, environmental protection, research and development (R&D), innovation, employment, etc. A Regulation was introduced in 1998 to enable the Commission to adopt group exemptions for certain categories of horizontal aid,[120] defining the criteria under which certain aid, such as for research and development, may be exempted from the notification obligation. The Commission used its powers under the enabling Regulation to introduce State aid block exemption Regulations in relation to small- and medium-sized enterprises, *de minimis* aid, training aid and employment aid, on the basis that aid for these horizontal

---

117 See Case C-24/95 *Land Rheinland Pfalz v Alcan Deutschland* [1997] ECR I-1591; [1997] 2 CMLR 1034.

118 Commission Notice on co-operation between national courts and the Commission in the State aid field, OJ 1995, C312/7.

119 Case 39/94 *La Poste* [1996] ECR I-3547; [1996] 3 CMLR 369; [1996] All ER (EC) 685.

120 Regulation 994/98/EC on the application of Arts 92 and 93 of the EC Treaty to certain categories of horizontal aid, OJ 1998, L142/1.

objectives contributes to overall Community objectives. Accordingly, the exemption of certain categories of aid from notification requirements was intended to allow the Commission to concentrate its resources on ad hoc schemes to assist particular companies.

The Competition Commissioner recognised in 2003 that a number of challenges faced the Community State aid regime.[121] A key issue was the enlargement of the Community and the accession of 10 new Member States on 1 May 2004. The application of the rules to economies in transition from centrally-planned to market-based economies was potentially problematic, particularly in relation to the perceived greater incidence of State rescue of ailing firms and the complex issue of compensation for provision of services in the general economic interest.[122] In addition, enlargement would also lead to additional Commission workload. Partly in anticipation of the increased workload, and with a view to allowing less but better targeted aid towards horizontal objectives of common interest across the Union, the Commission introduced its modernisation initiative at the end of 2003 with a view to identifying aid likely to produce significant effects on competition and impact on the internal market, thereby allowing a more effective prioritisation of scarce enforcement resources. The Commission launched a comprehensive reform of State aid rules and procedures in its State Aid Action Plan in June 2005.[123] The aim was to ensure the State aid rules focus aid measures in order to contribute to the Community Lisbon strategy to enhance the competitiveness of EU industry and create sustainable jobs. The overall policy goal can be defined as 'less and better targeted State aid', but it also included the following elements: a more refined economic approach; more streamlined and efficient procedures; better enforcement; greater predictability; and enhanced transparency. Since the adoption of the Plan, a number of new measures have been introduced, and other measures have been revised, or are under revision, with a view to completing the modernisation process by 2009. A key objective of the State Aid Action Plan was to create a coherent and user-friendly set of rules to apply to aid, which fulfilled the compatibility criteria in Article 87(3). Accordingly, the Commission consolidated the existing Block Exemption Regulations into a single instrument, the General Block Exemption ('GBER'). The GBER was adopted in July 2008,[124] and this key measure should contribute to achieving less and better targeted aid. It will cover certain types of horizontal aid already provided for by existing block

---

121 Monti, M, 'New developments in State aid policy', British Chamber of Commerce, Brussels, 1 December 2003.

122 Discussed above; see Hansen, Van Ysendyck and Zuhlke, fn 46, particularly at pp 225–29. See, also, Evans, A, 'Enlargement and State Aid in CEECs', CLaSF Working Paper 04, January 2004.

123 State Aid Action Plan, Less and Better targeted State aid: a roadmap for state aid reform 2005–2009, COM(2005) 107 final, Commission press release IP/05/680, 7 June 2005.

124 [2008] OJ L214/3.

exemption Regulations, such as training and regional aid, but it will also integrate into the GBER aid in the form of risk capital, and further enlarge the scope of existing BERs by extending the R&D aspect to large enterprises. The most significant inclusion is in relation to environmental aid, largely drawn from experience under the environmental guidelines published in 2001 and revised in 2008.

The key trends in the jurisprudence also demonstrate a tightening in the State aid rules: selectivity has been more difficult to disprove and advantage has been construed widely. Nonetheless, the interrelationship between the State aid regime and national tax systems is problematic and there are likely to be more confrontations between Member States and the Commission on this issue. It has been argued that the Commission has indirectly sought harmonisation of European tax regimes via the application of the State aid provisions,[125] but the European Court has clearly recognised the legitimate role of national taxation regimes in addressing legitimate policy objectives. Furthermore, the provision of services of general economic interest has been accommodated through the application of the State aid rules. An important future trend may be the increased role of the national courts as part of the general process of decentralisation of the Community workload, although the national courts' role is limited and will be fraught with difficulties.[126] One area of difficulty for national courts has been avoided by the Court's determination that State labour law regimes, which inevitably impact on the competitiveness of undertakings, are not covered by the State aid rules.[127]

Nonetheless, it has been argued that although State aid law has shifted from being a purely administrative procedure to a system of economic law enforcement involving legal challenges by competitors this development is limited. The role of national courts through the direct effect doctrine is limited, and the European Courts have not developed standing beyond market interests to include environmental or regional interest groups despite the important role that environmental and regional policy play in the State aid control regime.[128] However, a recent study on the enforcement of State aid at national level has confirmed that there has been a marked increase in the number of State aid cases raised before national courts.[129]

---

125 See Hansen, Van Ysendyck and Zuhlke, fn 46, particularly at pp 223–25.
126 See Ross, M, 'State aids and national courts: definitions and other problems – a case of premature emancipation' (2000) 37 CML Rev 401, which notes the 'mismatch' between the Court imposed duties and their impact at national level, p 421.
127 See Rodger, BJ, 'State aid – a fully level playing field' [1999] ECLR 251.
128 See Evans, A, 'Law, policy and equality in the European Union: the example of State aid control' (1998) 23 EL Rev 434.
129 Jestaedt, T, Derenne, J, & Ottervanger, T, 'Study on the Enforcement of State Aid Law at National Level' March 2006, accessible at http://ec.europa.eu/comm/competition/state_aid/ studies_reports/study_part_1.pdf

State regulation and intervention

In the first part of the chapter the potential effect of aid granted by a Member State was discussed, but State aid is not the only way in which the activities of States may distort competition.[130] Most Member States have 'mixed economies' in that the State may intervene in those industries which are considered 'essential' to the health of the national economy. For example, the importance of coal and steel to European economies was recognised by the Treaty of Paris of 1951, which formed the European Coal and Steel Community, the precursor to the European Economic Community. However, such recognition of State intervention does not sit well with a literal interpretation of Art 3(1)(g) of the Treaty which requires 'that competition in the common market is not distorted'. The involvement of Member States in their national economy will inevitably distort competition to some extent. The intervention of Member States will also be a particular problem as it leads to markets being organised within national boundaries, thereby hampering the creation of a single market. However, as market regulation, intervention or involvement, is so well recognised, and even protected to a degree by Art 295 EC,[131] it is not directly challenged. Although there is no direct challenge to State regulation there have been ways in which the Commission has used the Treaty to ensure that competition is distorted to the least extent possible. The interplay between the competition rules and State regulation is developing constantly and is likely to be given even greater scrutiny in the near future.

While most of the discussion of such situations stems from the application of Community law the interaction between the activities of the State and domestic competition law is also increasingly important. This is particularly the case where the State interacts with private individuals or undertakings in a commercial context. In such situations, are the actions of the State constrained by competition law? The growing importance of this area was stressed by John Vickers, the Chairman of the Office of Fair Trading (OFT), in 2003:

> The relationship between competition policy and government activities is perhaps one of the most interesting and potentially fruitful current issues. It has grown in importance as government bodies have increasingly operated in market environments, and as the will and the means of competition scrutiny of aspects of government activities have strengthened – both generally positive developments.[132]

---

130 For a comprehensive discussion of many of these issues see, Szyszczack, E, *The Regulation of the State in Competitive Markets in the EU*, Hart: Oxford, 2007.

131 Article 295 EC provides that nothing in the Treaty shall prejudice the ownership of property. This has been taken to cover the purchase of property, or industries, by States themselves.

132 Vickers, J, 'How does the prohibition of abuse of dominance fit with the rest of competition policy?', Paper for the Eighth Annual EU Competition Law and Policy Workshop at the EUI, Florence, 6 June 2003, p 6.

The main limit on the behaviour of States within Community law is enshrined in Art 10 of the EC Treaty. Article 10(2) obliges Member States to abstain from adopting measures which could jeopardise the attainment of the objectives of the Treaty. The Commission can enforce this obligation through Art 226 EC where the actions of Member States threaten to distort competition. This general power is expressed more clearly in Art 86(1) of the Treaty, in relation to 'public undertakings and undertakings to which Member States grant special or exclusive rights'. Member States are required to 'neither enact nor maintain in force any measure contrary to the rules contained in the Treaty'. This provision is unusual in that it relies, for its effect, on other Articles of the Treaty. Despite referring specifically to Arts 12 and 81–89 EC, Art 86(1) also applies to all the other provisions of the Treaty. Article 86(1) also gives a special defence to undertakings which have been granted 'special or exclusive rights' from challenge under the competition rules. We will deal with the application of the competition rules to Member States before considering the effect of Art 86 on undertakings.

Article 86(2) deals with situations in which undertakings are 'entrusted with the operation of services of general economic interest or having the character of a revenue-producing monopoly'. It is clear from this provision that such undertakings are subject to the competition rules, but only so far as the rules do not obstruct the 'particular tasks assigned to them'. This creates another potential defence for undertakings involved in some sectors of the economy where they are assigned a particular role by the State. Services of general interest are an increasingly important area of Community law. The Commission published Green and White Papers on services of general interest,[133] opening a consultation process on a wider framework for dealing with such services. That process resulted in the adoption of a Protocol on Services of General Interest to be annexed to the Treaty of Lisbon and a further Communication from the Commission in 2007.[134] It should be noted that these discussions, following the wider conception in the Protocol, focus on both services of general economic interest (SGEI), which are subject to the internal market and competition rules of the EC Treaty, and other non-economic services of general interest, such as justice and social security, which do not normally fall under the Treaty in the same way. It is already clear that the distinction between these two groups is politically sensitive and fraught with difficulty.

---

133 C(2003) 270 final and COM(2004) 374 final.
134 Communication from the Commission on Services of general interest, including social services of general interest: a new European Commitment, COM(2007) 725 final.

Measures adopted by the State

One of the first applications of the competition rules to measures adopted by Member States was in *Inno v ATAB*.[135] In that case the Dutch taxation of tobacco was challenged on the basis that it distorted competition. The Court's judgment focused on the relationship between Arts 3, 10, 81 and 82 of the Treaty, and stated in very broad terms that Member States should not adopt measures which deprived the competition rules of their effect. The subsequent case law has largely been used to refine the meaning of the Court's earlier judgments.

Article 81

In several cases the Court has challenged the sanctioning of private cartels by a Member State. In *BNIC v Yves Aubert*,[136] the Court examined the extension of a price-fixing agreement set up by BNIC, a trade organisation for cognac producers, to the entire industry through a ministerial order. An action had been brought against Yves Aubert for undercutting the fixed price and the national court referred the matter to the Court under Art 234. The Court was of the view that the ministerial order extended the impact of the private agreement and constituted a breach of France's obligations under the Treaty. It seems obvious that the Court was able to challenge the State support of a blatant price-fixing agreement, but the use of Art 81 has been extended to less obvious situations. There is no need for the State measure to support an existing agreement, only the need, as in *Vlaamse Reisbureaus*,[137] that the State measure be related to an agreement between private undertakings. In that case, the State measure prohibited travel agents from passing on commissions to their clients. The Court decided that the measure evolved from a pre-existing, though no longer operative, agreement which fell foul of Art 81.

A different use of Art 81 can be observed from *Van Eycke*.[138] The Court held that Member States could not 'deprive [their] own legislation of its official character by delegating to private traders responsibility for taking decisions affecting the economic sphere'. The danger with such delegation is that it may lead to traders disguising anti-competitive activity behind the veil of State regulation. As traders would represent only their own interests, rather than the interests of the State as a whole, traders should not be granted

---

135 Case 13/77 [1977] ECR 2115; [1978] 1 CMLR 283.

136 Case 136/86 [1987] ECR 4789; [1988] 4 CMLR 331.

137 Case 311/85 *Vereniging van Vlaamse Reisbureaus v Sociale Dienst* [1987] ECR 3801; [1989] 4 CMLR 213.

138 Case 267/86 [1988] ECR 4769; [1990] 4 CMLR 330. See also the related cases of Case C-35/96 *Commission v Italy* [1998] ECR I-3851 and Case T-513/93 *CNSD v Commission* [2000] ECR II-1807.

such powers. It can be seen that the grant of such powers would result in an organisation which would effectively operate as a cartel.

The operation of Art 81, in relation to State measures, is therefore dependent upon the activities of undertakings in the market. The acts of the State will not be challenged unless they come within one of the types of situations mentioned above. There has been academic debate about the conceptual basis of the Court's jurisprudence in this area[139] but the Court has confirmed its approach in a number of cases.[140]

Article 82

Article 82 has been applied most frequently in relation to State measures. Its application is usually in conjunction with Art 86(1) of the Treaty, which deals with public undertakings[141] or undertakings granted special or exclusive rights.[142] It is obvious how the granting of special or exclusive rights to an undertaking may bring it within the concept of dominance under Art 82. While it was considered that Art 86(1) and Art 82 did not challenge the grant of such rights,[143] it was assumed initially that they were designed to deal with State measures which required undertakings with such rights to act in an abusive manner. This view was challenged in a number of cases in the early 1990s.

In *Höffner & Elser v Macrotron*[144] the Court considered the grant of exclusive rights in the employment procurement market to a public undertaking, the Federal Employment Office. In reality, the Federal Employment Office did not have the resources to satisfy the demand of the German employment market and, as a result, several 'headhunting' agencies operated alongside the service provided by the Federal Employment Office. One of these unofficial agencies raised an action over a disputed fee and was met with a defence based on the illegality of its operation. The matter was referred to the Court. It decided that the grant of an exclusive right would breach Arts 82 and 86(1)

---

139 See Bacon, K, 'State regulation of the market and EC competition rules' [1997] 5 ECLR 283.

140 Case C-2/91 *Wolf Meng* [1993] ECR I-5751; Case C-185/91 *Bundessanstalt für den Güterfernverkehr v Gebruder Reiff* [1993] ECR I-5801; Case C-245/91 *Ohra Schadeverzekeringen* [1993] ECR I-5851; [1995] 5 CMLR 145; and Case C-35/99 *Criminal Proceedings v Manuele Arduino* [2002] ECR I-1529.

141 Undertakings owned or controlled by the State.

142 There is no authoritative definition of special or exclusive rights, but in the telecommunications sector the Council defined them as 'special or exclusive rights shall mean rights deriving from authorizations granted by a competent authority of the Member State concerned, by law, regulation or administrative action, having as their result the reservation for one or more entities of the exploitation of an activity', Art 2(3), Directive 93/38/EEC, OJ 1993, L199/84.

143 Case 155/73 *Sacchi* [1974] ECR 409.

144 Case C-41/90 [1991] ECR I-1979; [1993] 4 CMLR 306.

of the Treaty if the existence of that right would inevitably lead to an abuse under Art 82. This would be the outcome if the agency which was granted special rights could not satisfy demand whilst other competitors were barred from the market. The Court appeared to go further in *Porto di Genova*[145] when it suggested that there would be a breach not only where the undertaking in question cannot avoid abusing its dominant position, but also 'when such rights are liable to create a situation in which that undertaking is induced to commit such abuses'. However, in *Carra and Others*,[146] a case with similar facts to *Höffner*, the Court set out three cumulative criteria in order to establish a breach. Those criteria are as follows:

a   the public placement offices are manifestly unable to satisfy demand on the market for all types of activity;
b   the actual placement of employees by private companies is rendered impossible by the maintenance in force of statutory provisions; and
c   the placement activities in question could extend to the nationals, or the territory, of other Member States.

Therefore, where there is a necessary link between the grant of the right and the existence of an abuse the grant of the right can be challenged under Arts 86(1) and 82.

A second type of application of Arts 86(1) and 82 is evident in relation to the nature of special or exclusive rights granted by the Member State. This application of the provision allows the grant of such a right to be challenged but this time on a somewhat different basis. In *RTT v GB-Inno*,[147] the Court considered the Belgian telephone monopoly system. RTT had control over the public telephone network but its exclusive rights also extended over the market for telecommunications equipment. Before telephone equipment could be connected to the Belgian network the equipment had to be approved by RTT. GB-Inno had been importing telephone equipment and RTT asked for an injunction to stop the imports which were encouraging the connection of unapproved equipment. The Court held that the extension of the monopoly into the secondary market for the approval of equipment was a breach of Art 86(1). The Court so held on two grounds: first, the extension would have been an abuse of a dominant position as RTT could use its monopoly power to eliminate competitors from a secondary market; and secondly, Art 86(1) prohibits Member States from putting such undertakings 'in a position which the said undertakings could not themselves attain by their own conduct without infringing Art [82]'.

---

145   Case C-179/90 *Merci Convenzionali Porto di Genova v Siderurgica Gabrielli SpA* [1991] ECR I-5889; [1994] 4 CMLR 422.
146   Case C-258/98 *Giovanni Carra and Others* [2000] ECR I-4217.
147   Case C-18/88 [1991] ECR I-5941.

The reasoning in *RTT* was explained further by the Court in *Corbeau*.[148] Once more, the question concerned the inclusion of ancillary services within a State monopoly, in this case the inclusion of express courier services within the Belgian postal monopoly. The Court interpreted Art 86(1) alongside Art 86(2). Article 86(2) gives private undertakings, with exclusive rights, a defence to competition actions in so far as the exclusive rights are necessary to ensure the performance of the undertaking's particular tasks. When examining the nature of the monopoly in question it was apparent that the reservation of express courier services to the holder of the postal monopoly was not necessary for the maintenance of the general postal service. In that sense the Court was of the opinion that the reservation of the secondary market was inherently abusive and contrary to Art 86.[149]

The use of Art 86 to challenge State monopolies is a relatively recent concept and, therefore, the case law is in a formative stage of development. The doctrines introduced in *Höffner* and *RTT* have a potentially wide application to the way in which Member States organise their economies and it will be interesting to see how far the doctrines develop in the future.[150]

Article 86(3)

Under Art 86(3) of the Treaty, the Commission has the power to ensure the application of Art 86(1) and (2). To that end, the Commission can address Decisions to Member States and also produce Directives. The Commission's ability to issue Decisions and Directives in this context has been challenged on a number of occasions as the power enables the Commission to avoid the parallel and more complex procedure available to it under Art 226 of the Treaty. The Court has consistently held that Art 86(3) empowers the Commission to adopt Decisions or Directions where appropriate.[151]

The State entities as undertakings

In many areas of the global economy a process of 'liberalisation' is underway. That process means that areas of the economy, which were traditionally controlled by the State, are being opened up to private undertakings. Liberalisation may lead to the State exiting a particular sector of the economy, or it

---

148 Case C-320/91 [1993] ECR I-2533; [1995] 4 CMLR 621.
149 See, also, Case C-260/89 *ERT v DEP* [1991] ECR I-2925.
150 For a detailed discussion of these issues in a wider context see Szyszczak, E, *The Regulation of the State in Competitive Markets in the EU*, 2007, Oxford: Hart and Prosser, T, *The Limits of Competition Law. Markets and Public Services*, 2005, Oxford: OUP.
151 See, in particular, Cases 188–90/80 *France v Commission* [1982] ECR 2545; [1982] 3 CMLR 144; Case 226/87 *Commission v Greece* [1988] ECR 3611; [1989] 3 CMLR 569; Cases C-48/90 and C-66/90 *Netherlands and Others v Commission* [1992] ECR I-565; and Case C-163/99 *Portugal v Commission* [2001] ECR I-2613.

may result in a mix of public and private provision. It is in the latter situation where a number of interesting competition questions are raised. Where the State is involved in a commercial sector, either as a purchaser or a provider, it may become embroiled in disagreements with private undertakings who may seek to rely on the competition rules to protect their position. The type of situation which may arise, and the way in which the law responds, is best illustrated by a number of key cases.

The starting point for discussion is *Höffner*,[152] discussed above. In that case a State body, the Federal Employment Office, was considered to be an under-taking as it was involved in an economic activity – employment procurement. In such circumstances the issue is not a controversial one. A number of more recent cases, involving healthcare insurance or provision, have been much more sensitive. *FENIN*[153] concerned a complaint, from an association repre-senting the majority of suppliers of medical goods and equipment to the Spanish National Health Service, that several organisations within the health service had abused their dominant position by taking up to 300 days to pay invoices. The CFI followed the line set out in *Höffner*, that being that the concept of 'undertaking' covers any entity engaged in an economic activity regardless of the entity's legal status. Nonetheless, a distinction was drawn between a health service's ordinary purchasing of products, which was not an economic activity in itself, and the purchasing of products as part of a wider economic activity. It was made clear that it was the use of the purchased goods that would determine whether the entity was involved in an economic activity. As the health service had only purchased goods as part of its social function – providing healthcare – it was not involved in an economic activity, even though the total sum involved in those transactions was considerable. The provision of healthcare was not an economic activity as it operated 'according to the principle of solidarity in that it is funded from social secur-ity contributions and other State funding and in that it provides services free of charge to its members on the basis of universal cover'.[154] The question of the 'principle of solidarity' is vital in deciding whether State activity is a 'social function' or an economic activity.[155]

Similar questions arose in UK competition law in the *BetterCare* series of cases. BetterCare provides nursing home and residential care services in Northern Ireland. North and West Belfast Health and Social Services Trust (N & W) purchased services from BetterCare and also managed its own facilities. BetterCare made a complaint to the Director General of Fair

---

152 Case C-41/90 [1991] ECR I-1979; [1993] 4 CMLR 306.

153 Case T-319/99 *FENIN v Commission* [2003] ECR II-357; [2003] 5 CMLR 1 and Case C-205/03P *FENIN v Commission* [2006] ECR I-6295.

154 At para 39.

155 See, also, Cases C-159 and 160/91 *Poucet and Pistre* [1993] ECR I-637; Case C-244/94 *FFSA* [1995] ECR I-4013; and Case C-67/96 *Albany* [1999] ECR I-5751.

Trading (DGFT) that N & W was abusing its dominant position by offering unreasonably low contract prices and unfair terms that made it difficult for BetterCare to continue in business. The matter in this case was potentially more complex than in *FENIN* as N & W not only purchased residential care, but was also a provider of residential care, and it also recovered some of the costs of the provision from residents in certain circumstances. In its first Decision, which was made before the *FENIN* judgment, the DGFT decided that N & W was not an undertaking.[156] That Decision was then overturned by the Competition Appeal Tribunal (CAT) on appeal.[157] Following the successful appeal the case was remitted to the OFT which went on to produce a second Decision in late 2003.[158] The OFT decided, in light of the fluid position of Community law, not to make a finding as to whether N & W was an 'undertaking' but, in any event, found that N & W had not abused a dominant position. The OFT also considered that the setting of prices for social care by the DHSSPS and EHSSB, the two statutory bodies charged with that function, was not an economic activity. It was unusual that the OFT avoided coming to a conclusion in this case, but it does indicate the complexity and political sensitivity of decisions in relation to the position of a state entity as an undertaking.

One of the reasons that the OFT did not want to make any findings on the 'undertaking' issue in the second *BetterCare* Decision was the Court's imminent judgment in *AOK Bundesverband*.[159] In *AOK Bundesverband* the Düsseldorf Higher Regional Court referred a number of questions to the Court regarding the setting of maximum prices for the purchase of medicinal products by various compulsory medical insurance funds. The setting of maximum prices was supported by government measures. A number of pharmaceutical manufacturers challenged the setting of maximum prices as being contrary to Art 81 EC, before the German courts. The Court was of the opinion that the German statutory health insurance scheme fulfilled an exclusively social function, which was founded on the principle of national solidarity and was entirely non-profit-making. The medical insurance funds were also compelled, by law, to offer to their members identical obligatory benefits which did not depend on the amount of each member's contributions. The Government had introduced an element of competition but only in order to encourage the sickness funds to operate in the most effective and least costly manner possible. It was, however, possible that some operations fell outside

---

156 DGFT Decision CA/98/11/2002, Case CP/0829-01, *North & West Belfast Health and Social Services Trust*, 30 April 2002.

157 Case 1006/2/1/01 *BetterCare Group Ltd v DGFT* [2002] CAT 7.

158 OFT Decision CA98/09/2003, Case CE/1836-02 *BetterCare Group Ltd/North & West Belfast Health & Social Services Trust*, 18 December 2003.

159 Cases C-264, 306, 354 and 355/01, [2004] 4 CMLR 22. See Lasok, KPE, 'When is an undertaking not an undertaking?' [2004] ECLR 383.

this purely social nature, but as the setting of maximum prices was carried out within a legislative framework, the funds were not pursuing an interest 'separable from the exclusively social objective of the sickness funds'.

The judgment in *AOK Bundesverband* clarified the issues somewhat and allowed the OFT to issue new Guidance in the UK. The OFT Policy Note[160] stressed that where a public body is only a purchaser of goods or services and is not involved in their provision it will not be considered an undertaking. In cases where the public body was active as a provider the OFT described the law as being in a 'state of development'[161] and was unlikely to exercise its powers under the 1998 Act, preferring other means of regulation. One of the issues that were outstanding when the Policy Note was issued was the *FENIN* appeal.[162] In that appeal the Court of Justice confirmed the judgment of the CFI, but did not directly address the issue of undertakings which are active as purchasers and providers. Although the issue was not addressed by the Court it was discussed by AG Maduro. One of the issues canvassed in the appeal was that while the majority of healthcare offered in the SNS was provided free of charge, there was a small proportion of private care provided for remuneration. The issue was ruled out of time by the Court, but the AG suggested that this matter should be referred back to the CFI to investigate whether the private element of the SNS affected the 'solidarity' of the system.[163] The position of cases like *BetterCare II* is therefore still uncertain. What is clear is that such cases are likely to arise again and that the Court will, no doubt, be called upon to clarify the position further.

State regulation and undertakings

Although Art 86 of the Treaty refers to the activities of Member States, it may also have an important impact on private undertakings which undertake 'public' functions. As can be seen from the cases that have already been discussed, it may well be possible for an undertaking involved in a dispute before a national court to use Art 81 or 82, alongside Art 86, in order to indirectly challenge a State measure. This ability has been very important for the development of the Court's jurisprudence. Member States prefer to use informal methods to resolve disputes with the Commission but where private undertakings are involved in disputes before national courts the issues are more likely to be referred to the Court. Without those references it is unlikely that the law would have developed to the extent it already has.

---

160 Policy Note 1/2004, The Competition Act and public bodies, OFT 443.
161 Ibid, at para 28.
162 Case C-205/03 P *FENIN v Commission* [2006] ECR I-6295.
163 See Boeger, N, 'Solidarity and EC Competition Law' (2007) 32(3) ELRev 319, and Krajewski, M, and Farley, M, 'Non-Economic Activities in Upstream and Downstream Markets and the Scope of Competition Law after FENIN' (2007) 32(1) ELRev 111.

Article 86(2) contains provisions that relate directly to undertakings which are 'entrusted with the operation of services of general economic interest or having the character of revenue producing monopolies'. The Article states that the competition rules apply to those undertakings but only in so far as 'the application of such rules does not obstruct the performance, in law or in fact, of the particular task assigned to them'. There is also the general proviso that trade should not be affected in a manner which is contrary to the interests of the Community. This is, in effect, a defence against the application of the competition rules in favour of undertakings given special responsibilities by the State. It is thought that there is a correlation between the undertakings granted special or exclusive rights under Art 86(1) and undertakings entrusted with the operation of services of general economic interest under Art 86(2), although this is not explicit from the wording. It is important that the undertaking has been 'entrusted' with the operation of the service by a Member State. In *Uniform Eurocheques*,[164] the Commission decided that Art 86(2) did not apply as the founders of the Eurocheque system were private undertakings even though the system had been approved by several Member States.

As it is a defence, or derogation, from the competition rules, the Court has construed Art 86(2) very narrowly.[165] Before the defence is available the Court requires the anti-competitive behaviour to be necessary for the performance of the tasks assigned, not that it merely facilitates the performance of those tasks. That issue was considered by the Court in *Corbeau*.[166] Corbeau had set up an alternative express postal service in Liège. This service would collect mail and deliver it by noon the following day. Mail for outside the local area was placed in the normal postal system. Corbeau was prosecuted under Belgian law for breach of the postal monopoly system and he claimed, in defence, that Belgian law was contrary to Art 86. The Court considered whether the reservation of the postal services to the national postal monopoly was necessary for the performance of its tasks. It was recognised that the postal service would need to offset the losses entailed on less profitable services with the revenue from profitable sectors. If private undertakings could offer cheaper services in the profitable areas it would remove the ability to offset losses. However, the Court held that where there are services which could be dissociable from the general service, such as express services or the ability to change the destination in the course of transit, the exclusion of competition is not justified unless the ability to offer such services in a specific area compromised the general service. As this was a preliminary reference the Court left the final decision in this case to the national court. It would appear, however, that the defence will only be available when a service of general

164 Commission Decision 85/77/EEC, OJ 1985, L35/43.
165 Case 127/73 *BRT v SABAM* [1974] ECR 313; [1974] 2 CMLR 238. See, also, Case T-128/98 *Aéroports de Paris v Commission* [2000] ECR II-3929.
166 Case C-320/91 [1993] ECR I-2533; [1995] 4 CMLR 621.

economic importance is threatened by competitors who can 'cherry-pick' the profitable sectors of the business without bearing the costs involved in operating the general service. Competition will be allowed to operate in as many areas as possible unless the general service is threatened.[167]

Another postal case[168] was considered by the CFI in *Deutsche Post*.[169] Deutsche Post was making charges for the practice of ABA non-physical re-mailing, where bulk mail is sent electronically from a sender in country 'A' to country 'B' for re-mailing back into country 'A'. This is done to benefit from lower charges in country 'B'. In order to address this practice the destination country applied extra charges to recover costs similar to the normal domestic tariff. The key question for the CFI was whether the application of competition law would jeopardise the performance of the postal service which was seen to be in the general economic interest. The CFI decided that the additional charges applied by the destination country would be compatible with Art 86 as long as there was no double charging after other compensation from international mail Conventions was taken into account.

Further reading

General reading

Prosser, T, *The Limits of Competition Law. Markets and Public Services*, 2005, Oxford: OUP.

Szyszczak, E, *The Regulation of the State in Competitive Markets in the EU*, 2007, Oxford: Hart.

State aid

Abbamonte, G, 'Market economy investor principle: a legal analysis of an economic problem' [1996] 4 ECLR 258.

Biondi, A, Eckhout, P, and Flynn, J (eds), *The Law of State Aid in the European Union*, 2004, Oxford: OUP.

Bishop, SB, 'State aids: Europe's spreading cancer' [1995] ECLR 331.

Hancher, L, Ottervanger, TR, and Slot, PJ, *EC State Aids*, 3rd edn, 2006, London: Sweet & Maxwell.

Louis, F, and Vallery, A, 'Ferring Revisited: the *Altmark* Case and State Financing of Public Services Obligations' (2004) 57 World Competition 53.

Ross, M, 'State aids and national courts: definitions and other problems – a case of premature emancipation' (2000) 37 CML Rev 401.

---

167 See, also, Case C-340/99 *TNT Traco SpA v Poste Italiane SpA* [2001] ECR I-4109.

168 European postal markets have thrown up a number of interesting cases which are discussed in detail in, Diez Estella, F, 'Abusive Practices in the Postal Services' Part 1: [2006] ECLR 184, Part 2: [2006] ECLR 228.

169 Joined Cases C-147 and 148/97 *Deutsche Post AG v Gesellschaft für Zahlungssysteme mbH and Citicorp Kartenservice GmbH* [2000] ECR I-825; [2000] 4 CMLR 838.

State regulation

Bacon, K, 'State regulation of the market and EC competition rules: Articles 85 and 86 compared' [1997] 5 ECLR 283.

Boeger, N, 'Solidarity and EC Competition Law' (2007) 32(3) ELRev 319.

Ehle, D, 'State regulation under the US antitrust State action doctrine and under EC competition law: a comparative analysis' [1998] 6 ECLR 380.

Gagliardi, AF, 'United States and European Union antitrust versus State regulation of the economy: is there a better test?' (2000) 25 EL Rev 353.

Van de Gronden, JW, 'Purchasing care: economic activity or service of general (economic) interest?' [2004] ECLR 87.

Discussion

1   Does Community law intend to set up a level competitive playing field across all Member States? Is a completely level playing field feasible, desirable and politically acceptable?

2   What is State aid, and what has the Commission done to modernise the application of the State aid rules?

3   Explain the difference between illegal and incompatible State aid. To what extent can and should enforcement of the State aid rules be decentralised?

4   To what extent does Art 86 alter the way in which Member States can organise their national economies and provide social services?

Chapter 8

Overview: policy developments and practical implications

Introduction

The previous seven chapters have introduced the principal issues which are of interest to competition lawyers. Discussion focused on the substantive rules and enforcement regimes under the main competition laws of both the Community and the UK. This concluding chapter aims to provide a brief overview of certain topical policy issues and practical implications, which are relevant for Community and national competition practitioners, enforcement authorities, academics and industry, and of which students of competition law ought to be aware. The overview includes current debates and problems in addition to likely developments in the near future. Students should be conscious that certain issues in policy issues and practical implications may overlap to a degree.

At a policy level the following issues will be at the forefront of debate:

a continuing debate concerning the role of intervention by competition authorities as opposed to a laissez-faire approach based upon free markets;
b certainty and predictability in competition law and the relevance of economics and economic analysis;
c the increasing trend towards globalisation of markets and international co-operation in competition law enforcement;
d substantive reform of Community competition law;
e developments in enforcement of Community competition law;
f new directions in competition law, notably criminalisation; and
g development of the revised UK competition regime post-Competition and Enterprise Acts.

At a practical level, for businesses and their legal advisers, there are certain issues that are likely to develop and increase in importance. Those issues are as follows:

a   enhanced awareness of the need for effective compliance programmes;
b   the debate between the pigeon-holing of business activity and market analysis;
c   'whistle-blowing', which includes strategies of informing the competition authorities about breaches of competition law, and corresponding leniency programmes; and
d   development of the remedies for competitor and customer complainants.

Policy level

Laissez-faire competition laws?

The debate surrounding the nature and role of competition law and policy, outlined in Chapter 1, has both a national and international perspective. At the national level there have always been advocates of laissez-faire market economics, whose faith in free markets leads to a distrust of regulatory competition authorities. The principle of laissez-faire is based on the concepts of economic freedom and the limitation of governmental intervention. The implications for competition policy will depend to a great extent on any national system's historical, political and legal culture and the attitude towards markets and the role of the State.[1] Inevitably, therefore, competition law and policy reflect the prevailing political ideology. For instance, particularly in the United States, the debate over the last 40 years between the Chicago and Harvard schools generally mirrors the wider political debate on intervention or freedom of the market, although not all Harvard scholars were particularly interventionist and even most Chicago school proponents have agreed that some form of control over naked horizontal cartels is required. Accordingly, the debate in competition law has tended to concern the degree of intervention which is deemed appropriate. Recent political discussion in the UK and US has focused on a 'third way' in politics between capitalism and free markets, and the State economy. Although this 'third way' may in fact be little more than the traditional concept of the mixed economy, it may shed light on recent developments in competition and antitrust economic analysis which have tended to move away from the Chicago/Harvard dichotomy and look for practical economic theories, such as those found in industrial economics.[2]

---

1   See Helm, D, 'The economic borders of the state', in *The Economic Borders of the State*, 1989, New York: OUP, pp 1–45.
2   See, for example, Larner, RJ and Meehan, JW (Jr), 'The structural school, its critics, and its progeny: an assessment', in Larner, RJ and Meehan, JW (Jr), *Economics and Antitrust Policy*, New York: Quorum, 1989, pp 179–209; Kovacic, WE, 'The Intellectual DNA of Modern US Competition Law for Dominant Firm Conduct: The Chicago/Harvard Double Helix' [2007] Columbia Business Law Review 1; and, Averitt, NW, and Lande, RH, 'Using the "Consumer Choice" Approach to Antitrust Law' (2007) Antitrust Law Journal 175.

On an international perspective, it has been noted that even whilst international commerce is booming the number of systems of national competition law is increasing.[3] National competition laws are introduced to reflect domestic realities, yet national competition laws can lead to competitive distortions based on national protectionism.[4] Accordingly, it has been asserted that instead of creating globalised rules of competition or co-operation in enforcing national competition rules a new globalised market without competition laws and based on free trade would be preferable.[5]

Certainty and predictability v economic analysis

Although it is suggested below that a practical problem in competition law is the 'pigeon-holing' of commercial transactions to achieve fixed legal outcomes, many practitioners, reformists and certain academics, particularly in the UK, stress the need for certainty and predictability in competition law. This view informs the systems of competition law enforcement discussed in Chapter 2, and a notable critique of Regulation 1/2003 focused on the resulting lack of certainty for industry. The discussion of the substantive issues in Chapters 3–7 demonstrates the continuing debate over certainty and predictability in competition law and policy. We would suggest that achieving certainty and predictability is in the second order of importance and that recent economic analysis suggests that it is unattainable as a primary goal. It is clear that any set of competition laws arise necessarily as a result of political choice, and the chosen rules will reflect this first order rationale for their existence.[6] Accordingly, at least to a certain extent, the relevant rules are not mechanical, but discretionary, and require a degree of political value judgment.

Another difficulty in attaining certainty and predictability in practice is the role of economic theory and analysis. On the one hand, legal rules in competition law tend to rely upon the legalistic concept of identifying a wrong. This reliance on a 'wrong' does not fit particularly well with economic analysis. On the other hand, it has been generally noted that competition rules utilise economic theory, itself based on various unobservable assumptions, which seeks to provide fairly clearcut answers reliant on the abstract notions of perfect competition and monopoly. The economic theory of perfect competition forms the basis of the pure competition policy objective at the core of most competition laws. However, the difficulty now being

---

3 Baker, DI, 'US: international co-operation on competition law policy' (1997) International Business Lawyer 473–80.

4 See Nicolaides, P, 'Competition policy in the process of economic integration, an exploration of the forms and limits of co-operation' (1997) 21(1) World Competition 117–39.

5 De Leon, I, 'The dilemma of regulating international competition under the WTO system' [1997] ECLR 162.

6 See Fidler, D, 'Competition law and international relations' (1992) 41 ICLQ 563.

recognised is that, although economic analysis provides us with the general theory about monopoly, it should be used to identify particular behaviour that is harmful. Whether identification is possible, for instance, through law and economics or industrial economics, the implication is that individualised, predictive economic analysis of the particular market will be required to identify harmful behaviour. The most obvious example is in identifying the predictable effects of a merger. Nonetheless, economic analysis does not fit easily with providing certainty and predictability in the law. A final point to remember is that most forms of economic theory are founded on political ideology, for example, the approach based on law and economics is loosely identified with the Chicago school. It is also clear that the need for regulatory authorities to be able to defend their findings on appeal, in a legal setting, drives their policy choices and the manner in which they utilise economic theories.

Globalisation and international co-operation in competition law enforcement

One of the most important trends in recent years has been the globalisation of markets, as discussed in Chapter 2. The international nature of business activity and commerce is indicated by the number of recent competition cases which have involved more than one competition law system. Strangely, it has been observed that although national competition law generally reflects domestic politics and interests, the introduction of nationally-based competition laws has occurred during a period of market globalisation.[7] This increasing globalisation of markets has inevitably required some form of response from competition authorities facing the international aspects of competition law, such as international cartels, world-scale mergers and abuses of dominance on several markets. A competition authority may lack the appropriate remedies to tackle competition problems arising in its jurisdiction where those problems stem from organisations beyond its territory, or there may be the risk of taking action which affects the interests of a third country or is in conflict with measures adopted there. In order to overcome these difficulties, some form of international co-operation appears to be both necessary and desirable. The Organisation for Economic Co-operation and Development (OECD) recognised this in the 1960s and recommended that there should be increased co-operation on anti-competitive practices affecting international trade, a recommendation revised in 1995.[8] No formal system was instituted but many bilateral agreements have arisen consequently. The most important

---

7 See above, Baker, fn 3.

8 Revised recommendation of the Council concerning co-operation between member countries on anti-competitive practices affecting international trade, 27 and 28 July 1995, C(95) 130 final.

example of bilateral co-operation is the Agreement between the Community and the US.[9] This provides for notification of cases affecting the other authority's interests, co-operation and co-ordination of activities, and the agreement also contains provisions on the confidentiality of information exchanged. Importantly, it provides for both negative comity, that is, respect for the other party's enforcement, and positive comity, whereby either party can request the other to act in a matter which may affect its interests.[10] This Agreement was resorted to in recent years in relation to the activities of Microsoft. The Agreement has also been used extensively in merger cases, although the reaction to the *GE/Honeywell* merger and the Commission's 2004 *Microsoft* Decision revealed the limitations of the co-operation process.[11] However, the Agreement has been resorted to, with success, in major mergers including *AOL/Time Warner* and *Exxon/Mobil*. International co-operation is particularly important in the context of mergers because of the likelihood of multiple authorities considering significant mergers between parties with worldwide trading interests. Such large-scale mergers may lead to the requirement of multiple notifications or 'filings' with various competition authorities, and this may in turn result in international disagreements and uncertainty, as in *Boeing/McDonnell Douglas*[12] and *GE/Honeywell* where the Commission prohibited mergers permitted by the US authorities.

It is also in the interests of the private sector to promote co-operation between enforcement agencies in order to reduce uncertainty and delays in its international business transactions. A lingering doubt remains as to the range of co-operation that is possible. Beyond the confines of economic trading blocs, limited co-operation along the lines of the US/EC Agreement is all that seems possible, although perhaps the timescales for decisions and forms of notification could also be standardised. It has been suggested that deeper co-operation, reliant on the adoption of similar substantive rules, is unlikely except within regional blocs that have a degree of economic integration.[13] This integration within regional blocs is exemplified by the establishment of

---

9 Agreement between the Government of the United States of America and the European Communities regarding the application of their competition laws, OJ 1995, L95/47, as corrected by OJ 1995, L131/38 and amended by OJ 1998, L173/28. For a fuller discussion, see Cocuzza, C and Montini, M, 'International antitrust co-operation in a global economy' [1998] ECLR 156 and Canenbley, C and Rosenthal, M 'Co-operation between Antitrust authorities In- and Outside the EU: What does it mean for Multinational corporations?' Part 1 [2005] 2 ECLR 106; Part 2 [2005] 3 ECLR 178.

10 Ibid, Art V.

11 Case IV/M2220, Commission Decision 2004/134/EC *GE/Honeywell*, OJ 2004, L48/1. Commission Decision 2007/53/EC *Microsoft*, OJ 2007, L 32/23. See, also, Burnside, A, 'GE, honey, I sunk the merger' [2002] ECLR 107 and Case IV/M877, Commission Decision 1997/816/EC *Boeing/McDonnell Douglas*, OJ 1997, L336/16.

12 Case IV/M877, Commission Decision 1997/816/EC *Boeing/McDonnell Douglas*, OJ 1997, L336/16.

13 See above, Nicolaides, fn 4.

the European Competition Network (ECN) with its co-ordinated network of National Competition Authorities (NCAs) which applies Community law.[14] On a wider scale, co-operation at a global level is unlikely to proceed beyond basic co-operation in the absence of the convergence of competition laws. In particular, a world competition authority is unlikely to arise in the near or distant future, although the European Commission is seeking to develop matters on a multilateral level through the World Trade Organisation (WTO) and by expanding the scope of existing bilateral agreements.[15] In the near future, competition law convergence is likely to be developed through the auspices of the International Competition Network (ICN), launched in 2001 as a project-orientated, consensus-based informal network of antitrust agencies from developed and developing countries. The ICN does not seek to introduce any form of global competition law but, instead, gradual convergence through understanding of best practice in areas of competition law enforcement.

Changes in substantive Community competition law

This section will briefly review the key developments in relation to the principal Community competition law rules. Article 82 has been revitalised by reducing its focus on exploitative abuses, such as excessive, monopolistic prices. Instead of exploitative abuses, the Commission has been concentrating on exclusionary or anti-competitive types of abuse which are more likely to damage the longer-term competitive structure of the market. Nonetheless, the Community authorities have been criticised for developments under Art 82 which allegedly constitute unnecessary intrusions into lawful and legitimate competitive activity, and it has been argued that the Commission still needs to develop a clearer distinction between unlawful abuse and legitimate competition on the merits.[16] The Court, in *Irish Sugar* and *Microsoft*, emphasised that super-dominant undertakings have to be particularly

14 See Canenbley, C, and Rosenthal, M, 'Co-operation between Antitrust authorities In- and Outside the EU: What does it mean for Multinational corporations?' Part 1 [2005] 2 ECLR 106; Part 2 [2005] 3 ECLR 178.

15 Schaub, A (Director General for Competition), 'International co-operation in antitrust matters: making the point in the wake of the Boeing/MDD proceedings' (1998) EC Competition policy newsletter, Spring, p 3. See, also, Von Meibom, W and Geiger, A, 'A world competition law as an *ultima ratio*' [2002] ECLR 445; and Rodger, BJ, 'Competition policy, liberalism and globalism: a European perspective' (2000) 6 CJEL 289.

16 See Andrews, P, 'Is meeting competition a defence to predatory pricing? – the *Irish Sugar* decision suggests a new approach' [1998] ECLR 49. For critique, see, for instance, Ridyard, D, 'Exclusionary pricing and price discrimination abuses under Article 82 – an economic analysis' [2002] ECLR 286; Kallaugher, J and Sher, B, 'Rebates revisited: anti-competitive effects and exclusionary abuse under Art 82' [2004] ECLR 263.

cautious about their competitive behaviour.[17] In *Irish Sugar* the Court sought to set out a simpler method of demonstrating predatory pricing through selectivity, but the Commission's subsequent policy has been criticised as being confusing for undertakings that will have to decide what type of price competition is legitimate. Case law had suggested that meeting, but not beating, competition would be acceptable. Nonetheless, in *France Télécom v Commission*[18] the CFI made it clear that dominant undertakings had no 'absolute right' to align their prices with those of a competitor, especially where they are potentially abusive through being below cost.

The Commission has been criticised for, in effect, chilling competition but it is clear that the Community authorities are more sceptical about the market practices of 'monopolists' than their US counterparts.[19] In relation to the essential facilities doctrine, the judgment in *Oscar Bronner* certainly indicated the Court's caution regarding its application.[20] This issue is even more problematic when balancing the coexistence of IP rights and competition law. In this context, the *Microsoft* judgment went some way to explaining how a number of the elements of the *Magill/IMS* test should be applied.[21] The most controversial element of the *Magill/IMS* test has always been the 'new product' criteria. The CFI in *Microsoft* made it clear that problems may arise, 'where there is a limitation not only of production or markets, but also of technical development'.[22] It is now clear that those seeking supply must show that the refusal denies them the opportunity to supply a new product or market, or to innovate in the way they provide products or services. Both key aspects of the 2007 *Microsoft* case, interoperability and tying, are being re-examined by the Commission in another investigation into Microsoft.[23]

The Commission is undertaking a full-scale review of the application of exclusionary abuses under Art 82. The European Commission, in December 2005, published a discussion paper to begin a lengthy process of consultation and debate.[24] This review can seen as the end of a process of reform of much

---

17 Case T-228/97 *Irish Sugar v Commission* [1999] ECR II-2969 and Case T-201/04 *Microsoft v Commission*, judgment of 17 September 2007.

18 Case T-339/04 *France Télécom v Commission* [2007] ECR II-521.

19 See Sher, B, 'The last of the steam-powered trains: modernising Article 82' [2004] ECLR 243.

20 See Bergman, M, 'The *Bronner* case – a turning point for the essential facilities doctrine' [2000] ECLR 59. See, also, Case C-418/01 *IMS Health v NDC Health* [2004] ECR I-5039.

21 The *IMS* and *Microsoft* cases have generated an enormous amount of literature. A few of the more balanced examples are: Killick, J, '*IMS* and *Microsoft* Judged in the Cold Light of *IMS*' (2004) 1(2) CompLRev 23; Ong, B, 'Building Brick Barricades and other Barriers to Entry: Abusing a Dominant Position by Refusing to Licence Intellectual Property Rights' [2005] ECLR 213; and, Vezzoso, S, 'The Incentives Balance Test in the EU Microsoft Case: A Pro-Innovation "Economics Based" Approach' [2006] ECLR 382.

22 At para 647.

23 See Commission MEMO/08/19, 14 January 2008.

24 DG Competition discussion paper on the application of Article 82 of the Treaty to exclusionary abuses, Brussels, December 2005.

of EC competition law, including reform of the way the EC handles vertical restraints under Reg 2790/99,[25] the modernisation of the enforcement system under Reg 1/2003,[26] and the merger control provisions under Reg 139/2004.[27] The focus appears to be on moving towards enforcement methodologies that seek to identify when particular behaviour or conduct has demonstrable anti-competitive effects on particular markets, and away from rules that are based on the form of the behaviour or conduct.[28] It will be interesting to observe the result of the review process; a balance must be struck between economic sophistication and workable, enforceable, legal rules.

In relation to Art 81 the most important developments in recent years have been enforcement-related, as discussed below in relation to fines, leniency and the proposed settlements process, although there is a line of interesting cases, notably *Wouters*, on the scope of a Europeanised rule of reason approach within Article 81(1).[29]

The introduction of the new Merger Regulation, Regulation 139/2004,[30] has suggested three main themes in the development of merger policy in the Community. First is the increasing trend towards transparency. The publication of the Commission Guidelines on horizontal and non-horizontal mergers[31] demonstrated the Commission's greater willingness to open up its decision-making to allow the parties to mergers to shape their merger into an acceptable form before seeking Commission approval. The second theme is the development of a case referral system between the Commission and the NCAs. The prior-notification provisions in Art 4 of the Merger Regulation and the revision to Arts 9 and 21, alongside the Commission Notice on case referral,[32] have been utilised frequently and have allowed for more sensitive case handling. The final theme of development stems from the new substantive appraisal test of 'significant impediment to competition'. The introduction of the new test was ostensibly to bring oligopoly cases more clearly into

---

25 OJ 1999, L336/21.

26 OJ 2003, L1/1.

27 OJ 2004, L24/1.

28 For more detailed discussion see, Mertikopoulou, V, 'DG Competition's Discussion Paper on the Application of Article 82 EC to Exclusionary Abuses: the Proposed Economic Reform from a Legal Point of View' [2007] ECLR 241 and Dreher, M, and Adam, M, 'Abuse of Dominance Under Reform – Sound Economics and Established Case Law' [2007] ECLR 278.

29 Case C-309/99 *Wouters* [2002] ECR I-1577.

30 Regulation 139/2004/EC on the control of concentrations between undertakings (the EC Merger Regulation), OJ 2004, L24/1.

31 Commission Notice, Guidelines on the assessment of horizontal mergers under the Council Regulation on the control of concentrations between undertakings, OJ 2004, C31/3, and Commission Notice, Guidelines on the assessment of non-horizontal mergers under the Council Regulation on the control of concentrations between undertakings, 28 November 2007.

32 Commission Notice on case referral in respect of concentrations, OJ 2005, C56/2.

the Merger Regulation, particularly in light of the Commission's problems in the *Airtours* case.[33] The Commission sought to resist the 'substantial lessening of competition' test which has been preferred in several other jurisdictions, although the *Sony/Bertelsmann* saga involving the third party Impala has demonstrated the continuing difficulties for the Commission in the application of the new 'significant impediment' test.[34] An additional issue that has arisen concerns the availability of a damages remedy against the Commission for a party which claims to have suffered loss following an erroneous decision by a Commission to block a merger. We await ECJ clarification of the position.[35]

The State aid rules, outlined in Chapter 7, are potentially the most contentious aspect of Community competition law. The Commission's task, in relation to State aid, has inevitably increased with the enlargement of the Community following the accession of the new Member States, yet this is an area in which decentralised enforcement of the substantive rules continues to play only a limited role. The Commission is trying to balance two potentially conflicting objectives within its State aid remit. On the one hand, the Commission has stressed the need to restrict the availability of State aid, particularly for rescue and restructuring of inefficient firms. On the other hand, the Community recognises the benefits of supporting aid that benefits Community horizontal objectives, such as environmental and regional policy. The Competition Commissioner recognised in 2003 that a number of challenges faced the Community State aid regime. The Commission launched a comprehensive reform of State aid rules and procedures in its State Aid Action Plan in June 2005.[36] The aim was to ensure the State aid rules focus aid measures in order to contribute to the Community Lisbon strategy to enhance the competitiveness of EU industry and create sustainable jobs. The overall policy goal can be defined as 'less and better targeted State aid'. Since the adoption of the Plan, a number of new measures have been introduced, and other measures have been revised or are under revision with a view to completing the modernisation process by 2009. The Autumn 2007 State Aid Scoreboard, published in December 2007, demonstrated, in line with the State Aid Action Plan objective, that overall levels of aid are decreasing and that Member States have steadily reoriented their State aid towards horizontal objectives in the Community interest. Finally, there are two areas that are likely to remain problematic in the near future: the application of State

---

33 Case T-342/99 *Airtours v Commission* [2002] ECR II-2585.
34 Case T-464/04 *Impala v Commission* [2006] ECR II-2289. On appeal Case C-413/06 P *Bertelsmann and Sony Corporation of America v Impala*, judgment of 10 July 2008.
35 Case T-351/03 *Schneider Electric v Commission*, judgment of 11 July 2007. On appeal Case C-440/07 *Commission v Schneider Electric*, pending.
36 State Aid Action Plan, Less and Better targeted State aid: a roadmap for state aid reform 2005–2009, COM(2005) 107 final, Commission press release IP/05/680 7 June 2005.

aid to domestic tax regimes (and derogations or exemptions from such) and the interplay between State aid and public service obligations.[37]

Developments in the enforcement of Community competition law

The enforcement of Community competition law recently underwent dramatic reform in Regulation 1/2003.[38] Probably the most important aspect of Regulation 1/2003 was the provision for an increased level of co-operation between all the authorities involved in the enforcement of Community competition law.[39] This operates through the network of competition authorities, known as the 'European Competition Network' (ECN), incorporating the Commission and all the NCAs. The operation of the ECN is, therefore, central to the success of the new regime; it is notable that between 1 May 2004 and 31 December 2006, 670 cases were pursued under the Community competition rules, and the Commission was involved in the investigation in less than 25% of cases. At one stage it was considered that a future Modernisation II package, involving some form of harmonisation of national NCA powers, procedures and remedies in cases of Community law infringements, would be required. However, the ability to exchange information and engage in dialogue within the ECN has facilitated a certain degree of convergence already,[40] particularly in relation to leniency where virtually all Member States now have some form of leniency programme and the ECN has developed a Model Leniency Programme.[41]

The other important issue raised by modernisation is about the ability of those who suffer through violations of competition law to utilise 'self-help' remedies through the domestic courts, rather than seeking administrative help from the Commission or the NCAs. Private enforcement has proved to be vital for the development of the US enforcement system and it is hoped

---

37 See Communication from the Commission, Services of general interest, including social services of general interest: a new European commitment, COM(2007) 725 final.

38 Regulation 1/2003/EC on the implementation of the rules on competition laid down in Arts 81 and 82 of the EC Treaty, OJ 2003, L1/1.

39 See Dekeyser, K, and Jaspers, M, 'A New Era of ECN Cooperation, Achievements and Challenges with Special Focus on Work in the Leniency Field' (2007) 30(1) World Competition 3.

40 See ECN Working Group on Cooperation Issues, 'Results of the questionnaire on the reform of the Member States (MS) national competition laws after EC Regulation No. 1/2003', as of May 18, 2007, at http://ec.europa.eu/comm/competition/ecn/index_en.html, which demonstrates the increasing degree of convergence in Member States' procedural and remedial rules.

41 See Dekeyser, K, and Jaspers, M, 'A New Era of ECN Cooperation, Achievements and Challenges with Special Focus on Work in the Leniency Field' (2007) 30(1) World Competition 3. The ECN Model programme is published on the ECN website, http://ec.europa.eu/comm/competition/ecn/index_en.html. See, further discussion in Chapter 5.

that this will also be true for the Community.[42] Some steps have been taken to facilitate private enforcement in terms of both EC law[43] and UK law,[44] but the limited number of successful private actions to date tends to suggest that a great many issues will need to be clarified before private enforcement will play a major role in the development of either EC or UK competition law. The ongoing discussions following the Commission's Green Paper on private actions, the OFT's recommendations, and the Commission White Paper on Damages actions indicates the number of issues that potentially stand in the way of private litigants.[45]

The Commission's fining policy is a central pillar of its enforcement strategy and its 1998 Notice was revised in 2006 in three principal ways to further enhance deterrence.[46] There has been a dramatic increase in the overall fines imposed by the Commission, particularly in relation to cartels, in recent years. The Community leniency policy was also revised in 2006 to enhance transparency and further encourage leniency applications to destabilise cartels.

Following a public consultation the Commission adopted, in June 2008, a Regulation providing, in cartel cases, for a direct settlement process whereby infringing parties may be granted a fine rebate conditional upon acceptance, within a set deadline, of the commission of the infringement, admission of liability, and the level of fine. The faster and simplified procedure envisaged will, it is argued, lead to a more efficient use of enforcement resources.[47] The expedited procedure will provide for a 10% discount on

---

42 See Jones, CA, *Private Enforcement of Antitrust Law in the EU, UK, and USA*, 1999, Oxford: OUP.

43 See Case C-453/99 *Courage Ltd v Bernard Crehan* [2001] ECR I-6297; [2001] 5 CMLR 28, and Komninos, AP, 'New prospects for private enforcement of EC competition law: *Courage v Crehan* and the Community right to damages' (2002) 39 CML Rev 447. See the Ashurst Report, 'Study on the Conditions of claims for damages in case of infringement of EC competition rules', available at http://ec.europa.eu/comm/competition/antitrust/others/actions_for_damages/study.html; and subsequent Commission Green Paper on damages actions for breach of the EC antitrust rules, COM (2005) 672, 19 December 2005, and associated staff working document, SEC (2005) 1732. See, also, Pheasant, J, 'Damages Actions for Breach of the EC Antitrust Rules – The European Commission's Green Paper' [2006] ECLR 365.

44 See ss 17–20 of the Enterprise Act 2002.

45 Commission Green Paper – Damages actions for breach of the EC antitrust rules, COM(2005) 672 final; Private actions in competition law: effective redress for consumers and business. Recommendations from the Office of Fair Trading, OFT916resp; and, White Paper on Damages actions for breach of the EC antitrust rules, COM(2008) 165 final. See also Commission Staff Working Paper accompanying the White Paper on Damages actions for breach of the EC antitrust rules, SEC(2008) 404.

46 Guideline on the Method of setting fines imposed pursuant to Article 23(2) of Regulation 1/2003, OJ 2006 C 210/2.

47 Regulation 622/2008/EC, OJ 2008, L171/3. See Chapter 5 for further discussion.

the fine to be imposed; although there are clearly implications in such a system for: third party rights, due process and 'fair trial' objections, leniency incentives, and follow-on private enforcement actions.

New directions for competition law

There are a number of developing issues that competition law systems are beginning to confront and which are likely to be at the forefront of debate in the years ahead. At this early stage in the development of those issues it is only possible to outline core issues, rather than to undertake a fuller discussion.

Criminalisation

The criminalisation of aspects of competition law in the UK indicates that the enforcement model chosen by the UK, whilst drawing from the Community model in the 1998 Act, also borrows from the US model in the 2002 Act. Criminalisation should increase the deterrent effect of the competition law regime in the UK, subject to high-profile successful prosecutions,[48] but it also raises a number of more difficult questions.[49] By moving away from the Community model, the criminalisation of cartel involvement within the UK raises issues of concurrency. Prosecution of a cartel's ringleaders may come into conflict with other Member States', or the Commission's, attempts to rely on the Community prohibition.[50] Such problems could also become much more widespread if other Member States follow the UK's lead and adopt their own criminal sanctions. The adoption of national criminal sanctions may threaten the Commission's ability to act as the prime enforcer with regard to cartels, as the Commission may have to wait until the end of the various criminal procedures across the Community before it can take action. Discussions surrounding the need for criminalisation, and the form it should take, can also be seen in other jurisdictions, particularly Australia.[51]

---

48 The first prosecution under the Cartel Offence is now complete with 3 individuals being sentenced to between 2 and a half and 3 years, see OFT Press Release 72/08, 11 June 2008.

49 On the role of criminalisation in increasing deterrence see, Whelan, P, 'A Principled Argument for Personal Criminal Sanctions as Punishment under EC Cartel Law' (2007) 4(1) Comp LRev 7.

50 See, generally, Nazzini, R, 'Criminalisation of cartels and concurrent proceedings' [2003] ECLR 483.

51 Fisse, B, 'The Australian Cartel Criminalisation Proposals: An Overview and Critique' (2007) 4(1) Comp LRev 51 and Beaton-Wells, C, 'Capturing the Criminality of Hard-Core Cartels: The Australian Proposal' (2007) 31(3) Melbourne Uni LRev 674.

Human rights

As with any area involving the State's enforcement of legal provisions, human rights and the rights of the defence are becoming increasingly important. While competition law is rarely enforced against natural persons, it is clear that legal persons do have 'human' rights and can rely on the provisions of the European Convention on Human Rights and the Human Rights Act to protect them.[52] In a competition law context it is probably Art 6 of the Convention, the right to a fair trial, that is of the greatest importance, although other rights may also come into play.[53] The debate surrounding access to the file and the privilege against self-incrimination has already been discussed in Chapter 2, but there is scope for many more issues to come to the fore, particularly with regard to the new cartel offence in the UK.

Resale price maintenance

It is generally accepted in the European Community that resale price maintenance, where minimum prices are set in vertical relationships, for instance between manufacturer and retailer, are prohibited. However, the *Leegin* judgment of the US Supreme Court, advocated a more lenient approach to RPM. This approach is also reflected in a recent academic debate on the issue, which suggests that the practice can be pro-competitive by ensuring the provision of pre-sale promotional services and an increase in the number of retail outlets.[54] Nonetheless, probably the greatest publicity has been attracted by enforcement under the Chapter I prohibition in relation to RPM schemes, which the OFT has frequently condemned, and it will be interesting to observe whether UK and Community authorities and/or courts will move towards the newer more lenient approach taken by the US.

Competition in the 'new' economy

There is a range of issues at the interface between the development of the 'new economy' and competition law which is too detailed for this book to address, but which the Commission and Community law, in particular, are already starting to tackle. One of the key issues in many 'new economy' cases is the impact of markets that exhibit network effects. These are products where the value of a product to an individual user is increased the larger the

---

52 See, for example, Almeye, E, 'The interplay between human rights and competition law in the EU' [2004] ECLR 33.
53 See, Andreangeli, A, 'Toward an EU Competition Court: "Article-6-Proofing" Antitrust Proceedings before the Commission?' (2007) 30(4) World Comp 59.
54 US Supreme Court, June 28, 2007, *Leegin Creative Leather Products Inc. v PSKS Inc., DBA Kay's Closet . . . Kay's Shoes* 551 U.S. (2007). See Kneepens, M, 'Resale Price Maintenance: Economics Call for a More Balanced Approach' [2007] ECLR 656.

number of other users the product has. Essentially the user is buying into a network of products, often where the products can communicate with others, rather than buying a stand-alone product. In such markets one network can reach a 'critical mass' where a single network, through its ubiquity, provides a uniquely valuable offer. An example of the impact of such effects can be seen in *Microsoft*.[55] Rather than the old economy model of competition within a market, the new economy model tends to lead to cyclical competition for a market – competition occurring to decide the dominant provider in each generation of the technology.[56]

The State and the liberal professions

Competition law, at both the domestic and Community level, is being developed in relation to areas of the economy previously considered sacrosanct. First, there is the controversial debate concerning the extent to which competition law applies to State entities. Chapter 7, in particular, indicated the sensitivities involved in this area, particularly in assessing what types of market involvement render a State body's activities to be those of an undertaking and which are exposed to the full impact of competition law. It will be interesting to observe the application of the fact-specific solidarity basis across the range of state activity in 'social markets'. More straightforward is the debate on the application of competition law to the professions, notably including the legal profession. At the domestic level, the exclusion of certain professional rules from the Competition Act 1998 has been deemed to be no longer appropriate, and it is evident that both the Office of Fair Trading (OFT) and the European Commission are desperate to enhance competition generally in the professions and remove antiquated practices and restrictions.[57]

---

55 Case T-201/04 *Microsoft v Commission* [2007] 5 CMLR 846.
56 Consider the format wars in the video marketplace between VHS and Betamax in VCRs and between Blu-Ray and HD-DVD in HD video. See, also, Graham, C and Smith, F, *Competition, Regulation and the New Economy*, 2004, Oxford: Hart; Bishop, B and Caffarra, C, 'Merger control in "new markets" ' [2001] ECLR 31; Veljanovski, C, 'EC antitrust in the new economy: is the European Commission's view of the network economy right?' [2001] ECLR 115; and Ahlborn, C, Evans, DS and Padilla, AJ, 'Competition policy in the new economy: is European competition law up to the challenge?' [2001] ECLR 156.
57 See Commission Communication, Report on competition in professional services COM(2004) 83 final, 9 February 2004 followed in September 2005 by Report, Professional Services – Scope for More Reform COM (2005) 405 final, 5 September 2005; OFT Report, Competition in professions, OFT 328, March 2001; and, the super-complaint submitted by Which? in May 2007, relating to restrictions on business structures and access in the Scottish Legal Profession which resulted in OFT Response to Which?'s super-complaint: 'Restrictions on business structures and direct access in the Scottish legal profession', OFT 946 and a Scottish Government commitment to change the Scottish legal profession by removing a range of current restrictions, see OFT Press Release 178/07, 19 December 2007.

The revised UK competition regime post-Competition and Enterprise Acts

UK competition law has undergone major reform twice since 1998. The Competition Act 1998 radically altered UK competition law by introducing, as of 1 March 2000, the Chapter I and Chapter II prohibitions, modelled on Arts 81 and 82, respectively, with the primary objective of harmonising domestic law and Community law and avoiding double burdens on business. The main provisions of the Act were outlined in Chapters 1 and 2 of this book and the Chapter I and II prohibitions were discussed in Chapters 3–5.[58] In the first eight years there has been considerable practice under the Act; the OFT has adopted a number of decisions utilising its enhanced investigatory and fining powers,[59] and the Competition Appeal Tribunal (CAT) has dealt with a wide variety of issues through the appeals process. In 2001, the Government proposed further changes to the UK competition law structure.[60] The Enterprise Act 2002 was introduced and further reformed UK competition law, repealing the monopoly and merger provisions of the Fair Trading Act 1973 and making a number of other important changes, including the creation of a criminal offence for involvement in cartels. It also created a specialist competition tribunal, the CAT; the Act's provisions will allow the CAT to enhance private enforcement of both EC and UK competition law.[61] The 2002 Act also marked a more explicit recognition of the importance of the consumer interest in competition law: first, by providing enhanced rights to complain for consumer bodies ('super-complaints'); and secondly, by facilitating representative actions before the CAT and, more generally, by the requirement on the Competition Commission to assess any 'customer benefits' during a merger or market investigation. Interestingly, there has been a considerable focus on financial services in market investigations undertaken under the Enterprise Act 2002, with an emphasis on consumer protection and remedies aimed generally at reducing prices/interest rates by enhancing transparency and increasing consumer awareness.

In 2007, the OFT imposed a then record fine of £121.5m on British Airways for colluding with Virgin Atlantic in increasing prices payable for long-haul passenger fuel surcharges under the 1998 Act Chapter I prohibition. This

---

58 See Rodger, BJ and MacCulloch, A (eds), *The UK Competition Act: A New Era for UK Competition Law*, 2000, Oxford: Hart.

59 See, for instance, Rodger, B, 'Early steps to a mature competition law system: case law developments in the first eighteen months of the Competition Act 1998' [2002] ECLR 52 and Rodger, BJ, 'Competition Law Litigation in the UK Courts: A Study of All Cases to 2004' Part 1 [2006] ECLR 241, Part 2 [2006] ECLR 279, Part 3 [2006] ECLR 341.

60 HM Treasury and DTI, *Productivity in the UK: Enterprise and the Productivity Challenge*, June 2001, and *Productivity and Enterprise: A World Class Competition Regime*, Cm 5233, 31 July 2001.

61 See, in particular, Case 1078/7/9/0 *Consumers' Association v JJB Sports*, before the CAT, which settled in 2007.

case, together with a number of other decisions, highlights the important role played by the fining powers under the 1998 Act and that deterrence is a key aspect of the imposition of penalties. Furthermore, like the European Commission, the OFT has been developing its policy on remedies to enhance compliance and effective case management by considering the swift conclusion of enforcement proceedings by administrative settlements, loosely akin to plea-bargaining processes in criminal law. One key development relates to the role afforded the CAT to undertake judicial review of any decision by the OFT or CC. The possibility of review was demonstrated first in *IBA Health Ltd v OFT*;[62] the next two cases challenging OFT decisions also involved mergers in the pharmaceutical industry, successfully in *Celesio v OFT*.[63] The first challenge to a CC decision followed the September 2005 Report by the Commission in relation to the acquisition by Somerfield of 115 stores from Morrison supermarkets, which concluded that the acquisition would lead to a substantial lessening of competition in 12 local grocery markets in Great Britain, and was unsuccessful.[64]

Practical implications

Instituting an effective compliance programme

The practical importance of ensuring that competition laws are complied with cannot be underestimated.[65] Any undertaking must be aware of the potential impact of both national and Community competition rules. The laws of, for instance, other Member States or the US may be applicable to the activities of UK-based companies. This can affect an organisation in all aspects of its activities, such as its form of contracting for distribution and purchasing, any pricing policies adopted, its responses to competition in the market, any governmental funding acquired and also the purchase of assets or shares of another organisation. The implications of a lack of awareness or the inability to deal with the effect of competition law are significant. A restriction in an agreement for the distribution of products may be null and void. Governmental aid may need to be refunded with interest. A past takeover may be unravelled and fines may be imposed. A planned takeover may be prevented by the authorities. Parties may be required to divest certain assets for a merger to proceed or to give commitments as to future pricing

---

62 [2003] CAT 27; on appeal *OFT v IBA Health Ltd* [2004] EWCA Civ 142.

63 [2006] CAT 9. Cf *Unichem Ltd v OFT* [2005] CAT 8.

64 *Somerfield plc v Competition Commission* [2006] CAT 4. See, also, *Stericycle International LLC and others v Competition Commission* [2006] CAT 21. See, generally, Robertson, A, Lester, M, and Love, S, 'Judicial Review in the United Kingdom of Competition and State Aid Decisions' Pt I [2007] ECLR 553, Pt II [2007] ECLR 585.

65 See Armstrong, J, 'Compliance programmes' [1995] ECLR 147 and Rodger, BJ, 'Compliance with competition law: a view from industry' [2000] CLLR 249.

and market behaviour. An undertaking may be ordered, either by a court or a competition authority, to resume supplies to a competitor. The European Commission can impose fines of up to 10% of an undertaking's worldwide turnover, a very significant and practical threat, in addition to imposing daily penalties for noncompliance with Arts 81 and 82 EC.[66] Damages, and interim remedies, can be sought in the national courts in respect of breaches of Arts 81 and 82 and illegally provided State aid. The position is similar under the Competition Act 1998. For all of these reasons it is necessary for a company to establish an effective compliance programme and ensure that its directors and employees are both aware of competition law's existence and adequately prepared to follow it.

An effective compliance programme would include, at least, the following features:

a   effective communication to all staff, through a policy statement, of the fact that compliance with competition law is a core value of the organisation;
b   senior management should be knowledgable about, and keen to conform with, competition rules and discipline any breaches;
c   an established education programme that updates management on current competition law developments;
d   a system of reporting on compliance with competition law; and
e   a satisfactory policy on record-keeping to ensure the retention of relevant documentation.

It is obvious that companies are becoming increasingly aware of the need for effective in-house compliance programmes, and many conferences now provide advice on the effective implementation of such a policy. Effective compliance can be both costly and time consuming for employees and, particularly, directors. However, it is clear that the benefits of an effective programme may be significant in helping to avoid potentially illegal activity with all its associated uncertainty, costs and the resources wasted during a competition investigation. This is probably even more important in the UK following the introduction of the Competition Act 1998 with its increased enforcement powers. Indeed, it is clear that business practice in the UK is not nearly as well-evolved as in the US where antitrust compliance is taken very seriously.[67] This difference may be accounted for by the litigious nature of US

---

66 It is clear from the longstanding dispute between Microsoft and the Commission following its 2004 Decision that the penalties for noncompliance may exceed the penalties for the original infringement; see Commission Press Release IP/08/318, 'Antitrust: Commission imposes €899 million penalty on Microsoft for non-compliance with March 2004 Decision', 27 February 2008.
67 O'Meara, B, 'Corporate antitrust compliance programmes' [1998] ECLR 59.

antitrust lawyers, the longer history of antitrust enforcement and also the consideration given by enforcement authorities to the existence of an antitrust compliance programme within organisations. Nonetheless, it is clear that business compliance with both Community and UK competition law has increased considerably in recent years.[68] A final form of compliance education requires awareness of the effect of other competition law regimes. This is partly due to the increasing globalisation of markets and is also necessary as a result of the extraterritorial enforcement of certain competition laws.[69] In particular, with mergers there has to be practical awareness of the different filing requirements in each potentially applicable competition law system.[70]

Pigeon-holing in market analysis

Pigeon-holing is a common problem recognised by economists and practitioners in the field. This can refer to two related issues. The first is that competition laws tend to be fairly formalistic, although the public interest test under the Fair Trading Act 1973 was a notable exception. Although competition laws tend to be based, at least loosely, on economics, competition law has struggled to accurately translate the economic concern into the form of a legal wrong with which it can deal. A classic example of the translation problem is the way competition laws generally struggle to deal effectively with oligopolies. These issues are pigeon-holed into legal terminology, such as anti-competitive agreement and collective dominance. It is crucial when determining the existence of a dominant position to assess the market and market share of an undertaking, even though many economists would clearly argue that this is formalistic and unnecessary in assessing market power.

The pigeon-holing of types of conduct into legal forms is exemplified by the competition law treatment of vertical restraints and mergers discussed in Chapters 4 and 6, respectively. All competition practitioners should be aware of pigeon-holing. For instance, in relation to vertical restraints, the Commission's approach prior to the introduction of the vertical agreements Regulation, Regulation 2790/99, was criticised as formalistically pigeon-holing types of restriction and agreements, for reasons of convenience and without valid competition reasons.[71] The classic examples were the block exemptions in relation to, for example, exclusive distribution. These block exemptions set out the parameters for the exemption of a particular type of agreement. If parties were interested in a specific form of distribution

---

68 See above, Rodger, fn 65.
69 See Griffin, JP, 'Antitrust aspects of cross-border mergers and acquisitions' [1998] ECLR 12.
70 Ibid.
71 See Hawk, B, 'System failure: vertical restraints and EC competition law' (1995) 32 CML Rev 973.

agreement, most suited to their economic, distribution and other needs, their legal advisers would advise them that it would be preferable to adapt the agreement to the approved legal form. Otherwise, the parties would have to proceed according to the vagaries, uncertainty and delay of the individual exemption process. However, the sea change in vertical restraints policy, through the vertical agreements Regulation and Guidelines,[72] demonstrates the more recent emphasis on an economics-based approach focusing on market power and inter-brand competition. The new position is less formalistic and does not result in the same degree of pigeon-holing of commercial activities. A similar move away from formalism can be seen in the approach suggested by the Commission's Discussion Paper on Exclusionary Abuses.[73] This focuses on analysing the effects of certain behaviour on particular markets rather than the form of the behaviour itself.

Whistle-blowing and leniency

It is commonly accepted that the most pernicious type of competitive activity is the formation of a horizontal cartel, such as was uncovered by the Commission in *Polypropylene*.[74] It is evident that new cartels are regularly being uncovered by domestic competition authorities and the Commission. Accordingly, there have been efforts to enhance attempts to tackle cartels. In the UK, a Cartels Task Force was created in 1994 in order to increase general awareness of the problem and to encourage people to inform the OFT about any secret agreements or cartels they believe to be in operation.[75] The concern about deterring secret cartels was a primary reason for the introduction of the new Chapter I prohibition under the Competition Act 1998.[76] However, it is notoriously difficult to detect a secret cartel, especially as parties are unlikely to maintain any formal documentation of their collective conspiracy. For a number of years the US antitrust authorities have recognised that the best method to detect cartels is by an effective amnesty programme, providing amnesty or leniency to companies which approach the authorities to 'confess their sins' and to provide evidence of the cartel in which they participated. The US Corporate Leniency Programme (CLP) is considered to be the single greatest tool available to anti-cartel enforcers, and it works by destabilising cartels and creating distrust between participants

---

72 Regulation 2790/1999/EC, OJ 1999, L336/21 and Guidelines on vertical restraints, OJ 2000, C291/1.
73 DG Competition discussion paper on the application of Article 82 of the Treaty to exclusionary abuses, December 2005.
74 Commission Decision 86/398/EEC, OJ 1986, L230/1. Upheld, on appeal, in Case T-7/89 *Hercules NV v Commission* [1991] ECR II-1711; [1992] 4 CMLR 84.
75 See *Annual Report of the Director General of Fair Trading*, 1994, p 48.
76 See Peretz, G, 'Detection and deterrence of secret cartels under the UK Competition Bill' [1998] ECLR 145.

and, in effect, creating a race to the Department of Justice by informants.[77] Part of the reason for the success of the US CLP has been its transparency and the degree to which immunity can be predicted by the parties, as this transparency is a crucial factor in deliberations by a company's board as to whether to approach the authorities. One downside is that leniency provides no limited protection from private litigation being raised following a leniency application.[78] The Commission sought to take on the experience of the US CLP by introducing, in relation to Art 81 EC, a Notice on the reduction of fines in cartel cases in 1996.[79] Under the 1996 Notice, the Commission indicated that parties to a cartel in breach of Art 81(1) may have their fines reduced by the Commission, at its discretion, on the basis of criteria set out in the Notice. The Commission Notice provided a sliding scale of possible reductions in fine according to which of the various requirements in the Notice are complied with. The likelihood of a company making a leniency application and blowing the whistle on fellow conspirators depends on a number of factors. In any one case the company's decision-makers will have to consider the likely level of fines, the seriousness of the cartel and the importance of its role within the cartel, the likelihood of detection including the uncertain state of knowledge of the Commission, any continuing business relationships it may have with the other companies involved, any effects on its reputation, and the possibility that damages actions may subsequently be raised against it by parties allegedly suffering damages as a result of the operation of the cartel. In each case the company will have to undertake a cost/benefit analysis of these factors. The inherent uncertainties of such a process make any decision difficult to predict.[80] Criticisms of the 1996 Notice, in particular the lack of transparency and predictability in its application, ensured that it was a failure and very few applications were made. The Commission issued a revised Notice in 2002[81] in order to enhance the transparency and effectiveness of the leniency scheme.[82] The Notice was further revised in 2006.[83] The revised Notice makes it much clearer what information must be provided in order for full leniency to be granted, enough to trigger a

---

77 Riley, A, 'Cartel Whistleblowing: toward an American model' (2002) MJECL 67.

78 Since 2004 any company who is awarded US corporate leniency and co-operates also benefits when facing private compensation claims; they are only required to pay single, rather than treble, damages and are no longer jointly and severally liable with their co-conspirators.

79 Commission Notice on the non-imposition or reduction of fines in cartel cases, OJ 1996, C207/4.

80 See Hornsby, S and Hunter, J, 'New incentives for "whistle blowing": will the EC Commission's notice bear fruit?' [1997] ECLR 38.

81 Commission Notice on immunity from fines and reduction of fines in cartel cases, OJ 2002, C45/3.

82 Arbault, F and Peiro, F, 'The Commission's new notice on immunity and reduction of fines in cartel cases: building on success' (2002) ECN, June 2002, 17.

83 Commission Notice on Immunity from fines and reduction of fines in cartel cases, OJ 2006, C298/1.

'targeted investigation', and sets up a marker system allowing an applicant to place a marker while they gather together the necessary material.[84] The OFT has introduced a similar leniency programme for whistle-blowers in relation to the Competition Act 1998.[85] It should be noted that while the majority of Member States have introduced leniency programmes any divergences in their application could result in inconsistency in the application of Art 81 within the ECN. To harmonise the application of Art 81 and ensure that leniency policies are more coordinated the ECN published its Model Leniency Policy to guide the Member States in best practice in this area.[86]

The position of competitor and customer complainants

Complainants generally have two options as to how to proceed. The first is to complain to the relevant NCAs and/or the Commission in respect of alleged anti-competitive behaviour. The second is to seek a remedy through the appropriate national court. It should be noted that the Community has specific rules regarding the rights of complainants and the available remedies in relation to State aid and mergers.[87] Usually, the complainant can pursue both options of administrative complaint and/or litigation in the courts. If a domestic court deals with the issue after a Commission decision has been made, then the Commission decision is binding on the court.[88] Otherwise, the court has to be wary of taking a decision which may conflict with that of the Commission. However, the options may be more limited for the complainant if the Commission decides not to pursue the complaint. The rights of the complainant in this regard, under Arts 230 and 232, have been the subject of intense scrutiny. In *Automec (No 2)*,[89] the Court confirmed that the Commission has different priorities in dealing with complaints and may refuse to deal with cases that do not have sufficient Community interest. This would be the case where a claimant could secure adequate protection before their national courts. Following the adoption of Regulation 1/2003 the Commission issued a Notice on the handling of complaints by the Commission

---

84 See Sandhu, J, 'The European Commission's Leniency Policy: A Success' [2007] ECLR 148.

85 See *Leniency in Cartel Cases*, OFT 436.

86 ECN Model Leniency Programme, 29 September 2006.

87 See Nordberg, C, 'Judicial remedies for private parties under the State aid procedure' (1997) 24(1) LIEI 35; and Robertson, A, Lester, M, and Love, S, 'Judicial Review in the United Kingdom of Competition and State Aid Decisions' Pt I [2007] ECLR 553, Pt II [2007] ECLR 585.

88 See Cumming, G, '*Iberian UK Limited v BPB Industries plc*' [1997] 8 ECLR 534, regarding *Iberian UK Ltd v BPB Industries plc* [1996] 2 CMLR 601 and Case C-344/98 *Masterfoods v HB Ice Cream* [2001] 4 CMLR 14. Cf *Crehan v Inntrepreneur Pub Co (CPC)* [2006] UKHL 38, [2007] 1 AC 333, HL, see Hanley, C, 'The abandonment of deference' (2007) 44(3) CMLRev 817.

89 [1992] 5 CMLR 431.

under Arts 81 and 82 EC.[90] The Notice affirms the complementary nature of administrative and private enforcement action and encourages complainants to pursue remedies in the national courts. Finally, the Notice explains the procedure, and the limitations established in Court jurisprudence, notably *Automec*, for the treatment of complaints under Art 7(2) of Regulation 1/2003.

As complainants may only have the option of seeking remedies in the appropriate national court the Commission, in 1993, in the original Notice on co-operation between the Commission and national courts,[91] sought to enhance awareness of this option. Community jurisprudence during the late 1990s, in particular, sought to ensure that adequate and effective remedies were available in the national courts,[92] although there has been very little reported case law in relation to Community competition law throughout the Community. Although more actions are being raised and settled a number of outstanding issues needed to be resolved, such as what types of remedy are available, which third parties may sue for damages, and the appropriate basis for quantification of damages. Despite an increase in litigation in the national courts involving Community competition law, there has, as yet, been only one reported court decision awarding damages in the UK, in *Crehan*, although ultimately even this award was overturned by the House of Lords.[93] The Court of Justice's ruling in the *Crehan* reference,[94] discussed in Chapter 2, has, to an extent, clarified the requirement for national legal systems to make available appropriate legal redress in respect of breaches of Community competition law. In particular, the Court of Appeal subsequently noted that 'the effect of the ECJ decision was to put its imprimatur on the particular claim of Mr Crehan, holding that a right to the type of damages he claimed was conferred on him by Community law'.[95]

Nonetheless, the dearth of reported cases gives an understated impression of the number of competition-related actions, largely due to the frequency

---

90 OJ 2004, C101/65.

91 OJ 1993, C39/6.

92 See, for example, Cases C-46 and 48/93 *Brasserie du Pêcheur SA v Bundesrepublik Deutschland* [1996] ECR I-1029.

93 See *Crehan v Inntrepreneur Pub Co (CPC)* [2004] EWCA Civ 637, [2004] 2 Eu LR 693, CA. See Andreangeli, A, '*Courage Ltd v Crehan* and the Enforcement of Article 81 before National Courts' [2004] ECLR 758; *Crehan v Inntrepreneur Pub Co (CPC)* [2006] UKHL 38, [2007] 1 AC 333, HL, see Hanley, C, 'The abandonment of deference' (2007) 44(3) CMLRev 817. For general discussion of private litigation in the UK courts, see Rodger, B, 'Competition Law Litigation in the UK Courts: A Study of All Cases to 2004', Pt 1 [2006] ECLR 241, Pt II [2006] ECLR 279, Pt III [2006] ECLR 341.

94 Case C-453/99 *Courage Ltd v Crehan* [2001] ECR I-6297; [2001] 5 CMLR 28. Komninos, A, 'New Prospects for private enforcement of EC Competition Law: *Courage v Crehan* and the Community right to damages' (2002) 39 CML Rev 447–87.

95 *Crehan v Inntrepreneur Pub Co CPC* [2004] EWCA Civ 637, [2004] EuLR 693, at para 167.

with which actions are settled prior to a final hearing.[96] The European Court has also sought to ensure the effectiveness of national remedies, although this is a slow process.[97] Litigants have a number of obstacles to overcome in order to succeed in damages actions for breach of competition law,[98] including, but not limited to: gathering evidence and court discovery procedures; quantification of loss; causation; and establishing the jurisdiction of the court.[99] This was confirmed by the *Ashurst Report*,[100] which reported to the Commission that private damages actions were 'completely underdeveloped' throughout the Community. Following the *Ashurst Report*, the Commission published a Green Paper on damages actions for breach of the EC antitrust rules,[101] assessing a range of potential options to facilitate private competition law litigation in the national courts.[102] The OFT has published a series of recommendations which sets out these issues in a UK context.[103] A White Paper was published in April 2008 and makes a number of interesting suggestions that would require the adaptation of civil procedure within the Member States.[104] The proposals are based on the principle that all Community citizens who suffer damage through antitrust violations should be able to claim full compensation, enhanced deterrence through private actions being incidental to the compensation principle. The proposals include: guaranteed standing for all indirect purchasers, potentially through representative and opt-in collective actions; a minimum level of disclosure *inter partes*; the binding effect of NCA Decisions, when enforcing the Community prohibitions, across the Community; the limitation of the requirement of fault within a

---

96 See Rodger, B, 'Private Enforcement of Competition Law, The Hidden Story: Competition Litigation Settlements in the UK 2000–2005' [2008] 29(2) ECLR 96.

97 See, for instance, Case C-295/04 *Manfredi v Lloyd Adriatico Assicurazioni SpA* [2006] ECR I-6619.

98 Kon, S and Maxwell, A, 'Enforcement in national courts of the EC and new UK competition rules: obstacles to effective enforcement' [1998] ECLR 443.

99 See *Provimi Ltd v Aventis Animal Nutrition SA* [2003] EWHC 961, [2003] 2 All ER (Comm) 683.

100 Study on the Conditions of claims for damages in case of infringement of EC competition rules, available at http://ec.europa.eu/comm/competition/antitrust/others/actions_for_damages/study.html.

101 COM (2005) 672, 19 December 2005, and associated staff working document, SEC (2005) 1732.

102 Pheasant, J, 'Damages Actions for Breach of the EC Antitrust Rules – The European Commission's Green Paper' [2006] ECLR 365; Brkan, M, 'Procedural Aspects of Private Enforcement of EC Antitrust Law: Heading Toward New Reforms?' (2005) 28(4) World Competition 479; and, Hodges, C, 'Competition Enforcement, Regulation and Civil Justice: What is the Case? (2006) 43(5) CMLRev 1381.

103 Private actions in competition law: effective redress for consumers and business. Recommendations from the Office of Fair Trading, OFT916resp.

104 White Paper on Damages actions for breach of the EC antitrust rules, COM(2008) 165 final. See also, Commission Staff Working Paper accompanying the White Paper on Damages actions for breach of the EC antitrust rules, SEC(2008) 404.

private action; a non-binding framework to facilitate the calculation of damages; the availability of the passing-on defence to defendants, but a rebuttable presumption that damage has been passed on to indirect purchasers; the extension of limitation periods to account for administrative enforcement procedures; cost allocations rules; and protection for leniency applicants.

In the UK, prior to the Competition Act 1998, a complainant enjoyed virtually no means of redress. For instance, under the Fair Trading Act a complaint could be made about some form of monopoly behaviour or merger. However, thereafter there was little possibility of action. At all stages the exercise of discretion was involved in determining whether to refer an issue to the Competition Commission, whether behaviour was against the public interest and ultimately as to whether enforcement action could be taken. The position remains broadly similar under the Enterprise Act 2002, in relation to merger and market investigations, although there is specific provision for judicial review of decisions taken in relation to both types of investigation; this has been resorted to with increasing frequency, as outlined above.

Under the Competition Act 1998 the position has clearly improved for complainants. If they can satisfy the criteria of being interested third parties[105] they can appeal against OFT decisions in relation to the prohibitions. More importantly, the Act was intended to provide for effective enforcement by allowing third parties to sue, and there is a developing, albeit limited, body of case law in relation to the prohibitions.[106] Furthermore, the Enterprise Act 2002 made further provision for encouraging private actions in relation to breaches of the 1998 Act prohibitions, and, under the provisions in the 2002 Act, the CAT is likely to develop as the specialist competition court for the UK in the years ahead.[107] An example is the follow-on consumer representative action under these provisions in relation to Replica Kits, *The Consumers' Association v JJB Sports plc*, which was settled out of court in January 2008 following an agreement by JJB to pay consumers who were unlawfully overcharged £20 each. It demonstrates the potential for private enforcement via the CAT under these provisions.[108]

---

105 Section 47 provides that third parties with a sufficient interest, and bodies representing such persons, may appeal to the CAT in connection with decisions taken by the OFT in relation to the prohibitions.

106 See, Robertson, A, 'Litigating under the Competition Act 1998: the early case law' [2002] Comp LJ 335. See also Rodger, B, 'Competition Law Litigation in the UK Courts: A Study of All Cases to 2004', Pt 1 [2006] ECLR 241, Pt II [2006] ECLR 279, Pt III [2006] ECLR 341.

107 See, for instance, *HealthCare at Home Ltd v Genzyme Ltd* [2006] CAT 29, a judgment for interim relief by the CAT, although the case subsequently settled out of court.

108 Case 1078/7/9/07 *Consumers' Association v JJB Sports*. See also 'Private Actions in Competition Law: effective redress for consumers and business' OFT 916resp; see OFT press release 162/07, 26 November 2007.

Discussion

1   Should competition law provide settled rules or does it need to constantly adapt and reinvent itself?
2   What do you consider to be the key issues and challenges facing EC and UK competition law?
3   Consider what issues are relevant for an effective competition law compliance programme and devise the format of such a programme.

Glossary of key competition related terms

allocative efficiency A distribution of resources whereby the resources are put into the production of goods that customers want most, in the quantities they require. Through the most efficient allocation of resources, goods will be produced to meet demand at the lowest possible price.

anti-competitive Behaviour that is considered to be contrary to the prevailing competition rules. For instance, under Community law, note the possibility of anti-competitive agreements or anti-competitive abusive conduct. The term anti-competitive has no fixed meaning and depends largely on the rules of the relevant legal system.

antitrust US competition law is usually known as antitrust law. The name is taken from the trust companies that were prevalent at the time of the adoption of the Sherman Act in 1890. Trust companies formalised large cartels which antitrust law was designed to prevent.

barrier to entry A cost or obstacle that falls upon entrants to a market but which does not fall on existing market operators. There is a debate whether a barrier to entry is restricted to a cost that was not borne by existing operators when they entered the market, or is simply a cost that must be borne by new entrants before they can enter a market.

cartel A group of undertakings which, usually through agreement or understanding, act together in a market. By acting together they can, in effect, act as a monopoly and fix prices or allocate markets.

Chicago school A school of antitrust economics which developed at the University of Chicago and came to prominence in the 1960s. Its proponents believe that free markets are the most effective way to decide upon the allocation of resources. They also take a noninterventionist stance over the regulation of 'free' markets through the law.

collective dominance An alternative term, adopted under Community competition law, to denote the collective power of oligopolists. Collective dominance by a group of undertakings may, where there is abusive conduct, be dealt with under Art 82 EC.

collusion   A generic term for any form of agreement or understanding reached between competitors.

compartmentalisation of markets   A concept related to the primary goal under Community competition law of market integration. The concern is that certain types of agreement, for example, networks of distribution agreements, will be organised along national boundaries, in effect separating national markets from each other, thereby defeating the aim of a single Community market.

concentration   The generic term adopted under Community law to cover mergers, takeovers and joint ventures. What constitutes a concentration is determined under the Merger Regulation.

consumer welfare   The description given to the economic goal of much contemporary antitrust law. Its exact meaning is a matter of controversy and debate, but in the European conception it is usually taken to mean all forms of efficiency in markets that generate benefits for customers and final consumers in the marketplace in the medium term.

cross-elasticity of demand   The degree of influence the price of one good has on the demand for another. If cross-elasticity between goods is high the reduction in price of good X will cause a drop in demand for good Y. The fall in price of good X encourages customers to use it at the expense of good Y. A high cross-elasticity of demand indicates that goods are substitutable.

demand-side substitutability   The extent to which the consumer will regard different products as substitutes for each other. The legal test adopted on the basis of this economic test is referred to as interchangeability.

direct effect   This doctrine means that certain Community law provisions give rise to rights and obligations that may be enforced by individuals before their national courts.

dominant position   The classic definition is that it is a position of economic strength enjoyed by an undertaking, which enables the undertaking to prevent effective competition being maintained on the relevant market by affording the undertaking the power to behave, to an appreciable extent, independently of its competitors, customers and ultimately of its consumers.

economic entity doctrine   This doctrine may require legally distinct companies to be considered as one undertaking, for the purposes of Community law, where they are not independent from each other, for example, in a parent/subsidiary situation. The doctrine requires an examination of the managerial and economic independence of the undertakings in question.

effects doctrine   This doctrine provides that a legal system's competition laws are applicable where the action or behaviour takes place outside the jurisdiction but produces economic effects on markets within the jurisdiction. It is unclear whether or not the doctrine applies under Community competition law. It is inapplicable under UK competition law.

essential facility This concept is relevant under Community competition law in the context of refusals to supply, which may be deemed abusive under Art 82 EC. Certain types of infrastructure, such as a national electricity grid or computer reservation systems, may be considered to constitute an essential facility, such that access is essential for competition to develop, and the refusal to allow access to the facility may amount to abusive behaviour.

exclusive distribution This is a form of distribution whereby a producer agrees with a distributor to supply only to that distributor within a particular territory. This is a type of agreement involving vertical restraints.

exclusive purchasing This is a type of agreement requiring an exclusive commitment by the purchaser to purchase goods of that type only from the vendor. It is often known as a 'single-branding' agreement. Such commitments are frequently associated with exclusive distribution agreements.

free-rider The free-rider rationale is associated with the debate on the merits of vertical restraints and the rationale suggests that some form of intra-brand protection is necessary to allow a distributor to promote a brand effectively and thereby enhance inter-brand competition. The basic idea is that, without a degree of exclusivity, competitors of the distributor would take a free-ride on the distributor's advertising and promotional outlays and be able to sell the product at a cheaper price.

game theory A mathematical or economic analysis of decision-making, which attempts to predict the results of a situation as if it were a game of strategy. For each event, a prediction can be made based on the state of knowledge of the players at the time of the decision and their knowledge of earlier events.

Harvard school This school of antitrust analysis had its origins in the 1930s and it placed emphasis on market structure as the root of market failure, by exploring the link between market structure, conduct and performance, stressing that excessive concentration of market power resulted in undeservedly high profits.

intellectual property rights These are types of property rights, normally granted by national legal systems, which give the holder or owner the exclusive power to exploit the property. Examples are patents, trademarks and copyright. These exclusive property rights may come into conflict with the application of competition law.

inter-brand competition The competition between different brands of competing goods.

intra-brand competition Competition, normally between market operators at the same level of the market, for example, between two distributors, in relation to one brand of product.

joint ventures (concentrative and co-operative)   These involve the setting up of a company by two or more separate parent companies. The formation of the joint venture and the roles undertaken by the various parties can vary greatly. The distinction between concentrative and co-operative joint ventures, made by the Commission under the Merger Regulation, is now less significant. A concentrative joint venture is a full function joint venture performing, on a lasting basis, all the functions of an autonomous economic entity, and will be assessed by the Commission under the Merger Regulation. All other joint ventures are co-operative as they give rise to the threat of the co-ordination of competitive behaviour between the parent companies or between the parent companies and the joint venture and are considered under Art 81 EC.

market integration   One of the key goals of Community competition policy to create an integrated Single Market across all the Member States. The desire to create such a market shapes the Community's definition of, and response to, anti-competitive conduct.

merger (horizontal, vertical, conglomerate)   The term connotes both a welcome uncontested union between two or more parties and, equally, a hostile takeover. In addition, merger control will normally also cover differing degrees and forms of transfer of control of an undertaking, normally via the transfer of shares or assets. A horizontal merger involves parties at the same level of the market, such as two producers. Vertical mergers involve parties at different levels of the market, such as a producer and a distributor. Conglomerate mergers bring together unassociated types of business, often in a portfolio of company purchases by a holding company.

monopoly   A market structure where, in theoretical terms, one producer controls 100% of production or the supply of services (monopsony exists where one purchaser takes 100% of the goods produced or services supplied). Such a level of control is unlikely to exist in practice without governmental involvement, and the term is more generally used to refer to producers or service providers who have achieved a high level of control of a market.

multiple filing   A situation in which a business is forced to go through a number of similar administrative procedures for a single transaction in more than one national or supranational jurisdiction, for instance, in several Member States regarding the same merger. The requirement to file similar notifications in more than one jurisdiction is seen as wasteful and likely to encourage divergent results. Its avoidance is one of the benefits of the 'one stop shop'.

oligopolistic interdependence   The theory of oligopolistic interdependence asserts that, due to the limited number of parties involved in an oligopolistic market, the parties will each be able to derive a monopolist's excess profit without having to conspire together or form a prohibited cartel, as a result of the combination of the profit maximising motive and their mutual self-awareness on the market.

oligopoly A type of market where the majority of production is by a group of a few suppliers, none of which is dominant, but all of which are relatively large (oligopsony involves a limited number of purchasers and duopoly exists where there are only two producers). A market that is characterised by the existence of an oligopoly is known as an oligopolistic market. Although oligopolistic markets will be different, they will tend to have similar features. There will usually be a small number of sizeable undertakings operating in a market with homogeneous products. The market may also be characterised by limited price competition and parallel behaviour.

one stop shop A single agency that deals with all the regulatory matters in an area. The term is usually connected with Community merger control where the Commission took over responsibility for Community scale mergers from the Member States' national authorities, creating a single regulatory system.

passing off A common law action in the UK providing a remedy where the public are confused into thinking that the goods marketed are, in fact, produced by someone else, thereby unfairly benefiting the party marketing the goods, which profits from the goodwill of someone else.

per se A Latin phrase meaning 'by or in itself or themselves'. In a competition law context this phrase normally suggests that a particular type of market activity or agreement will be illegal without any further requirement to investigate and assess its economic impact.

perfect competition The theoretical neoclassical model of competition, which results in optimum allocative and productive efficiency. The model has certain prerequisites. It must be in relation to a homogeneous product, there must exist an infinite number of buyers and sellers, there must be free entry to and free exit from the market, and there must be full information available to consumers, allowing them to make rational decisions. Because real markets rarely meet the prerequisites, the model is virtually unknown in practice.

predatory pricing A pricing strategy whereby a powerful operator reduces its prices to near or below cost to drive a competitor out of the market.

relevant market In order to determine an undertaking's market strength one must define exactly which market the undertaking is competing in; that market is known as the relevant market. This is normally the first stage in any competition inquiry into dominance, particularly under Community law. It is also relevant for merger inquiries and under

Art 81. The relevant market is itself divided into three parts: product market, geographical market and temporal market.

restrictive trade practices legislation   In the UK the area of law dealing with the problems associated with cartels and other anti-competitive agreements has traditionally been known as restrictive trade practices legislation. This legislation has been repealed by the Competition Act 1998.

rule of reason   A term derived from US antitrust law, the rule of reason approach runs counter to the per se approach. It requires a detailed economic analysis of an agreement, the market structure and market conditions in order to assess the likely pro- and anti-competitive effects. It increases the complexity of antitrust/competition law enforcement and reduces certainty and predictability. It has been partially adopted by the Community authorities.

selective distribution   A type of distribution system whereby a manufacturer chooses its authorised distributors according to qualitative criteria. If a potential distributor meets the criteria, the potential distributor should be allowed to distribute the product.

State aid   There are specific Community rules, in the Treaty, on State aid. It is defined as aid, normally financial, to companies by public authorities of Member States. The aid can vary from State subsidies and capital injections to exemptions from taxation and loan guarantees. State aid can jeopardise the level competitive playing field in the Community.

supply-side substitutability   Otherwise referred to as supply-side interchangeability. This involves consideration by the competition authorities of the extent to which other suppliers, currently manufacturing other products, can quickly, and without major expenditure, begin producing a product which is substitutable. This possible alternative supply is known as potential competition and is relevant in assessing the likely competitive pressures on the supplier under consideration.

tacit collusion   A phenomenon found in oligopolistic markets whereby the undertakings involved act in a parallel manner through enlightened self-interest after they become aware that they are highly interdependent. There is no need for communication between the undertakings for tacit collusion to occur.

tie-ins   Transactions where a seller insists on selling additional products, tied products, to buyers of another product, tying products. Such a transaction forces the buyer to accept products that it did not want or could have acquired at a lower price elsewhere.

vertical integration   Where a producer has control over many stages of the production and/or marketing of a product. For instance, the producer may control the supply of raw materials, processing, manufacture, transport and distribution, rather than operating at only one level of the market.

vertical restraints These are the contractual restrictions employed in vertical agreements, made between undertakings operating at different levels of the market, to facilitate the distribution of goods and services. An example would be an exclusive distributorship requirement in a distribution agreement.

workable competition A level of competition that falls short of 'perfect competition', but which produces a reasonable level of allocative efficiency. The prerequisites of perfect competition do not have to be present, but an efficient scale of production will be reached with genuine alternatives for consumers and without overcapacity for producers. The concept is difficult to define in detailed terms, but is an obtainable policy goal somewhere between perfect competition and monopoly.

Index

Abuse of dominant position *see*
    Dominant position abuse
Advantage, definition of 344–5
Agreements of minor importance 189
Airlines
    cartels 7
    flag carriers 10, 343, 358
    incentives to use airports 10, 343
    regional aid 357
    State aid 10, 351
Allocative efficiency 11–12
Anti-competitive agreements 171–238
    abolition of notification 193
    agreements 173–4
    appreciability 207, 212
    Art 1 prohibition 171–90
    association of undertakings 188
    black list 198, 199, 227, 229
    block exemptions 187, 193, 195, 196–9
    breach of prohibition 190–2
    collusion 175–8
    concerted practices 174–6
    consequences of breach 190–2
    dawn raids 51, 52
    effect of agreement 184–9
    exception rule 193–6
    exclusive distribution agreements 193,
        217, 221–5, 226, 232
    exclusive purchasing agreements 234–6
    exemptions 192–3, 226
    export bans 221, 223, 225
    grey list 198
    horizontal 172, 173
    inapplicability
        benefit-efficiency gains 194–5
        conditions 194–6
        fair share to consumers 195–6
        no indispensable restrictions 195
        no substantial elimination of
            competition 196
    inter-brand competition 219
    interstate trade 179–80
    intra-brand competition 217–8
    jurisprudence 187
    market analysis 187, 207
    market share test 182, 189
    mergers 210
    minor importance agreements 189
    national courts 199–200
    new technology transfer 197
    notification requirement 193
    nullity sanction 190–2, 278
    object of agreement 181–4
    prevention, restriction or distortion of
        competition 157–8, 180–1
    price-fixing 172, 182
    resale price maintenance 214
    selective distribution agreements 225
    technology licensing 221
    territorial restrictions 222–3, 229–30,
        232–3
    UK *see* Anti-competitive agreements,
        UK
    undertakings, definition of 178–9
    unilateral behaviour 174
    vertical *see* Vertical agreements;
        Vertical Agreements Regulation
    void agreements 190–2, 208
    white list 197
    within Common Market requirement
        190
Anti-competitive agreements, UK 200
    advice and information 205
    appreciability concept 207, 212
    association of undertakings 203
    block exemptions 209

cartels 201–2, 210–11
case law 216
Chapter 1 prohibition
    operation of 204–9
    outline 203–4
    vertical agreements and 209
Competition Act 1998 203–11
Competition Appeal Tribunal (CAT)
    203–4
Competition Commission Appeal
    Tribunal 212
compliance 210–11
concerted practices 206
criminal cartel offence 25, 66, 394
    dishonesty test 259
damages 204
deterrence 210–11
enforcement 210–11
Enterprise Act 2002 203–4, 210
evidence gathering 201
exclusive distribution agreements 232
exemptions 208–9, 212–14
extraterritoriality 207–8
harmonisation with Community law
    204–6
horizontal agreements 205
inter-brand competition 209, 219
intra-brand competition 209,
    217–18
investigations 203, 211
land agreements 210
market-sharing agreement 207
mergers 210
negative clearances 208
non-binding opinions 209
notification 208–9, 212–14
nullity sanction 190–2
Office of Fair Trading (OFT) 203–4
Opening Markets: New Policy on
    Restrictive Trade Practices
    (White Paper) 202
practice 211–16
price fixing 214–16
professional rules 210
public transport ticketing schemes
    209
reasonable suspicion 203
representations 203
resale price maintenance 214–16
Resale Prices Act 1976 200
Restrictive Trade Practices Act 1976
    200

restrictive trade practices
    legislation 200–2
    reform of 202
rule of reason 212, 220
small agreements 204, 215
specialisation agreements 205
vertical agreements 206, 209, 217
void agreements 208
Anti-competitive behaviour 1
Appeals
    CAT see Competition Appeal Tribunal
        (CAT)
    CCAT see Competition Commission
        Appeal Tribunal (CCAT)
    Court of Appeal 75, 145, 168, 204,
        337
    Court of First Instance 36, 62
    Court of Justice 62–3
    European Community enforcement
        62–6
    financial penalties 69, 70–3
    judicial review 337–8
    merger control 313, 320–1
    preliminary rulings 65
    review of legality 63–4
Appreciability concept 207, 212
Association of undertakings
    Art 81 176
    UK 203
Austrian school 13

Barriers to entry 112–16
    access to capital 114
    conduct 116
    economies of scale 115
    financial resources 114–15
    legal provisions 114
    product differentiation 115–16
    technological advantage 114
    vertical integration 115
Black list 198, 199, 227, 229
Block exemptions
    anti-competitive agreements 187, 193,
        195, 196–9
    black list 198, 199, 227, 229
    exclusive distribution agreements
        226
    grey list 198
    safe-harbours 196, 234, 297
    State aid 367
    vertical restraints 221, 224, 226, 227,
        230

white list 197
withdrawal of regime 230
Bork, Robert 15, 21, 219

Canada, co-operation agreement with
  European Community 96
Cartels 241–73
  airline 7
  American experience 243–4
  anti-competitive agreements 182
  bid-rigging 242, 259
  cartel offence in UK 258–60
  chemicals industry 245
  chiselling 262–3
  compensation claims 254–8
  Competition Disqualification Orders
    260
  co-ordination in control 246–7
  criminal offence 25, 29, 66, 271, 394
    dishonesty test 259
  crisis cartels 14
  definition 2, 242
  detection of 261–2
  deterrence
    concept of 247
    optimal 247–9
  dishonesty 259–60
  distrust within undertaking 263–4,
    268–9
  early EC provisions 244–5
  EC block exemption 241–2
  Enterprise Act 2002 81–3
  European Coal and Steel Community
    (ECSC) 244
  fines 248–9
    calculation in UK 252–3
    calculation of EC corporate
      249–52
    inability to pay 252, 254
    level of 249–50
    OFT guidance to calculating 252
    problem with corporate 253–4
    relevant turnover 252
    review of by CFI 250
  Geneva Declaration on Cartels 243
  Germany 242–3
  history of European 242–4
  imprisonment for offence 259
  increasing financial penalties 254–8
  indirect purchasers' claims 256–7
  individual penalties 258–61
  international 30, 243, 246, 386

  legal challenges to Commission
    decisions 246
  leniency programmes 50–1, 71–2, 205,
    211, 262–6, 268
  Monopolies Commission 244
  Net Book Agreement (NBA) 5
  Noorwijks Cement Accord 245
  policy
    within EC 264–6
    within UK 244, 266–9
  price-fixing 81
  punishment 248, 249
  R&D agreements 241
  representative actions 257
  Restrictive Practices Court 244
  social cost of penalties 258
  State intervention 372–3
  whistle-blowers 262
Certainty 385–6
Certification free-rider issue 219
Chapter I prohibition
  see also Anti-competitive agreements,
    UK
  operation of 204–9
  vertical restraints 236–8
Chapter II prohibition
  see also Dominant position abuse, UK
  case law 147–55
  guidelines 146–7
  tribunal judgments 147–55
Chicago school 13, 15, 16, 18, 21–2, 29,
  219, 384, 386
Clayton Act (US) 20
Collective dominance 94, 300, 301, 409
  oligopolistic markets 136–41
Collusion 410
  tacit 414
Comfort letters 50
Community dimension, Merger
  Regulation 45, 314–5
Compartmentalisation of markets 218,
  410
Competition
  perfect see Perfect competition
  pure see Pure competition
  workable 12, 13, 415
Competition Act 1998 28, 32–3
  anti-competitive agreements 203–11
  Chapter I prohibition 28
    vertical restraints 236, 237
  Chapter II prohibition 28, 143–4
  dominant position abuse 143–4

enforcement in the UK 66, 67–74
merger control 309
vertical restraints 236, 237
Competition Appeal Tribunal (CAT) 397
  anti-competitive agreements 203–4
  consumer bodies 75–6
  dominant position abuse 144
  Enterprise Act 2002 26, 74–6
  financial penalties 75
  further right of appeal 75
  jurisdiction 75
  membership 75
  merger control 313, 320–1
  oral hearings 75
  President 74–5
  procedural rules 75
  reference to European Court 75
  third party appeals 74
Competition Commission
  assessment of competition 161
  competition test 159–65
  conduct 163
  customer benefits 397
  excessive or unfair prices or profits
    163–5
  investigation and reporting 79–80
  market structure 161
  membership 79
  merger control 313, 320–1
    acceptance of undertakings 323–4,
      335–7
    inquiry 327–9
    investigations 309
    judicial review 338
    remedies 310
    report 327
  non-binding recommendations 80
  remedial action 166–8
  reporting stage 158–9
  Secretary of State, reference to 79
  undertakings, power to receive 81
  utilities panels 79
Competition Commission Appeal
    Tribunal (CCAT) 71, 212
  anti-competitive agreements 212
  dominant position abuse 144
Competition law
  abuse of dominant position see
    Dominant position abuse
  anti-competitive agreements see
    Anti-competitive agreements
  background 1–10

changes in 388–92
compliance programmes 398–400
development of 22–9
economics see Economic theory and
    analysis
enforcement see Enforcement
extraterritoriality 92–5
merger control see Merger control;
    Mergers
National Competition Authorities
    (NCAs) 24, 36, 65, 193, 285, 388
politics of see Politics
pure competition objective 3–4
Treaty background 22–4
UK see Competition law, UK
US see US antitrust law
Competition law, UK
  see also Competition Act 1998;
    Enterprise Act 2002
  abolition of notification system 29
  abuse of dominant position see
    Dominant position abuse, UK
  anti-competitive agreements see Anti-
    competitive agreements, UK
  Community law and 83–8
  compliance programme 398–400
  extraterritoriality 90–2
  merger control see Merger control,
    UK
  statutory development 27–9
Competition policy
  Community 19–20
  consumer protection 18, 165–6,
    195–6
  countervailing power 19
  criminalisation 394
  efficiency see Efficiency
  enforcement 392–4
  extra-competition policies 16
  fairer distribution of wealth 17
  globalisation 386–8
  human rights 395
  internal market 19, 23
  laissez-faire competition laws 384–5
  objectives 29–31
  political objectives 16–20
  prevention of concentration of power
    16–17
  pure competition 16
  regional policy 18
  regulation of excessive profits 17
  State aid 4, 10, 23, 391

State regulation 4–10
unified market creation 19
Competition policy, UK 397–8
  changes in 24–9
  conspiracy to defraud 24
  criminal law 24–5, 66, 394
  delict 25–6
  depoliticisation 32
  objectives 31–3
  public interest test 28, 155, 159–60,
    312–13, 329–32
  restraint of trade 26–7
  restrictive trade practices 27
  torts 25–6
Competition service 74
Competition test 159–65, 168, 310, 318,
  321, 330, 391
Competitors
  complainants 49, 403–6
  state aid remedies 364–7
Complainants
  competitors 49, 403–6
  OFT 67–8
Compliance
  institution of programme 398–400
  OFT Compliance and Education Unit
    70, 211
Concentrations
  see also Merger control; Mergers
  appraisal procedure 289–95
  basis of appraisal 295–304
  case allocation and referral 285–6
  Community dimension 282–3, 284,
    288
  control of 280
  form of 281
Concerted practices
  agreements and 206–7
  anti-competitive agreements 173,
    174–6
  Art 81 172
  parallelism and oligopoly 176–8
Conditions, unfair 120
Conglomerate mergers 276–7, 302–3,
  316, 320, 338
Conspiracy to defraud 24
Conspiracy to injure 25
Consumer protection 18, 164, 397
  Office of Fair Trading 165–6
Copyright 120, 134–5, 191
Corporate Leniency Programme (US)
  401–3

Countervailing power 19
Court of Appeal 75, 145, 168, 204, 337
Criminal Offences
  cartels 25, 29, 66, 271, 397
  obstruction of OFT 69
  UK 24–5
Crisis cartels 14, 195, 196
Cross-elasticity of demand 107, 410

Damages
  cartels 254–8, 402
  Chapter II prohibition 154–5
  Community law 83–8, 404–5
  competitors' remedies 366
  compliance with competition laws
    399
  UK law 88–9
Dawn raids 51, 52
De minimis policy
  State aid 348–9
  vertical restraints 220–1
Defence, right of 60–2
  access to file 61–2
  Art 6 European Convention for the
    Protection of Human Rights and
    Fundamental Freedoms 60
  business secrets 61, 62
  Court of First Instance 60, 62
  disclosure of documents 61–2
  duty of confidentiality 61, 62
  European Human Rights Commission
    (EHRC) 60
  fair and public hearing 60
  Hearing Officer 60
  professional privilege 60
  professional secrecy 61, 61
Delicts 25–6
Demand
  cross-elasticity of 107, 410
  substitution 105–6
Director disqualification 81–3
Director General of Fair Trading
  creation of position 27, 308
  merger control 318
  transfer of functions to OFT 27–9, 66,
    67, 155, 312
Directorate General for Competition 36,
  187, 280, 342
Dishonesty
  cartel offence 259–60
  Ghosh test 259
Disqualification of directors 260

Distribution agreements
  efficiency gains 218
  exclusive *see* Exclusive distribution
    agreements
  selective *see* Selective distribution
    agreements
  single-branding commitments 218
  vertical restraints 217, 228
Dominant position, meaning 410
Dominant position abuse
  abuse of position 117–19
    examples 117
    exclusionary abuses 110, 118, 120,
      121–2
    exploitative abuses 118, 119–21
  access to capital 114
  anti-competitive abuses 121
  Art 82 101–2
  barriers to entry 112–16
  collective dominance 136–41, 300–1
  cross-elasticity of demand 107, 410
  definition 110
  demand substitution 105–6
  discounts and rebates 124–6
  economies of scale 115
  effect on trade test 102–4
  examples of abusive conduct 117
  excessive prices 119–20
  exclusionary abuses 110, 118, 120,
    121–2
  exploitative abuses 118, 119–21
  export bans 123
  financial resources 114–15
  intellectual property rights 134–6
  jurisdictional test 103
  legitimate competition 388
  leverage 128–9
  market strength 110–12
  mergers 129
  new competitors 131
  predatory pricing 126–8
  pricing strategies 123–4
  product differentiation 115–16
  quiet life 121
  refusal to supply 130–34
  relevant markets 412–3
    geographical market 109
    product market 105–6
    temporal market 109
  super-dominant position 127
  supply side substitutability 108–9, 319
  technological advantage 114

  tying and leverage 128–9
  UK *see* Dominant position abuse, UK
  undertakings, meaning 101, 102
  unfair conditions 120
  vertical integration 115, 414
Dominant position abuse, UK
  abuse of market power 141–2
  acceptance of undertakings 166–8
  adverse effect on competition 160,
    166–8
  case law 147–53
  Chapter II prohibition 143–5, 397–8
    case law 147–53
    guidelines 146–7
  Competition Act 1998 141, 143–55
  Competition Appeal Tribunal 145
  competition test 159–65
  conduct 163
  consistency with Community law
    145–6
  consumer protection 165–6
  court case law 153–5
  DGFT's role 144–5
  enforcement 144–5
  Enterprise Act 2002 143, 155–68
  excessive or unfair prices or profits
    163–5
  Fair Trading Act 1973 168
  guidelines 146–7
  information gathering 155–6
  investigation 155–6
  legislative developments 142–3
  market investigation references
    156–7
  Office of Fair Trading 144–5, 147,
    155–8
  prevention, restriction or distortion of
    competition 157–8
  public interest test 159–60
  reference test 157–8
  reform of anti-monopoly laws 141–3
  remedial action 166–8
  reporting stage 158–9
  Secretary of State role 155
  Trade and Industry Committee report
    142
  tribunal judgements 147–53

EC Treaty
  Art 81 *see* Anti-competitive
    agreements
  Art 82 *see* Dominant position abuse

Art 87 *see* State aid
background 22–4
Economic delicts 25
Economic efficiency 172
Economic entity doctrine 92, 103, 178–9, 410
Economic theory and analysis 11–14
  Austrian school 13
  certainty and predictability 385–6
  Chicago school 13, 15, 16, 18, 21–2, 29, 219, 384, 386
  cross-elasticity of demand 107, 410
  demand substitution 105–6
  detrimental behaviour 13
  game theory 137, 138, 411
  Harvard school 21, 384, 411
  laissez-faire 13, 24, 384–5
  market power 12
  neoclassical model 11–13, 17, 171
  perfect competition 11–12, 15, 385, 413
  pure competition objective 3–4, 11–14, 16, 17, 310
  supply side substitutability 108–9, 319
Economies of scale 115
Effect on trade test 102–4
Effects doctrine 92–4, 410
Efficiency
  allocative 11–12, 409
  audits for nationalised industries 28
  Chicago school 16, 21
  conduct, of 13
  mergers 12
  monopolies 3, 12
  productive 11
Efficiency defence, merger control 298–9
Employment, State aid 367
Enforcement
  appeals 62–5
    Court of First Instance 36, 62
    Court of Justice 62–3
    preliminary rulings 65
    review of legality 63–4
  calling-in investigation 41–2
  comfort letters 50
  Commission role 46–60
  complaints 49–51
  consistency and uniformity 41
  co-operation with national authorities 39–40
  decentralisation 47, 83–8, 266, 369
  decision-making 56–60

defence, right of 60–2
Directorate General for Competition 36, 187, 280, 342
enlargement of Community 37–8
European Competition Network (ECN) 35, 39–42, 46
extraterritoriality 90–4
fact finding stage 48–9
finding of inapplicability 50, 56
fines 58–60
global competition rules 95–7
human rights aspects 55–6
implementing Regulations 65
information sharing 96, 263
infringement proceedings 56, 57
inspections 52–3
interim measures 56–7
international co-operation 95–7, 386–8
investigatory powers 51, 82, 156
National Competition Authorities (NCAs) 24, 36, 39, 65, 193, 285, 388
national courts 83–8, 90
negative clearance 69, 208
outline 36–8
Regulation 1/2003 36, 65–6
Regulation 17/62 36–8
requests for information 51
taking of statements 52
whistle-blower 51, 70, 211, 403
Enforcement, UK
  appeals
    Competition Appeal Tribunal 74–6, 89
    Court of Appeal 75, 145, 168, 204, 337
  by individuals 88–9
  cartels 81–3
  Competition Act 1998 67–74
  Competition Commission 79–80
  damages awards 89, 95
  director disqualification 81–3
  Enterprise Act 2002 66, 76, 81
  financial penalties 69, 70–1, 73
  information gathering 51
  initiation 48–9
  leniency programme 69, 211
  National Competition Authorities (NCAs) 89–90
  Office of Fair Trading 67–70, 73–4, 88, 90
  penalties 70–3

pre-Enterprise Act 2002 80
private law actions 88
Secretary of State 78
utility regulators 73
Enterprise Act 2002 28, 397
anti-competitive agreements 203–4,
210
cartel offence investigations 81–3
Competition Appeal Tribunal (CAT)
26, 74–7
enforcement 66, 76, 81
guidance 325
merger control 308, 310, 312–26
notification 325
Office of Fair Trading 28
private actions 406
Secretary of State, reduction in role 81
undertakings in lieu of reference 324–5
vertical restraints 238
Environmental protection, State aid 376
Essential facilities 132–4, 154, 389
Euro-defence 191
European Commission
calling-in investigation 41–2
decentralisation 47–8
decision making 56–66
appeals 62–5
Directorate General for Competition
36, 46–7, 342
enforcement process by 48–66
see also Enforcement
guardian of the Treaty 46
investigation powers 51
Legal Service 47
membership 46
powers unfair 48
protect rights of the defence 48
staff 46–7
supervisory powers under Treaty 46,
48
European Community, enlargement of
367–8
European Community competition law
abuse of dominant position see
Dominant position abuse
anti-competitve agreements see
Anti-competitve agreements
changes in 388–91
compliance programme 398–400
development of 22–4
enforcement see Enforcement
merger control see Merger control

National Competition Authorities
(NCAs) 24, 36, 39, 193, 276, 285,
388
supremacy 43–4
Treaty background 22–3
UK competition law and 43–6
European Community policy
criminalisation 394
enforcement 392–4
globalisation 386–8
human rights 395
objectives 29–31
State aid 4, 10, 14, 18
State regulation 4–10
unified market creation 19
European Competition Network (ECN)
35, 39–42, 46, 266, 286, 287–8,
392, 403
European Economic Area (EEA) 96
European Free Trade Association
(EFTA) 96
Excessive price 119–20, 164
Exclusionary abuses 118, 121–36
export bans 123
mergers 129
pricing strategies 123–8
refusal to supply 130–6
tying and leverage 128–9
Exclusive distribution agreements 193,
217, 221, 223, 225, 226
treatment of under Art 81 232
Exclusive purchasing agreements
234–6
Exploitative abuse
excessive prices 119–20
quiet life 121
unfair conditions 120
Export bans 123, 221
vertical restraints 225
'Extra-competition' policies 16
Extraterritoriality 90–4

Fact finding
European Commission 48–9, 84
Fair Trading Act 1973 27, 66, 76, 308–12
competition related inquiries 330–2
DGFT functions 200
public interest issues 329–30
Federal Trade Commission Act (US) 20
Financial penalties
see also Fines
anti-competitive agreements 214–16

Competition Appeal Tribunal (CAT) 75
Office of Fair Trading 70–3
Finding of inapplicability 50, 56, 234
Fines 58–60, 248–9
  see also Financial penalties
  Chapter I prohibition 72
  Competition Act 1998 70–3
  enforcement 58–60
  leniency *see* Leniency Programmes
  merger control 288, 293, 294
  OFT guidance 70–3
Flynn, John 15
Free-riders 174, 233

Game theory 137, 13
Global competition rules 95–7
Globalisation 90–7, 306–7, 386–8

Hard core restraints 229–30, 237
Harvard school 15, 21, 384
Herfindahl-Hirschman Index (HHI) 297
Horizontal agreements 172, 183, 184, 205, 241
Horizontal aid 356, 357, 361, 367, 368
Horizontal mergers 276–7, 320, 333
Horizontal price-fixing 58, 81, 172
Human rights 55–6, 395

Information
  see also Fact finding; Investigation powers
  privileged status 54
Inspections 52–3, 361
Integration
  market 19, 29–30, 172, 183, 192, 206, 218, 229, 232, 233, 236
  vertical 115, 414
Intellectual property rights 114, 134–6, 411
  abuse of dominant position 134–6
  anti-competitive agreements 225
  essential facility test 136
  licensing agreements 191
  licencing of IP rights 135–6
  new product criteria 135, 136
  tv guides 134–5
Intended use of product 108
Inter-brand competition 411
  increase in 219
  mergers 276
  vertical agreements 174, 209

vertical restraints 219–20, 226, 231, 232, 401
Interdependence, oligopolies 137–40, 162–3, 412
Interim interdict 366
Interim relief 287, 366
International cartels 246, 386
International co-operation 386–8
  bilateral agreements 386–8
  Canada–European Community 96
  enforcement 95–7
  multilateral agreements 388
  notification of cases 387
  US–European Community 95
International Competition Network (ICN) 97, 388
International Competition Policy Advisory Committee 96
Interstate trade 44, 45, 92, 103, 179–80, 182, 189, 209, 237
Intra-brand competition 411
  export bans 123
  restriction of 217–8
  vertical agreements 174, 209
  vertical restraints 220, 226, 231, 232
Intra-Community trade, state aid and 347–8
Investigation powers
  calling-in investigation by Commission 41–2
  co-operation between EC and national authorities 39–42
  enforcement 35, 36–8
  European Competition Network 24
  inspections 52–3
  merger control 290–1
  professional legal privilege 54, 60
  requests for information 51–2
  self-incrimination privilege 54, 55–6, 60
  taking statements 52

Joint ventures 281, 282, 296
  merger control 304–6
Judicial review 168, 337, 338

Laissez-faire 13, 24, 384–5
Land agreements 210
Legitimate expectations 364, 367
Leniency programmes 262–6, 393
  cartels 50, 59, 401–3

Corporate Leniency Programme
(CLP) 401–2
EC 264–6
Model Leniency Programme 42, 392,
403
Office of Fair Trading 7, 71–3, 266–9
UK 266
whistle-blowing 6–7, 22, 51, 59, 70
Leverage 128–9
Licensing arrangements 221, 225
Liesner Report 308
Lilley doctrine 319
Loan financing 352
Loan guarantees 351–2

Market economy investor principle
349–52
Market share tests 182, 189, 317–8
Market share threshold 228–9
Market-sharing 58, 81, 182, 245
Market strength 110–12
Markets
analysis, pigeon-holing 385, 400–1
barriers to entry *see* Barriers to entry
compartmentalisation 218
demand substitution 105, 106, 108
failure 1
foreclosure 218
globalisation 90, 386–8
Herfindahl-Hirschman Index (HHI)
297
integration 9, 29–30, 172, 183, 192,
206, 218, 229, 232, 233, 236
investigations 76
oligopolistic structure 296
power 12, 13
relevant geographical 109
relevant product 105–6
secondary 132, 135
SSNIP tests 105–6
super-dominance 111–12, 117, 149
temporal 109
temporary strength 112
Markets and Projects Division, OFT 68
Media mergers 311, 323
Medium-sized enterprises 19, 29
access to capital 114–15
State aid 356, 367
Merger control
anti-competitive agreements 210
appraisal procedure 289–95
back referral 286–7

case allocation 285–8
case referral 285–8
collective dominance 136–41
community dimension 282–8
compatibility with Common Market
291, 292, 295
control of concentrations 280
decision of incompatibility 294, 362
defences 298
dominant position abuse 129, 277
efficiency defence 298–9
examples 8–10
failing firm defence 299, 320
fines 290
historical background 277–80
industrial control 299–300
initiation of proceedings 289–90
international mergers 306–7
investigative powers 290–5
joint control 282, 291, 293
joint ventures 282, 291, 293
mandatory notification 288–9
market analysis 296
merger regulation 280–307
multiple filing 279, 284, 285, 412
negotiated clearance 294
notification 288–9
nullity sanction 278
oligopolistic markets 300–2
'one stop shop' principle 280, 282, 284,
287, 413
prior notification 390
prohibited concentrations 295–6
referral back 286–7
remedies 292
significant impediment to competition
296, 390
social goals 299
substantial lessening of competition
test 330
suspension of concentrations 289
threshold test 283
time limits 289, 290, 292–3, 294, 304,
306, 327
Merger control, UK
acceptance of undertakings 323–5
anti-competitive agreement exclusion
210
appeals 313, 321
background 307–8
ceasing to be distinct enterprises
315

Community merger control and 282, 314
Competition Act 1998 309
Competition Appeal Tribunal (CAT) 313
Competition Commission 309, 310, 314
  acceptance of undertakings 323–5, 335–7
  inquiry 327–9
  investigations 309
  judicial review 338
  remedies 310
  report 327
counterfactual 333
deregulation and 308–9
Director General of Fair Trading 318
duty to refer 320–2
  exceptions 322–3
efficiency gains 333
Enterprrise Act 2002 308, 310, 312–26
examples 8–9
Fair Trading Act 1973 308–10, 315–16, 325, 329–32, 335
guidance 325
informal advice 325
informal submission 325–6
inquiries
  1973 Act 330–2
  Competition Commission 327–9
investigations 312–13, 327
investor protection 312
judicial review 337
Liesner Report 308
Lilley doctrine 319
market share test 315
Monopolies and Restrictive Practices Commission 307
newspaper mergers 311
notification 325
Office of Fair Trading 309, 312
  referrals 313–4
Productivity and Enterprise; A World Class Competition Regime (White Paper) 309
public interest 312–13, 329–30
referrals 313–26
  duty to refer 320–2
  making a reference 323
  under 1973 Act 318–19
  undertakings in lieu 323–5
reform 308–10

relevant merger situation 314–15
remedial action 335–7
review of decisions 313, 320–1
Secretary of State 312
statutory pre-notification 325–6
substantial lessening of competition test 310, 317–18, 319–20, 332–5
Tebbit doctrine 32, 313, 318–19, 329
undertakings in lieu of a reference 323–5
value of turnover test 316–17
Merger Regulation 280–307
  collective dominance theory 94
  threshold level 45
Mergers
  abuse of dominant position 129
  anti-competitive agreements 210
  benefits 275–6
  conglomerate 276–7, 278, 302–4
  controls *see* Merger Control; Merger Control UK
  disadvantages 276
  efficiency 3–4
  horizontal 276–7
  international 306–7
  interventions 275, 276
  large-scale 279, 280, 295, 387
  meaning 3
  newspapers 311
  State intervention 5
  vertical 302–4
  world-scale 386
Minor importance, agreements of 189
Monopolies
  see also Dominant position abuse
  bans 3
  efficiency 3–4
  meaning 2
  State intervention 5
  State monopolies 375
  Trade and Industry Report on UK policy 142
Monopolies and Mergers Commission 79
Monopolies and Restrictive Practices Commission 27
Monopoly price/rent 119–20
Multiple filing 279, 284, 285, 412

National Competition Authorities (NCAs) 24, 36, 65, 193, 285, 388

co-operation between Commission
and 39–42
decentralisation of enforcement 39–42
enforcement by 39–42
merger referrals 286
Office of Fair Trading 42
UK 42
National Courts
anti-competitive agreements in
199–200
breach of statutory duty 26
Community law 83–8
damages 83
enforcement in by individuals 83–8
guidance from Commission 84
State aid 367
third parties 88
Nationalised industries 5
efficiency audits 28
Negative clearance
enforcement 69
Office of Fair Trading 208
Neo-classical model 11–14, 17, 121
Net Book Agreement (NBA) 5–6
Northern Irish Office for the Regulation
of Electricity and Gas (OFREG)
73
Notification
abolition 29, 69
anti-competitive agreements 193,
208–9, 212–14
merger control 288–9, 325, 326, 390
State aid 361–4

Office of Fair Trading
advice and information 69–70
anti-competitive agreements 203–4
Board 67–8
cartels 201–2, 211
Chapter I prohibitions 212
Competition Act 1998 67
Compliance and Education Unit 70,
211
concurrent powers 73–4
consumer protection role 165–6
dominant position abuse 144
Enterprise Act role 155
reference to Competition
Commission 155
enforcement of prohibitions 68–9
Enterprise Act 2002 28, 155–68
financial penalties 69, 70–3

guidelines 69–70
informal guidance 69, 209
information gathering 155–6
investigation powers 210–11
Markets and Projects Division 68
merger control 312–13
referrals 313–4
negative clearances 69
notification, withdrawal of scheme 69
obstruction of 69
Policy and Strategy Division 68
representations 69, 144, 203
Rule 7 notice 69
vertical restraints 237–8
Office of Communications (OFCOM)
73
Office of Gas and Electricity Markets
(OFGEM) 73
Office of the Rail Regulator (ORR) 73
Office of Water Services (OFWAT) 73
Oligopolies 12, 15
collective dominance 136–41
interdependence 137, 138, 162–3, 412
market structure 296
parallelism and 137, 138, 176–8
pricing 162–3
One stop shop principle 280, 282, 284,
287, 413
Opening Markets; New Policy on
Restrictive Trade Practices (White
Paper) 202
Organisation for Economic
Co-operation and Development
(OECD) 386
Ought assumptions 15

Parent company 92, 93, 103, 179, 315
passing off 26, 413
Perfect competition 11–12, 15, 385, 413
Pigeon-holing 384, 385, 400–1
Policy and Strategy Division OFT 68
Politics 14–16
fairer distribution of wealth 17
industrial policy 14, 29
prevention of concentration of
economic power 16–17
regional policy 18
small and medium sized enterprises
19–20
unified market creation 19
Predatory pricing 126–8, 413
Predictability 385–6

Prevention, restriction or distortion of competition 180–9
  Art 81(1) 172
  effect on competition and appreciability 207
  reference test 157–8
  vertical restraints 220
Price fixing
  anti-competitive agreements 182, 214–6
  conspiracy to defraud 24
  conspiracy to injure 25
  horizontal 58, 81, 172
Price maintenance agreements 6, 8
Price maker 12
Price taker 11, 110
Prices
  discounts and rebates 124–6
  excessive 119–20, 163–5
  exclusionary abuses 121–3
  monopoly price 119
  oligopolistic pricing 162–3
  predatory pricing 126–8
  relevant product market 105–6
Private enforcement
  Ashurst Report 86, 87
  Commission priorities in enforcement 83
  damages 86
  decentralisation 83
    difficulties to overcome 88
  direct effect doctrine 83
  disparities between court procedures 87
  indirect purchasers 87
  Milk Marketing Board 84
  national courts 86
  principle of effectiveness 86
  principle of equivalence 85
  subsidiarity 83
  Treaty of Amsterdam 87
Product differentiation 115–16
Productive efficiency 11
Productivity and Enterprise; A World Class Competition Regime (White Paper) 237–8, 309
Professional legal privilege 54–5
Professions
  competition law and 396
  rules as anti-competitive agreements 209–10
Profits, regulation of excessive 17

Protection of consumers 17–18
Public interest
  dominant position abuse 159–60
  merger control 312, 329–32
  test 32
Public service obligations, State aid 353, 392
Public Transport ticketing schemes 209
Purchasing agreements, exclusive 234–6
Pure competition
  free market stance 13
  minimal intervention 13
  objective 3–4, 11–14, 16

R&D agreements 241
Refusal to supply
  abuse of dominant position 130–3
  access to essential facilities 132–4
  examples 130–4
  intellectual property rights 134–6
  new markets 132–4
  to damage or deter competitor 130
Regional aid 357
Relevant geographical market 109
Relevant product market 105–7
Resale price maintenance 214–7, 221, 223, 224, 229, 395
Resale Prices Act 1976 28, 200
Restrictive Practices Court (RPC) 66, 201, 244
Restrictive Practices Court Act 1976 28
Restrictive trade practices legislation 5, 200, 414
Revenue producing monopolies 379
Rule of reason 414
  anti-competitive agreements 212
  court and 224–5
  US 223–4

Safe harbour, block exemptions 196, 234, 297
Secondary markets 129, 132, 135, 374–5
Secretary of State
  merger control 312
  public interest cases 155
  reduction of role 81, 155
Selective distribution agreements 225
Self incriminating privilege 55–6
Sherman Act (US) 2, 19, 20–1, 223, 224
Significant impediment test 391
Single-branding agreements 217, 234–6

Small and medium-sized enterprises
(SMEs) 19, 29
access to capital 114–15
State aid 356, 367
Small but Significant Non-transitory
Increase in Price (SSNIP) test 105
State, as undertaking 102–4
State aid
advantage 344–5
air transport 358
Art 87
exemptions 354–6
prohibitions 344–54
block exemptions 400
capital injections 344
Community objectives and 355, 368
compensating factors 341
competitors' remedies 364–7
damages 366
de minimis rule 361, 362, 367
developments 367–9
discretionary exemptions 355–6
distortion of competition 348–9
economies in transition 368
employment 367
enabling Regulation 361
energy saving 355
enlargement of Community and 342,
368
environmental protection 367–8
equity injections 349, 350
exemptions 354–6
discretionary 355–6
mandatory 354–5
expedited procedures 393–4
frameworks and guidelines 356–60
heritage conservation 356
horizontal 357, 361, 367, 378
interim interdict 366
interim relief 366
interlocutory injunction 366
intra-Community trade 347–8
investigation, preliminary 362
justification 341
legitimate expectations and 364, 367
loan financing 352
loan guarantees 351–2
mandatory exemptions 354–5
market economy investor principle
349–52
meaning 341–3
national courts 367

notification 361–4
procedure 360–4
public service obligations 353, 392
recovery 363–4
regional aid 357
remedies, competitors 364–7
rescue and restructuring 357–60
sectoral aid 356
selectivity 346–7
small and medium-sized companies
356, 367
State source of funding 345–6
tax schemes 347, 369
training 367, 3691
welfare gains 367
State intervention 370–2
anti-competitive behaviour 379, 403
cartels 5–8
challenging State monopolies 375
Community law 22
defence 379
derogation from competition rules
379
dominant position abuse 374
general economic interest 368, 369,
371, 379, 380
measures adopted by the State 372–8
mergers 8–10
monopolies 5
postal cases 379
private cartels 372
revenue producing monopolies 379
services of general interest 371
special or exclusive rights granted 374
undertakings with public function
378
vertical restraints 7–8
Substantial lessening of competition test
330, 391
Super-dominance 111–12, 117, 149
Supply side substitutability 108–9, 319,
414
Supremacy of Community Law 43, 44

Tacit collusion 178, 298, 303, 414
Tax schemes 347, 369
Tebbit Doctrine 32, 313, 318–19, 329
Temporal market 109
Territorial restrictions 221, 222–3,
229–30, 232–3
Tie-ins 128–9, 414
Torts 25–6

Trade
    interstate 44, 45, 103, 179–80, 182, 189,
        209, 237
    intra-Community 347–8
Trade associations 27
Training, State aid 367, 369

Undertakings (binding commitments)
    given to Competition Commission 81,
        166–7
    merger control 323–5, 335–7
Undertakings (commercial entities)
    Article 81 definition 178–9
    association of 206
    dominant position abuse law and 101,
        102
    State as 102–3
    State entities as 375–8
    State regulation 378–80
    trade between states 102–4
Unfair conditions, dominant position
        abuse and 120
United Kingdom
    see Anti-competitive agreements, UK;
        Competition law, UK;
        Competition policy, UK;
        Dominant position abuse, UK;
        Merger control, UK
United Nations Conference on Trade
        and Development (UNCTAD) 95
US antitrust law 20–2, 409
    Chicago school 13, 15, 16, 18, 21–2,
        29, 219, 384, 386, 409
    Clayton Act 20
    co-operation agreement with
        European Community 95
    Corporate Leniency Programme
        (CLP) 401–3
    extraterritoriality 90–1, 92–4
    Federal Trade Commission Act 20
    Harvard school 21, 411
    rule of reason 223–4, 414
    Sherman Act 2, 19, 20–1, 223, 224
Utilities
    Competition Commission panels
        79
    enforcement powers 73
    regulators 73

Value of turnover test 316
Vertical Agreements 173–4, 217
    see also Vertical restraints

anti-competitive agreements 206, 209
    meaning 173
Vertical Agreements Regulation
    black list 198, 199, 227, 239
    block exemption withdrawal 230
    definition of vertical agreements 228
    excluded obligations 230
    exclusive distribution agreements
        232
    hard core restraints 229–30
    market share threshold test 228–9
    resale price maintenance 229
    selective distribution agreements 225
    single-branding agreements 234–6
    territorial restrictions 222–3
Vertical Integration 115, 414
Vertical mergers 276, 303, 320
Vertical restraints
    see also Vertical Agreements
        Regulation
    2000 order 237
    2004 order 237–8
    ancillary restraints 188, 225
    block exemptions 221, 224, 226, 227,
        230
    certification free-rider issue 219
    Chapter I prohibition 236, 237
    compartmentalisation of markets 218,
        410
    Competition Act 1998 236–7
    de minimis doctrine 220–1
    distribution agreements 217, 218
    efficiency gains 218
    exclusive distribution agreements 217,
        411
        Article 81 treatment 232
        parallel imports 223, 233
        Post-Regulation 2790 233–4
        reasons for adopting 232
        reform 231–2
        territorial restrictions 232–3
    export bans 221
    foreclosure of competition 218
    franchising 217
    free-rider problems 219–20
    hard core restraints 195, 198, 229, 230,
        237
    hold-up problem 219
    intellectual property rights 225
    inter-brand competition 219
    intra-brand competition 217–8
    market share threshold 228–9

meaning 217
network of 207, 221
objections 218
Office of Fair Trading 237–8
pigeon-holing 400–1
pro-competitive effects 194, 218
purpose 237
reform 226–7
resale price maintenance 229
rule of reason 414
   court and 224–5
   US 223–4
selective distribution 188, 217, 219,
   225, 414

significant market power 303
single-branding commitments 217, 218
small and medium sized undertakings
   189
technology licensing 221
territorial restrictions 222–3
UK competition law 236–8

Wealth, fairer distribution of 17
Whistle-blowers, leniency programmes
   6, 22, 50–1, 70, 211, 262–70,
   401–3
Workable competition 12, 13, 415
World Trade Organisation (WTO) 95, 96,
   388